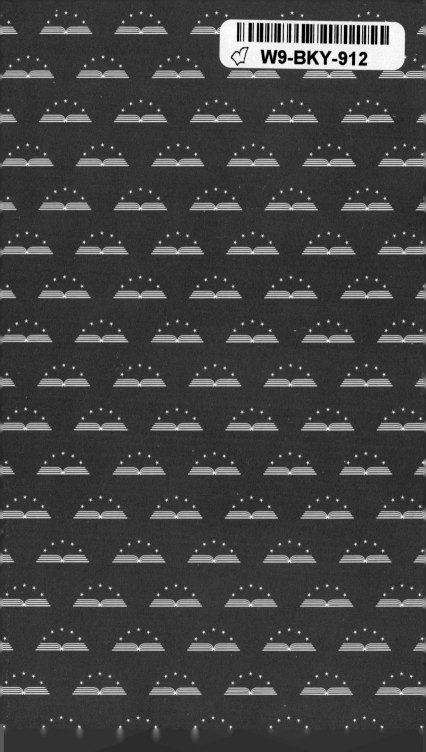

AMERICAN POETRY:
THE SEVENTEENTH AND
EIGHTEENTH CENTURIES

AMERICAN POETRY:
THE SEVENTEENTH AND EIGHTEENTH CENTURIES

THE LIBRARY OF AMERICA

Some of the material in this volume is reprinted by permission
of the holders of copyright and publication rights.
Acknowledgments are on pages 894–97.

The paper used in this publication meets the
minimum requirements of the American National Standard for
Information Sciences—Permanence of Paper for Printed
Library Materials, ANSI Z39.48—1984.

Distributed to the trade
in the United States by Penguin Putnam Inc.
and in Canada by Penguin Books Canada Ltd.

Library of Congress Control Number: 2007929763
ISBN: 978–1–931082–90–7

First Printing
The Library of America—178

Manufactured in the United States of America

DAVID S. SHIELDS

SELECTED THE CONTENTS AND WROTE THE NOTES
FOR THIS VOLUME

American Poetry:
The Seventeenth and Eighteenth Centuries
is published with support from the
National Endowment for the Humanities.

Contents

GEORGE SANDYS (1578–1644)
  from Ovid's Metamorphoses, 1

THOMAS MORTON (c. 1580–c. 1646)
  from New English Canaan, or New Canaan
    The Authors Prologue, 4
    The Poem, 4
    The Songe, 5

JOHN SMITH (1580–1631)
  The Sea Marke, 7

JOHN WILSON (1588–1667)
  To God our twice-Revenger, 8
  Anagram made by mr John Willson of Boston upon
    the Death of Mrs Abigaill Tompson, 9

WILLIAM BRADFORD (1590–1657)
  A Word to New England, 12
  Of Boston in New England, 12
  "Certain Verses left by the Honoured William
    Bradford Esq;," 14

CHRISTOPHER GARDINER (c. 1596–c. 1662)
  "Wolfes in Sheeps clothing why will ye," 16

EDWARD JOHNSON (1598–1672)
  New England's Annoyances, 17
  "You that have seen these wondrous works by *Sions* Savior
    don," 20

from THE BAY PSALM BOOK (1640)
  Psalme 19, 23
  Psalme 23, 24
  Psalme 107, 25

ROGER WILLIAMS (c. 1606–1683)
  from A Key into the Language of America, 30

JOHN FISKE (1608–1677)
  John Kotton : O, Honie Knott, 32
  John Wilson : W'on Sion-hil, 35

ANNE BRADSTREET (1612–1672)
    The Prologue (from *The Tenth Muse*), 36
    A Dialogue between Old England and New, 38
    The Author to her Book, 45
    Contemplations, 46
    Before the Birth of one of her Children, 55
    To my Dear and loving Husband, 55
    In memory of my dear grand-child Elizabeth Bradstreet, 56
    On my dear Grand-child Simon Bradstreet, 57
    "As weary pilgrim, now at rest," 57
    To my dear children, 58
    May. 13. 1657, 59
    Upon my dear & loving husband his goeing into England, 60
    "In silent night when rest I took," 61

JOHN SAFFIN (1626–1710)
    "Sweetly (my Dearest) I left thee asleep," 63
    To his Excellency Joseph Dudley Eqr Gover: &c, 64

EDMUND HICKERINGILL (1631–1708)
    from Jamaica Viewed, 67

MICHAEL WIGGLESWORTH (1631–1705)
    A Song of Emptiness, 71
    from The Day of Doom, 74
    God's Controversy with New-England, 111
    from Meat out of the Eater, 124
    "I Walk'd and did a little *Mole-hill* view," 128

URIAN OAKES (c. 1631–1681)
    An Elegie Upon that Reverend, Learned, Eminently Pious,
        and Singularly Accomplished Divine, my ever Honoured
        Brother, Mr. Thomas Shepard, 132

GEORGE ALSOP (1636–c. 1673)
    The Author to His Book, 144
    "Trafique is Earth's great *Atlas*, that supports," 146
    "Heavens bright Lamp, shine forth some of thy Light," 146

BENJAMIN TOMPSON (1642–1714)
    The Grammarians Funeral, 148
    from New-Englands Crisis, 150
    To Lord Bellamont when entering Governour of the
        Massachusetts, 153
    "Some of his last lines," 155

JAMES REVEL (fl. c. 1659–1680)

 The Poor Unhappy Transported Felon's Sorrowful Account
  of His fourteen Years Transportation at Virginia, 156

EDWARD TAYLOR (c. 1642–1729)

 from *Preparatory Meditations* (*First Series*)

  1. Meditation, 164

  3. Meditation. Can. 1.3. Thy Good Ointment, 164

  4. Meditation. Cant. 2.1. I am the Rose of Sharon, 166

  The Reflexion, 168

  9. Meditation. Joh. 6.51. I am the Living Bread, 169

  23. Meditation. Cant. 4.8. My Spouse, 170

  24. Meditation. Eph. 2.18. Through him we have—an
   Access—unto the Father, 172

  32. Meditation. 1 Cor. 3.22. Whether Paul or Apollos, or
   Cephas, 173

  39. Meditation. from 1 Joh. 2.1. If any man sin, we have
   an Advocate, 175

  46. Meditation. Rev. 3.5. The same shall be cloathed in
   White Raiment, 176

 from *Preparatory Meditations* (*Second Series*)

  1. Meditation. Col. 2.17. Which are Shaddows of things
   to come and the body is Christs, 178

  4. Meditation. Gal. 4.24. Which things are an
   Allegorie, 179

  12. Meditation. Ezek. 37.24. David my Servant shall be
   their King, 180

  14. Meditation. Col. 2.3. In whom are hid all the
   Treasures of Wisdom, and Knowledge, 182

  18. Meditation. Heb 13.10. Wee have an Altar, 183

  Meditation 24. Joh. 1.14. ἐσκήνωσεν ἐν ἡμῖν
   Tabernacled amongst us, 185

  34. Meditation. Rev. 1.5. Who loved us and washed away
   our Sins in his Blood, 187

  60a. Meditation. Joh. 6.51. I am the Living Bread, that
   came down from Heaven, 189

  150. Meditation. Cant. 7.3. Thy two breasts are like two
   young Roes that are twins, 190

 from *Gods Determinations*

  The Preface, 191

  The Accusation of the Inward Man, 192

  The Glory of and Grace in the Church set out, 194

Upon a Spider Catching a Fly, 195
Upon a Wasp Child with Cold, 196
Huswifery, 198
The Ebb and Flow, 198
Upon the Sweeping Flood. Aug: 13.14. 1683, 199

FRANCIS DANIEL PASTORIUS (1651–1719)
"In these Seven Languages I this my book do own," 200
A Token of Love and Gratitude, 200
Rachel Preston, Hannah Hill & Mary Norris, 202
"As often as some where before my Feet," 207
"Delight in Books from Evening," 207
"When I solidly do ponder," 207
Epibaterium, Or a hearty Congratulation to William Penn, 209
"If any honest Friend be pleased to walk into my poor
    Garden," 214

JOHN NORTON JR. (1651–1716)
A Funeral Elogy, Upon that Pattern and Patron of Virtue, the
    truely pious, peerless & matchless Gentlewoman, Mrs.
    Anne Bradstreet, 216

SAMUEL SEWALL (1652–1730)
"Once more! Our GOD, vouchsafe to Shine," 219
Upon the drying up that Ancient River, the River
    Merrimak, 220

BENJAMIN HARRIS (c. 1655–c. 1720)
"In Adam's Fall," 221

JOHN DANFORTH (1660–1730)
A few Lines to fill up a Vacant Page, 224

COTTON MATHER (1663–1728)
"Go then, my Dove, but now no longer Mine!" 225
Gratitudinis Ergo, 225
Singing at the Plow, 232
The Songs of Harvest, 233

SARAH KEMBLE KNIGHT (1666–1727)
from The Journal of Madam Knight
    "I ask thy Aid, O Potent Rum!" 234
    "Tho' Ill at ease, A stranger and alone," 234

ROBERT HUNTER (1666–1734)
    from Androboros: A Biographical Farce, 235

EBENEZER COOK (c. 1667–c. 1733)
    The Sot-Weed Factor; or, A Voyage to Maryland, &c., 239

LEWIS MORRIS II (1671–1746)
    The Mock Monarchy; or, the Kingdom of the Apes, 259

BENJAMIN COLMAN (1673–1747)
    A Quarrel with Fortune, 271
    A Poem, on Elijahs Translation, 271

TOM LAW (fl. 1720s)
    Lovewell's Fight, 280

CHRISTOPHER WITT (1675–1765)
    From the Hymn-Book of Johannes Kelpius
        Of the Wilderness of the Secret, or Private
            Virgin-Cross-Love, 284
        The Paradox and Seldom Contentment of the God
            loving Soul, 293
        Of the Power of the New Virgin-Body, Wherein the Lord
            himself dwelleth and Revealeth his Mysteries, 297

HENRY BROOKE (1678–1736)
    The New Metamorphosis, or Fable of the Bald Eagle, 299
    To my Bottle-friends, 303
    Modern Politeness, 304
    An unwilling Farewel to Poesy, 306

ROGER WOLCOTT (1679–1767)
    from Meditations on Man's First and Fallen Estate, and the
        Wonderful Love of God Exhibited in a Redeemer, 310
    from A Brief Account of the Agency of the Honourable
        John Winthrop, Esq; in the Court of King Charles the
        Second, 313

CHARLES HANSFORD (c. 1685–1761)
    My Country's Worth, 329

GEORGE BERKELEY (1685–1753)
    Verses on the Prospect of planting Arts and Learning in
        America, 346

GEORGE SEAGOOD (c. 1685–1724)
Mr. Blackmore's Expeditio Ultramontana, 347

JOSEPH BREINTNALL (c. 1695–1746)
"A plain Description of one single Street in this City," 353
The Rape of Fewel, 354
To the Memory of Aquila Rose, Deceas'd, 357

JAMES KIRKPATRICK (1696–1770)
The Nonpareil, 366

SUSANNA WRIGHT (1697–1784)
Anna Boylens Letter to King Henry the 8th, 371
On the Benefit of Labour, 373
On the Death of a little Girl, 374
My own Birth Day, 376
To Eliza Norris—at Fairhill, 377

RICHARD LEWIS (c. 1699–1734)
To Mr. Samuel Hastings, (Ship-wright of Philadelphia) on his
    launching the Maryland-Merchant, a large ship built by
    him at Annapolis, 380
A Journey from Patapsco to Annapolis, 386
Food for Criticks, 396

THOMAS DALE (1700–1750)
Prologue spoken to the Orphan, 401
Epilogue to the Orphan, 402

"RALPHO COBBLE" (fl. 1732)
"Learning that Cobweb of the Brain," 403

JAMES STERLING (1701–1763)
from An Epistle to the Hon. Arthur Dobbs, Esq. in Europe
    from a Clergyman in America, 405

WILLIAM DAWSON (1704–1752)
The Wager, 413
On the Corruptions of the Stage, 420
To a Friend, Who recommended a Wife to Him, 421
To a Lady, on a Screen of Her Working, 421

JOHN ADAMS (1705–1740)
Melancholly discrib'd and dispell'd, 423

ARCHIBALD HOME (c. 1705–1744)
An Elegy On the much to be lamented Death of George
      Fraser of Elizabeth Town, 425
The Ear-Ring, 427
Black-Joke: A Song, 428
On killing a Book-Worm, 429

JOSEPH GREEN (1706–1780)
To Mr. B occasioned by his Verse, to Mr. Smibert on
      seeing his Pictures, 430
The Poet's Lamentation for the Loss of his Cat, which he us'd
      to call his Muse, 430
On Mr. B—s's singing an Hymn of his own composing, 432
To the Author of the Poetry in the last *Weekly Journal*, 434
A True Impartial Account of the Celebration of the Prince of
      Orange's Nuptials at Portsmouth, 435
Inscription under Revd. Jn. Checkley's Picture, 437
"A fig for your learning, I tell you the Town," 437
The Disappointed Cooper, 437
"Hail! *D—p—t* of wondrous fame," 440

BENJAMIN FRANKLIN (1706–1790)
Drinking Song, 443
I Sing My Plain Country Joan, 444
Three Precepts, 446

MATHER BYLES (1707–1788)
Hymn to Christ for our Regeneration and Resurrection, 447
To Pictorio, on the Sight of his Pictures, 448
The Conflagration, 450

JANE COLMAN TURELL (1708–1735)
To my Muse, December 29. 1725, 454
An Invitation into the Country, 454
"*Phoebus* has thrice his Yearly Circuit run," 456

MARY HIRST PEPPERELL (1708–1789)
A Lamentation &c. On the Death of a Child, 458

JOHN SECCOMB (1708–1792)
Father Abbey's Will, 459
Proposal to Mistress Abbey, 462

ANON.
The Convert to Tobacco, 466

"POOR JULIAN"
    Poor Julleyoun's Warnings to Children and Servants, 470
    Advice from the Dead to the Living, 473

JUPITER HAMMON (1711–c. 1806)
    An Address to Miss Phillis Wheatly, Ethiopian Poetess, in
        Boston, 477

JOHN OSBORN (1713–1753)
    A Whaling Song, 481

THOMAS CRADOCK (1718–1770)
    Hymn for Ascension, 484
    from Maryland Eclogues in Imitation of Virgil's, 485

CHARLES WOODMASON (c. 1720–c. 1777)
    To Benjamin Franklin Esq; of Philadelphia, on his Experiments
        and Discoveries of Electricity, 489

JAMES GRAINGER (c. 1721–1766)
    from *The Sugar-Cane*, 492

SAMUEL DAVIES (1723–1761)
    "What IS great *God*! and what IS NOT," 516
    "While o'er our guilty Land, O Lord," 517
    "While various Rumours spread abroad," 519
    The Invitations of the Gospel, 520
    Self-Dedication at the Table of the Lord, 521

A.L.M. (fl. 1744)
    A College Room, 523

THOMAS CLEMSON (fl. 1746)
    "From Thomas Clemson ran away," 526

"CAROLINA, A YOUNG LADY"
    On her Father having desired her to forbid all young Men the
        House, 528

JOSEPH DUMBLETON (fl. 1744–1749)
    A Rhapsody on Rum, 529

WILLIAM LIVINGSTON (1723–1790)
    from Philosophic Solitude, 531
    Proclamation, 538

SAMSON OCCOM (1723–1792)
  The Sufferings of Christ, 543
  A Morning Hymn, 544
  A Son's Farewell, 545
  The Slow Traveller, 546

ANON.
  A Description of a Winter's Morning, 548

ANON.
  The Petition, 549

WILLIAM SMITH (1727–1803)
  The Mock Bird and Red Bird, 550
  The Cherry-Tree and Peach-Tree, 552
  The Birds of different Feather, 554

HANNAH GRIFFITTS (1727–1817)
  The female Patriots. Address'd to the Daughters
      of Liberty in America, 558
  To Sophronia. In answer to some Lines she directed to be
      wrote on my Fan, 559
  The Cits Return from the Wilderness to the City, 559
  Wrote on the last Day of February 1775, 561
  Upon Reading a Book entituled Common Sense, 561
  On reading a few Paragraphs in the Crisis, 562

MARY NELSON (fl. 1769)
  Forty Shillings Reward, 564

MERCY OTIS WARREN (1728–1814)
  A Thought on the Inestimable Blessing of Reason,
      occcasioned by its privation to a friend of very
      superior talents and virtues, 566
  To Mr. ——, 567

LUCY TERRY (c. 1730–1821)
  Bars Fight, 570

NED BOTWOOD (c. 1730–1759)
  Hot Stuff, 571

HENRY TIMBERLAKE (1730–1765)
  A Translation of the War-Song, 572

BENJAMIN BANNEKER (1731–1806)
    The Puzzle of the Hare and Hound, 574

THOMAS GODFREY JR. (1736–1763)
    Verses Occasioned by a Young Lady's asking the Author, What
        was a Cure for Love?, 576
    Epistle to a Friend; from Fort Henry, 577
    A Dithyrambic on Wine, 578

ANNIS BOUDINOT STOCKTON (1736–1801)
    A Satire on the fashionable pompoons worn by the Ladies in
        the year 1753. by a Gentleman; Answered by a young Lady
        of sixteen, 581
    A Sarcasm against the ladies in a newspaper; An impromptu
        answer, 582
    Compos'd in a dancing room, 583
    A Poetical Epistle, addressed by a Lady of New-Jersey, to her
        Niece, upon her Marriage, in this City, 584
    To Miss Mary Stockton, 587
    Sensibility, an ode, 588

JOHN SINGLETON (fl. c. 1750–1767)
    from A General Description of the West-Indian Islands, 590

FRANCIS HOPKINSON (1737–1791)
    "My gen'rous heart disdains," 598
    An Epitaph for an Infant, 599
    The Battle of the Kegs, 599
    A Camp Ballad, 602

JONATHAN ODELL (1737–1818)
    The Word of Congress, 604

THOMAS PAINE (1737–1809)
    Liberty Tree, 614

YANKEE DOODLE
    Yankee Doodle, or (as now christened by the Saints of New
        England), The Lexington March, 616
    The Yankey's return from Camp, 618

ELIZABETH GRAEME FERGUSSON (1737–1801)
    To Doctor Fothergill, 621

ROBERT BOLLING (1738–1775)
    Neanthe, 625
    Occlusion, 639

NATHANIEL EVANS (1742–1767)
    To Benjamin Franklin, Esq: L.L.D., Occasioned by hearing
        him play on the Harmonica, 641

JOSEPH STANSBURY (1742–1809)
    Verses to the Tories, 643
    The United States, 643
    To Cordelia, 644

WILLIAM BILLINGS (1746–1800)
    Chester, 646

JOHN ANDRÉ (1750–1780)
    Cow-Chace, 647

JOHN TRUMBULL (1750–1831)
    from The Progress of Dulness (from Part Third: The
        Progress of Coquetry, or, The Adventures of Miss
        Harriet Simper), 657
    from M'Fingal (from Canto Third, The Liberty Pole), 668

ANN ELIZA BLEECKER (1752–1783)
    Written in the Retreat from Burgoyne, 680
    On Reading Dryden's Virgil, 681
    Return to Tomhanick, 682

TIMOTHY DWIGHT (1752–1817)
    from The Triumph of Infidelity, 684
    from Greenfield Hill (Part II, The Flourishing Village), 687
    from The Psalms of David
        "Shall man, O God of light, and life," 708
        "While life prolongs its precious light," 710
        "I love thy kingdom, Lord," 711

ANON.
    from The Philadelphiad
        Country Clown, 713
        Quaker, 714
        The Universal Motive, 715
        Bagnio, 716
        The Emigrant, 717
        Miss Kitty Cut-a-dash, 718

ANNE HECHT (fl. 1780s)
    Advice to Mrs. Mowat, 720

PHILIP FRENEAU (1752–1832)
    American Liberty, 723
    Libera nos, Domine—Deliver us, O Lord, 732
    Female Frailty, 733
    Stanzas Occasioned by the Ruins of a Country Inn, 739
    The Dying Indian, 740
    The Wild Honey Suckle, 742
    The Indian Student, or Force of Nature, 743
    Lines occasioned by a Visit to an old Indian Burying
        Ground, 746
    The Country Printer, 747
    To Sir Toby, a Sugar-Planter in the interior parts of
        Jamaica, 752
    To Mr. Blanchard, 754
    The Republican Genius of Europe, 755
    On a Honey Bee, Drinking from a Glass of Wine, and
        Drowned Therein, 756

DAVID HUMPHREYS (1752–1818)
    Mount-Vernon: An Ode, 758
    The Genius of America, 760
    The Monkey, Who Shaved Himself and His Friends, 761

ST. GEORGE TUCKER (1752–1827)
    A Dream on Bridecake, 763
    A Second Dream on Bridecake, 764

GEORGE OGILVIE (c. 1753–1801)
    from Carolina; or, The Planter, 767

PHILLIS WHEATLEY (c. 1753–1784)
    To Mæcenas, 774
    To the University of Cambridge, in New-England, 775
    On being brought from Africa to America, 776
    On the Death of the Rev. Mr. George Whitefield, 777
    To the Right Honourable William, Earl of Dartmouth, 778
    To S. M., a young African Painter, on seeing his Works, 780
    A Farewel to America, 781
    To a Gentleman of the Navy, 783
    Philis's Reply to the Answer in our last by the Gentleman in
        the Navy, 784
    To His Excellency General Washington, 786
    Liberty and Peace, 787

LEMUEL HAYNES (1753–1833)
    The Battle of Lexington, 789

JOEL BARLOW (1754–1812)
    Innumerable mercies acknowledged, 796
    from The Conspiracy of Kings, 796
    The Hasty-Pudding, 799

ROYALL TYLER (1757–1826)
    The Origin of Evil. An Elegy, 809
    Ode Composed for the Fourth of July, 813
    An Irregular Supplicatory Address to the American Academies
        of Arts and Sciences, 815

MARGARET LOWTHER PAGE (1759–1835)
    To Miss J. L.—, 818

SARAH WENTWORTH MORTON (1759–1846)
    The African Chief, 820
    Memento, 822

JOSEPH HOPKINSON (1770–1842)
    Song, Adapted to the President's March
        ("Hail Columbia!"), 823

THOMAS GREEN FESSENDEN (1771–1837)
    Jonathan's Courtship, 825

CHARLES BROCKDEN BROWN (1771–1810)
    Monody, On the death of Gen. George Washington, 828

ROBERT TREAT PAINE JR. (1773–1811)
    Adams and Liberty, 831

WILLIAM MUNFORD (1775–1825)
    The Disasters of Richland, 834

Biographical Notes, 839
Note on the Texts, 881
Acknowledgements, 894
Notes, 898
Index of Titles and First Lines, 942
Index of Poets, 951

GEORGE SANDYS

(1578–1644)

FROM

Ovid's Metamorphoses

FROM

The Sixth Booke

Both settle to their tasks apart: both spread
At once their warps, consisting of fine thred,
Ty'd to their beames: a reed the thred divides,
Through which the quick-returning shuttle glides,
Shot by swift hands. The combs inserted tooth
Betweene the warp supprest the rising woofe:
Strife less'ning toyle. With skirts tuckt to their waste,
Both move their cunning armes with nimble haste.
Here crimson, dyde in *Tyrian* brasse, they weave:
The scarce distinguisht shadowes sight deceave.
So watry clowds, shot by *Apollo,* showe;
The vast sky painted with a mightie Bowe:
Where, though a thousand severall colours shine,
No eye their close transition can define:
What touch, the same so neerely represents;
And by degrees, scarce sensible, dissents.
Through-out imbellished with ductil gold:
And both reviv'd antiquities unfold.
  Pallas, in *Athens, Marse's* Rock doth frame:
And that old strife about the Cittyes name.
Twice six Cœlestialls sit inthron'd on hie,
Repleat with awe-infusing gravitie:
Jove in the midst. The suted figures tooke
Their lively formes: *Jove* had a regall looke.
The Sea-god stood, and with his Trident strake
The cleaving rock, from whence a fountayn brake:
Whereon he grounds his clame. With speare and shield
Her selfe she armes: her head a murrion steild:
Her brest her *Ægis* guards. Her lance the ground

Appeares to strike; and from that pregnant wound
The hoary olive, chargd with fruit, ascends.
The Gods admire: with victory she ends.
Yet she, to show the Rivall of her prayse
What hopes to cherish for such bold assayes,
Add's foure contentions in the utmost bounds
Of every angle, wrought in little Rounds.
One, *Thracian Rhodope* and *Hæmus* showes,
Now mountaines, topt with never-melting snowes,
Once humane bodyes: who durst emulate
The blest Cœlestialls both in stile and state.
The next containes the miserable doome
Of that *Pygmæan* matron, over-come
By *Juno*; made a Crane, and forc't to jar
With her owne nation in perpetuall war.
A third presents *Antigone,* who strove
For unmatcht beautie with the wife of *Jove.*
Not *Ilium*, nor *Laomedon* her sire,
Prevail'd with violent *Saturnia's* ire.
Turnd to a Stork; who, with white pinions rais'd,
Is ever by her creaking bill selfe-prais'd.
In the last circle *Cynaras* was plac't;
Who, on the temples, staires, the formes imbrac't
Of his late daughters, by their pride o're-throwne:
And seemes himselfe to be a weeping stone.
The web a wreathe of peacefull olive bounds:
And her owne tree her work both ends and crownes.
    Arachne weaves *Europa's* rape by *Jove*:
The Bull appeares to live, the Sea to move.
Back to the shore she casts a heavy eye;
To her distracted damsels seemes to cry:
And from the sprinkling waves, that skip to meete
With such a burden, shrinks her trembling feete.
Asteria there a strugling Eagle prest:
A Swan here spreds his wings o're *Leda's* brest.
Jove, Satyr-like, *Antiope* compels;
Whose fruitfull womb with double issue swels:
Amphitryo for *Alcmena's* love became:
A showre for *Danaë;* for *Ægina* flame:
For beautifull *Mnemosyne* he takes

A pastors forme; for *Deois* a snakes.
Thee also, *Neptune,* like a lustfull Stere,
She makes the faire *Æolian* Virgin beare:
To get th' *Aloides* in *Enipe's* shape:
Now turn'd t'a Ram in sad *Bisaltis* rape.
The gold-haird mother of life-strengthning Seede,
The snake-hair'd mother of the winged Steede,
Found thee a Stalion: thee *Melantho* findes
A Delphin. She to every forme assignes
Life-equald looks; to every place their sites.
Here *Phœbus* in a Heards-mans shape delights;
A Lyon's now; now falcons wings displayes:
Macarean Issa shepheard-like betrayes.
Liber, a grape, *Erigone* comprest:
And *Saturne,* horse-like, *Chiron* gets, halfe-beast.
A slender wreathe her finisht web confines;
Flowres intermixt with clasping ivy twines.
   Not *Pallas* this, not Envy this reproves:
Her faire successe the vext Virago moves;
Who teares the web, with crimes cœlestiall fraught:
With shuttle from *Cytorian* mountaines brought,
Arachne thrice upon the fore-head hits.
Her great heart brooks it not. A cord she knits
About her neck. Remorsefull *Pallas* stayd
Her falling waight: Live wretch, yet hang, she said.
This curse (least after times thy pride secure)
Still to thy issue, and their race, indure.
Sprinkled with *Hecat's* banefull weeds, her haire
She forthwith sheds: her nose and eares impaire;
Her head growes little; her whole body so;
Her thighs and legs to spiny fingers grow:
The rest all belly. Whence a thred she sends:
And now, a Spider, her old webs extends.

THOMAS MORTON

(c. 1580–c. 1646)

FROM

New English Canaan,
or New Canaan

The Authors Prologue

If art & industry should doe as much
As Nature hath for Canaan, not such
Another place, for benefit and rest,
In all the universe can be possest,
The more we proove it by discovery,
The more delight each object to the eye
Procures, as if the elements had here
Bin reconcil'd, and pleas'd it should appeare,
Like a faire virgin, longing to be sped,
And meete her lover in a Nuptiall bed,
Deck'd in right ornaments t' advaunce her state
And excellence, being most fortunate,
When most enjoy'd, so would our Canaan be
If well imploy'd by art & industry
Whose offspring, now shewes that her fruitfull wombe
Not being enjoy'd, is like a glorious tombe,
Admired things producing which there dye,
And ly fast bound in darck obscurity,
The worth of which in each particuler,
Who list to know, this abstract will declare.

The Poem

Rise Oedipeus, and if thou canst unfould,
What meanes Caribdis underneath the mould,
When Scilla sollitary on the ground,
(Sitting in forme of Niobe) was found;
Till Amphitrites Darling did acquaint,

4

Grim Neptune with the Tenor of her plaint,
And causd him send forth Triton with the sound,
Of Trumpet lowd, at which the Seas were found,
So full of Protean formes, that the bold shore,
Presented Scilla a new parramore,
So stronge as Sampson and so patient,
As Job himselfe, directed thus, by fate,
To comfort Scilla so unfortunate.
I doe professe by Cupids beautious mother,
Heres Scogans choise for Scilla, and none other;
Though Scilla's sick with greife because no signe,
Can there be found of vertue masculine.
Esculapius come, I know right well,
His laboure's lost when you may ring her Knell,
The fatall sisters doome none can withstand,
Nor Cithareas powre, who poynts to land,
With proclamation that the first of May,
At Ma-re Mount shall be kept holly day.

The man who brought her over was named Samson Job.

The Songe

Drink and be merry, merry, merry boyes,
Let all your delight be in Hymens joyes,
Iô to Hymen now the day is come,
About the merry Maypole take a Roome.
  Make greene garlons, bring bottles out;
  And fill sweet Nectar, freely about,
  Uncover thy head, and feare no harme,
  For hers good liquor to keepe it warme.
Then drinke and be merry, &c.
Iô to Hymen, &c.
  Nectar is a thing assign'd,
  By the Deities owne minde,
  To cure the hart opprest with greife,
  And of good liquors is the cheife,
Then drinke, &c.
Iô to Hymen, &c.
  Give to the Mellancolly man,
  A cup or two of 't now and than;

This physick' will soone revive his bloud
And make him be of a merrier moode.
Then drinke &c.
Iô to Hymen &c.
Give to the Nymphe thats free from scorne,
No Irish stuff nor Scotch over worne,
Lasses in beaver coats come away,
Yee shall be welcome to us night and day.
To drinke and be merry &c.
Iô to Hymen, &c.

JOHN SMITH

(1580–1631)

The Sea Marke

Aloofe, aloofe, and come no neare,
   the dangers doe appeare;
Which if my ruine had not beene
   you had not seene:
I onely lie upon this shelfe
   to be a marke to all
   which on the same might fall,
That none may perish but my selfe.

If in or outward you be bound,
   doe not forget to sound;
Neglect of that was cause of this
   to steare amisse.
The Seas were calme, the wind was faire,
   that made me so secure,
   that now I must indure
All weathers be they foule or faire.

The Winters cold, the Summers heat,
   alternatively beat
Upon my bruised sides, that rue
   because too true
That no releefe can ever come.
   But why should I despaire
   being promised so faire
That there shall be a day of Dome.

JOHN WILSON

(1588–1667)

To God our twice-Revenger

We saw, but oh! how sad were we to see,
Spaines (prouder) Fleete on the proud Ocean spred:
An hundred ships there were, and eight times three,
Which made it deem'd and nam'd unconquered.
   The ancient Pilots were amaz'd to see 't,
   When they beheld this new-huge-bodied fleete.
The Sea with mazed smile saw in her bounds,
All the Earths wealth and honor brought by ships,
But we all trembled at the frequent sounds
Of Trumpets, Drummes: at naked Swords and Whips
   (Sore threatned) wherewith all the Spaniard fell
   Came arm'd this Brittaine nation to quell.
Our hopes are in a lone-torne ship (befitted,
With fire and Brimstone as her chiefest loade)
Shee, without guide, is to the windes committed,
And forth with cruell destinie she roade;
   (Them and herselfe with her own flames to spoile)
   Windes ferve; she burnt herselfe, put them to foile.
Heere were we cheer'd to see the Ocean maine,
All white before with sailes, now purple growne.
As suddenly with bloud of Spainards slaine:
Their fleete is scattred, and their ships o're throwne,
   Some sinke, some burne i' th' Sea, and some at last,
   After long wandring, on strange shores are cast.

We saw, but oh! how glad were we to see,
O cruell Rome, out of thy darkesome den,
So many weapons of thy villanie
And mightie engines, pluckt by hands of men?
   Stones, Faggots, Crowes, Gun-powder-tubs we saw,
   Those wines *The whore* doth from her vessels draw.
Long were they hid under the secret vaulte,
Of that Great house; and there they were to lye,

Till they were made (O horrible assault!)
By wicked *Faux* his hand, aloft to flye.
  Those sacred roomes where lawes were wont to breed,
  To sudden wracke and ruine were decreed.
King, Prince, Peeres, Prelates, Commons, Gospell bright,
All at one blow together were to fall:
Match was in hand to give the traines their light,
But God reveal'd, destroy'd reveng'd them all.
  Hell needes not blush: for this impiety
  Doth worst of men, fiendes, furies, justifie.
Hell never knew such wickednesse as this,
Another hell, (like it) there need a'-bin.
Should plot and pay be like? for both there is
One measure: none of pay; for, none of sinne.
  Should praise be like Gods grace? there is but one
  Measure for both: Grace had, praise must have none!

Anagram made by mr John Willson of Boston upon the Death of Mrs. Abigaill Tompson

And sent to her husband in virginia, while he was sent to preach the gospell there.

i am gon to all bliss
The blessed news i send to the is this:
That i am goon from the unto all bliss,
Such as the saints & angells do enjoy,
Whom neither Devill, world, nor flesh anoiy.
To bliss of blisses i am goon: to him
Who as a bride did for him selfe me trimm.
Thy bride i was, a most unworthy one,
But to a better bridegroom i am gon,
Who doth a Count me worthy of him selfe,
Tho i was never such a worthles elfe.
He hath me Cladd with his own Righteousness,
And for the sake of it he doth me bless.
Thou didst thy part to wash me, but his grace
Hath left no spott nor wrincle on my face.

Thou little thinkst, or Canst at all Conceive,
What is the bliss that i do now receive.
When oft i herd thee preach & pray & sing
I thought that heaven was a glorious thing,
And i believed, if any knew, twas thou
That knewest what a thing it was; but now
I se thou sawest but a glimps, and hast
No more of heaven but a little tast,
Compared with that which hear we see & have,
Nor Canst have more till thou art past the grave.
Thou never touldst me of the Tyth, nor yet
The hundred thousand thousand part of it.
Alas, Dear Soule, how short is all the fame
Of the third heavens, where i translated amm!
O, if thou ever lovest me at all,
Whom thou didst by such loveing titles Call,
Yea, if thou lovest Christ, (as who doth more?)
Then do not thou my Death too much deplore.
Wring not thy hand, nor sigh, nor mourn, nor weep,
All tho thine Abigaill be faln a sleep.
Tis but her body—that shall ryse again;
In Christs sweet bosomb doth her soule remain.
Mourn not as if thou hadst no hope of me;
Tis i, tis i have Caus to pitty thee.
O turne thy sighings into songs of prais
Unto the name of god; lett all thy Days
Be spent in blessing of his name for thiss:
That he hath brought me to this place of bliss.
It was a blessed, a thrice blessed, snow
Which to the meeting i then waded through,
When piercd i was upon my naked skinn
Up to the middle, the deep snow within.
There never was more happie way i trodd,
That brought me home so soone unto my god
Instead of Braintry Church; Conducting mee
Into a better Church, where now i see,
Not sinfull men, But Christ & those that are
Fully exempt from every spot & skarr
Of sinfull guilt, where i no longer need
Or word or seale my feeble soul to feede,

But face to face i do behould the lamb,
Who down from heaven for my salvation Came,
And thither is asended up again,
Me to prepare a place whear in to Raign,
Where we do allways hallaluiahs sing,
Where i do hope for the to Come err long
To sing thy part in this most glorious song.

WILLIAM BRADFORD

(1590–1657)

A Word to New England

Oh New England, thou canst not boast;
Thy former glory thou hast lost.
When Hooker, Winthrop, Cotton died,
And many precious ones beside,
Thy beauty then it did decay,
And still doth languish more away.
Love, truth, goodness, mercy and grace—
Wealth and the world have took their place.
Thy open sins none can them hide:
Fraud, drunkenness, whoredom and pride.
The great oppressors slay the poor,
But whimsy errors they kill more.
Yet some thou hast which mourn and weep,
And their garments unspotted keep;
Who seek God's honor to maintain,
That true religion may remain.
These do invite, and sweetly call,
Each to other, and say to all;
Repent, amend, and turn to God,
That we may prevent his sharp rod.
Yet time thou hast; improve it well,
That God's presence may with ye dwell.

Of Boston in New England

Oh Boston, though thou now art grown
To be a great and wealthy town,
Yet I have seen thee a void place,
Shrubs and bushes covering thy face.

No houses then in thee there were,
Nor such as gold and silk did wear.
No drunkenness was then in thee,
Nor such excess as now we see.

We then drunk freely of thy spring,
Without paying of anything.
We lodged freely, where we would.
All things were free, and nothing sold.

And they that did thee first begin
Had hearts as free, and as willing,
Their poor friends for to entertain,
And never looked at sordid gain.

Some thou hast had, whom I did know,
Who spent themselves to make thee grow.
Thy foundations they did lay,
Which do remain unto this day.

When thou wast weak, they did thee nurse;
Or else with thee it had been worse.
They left thee not, but did defend
And succor thee, unto their end.

Thou now art grown in wealth and store.
Do not forget that thou wast poor,
And lift not up thyself in pride.
From truth and justice turn not aside.

Remember thou a Cotton had,
Who made the hearts of many glad.
What he thee taught bear thou in mind;
It's hard another such to find.

A Winthrop once in thee was known,
Who unto thee was as a crown.
Such ornaments are very rare,
Yet thou enjoyed this blessed pair.

But these are gone; their work is done.
Their day is past; set is their sun.
Yet faithful Wilson still remains,
And learned Norton doth take pains.

Live thee in peace; I could say more.
Oppress not the weak and poor.
The trade is all in your own hand;
Take heed thee do not wrong the land.

Lest He that hath lift you on high,
When as the poor to him to cry,
Do throw you down from your high state,
And make you low, and desolate.

———

Certain Verses left by the Honoured *William
Bradford* Esq; Governour of the Jurisdiction of
Plimouth, penned by his own hand, declaring the
gracious dispensation of Gods Providence towards
him in the time of his Life, and his preparation
and fittedness for Death

From my years young in dayes of Youth,
God did make known to me his Truth,
And call'd me from my Native place
For to enjoy the Means of Grace.
In *Wilderness* he did me guide,
And in *strange Lands* for me provide.
In *Fears* and *Wants*, through *Weal* and *Woe*,
As *Pilgrim* past I to and fro:
Oft left of them whom I did trust;
How vain it is to rest on *Dust*!
A man of *Sorrows* I have been,
And many *Changes* I have seen.
Wars, Wants, Peace, Plenty have I known;
And some *advanc'd*, others *thrown down*.
The *humble, poor, cheerful* and *glad*;
Rich, discontent, sower and *sad*:

When *Fears* with *Sorrows* have been mixt,
Consolations came betwixt.
Faint not, *poor Soul*, in God still trust,
Fear not the things thou suffer must;
For, *whom he loves he doth chastise*,
And then *all Tears wipes from their eyes.*
Farwell, *dear Children*, whom I love,
Your *better Father* is above:
When I am gone, he can supply;
To him I leave you when I dye.
Fear him in *Truth*, walk in his *Wayes*,
And he will bless you all your dayes.
My dayes are spent, *Old Age* is come,
My *Strength* it fails, my *Glass* near run:
Now I will wait when work is done,
Untill my *happy Change* shall come,
When from my labours I shall rest
With Christ above for to be blest.

CHRISTOPHER GARDINER

(c. 1596–c. 1662)

Wolfes in Sheeps clothing why will ye,
Think to deceave God that doth see,
Your simulated sartinty.
   For my part I doe wish you could,
Your owne infirmities behold,
For then you would not be so bold,
Like Sophists why will you dispute,
With wisdome so, you doe confute,
None but your selves: for shame be mute.
   Least great Jehovah with his powre,
Do come upon you in an howre,
When you least think and you devoure.

EDWARD JOHNSON

(1598–1672)

New England's Annoyances

I

New England's annoyances you that would know them,
Pray ponder these verses which briefly doth show them.
The place where we live is a wilderness wood,
Where grass is much wanting that's fruitful and good.

2

From the end of November till three months are gone,
The ground is all frozen as hard as a stone,
Our mountains and hills and vallies below,
Being commonly covered with ice and with snow.

3

And when the north-wester with violence blows,
Then every man pulls his cap over his nose;
But if any's so hardy and will it withstand,
He forfeits a finger, a foot, or a hand.

4

When the ground opens we then take the hoe,
And make the ground ready to plant and to sow;
Our corn being planted and seed being sown,
The worms destroy much before it is grown.

5

While it is growing much spoil there is made,
By birds and by squirrels that pluck up the blade;
Even when it is grown to full corn in the ear,
It's apt to be spoil'd by hog, racoon, and deer.

6

Our money's soon counted, for we have just none,
All that we brought with us is wasted and gone.
We buy and sell nothing but upon exchange,
Which makes all our dealings uncertain and strange.

7

And now our garments begin to grow thin,
And wool is much wanted to card and to spin;
If we can get a garment to cover without,
Our innermost garment is clout upon clout.

8

Our clothes we brought with us are apt to be torn,
They need to be clouted before they are worn,
For clouting our garments does injure us nothing:
Clouts double are warmer than single whole clothing.

9

If flesh meat be wanting to fill up our dish,
We have carrots and pumpkins and turnips and fish;
And when we have a mind for a delicate dish,
We repair to the clam banks, and there we catch fish.

10

Instead of pottage and puddings and custards and pies,
Our pumpkins and parsnips are common supplies;
We have pumpkin at morning and pumpkin at noon;
If it was not for pumpkins we should be undone.

11

If barley be wanting to make into malt,
We must be contented and think it no fault;
For we can make liquor to sweeten our lips,
Of pumpkins and parsnips and walnut tree chips.

12

And of our green corn-stalks we make our best beer,
We put it in barrels to drink all the year:
Yet I am as healthy, I verily think,
Who make the spring-water my commonest drink.

13

And we have a Cov'nant one with another,
Which makes a division 'twixt brother and brother:
For some are rejected, and others made Saints,
Of those that are equal in virtues and wants.

14

For such like annoyance we've many mad fellows
Find fault with our apples before they are mellow;
And they are for England, they will not stay here,
But meet with a lion in shunning a bear.

15

Now while some are going let others be coming,
For while liquor is boiling it must have a scumming;
But we will not blame them, for birds of a feather,
By seeking their fellows are flocking together.

16

But you who the Lord intends hither to bring,
Forsake not the honey for fear of the sting;
But bring both a quiet and contented mind,
And all needful blessings you surely shall find.

———

You that have seen these wondrous works by *Sions* Savior don,
Expect not miracle, lest means thereby you over-run;
The noble Acts *Jehovah* wrought, his *Israel* to redeem,
Surely this second work of his shall far more glorious seem;
Not only *Egypt*, but all Lands, where Antichrist doth raign,
Shall from Jehovahs heavy hand ten times ten plagues
sustain:
Bright shining shall this Gospel come, Oh glorious King of
Saints,
Thy blessed breath confounds thy foes, all mortal power
faints,
The ratling bones together run with self-same breath that
blows,
Of *Israels* sons long dead and dry, each joynt their sinew
grows,
Fair flesh doth cover them, & veins (lifes fountain) takes there
place.
Smooth seamless coats doth cloath their flesh, and all their
structure grace.
The breath of Life is added, they no *Antinomians* are,
But loving him who gives them life, more zealous are by far
To keep his Law, then formerly when righteousnesse they
sought,
In keeping that they could not keep, which then their
downfal brought.
Their ceremonies vanisht are, on Christ's all their desires,
Their zeal all Nations doth provoke, inkindled are loves
fires:
With hast on horseback, bringing home their sons &
daughters, they
Rejoyce to see this glorious sight, like Resurrections day;
Up and be doing, you young plants, Christ calls his work
unto,
Polluted lips, touch'd with heav'ns fire, about this work
shall go.
Prostrate in prayer parents, and you young ones on Christ call,

Suppose of you he will make use, whereby that beast shall
    fall:
So be it Lord thy servants say, who are at thy disposing,
    With outward word work inward grace, by heavenly truths
    disclosing.
Awake, stand up from death to life, in Christ your studies
    enter,
    The Scriptures search, bright light bring forth, upon this
    hardship venter.
Sound doctrine shall your lips preach out, all errors to
    confound
    And rid Christ's Temple from this smoke, his glory shall
    abound;
Precipitant doth *Dagon* fall, his triple head off cut,
    The Beast that all the world admires, by you to death is
    put:
Put hand to mouth, with vehement blast your silver Trumpets
    sound,
    Christ calls to mind his peoples wrongs, their foes hee'l
    now confound:
Be strong in God, and his great might, his wondrous works
    do tell,
    You raised are unwonted ways, observe his workings well.
As *Jordans* streams congeal'd in heaps, and *Jerico's* high
    walls
    With Rams horns blast, and *Midians* Host, with pitcher
    breaking falls;
Like works your faith, for to confirm in these great works to
    come,
    That nothing now too hard may seem, *Jehovah* would have
    don.
The rage of Seas, and hunger sharp, wants of a desart Land,
    Your noble hearts have overcom, what shall this work
    withstand?
Not persecutors pride and rage, strong multitudes do fall,
    But little handfuls of least dust, your Christ confounds
    them all;
Not Satan and his subtil train with seeming shew reforming,

Another Gospel to bring forth, brings damned errors
    swarming;
Your selves have seen his paint washt off, his hidden poysons
    found,
    Christ you provides with Antidotes, to keep his people
    sound:
There's nought remains but conquest now, through Christ's
    continued power,
    His hardest works have honors most attend them every
    hour.
What greater honor then on earth, Christ's Legat for to be,
    Attended with his glorious Saints in Church fraternity.
Christ to behold adorning now his Bride in bright array,
    And you his friends him to attend upon his Nuptial day,
With crowned heads, as Conquerors triumphant by his side;
    In's presence is your lasting joy, and pleasures ever bide.

THE BAY PSALM BOOK

Psalme 19

To the chiefe musician a psalme of David.

The heavens doe declare
   the majesty of God:
also the firmament shews forth
   his handy-work abroad.
2 Day speaks to day, knowledge
   night hath to night declar'd.
3 There neither speach nor language is,
   where their voyce is not heard.
4 Through all the earth their line
   is gone forth, & unto
the utmost end of all the world,
   their speaches reach also:
A Tabernacle hee
   in them pitcht for the Sun.
5 Who Bridegroom like from's chamber goes
   glad Giants-race to run.
6 From heavens utmost end,
   his course and compassing;
to ends of it, & from the heat
   thereof is hid nothing.

2

7 The Lords law perfect is,
   the soule converting back:
Gods testimony faithfull is,
   makes wise who-wisdome-lack.
8 The statutes of the Lord,
   are right, & glad the heart:
the Lords commandement is pure,
   light doth to eyes impart.

9 Jehovahs feare is cleane,
and doth indure for ever:
the judgements of the Lord are true,
and righteous altogether.

10 Then gold, then much fine gold,
more to be prized are,
then hony, & the hony-comb,
sweeter they are by farre.

11 Also thy servant is
admonished from hence:
and in the keeping of the same
is a full recompence.

12 Who can his errors know?
from secret faults cleanse mee.

13 And from presumptuous-sins, let thou
kept back thy servant bee:
Let them not beare the rule
in me, & then shall I
be perfect, and shall cleansed bee
from much iniquity.

14 Let the words of my mouth,
and the thoughts of my heart,
be pleasing with thee, Lord, my Rock
who my redeemer art.

*

Psalme 23

A Psalme of David.

The Lord to mee a shepheard is,
want therefore shall not I.

2 Hee in the folds of tender-grasse,
doth cause mee downe to lie:
To waters calme me gently leads

3 Restore my soule doth hee:
he doth in paths of righteousnes:
for his names sake leade mee.

4   Yea though in valley of deaths shade
     I walk, none ill I'le feare:
     because thou art with mee, thy rod,
     and staffe my comfort are.
5   For mee a table thou hast spread,
     in presence of my foes:
     thou dost annoynt my head with oyle,
     my cup it over-flowes.
6   Goodnes & mercy surely shall
     all my dayes follow mee:
     and in the Lords house I shall dwell
     so long as dayes shall bee.

Psalme 107

O give yee thanks unto the Lord,
     because that good is hee:
because his loving kindnes lasts
     to perpetuitee.
2   So let the Lords redeem'd say: whom
     hee freed from th' enemies hands:
3   and gathred from East, & West,
     from South, & Northerne lands.
4   I th' desart, in a desart way
     they wandred: no towne finde,
5   to dwell in. Hungry & thirsty:
     their soule within them pinde.
6   Then did they to Jehovah cry
     when they were in distresse:
     who did them set at liberty
     out of their anguishes.
7   In such a way that was most right
     he led them forth also:
     that to a citty which they might
     inhabit they might go.
8   O that men would Jehovah prayse
     for his great goodnes *then:*

    & for his workings wonderfull
       unto the sonnes of men.

9 Because that he the longing soule
       doth throughly satisfy:
    the hungry soule he also fills
       with good abundantly.

2

10 Such as in darknes' and within
       the shade of death abide;
    who are in sore affliction,
       also in yron tyde:

11 By reason that against the words
       of God they did rebell;
    also of him that is most high
       contemned the counsell.

12 Therefore with molestation
       hee did bring downe their heart:
    downe did they fall, & none their was
       could help them to impart.

13 Then did they to Jehovah cry
       when they were in distress:
    who did them set at liberty
       out of their anguishes.

14 He did them out of darknes bring,
       also deaths shade from under:
    as for the bands that they were in
       he did them break asunder.

15 O that men would Jehovah prayse
       for his great goodness *then*:
    and for his workings wonderfull
       unto the sonnes of men.

16 For he hath all to shivers broke
       the gates that were of brasse:
    & hee asunder cut each barre
       that made of yron was.

3

17 For their transgressions & their sins,
        fooles doe affliction beare.
18 All kinde of meate their soule abhorres:
        to deaths gate they draw neare.
19 Then did they to Jehovah cry
        when they were in distress:
    who did them set at liberty
        out of their anguishes.
20 He, sent his word, & therewithall
        healing to them he gave:
    from out of their destructions
        he did them also save.
21 O that men would Jehovah prayse,
        for his great goodness *then:*
    & for his workings wonderfull
        unto the sons of men.
22 And sacrifices sacrifice
        let them of thanksgiving:
    & while his works they doe declare
        let them for gladnes sing.

4

23 They that goe downe to th' sea in ships:
        their busines there to doo
24 in waters great. The Lords work see,
        i'th' deep his wonders too.
25 Because that he the stormy winde
        commandeth to arise:
    which lifteth up the waves thereof,
26   They mount up to the skyes:
    Downe goe they to the depths againe,
        their soule with ill doth quaile.
27 They reele, & stagger, drunkard like,
        and all their wirt doth faile.
28 Then did they to Jehovah cry
        when they were in distress:
    and therupon he bringeth them
        out of their anguishes.

29   Hee makes the storme a calme: so that
      the waves thereof are still.

30   Their rest then glads them; he them brings
      to th' hav'n which they did will.

31   O that men would Jehovah prayse
      for his great goodnes *then*:
      & for his workings wonderfull
      unto the sons of men.

32   Also within the peoples Church
      him let them highly rayse:
      where Elders are assembled, there
      him also let them prayse.

5

33   He rivers to a desart turnes,
      to drought the springing well:

34   A fruitful soyle to barrennes;
      for their sin there that dwell.

35   The desart to a poole he turnes;
      and dry ground to a spring.

36   Seates there the hungry; who prepare
      their towne of habiting,

37   Vineyards there also for to plant,
      also to sow the field;
      which may unto them fruitfull things
      of much revenue yield.

38   Also he blesseth them, so that
      they greatly are increast:
      and for to be diminished
      he suffers not their beast.

39   Againe they are diminished
      & they are brought downe low,
      by reason of their pressing-streights,
      affliction & sorrow.

6

40   On Princes he comtempt doth powre;
      and causeth them to stray

      i'th' solitary wildernes,
        wherin there is no way.
41 Yet hee out of affliction
        doth make the poore to rise:
      & like as if it were a flock
        doth make him families.
42 The righteous shall it behold,
        and he shall joyfull bee:
      in silence stop her mouth also
        shall all iniquitee.
43 Who so is wise, & who so will
        these things attentive learne:
      the living kindenes of the Lord
        they clearely shall discerne.

ROGER WILLIAMS

(c. 1604–1683)

A Key into the Language of America

The Courteous *Pagan* shall condemne
Uncourteous Englishmen,
Who live like Foxes, Beares and Wolves.
Or Lyon in his Den.

Let none sing *blessings* to their soules,
For that they Courteous are:
The wild *Barbarians* with no more
Then Nature, goe so farre:

If Natures Sons both *wild* and *tame,*
Humane and Courteous be:
How ill becomes it Sonnes of God
To want Humanity?

—

Course *bread* and *water's* most their fare,
O *Englands* diet fine;
Thy *cup* runs ore with plenteous store
Of wholesome *beare* and *wine.*

Sometimes *God* gives them *Fish* or *Flesh,*
Yet they're *content* without;
And what comes in, they *part* to *friends*
And *strangers* round about.

Gods *providence* is rich to his,
Let none *distrustfull* be;
In *wildernesse,* in great *distresse,*
These *Ravens* have fed me.

—

Boast not proud *English*, of thy birth & blood,
Thy brother *Indian* is by birth as Good.
Of one blood God made Him, and Thee & All,
As wise, as faire, as strong, as personall.

By nature wrath's his portion, thine no more
Till Grace *his* soule and *thine* in Christ restore,
Make sure thy second birth, else thou shalt see,
Heaven ope to *Indians* wild, but shut to thee.

—

Adulteries, Murthers, Robberies, Thefts,
Wild *Indians* punish these!
And hold the Scales of Justice so,
That no man farthing leese.

When *Indians* heare the horrid filths,
of *Irish, English* Men,
The horrid Oaths and Murthers late,
Thus say these *Indians* then:

We weare no Cloaths, have many Gods,
And yet our sinnes are lesse:
You are Barbarians, Pagans wild,
Your Land's the Wildernesse.

—

The *Indians* prize not *English* gold,
Nor *English Indians* shell:
Each in his place will passe for ought,
What ere men buy or sell.

English and *Indians* all passe hence,
To an eternall place,
Where shels nor finest gold's worth ought,
Where nought's worth ought but Grace.

This Coyne the *Indians* know not of,
Who knowes how soon they may?
The *English* knowing, prize it not,
But fling't like drosse away.

JOHN FISKE

(1608–1677)

*Upon the much-to be lamented desease
of the Reverend Mr John Cotton
late Teacher to the church at Boston N. E.
who departed this Life 23 of 10. 52.*

John { *Cotton*
{ *Kotton after the old English writi'g*
Anagr:
O, Honie knott

With Joy erst while, (when knotty doubts arose)
To Thee we calld, o Sir, the knott disclose:
But now o and alasse to thee to call
In vayne tis thou no Answer give or shall.
Could loud Shrickes, could crys recall thee back
From deaths estate we wold our eye ne're slack
O, this our greife it is, lament shall we
A Father in our Israel's cea'st to be
even hee that in the Church a pillar was
A gurdeon knot of sweetest graces as
He who set fast to Truths so clossly knitt
as loosen him could ne're the keenest witt
Hee who his Flesh together bound ful-fast
no knott more sure whilest his life did last
Hee who the knotts of Truth, of Mysteries
sacred, most cleerely did ope' fore our eyes
even hee who such a one, is ceas'd to bee
'twixt whose life, death, the most sweete harmony
Knotts we doe meet with many a cue daily
which crabbed anggry tough unpleasing bee
But we as in a honi-comb a knott
of Hony sweete, here had such sweetenes Gott
the knotts and knobbs that on the Trees doe grow
the bitterest excressences we know.

> his soule Embalmd with grace
>   was fit to soare on high
> and to receive its place
>   above the starry skie.
> now grant O God that we
>   may follow after him
> surviving worlds ocean unto thee
>   our passage safe may swim.

A vine tree seene, a plant of Gods owne hand
In it this knott of sweetest parts did stand.
The knott in place sublime: most eminent
As, his, no Branch could challeng like extent
The knott sometimes seems a deformity
It's a mistake, tho such be light set by
The knott it is the Joynt, the strength of parts
the bodies-beauty, so this knott out-starts
What others in that place, they ought to bee
even such a knott exemplar'ly was hee
Knotts now adayes affrayd of are most men
of Hony it expose'd feare none would then
I guesse why knotty Learning downe does goe
'twould not, if as in him 'twere sweetned soe
Meeknes Humility forbearance too
this lovely knott to love the most did woe
In knotts what greate adoe to gayne the hearte
yee had it heere, he did it free impart
When knotty theames and paynes some meet with then
as knotty and uncouth their tongue and pen
so 'twas not heere, he caus'd us understand
and tast the sweetnes of the knott in hand.
When knotty querks and quiddities broacht were
by witt of man he sweetely Breathed there.
His charity his wisdom meeknes eke
left none that loved light, in knotts to seeke
Hee tho invincible through softnes did
the knottiest peeces calme and cleave amid
Such was hee of such use in these last dayes
Whose want bewayle, o, and alas alwaies
This knott so we have seen lien broknly

By knotts so breathlesse, so crookt, crackt, or fly
This knott thereof so surfetted we see
By hony surfetted we know som bee
The cause nor in the knott nor hony say
Through Temper bad, unskilfulnes this may
O knott of Hony most delightfull when
Thou livd'st, thi death a sad presage hath ben
Have Ben? yea is, and is, and is alas
For woe to us, so greate a Breach when was
Woe to that knotty pride hee ne're subdude
Woe they who doe his Truthes dispenct exclude
and woe to them that factions there contrive
woe them whose wayes unrighteous survive
Woe they that by him warning did not take
Woe to us all if mercy us forsake
A Mercy once New England thou hast had
(you Boston cheifly) in thi Cotton clad
Some 'gan to count't too meane a dresse and sought
Silk Velvetts Taffeties best could be bought
these last will soyle, if first doe soyle also
how can we think but Naked we shall goe
must silken witts, must velvet tongues be had
and shall playne preaching be accounted bad
I feare a famine, pinching times t'ensue
Time Such may have, slighted mercy to Rue
My wakened muse to rest, my moystned pen
mye eye, my hearte which powred out this have ben
cease try no more, for Hee hath gayn'd his prize
His heavenly mansion 'bove the starry skie
Returne thee home and wayle the evills there
Repent breake off thi sins Jehovah feare

    O Jehovah feare: this will thi wisdom bee
    And thou his waies of mercy yet maust see
    Returne thou mee;   And turned bie
    Lord unto thee: even so shall I.

Reverendo viro Domino Joanni Wilsono
Ecclesiae Bostoniensis pastori fidelissimo
Fratri ac Amico plurimum observando

John Wilson
Anagr.
W'on Sion-hil

When Jah so rare a Gem pleas'd to distrayne
as once thee Gave, what priviledge remaine?
That Blessed pearle enjoy'd w'on Sion-hil
Him though translated hence, yet heere we still:
What doe we heere when such a one is gone!
What? heere's that Lamb, who may suffice alone
As then that presence of rich grace we had
He graunt it now, a double blessing adde.

Tuus συνκοινωνοπενθής

Wenh. 7. of 11th   Tibique addictissimus

52

ANNE BRADSTREET

(1612–1672)

The Prologue

(from *The Tenth Muse*)

1.

To sing of Wars, of Captaines, and of Kings,
Of Cities founded, Common-wealths begun,
For my mean Pen, are too superiour things,
And how they all, or each, their dates have run:
Let Poets, and Historians set these forth,
My obscure Verse, shal not so dim their worth.

2.

But when my wondring eyes, and envious heart,
Great *Bartas* sugar'd lines doe but read o're;
Foole, I doe grudge, the Muses did not part
'Twixt him and me, that over-fluent store;
A *Bartas* can, doe what a *Bartas* wil,
But simple I, according to my skill.

3.

From School-boyes tongue, no Rhethorick we expect,
Nor yet a sweet Consort, from broken strings,
Nor perfect beauty, where's a maine defect,
My foolish, broken, blemish'd Muse so sings;
And this to mend, alas, no Art is able,
'Cause Nature made it so irreparable.

4.

Nor can I, like that fluent sweet tongu'd *Greek*
Who lisp'd at first, speake afterwards more plaine
By Art, he gladly found what he did seeke,

A full requitall of his striving paine:
Art can doe much, but this maxime's most sure,
A weake or wounded braine admits no cure.

5.

I am obnoxious to each carping tongue,
Who sayes, my hand a needle better fits,
A Poets Pen, all scorne, I should thus wrong;
For such despight they cast on female wits:
If what I doe prove well, it wo'nt advance,
They'l say its stolne, or else, it was by chance.

6.

But sure the antick *Greeks* were far more milde,
Else of our Sex, why feigned they those nine,
And poesy made, *Calliope's* owne childe,
So 'mongst the rest, they plac'd the Arts divine:
But this weake knot they will full soone untye,
The *Greeks* did nought, but play the foole and lye.

7.

Let *Greeks* be *Greeks*, and Women what they are,
Men have precedency, and still excell,
It is but vaine, unjustly to wage war,
Men can doe best, and Women know it well;
Preheminence in each, and all is yours,
Yet grant some small acknowledgement of ours.

8.

And oh, ye high flown quils, that soare the skies,
And ever with your prey, still catch your praise,
If e're you daigne these lowly lines, your eyes
Give wholsome Parsley wreath, I aske no Bayes:
This meane and unrefined stuffe of mine,
Will make your glistering gold but more to shine.

A Dialogue between Old England and New

concerning their present troubles.
Anno 1642.

New England.

Alas, deare Mother, fairest Queen, and best,
With honour, wealth, and peace, happy and blest;
What ayles thee hang thy head, and crosse thine armes?
And sit i'th dust, to sigh these sad alarms?
What deluge of new woes thus over-whelme
The glories of thy ever famous Realme?
What meanes this wailing tone, this mourning guise?
Ah, tell thy Daughter, she may simpathize.

Old England.

Art ignorant indeed, of these my woes?
Or must my forced tongue these griefes disclose?
And must my selfe dissect my tatter'd state,
Which 'mazed Christendome stands wondring at?
And thou a childe, a Limbe, and dost not feele
My weakned fainting body now to reele?
This Phisick-purging-potion I have taken,
Will bring Consumption, or an Ague quaking,
Unlesse some Cordial thou fetch from high,
Which present help may ease this malady.
If I decease, dost think thou shalt survive?
Or by my wasting state, dost think to thrive?
Then weigh our case, if't be not justly sad,
Let me lament alone, while thou art glad.

New England.

And thus, alas, your state you much deplore,
In generall terms, but will not say wherefore:
What Medicine shall I seek to cure this woe,
If th' wound's so dangerous I may not know?
But you perhaps would have me guesse it out,
What, hath some *Hengist*, like that *Saxon* stout,
By fraud, and force, usurp'd thy flowring crown,
And by tempestuous Wars thy fields trod down?
Or hath *Canutus*, that brave valiant *Dane*,

The regall, peacefull Scepter from thee tane?
Or is't a *Norman*, whose victorious hand
With *English* blood bedews thy conquered Land?
Or is't intestine Wars that thus offend?
Doe *Maud*, and *Stephen* for the Crown contend?
Doe Barons rise, and side against their King?
And call in Forreign ayde, to help the thing?
Must *Edward* be depos'd, or is't the houre
That second *Richard* must be clapt i'th' Tower?
Or is the fatall jarre againe begun,
That from the red, white pricking Roses sprung?
Must *Richmonds* ayd, the Nobles now implore,
To come, and break the tushes of the Boar?
If none of these, deare Mother, what's your woe?
Pray, doe not feare *Spaines* bragging Armado?
Doth your Allye, faire *France*, conspire your wrack?
Or, doth the *Scots* play false behind your back?
Doth *Holland* quit you ill, for all your love?
Whence is this storme, from Earth, or Heaven above?
Is't Drought, is't Famine, or is't Pestilence?
Dost feele the smart, or feare the consequence?
Your humble Childe intreats you, shew your grief,
Though Armes, no Purse she hath, for your releif:
Such is her poverty, yet shall be found
A supplyant for your help, as she is bound.

Old England.
I must confesse, some of those Sores you name,
My beauteous Body at this present maime;
But forraigne Foe, nor fained friend I feare,
For they have work enough (thou knowst) elsewhere;
Nor is it *Alcies* Son, and *Henries* Daughter,
Whose proud contention cause this slaughter;
Nor Nobles siding, to make *John* no King
French *Lewis* unjustly to the Crown to bring;
No *Edward*, *Richard*, to lose rule, and life,
Nor no *Lancastrians*, to renew old strife;
No Crook-backt Tyrant, now usurps the Seat,
Whose tearing tusks did wound, and kill, and threat:
No Duke of *York*, nor Earle of *March*, to soyle

Their hands in Kindreds blood, whom they did foyle:
No need of *Tudor*, Roses to unite,
None knowes which is the Red, or which the White:
Spaines braving Fleet a second time is sunke,
France knowes, how of my fury she hath drunk;
By *Edward* third, and *Henry* fifth of fame,
Her Lillies in mine Armes avouch the same.
My Sister *Scotland* hurts me now no more,
Though she hath bin injurious heretofore.
What *Holland* is, I am in some suspence,
But trust not much unto his Excellence;
For wants, sure some I feele, but more I feare,
And for the Pestilence, who knowes how neare;
Famine, and Plague, two sisters of the Sword,
Destruction to a Land doth soone afford;
They're for my punishments ordain'd on high,
Unlesse thy teares prevent it speedily.
But yet, I answer not what you demand,
To shew the grievance of my troubled Land;
Before I tell the effect, ile shew the cause,
Which are my Sins, the breach of sacred Lawes;
Idolatry, supplanter of a Nation,
With foolish superstitious adoration;
And lik'd, and countenanc'd by men of might,
The Gospel is trod down, and hath no right;
Church Offices are sold, and bought, for gaine,
That Pope, had hope, to find *Rome* here againe;
For Oathes, and Blasphemies did ever eare
From *Beelzebub* himself, such language heare?
What scorning of the Saints of the most high,
What injuries did daily on them lye;
What false reports, which nick-names did they take,
Nor for their owne, but for their Masters sake;
And thou, poore soule, wast jeer'd among the rest,
Thy flying for the Truth I made a jeast;
For Sabbath-breaking, and for Drunkennesse,
Did ever Land prophannesse more expresse?
From crying bloods, yet cleansed am not I,
Martyrs, and others, dying causelesly:
How many Princely heads on blocks laid down,

For nought, but title to a fading Crown?
'Mongst all the cruelties which I have done,
Oh, *Edwards* Babes, and *Clarence* haplesse Son,
O *Jane*, why didst thou dye in flowring prime,
Because of Royall Stem, that was thy crime;
For Bribery, Adultery, for Thefts, and Lyes,
Where is the Nation, I cann't paralize;
With Usury, Extortion, and Oppression,
These be the *Hydra's* of my stout transgression;
These be the bitter fountains, heads, and roots,
Whence flow'd the source, the sprigs, the boughs, and fruits;
Of more then thou canst heare, or I relate,
That with high hand I still did perpetrate;
For these, were threatned the wofull day,
I mock'd the Preachers, put it farre away;
The Sermons yet upon record doe stand,
That cry'd, destruction to my wicked Land:
These Prophets mouthes (alas the while) was stopt,
Unworthily, some backs whipt, and eares cropt,
Their reverent cheeks, did beare the glorious markes
Of stinking, stigmatizing, Romish Clerkes;
Some lost their livings, some in prison pent,
Some grossely fin'd, from friends to exile went:
Their silent tongues to heaven did vengeance cry,
Who heard their cause, and wrongs judg'd righteously,
And will repay it sevenfold in my lap,
This is fore-runner of my after clap,
Nor took I warning by my neighbours falls,
I saw sad *Germanie's* dismantled walls.
I saw her people famish'd, Nobles slain,
Her fruitfull land, a barren heath remain.
I saw (unmov'd) her Armies foil'd and fled,
Wives forc'd, babes toss'd, her houses calcined,
I saw strong *Rochel* yeelding to her foe,
Thousands of starved Christian there also.
I saw poore *Ireland* bleeding out her last,
Such cruelty as all reports have past.
My heart obdurate, stood not yet agast.
Nor sip I of that cup, and just 't may be,
The bottome dregs reserved are for me.

New England.

To all you've said, sad mother, I assent
Your fearfull sinnes, great cause there's to lament,
My guilty hands (in part) hold up with you,
A sharer in your punishment's my due,
But all you say, amounts to this effect,
Not what you feel, but what you do expect.
Pray in plain termes, what is your present grief,
Then let's join heads, and hands for your relief.

Old England.

Well, to the matter then, there's grown of late,
'Twixt King and Peeres a question of state,
Which is the chief, the law, or else the King,
One saith its he, the other no such thing.
My better part in Court of Parliament,
To ease my groaning land shew their intent,
To crush the proud, and right to each man deal.
To help the Church, and stay the Common-Weal,
So many obstacles comes in their way,
As puts me to a stand what I should say,
Old customes, new Prerogatives stood on,
Had they not held law fast, all had been gone,
Which by their prudence stood them in such stead,
They took high *Strafford* lower by the head,
And to their *Laud* be't spoke, they held i'th' Tower,
All *Englands* Metropolitane that houre,
This done, an Act they would have passed fain,
No prelate should his Bishoprick retain;
Here tugg'd they hard indeed, for all men saw,
This must be done by Gospel, not by law.
Next the *Militia* they urged sore,
This was deny'd, I need not say wherefore.
The King displeas'd, at *York* himself absents,
They humbly beg return, shew their intents,
The writing, printing, posting to and fro,
Shews all was done, I'll therefore let it go.
But now I come to speak of my disaster,
Contention's grown 'twixt Subjects and their Master:
They worded it so long, they fell to blows,

That thousands lay on heaps, here bleeds my woes.
I that no warres, so many yeares have known,
Am now destroy'd, and slaughter'd by mine own,
But could the field alone this cause decide,
One battell, two or three I might abide,
But these may be beginnings of more woe,
Who knows, the worst, the best may overthrow;
Religion, Gospell, here lies at the stake,
Pray now dear child, for sacred *Zion's* sake,
Oh pity me, in this sad perturbation,
My plundered Townes, my houses devastation,
My ravisht virgins, and my young men slain,
My wealthy trading faln, my dearth of grain,
The seed time's come, but Ploughman hath no hope,
Because he knows not, who shall inn his crop:
The poore they want their pay, their children bread,
Their wofull mother's tears unpitied.
If any pity in thy heart remain,
Or any child-like love thou dost retain,
For my relief now use thy utmost skill,
And recompence me good, for all my ill.

New England.
Dear mother cease complaints, and wipe your eyes,
Shake off your dust, chear up, and now arise,
You are my mother, nurse, I once your flesh,
Your sunken bowels gladly would refresh:
Your griefs I pity much, but should do wrong,
To weep for that we both have pray'd for long,
To see these latter dayes of hop'd for good,
That Right may have its right, though't be with blood;
After dark Popery the day did clear,
But now the Sun in's brightnesse shall appear,
Blest be the Nobles of thy Noble Land,
With (ventur'd lives) for truths defence that stand,
Blest be thy Commons, who for Common good,
And thine infringed Lawes have boldly stood.
Blest be thy Counties which do aid thee still
With hearts, and states, to testifie their will.
Blest be thy Preachers, who do chear thee on,

O cry: the sword of God, and *Gideon*:
And shall I not on those with *Mero's* curse,
That help thee not with prayers, arms, and purse,
And for my self, let miseries abound,
If mindlesse of thy state I e'r be found.
These are the dayes, the Churches foes to crush,
To root out Prelates, head, tail, branch, and rush.
Let's bring *Baals* vestments out, to make a fire,
Their Myters, Surplices, and all their tire,
Copes, Rochets, Crossiers, and such trash,
And let their names consume, but let the flash
Light Christendome, and all the world to see,
We hate *Romes* Whore, with all her trumperie.
Go on brave *Essex*, shew whose son thou art,
Not false to King, nor Countrey in thy heart,
But those that hurt his people and his Crown,
By force expell, destroy, and tread them down:
Let Gaoles be fill'd with th' remnant of that pack,
And sturdy *Tyburn* loaded till it crack,
And yee brave Nobles, chase away all fear,
And to this blessed Cause closely adhere
O mother, can you weep, and have such Peeres.
When they are gone, then drown your self in teares.
If now you weep so much, that then no more,
The briny Ocean will o'rflow your shore,
These, these, are they (I trust) with *Charles* our King,
Out of all mists, such glorious dayes will bring,
That dazzled eyes beholding much shall wonder
At that thy setled Peace, thy wealth and splendour,
Thy Church and Weal, establish'd in such manner,
That all shall joy that thou display'dst thy banner,
And discipline erected, so I trust,
That nursing Kings, shall come and lick thy dust:
Then Justice shall in all thy Courts take place,
Without respect of persons, or of case,
Then bribes shall cease, and suits shall not stick long,
Patience, and purse of Clients for to wrong:
Then High Commissions shall fall to decay,
And Pursevants and Catchpoles want their pay,
So shall thy happy Nation ever flourish,

When truth and righteousnesse they thus shall nourish.
When thus in Peace: thine Armies brave send out,
To sack proud *Rome*, and all her vassalls rout:
There let thy name, thy fame, thy valour shine,
As did thine Ancestours in *Palestine*,
And let her spoils, full pay, with int'rest be,
Of what unjustly once she poll'd from thee,
Of all the woes thou canst let her be sped,
Execute toth' full the vengeance threatned.
Bring forth the beast that rul'd the world with's beck,
And tear his flesh, and set your feet on's neck,
And make his filthy den so desolate,
To th' 'stonishment of all that knew his state,
This done, with brandish'd swords, to *Turky* go,
(For then what is't, but English blades dare do)
And lay her wast, for so's the sacred doom,
And do to *Gog*, as thou hast done to *Rome*.
Oh *Abrahams* seed lift up your heads on high.
For sure the day of your redemption's nigh;
The scales shall fall from your long blinded eyes,
And him you shall adore, who now despise,
Then fulness of the Nations in shall flow,
And Jew and Gentile, to one worship go,
Then follows dayes of happinesse and rest,
Whose lot doth fall to live therein is blest:
No Canaanite shall then be found ith' land,
And holinesse, on horses bells shall stand,
If this make way thereto, then sigh no more,
But if at all, thou didst not see't before.
Farewell dear mother, Parliament, prevail,
And in a while you'l tell another tale.

The Author to her Book

Thou ill-form'd offspring of my feeble brain,
Who after birth did'st by my side remain,
Till snatcht from thence by friends, less wise then true
Who thee abroad, expos'd to publick view,

Made thee in raggs, halting to th' press to trudge,
Where errors were not lessened (all may judg).
At thy return my blushing was not small,
My rambling brat (in print) should mother call.
I cast thee by as one unfit for light,
Thy Visage was so irksome in my sight;
Yet being mine own, at length affection would
Thy blemishes amend, if so I could:
I wash'd thy face, but more defects I saw,
And rubbing off a spot, still made a flaw.
I stretcht thy joynts to make thee even feet,
Yet still thou run'st more hobling then is meet;
In better dress to trim thee was my mind,
But nought save home-spun Cloth, i' th' house I find.
In this array, 'mongst Vulgars mayst thou roam,
In Criticks hands, beware thou dost not come;
And take thy way where yet thou are not known,
If for thy Father askt, say, thou hadst none:
And for thy Mother, she alas is poor,
Which caus'd her thus to send thee out of door.

Contemplations

Sometimes now past in the Autumnal Tide,
When *Phœbus* wanted but one hour to bed,
The trees all richly clad, yet void of pride,
Were gilded o're by his rich golden head.
Their leaves & fruits seem'd painted, but was true
Of green, of red, of yellow, mixed hew,
Rapt were my sences at this delectable view.

2

I wist not what to wish, yet sure thought I,
If so much excellence abide below;
How excellent is he that dwells on high?
Whose power and beauty by his works we know.
Sure he is goodness, wisdome, glory, light,
That hath this under world so richly dight:
More Heaven then Earth was here, no winter & no night.

3

Then on a stately Oak I cast mine Eye,
Whose ruffling top the Clouds seem'd to aspire;
How long since thou wast in thine Infancy?
Thy strength, and stature, more thy years admire,
Hath hundred winters past since thou wast born?
Or thousand since thou brakest thy shell of horn,
If so, all these as nought, Eternity doth scorn.

4

Then higher on the glistering Sun I gaz'd,
Whose beams was shaded by the leavie Tree,
The more I look'd, the more I grew amaz'd,
And softly said, what glory's like to thee?
Soul of this world, this Universes Eye,
No wonder, some made thee a Deity:
Had I not better known, (alas) the same had I.

5

Thou as a Bridegroom from thy Chamber rushes,
And as a strong man, joyes to run a race,
The morn doth usher thee, with smiles & blushes,
The Earth reflects her glances in thy face.
Birds, insects, Animals with Vegative,
Thy heat from death and dulness doth revive:
And in the darksome womb of fruitful nature dive.

6

Thy swift Annual, and diurnal Course,
Thy daily streight, and yearly oblique path,
Thy pleasing fervor, and thy scorching force,
All mortals here the feeling knowledg hath.
Thy presence makes it day, thy absence night,
Quaternal Seasons caused by thy might:
Hail Creature, full of sweetness, beauty & delight.

7

Art thou so full of glory, that no Eye
Hath strength, thy shining Rayes once to behold?
And is thy splendid Throne erect so high?
As to approach it, can no earthly mould.
How full of glory then must thy Creator be?
Who gave this bright light luster unto thee:
Admir'd, ador'd for ever, be that Majesty.

8

Silent alone, where none or saw, or heard,
In pathless paths I lead my wandring feet,
My humble Eyes to lofty Skyes I rear'd
To sing some Song, my mazed Muse thought meet.
My great Creator I would magnifie,
That nature had, thus decked liberally:
But Ah, and Ah, again, my imbecility!

9

I heard the merry grashopper then sing,
The black clad Cricket, bear a second part,
They kept one tune, and plaid on the same string,
Seeming to glory in their little Art.
Shall Creatures abject, thus their voices raise?
And in their kind resound their makers praise:
Whilst I as mute, can warble forth no higher layes.

10

When present times look back to Ages past,
And men in being fancy those are dead,
It makes things gone perpetually to last,
And calls back moneths and years that long since fled
It makes a man more aged in conceit,
Then was *Methuselah*, or's grand-sire great:
While of their persons & their acts his mind doth treat.

11

Sometimes in *Eden* fair, he seems to be,
Sees glorious *Adam* there made Lord of all,
Fancyes the Apple, dangle on the Tree,
That turn'd his Sovereign to a naked thral.
Who like a miscreant's driven from that place,
To get his bread with pain, and sweat of face:
A penalty impos'd on his backsliding Race.

12

Here sits our Grandame in retired place,
And in her lap, her bloody *Cain* new born,
The weeping Imp oft looks her in the face,
Bewails his unknown hap, and fate forlorn;
His Mother sighs, to think of Paradise,
And how she lost her bliss, to be more wise,
Believing him that was, and is, Father of lyes.

13

Here *Cain* and *Abel* come to sacrifice,
Fruits of the Earth, and Fatlings each do bring,
On *Abels* gift the fire descends from Skies,
But no such sign on false *Cain's* offering;
With sullen hateful looks he goes his wayes.
Hath thousand thoughts to end his brothers dayes,
Upon whose blood his future good he hopes to raise.

14

There *Abel* keeps his sheep, no ill he thinks,
His brother comes, then acts his fratricide,
The Virgin Earth, of blood her first draught drinks
But since that time she often hath been cloy'd;
The wretch with gastly face and dreadful mind,
Thinks each he sees will serve him in his kind,
Though none on Earth but kindred near then could he find.

15

Who fancyes not his looks now at the Barr,
His face like death, his heart with horror fraught,
Nor Male-factor ever felt like warr,
When deep dispair, with wish of life hath fought,
Branded with guilt, and crusht with treble woes,
A Vagabond to Land of *Nod* he goes,
A City builds, that wals might him secure from foes.

16

Who thinks not oft upon the Fathers ages.
Their long descent, how nephews sons they saw,
The starry observations of those Sages,
And how their precepts to their sons were law,
How Adam sigh'd to see his Progeny,
Cloath'd all in his black sinfull Livery,
Who neither guilt, nor yet the punishment could fly.

17

Our life compare we with their length of dayes
Who to the tenth of theirs doth now arrive?
And though thus short, we shorten many wayes,
Living so little while we are alive;
In eating, drinking, sleeping, vain delight
So unawares comes on perpetual night,
And puts all pleasures vain unto eternal flight.

18

When I behold the heavens as in their prime,
And then the earth (though old) stil clad in green,
The stones and trees, insensible of time,
Nor age nor wrinkle on their front are seen;
If winter come, and greeness then do fade,
A Spring returns, and they more youthfull made;
But Man grows old, lies down, remains where once he's laid.

19

By birth more noble then those creatures all,
Yet seems by nature and by custome curs'd,
No sooner born, but grief and care makes fall
That state obliterate he had at first:
Nor youth, nor strength, nor wisdom spring again
Nor habitations long their names retain,
But in oblivion to the final day remain.

20

Shall I then praise the heavens, the trees, the earth
Because their beauty and their strength last longer
Shall I wish there, or never to had birth,
Because they're bigger, & their bodyes stronger?
Nay, they shall darken, perish, fade and dye,
And when unmade, so ever shall they lye,
But man was made for endless immortality.

21

Under the cooling shadow of a stately Elm
Close sate I by a goodly Rivers side,
Where gliding streams the Rocks did overwhelm;
A lonely place, with pleasures dignifi'd.
I once that lov'd the shady woods so well,
Now thought the rivers did the trees excel,
And if the sun would ever shine, there would I dwell.

22

While on the stealing stream I fixt mine eye,
Which to the long'd for Ocean held its course,
I markt, nor crooks, nor rubs that there did lye
Could hinder ought, but still augment its force:
O happy Flood, quoth I, that holds thy race
Till thou arrive at thy beloved place,
Nor is it rocks or shoals that can obstruct thy pace.

23

Nor is't enough, that thou alone may'st slide,
But hundred brooks in thy cleer waves do meet,
So hand in hand along with thee they glide
To *Thetis* house, where all imbrace and greet:
Thou Emblem true, of what I count the best,
O could I lead my Rivolets to rest,
So may we press to that vast mansion, ever blest.

24

Ye Fish which in this liquid Region 'bide,
That for each season, have your habitation,
Now salt, now fresh where you think best to glide
To unknown coasts to give a visitation,
In Lakes and ponds, you leave your numerous fry,
So nature taught, and yet you know not why,
You watry folk that know not your felicity.

25

Look how the wantons frisk to task the air,
Then to the colder bottome streight they dive,
Eftsoon to *Neptun's* glassie Hall repair
To see what trade they great ones there do drive,
Who forrage o're the spacious sea-green field,
And take the trembling prey before it yield,
Whose armour is their scales, their spreading fins their shield.

26

While musing thus with contemplation fed,
And thousand fancies buzzing in my brain,
The sweet-tongu'd Philomel percht ore my head,
And chanted forth a most melodious strain
Which rapt me so with wonder and delight,
I judg'd my hearing better then my sight,
And wisht me wings with her a while to take my flight.

27

O merry Bird (said I) that fears no snares,
That neither toyles nor hoards up in thy barn,
Feels no sad thoughts, nor cruciating cares
To gain more good, or shun what might thee harm
Thy cloaths ne're wear, thy meat is every where,
Thy bed a bough, thy drink the water cleer,
Reminds not what is past, nor whats to come dost fear.

28

The dawning morn with songs thou dost prevent,
Sets hundred notes unto thy feathered crew,
So each one tunes his pretty instrument,
And warbling out the old, begin anew,
And thus they pass their youth in summer season,
Then follow thee into a better Region,
Where winter's never felt by that sweet airy legion.

29

Man at the best a creature frail and vain,
In knowledg ignorant, in strength but weak,
Subject to sorrows, losses, sickness, pain,
Each storm his state, his mind, his body break,
From some of these he never finds cessation,
But day or night, within, without, vexation,
Troubles from foes, from friends, from dearest, near'st
     Relation.

30

And yet this sinfull creature, frail and vain,
This lump of wretchedness, of sin and sorrow,
This weather-beaten vessel wrackt with pain,
Joyes not in hope of an eternal morrow;
Nor all his losses, crosses and vexation,
In weight, in frequency and long duration
Can make him deeply groan for that divine Translation.

31

The Mariner that on smooth waves doth glide,
Sings merrily, and steers his Barque with ease,
As if he had command of wind and tide,
And now becomes great Master of the seas;
But suddenly a storm spoiles all the sport,
And makes him long for a more quiet port,
Which 'gainst all adverse winds may serve for fort.

32

So he that faileth in this world of pleasure,
Feeding on sweets, that never bit of th' sowre,
That's full of friends, of honour and of treasure,
Fond fool, he takes this earth ev'n for heav'ns bower.
But sad affliction comes & makes him see
Here's neither honour, wealth, or safety;
Only above is found all with security.

33

O Time the fatal wrack of mortal things,
That draws oblivions curtains over kings,
Their sumptuous monuments, men know them not,
Their names without a Record are forgot,
Their parts, their ports, their pomp's all laid in th' dust
Nor wit nor gold, nor buildings scape times rust;
But he whose name is grav'd in the white stone
Shall last and shine when all of these are gone.

Before the Birth of one of her Children

All things within this fading world hath end,
Adversity doth still our joyes attend;
No tyes so strong, no friends so clear and sweet,
But with deaths parting blow is sure to meet.
The sentence past is most irrevocable,
A common thing, yet oh inevitable;
How soon, my Dear, death may my steps attend,
How soon't may be thy Lot to lose thy friend,
We both are ignorant, yet love bids me
These farewell lines to recommend to thee,
That when that knot's unty'd that made us one,
I may seem thine, who in effect am none.
And if I see not half my dayes that's due,
What nature would, God grant to yours and you;
The many faults that well you know I have,
Let be interr'd in my oblivious grave;
If any worth or virtue were in me,
Let that live freshly in thy memory
And when thou feel'st no grief, as I no harms,
Yet love thy dead, who long lay in thine arms:
And when thy loss shall be repaid with gains
Look to my little babes my dear remains.
And if thou love thy self, or loved'st me
These O protect from step Dames injury.
And if chance to thine eyes shall bring this verse,
With some sad sighs honour my absent Herse;
And kiss this paper for thy loves dear sake,
Who with salt tears this last Farewel did take.

To my Dear and loving Husband

If ever two were one, then surely we.
If ever man were lov'd by wife, then thee;
If ever wife was happy in a man,
Compare with me ye women if you can.
I prize thy love more then whole Mines of gold,

Or all the riches that the East doth hold.
My love is such that Rivers cannot quench,
Nor ought but love from thee, give recompence.
Thy love is such I can no way repay,
The heavens reward thee manifold I pray.
Then while we live, in love lets so persever,
That when we live no more, we may live ever.

In memory of my dear
grand-child Elizabeth Bradstreet

who deceased August, 1665 being a year and half old

Farewel dear babe, my hearts too much content,
Farewel sweet babe, the pleasure of mine eye,
Farewel fair flower that for a space was lent,
Then ta'en away unto Eternity.
Blest babe why should I once bewail thy fate,
Or sigh thy dayes so soon were terminate;
Sith thou art setled in an Everlasting state.

2.

By nature Trees do rot when they are grown.
And Plumbs and Apples throughly ripe do fall,
And Corn and grass are in their season mown,
And time brings down what is both strong and tall.
But plants new set to be eradicate,
And buds new blown, to have so short a date,
Is by his hand alone that guides nature and fate.

On my dear Grand-child Simon Bradstreet

*Who dyed on 16. Novemb. 1669. being but
a moneth, and one day old*

No sooner come, but gone, and fal'n asleep,
Acquaintance short, yet parting caus'd us weep,
Three flours, two scarcely blown, the last i'th' bud,
Cropt by th' Almighties hand; yet is he good,
With dreadful awe before him let's be mute,
Such was his will, but why, let's not dispute,
With humble hearts and mouths put in the dust,
Let's say he's merciful, as well as just,
He will return, and make up all our losses,
And smile again, after our bitter crosses.
Go pretty babe, go rest with Sisters twain
Among the blest in endless joyes remain.

———

As weary pilgrim, now at rest
Hugs with delight his silent nest
His wasted limbes, now lye full soft
That myrie steps, have troden oft
Blesses himself, to think upon
his dangers past, and travailes done
The burning sun no more shall heat
Nor stormy raines, on him shall beat
The bryars and thornes no more shall scrat
nor hungry wolves at him shall catch
He erring pathes no more shall tread
Nor wild fruits eate, in stead of bread
for waters cold he doth not long
for thirst no more shall parch his tongue
No rugged stones his feet shall gaule
nor stumps nor rocks cause him to fall
All Cares and feares, he bids farwell
and meanes in safity now to dwell.
A pilgrim I, on earth, perplext
With sinns with cares and sorrows vext

By age and paines brought to decay
and my Clay house mouldring away
Oh how I long to be at rest
And soare on high among the blest.
This body shall in silence sleep,
Mine eyes no more shall ever weep
No fainting fits shall me assaile
nor grinding paines, my body fraile,
With cares and fears ner' cumbred be
Nor losses know, nor sorrowes see.
What tho my flesh shall there consume
it is the bed Christ did perfume
And when a few yeares shall be gone
this mortall shall be cloth'd upon
A Corrupt Carcasse downe it lyes
a glorious body it shall rise
In weaknes and dishonour sowne
in power 'tis rais'd by Christ alone
Then soule and body shall unite
and of their maker have the sight
Such lasting joyes, shall there behold
as eare ner' heard nor tongue ere told
Lord make me ready for that day
then Come deare bridgrome Come away

Aug: 31 69

To my dear children

This Book by Any yet unread,
I leave for you when I am dead,
That being gone, here you may find
What was your liveing mothers mind.
Make use of what I leave in Love
And God shall blesse you from above.

May. 13. 1657

As spring the winter doth succeed
And leaves the naked Trees doe dresse
The earth all black is cloth'd in green
At Sun-shine each their joy expresse.

My Suns return'd with healing wings
My Soul and Body doth rejoice,
My heart exults & praises sings
To him that heard my wailing Voice.

My winters past my stormes are gone
And former clowdes seem now all fled
But if they must eclipse again
I'le run where I was succoured.

I have a shelter from the storm
A shadow from the fainting heat
I have accesse unto his Throne,
Who is a God so wondrous great.

O hast thou made my pilgrimage
Thus pleasant fair and good,
Blessd me in Youth, and elder Age
My Baca made a springing flood?

I studious am what I shall doe
To show my Duty with delight
All I can give is but thine own
And at the most a simple mite.

Upon my dear & loving husband his goeing into England

Jan. 16. 1661

O thou most high who rulest All
And hear'st the prayers of Thine
O hearken Lord unto my suit
And my petition signe.

Into thy Everlasting Armes
Of mercy I commend
Thy servant Lord. Keep & preserve
My husband, my dear freind.

At thy comand O Lord he went
Nor nought could keep him back
Then let thy promis joy his heart
O help and bee not slack.

Uphold my heart in Thee O God
Thou art my strenght and stay;
Thou see'st how weak & frail I am,
Hide not thy face Away.

I in obedience to thy Will
Thou knowest did submitt
It was my Duty so to doe
O Lord accept of it.

Unthankfullnes for mercyes past
Impute thou not to me
O Lord thou know'st my weak desires
Was to sing praise to Thee.

Lord bee thou pilott to the ship
And send them prosperous gailes
In stormes and sicknes Lord preserve.
Thy Goodnes never failes.

Unto thy Work he hath in hand
Lord graunt thou good Successe
And favour in their eyes to whom
He shall make his Addresse.

Rember Lord thy folk whom thou
To Wildernesse ha'st brought
Let not thine own Inheritance
Bee sold away for Nought.

But Tokens of thy favour Give,
With Joy lend back my Dear
That I and all thy servants may
Rejoice with heavenly chear—

Lord let my Eyes see once Again
Him whom thou gavest me
That wee together may sing praise
For ever unto Thee.

And the Remainder of our Dayes
Shall consecrated bee
With an Engaged heart to sing
All praises unto Thee.

———

In silent night when rest I took
For sorrow neer I did not look,
I waken'd was with thundring nois
And piteous shreiks of dreadfull voice.
That fearfull sound of fire and fire,
Let no man know is my Desire.
I starting up the light did spye,
And to my God my heard did cry
To strenghten me in my Distresse
And not to leave me succourlesse.
Then coming out beheld a space
The flame consume my dwelling place,
And when I could no longer look
I blest his Name that gave & took,

That layd my goods now in the dust
Yea so it was, and so 'twas just.
It was his own it was not mine
Far be it that I should repine,
He might of All justly bereft,
But yet sufficient for us left.
When by the Ruines oft I past
My sorrowing eyes aside did cast
And here and there the places spye
Where oft I sate and long did lye,
Here stood that Trunk, and there that chest
There lay that store I counted best
My pleasant things in ashes lye
And them behold no more shall I.
Under thy roof no guest shall sitt,
Nor at thy Table eat a bitt.
No pleasant tale shall 'ere be told
Nor things recounted done of old.
No Candle 'ere shall shine in Thee
Nor bridegroom's voice ere heard shall bee.
In silence ever shalt thou lye
Adeiu, Adeiu, All's Vanity.
Then streight I 'gin my heart to chide,
And did thy wealth on earth abide,
Didst fix thy hope on mouldring dust,
The arm of flesh didst make thy trust?
Raise up thy thoughts above the skye
That dunghill mists away may flie.
Thou hast an house on high erect
Fram'd by that mighty Architect,
With glory richly furnished
Stands permanent tho: this bee fled.
'Its purchased & paid for too
By him who hath Enough to doe.
A prise so vast as is unknown
Yet by his Gift is made thine own.
Ther's wealth enough I need no more,
Farewell my pelf, farewell my Store.
The world no longer let me Love
My hope, and Treasure lyes Above.

JOHN SAFFIN

(1626–1710)

Sweetly (my Dearest) I left thee asleep
Which Silent parting made my heart to weep,
Faine would I wake her, but Love did Reply
O wake her not, So sweetly let her Lye.
But must I goe, O must I Leave her So,
So ill at Ease: involv'd in Slumbering wo
Must I goe hence: and thus my Love desert
Unknown to Her, O must I now Depart;
Thus was I hurried with such thoughts as these,
Yet loath to Rob the of thy present Ease,
Or rather senceless payn: farewell thought I,
My Joy my Deare in whom I live or Dye
Farewell Content, farewell fare Beauty's light
And the most pleasing Object of my Sight;
I must begone, Adieu my Dear, Adieu
Heavens grant good Tideings I next heare from you
Thus in sad Silence I alone and mute,
My lips bad thee farewell, with a Salute.
And so went from thee; turning back againe
I thought one kiss to little then Stole twaine
And then another: but no more of this,
Count with your Self how many of them you miss.
And now my love soon let me from the heare
Of thy good health, that may my Spirits Cheare
Acquaint me with such passages as may
Present themselves since I am come away
And above all things let me thee Request
To bee both Chearfull quiet and at Rest
In thine own Spirit, and let nothing move
Thee unto Discontent my Joy my Love.
Hopeing that all things shall at last Conduce
Unto our Comfort and a Blessed use
Considering that those things are hardly gain'd
Are most Delightfull when they are Attain'd.
Gold Crowns are heavy: Idalian Burn's

And Lovers Days are good, and bad by turn's
But yet the Consummation will Repay
The Debt that's due many a happy Day
Which that it may so be, Ile Heaven Implore
To grant the fame henceforth forever more
And so farewell, farewell fair Beautys light
Ten thousand times Adieu my Dear Delight.
   Your Ever loveing friend whilest Hee
   Desolved is: or Cease to bee.

To his Excellency Joseph Dudley Eqr Gover: &c

Sr: My humble Muse Sad, and in lonely State
   On various things doth meekly Contemplate
   And now presumes to give Her sober Sence
   Of what She deemes concerns your Excellence.
   Yet some perhaps more gratefull might Reveale
   What they through fear, or bye Respects Conseale.
   When Erst that Noble Bassa dar'd to tell
   The Grand Amurath (plaine) he did not well
   T' Omit his great Affaires of State (unarm'd)
   Was by the Beauty of his Captive Charm'd;
   On which (adds he) your Vassalls all amated,
   Say you your Ancestors han't Imitated;
   In Glorious Atchievements.
   And now Great Sir, my loyalty Comands
   Me thus to put my life into your hands:
   To act towards me as you please at Leasure
   I humbly Bow unto your Royall Pleasure.
   Thus Said, the Sultan gravely did Reply,
   I pardon this thy Bold Temerity;
   And thee Comand forth with the Estates Convene
   And thou shalt Shortly see another Seene.
   Then why may'nt I by way of Imitation
   Speak Truth to you, though in a lower Station
   And through unfeined love presume to Say
   What may be usefull unto you this Day:
   Who am your faithfull Servant, (though forsaken)

Your Excellence hath not fitt Measures taken;
In the due Conduct of your Government,
Which has Occasiond so much discontent
Among your people: if you they have not hated,
Yet to your Self, their Love is much abated;
I need not name particulars, They Strang
In Church and Comon weale there's such a Chang
Made, and Endeavour'd, in so Short a Space
Which threatens all Our Priviledge to Rase;
And if Accomplished would surely then:
Cause us to Cease to be Right Englishman.

Now if you think these Hints proceed from mee
I doe assure you tis Vox Populi:
And if I miss not much in my Account
If you persist therein, 'Twill you Dismount;
Sure Wisest Princes all Endeavours prove
To gaine and keep their loyall Subjects Love
For as Lord Burleigh to that Queen said do
But gaine their Hearts, you've hands, and purses to.
And that wise Queen in working Reformation,
Wrought gradually, not Sudden Alteration.
And tis a Rule to which all men Consent,
That violent motions are not Permanent.
And he that manageth Affaires of State
Had need beware, he Don't Precipitate.

You know what Phoebus Said to Phaeton,
When he would Rule the Chariot of the Sun:
Me Imitate, the Tracts thy wheeles will guide
For bear the whip, and doe not over Ride.

And now, Sir, Though my life's not in your hand,
Yet is my welfare much at your Comand:
Zeale me incites these Memoires (as tis meet)
To lay them at your Excellencys feet;
It may perhaps Displease, if so it do
Sure love and honour me Constraines thereto:
And I Remember what the Wiseman Sed,
Tis better be Reprov'd, than flattered;

And he more favouer afterwards shall finde
Than he that Sailes with Every Blast of winde
But if to speak the Truth be Deem'd a Crime,
We may conclude it is an Evil time.

From him who honoureth your Excellence
Though not Regarded with that Recompence
John Saffin

or

From him though Aged, is not whimsey Pated,
Or prone to Dote, nor Superannuated.

EDMUND HICKERINGILL

(1631–1708)

FROM

Jamaica Viewed

Under the Line that equal's night and day
Guiana stands, part of *America*:
On whose head *Phœbus* shoots his fiery steams,
Twice every year, with down-right darted beams.
In his *Twelve Houses*, as he travells forth
Alongst the *Zodiack*, 'twixt the South and North.
Whose Native *Indian* hath not, nor needs Art
To clothe himself, Nature supplies that Part.
They're true Philosophers, not much they have,
Nor do they want much, nor much do they crave.
They care not for the morrow; no supply
But just from hand to mouth, no Granary:
If they want Flesh, they take their bow in hand.
And then for Hare or Deer, hunt o're the Land.
For all Game here most eas'ly take be,
Since they take Covert in some hollow Tree.
Or some such crazie Refuge, whence they are
Dig'd forth at leisure for the Hunters fare.
Or if the stomach do in Fish delight,
With wily Feats he gluts his appetite.
His Bread and drink both made of one root are,
Cassawder call'd, cook'd by the womens care;
Who shew their best of duty to their Home,
When their Mates wearied with their Booties come.
For every man in's House is Lord and King,
Hath pow'r of life and death, and every thing:
His will's his law, from him there's no appeal,
No other Monarchy or Commonweale.
If Wives and Children offenders are,
His will's the Judge, hand, Executioner:
To none but to their chief, they Homage owe,
That's th' Eldest Son, when marry'd, t'him they bowe,

His Father, Mother, Brethren, Nephews, all;
Must low'r to him, and on the knee must fall:
Till his first Son be married, then he
(Depos'd) must to his own Son bend the knee.
Thus do they live by families, thus then
They're alwaies govern'd by middle-ag'd men.
When any dyes, into his Urne is hurl'd
All that he hath; (to use, i' th' other world:)
His Axe, Bill, Knife, his Bow and Hammock too,
And this the best of service they can doe
For their dead Friend. If he a Captain be,
Then if he have a Slave, he then must die;
And the same Roge burn both; thus is supply'd
Each one i' th' other world, as 'fore he dy'd.
But usually their Slaves when captive ta'ne,
Are to the *English* sold; and some are slain,
And their flesh forthwith Barbacu'd and eat
By them, their Wives and Children as choice meat.
Thence are they call'd *Caribs*, or *Cannibals*;
The very same that we *Man-eaters* cal.
And yet herein lies not their chief content
To eat for food, but as a Sacrament;
To bind them and their Children to be fierce,
And into th'entrails of their foes to pierce.
Though in the world no greater Cowards be,
Managing all their Fights with treachery,
Most of their feats by stealth and night are done,
If once it come to handy-gripes, they run.
Thus much I'le say; I would not wish to have
A better friend, or foe, or better slave
Than is an *Indian*; where he once affects,
In love and service shall be no neglects.
Command him as your slave, his life, his All,
If he do once you, but *Bone-aree* call;
And who would wish an easier foe, then he,
That (like a Buck) at noise of Guns will flie,
But then your slave if that an *Indian* be,
No other Caterer you need but he.
He plenty shall provide for yours and you,
With his Dogs only, and his Bill and Bow.

And thus much for their Men. Their Women are
Lovely, though brown; modest, hiding their Ware,
With several colour'd Beads together knit,
With Art methodical together set;
And this they use whilest they are young and fair,
But when they're old, their heedlesse, all is bare.
If of your Wine and Brandee, youl'e be free,
The'le not leave till they drunk as beggars be.
They call the Devil *Yerkin*, him alone
They worship, saying, God wills harm to none,
But is intirely good; and therefore they,
The mercy of their *Yerkin* only pray.
When they are sick, *Yerkin* doth bear the blame,
Of him they beg deliverance from the same,
The Muses and their Flamens they cashiere,
Only *Diana*'s Troops are 'stablish'd here
Except some Priests, which they do call *Peei*,
With mumbling Charms *Yerkin* to pacifie.
(In sum to say) They're all simplicity,
Almost like *Adam*, in's innocency.
Whatever Nature or their Appetite
Does dictate; they do follow with delight,
Not once with conscience check embittered,
Being by the law of nature only led.
Not coveting large Barns, with hoards to stuffe,
When once their belly's full, they have enough;
For *Avarice*, here never makes them jarre,
Nor warrants, by religion's varnish, warre.
His pride so natural, (if't be a vice,)
Yet costs him nothing or but little Price;
It never makes him sell his land, nor shut
Shop-windows up, nor a spare Jewel put
To trouble, in a Pawne for Cloak or Gown.
His only pride's a Feather in his Crown:
The cast-clothes of some gaudy Bird fits him,
For which he needs not venture life nor limb,
Nor *Hector* it, nor list under Sir *Hugh*,
(When known by the old suit, to fish for new;)
Nor crindge to Velvet Title, with a gape,
Like fawning Curre, or mopping Jack-an-Ape:

Nor need to be light-finger'd in a crowd;
Nor light heel'd to procure a Scarfe or Hood
Nor with stretch'd Fancies beg a Ladies smile,
Which she (poor soul) scarce understands the while.
They make no Mintage here of Braines, nor be
The *sterling* Pence coyn'd with a Comœdie.
For pomp and fine clothes only are the cause
Of all our shirking Trades, and endlesse lawes.
Since Nature ne're brought forth a Creature yet,
Unfurnish'd, with what Coverlets were fit.
The Back (if not misus'd) in coldest Land,
Craving no waste cloathes, more then face or hands.

MICHAEL WIGGLESWORTH

(1631–1705)

A Song of Emptiness
To fill up the Empty Pages following

Vanity of Vanities

Vain, frail, short liv'd, and miserable Man,
Learn what thou art when thine estate is best:
A restless Wave o'th' troubled Ocean,
A Dream, a lifeless Picture finely drest:

A Wind, a Flower, a Vapour, and a Bubble,
A Wheel that stands not still, a trembling Reed,
A rolling Stone, dry Dust, light Chaff, and Stubble,
A Shadow of Something, but nought indeed.

Learn what deceitful toyes, and empty things,
This World, and all its best Enjoyments bee:
Out of the Earth no true Contentment springs,
But all things here are vexing Vanitee.

For what is *Beauty*, but a fading Flower?
Or what is *Pleasure*, but the Devils bait,
Whereby he catcheth whom he would devour,
And multitudes of Souls doth ruinate?

And what are *Friends* but mortal men, as we?
Whom Death from us may quickly separate;
Or else their hearts may quite estranged be,
And all their love be turned into hate.

And what are *Riches* to be doted on?
Uncertain, fickle, and ensnaring things;
They draw Mens Souls into Perdition,
And when most needed, take them to their wings.

Ah foolish Man! that sets his heart upon
Such empty Shadows, such wild Fowl as these,
That being gotten will be quickly gone,
And whilst they stay increase but his disease

As in a Dropsie, drinking draughts begets,
The more he drinks, the more he still requires:
So on this World whoso affection sets,
His Wealths encrease encreaseth his desires.

O happy Man, whose portion is above,
Where Floods, where Flames, where Foes cannot bereave him;
Most wretched man, that fixed hath his love
Upon this World, that surely will deceive him!

For, what is *Honour*? What is *Sov'raignty*,
Whereto mens hearts so restlessly aspire?
Whom have they Crowned with Felicity?
When did they ever satisfie desire?

The Ear of Man with hearing is not fill'd:
To see new sights still coveteth the Eye:
The craving Stomack though it may be still'd,
Yet craves again without a new supply.

All Earthly things, man's Cravings answer not,
Whose little heart would all the World contain,
(If all the World should fall to one man's Lot)
And notwithstanding empty still remain.

The *Eastern Conquerour* was said to weep,
When he the *Indian* Ocean did view,
To see his Conquest bounded by the Deep,
And no more Worlds remaining to subdue.

Who would that man in his Enjoyments bless,
Or envy him, or covet his estate,
Whose gettings do augment his greediness,
And make his wishes more intemperate?

Such is the wonted and the common guise
Of those on Earth that bear the greatest Sway:
If with a few the case be otherwise
They seek a Kingdom that abides for ay.

Moreover they, of all the Sons of men,
that Rule, and are in highest places set,
Are most inclin'd to scorn their Bretheren
And God himself (without great grace) forget.

For as the Sun doth blind the gazer's eyes,
That for a time they nought discern aright:
So Honour doth befool and blind the Wise,
And their own Lustre 'reaves them of their sight.

Great are their Dangers, manifold their Cares,
Thro which, whilst others Sleep, they scarcely Nap;
And yet are oft surprized unawares,
And fall unweeting into Envies Trap.

The mean Mechanick finds his kindly rest,
All void of fear Sleepeth the County-Clown,
When greatest Princes often are distrest,
And cannot Sleep upon their Beds of Down.

Could *Strength* or *Valour* men Immortalize,
Could *Wealth* or *Honour* keep them from decay,
There were some cause the same to Idolize,
And give the lye to that which I do say.

But neither can such things themselves endure
Without the hazard of a Change one hour,
Nor such as trust in them can they secure
From dismal dayes, or Deaths prevailing pow'r.

If *Beauty* could the beautiful defend
From Death's dominion, than fair *Absalom*
Had not been brought to such a shameful end:
But fair and foul into the Grave must come.

If *Wealth* or *Scepters* could Immortal make,
then wealthy *Croesus*, wherefore art thou dead?
If *Warlike force*, which makes the World to quake,
Then why is *Julius Caesar* perished?

Where are the *Scipio's* Thunder-bolts of War?
Renowned *Pompey*, *Caesars* Enemie?
Stout *Hannibal*, *Romes* Terror known so far?
Great *Alexander*, what's become of thee?

If *Gifts* and *Bribes* Death's favour might but win,
If *Power*, if force, or *Threatnings* might it fray,
All these, and more, had still surviving been:
But all are gone, for Death will have no Nay.

Such is this World with all her Pomp and Glory,
Such are the men whom worldly eyes admire:
Cut down by Time, and now become a Story,
That we might after better things aspire.

Go boast thy self of what thy heart enjoyes,
Vain Man! triumph in all thy worldly Bliss:
Thy best enjoyments are but Trash and Toyes:
Delight thy self in that which worthless is.

Omnia praetereunt praeter amare Deum.

FROM
The Day of Doom

I

Still was the night, Serene and Bright,
   When all Men sleeping lay;
Calm was the season, and carnal reason
   Thought so 'twould last for ay.

The security
of the World
before Christs
coming to
Judgment.
Luke 12:19.

Soul, take thine ease, let sorrow cease,
   much good thou has in store:
This was their Song, their Cups among,
   the Evening before.

2

Wallowing in all kind of sin,
   vile wretches lay secure:
The best of men had scarcely then
   their Lamps kept in good ure.   Matt. 25:5.
Virgins unwise, who through disguise
   amongst the best were number'd,
Had clos'd their eyes; yea, and the wise
   through sloth and frailty slumber'd.

3

Like as of old, when Men grow bold
   God's threatnings to contemn,   Matt. 24:37,
Who stopt their Ear, and would not hear,   38.
   when Mercy warned them:
But took their course, without remorse,
   till God began to powre
Destruction the World upon
   in a tempestuous showre.

4

They put away the evil day,
   And drown'd their care and fears,
Till drown'd were they, and swept away
   by vengeance unawares:
So at the last, whilst Men sleep fast   1 Thess. 5:3.
   in their security,
Surpriz'd they are in such a snare
   as cometh suddenly.

5

For at midnight brake forth a Light,
    which turn'd the night to day,
And speedily an hideous cry
    did all the world dismay.
Sinners awake, their hearts do ake,
    trembling their loynes surprizeth;
Amaz'd with fear, by what they hear,
    each one of them ariseth.

*The Sudden-
ness, Majesty,
& Terrour of
Christ's ap-
pearing.
Matt. 25:6.
2 Pet. 3:10.*

6

They rush from Beds with giddy heads,
    and to their windows run,
Viewing this light, which shines more bright
    then doth the Noon-day Sun.
Straightway appears (they see't with tears)
    the Son of God most dread;
Who with his Train comes on amain
    To Judge both Quick and Dead.

*Matt. 24:29,
30.*

7

Before his face the Heav'ns gave place,
    and Skies are rent asunder,
With mighty voice, and hideous noise,
    more terrible than Thunder.
His brightness damps heav'ns glorious lamps
    and makes them hide their heads,
As if afraid and quite dismay'd,
    they quit their wonted steads.

2 Pet. 3:10.

8

Ye sons of men that durst contemn
    the Threatnings of Gods Word,
How cheer you now? your hearts, I trow,
    are thrill'd as with a sword.

Now Atheist blind, whose brutish mind
  a God could never see,
Dost thou perceive, dost now believe,
  that Christ thy Judge shall be?

9

Stout Courages, (whose hardiness
  could Death and Hell out-face)
Are you as bold now you behold
  your Judge draw near apace?
They cry, no, no: Alas! and wo!
  our Courage all is gone:
Our hardiness (fool hardiness)
  hath us undone, undone.

10

No heart so bold, but now grows cold
  and almost dead with fear:
No eye so dry, but now can cry,   Rev. 6:16.
  and pour out many a tear.
Earths Potentates and pow'rful States,
  Captains and Men of Might
Are quite abasht, their courage dasht
  at this most dreadful sight.

11

Mean men lament, great men do rent
  their Robes, and tear their hair:
They do not spare their flesh to tear   Matt. 24:30.
  through horrible despair.
All Kindreds wail: all hearts do fail:
  horror the world doth fill
With weeping eyes, and loud out-cries,
  yet knows not how to kill.

12

Some hide themselves in Caves and Delves,   Rev. 6:15, 16.
  in places under ground:
Some rashly leap into the Deap,
  to scape by being drown'd:
Some to the Rocks (O sensless blocks!)
  and woody Mountains run,
That there they might this fearful sight,
  and dreaded Presence shun.

13

In vain do they to Mountains say,
  Fall on us, and us hide
From Judges ire, more hot than fire,
  for who may it abide?
No hiding place can from his Face,
  sinners at all conceal,
Whose flaming Eyes hid things doth 'spy,
  and darkest things reveal.

14

The Judge draws nigh, exalted high
  upon a lofty Throne,
Amidst the throng of Angels strong,   Matt. 25:31.
  lo, Israel's Holy One!
The excellence of whose presence
  and awful Majesty
Amazeth nature, and every Creature,
  doth more than terrify.

15

The Mountains smoak, the Hills are shook,   Rev. 6:14.
  the Earth is rent and torn,
As if she should be clean dissolv'd,
  or from the center born.

The Sea doth roar, forsakes the shore,
   and shrinks away for fear;
The wild Beasts flee into the Sea,
   so soon as he draws near.

16

Whose Glory bright, whose wondrous might,
   whose Power Imperial,
So far surpass whatever was
   in Realms Terrestrial;
That tongues of mean (nor Angels pen)
   cannot the same express,
And therefore I must pass it by,
   lest speaking should transgress.

17

Before his Throne a Trump is blown,
   Proclaiming th' Day of Doom:
Forthwith he cries, Ye Dead arise,
   and unto Judgment come.
No sooner said, but 'tis obey'd;
   Sepulchers open'd are:
Dead Bodies all rise at his call,
   and's mighty power declare.

1 Thess. 4:16.
Resurrection
of the Dead.
John 5:28, 29.

18

Both Sea and Land, at his Command,
   their Dead at once surrender:
The Fire and Air constrained are
   also their dead to tender.
The mighty word of this great Lord
   links Body and Soul together
Both of the Just, and the unjust,
   to part no more for ever.

19

The same translates, from Mortal states
   to Immortality,
All that survive, and be alive,
   i'th' twinkling of an eye:
That so they may abide for ay
   to endless weal or woe;
Both the Renate and Reprobate
   are made to dy no more.

*The living
Changed.*

*Luke 20:36.
1 Cor. 15:52.*

20

His winged Hosts flie through all Coasts,
   together gathering
Both good and bad, both quick and dead,
   and all to Judgment bring.
Out of their holes those creeping Moles,
   that hid themselves for fear,
By force they take, and quickly make
   before the Judge appear.

*All brought
to Judgment.
Matt. 24:31.*

21

Thus every one before the Throne
   of Christ the Judge is brought,
Both righteous and impious
   that good or ill had wrought.
A separation, and diff'ring station
   by Christ appointed is
(To sinners sad) 'twixt good and bad,
   'twixt Heirs of woe and bliss.

*2 Cor. 5:10.
The Sheep
separated
from the
Goats.
Matt. 25:32.*

22

At Christ's right hand the Sheep do stand,
   his holy Martyrs, who
For his dear Name suffering shame,
   calamity and woe,

*Who are
Christ's
Sheep.
Matt. 5:10, 11.*

Like Champions stood, & with their Blood
    their testimony sealed;
Whose innocence without offence,
    to Christ their Judge appealed.

23

Next unto whom there find a room
    all Christ's afflicted ones,
Who being chastised, neither despised
    nor sank amidst their groans:
Who by the Rod were turn'd to God,
    and loved him the more,
Not murmuring nor quarrelling
    when they were chast'ned sore.

Heb. 12:5, 6, 7.

24

Moreover, such as loved much,
    that had not such a tryal,
As might constrain to so great pain,
    and such deep self denyal:
Yet ready were the Cross to bear,
    when Christ them call'd thereto,
And did rejoyce to hear his voice,
    they're counted Sheep also.

Luke 7:41, 47.

25

Christ's Flock of Lambs there also stands,
    whose Faith was weak, yet true;
All sound Believers (Gospel receivers)
    whose Grace was small, but grew:
And them among an Infant throng
    of Babes, for whom Christ dy'd;
Whom for his own, by wayes unknown
    to men, he sanctify'd.

John 21:15.
Matt. 19:14.
John 3:3.

26

All stand before their Saviour
    in long white Robes yclad,
Their countenance full of pleasance,
    appearing wondrous glad.
O glorious sight! Behold how bright
    dust heaps are made to shine,
Conformed so their Lord unto,
    whose Glory is Divine.

Rev. 6:11.
Phil. 3:21.

27

At Christ's left hand the Goats do stand,
    all whining hypocrites,
Who for self-ends did seem Christ's friends,
    but foster'd guileful sprites:
Who Sheep resembled, but they dissembled
    (their hearts were non sincere);
Who once did throng Christ's Lambs among,
    but now must not come near.

*The Goats
described or
the several
sorts of
Reprobates
on the left
hand.
Matt. 24:51.*

28

Apostates and Run-awayes,
    such as have Christ forsaken,
Of whom the devil, with seven more evil,
    hath fresh possession taken:
Sinners in grain, reserv'd to pain
    and torments more severe:
Because 'gainst light they sinn'd with spight,
    are also placed there.

*Luke 11:24,
26.
Heb. 6:4,
5, 6.
Heb. 10:29.*

29

There also stand a num'rous band,
    that no Profession made
Of Godliness, nor to redress
    their wayes at all essay'd:

*Luke 12:47.
Prov. 1:24, 26.
John 3:19.*

Who better knew, but (sinful Crew)
   Gospel and Law despised;
Who all Christ's knocks withstood like blocks
   and would not be advised.

30

Moreover, there with them appear
   a number, numberless
Of great and small, vile wretches all,
   that did Gods Law transgress:
Idolaters, false worshippers,
   Prophaners of Gods Name,
Who not at all thereon did call,
   or took in vain the same.

Gal. 3:10.
1 Cor. 6:9.
Rev. 21:8.

31

Blasphemers lewd, and Swearers shrewd,
   Scoffers at Purity
That hated God, contemn'd his Rod,
   and lov'd Security;
Sabbath-polluters, Saints persecuters,
   Presumptuous men and Proud,
Who never lov'd those that reprov'd;
   all stand amongst this Crowd.

Exod. 20:7, 8.

2 Thess. 1:6,
8, 9.

32

Adulterers and Whoremongers
   were there, with all unchast:
There Covetous, and Ravenous,
   that Riches got too fast:
Who us'd vile ways themselves to raise
   t'Estates and worldly wealth,
Oppression by, or Knavery
   by force, or fraud, or stealth.

Heb. 13:4.
1 Cor. 6:10.

33

Moreover, there together were
   Children flagitious,
And Parents who did them undo   Zech. 5:3, 4.
   by Nurture vicious.   Gal. 5:19, 20,
False-witness-bearers, and self-forswearers   21.
   Murd'rers, and Men of blood,
Witches, Inchanters, & Ale-house-haunters,
   beyond account there stood.

34

Their place there find all Heathen blind,
   that Natures light abused,
Although they had no tydings glad   Rom. 2:13.
   of Gospel-grace refused.
There stands all Nations and Generations
   of *Adam's* Progeny,
Whom Christ redeem'd not, who Christ esteem'd not,
   through Infidelity.

35

Who no Peace-maker, no Undertaker,   Acts. 4:12.
   to shrow'd them from Gods ire
Ever obtain'd; they must be pained
   with everlasting fire.
These num'rous bands, wringing their hands,
   and weeping, all stand there,
Filled with anguish, whose hearts do languish
   through self-tormenting fear.

36

Fast by them stand at Christ's left hand
   the Lion fierce and fell,
The Dragon bold, that Serpent old,
   that hurried Souls to Hell.

There also stand, under command,   1 Cor. 6:3.
   Legions of Sprights unclean,
And hellish Fiends, that are no friends
   to God, nor unto Men.

37

With dismal chains, and strongest reins,
   like Prisoners of Hell,
They're held in place before Christ's face,   Jude 6.
   till He their Doom shall tell.
These void of tears, but fill'd with fears,
   and dreadful expectation
Of endless pains, and scalding flames,
   stand waiting for Damnation.

38

All silence keep, both Goats and Sheep,
   before the Judge's Throne;
With mild aspect to his Elect   The Saints
   then spake the Holy One;   cleared
                                                 & justified.
My Sheep draw near, your Sentence hear,
   which is to you no dread,
Who clearly now discern, and know
   your sins are pardoned.

39

'Twas meet that ye should judged be,   2 Cor. 5:10.
   that so the world may spy   Eccles. 3:17.
                                                 John 3:18.
No cause of grudge, when as I Judge
   and deal impartially.
Know therefore all, both great and small,
   the ground and reason why
These Men do stand at my right hand,
   and look so chearfully.

40

These Men be those my Father chose   John 17:6.
   before the worlds foundation,   Eph. 1:4.
And to me gave, that I should save
   from Death and Condemnation.
For whose dear sake I flesh did take,
   was of a Woman born,
And did inure my self t'indure,
   unjust reproach and scorn.

41

For them it was that I did pass
   through sorrows many one:
That I drank up that bitter Cup,
   which made me sigh and groan.   Rev. 1:5.
The Cross his pain I did sustain;
   yea more, my Fathers ire
I underwent, my Blood I spent
   to save them from Hell fire.

42

Thus I esteem'd, thus I redeem'd
   all these from every Nation,
That they may be (as now you see)
   a chosen Generation.
What if ere-while they were as vile,
   and bad as any be,   Eph. 2:1, 3.
And yet from all their guilt and thrall
   at once I set them free?

43

My grace to one is wrong to none:
   none can Election claim,   Matt. 20:13,
Amongst all those their souls that lose,   15.
   none can Rejection blame.   Rom. 9:20,
                                                 21.

He that may chuse, or else refuse,
   all men to save or spill,
May this Man chuse, and that refuse,
   redeeming whom he will.

    44

But as for those whom I have chose   Isa. 53:4, 5, 11.
   Salvations heirs to be,
I underwent their punishment,
   and therefore set them free;
I bore their grief, and their relief
   by suffering procur'd,
That they of bliss and happiness
   might firmly be assur'd.

    45

And this my grace they did imbrace,   Acts. 13:48.
   believing on my Name;   James 2:18.
Which Faith was true, the fruits do shew   Heb. 12:7.
   proceeding from the same: Matt. 19:29.
Their Penitence, their Patience,
   their Love and Self-denial
In suffering losses, and bearing Crosses,
   when put upon the tryal.

    46

Their sin forsaking, their chearful taking
   my yoke, their Charity
Unto the Saints in all their wants,   1 John 3:3.
   and in them unto me,   Matt. 25:39,
These things do clear, and make appear 40.
   their Faith to be unfaigned,
And that a part in my desert
   and purchase they have gained.

47

Their debts are paid, their peace is made,
    their sins remitted are;
Therefore at once I do pronounce,
    and openly declare:
That Heav'n is theirs, that they be Heirs
    of Life and of Salvation!
Nor ever shall they come at all
    to Death or to Damnation.

Isa. 53:11, 12.
Rom. 8:16, 17, 33, 34.

John. 3:18.

48

Come, Blessed Ones, and sit on Thrones,
    Judging the World with me:
Come, and possess your happiness,
    and bought felicitie.
Henceforth no fears, no care, no tears,
    no sin shall you annoy,
Nor any thing that grief doth bring:
    Eternal Rest enjoy.

Luke 22:29, 30.
Matt. 19:28.

49

You bore the Cross, you suffered loss
    of all for my Names sake:
Receive the Crown that's now your own;
    come, and a Kingdom take.
Thus spake the Judge; the wicked grudge,
    and grind their teeth in vain;
They see with groans these plac't on Thrones
    which addeth to their pain:

Matt. 25:34.
They are placed on Thrones to joyn with Christ in judging the wicked.

50

That those whom they did wrong & slay,
    must now their judgment see!
Such whom they slighted, & once despighted,
    must now their Judges be!

Thus 'tis decreed, such is their meed,
   and guerdon glorious!   1 Cor. 6:2.
With Christ they sit, Judging is fit
   to plague the Impious.

51

The wicked are brought to the Bar,   The wicked
   like guilty Malefactors,   brought
                                        to the Bar.
That oftentimes of bloody Crimes   Rom. 2:3,
   and Treasons have been Actors.   6, 11.
Of wicked Men, none are so mean
   as there to be neglected:
Nor none so high in dignity,
   as there to be respected.

52

The glorious Judge will priviledge   Rev. 6:15, 16.
   nor Emperour, nor King: Isa. 30:33.
But every one that hath mis-done
   doth unto Judgment bring.
And every one that hath mis-done,
   the Judge impartially
Condemneth to eternal wo,
   and endless misery.

53

Thus one and all, thus great and small,
   the Rich as well as Poor,
And those of place as the most base,
   do stand the Judge before.
They are arraign'd, and there detain'd,
   before Christ's Judgement-seat
With trembling fear, their Doom to hear
   and feel his angers heat.

54

There Christ demands at all their hands
   a strict and strait account
Of all things done under the Sun,
   whose number far surmount
Man's wit & thought: yet all are brought
   unto this solemn Tryal;
And each offence with evidence,
   so that there's no denial.

Eccles. 11:9;
12:14.

55

There's no excuses for their abuses,
   since their own Consciences
More proof give in of each Man's sin,
   than thousand Witnesses,
Though formerly this faculty
   had grosly been abused,
Men could it stifle, or with it trifle,
   when as it them accused.

56

Now it comes in, and every sin
   unto Mens charge doth lay:
It judgeth them, and doth condemn,
   though all the world say nay.
It so stingeth and tortureth,
   it worketh such distress,
That each Man's self against himself,
   is forced to confess.

57

It's vain, moreover, for Men to cover
   the least iniquity:
The Judge hath seen, and privy been
   to all their villany.

Secret sins
and works
of darkness
brought
to light.

He unto light, and open sight
  the works of darkness brings:
He doth unfold both new and old,
  both known and hidden things.

Ps. 139:2,
4, 12.
Rom. 2:16.

58

All filthy facts, and secret acts,
  however closely done,
And long conceal'd, are there reveal'd
  before the mid-day Sun.
Deeds of the night shunning the light,
  which darkest corners sought,
To fearful blame, and endless shame,
  are there most justly brought.

Eccles. 12:14.

59

And as all facts and grosser acts,
  so every word and thought,
Erroneous notion, and lustful motion,
  are unto judgment brought,
No sin so small and trivial
  but hither it must come:
Nor so long past, but now at last
  it must receive a doom.

Matt. 12:36.
Rom. 7:7.

60

At this sad season, Christ asks a Reason
  (with just Austerity)
Of Grace refused, of light abus'd
  so oft, so wilfully:
Of Talents lent by them mispent,
  and on their Lust bestown;
Which if improv'd, as it behov'd,
  Heav'n might have been their own!

An account
demanded
of all their
actions.
John 5:40;
3:19.
Matt. 25:19,
27.

61

Of times neglected, of means rejected,
  of God's long-suffering,
And Patience, to Penitence   Rom. 2:4, 5.
  that sought hard hearts to bring.
Why Cords of love did nothing move
  to shame or to remorse?
Why warnings grave, and counsels, have
  nought chang'd their sinful course?

62

Why chastenings, and evil things,
  why judgments so severe
Prevailed not with them a jot,   Isa. 1:5.
  nor wrought an awful fear?
Why Promises of Holiness,   Jer. 2:20.
  and new Obedience,
They oft did make, but always brake
  the same, to God's offence?

63

Why still Hell-ward, without regard,
  they boldly ventured,   John 3:19, 20.
And chose Damnation before Salvation,   Prov. 8:36.
  when it was offered: Luke 1:20, 21.
Why sinful pleasures, & earthly treasures,
  like fools, they prized more
Than heav'nly wealth, Eternal health,
  and all Christ's Royal store.

64

Why, when he stood off'ring his Blood   Luke 13:34.
  to wash them from their sin,   John 5:40;
They would embrace no saving Grace,   15:22.
  but liv'd and dy'd therein?

Such aggravations, where no evasions,
    nor false pretences hold,
Exaggerate and cumulate
    guilt more than can be told.

65

They multiply and magnify
    mens gross iniquities,
They draw down wrath (as Scripture saith)
    out of Gods treasuries.
Thus all their ways Christ opens lays
    to men and Angels view,
And, as they were, makes them appear
    in their own proper hew.

66

Thus he doth find all of Mankind,
    that stand at his left hand,   Rom. 3:10, 12.
No Mothers Son, but hath mis-done,
    and broken God's Command.
All have transgrest, even the best,
    and merited God's wrath
Unto their own perdition,
    and everlasting scath.

67

Earths dwellers all, both great and small,   Rom. 6:23.
    have wrought iniquity,
And suffer must, for it is just,
    Eternal misery.
Amongst the many there come not any,
    before the Judge's face,
That able are themselves to clear,
    of all this cursed race.

68

Nevertheless, they all express,
   Christ granting liberty,
What for their way they have to say
   how they have liv'd, and why.
They all draw near, and seek to clear
   themselves by making pleas.
There Hypocrites, false-hearted wights,
   do make such pleas as these:

Hypocrites plead for themselves.

69

Lord, in thy Name, and by the same,
   we Devils dispossest,
We rais'd the dead, and ministred
   succour to the distrest.
Our painful teaching, & pow'rful preaching
   by thine own wondrous might,
Did throughly win to God from sin
   many a wretched wight.

Matt. 7:21, 22, 23.

70

All this, quoth he, may granted be,
   and your case little better'd,
Who still remain under a chain,
   and many irons fetter'd.
You that the dead have quickened,
   and rescu'd from the grave,
Your selves were dead, yet never ned,
   a Christ your Souls to save.

The judge replyeth. John 6:70. 1 Cor. 9:27.

71

You that could preach, and others teach
   what way to life doth lead;
Why were you slack to find that track
   and in that way to tread?

Rom. 2:19, 21, 22, 23.

How could you bear to see or hear
   of others freed at last,
From Satan's pawes, whilst in his jawes
   your selves were held more fast?

72

Who though you knew Repentance true,
   and Faith in my great Name,
The only mean to quit you clean,
   from punishment and blame,
Yet took no pain true Faith to gain,
   such as might not deceive,
Nor would repent, with true intent,
   your evil deeds to leave.

John 9:41.

Rev. 2:21, 22.

73

His Masters will how to fulfill
   the servant that well knew,
Yet left undone his duty known,
   more plagues to him are due.
You against light perverted right;
   wherefore it shall be now
For Sidon and for Sodoms Land
   more easie than for you.

Luke 12:47.
Matt. 11:21,
22, 24.

74

But we have in thy presence been,
   say some, and eaten there.
Did we not eat thy Flesh for meat,
   and feed on heavenly Cheer?
Whereon who feed shall never need,
   as thou thy self dost say,
Nor shall they dy eternally,
   but live with Christ for ay.

Another plea
of hypocrites.
Luke 13:26.

75

We may alledge, thou gav'st a pledge
    of thy dear love to us
In Wine and Bread, which figured
    thy Grace bestowed thus.
Of strengthning Seals, of sweetest Meals,
    have we so oft partaken;
And shall we be cast off by thee,
    and utterly forsaken?

76

To whom the Lord thus in a word
    returns a short reply,
I never knew any of you
    that wrought iniquity.
You say y'have been my Presence in;
    but friends, how came you there
With Raiment vile that did defile
    and quite disgrace my Cheer?

Is Answered.
Luke 13:27.
Matt. 22:12.

77

Durst you draw near without due fear
    unto my holy Table?
Durst you prophane, and render vain
    so far as you were able,
Those Mysteries? which whoso prize
    and carefully improve,
Shall saved be undoubtedly,
    and nothing shall them move.

78

How durst you venture, bold guests, to enter
    in such a sordid hew,
Amongst my guests, unto those Feasts
    that were not made for you?

1 Cor. 11:27,
29.

How durst you eat for spiritual meat
  your bane, and drink damnation,
Whilst by your guile you rendred vile
  so rare and great Salvation?

79

Your fancies fed on heav'nly Bread,
  your hearts fed on some Lust:
You lov'd the Creature more than th' Creator,
  your Souls clave to the dust.
And think you by Hypocrisie,
  and cloaked Wickedness,
To enter in, laden with sin,
  to lasting happiness?

Matt. 6:21, 24.
Rom. 1:25.

80

This your excuse shews your abuse
  of things ordain'd for good;
And doth declare you guilty are
  of my dear Flesh and Blood.
Wherefore those Seals and precious Meals
  you put so much upon
As things divine, they seal and sign
  you to Perdition.

1 Cor. 11:27, 29.

81

Then forth issue another Crew
  (those being silenced)
Who drawing high to the most High
  adventure thus to plead:
We sinners were, say they, it's clear,
  deserving Condemnation:
But did not we rely on thee,
  O Christ, for whole Salvation?

Another sort
of hypocrites
make their
pleas.

82

We did believe and oft receive
   thy gracious promises:
We took great care to get a share   Acts. 8:13.
   in endless happiness.   Isa. 58:2, 3.
      Heb. 64:5.
We pray'd & wept, we Fast-dayes kept,
   lewd ways we did eschew:
We joyful were thy Word to hear;
   we form'd our lives anew.

83

We thought our sin had pard'ned been;
   that our Estate was good,
Our debts all paid, our peace well made,
   our Souls wash'd with thy Blood.
Lord, why dost thou reject us now,   2 Pet. 2:20.
   who have not thee rejected,
Nor utterly true sanctity
   and holy life neglected.

84

The Judge incensed at their pretenced   The Judge
   self-vanting Piety,   uncaseth
      them.
With such a look as trembling strook
   into them, made reply;
O impudent, impenitent,   John 2:24, 25.
   and guileful generation!
Think you that I cannot descry
   your hearts abomination?

85

You nor receiv'd, nor yet believ'd
   my Promises of Grace;
Nor were you wise enough to prize   John 6:64.
   my reconciled Face:

But did presume that to assume
   which was not your to take,
And challenged the Children's bread,
   yet would not sin forsake.

Ps. 50:16.
Matt. 15:26.

86

Being too bold you laid fast hold,
   where int'rest you had none,
Your selves deceiving by your believing,
   all which you might have known.
You ran away, but ran astray,
   with Gospel-promises,
And perished, being still dead
   in sins and trespasses.

Rev. 3:17.

Matt. 13:20.

87

How oft did I Hypocrisie
   and Hearts deceit unmask
Before your sight, giving you light
   to know a Christians task?
But you held fast unto the last
   your own Conceits so vain:
No warning could prevail, you would
   your own Deceits retain.

Matt. 6:2,
4, 24.
Jer. 8:5, 6,
7, 8.

88

As for your care to get a share
   in bliss; the fear of Hell,
And of a part in endless smart,
   did thereunto compel.
Your holiness and ways redress,
   such as it was, did spring
From no true love to things above,
   but from some other thing.

Ps. 78:34, 35,
36, 37.

89

You pray'd & wept, you Fast-days kept;
    but did you this to me?
No, but for sin, you sought to win,
    the greater libertie.
For all your vaunts, you had vile haunts,
    for which your Consciences
Did you alarm, whose voice to charm
    you us'd these practices.

Zech. 7:5, 6.
Isa. 58:3, 4.
1 Sam. 15:13,
21.
Isa. 1:11, 15.

90

Your Penitence, your diligence
    to Read, to Pray, to Hear,
Were but to drown'd the clamorous sound
    of Conscience in your ear.
If light you lov'd, vain glory mov'd
    your selves therewith to store,
That seeming wise, men might you prize,
    and honour you the more.

Matt. 6:2, 5.
John 5:44.

91

Thus from your selves unto your selves,
    your duties all do tend;
And as self-love the wheels doth move,
    so in self-love they end.
Thus Christ detects their vain projects,
    and close Impiety,
And plainly shews that all their shows
    were but Hypocrisy.

Zech. 7:5, 6.
Hos. 10:1.

92

Then were brought nigh a Company
    of Civil honest Men,
That lov'd true dealing, and hated stealing,
    ne'r wrong'd their Bretheren;

Civil honest
mens pleas.
Luke 18:11.

Who pleaded thus, Thou knowest us
    that we were blameless livers;
No Whoremongers, no Murderers,
    no quarrelers nor strivers.

93

Idolaters, Adulterers,
    Church-robbers we were none,
Nor false-dealers, no couzeners,
    but paid each man his own.
Our way was fair, our dealing square,
    we were no wastful spenders,
No lewd toss-pots, no drunken sots,
    no scandalous offenders.

94

We hated vice, and set great price,
    by vertuous conversation:
And by the same we got a name,
    and no small commendation.
Gods Laws express that righteousness,   1 Sam. 15:22.
    is that which he doth prize;
And to obey, as he doth say,
    is more than sacrifice.

95

Thus to obey, hath been our way,
    let our good deeds, we pray,
Find some regard and some reward
    with thee, O Lord, this day.
And whereas we transgressors be,   Eccles. 7:20.
    of *Adam's* Race were none,
No not the best, but have confest
    themselves to have mis-done.

96

Then answered unto their dread,
   the Judge: True Piety
God doth desire and eke require
   no less than honesty.
Justice demands at all your hands
   perfect Obedience:
If but in part you have come short,
   that is just offence.

Are taken off
& rendred
invalid.
Deut. 10:12.
Titus 2:12.
James 2:10.

97

On Earth below, where men did ow
   a thousand pounds and more,
Could twenty pence it recompence?
   could that have clear'd the score?
Think you to buy felicity
   with part of what's due debt?
Or for desert of one small part,
   the whole should off be set?

98

And yet that part, whose great desert
   you think to reach so far
For your excuse, doth you accuse,
   and will your boasting mar.
However fair, however square,
   your way and work hath been,
Before mens eyes, yet God espies
   iniquity therein.

Luke 18:11,
14.

99

God looks upon th' affection
   and temper of the heart;
Not only on the action,
   and the external part.

1 Sam. 16:7.
2 Chron. 25:2.

Whatever end vain men pretend,
 God knows the verity;
And by the end which they intend
 their words and deeds doth try.

100

Without true Faith, the Scripture saith   Heb. 11:6.
 God cannot take delight
In any deed, that doth proceed
 from any sinful wight.
And without love all actions prove   1 Cor 13:1,
 but barren empty things.   2, 3.
Dead works they be, and vanitie,
 the which vexation brings.

101

Nor from true faith, which quencheth wrath,
 hath your obedience flown:
Nor from true love, which wont to move
 Believers, hath it grown.
Your argument shews your intent,
 in all that you have done:
You thought to scale Heav'ns lofty Wall
 by Ladders of your own.

102

Your blinded spirit, hoping to merit   Rom. 10:3.
 by your own Righteousness,
Needed no Saviour, but your behaviour,
 and blameless carriages;
You trusted to what you could do,
 and in no need you stood:
Your haughty pride laid me aside,
 and trampled on my Blood.

103

All men have gone astray, and done,
    that which Gods Laws condemn:
But my Purchase and offered Grace
    all men did not contemn.   Rom. 9:30,
The *Ninevites*, and *Sodomites*,   32.
                                       Matt. 11:23,
    had no such sin as this: 24; 12:41.
Yet as if all your sins were small,
    you say, All did amiss.

104

Again you thought and mainly sought   Matt. 6:5.
    a name with men t'acquire.
Pride bare the Bell, that made you swell,
    and your own selves admire.
Mean fruit it is, and vile, I wiss,
    that springs from such a root:
Vertue divine and genuine
    wonts not from pride to shoot.

105

Such deeds as your are worse than poor;
    they are but sins guilt over
With silver dross, whose glistering gloss
    can them no longer cover.   Prov. 26:23.
The best of them would you condemn,   Matt. 23:27.
    and ruine you alone,
Although you were from faults so clear,
    that other you had none.

106

Your Gold is brass, your silver dross,
    your righteousness is sin: Prov. 15:8.
And think you by such honesty   Rom. 3:20.
    eternal life to win?

You make mistake, if for its sake
   you dream of acceptation;
Whereas the same deserveth shame,
   and meriteth Damnation.

*   *   *

205

They wring their hands, their caitiff-hands,   Luke 13:28.
   and gnash their teeth for terrour;
They cry, they roar for anguish sore,
   and gnaw their tongues for horrour.
But get away without delay,
   Christ pitties not your cry:
Depart to Hell, there may you yell,
   and roar Eternally.   Prov. 1:26.

206

That word, *Depart*, maugre their heart,   It is put in
   drives every wicked one,   Execution.
With mighty pow'r, the self-same hour,
   far from the Judge's Throne.
Away they're chaste by the strong blast   Matt. 25:46.
   of his Death-threatning mouth:
They flee full fast, as if in haste,
   although they be full loath.

207

As chaff that's dry, and dust doth fly
   before the Northern wind:
Right so are they chased away,
   and can no Refuge find.
They hasten to the Pit of Wo,
   guarded by Angels stout;   Matt. 13:41,
Who to fulfil Christ's holy will,   42.
   attend this wicked Rout.

208

Whom having brought, as they are taught,
    unto the brink of Hell
(That dismal place far from Christ's face,
    where Death and Darkness dwell:
Where Gods fierce Ire kindleth the fire,
    and vengeance feeds the flame
With piles of Wood, and Brimstone Flood,
    that none can quench the same.)

HELL.
Matt. 25:30.
Mark 9:43.
Isa. 30:33.
Rev. 21.8.

209

With Iron bands they bind their hands,
    and cursed feet together,
And cast them all, both great and small,
    into that Lake for ever.
Where day and night, without respite,
    they wail, and cry, and howl
For tort'ring pain, which they sustain
    in Body and in Soul.

Wicked Men
and Devils
cast into it for
ever.
Matt. 22:13;
25:46.

210

For day and night, in their despight,
    their torments smoak ascendeth.
Their pain and grief have no relief,
    their anguish never endeth.
There must they ly, and never dy,
    though dying every day:
There must they dying ever ly,
    and not consume away.

Rev. 14:10, 11.

211

Dy fain they would, if dy they could,
    but Death will not be had.
God's direful wrath their bodies hath
    for ev'r Immortal made.

They live to ly in misery,
   and bear eternal wo;
And live they must whilst God is just,
   that he may plague them so.

212

But who can tell the plagues of Hell,
   and torments exquisite?
Who can relate their dismal state,
   and terrours infinite?
Who fare the best, and feel the least,
   yet feel that punishment
Whereby to nought they should be brought,
   if God did not prevent.

The unsuffer-
able torments
of the
damned.
Luke 16:24.
Jude 7.

213

The least degree of miserie
   there felt's incomparable,
The lightest pain they there sustain
   more than intolerable.
But God's great pow'r from hour to hour
   upholds them in the fire,
That they shall not consume a jot,
   nor by it's force expire.

Isa. 33:14.
Mark 9:43,
44.

214

But ah, the wo they undergo
   (they more than all besides)
Who had the light, and knew the right,
   yet would not it abide.
The sev'n-fold smart, which to their part,
   and portion doth fall,
Who Christ his Grace would not imbrace,
   nor hearken to his call.

Luke 12:47.

215

The *Amorites* and *Sodomites*
    although their plagues be sore,   Matt. 11:24.
Yet find some ease, compar'd to these,
    who feel a great deal more.
Almighty God, whose Iron Rod,
    to smite them never lins,
Doth most declare his Justice rare
    in plaguing these mens sins.

216

The pain of loss their Souls doth toss,   Luke 16:23,
    and wond'rously distress,   25.
                                                    Luke 13:28.
To think what they have cast away
    by wilful wickedness.
We might have been redeem'd from sin
    think they, and liv'd above,
Being possest of heav'nly rest,
    and joying in God's love.

217

But wo, wo, wo our Souls into!   Luke 13:34.
    we would not happy be;
And therefore bear Gods Vengeance here
    to all Eternitee.
Experience and woful sense
    must be our painful teachers
Who n'ould believe, nor credit give,
    unto our faithful Preachers.

218

Thus shall they ly, and wail, and cry,   Mark 9:44.
    tormented, and tormenting   Rom. 2:15.
Their galled hearts with pois'ned darts
    but now too late repenting.

There let them dwell i'th' Flames of Hell:
　　there leave we them to burn,
And back agen unto the men
　　whom Christ acquits, return.

219

The Saints behold with courage bold,
　　and thankful wonderment,
To see all those that were their foes
　　thus sent to punishment:
Then do they sing unto their King
　　a Song of endless Praise:
They praise his Name, and do proclaim
　　that just are all his ways.

The Saints re-
joyce to see
Judgment ex-
ecuted upon
the wicked
World.
Ps. 58:10.
Rev. 19:1, 2, 3.

220

Thus with great joy and melody
　　to Heav'n they all ascend,
Him there to praise with sweetest layes,
　　and Hymns that never end:
Where with long Rest they shall be blest,
　　and nought shall them annoy:
Where they shall see as seen they be,
　　and whom they love enjoy.

They ascend
with Christ
into Heaven
triumphing.
Matt. 25:46.
1 John 3:2.
1 Cor. 13:12.

221

O glorious Place! where face to face
　　Jehovah may be seen,
By such as were sinners whilere
　　and no dark vail between.
Where the Sun shine, and light Divine,
　　of Gods bright Countenance,
Doth rest upon them every one,
　　with sweetest influence.

Their Eternal
happiness
and incompa-
rable Glory
there.

222

O blessed state of the Renate!
  O wondrous Happiness,
To which they're brought, beyond what thought
  can reach, or words express!
Griefs water-course, and sorrows sourse,   Rev. 21:4.
  are turn'd to joyful streams.
Their old distress and heaviness
  are vanished like dreams.

223

For God above in arms of love
  doth dearly them embrace,
And fills their sprights with such delights,   Ps. 16:11.
  and pleasures in his grace;
As shall not fail, nor yet grow stale
  through frequency of use:
Nor do they fear Gods favour there,
  to forfeit by abuse.

224

For there the Saints are perfect Saints,   Heb. 12:23.
  and holy ones indeed,
From all the sin that dwelt within
  their mortal bodies freed:
Made Kings and Priests to God through Christs
  dear loves transcendency,   Rev. 1:6; 22:5.
There to remain, and there to reign
  with him Eternally.

God's Controversy with New-England

Written in the time of the great drought
Anno 1662
By a lover of New-England's Prosperity

Isaiah 5.4
What could have been done more to my vineyard,
that I have not done in it? wherefore, when I
looked that it should bring forth grapes,
brought it forth wilde grapes?

The Author's request unto the Reader

Good christian Reader judge me not
    As too Censorious,
For pointing at those faults of thine
    Which are notorious.
For if those faults be none of thine
    I do not thee accuse:
But if they be, to hear thy faults
    Why shouldest thou refuse.

I blame not thee to spare my self:
    But first at home begin,
And judge my self, before that I
    Reproove anothers sin.
Nor is it I that thee reproove
    Let God himself be heard
Whose awfull providence's voice
    No man may disregard.

Quod Deus omnipotens regali voce minatur,
Quod tibi proclamant uno simul ore prophetae,
Quodq' ego cum lachrymis testor de numinis irâ,
Tu leve comentu ne ducas, Lector Amice.

New-England planted, prospered,
declining, threatned, punished.

Beyond the great Atlantick flood
   There is a region vast,
A country where no English foot
   In former ages past:
A waste and howling wilderness,
   Where none inhabited
But hellish fiends, and brutish men
   That Devils worshiped.

This region was in darkness plac't
   Far off from heavens light,
Amidst the shaddows of grim death
   And of Eternal night.
For there the Sun of righteousness
   Had never made to shine
The light of his sweet countenance,
   And grace which is divine:

Until the time drew nigh wherein
   The glorious Lord of hostes
Was pleasd to lead his armies forth
   Into those forrein coastes.
At whose approach the darkness sad
   Soon vanished away,
And all the shaddows of the night
   Were turnd to lightsome day.

The dark and dismal western woods
   (The Devils den whilere)
Beheld such glorious Gospel-shine,
   As none beheld more cleare.
Where sathan had his scepted sway'd
   For many generations,
The King of Kings set up his throne
   To rule amongst the nations.

The stubborn he in pieces brake,
　　Like vessels made of clay:
And those that sought his peoples hurt
　　He turned to decay.
Those curst Amalekites, that first
　　Lift up their hand on high
To fight against Gods Israel,
　　Were ruin'd fearfully.

Thy terrours on the Heathen folk,
　　O Great Jehovah, fell:
The fame of thy great acts, o Lord,
　　Did all the nations quell.
Some hid themselves for fear of thee
　　In forrests wide & great:
Some to thy people croutching came,
　　For favour to entreat.

Some were desirous to be taught
　　The knowledge of thy wayes,
And being taught, did soon accord
　　Therein to spend their dayes.
Thus were the fierce and barbarous
　　Brought to civility,
And those that liv'd like beasts (or worse)
　　To live religiously.

O happiest of dayes wherein
　　The blind received sight,
And those that had no eyes before
　　Were made to see the light!
The wilderness hereat rejoyc't,
　　The woods for joy did sing,
The vallys & the little hills
　　Thy praises ecchoing.

Here was the hiding place, which thou,
　　Jehovah, didst provide
For thy redeemed ones, and where
　　Thou didst thy jewels hide

In per'lous times, and saddest dayes
    Of sack-cloth and of blood,
When th' overflowing scourge did pass
    Through Europe, like a flood.

While almost all the world beside
    Lay weltring in their gore:
We, only we, enjoyd such peace
    As none enjoyd before.
No forrein foeman did us fray,
    Nor threat'ned us with warrs:
We had no enemyes at home,
    Nor no domestick jarrs.

The Lord had made (such was his grace)
    For us a Covenant
Both with the men, and with the beasts,
    That in this desart haunt:
So that through places wilde and waste
    A single man, disarm'd,
Might journey many hundred miles,
    And not at all be harm'd.

Amidst the solitary woods
    Poor travellers might sleep
As free from danger as at home,
    Though no man watch did keep.
Thus were we priviledg'd with peace,
    Beyond what others were.
Truth, Mercy, Peace, with Righteousness,
    Took up their dwelling here.

Our Governour was of our selves,
    And all his Bretheren,
For wisdom and true piety,
    Select, & chosen men.
Who, Ruling in the fear of God,
    The righteous cause maintained,
And all injurious violence,
    And wickedness, restrained.

Our temp'rall blessings did abound:
    But spirituall good things
Much more abounded, to the praise
    Of that great King of Kings.
Gods throne was here set up; here was
    His tabernacle pight:
This was the place, and these the folk
    In whom he took delight.

Our morning starrs shone all day long:
    Their beams gave forth such light,
As did the noon-day sun abash,
    And's glory dazle quite.
Our day continued many yeers,
    And had no night at all:
Yea many thought the light would last,
    And be perpetuall.

Such, O New-England, was thy first,
    Such was thy best estate:
But, Loe! a strange and suddain change
    My courage did amate.
The brightest of our morning starrs
    Did wholly disappeare:
And those that tarried behind
    With sack-cloth covered were.

Moreover, I beheld & saw
    Our welkin overkest,
And dismal clouds for sun-shine late
    O'respread from East to West.
The air became tempestuous;
    The wilderness gan quake:
And from above with awfull voice
    Th' Almighty thundring spake.

Are these the men that erst at my command
Forsook their ancient seats and native soile,
To follow me into a desart land,
Contemning all the travell and the toile,
Whose love was such to purest ordinances
As made them set at nought their fair inheritances?

Are these the men that prized libertee
To walk with God according to their light,
To be as good as he would have them bee,
To serve and worship him with all their might,
Before the pleasures which a fruitfull field,
And Country flowing-full of all good things, could yield?

Are these the folk whom from the brittish Iles,
Through the stern billows of the watry main,
I safely led so many thousand miles,
As if their journey had been through a plain?
Whom having from all enemies protected,
And through so many deaths and dangers well directed,

I brought and planted on the Western-shore,
Where nought but bruits and salvage wights did swarm
(Untaught, untrain'd, untam'd by Vertue's lore)
That sought their blood, yet could not do them harm?
My fury's flaile them thresht, my fatall broom
Did sweep them hence, to make my people elbow-room.

Are these the men whose gates with peace I crown'd,
To whom for bulwarks I Salvation gave,
Whilst all things else with rattling tumults sound,
And mortall frayes send thousands to the grave:
Whilest their own brethren bloody hands embrewed
In brothers blood, and fields with carcases bestrewed?

Is this the people blest with bounteous store,
By land and sea full richly clad and fed,
Whom plenty's self stands waiting still before,

And powreth out their cups well tempered?
For whose dear sake an howling wildernes
I lately turned into a fruitfull paradeis?

Are these the people in whose hemisphere
Such bright-beam'd, glist'ring, sun-like starrs I placed,
As by their influence did all things cheere,
As by their light blind ignorance defaced,
As errours into lurking holes did fray,
As turn'd the late dark night into a lightsome day?

Are these the folk to whom I milked out
And sweetnes stream'd from Consolations brest;
Whose soules I fed and strengthened throughout
With finest spirituall food most finely drest?
On whom I rained living bread from Heaven,
Withouten Errour's bane, or Superstition's leaven?

With whom I made a Covenant of peace,
And unto whom I did most firmly plight
My faithfulness, If whilst I live I cease
To be their Guide, their God, their full delight;
Since them with cords of love to me I drew,
Enwrapping in my grace such as should them ensew.

Are these the men, that now mine eyes behold,
Concerning whom I thought, and whilome spake,
First Heaven shall pass away together scrold,
Ere they my lawes and righteous wayes forsake,
Or that they slack to runn their heavenly race?
Are these the same? or are some others come in place?

If these be they, how is it that I find
In stead of holyness Carnality,
In stead of heavenly frames an Earthly mind,
For burning zeal luke-warm Indifferency,
For flaming Love, key-cold Dead-heartedness,
For temperance (in meat, and drink, and cloaths) excess?

Whence cometh it, that Pride, and Luxurie
Debate, Deceit, Contention and Strife,
False-dealing, Covetousness, Hypocrisie
(With such like Crimes) amongst them are so rife,
That one of them doth over-reach another?
And that an honest man can hardly trust his Brother?

How is it, that Security, and Sloth,
Amongst the best are Common to be found?
That grosser sinns, in stead of Graces growth,
Amongst the many more and more abound?
I hate dissembling shews of Holiness.
O practise as you talk, or never more profess.

Judge not, vain world, that all are hypocrites
That do profess more holiness then thou:
All foster not dissembling, guilefull sprites,
Nor love their lusts, though very many do.
Some sin through want of care and constant watch,
Some with the sick converse, till they the sickness catch.

Some, that maintian a reall root of grace,
Are overgrown with many noysome weeds,
Whose heart, that those no longer may take place,
The benefit of due correction needs.
And such as these however gone astray
I shall by stripes reduce into a better way.

Moreover some there be that still retain
Their ancient vigour and sincerity;
Whom both their own, and others sins, constrain
To sigh, and mourn, and weep, and wail, and cry:
And for their sakes I have forborn to powre
My wrath upon Revolters to this present houre.

To praying Saints I always have respect,
And tender love, and pittifull regard:
Nor will I now in any wise neglect

Their love and faithfull service to reward;
Although I deal with others for their folly,
And turn their mirth to tears that have been too too jolly.

For thinke not, O Backsliders, in your heart,
That I shall still your evill manners beare:
Your sinns me press as sheaves do load a cart;
And therefore I will plague you for this geare.
Except you seriously, and soon, repent,
Ile not delay your pain and heavy punishment.

And who be those themselves that yonder shew?
The seed of such as name by dreadfull Name!
On whom whilere compassions skirt I threw
Whilest in their blood they were, to hide their shame!
Whom my preventing love did neer me take!
Whom for mine own I mark't, lest they should me forsake!

I look't that such as these to vertue's Lore
(Though none but they) would have Enclin'd their ear:
That they at least mine image should have bore,
And sanctify'd my name with awfull fear.
Let pagan's Bratts pursue their lusts, whose meed
Is Death: For christians children are an holy seed.

But hear O heavens! Let Earth amazed stand;
Ye Mountains melt, and Hills come flowing down:
Let horrour seize upon both Sea and Land;
Let Natures self be cast into a stown.
I children nourisht, nurtur'd and upheld:
But they against a tender father have rebell'd.

What could have been by me performed more?
Or wherein fell I short of your desire?
Had you but askt, I would have op't my store,
And given what lawfull wishes could require.
For all this bounteous cost I lookt to see
Heaven-reaching-hearts, and thoughts, Meekness, Humility.

But lo, a sensuall Heart all void of grace,
An Iron neck, a proud presumptuous Hand;
A self-conceited, still, stout, stubborn Race,
That fears no threats, submitts to no command:
Self-will'd, perverse, such as can beare no yoke;
A generation even ripe for Vengeance stroke.

Such were the Carnall Brood of Israelites
That Josua and the Elders did ensue,
Who growing like the cursed Cananites
Upon themselves my heavy judgements drew.
Such also was that fleshly Generation,
Whom I o'rewhelm'd by waters deadly inundation.

They darker light, and lesser meanes misused;
They had not such Examples them to warn:
You clearer Rules, and precepts, have abused;
And dreadfull monuments of others harm.
My gospels glorious light you do not prize:
My Gospels endless, boundless grace you clean despize.

My painfull messengers you disrespect,
Who toile and sweat and sweale themselves away,
Yet nought at all with you can take effect,
Who hurrie headlong to your own decay.
In vain the Founder melts, and taketh pains:
Bellows and Lead's consum'd, but still your dross remains.

What should I do with such a stiff-neckt race?
How shall I ease me of such Foes as they?
What shall befall despizers of my Grace?
I'le surely beare their Candle-stick away,
And Lamps put out. Their glorious noon-day light
I'le quickly turn into a dark Egyptian night.

Oft have I charg'd you by my Ministers
To gird your selves with sack cloth, and repent.
Oft have I warnd you by my Messengers;

That so you might my wrathfull ire prevent:
But who among you hath this warning taken?
Who hath his crooked wayes, and wicked works forsaken?

Yea many grow to more and more excess;
More light and loose, more Carnall and prophane.
The sins of Sodom, Pride, and Wantonness,
Among the multitude spring up amain.
Are these the fruits of pious Education,
To run with greater speed and Courage to Damnation?

If here and there some two, or three, shall steere
A wiser Course, then their Companions do,
You make a mock of such; and scoff, and jeere
Becaus they will not be so bad as you.
Such is the Generation that succeeds
The men, whose eyes have seen my great and awfull deeds.

Now therefore hearken and encline your ear,
In judgement I will henceforth with you plead;
And if by that you will not learn to fear,
But still go on a sensuall life to lead:
I'le strike at once an All-Consuming stroke;
Nor cries nor tears shall then my fierce intent revoke.

Thus ceast his Dreadful-threatning voice
    The High & lofty-One.
The Heavens stood still Appal'd thereat;
    The Earth beneath did groane:
Soon after I beheld and saw
    A mortall dart come flying:
I lookt again, & quickly saw
    Some fainting, others dying.

The Heavens more began to lowre,
    The welkin Blacker grew:
And all things seemed to forebode
    Sad changes to ensew.

From that day forward hath the Lord
   Apparently contended
With us in Anger, and in Wrath;
   But we have not amended.

Our healthfull dayes are at an end,
   And sicknesses come on
From yeer to yeer, becaus our hearts
   Away from God are gone.
New-England, where for many yeers
   You scarcely heard a cough,
And where Physicians had no work,
   Now finds them work enough.

Now colds and coughs, Rhewms, and sore-throats,
   Do more and more abound:
Now Agues sore & Feavers strong
   In every place are found.
How many houses have we seen
   Last Autumn, and this spring,
Wherein the healthful were too few
   To help the languishing.

One wave another followeth,
   And one disease begins
Before another cease, becaus
   We turn not from our sins.
We stopp our ear against reproof,
   And hearken not to God:
God stops his ear against our prayer,
   And takes not off his rod.

Our fruitful seasons have been turnd
   Of late to barrenness,
Sometimes through great & parching drought,
   Sometimes through rain's excess.
Yea not the pastures & corn fields
   For want of rain do languish:
The cattell mourn, and hearts of men
   Are fill'd with fear and anguish.

The clouds are often gathered,
 As if we should have rain:
But for our great unworthiness
 Are scattered again.
We pray & fast, & make fair shewes,
 As if we meant to turn:
But whilest we turn not, God goes on
 Our fields & fruits to burn.

And burnt are all things in such sort,
 That nothing now appeares,
But what may wound our hearts with grief,
 And draw foorth floods of teares.
All things a famine do presage
 In that extremity,
As if both men, and also beasts,
 Should soon be done to dy.

This O New-England hast thou got
 By riot, and excess:
This hast thou brought upon thy self
 By pride and wantonness.
Thus must thy worldlyness be whipt.
 They, that too much do crave,
Provoke the Lord to take away
 Such blessings as they have.

We have been also threatened
 With worser things then these:
And God can bring them on us still,
 To morrow if he please.
For if his mercy be abus'd,
 Which holpe us at our need
And mov'd his heart to pitty us,
 We shall be plagu'd indeed.

Beware, O sinful-Land, beware;
 And do not think it strange
That sorer judgements are at hand,
 Unless thou quickly change.

Or God, or thou, must quickly change;
   Or else thou art undon:
Wrath cannot cease, if sin remain,
   Where judgement is begun.

Ah dear New England! dearest land to me:
Which unto God hast hitherto been dear,
And mayst be still more dear than formerlie,
If to his voice thou wilt incline thine ear.

Consider wel & wisely what the rod,
Wherewith thou art from yeer to yeer chastized,
Instructeth thee: Repent, and turn to God,
Who wil not have his nurture be despized.

Thou still hast in thee many praying saints,
Of great account, and precious with the Lord,
Who dayly powre out unto him their plaints,
And strive to please him both in deed and word.

Cheer on, sweet souls, my heart is with you all,
And shall be with you, maugre Sathan's might:
And whereso'ere this body be a Thrall,
Still in New-England shall be my delight.

FROM
Meat out of the Eater

Song I

I

Men's Strength meer Weakness is,
   As frail as *Venice* Glass:
And all his Excellency like
   The flower upon the grass.   Isa. 40:67.
   Adam in Paradise,
   And in his perfect state,
When left of God unto himself,   Gen. 3:6.
   Could soon degenerate.

2

He that was strong at first
   Immediately grew weak;
And let the stock of Grace run out,
   Like vessels that do leak.
Hence we are all made weak,   Rom. 5:6,
   And neither have Free-will   12, 14.
To chuse, nor Power to do what's good,
   But only what is ill.

3

But God, the God of Grace,
   His Blessed Son imploy'd
And sent to ransome and restore   John 3:17.
   What Adam had destroy'd.
He having us Redeem'd
   And Ransom'd with his Blood,
And also purchased for us   Rev. 1:5, 6.
   All grace and saving good.

4

Restoreth us to life,   Eph. 2:5, 6,
   Createth us anew,   10.
Enableth us to do what's good
   And evil to eschew.
But still he keeps the Stock   John 15:4, 5.
   Of grace in his own hand,
And hath not left it unto us
   To be at our command.

5

The strongest Saints have need   Phil. 4:13.
   Of daily fresh supplies;
And Christ will teach them where their strength
   And all their power lies.

Unless the Sun do shine,
  Soon vanisheth the Beam:
Unless the Fountain feed it still,
  Soon dry'd up is the Stream.

6

Hence if the strongest Saints
  Begin to grow secure,
Neglect their watch, trust in themselves;
  Christ will not this endure.
  He leaves them to themselves,
    And lets them trie their strength:
They fall and feel their weaknesses
  Unto their cost at length.

7

Thus *David* sadly fell;
  And who more strong then *David*?
Or who more graciously himself
  In all his straits behaved?
  David, while weak, was strong,
    And kept his hands most pure:
But in his strength he grew most weak
  By being too secure.

2 Sam. 11:2,
3, 4.

8

Peter was confident
  And thought he had much strength
To follow Christ through thick and thin:
  But what came on't at length?
  He thought his Love so great,
    He could with Christ have dy'd:
But ah frail man! e're morning light
  He Christ three times deny'd.

Luke 22:33,
56, 57, 58, 60.

9

Obj.
  Some haply here will say;
  If Saints of such renown

Have been so foil'd, and to the ground
   In time of Trial thrown;
   What will become of me,
   That am so weak and frail!
How shall I stand, when violent
   Temptations me assail?

10

Sol.

   Though God sometimes permit
   The strongest Saints to fall,
To stain the glory of all Flesh,
   And to awaken all:
   Yet let not weak ones faint,
   Nor be discouraged,
Who feel their wants and weaknesses,
   And flee to Christ their Head.

11

   For Christ hath strength enough:
   Do thou on him depend,
And he will make thee stand in storms,
   And hold out to the end.
   For in our weakness great
   Christ's strength doth more appear:
We never are so safe, as when
   We get to him most near.

Isa. 40:29, 30.

12

   When sense of our own wants,
   And manifold defects,
Drives us to Christ our only strength;
   Then he the weak protects.
   Hence we are never stronger,
   Then when we are most weak
Because we then most heartily
   Christ's help and succour seek.

13

Thus *Paul* that great Apostle,   2 Cor. 12:5, 7,
  when I am weak, saith he,   9, 10, 11.
Then am I strong; because the strength
  Of Christ then rests on me.
  Therefore I rather chuse
  In weaknesses to glory,
Then of my Revelations great
  To tell an ample story.

————

I Walk'd and did a little *Mole-hill* view,
Full peopled with a most industrious crew
Of busie *Ants*, where each one labour'd more,
Than if he were to bring home *Indian* Ore;
Here wrought the *Pioneers*, there march'd the *Bands*,
Here *Colonies* went forth to plant new *Lands*:
These hasted *out*, and those supplies brought *in*,
As if they had some sudden *Siege* foreseen:
Until there came an angry *Spade*, and cast
Country and *People* to a *Pit* at last.
  Again, I view'd a *Kingdom* in a *Hive*,
Where every own did *work*, and so all *thrive*;
Some go, some come, some war, some watch and ward,
Some make the works, and some the works do guard.
These frame their curious waxen cells, & those
Do into them their *Nector drops* dispose:
Until the greedy *Gardner* brought his smoke,
And, for the work, did all the workmen choke.
  Lo here, frail Mortals may fit Emblems see
Of their great toil, and greater vanity.
They weary out their brain, their strength, their time,
While some to Arts, and some to Honours climb:
They search earths bowels, cross the roring seas,
Mortgage their Souls, and forfeit all their ease,
Grudge night her sleep, & lengthen out the day,
To fat these bags, & cram those chests with clay,
They rack and charm each creature to explore

Some latent *Quintessence*, not known before:
Torture and squeez out all its juice and blood,
To try if they can now find out that GOOD
Which *Solomon* despair'd of, but at last
On the same shore of *Vanity* are cast;
The spade stops their career of *Pride* and *Lust*,
And calls them from their *Clay* unto their *Dust*.
Leave off your Circles, *Archimede*, away,
The *King* of *Terrour* calls, and will not stay:
Miser, kiss all your *Bags*, and then ly down;
Scholar, your *Books*; *Monarch*, yield up your *Crown*:
Give way Wealth, Honour, Arts, Thrones; back, make room,
That these pale *Souls* may come unto their doom.
    Nor shew *vain men* the fruit of all that pain,
Which in the end nothing but *Loss* did gain:
Compute your *lives*, and all your *hours* up cast,
Lo here's the *total sum* of all at last.
    I rose up early, sat up late, to *know*
As much as man, as tongues, as books could show;
I toil'd to search all *Science* and all *Art*,
But died *ignorant* of mine own *Heart*.
I got great *Honour*, and my *Fame* did stream
As far as doth the Mornings shining Beam;
My *Name* into a page of *Titles* swell'd,
My *head* a *Crown*, my *hand* a *Scepter* held:
Ador'd without, but shameful *lusts* within;
Adorn'd with *Titles*, but defil'd with *sin*.
    With anxious thoughts, with saddest cares & cost
I gain'd these *Lordships*, and this *Soul* I lost:
My greedy Heir now hovers o're my pelf,
I purchase *Land* for him, *Hell* for my self.
Go on you *nobler Brains*, and fill your sight
As full of *Learning* as the Sun's of light;
Expand your Souls to *Truth* as wide as Day,
Know all that *Men*, know all that *Angels* say:
Write shops of *Volumns*, and let every *Book*
Be fill'd with lustre as was *Moses* look:
Yet know, all this is but a better kind
Of *sublime vanity*, and more refin'd:
Except a saving knowledge crown the rest,

Devils know more, and yet shall ne'r be blest.
   Go on, *ambitious Worms*, yet, yet aspire,
Lay a sure Scene how you may yet rise higher:
March forward, *Macedonian Horn*, add on
Gaza to *Tyre*, *Indies* to *Babylon*;
Make *stirrups* of the peoples *backs* and *bones*,
Climb up by them to *Diadems* and *Thrones*:
Thy *Crowns* are all but *grass*; thine was the *toil*,
Thy *Captains* come and they divide the *spoil*.
Except one heav'nly Crown crown all the rest,
Devils are Potentates, and yet not blest.

   Go on, base *dunghil-souls*, heap gold as mire,
Sweep silver as the dust, emulate *Tyre*,
Fill every Ware-house, purchase every Field,
Add house to house, *Pelion* on *Ossa* build;
Get *Mida*'s vote to transubstantiate
Whate're you please all into golden plate;
Build wider barns, sing *requiem* to your heart,
Feel your wealths pleasures only, not their smart.
Except his Riches who for us was poor,
Do sweeten those which Mortals so adore;
Except sublimer wealth crown all the rest,
Devils have nobler Treasures, yet not blest.

   Cease then from vain delights, & set your mind
That solid and enduring GOOD to find,
Which sweetens life and death, which will encrease
On an immortal Soul immortal peace;
Which will replenish and advance you higher
Then e're your own Ambition could aspire.
Fear your great Maker with a child-like aw,
Believe his Grace, love and obey his Law.
This is the *total work of man*, and this
Will crown you here with *Peace*, and there with *Bliss*.

   Be kind unto your selves, believe and try:
If not, go on, fill up your lusts and die.
Sing peace unto your selves; 'twill once be known
Whose word shall stand, your *Judg*'s, or your *own*.
Crown thee with Rose-buds, satiate thine eyes,
Glut every sense with her own *vanities*:
Melt into pleasures, until that which Lust

Did not before consume, rot into dust:
The *Thrones* are set, the *Books* wil strait be read,
Hell will her souls, & gravs give up their dead;
Then there will be (and the time is not far)
Fire on the *Bench*, and *Stubble* at the *Bar*.
   O sinners ruminate these thoughts agen,
You have been *Beasts* enough, at last be *Men*.
Christ yet intreats, but if you will not turn,
Where grace will not convert, there fire wil burn.

URIAN OAKES

(c. 1631–1681)

An Elegie
Upon that Reverend, Learned, Eminently Pious, and Singularly Accomplished Divine, my ever Honoured Brother
Mr. Thomas Shepard

*The late Faithful and Worthy Teacher of the Church of Christ
at Charlstown in New-England,
Who finished his Course on Earth, and went to receive
his Crown, December 22. 1677.
In the 43d Year of his Age.*

1

Oh! that I were a Poet now in grain!
How would I invocate the Muses all
To deign their presence, lend their flowing Vein,
And help to grace dear *Shepard's* Funeral!
   How would I paint our griefs, and succours borrow
   From Art and Fancy, to limn out our sorrow!

2

Now could I wish (if wishing would obtain)
The sprightli'est Efforts of Poetick Rage,
To vent my Griefs, make others feel my pain,
For this loss of the Glory of our Age.
   Here is a subject for the loftiest Verse
   That ever waited on the bravest Hearse.

3

And could my Pen ingeniously distill
The purest Spirits of a sparkling wit
In rare conceits, the quintessence of skill

In *Elegiack Strains*, none like to it:
   I should think all too little to condole
   The fatal loss (to us) of such a Soul.

4

Could I take highest Flights of Fancy, soar
Aloft; If Wits Monopoly were mine:
All would be much too low, too light, too poor,
To pay due tribute to this great Divine.
   Ah! Wit avails not, when th' Heart's like to break,
   Great griefs are Tongue-ti'ed, when the lesser speak.

5

Away loose rein'd Careers of Poetry,
The celebrated Sisters may be gone;
We need no *Mourning Womens* Elegy,
No forc'd, affected, artificial Tone.
   Great and good *Shepard's* Dead! Ah! this alone
   Will set our eyes abroach, dissolve a stone.

6

Poetick Raptures are of no esteem,
Daring *Hyperboles* have here no place,
Luxuriant Wits on such a copious Theme,
Would shame themselves, and blush to shew their face
   Here's worth enough to overmatch the skill
   Of the most stately Poet *Laureat's Quill*.

7

Exube'rant Fancies useless here I deem,
Transcendant vertue scorns feign'd Elogies:
He that gives *Shepard* half his due, may seem,
If Strangers hear it, to Hyperbolize.
   Let him that can, tell what his vertues were,
   And say, this Star mov'd in no common Sphere.

8

Here need no Spices, Odours, curious Arts,
No skill of *Egypt*, to embalm the Name
Of such a Worthy: let men speak their hearts,
They'l say, He merits an Immortal Fame,
    When *Shepard* is forgot, all must conclude,
    This is prodigious ingratitude.

9

But live he shall in many a gratefull Breast,
Where he hath rear'd himself a Monument,
A Monument more stately than the best,
On which Immensest Treasures have been spent.
    Could you but into th' Hearts of thousands peep,
    There would you read his Name engraven deep.

10

Oh! that my head were Waters, and mine Eyes
A flowing Spring of Tears, still issuing forth
In streams of bitterness, to solemnize
The *Obits* of this Man of matchless worth!
    Next to the Tears our sins do need and crave,
    I would bestow my Tears on *Shepards* Grave.

11

Not that he needs our Tears: for he hath dropt
His measure full; not one Tear more shall fall
Into God's Bottle from his eyes; *Death* stopt
That water-course, his sorrows ending all.
    He Fears, he Cares, he Sighs, he Weeps no more:
    Hee's past all storms, Arriv'd at th' wished Shoar.

12

Dear *Shepard* could we reach so high a strain
Of pure Seraphick love, as to devest
Our selves, and love, of self-respects, thy gain

Would joy us, though it cross our interest.
   Then would we silence all complaints with this,
   Our Dearest Friend is doubtless gone to Bliss.

13

Ah! but the Lesson's hard, thus to deny
Our own dear selves, to part with such a Loan
Of Heaven (in time of such necessity)
And love thy comforts better than our own.
   Then let us moan our loss, adjourn our glee,
   Till we come thither to rejoice with thee.

14

As when some formidable Comets blaze,
As when Portentous Prodigies appear,
Poor Mortals with amazement stand and gaze,
With hearts affrighted, and with trembling fear:
   So are we all amazed at this blow,
   Sadly portending some approaching woe.

15

We shall not summon bold Astrologers,
To tell us what the Stars say in the case,
(Those Cousin-Germans to black Conjurers)
We have a sacred Oracle that says,
   When th' Righteous perish, men of mercy go,
   It is a sure presage of coming wo.

16

He was (ah woful word! to say he was)
Our wrestling *Israel*, second unto none,
The man that stood i' th' gap, to keep the pass,
To stop the Troops of Judgements rushing on.
   This man the honour had to hold the hand
   Of an incensed God against our Land.

17

When such a Pillar's faln (Oh such an one!)
When such a glorious, shining Light's put out,
When Chariot and Horsemen thus are gone;
Well may we fear some Downfal, Darkness, Rout.
    When such a Bank's broke down, there's sad occasion
    To wail, and dread some grievous Inundation.

18

What! must we with our God, and Glory part?
Lord! Is thy Treaty with *New-England* come
Thus to an end? And is War in thy Heart?
That this Ambassadour is called home.
    So Earthly Gods (Kings) when they War intend,
    Call home their Ministers, and Treaties end.

19

Oh for the Raptures, Transports, Inspirations
Of *Israel's Singer*, when his *Jon'athan's* Fall
So tun'd his mourning Harp! what Lamentations
Then would I make for *Shepards* Funeral!
    How truly can I say, as well as He?
    My *Dearest Brother I'm distress'd for thee*.

20

How Lovely, Worthy, Peerless, in my view?
How Precious, Pleasant hast thou been to me?
How Learned, Prudent, Pious, Grave, and True?
And what a Faithful Friend? who like to thee?
    Mine Eye's desire is vanish'd; who can tell
    Where lives my dearest *Shepard's* Parallel?

21

'Tis strange to think: but we may well believe,
That not a few of different Perswasions
From this great Worthy, do now truly grieve

I' th' Mourning croud, and joyn their Lamentations.
    Such Powers Magnetick had He to draw to Him
    The very Hearts, and Souls, of all that knew Him!

22

Art, Nature, Grace, in Him were all combin'd
To shew the World a matchless *Paragon*:
In whom of Radiant Virtues no less shin'd,
Than a whole Constellation: but hee's gone!
    Hee's gone alas! Down in the Dust must ly
    As much of this rare Person as could dy.

23

If to have solid Judgement, Pregnant Parts,
A piercing Wit, and comprehensive Brain;
If to have gone the *Round* of all the Arts,
Immunity from Deaths Arrest would gain,
    Shepard would have been Death-proof, and secure
    From that All conquering Hand, I'm very sure.

24

If Holy Life, and Deeds of Charity,
If Grace illustrious, and Virtue tri'ed,
If modest Carriage, rare Humility,
Could have brib'd Death, good *Shepard* had not di'ed.
    Oh! but inexorable Death attacks
    The best Men, and promiscu'ous havock makes.

25

Come tell me, Criticks, have you ever known
Such Zeal, so temper'd well with moderation?
Such Prudence, and such Inno'cence met in one?
Such Parts, so little Pride and Ostentation?
    Let *Momus* carp, and *Envy* do her worst,
    And swell with *Spleen* and *Rancour* till she burst.

26

To be descended well, doth *that* commend?
Can Sons their Fathers Glory call their own?
Our *Shepard* justly might to this pretend,
(His Blessed Father was of high Renown,
  Both *Englands* speak him great, admire his Name)
  But his own pers'onal worth's a better claim.

27

Great was the Father, once a glorious Light
Among us, Famous to an high Degree:
Great was this Son: indeed (to do him right)
As Great and Good (to say no more) as He.
  A double portion of his Fathers Spirit
  Did this (his Eldest) Son, through Grace, inherit.

28

His Look commanded Reverence and Awe,
Though Mild and Amiable, not Austere:
Well Humour'd was He (as I ever saw)
And rul'd by Love and Wisdome, more than Fear.
  The Muses, and the Graces too, conspir'd
  To set forth this Rare Piece, to be admir'd.

29

He govern'd well the Tongue (that busie thing,
Unruly, Lawless and Pragmatical)
Gravely Reserv'd, in Speech not lavishing,
Neither too sparing, nor too liberal.
  His Words were few, well season'd, wisely weigh'd
  And in his Tongue the Law of kindness sway'd.

30

Learned he was beyond the common Size,
Befriended much by Nature in his Wit,
And Temper, (Sweet, Sedate, Ingenious, Wise)

And (which crown'd all) he was Heav'ens Favourite:
  On whom the God of all Grace did command,
  And show'r down Blessings with a lib'eral hand.

31

Wise He, not wily, was; Grave, not Morose;
Not stiffe, but steady; Seri'ous, but not Sowre;
Concern'd for all, as if he had no Foes;
(Strange if he had!) and would not wast an Hour.
  Thoughtful and Active for the common good:
  And yet his own place wisely understood.

32

Nothing could make him stray from Duty; Death
Was not so frightful to him, as Omission
Of Ministerial work; he fear'd no breath
Infecti'ous, i'th' discharge of his Commission.
  Rather than run from's work, he chose to dy,
  Boldly to run on Death, than duty fly.

33

(Cruel Disease! that didst (like *High-way-men*)
Assault the honest Trav'eller in his way,
And rob dear *Shepard* of his life (Ah!) then,
When he was on the Road, where Duty lay.
  Forbear, bold Pen! 'twas God that took him thus,
  To give him great Reward, and punish us.)

34

Zealous in God's cause, but meek in his own;
Modest of Nature, bold as any Lion,
Where Consc'ience was concern'd: and there was none
More constant Mourners for afflicted Sion:
  So gene'ral was his care for th' Churches all,
  His Spirit seemed Apostolical.

35

Large was his Heart, to spend without regret,
Rejoycing to do good: not like those *Moles*
That root i' th' Earth, or roam abroad, to get
All for themselves (those sorry, narrow Souls!)
    But He, like th' Sun (i' th' Center, as some say)
    Diffus'd his Rayes of Goodness every way.

36

He breath'd Love, and pursu'd Peace in his day,
As if his Soul were made of Harmony:
Scarce ever more of Goodness crouded lay
In such a piece of frail Mortality.
    Sure Father *Wilsons* genuine Son was he,
    New-England's Paul had such a *Timothy*.

37

No Slave to th' Worlds grand *Idols*; but he flew
At *Fairer Quarries*, without stooping down
To Sublunary prey: his great Soul knew
Ambition none, but of the Heave'nly Crown.
    Now he hath won it, and shall wear't with Honour,
    Adoring Grace, and God in Christ, the Donour.

38

A Friend to Truth, a constant Foe to Errour,
Pow'erful i' th' *Pulpit*, and sweet in converse,
To weak ones gentle, to th' Profane a Terrour.
Who can his vertues, and good works rehearse?
    The Scripture—Bishops-Character read o're,
    Say this was *Shepards*: what need I say more?

39

I say no more, let them that can declare
His rich and rare endowments, paint this Sun,
With all its dazling Rayes: But I despair,

Hopeless by any hand to see it done.
    They that can *Shepards* goodness well display,
    Must be as good as he: But who are they?

40

See where our Sister *Charlstown* sits and Moans!
Poor Widowed *Charlstown!* all in Dust, in Tears!
Mark how she wrings her hands! hear how she groans!
See how she weeps! what sorrow like to hers!
    Charlstown, that might for joy compare of late
    With all about her, now looks desolate.

41

As you have seen some Pale, Wan, Ghastly look,
When grisly Death, that will not be said nay,
Hath seiz'd all for it self, Possession took,
And turn'd the Soul out of its house of Clay:
    So Visag'd is poor *Charlstown* at this day;
    Shepard, her very Soul, is torn away.

42

Cambridge groans under this so heavy cross,
And Sympathizes with her Sister dear;
Renews her Griefs afresh for her old loss
Of her own *Shepard*, and drops many a Tear.
    Cambridge and *Charlstown* now joint Mourners are,
    And this tremendous loss between them share.

43

Must Learnings Friend (Ah! worth us all) go thus?
That Great Support to *Harvards* Nursery!
Our *Fellow* (that no Fellow had with us)
Is gone to Heave'ns great University.
    Our's now indeed's a lifeless *Corporation*,
    The Soul is fled, that gave it *Animation*!

44

Poor *Harvard's* Sons are in their Mourning Dress:
Their sure Friend's gone! their Hearts have *put on Mourning*;
Within their Walls are Sighs, Tears, Pensiveness;
Their new Foundations dread an overturning.
    Harvard! where's such a fast Friend left to thee?
    Unless thy great Friend, *LEVERET*, it be.

45

We must not with our greatest Soveraign strive,
Who dare find fault with him that is most High?
That hath an absolute Prerogative,
And doth his pleasure: none may ask him, why?
    We're Clay-lumps, Dust-heaps, nothings in his sight:
    The Judge of all the Earth doth always right.

46

Ah! could not Prayers and Tears prevail with God!
Was there no warding off that dreadful Blow!
And was there no averting of that Rod!
Must *Shepard* dy! and that good Angel go!
    Alas! Out heinous sins (more than our hairs)
    It seems, were louder, and out-crie'd our Prayers.

47

See what our sins have done! what Ruines wrought
And how they have pluck'd out our very eyes!
Our sins have slain our *Shepard!* we have bought,
And dearly paid for, our Enormities.
    Ah Cursed sins! that strike at God, and kill
    His *Servants*, and the Blood of *Prophets* spill.

48

As you would loath the Sword that's warm and red,
As you would hate the hands that are embru'd
I'th' Hearts-blood of your dearest Friends: so dread,

And hate your sins; Oh! let them be pursu'd:
  Revenges take on bloody sins: for there's
  No Refuge-City for these Murtherers.

49

In vain we build the Prophets Sepulchers,
In vain bedew their Tombs with Tears, when Dead;
In vain bewail the Deaths of Ministers,
Whilest Prophet-killing sins are harboured.
  Those that these Murth'erous Traitors favour, hide;
  And with the blood of Prophets deeply di'ed.

50

New-England! know thy Heart-plague: feel this blow;
A blow that sorely wounds both Head and Heart,
A blow that reaches All, both high and low,
A blow that may be felt in every part.
  Mourn that this *Great Man's* faln in *Israel*:
  Lest it be said, *with him New-England fell!*

51

Farewel, Dear *Shepard!* Thou art gone before,
Made free of *Heaven*, where thou shalt sing loud *Hymns*
Of *High triumphant Praises* evermore,
In the sweet Quire of *Saints* and *Seraphims.*
  Lord! look on us here, clogg'd with sin and clay,
  And we, through Grace, shall be as happy as they.

52

My Dearest, Inmost, Bosome-Friend is Gone!
Gone is my sweet Companion, Soul's delight!
Now in an Huddling Croud I'm all alone,
And almost could bid all the World *Goodnight*:
  Blest be my Rock! God lives: Oh let him be,
  As He is All, so All in All to me.

                    The Bereaved, Sorrowful
                    URIAN OAKES.

GEORGE ALSOP

(1636–c. 1673)

The Author to His Book

When first *Apollo* got my brain with Childe,
He made large promise never to beguile,
But like an honest Father, he would keep
Whatever Issue from my Brain did creep:
With that I gave consent, and up he threw
Me on a Bench, and strangely he did do;
Then every week he daily came to see
How his new Physick still did work with me,
And when he did perceive he'd don the feat,
Like an unworthy man he made retreat,
Left me in desolation, and where none
Compassionated when they heard me groan.
What could he judge the Parish then would think,
To see me fair, his Brat as black as Ink?
If they had eyes, they'd swear I were no Nun,
But got with Child by some black *Africk* Son,
And so condemn me for my Fornication,
To beat them Hemp to stifle half the Nation.
Well, since 'tis so, I'le alter this base Fate,
And lay his Bastard at some Nobel's Gate;
Withdraw my self from Beadles, and from such,
Who would give twelve pence I were in their clutch:
Then, who can tell? this Child which I do hide,
May be in time a Small-beer Col'nel *Pride*.
But while I talk, my business it is dumb,
I must lay double-clothes unto thy Bum,
Then lap thee warm, and to the World commit
The Bastard Off-spring of a New-born wit.
Farewel, poor Brat, thou in a monstrous World,
In swadling bands, thus up and down art hurl'd;
There to receive what Destiny doth contrive,
Either to perish, or be sav'd alive.
Good Fate protect thee from a Criticks power,

For if he comes, thou'rt gon in half an hour,
Stifl'd and blasted, 'tis their usual way,
To make that Night, which is as bright as Day.
For if they once but wring, and skrew their mouth,
Cock up their Hats, and set the point Due South,
Armes all a kimbo, and with belly strut,
As if they had *Parnassus* in their gut:
These are the Symtomes of the murthering fall
Of my poor Infant, and his burial.
Say he should miss thee, and some ign'rant Asse
Should find thee out, as he along doth pass,
It were all one, he'd look into thy Tayle,
To see if thou wert Feminine or Male;
When he'd half starv'd thee, for to satisfie
His peeping Ign'rance, he'd then let thee lie;
And vow by's wit he ne're could understand,
The Heathen dresses of another Land:
Well, 'tis no matter, wherever such as he
Knows one grain, more then his simplicity.
Now, how the pulses of my Senses beat,
To think the rigid Fortune thou wilt meet:
Asses and captious Fools, not six in ten
Of thy Spectators will be real men,
To Umpire up the badness of the Cause,
And screen my weakness from the rav'nous Laws,
Of those that will undoubted sit to see
How they might blast this new-born Infancy:
If they should burn him, they'd conclude hereafter,
'Twere too good death for him to dye a Martyr;
And if they let him live, they think it will
Be but a means for to encourage ill,
And bring in time some strange *Antipod'ans*,
A thousand Leagues beyond *Philippians*,
To storm our Wits; therefore he must not rest,
But shall be hang'd, for all he has been prest:
Thus they conclude.—My Genius comforts give,
In Resurrection he will surely live.

———

Trafique is Earth's great *Atlas*, that supports
The pay of Armies, and the height of Courts,
And makes Mechanicks live, that else would die
Meer starving Martyrs to their penury:
None but the Merchant of this thing can boast,
He, like the Bee, comes loaden from each Coast,
And to all Kingdoms, as within a Hive,
Stows up those Riches that doth make them thrive:
Be thrifty, *Mary-Land*, keep what thou hast in store,
And each years Trafique to thy self get more.

————

Heavens bright Lamp, shine forth some of thy Light,
But just so long to paint this dismal Night;
Then draw thy beams, and hide thy glorious face,
From the dark sable Actions of this place;
Leaving these lustful *Sodomites* groping still,
To satisfie each dark unsatiate will,
Untill at length the crimes that they commit,
May sink them down to Hells Infernal pit.
Base and degenerate Earth, how dost thou lye,
That all that pass hiss, at thy Treachery?
Thou which couldst boast once of thy King and Crown,
By base Mechanicks now art tumbled down:
Brewers and *Coblers*, that have scarce an Eye,
Walk hand in hand in thy Supremacy;
And all those Courts where Majesty did Throne,
Are now the Seats for *Oliver* and *Joan*:
Persons of Honour, which did before inherit
Their glorious Titles from deserved merit,
Are all grown silent, and with wonder gaze,
To view such Slaves drest in their Courtly rayes;
To see a *Drayman* that knows nought but Yeast,
Set in a Throne like *Babylons* red Beast,
While heaps of Parasites do idolize
This red-nos'd *Bell*, with fawning Sacrifice.
What can we say? our King they've murthered,
And those well born, are basely buried:
Nobles are slain, and Royalists in each street

Are scorn'd, and kick'd by most men that they meet:
Religion's banisht, and Heresie survives,
And none but Conventicks in this Age thrives.
Oh could those *Romans* from their Ashes rise,
That liv'd in *Nero*'s time: Oh how their cries
Would our perfidious Island shake, nay rend,
With clamorous screaks unto the Heaven send:
Oh how they'd blush to see our Crimson crimes,
And know the Subjects Authors of these times:
When as the Peasant he shall take his King,
And without cause shall fall a murthering him;
And when that's done, with Pride assume the Chair,
And *Nimrod*-like, himself to Heaven rear;
Command the People, make the Land obey
His baser will, and swear to what he'l say.
Sure, sure our God has not these evils sent
To please himself, but for mans punishment:
And when he shall from our dark sable Skies
Withdraw these Clouds, and let our Sun arise,
Our dayes will surely then in Glory shine,
Both in our Temporal, and our State divine:
May this come quickly, though I may never see
This glorious day, yet I would sympathie,
And feel a joy run through each vain of blood,
Though Vassalled on t'other side the Floud.
Heavens protect his Sacred Majesty,
From secret Plots, & treacherous Villany.
And that those Slaves that now predominate,
Hang'd and destroy'd may be their best of Fate;
And though Great *Charles* be distant from his own,
Heaven I hope will seat him on his Throne.

                                    Vale.
                          Yours what I may,
                                    G. A.

From the Chimney-
corner upon a low
Cricket, where I
writ this in the noise
of some six Women,
Aug. 19. Anno

BENJAMIN TOMPSON

(1642–1714)

The Grammarians Funeral

OR,

An ELEGY composed upon the Death of Mr. John Woodmancy,
formerly a School-Master in Boston: *But now Published upon
the DEATH of the Venerable
Mr. Ezekiel Chevers,
The late and famous School-Master of* Boston *in* New-England;
Who Departed this Life the Twenty-first *of* August 1708. *Early
in the Morning. In the Ninety-fourth Year of his Age.*

Eight Parts of *Speech* this Day wear *Mourning Gowns*
Declin'd *Verbs, Pronouns, Participles, Nouns.*
And not declined, *Adverbs* and *Conjunctions,*
In *Lillies* Porch they stand to do their functions.
With *Preposition*; but the most affection
Was still observed in the *Interjection.*
The *Substantive* seeming the limbed best,
Would set an hand to bear him to his Rest.
The *Adjective* with very grief did say,
Hold me by strength, or I shall faint away.
The Clouds of Tears did over-cast their faces,
Yea all were in most lamentable *Cases.*
The five *Declensions* did the Work decline,
And *Told* the *Pronoun Tu,* The work is thine:
But in this case those have no call to go
That want the *Vocative,* and can't say O!
The *Pronouns* said that if the *Nouns* were there,
There was no need of them, they might them spare:
But for the sake of *Emphasis* they would,
In their Discretion do what ere they could.
Great honour was confer'd on *Conjugations,*
They were to follow next to the *Relations.*
Amo did love him best, and *Doceo* might
Alledge he was his Glory and Delight.
But *Lego* said by me he got his skill,

148

And therefore next the *Herse* I follow will.
Audio said little, hearing them so hot,
Yet knew by him much Learning he had got.
O *Verbs* the *Active* were, Or *Passive* sure,
Sum to be *Neuter* could not well endure.
But this was common to them all to Moan
Their load of grief they could not soon *Depone*.
A doleful Day for *Verbs*, they look so *moody*,
They drove Spectators to a Mournful Study.
The *Verbs* irregular, 'twas thought by some,
Would break no rule, if they were pleas'd to come.
Gaudeo could not be found; fearing disgrace
He had with-drawn, sent *Maereo* in his Place.
Possum did to the utmost he was able,
And bore as Stout as if he'd been A *Table*.
Volo was willing, *Nolo* some-what stout,
But *Malo* rather chose, not to stand out.
Possum and *Volo* wish'd all might afford
Their help, but had not an *Imperative Word*.
Edo from Service would by no means Swerve,
Rather than fail, he thought the *Cakes* to Serve.
Fio was taken in a fit, and said,
By him a Mournful *POEM* should be made.
Fero was willing for to bear a part,
Altho' he did it with an aking heart.
Feror excus'd, with grief he was so Torn,
He could not bear, he needed to be born.

Such *Nouns* and *Verbs* as we defective find,
No *Grammar* Rule did their attendance bind.
They were excepted, and exempted hence,
But *Supines*, all did blame for negligence.
Verbs Offspring, *Participles* hand-in-hand,
Follow, and by the same direction stand:
The rest Promiscuously did croud and cumber,
Such Multitudes of each, they wanted Number.
Next to the Corpse to make th' attendance even,
Jove, Mercury, Apollo came from heaven.
And *Virgil, Cato*, gods, men, Rivers, Winds,
With *Elegies*, Tears, Sighs, came in their kinds.

Ovid from *Pontus* hast's Apparrell'd thus,
In Exile-weeds bringing *De Tristibus.*
And *Homer* sure had been among the Rout,
But that the Stories say his Eyes were out.
Queens, Cities, Countries, Islands, Come
All Trees, Birds, Fishes, and each Word in *Um.*

What *Syntax* here can you expect to find?
Where each one bears such discomposed mind.
Figures of Diction and Construction,
Do little: Yet stand sadly looking on.
That such a Train may in their motion *chord,*
Prosodia gives the measure Word for Word.
                              Sic Maestus Cecinit,
                              Benj. Tompson.

FROM
New Englands Crisis

The Prologue

The times wherein old *Pompion* was a Saint,
When men far'd hardly yet without complaint
On vilest *Cates*, the dainty *Indian Maize*
Was eat with *Clamp-shells* out of wooden Trayes
Under thatcht *Hutts* without the cry of *Rent,*
And the best *Sawce* to every Dish, *Content.*
When Flesh was food, and hairy skins made coats,
And men as wel as birds had chirping Notes.
When Cimnels were accounted noble bloud
Among the tribes of common herbage food.
Of *Ceres* bounty form'd was many a knack
Enough to fill *poor Robins Almanack.*
These golden times (too fortunate to hold)
Were quickly sin'd away for love of gold.
Twas then among the bushes, not the street
If one in place did an inferiour meet,
Good morrow Brother, is there ought you want?

Take freely of me, what I have you ha'nt.
Plain *Tom* and *Dick* would pass as currant now,
As ever since *Your Servant Sir* and bow.
Deep-skirted doublets, *puritanick* capes
Which now would render men like upright Apes,
Was comlier wear our wiser Fathers thought
Than the cast fashions from all *Europe* brought.
Twas in those dayes an honest *Grace* would hold
Till an hot puddin grew at heart a cold.
And men had better stomachs to religion
Than I to capon, turkey-cock or pigeon.
When honest Sisters met to pray not prate
About their own and not their neighbours state.
During *Plain Dealings* Reign, that worthy Stud
Of th' ancient planters race before the flood
These times were good, Merchants car'd not a rush
For other fare than *Jonakin and Mush.*
Although men far'd and lodged very hard
Yet Innocence was better than a Guard.
Twas long before spiders and wormes had drawn
Their dungy webs or hid with cheating Lawne
New-Englands beautyes, which stil seem'd to me
Illustrious in their own simplicity.
Twas ere the neighbouring *Virgin-land* had broke
The Hogsheads of her worse than hellish smoak.
Twas ere the Islands sent their Presents in,
Which but to use was counted next to sin.
Twas ere a *Barge* had made so rich a fraight
As *Chocholatte*, dust-gold and bitts of eight.
Ere wines from *France* and *Moscovadoe* too
Without the which the drink will scarsly doe,
From western Isles, ere fruits and dilicacies,
Did rot maids teeth and spoil their hansome faces.
Or ere these times did chance the noise of war
Was from our towns and hearts removed far.
No Bugbear Comets in the chrystal air
To drive our christian Planters to despair.
No sooner pagan malice peeped forth
But Valour snib'd it; then were men of worth
Who by their prayers slew thousands Angel like,

Their weapons are unseen with which they strike.
Then had the Churches rest, as yet the coales
Were covered up in most contentious souls.
Freeness in Judgment, union in affection,
Dear love, sound truth they were our grand protection.
These were the twins which in our Councells sate,
These gave prognosticks of our future fate,
If these be longer liv'd our hopes increase,
These warrs will usher in a longer peace:
But if *New-Englands* love die in its youth
The grave will open next for blessed Truth.
This *Theame* is out of date, the peacefull hours
When Castles needed not but pleasant bowers.
Not ink, but bloud and tears now serve the turn
To draw the figure of *New-Englands* Urne.
New Englands hour of passion is at hand,
No power except Divine can it withstand;
Scarce hath her glass of fifty years run out,
But her old prosperous Steeds turn heads about,
Tracking themselves back to their poor beginnings,
To fear and fare upon their fruits of sinnings:
So that the mirrour of the Christian world
Lyes burnt to heaps in part, her Streamers furl'd
Grief reigns, joyes flee and dismal fears surprize,
Not dastard spirits only but the wise.
Thus have the fairest hopes deceiv'd the eye
Of the big swoln Expectant standing by.
Thus the proud Ship after a little turn
Sinks into *Neptunes* arms to find its Urn.
Thus hath the heir to many thousands born
Been in an instant from the mother torn.
Ev'n thus thine infant cheeks begin to pale,
And thy supporters through great losses fail.
This is the *Prologue* to thy future woe,
The *Epilogue* no mortal yet can know.

To Lord Bellamont when entering
Governour of the Massachusetts

Were I sole sov'reign of rare Fancies now,
All to your Merits Should with Rev'rence bow.

Transcendent Sir,

Your Stamp is royal; Your Commissions Rays
From loyal Hearts demand loud Thanks, high Praise.
Our Senators with publick Cares so tir'd,
With chearfullness resign to you desird.
Accept a poor Mans Thanks, a rural Bitt,
E're you arrive the Festivalls of Witt.
The Traveller where Wine's not to be had,
With a Cup of cold Water's often glad.
Since Harvards Libertys we fear are lost,
And Hasty-Pudding's Servd in stead of roast.
I've seen some feasted and placd in the Chair
And treated as I thought with Treatment rare:
But what was in the Pot he who this writ,
Tasting not once thereof, Still turnd the Spit.
We hope your Grandeur, for whom all have prayd,
Shall never lack our Love, our Purse, our Aid.
We bless our King; we thank the Waves and Wind,
That to our Sinking State have been So kind:
To land your Person, Ship'd by Grace of God.
Our loyal Hearts bespeak your long Abode.

Had you arriv'd Some hundred Years agoe,
The naked Tribes with knotty Clubbs and Bow
Storming your canvas'd Whale, with spears Head tryd
Whether your Timber had been Soul-ifyd.
An antient Chicataubuts Smoaky Ghost,
Once Lord of all this Soil and dreary Coast
Awakend by the Triumph of this Day
Hearing your Lordship was to come this Way,
Beggd Pluto's Leave, but that it would affright
To testifie his Joy at this fair Sight.

Here's running, riding, pressing hard to See
A blazing Beam darting from Majesty.
And who among whole thousands can do less,
Than for this Voi'ge thank you and Heav'n bless?
Whilst to your Lordship we our Gratias render,
Poor Emmett I tremble as an Offender.
But gen'rous Souls o'er look a World of Faults.
The Heart well trimd, the Pen more rarely halts.

Fam'd Agawam, who once drew salem Fair
Sure prophecyd this Interview so rare.
So what in jest with his Sharp Awl he wrote
Is in good Earnest to our Quarters brought.

Mountains bare-headed Stand; Each fertile Field,
When washd with Showers will rich presents yield.
Adopt this People as we ready be;
An Eden So long hid you'll quickly See.
Deep Mines their Riches tender; Gardens Flowers;
Their Sprawling Vines Stretch out to make you Bowers.
Charles River Swoln with Joys, o'er flows with Thanks:
And Sends his golden *Trouts* up winding Banks.
Old Merimack was ne'er So glad before:
And casts up *Salmon* free cost on the Shore.
Deep Conges drop the *Elm*; tall *Cedars* bow—
And Corydon to gaze deserts the Plough.
Damoetas his Nown Self, had hither rid,
But that he's run with Speed to fetch a Kid.
To make this Country Treat more Solemn up
Brisk Thesiylis comes panting with a Cup
Of dainty Syllabub: Sweet Amaryllis
Her Flask replete with Rose and Daffodyl.
Down at your Ladys Feet her self she flings;
Whilst Daphne, in her Strains, your Welcome sings.
And not one Face in all this Grand Convent
But Smiles forth Tokens of their full Content.
Brisk sons of Mars, Valours right Heirs, all round,
Your modest Arms this Day are richly crownd.
A General you have from Europe blown

Whose very Sight might make *Quebeck* your own
Although With Wrinkled Age my Colours furld,
Under his Conduct we'd soon storm that World.

Pardon, fair Sir, that many Thousand Meet
To lay a Province' Welcomes at your Feet.
A City Treaty for your Worth remains
By Potent Purses and more Powerfull Brains.
I'll to my Coblers Den, with Leave retire:
And if your Grandeur Frowns, there I'll expire.

———

The following Verses were made by
Mr. Benjamin Tompson
Roxbury June 20th. 1713.
being some of his last lines.

I feel this World too mean, and low.
Patron's a lie: Friendship a Show
Preferment trouble: Grandure Vaine
Law a pretence: a Bubble Gaine
Merit a flash: a Blaze Esteem
Promise a Rush: and Hope a Dream
Faith a Disguise: a Truth Deceit
Wealth but a Trap: and Health a Cheat
These dangerous Rocks, Lord help me Shun
Age tells me my Days work is done.

JAMES REVEL

(fl. c. 1659–1680)

The Poor Unhappy Transported Felon's Sorrowful Account of His fourteen Years Transportation at Virginia in America

PART I.

My loving countrymen pray lend an ear,
To this relation that I bring you here,
My present sufferings at large I will unfold,
Altho' its strange, 'tis true as e'er was told.

Of honest parents I did come tho' poor,
Who besides me had children never more,
Near temple-bar was born their darling son,
In virtue's paths he for some time did run.

My parents in me took a vast delight,
And sent me unto school to read and write,
And cast accompts likewise as it appears,
Until that I was aged thirteen years.

Then to a tin man I was apprentice bound,
My master and my mistress good I found,
They lik'd me well, my business I did mind,
From me my parents comfort hop'd to find.

My master near unto Moorfields did dwell,
Here into wicked company I fell,
To wickedness I quickly was inclin'd,
So soon is tainted any youthful mind.

I from my master then did run away,
And rov'd about the streets both night and day,
Did with a gang of thieves a robbing go,
Which fill'd my parents hearts with grief and woe.

At length my master got me home again,
And us'd me well in hopes I might reclaim,
My father tenderly to me did say,
My dearest child why did you run away.

If you had any cause at all for grief,
Why came you not to me to seek relief,

I well do know you did for nothing lack,
Food for the belly, and cloaths for the back.

   My mother said, son, I did implore,
That you will from your master go no more,
Your business mind, your master don't forsake,
Lest you again to wicked courses take.

   I promis'd fair, but yet could not refrain,
But to my old companions went again;
For vice when once, alas! it taints the mind,
Is not soon rooted out again we find.

   With them a thieving I again did go,
But little did my tender parents know,
I followed courses which did seem most vile,
My absence griev'd them being their only child.

   A wicked life I liv'd I must confess,
In fear and dread, and great uneasiness,
Which does attend those actions most unjust,
For thieves can never one another trust.

   Strong liquor banished the thoughts of fear,
But justice stopped us in our full career,
One night was taken up one of our gang,
Who five impeach'd, and three of them were hang'd.

   I was one of the five was try'd and cast,
Yet transportation I did get at last,
A just reward for my vile actions base,
So justice overtook me at the last.

   My father vex'd, my mother she took on,
And said, alas! alas! my only son,
My father said, it cuts me to the heart,
To think on such a cause as this we part.

   To see him grieve pierced my very soul,
My wicked case I sadly did condole,
With grief and shame my eyes did overflow,
And had much rather choose to die than go.

   In vain I grieved and in vain my parents wept,
For I was quickly sent on board the ship,
With melting kisses, and a heavy heart,
I from my parents then did part.

PART II.

In a few days we left the river quite,
And in short time of land we lost the sight,
The captain and the sailors us'd us well,
But kept us under lest we should rebel.

   We were in number much about threescore
A wicked lousy crew as e'er went o'er,
Oaths and tobacco with us plenty were,
Most did smoak, but all did curse and swear

   Five of our number in the passage dy'd,
Who were cast into the ocean wide,
And, after sailing seven weeks and more,
We at Virginia all were put on shore.

   Then to refresh us we were all well clean'd,
That to our buyers we might the better seem;
The things were given that did to each belong,
And they that had clean linen put it on.

   Our faces shav'd, comb'd our wigs and hair,
That we in decent order might appear,
Against the Planters did come us to view,
How well they lik'd this fresh transported crew.

   The women from us separated stood,
As well as we by them to be thus view'd,
And in short time some men up to us came,
Some ask'd our trade, others ask'd our name.

   Some view'd our limbs turning us round,
Examining like horses if we were sound,
What trade my lad, said one to me,
A tin-man sir. That will not do for me.

   Some felt our hands, others our legs and feet,
And made us walk to see if we were compleat.
Some view'd our teeth, to see if they were good,
And fit to chew our hard and homely food.

   If any like our limbs, our looks and trades,
Our captain then a good advantage make,
For they a difference make it doth appear,
'Twixt those of seven and those of fourteen years.

   Another difference too there is allow'd,
Those who have money will have favour shew'd;
But if no cloaths nor money they have got,

Hard is their fate, and hard will be their lot.
  At length a grim old man unto me came,
He ask'd my trade, likewise my name,
I told him I a tin-man was by trade,
And not eighteen years of age I said.
  Likewise the cause I told which brought me here,
And for fourteen years transported were;
And when from me he this did understand,
He bought me of the captain out of hand.

PART III.

Down to the harbour I was took again,
On board a ship loaded with chains;
Which I was forc'd to wear both night and day,
For fear I from the sloop should run away.
  My master was a man but of ill fame,
Who first of all a transport thither came,
In Rapahannock county he did dwell,
In Rapahannock river known full well.
  When the ship was laden and home sent,
An hundred miles we up the river went,
The weather cold, and very hard my fare,
My lodgings on the deck both hard and bare.
  At last to my new master's house I came,
To the town of Wicowoco call'd by name,
Here my European cloaths were took from me,
Which never after I could ever see.
  A canvas shirt and trowzers me they gave,
A hop sack frock in which I was a slave,
No shoes or stockings had I for to wear,
Nor hat nor cap my head and feet were bare.
  Thus dress'd, into the field I next did go,
Among tobacco plants all day to hoe,
At day break in the morn our work begun,
And lasted till the setting of the sun.
  My fellow slaves were five transports more,
With eighteen negroes which is twenty four,
Besides four transport women in the house,
To wait upon his daughter and his spouse.
  We and the negroes both alike did fare,

Of work and food we had an equal share,
And in a piece of ground called our own,
The food we eat first by ourselves is sown.

   No other time to us they will allow,
But on a Sunday we the same must do,
Six days we slave for our master's good,
The seventh is to produce our homely food,

   And when we a hard day's work have done,
Away unto the mill we must be gone,
'Till twelve or one o'clock a grinding corn,
And must be up by day light in the morn.

   And if you get in debt with any one,
It must be paid before from thence you come,
In publick places they'll put up your name,
As every one their just demands may claim.

   But if we offer for to run away,
For every hour we must serve a day,
For every day a week, they're so severe,
Every week a month, every month a year.

   But if they murder, rob or steal while there,
They're straitway hang'd the laws are so severe,
For by the rigour of that very law,
They are kept under and do stand in awe.

PART IV.

At last it pleased God I sick did fall,
But I no favour could receive at all,
For I was forc'd to work while I could stand,
Or hold the hoe within my feeble hand.

   Much hardship then I did endure,
No dog was ever nursed so before,
More pity then the negro slaves bestow'd,
Than my inhuman brutal master show'd.

   Oft on my knees the Lord I did implore,
To let me see my native land once more,
For through his grace my life I would amend,
And be a comfort to my dearest friends.

   Helpless and sick and left alone,
I by myself did use to make my moan,
And think upon my former wicked ways,

That had brought me to this wretched case.
 The Lord who saw my grief and smart,
And my complaint, he knew my contrite heart,
His gracious mercy did to me afford,
My health again was unto me restor'd.

 It pleas'd the Lord to grant to me such grace,
That tho' I was in such a barbarous place,
I serv'd the Lord with fervency and zeal,
By which I did much inward comfort feel.

 Now twelve years had passed thus away,
And but two more by law I had to stay,
When death did my cruel master call,
But that was no relief to me at all.

 The Widow would not the plantation hold,
So we and that were to be sold,
A Lawyer who at James town did dwell,
Came for to see and lik'd it very well.

 He bought the negroes who for life are slaves,
But no transported felons would he have,
So we were put like sheep into the fold,
Unto the best bidder to be sold.

PART V.

A Gentleman who seemed very grave,
Said unto me, how long are you a slave,
Not two years quite, I unto him reply'd,
That is but very short indeed, he cry'd.

 He ask'd my trade, name and whence I came,
And what vile fact had brought me to this shame,
I told him all, at which he shook his head,
I hope you have seen your folly now he said.

 I told him yes, and truly did repent,
But what made me most of all relent,
That I should to my parents prove so wild,
Being their darling and their only child.

 He said no more but from me short did turn,
While from my eyes the tears did trickling run,
To see him to my overseer to go,
But what he said to him, I do not know,
 He straitway came unto me again,

And said, no longer you must here remain,
For I have bought you of this man said he,
Therefore prepare yourself to go with me.

    I went with him, my heart opprest with woe,
Not knowing him or where I must go,
But was surprized very much to find,
He used me so tenderly and kind.

    He said he would not use me as a slave,
But as a servant if I'd well behave,
And if I pleas'd him when my time expir'd,
He'd send me home again if I requir'd.

    My kind new master did at James-town dwell,
By trade a cooper and liv'd very well,
I was his servant on him to attend,
Thus God unlook'd for raised me a friend.

PART VI.

Thus did I live in plenty, peace and ease,
Having none but my master to please,
And if at any time he did ride out,
I with him rode the country round about.

    And in my heart I often griev'd to see,
So many transport felons there to be,
Some who in England have liv'd fine and brave,
Were like horses forc'd to trudge and slave.

    At length my fourteen years expir'd quite,
Which fill'd my very soul with fond delight,
To think I should no longer there remain,
But to old England once return again.

    My master for me did express much love,
And as good as his promise he did prove,
He got me ship'd and I came home again,
With joy and comfort tho' I went with pain.

    My father and mother well I found,
Who to see me with joy did abound,
My mother over me did weep with joy,
My father cry'd, once more I see my boy.

    Whom I thought dead, but does alive remain,
And is returned to me once again,

I hope God has so wrought upon thy mind,
No more to wickedness thoul't be inclin'd,
   I told him all the dangers I went thro',
Likewise my sickness, and my hardships too,
Which fill'd their tender hearts with sad surprize,
While melting tears ran trickling from their eyes,
   I begg'd of them from all grief to refrain,
Since God had brought me to their home again,
The Lord unto me so much grace would give,
To work for you both while I do live.
   My countrymen take warning e'er too late,
Lest you shou'd share my unhappy fate,
Altho' but little crimes you here have done,
Think of seven or fourteen years to come.
   Forc'd from your friends and country to go,
Among the Negroes to work at the hoe,
Indifferent countries void of all relief,
Sold for a slave because you prov'd a thief.
   Now young men all with speed your lives amend
Take my advice, as one that is your friend,
For tho' so slight you do make of it here,
Hard is your lot if you once get there.

EDWARD TAYLOR

(c. 1645–1729)

Preparatory Meditations (First Series)

1. Meditation

Westfield 23.5m 1682.

What Love is this of thine, that Cannot bee
   In thine Infinity, O Lord, Confinde,
Unless it in thy very Person see,
    Infinity, and Finity Conjoyn'd?
    What hath thy Godhead, as not satisfide
    Marri'de our Manhood, making it its Bride?

Oh, Matchless Love! filling Heaven to the brim!
   O're running it: all running o're beside
This World! Nay Overflowing Hell; wherein
    For thine Elect, there rose a mighty Tide!
    That there our Veans might through thy Person bleed,
    To quench those flames, that else would on us feed.

Oh! that thy Love might overflow my Heart!
   To fire the same with Love: for Love I would.
But oh! my streight'ned Breast! my Lifeless Sparke!
    My Fireless Flame! What Chilly Love, and Cold?
    In measure small! In Manner Chilly! See.
    Lord blow the Coal: Thy Love Enflame in mee.

3. Meditation. Can. 1.3. Thy Good Ointment

11.12m 1682.

How sweet a Lord is mine? If any should
   Guarded, Engarden'd, nay, Imbosomd bee
In reechs of Odours, Gales of Spices, Folds
   Of Aromaticks, Oh! how sweet was hee?

164

He would be sweet, and yet his sweetest Wave
Compar'de to thee my Lord, no Sweet would have.

A Box of Ointments, broke; sweetness most sweet.
  A surge of spices: Odours Common Wealth,
A Pillar of Perfume: a steaming Reech
  Of Aromatick Clouds: All Saving Health.
  Sweetness itselfe thou art: And I presume
  In Calling of thee Sweet, who art Perfume.

But Woe is mee! who have so quick a Sent
  To Catch perfumes pufft out from Pincks, and Roses
And other Muscadalls, as they get Vent,
  Out of their Mothers Wombs to bob our noses.
  And yet thy sweet perfume doth seldom latch
  My Lord, within my Mammulary Catch.

Am I denos'de? or doth the Worlds ill sents
  Engarison my nosthrills narrow bore?
Or is my smell lost in these Damps it Vents?
  And shall I never finde it any more?
  Or is it like the Hawks, or Hownds whose breed
  Take stincking Carrion for Perfume indeed?

This is my Case. All things smell sweet to mee:
  Except thy sweetness, Lord. Expell these damps.
Breake up this Garison: and let me see
  Thy Aromaticks pitching in these Camps.
  Oh! let the Clouds of thy sweet Vapours rise,
  And both my Mammularies Circumcise.

Shall Spirits thus my Mammularies suck?
  (As Witches Elves their teats,) and draw from thee
My Dear, Dear Spirit after fumes of muck?
  Be Dunghill Damps more sweet than Graces bee?
  Lord, clear these Caves. These Passes take, and keep.
  And in these Quarters lodge thy Odours sweet.

Lord, breake thy Box of Ointment on my Head;
  Let thy sweet Powder powder all my hair:

My Spirits let with thy perfumes be fed
   And make thy Odours, Lord, my nosthrills fare.
   My Soule shall in thy sweets then soar to thee:
   I'le be thy Love, thou my sweet Lord shalt bee.

4. Meditation. Cant. 2.1. I am the Rose of Sharon

22.2m 1683.

My Silver Chest a Sparke of Love up locks:
   And out will let it when I can't well Use.
The gawdy World me Courts t'unlock the Box,
   A motion makes, where Love may pick and choose.
   Her Downy Bosom opes, that pedlars Stall,
   Of Wealth, Sports, Honours, Beauty, slickt up all.

Love pausing on't, these Clayey Faces she
   Disdains to Court; but Pilgrims life designs,
And Walkes in Gilliads Land, and there doth see
   The Rose of Sharon which with Beauty shines.
   Her Chest Unlocks; the Sparke of Love out breaths
   To Court this Rose: and lodgeth in its leaves.

No flower in Garzia Horti shines like this:
   No Beauty sweet in all the World so Choice:
It is the Rose of Sharon sweet, that is
   The Fairest Rose that Grows in Paradise.
   Blushes of Beauty bright, Pure White, and Red
   In Sweats of Glory on Each Leafe doth bed.

Lord lead me into this sweet Rosy Bower:
   Oh! Lodge my Soul in this Sweet Rosy bed:
Array my Soul with this sweet Sharon flower:
   Perfume me with the Odours it doth shed.
   Wealth, Pleasure, Beauty Spirituall will line
   My pretious Soul, if Sharons Rose be mine.

The Blood Red Pretious Syrup of this Rose
   Doth all Catholicons excell what ere.

Ill Humours all that do the Soule inclose
   When rightly usd, it purgeth out most clear.
   Lord purge my Soul with this Choice Syrup, and
   Chase all thine Enemies out of my land.

The Rosy Oyle, from Sharons Rose extract
   Better than Palma Christi far is found.
Its Gilliads Balm for Conscience when she's wrackt
   Unguent Apostolorum for each Wound.
   Let me thy Patient, thou my Surgeon bee.
   Lord, with thy Oyle of Roses Supple mee.

No Flower there is in Paradise that grows
   Whose Virtues Can Consumptive Souls restore
But Shugar of Roses made of Sharons Rose
   When Dayly usd, doth never fail to Cure.
   Lord let my Dwindling Soul be dayly fed
   With Sugar of Sharons Rose, its dayly Bread.

God Chymist is, doth Sharons Rose distill.
   Oh! Choice Rose Water! Swim my Soul herein.
Let Conscience bibble in it with her Bill.
   Its Cordiall, ease doth Heart burns Causd by Sin.
   Oyle, Syrup, Sugar, and Rose Water such.
   Lord, give, give, give; I cannot have too much.

But, oh! alas! that such should be my need
   That this Brave Flower must Pluckt, stampt, squeezed bee,
And boyld up in its Blood, its Spirits sheed,
   To make a Physick sweet, sure, safe for mee.
   But yet this mangled Rose rose up again
   And in its pristine glory, doth remain.

All Sweets, and Beauties of all Flowers appeare
   In Sharons Rose, whose Glorious Leaves out vie
In Vertue, Beauty, Sweetness, Glory Cleare,
   The Spangled Leaves of Heavens cleare Chrystall Sky.
   Thou Rose of Heaven, Glory's Blossom Cleare
   Open thy Rosie Leaves, and lodge mee there.

My Dear-Sweet Lord, shall I thy Glory meet
    Lodg'd in a Rose, that out a sweet Breath breaths.
What is my way to Glory made thus sweet,
    Strewd all along with Sharons Rosy Leaves.
    I'le walk this Rosy Path: World fawn, or frown
    And Sharons Rose shall be my Rose, and Crown.

The Reflexion

Lord, art thou at the Table Head above
    Meat, Med'cine, sweetness, sparkling Beautys to
Enamour Souls with Flaming Flakes of Love,
    And not my Trencher, nor my Cup o'reflow?
    Be n't I a bidden Guest? Oh! sweat mine Eye.
    Oreflow with Teares: Oh! draw thy fountains dry.

Shall I not smell thy sweet, oh! Sharons Rose?
    Shall not mine Eye salute thy Beauty? Why?
Shall thy sweet leaves their Beautious sweets upclose?
    As halfe ashamde my sight should on them ly?
    Woe's me! for this my sighs shall be in grain
    Offer'd on Sorrows Altar for the same.

Had not my Soule's thy Conduit, Pipes stopt bin
    With mud, what Ravishment would'st thou Convay?
Let Graces Golden Spade dig till the Spring
    Of tears arise, and cleare this filth away.
    Lord, let thy spirit raise my sighings till
    These Pipes my soule do with thy sweetness fill.

Earth once was Paradise of Heaven below
    Till inkefac'd sin had it with poyson stockt
And Chast this Paradise away into
    Heav'ns upmost Loft, and it in Glory Lockt.
    But thou, sweet Lord, hast with thy golden Key
    Unlockt the Doore, and made, a golden day.

Once at thy Feast, I saw thee Pearle-like stand
    'Tween Heaven, and Earth where Heavens Bright glory all

In streams fell on thee, as a floodgate and,
   Like Sun Beams through thee on the World to Fall.
   Oh! sugar sweet then! my Deare sweet Lord, I see
   Saints Heavens-lost Happiness restor'd by thee.

Shall Heaven, and Earth's bright Glory all up lie
   Like Sun Beams bundled in the sun, in thee?
Dost thou sit Rose at Table Head, where I
   Do sit, and Carv'st no morsell sweet for mee?
   So much before, so little now! Sprindge, Lord,
   Thy Rosie Leaves, and me their Glee afford.

Shall not thy Rose my Garden fresh perfume?
   Shall not thy Beauty my dull Heart assaile?
Shall not thy golden gleams run through this gloom?
   Shall my black Velvet Mask thy fair Face Vaile?
   Pass o're my Faults: shine forth, bright sun: arise
   Enthrone thy Rosy-selfe within mine Eyes.

9. Meditation. Joh. 6.51. I am the Living Bread

7.7m 1684.

Did Ever Lord such noble house mentain,
   As my Lord doth? Or such a noble Table?
'T would breake the back of kings, nay, Monarchs brain
   To do it. Pish, the Worlds Estate's not able.
   I'le bet a boast with any that this Bread
   I eate excells what ever Caesar had.

Take earth's Brightst Darlings, in whose mouths all flakes
   Of Lushous Sweets she hath do croude their Head,
Their Spiced Cups, sweet Meats, and Sugar Cakes
   Are but dry Sawdust to this Living Bread.
   I'le pawn my part in Christ, this Dainti'st Meate,
   Is Gall, and Wormwood unto what I eate.

The Boasting Spagyrist (Insipid Phlegm,
   Whose Words out strut the Sky) vaunts he hath rife

The Water, Tincture, Lozenge, Gold, and Gem,
   Of Life itselfe. But here's the Bread of Life.
I'le lay my Life, his Aurum Vitae Red
   Is to my Bread of Life, worse than DEAD HEAD.

The Dainti'st Dish of Earthly Cookery
   Is but to fat the body up in print.
This Bread of Life doth feed the Soule, whereby
   Its made the Temple of Jehovah in't.
   I'le Venture Heav'n upon't that Low or High
   That eate this Living Bread shall never dy.

This Bread of Life, so excellent, I see
   The Holy Angells doubtless would, if they
Were prone unto base Envie, Envie't mee.
   But oh! come, tast how sweet it is. I say,
   I'le Wage my Soule and all therein uplaid,
   This is the sweetest Bread that e're God made.

What wonder's here, that Bread of Life should come
   To feed Dead Dust? Dry Dust eate Living Bread?
Yet Wonder more by far may all, and some
   That my Dull Heart's so dumpish when thus fed.
   Lord Pardon this, and feed mee all my dayes,
   With Living Bread to thy Eternall Prayse.

23. Meditation. Cant. 4.8. My Spouse

21.6m 1687.

Would God I in that Golden City were,
   With Jaspers Walld, all garnisht, and made swash,
With Pretious Stones, whose Gates are Pearles most cleare
   And Street Pure Gold, like to transparent Glass.
   That my dull Soule, might be inflamde to see
   How Saints and Angells ravisht are in Glee.

Were I but there, and could but tell my Story,
   'Twould rub those Walls of Pretious Stones more bright:

And glaze those Gates of Pearle, with brighter Glory;
   And pave the golden Street with greater light.
   'Twould in fresh Raptures Saints, and Angells fling.
   But I poore Snake Crawl here, scarce mudwalld in.

May my Rough Voice, and my blunt Tongue but spell
   My Tale (for tune they can't) perhaps there may
Some Angell catch an end of't up, and tell
   In Heaven, when he doth return that way,
   He'l make thy Palace, Lord, all over ring,
   With it in Songs, thy Saint, and Angells sing.

I know not how to speak't, it is so good:
   Shall Mortall, and Immortall marry? nay,
Man marry God? God be a Match for Mud?
   The King of Glory Wed a Worm? mere Clay?
   This is the Case. The Wonder too in Bliss.
   Thy Maker is thy Husband. Hearst thou this?

My Maker, he my Husband? Oh! strange joy!
   If Kings wed Worms, and Monarchs Mites wed should,
Glory spouse Shame, a Prince a Snake or Fly
   An Angell Court an Ant, all Wonder would.
   Let such wed Worms, Snakes, Serpents, Divells, Flyes.
   Less Wonder than the Wedden in our Eyes.

I am to Christ more base, than to a King
   A Mite, Fly, Worm, Ant, Serpent, Divell is,
Or Can be, being tumbled all in Sin,
   And shall I be his Spouse? How good is this?
   It is too good to be declar'de to thee.
   But not too good to be believ'de by mee.

Yet to this Wonder, this is found in mee,
   I am not onely base but backward Clay,
When Christ doth Wooe: and till his Spirit bee
   His Spokes man to Compell me I deny.
   I am so base and Froward to him, Hee
   Appears as Wonders Wonder, wedding mee.

Seing, Dear Lord, its thus, thy Spirit take
 And send thy Spokes man, to my Soul, I pray.
Thy Saving Grace my Wedden Garment make:
 Thy Spouses Frame into my Soul Convay.
 I then shall be thy Bride Espousd by thee
 And thou my Bridesgroom Deare Espousde shalt bee.

   24. Meditation. Eph. 2.18. Through him we
    have—an Access—unto the Father

6.9m 1687.

Was there a Palace of Pure Gold, all Ston'de
 And pav'de with Pearles, whose Gates Rich Jaspers were,
And Throne a Carbuncle, whose King Enthronde
 Sat on a Cushion all of Sunshine Cleare;
 Whose Crown a Bunch of Sun Beams was: I should
 Prize such as in his favour shrine me Would.

Thy Milke white Hand, my Glorious Lord, doth this:
 It opes this Gate, and me Conducts into
This Golden Palace whose rich Pavement is
 Of Pretious Pearles: and to this King also.
 Thus Thron'de, and Crown'd: whose Words are 'bellisht all
 With brighter Beams, than e're the Sun let fall.

But oh! Poore mee, thy sluggish Servant, I
 More blockish than a block, as blockhead, stand.
Though mine Affections Quick as Lightning fly
 On toys, they Snaile like move to kiss thy hand.
 My Coal-black doth thy Milke White hand avoide,
 That would above the Milky Way me guide.

What aim'st at, Lord? that I should be so Cross.
 My minde is Leaden in thy Golden Shine.
Though all o're Spirit, when this dirty Dross
 Doth touch it with its smutting leaden lines.
 What shall an Eagle t'catch a Fly thus run?
 Or Angell Dive after a Mote ith'Sun?

What Folly's this? I fain would take, I thinke,
  Vengeance upon myselfe: But I Confess,
I can't. Mine Eyes, Lord, shed no Tears but inke.
  My handy Works, are Words, and Wordiness.
  Earth's Toyes ware Knots of my Affections, nay,
  Though from thy Glorious Selfe they're Stoole away.

Oh! that my heart was made thy Golden Box
  Full of Affections, and of Love Divine
Knit all in Tassles, and in True-Love Knots,
  To garnish o're this Worthy Worke of thine.
  This Box and all therein more rich than Gold,
  In sacred Flames, I to thee offer would.

With thy rich Tissue my poore Soule array:
  And lead me to thy Fathers House above.
Thy Graces Storehouse make my Soule I pray.
  Thy Praise shall then ware Tassles of my Love.
  If thou Conduct mee in thy Fathers Wayes,
  I'le be the Golden Trumpet of thy Praise.

32. Meditation. 1 Cor. 3.22.
Whether Paul or Apollos, or Cephas

28.2m 1689.

Thy Grace, Dear Lord's my golden Wrack, I finde
  Screwing my Phancy into ragged Rhimes,
Tuning thy Praises in my feeble minde
  Untill I come to strike them on my Chimes.
  Were I an Angell bright, and borrow could
  King Davids Harp, I would them play on gold.

But plung'd I am, my minde is puzzled,
  When I would spin my Phancy thus unspun,
In finest Twine of Praise I'm muzzled.
  My tazzled Thoughts twirld into Snick-Snarls run.
  Thy Grace, my Lord, is such a glorious thing,
  It doth Confound me when I would it sing.

Eternall Love an Object mean did smite
　　Which by the Prince of Darkness was beguilde,
That from this Love it ran and sweld with spite
　　And in the way with filth was all defilde
　　Yet must be reconcild, cleansd, and begrac'te
　　Or from the fruits of Gods first Love displac'te.

Then Grace, my Lord, wrought in thy Heart a vent,
　　Thy Soft Soft hand to this hard worke did goe,
And to the Milke White Throne of Justice went
　　And entred bond that Grace might overflow.
　　Hence did thy Person to my Nature ty
　　And bleed through humane Veans to satisfy.

Oh! Grace, Grace, Grace! this Wealthy Grace doth lay
　　Her Golden Channells from thy Fathers throne,
Into our Earthen Pitchers to Convay
　　Heavens Aqua Vitae to us for our own.
　　O! let thy Golden Gutters run into
　　My Cup this Liquour till it overflow.

Thine Ordinances, Graces Wine-fats where
　　Thy Spirits Walkes, and Graces runs doe ly
And Angells waiting stand with holy Cheere
　　From Graces Conduite Head, with all Supply.
　　These Vessells full of Grace are, and the Bowls
　　In which their Taps do run, are pretious Souls.

Thou to the Cups dost say (that Catch this Wine,)
　　This Liquour, Golden Pipes, and Wine-fats plain,
Whether Paul, Apollos, Cephas, all are thine.
　　Oh Golden Word! Lord speake it ore again.
　　Lord speake it home to me, say these are mine.
　　My Bells shall then thy Praises bravely chime.

39. Meditation. from 1 Joh. 2.1.
If any man sin, we have an Advocate

9.9m 1690.

My Sin! my Sin, My God, these Cursed Dregs,
　　Green, Yellow, Blew streakt Poyson hellish, ranck,
Bubs hatcht in natures nest on Serpents Eggs,
　　Yelp, Cherp and Cry; they set my Soule a Cramp.
　　I frown, Chide, strik and fight them, mourn and Cry
　　To Conquour them, but cannot them destroy.

I cannot kill nor Coop them up: my Curb
　　'S less than a Snaffle in their mouth: my Rains
They as a twine thrid, snap: by hell they're spurd:
　　And load my Soule with swagging loads of pains.
　　Black Imps, young Divells, snap, bite, drag to bring
　　And pick mee headlong hells dread Whirle Poole in.

Lord, hold thy hand: for handle mee thou may'st
　　In Wrath: but, oh, a twinckling Ray of hope
Methinks I spie thou graciously display'st.
　　There is an Advocate: a doore is ope.
　　Sin's poyson swell my heart would till it burst,
　　Did not a hope hence creep in't thus, and nurse't.

Joy, joy, Gods Son's the Sinners Advocate
　　Doth plead the Sinner guiltless, and a Saint.
But yet Atturnies pleas spring from the State
　　The Case is in: if bad its bad in plaint.
　　My Papers do contain no pleas that do
　　Secure mee from, but knock me down to, woe.

I have no plea mine Advocate to give:
　　What now? He'l anvill Arguments greate Store
Out of his Flesh and Blood to make thee live.
　　O Deare bought Arguments: Good pleas therefore.
　　Nails made of heavenly Steel, more Choice than gold
　　Drove home, Well Clencht, eternally will hold.

Oh! Dear bought Plea, Deare Lord, what buy't so deare?
   What with thy blood purchase thy plea for me?
Take Argument out of thy Grave t'appeare
   And plead my Case with, me from Guilt to free.
   These maule both Sins, and Divells, and amaze
   Both Saints, and Angells; Wreath their mouths with praise.

What shall I doe, my Lord? what do, that I
   May have thee plead my Case? I fee thee will
With Faith, Repentance, and obediently
   Thy Service gainst Satanick Sins fulfill.
   I'l fight thy fields while Live I do, although
   I should be hackt in pieces by thy foe.

Make me thy Friend, Lord, be my Surety: I
   Will be thy Client, be my Advocate:
My Sins make thine, thy Pleas make mine hereby.
   Thou wilt mee save, I will thee Celebrate.
   Thou'lt kill my Sins that cut my heart within:
   And my rough Feet shall thy smooth praises sing.

46. Meditation. Rev. 3.5.
The same shall be cloathed in White Raiment

17.5m 1692.

Nay, may I, Lord, believe it? Shall my Skeg
   Be ray'd in thy White Robes? My thatcht old Cribb
(Immortal Purss hung on a mortall Peg,)
   Wilt thou with fair'st array in heaven rig?
   I'm but a jumble of gross Elements
   A Snaile Horn where an Evill Spirit tents.

A Dirt ball dresst in milk white Lawn, and deckt
   In Tissue tagd with gold, or Ermins flush,
That mocks the Starrs, and sets them in a fret
   To se themselves out shone thus. Oh they blush.
   Wonders stand gastard here. But yet my Lord,
   This is but faint to what thou dost afford.

I'm but a Ball of dirt. Wilt thou adorn
   Mee with thy Web wove in thy Loom Divine
The Whitest Web in Glory, that the morn
   Nay, that all Angell glory, doth ore shine?
   They ware no such. This whitest Lawn most fine
   Is onely worn, my Lord, by thee and thine.

This Saye's no flurr of Wit, nor new Coin'd Shape
   Of frollick Fancie in a Rampant Brain.
It's juyce Divine bled from the Choicest Grape
   That ever Zions Vinyarde did mentain.
   Such Mortall bits immortalliz'de shall ware
   More glorious robes, than glorious Angells bare.

Their Web is wealthy, wove of Wealthy Silke
   Well wrought indeed, its all brancht Taffity.
But this thy Web more white by far than milke
   Spun on thy Wheele twine of thy Diety
   Wove in thy Web, Fulld in thy mill by hand
   Makes them in all their bravery seem tand.

This Web is wrought by best, and noblest Art
   That heaven doth afford of twine most choice
All brancht, and richly flowerd in every part
   With all the sparkling flowers of Paradise
   To be thy Ware alone, who hast no peere
   And Robes for glorious Saints to thee most deare.

Wilt thou, my Lord, dress my poore wither'd Stump
   In this rich web whose whiteness doth excell
The Snow, though 'tis most black? And shall my Lump
   Of Clay ware more than e're on Angells fell?
   What shall my bit of Dirt be deckt so fine
   That shall Angelick glory all out shine?

Shall things run thus? Then Lord, my tumberill
   Unload of all its Dung, and make it cleane.
And load it with thy wealthi'st Grace untill
   Its Wheeles do crack, or Axletree complain.
   I fain would have it cart thy harvest in,
   Before its loosed from its Axlepin.

Then screw my Strings up to thy tune that I
　May load thy Glory with my Songs of praise.
Make me thy Shalm, thy praise my Songs, whereby
　My mean Shoshannim may thy Michtams raise.
　And when my Clay ball's in thy White robes dresst
　My tune perfume thy praise shall with the best.

FROM

Preparatory Meditations (Second Series)

1. Meditation. Col. 2.17. Which are
Shaddows of things to come and the body is Christs

1693.

Oh Leaden heeld. Lord, give, forgive I pray.
　Infire my Heart: it bedded is in Snow.
I Chide myselfe seing myselfe decay.
　In heate and Zeale to thee, I frozen grow.
　File my dull Spirits: make them sharp and bright:
　Them firbush for thyselfe, and thy delight.

My Stains are such, and sinke so deep, that all
　The Excellency in Created Shells
Too low, and little is to make it fall
　Out of my leather Coate wherein it dwells.
　This Excellence is but a Shade to that
　Which is enough to make my Stains go back.

The glory of the world slickt up in types
　In all Choise things chosen to typify,
His glory upon whom the worke doth light,
　To thine's a Shaddow, or a butterfly.
　How glorious then, my Lord, art thou to mee
　Seing to cleanse me, 's worke alone for thee.

The glory of all Types doth meet in thee.
　Thy glory doth their glory quite excell:

More than the Sun excells in its bright glee
   A nat, an Earewig, Weevill, Snaile, or Shell.
   Wonders in Crowds start up; your eyes may strut
   Viewing his Excellence, and's bleeding cut.

Oh! that I had but halfe an eye to view
   This excellence of thine, undazled: so
Therewith to give my heart a touch anew
   Untill I quickned am, and made to glow.
   All is too little for thee: but alass
   Most of my little all hath other pass.

Then Pardon, Lord, my fault: and let thy beams
   Of Holiness pierce through this Heart of mine.
Ope to thy Blood a passage through my veans.
   Let thy pure blood my impure blood refine.
   Then with new blood and spirits I will dub
   My tunes upon thy Excellency good.

4. Meditation. Gal. 4.24.
Which things are an Allegorie

24.10m 1693.

My Gracious Lord, I would thee glory doe:
   But finde my Garden over grown with weeds:
My Soile is sandy; brambles o're it grow;
   My Stock is stunted; branch no good Fruits breeds.
   My Garden weed: Fatten my Soile, and prune
   My Stock, and make it with thy glory bloome.

O Glorious One, the gloriou'st thought I thincke
   Of thee falls black as Inck upon thy Glory.
The brightest Saints that rose, do Star like, pinck.
   Nay, Abrams Shine to thee's an Allegory,
   Or fleeting Sparke in th'Smoke, to typify
   Thee, and thy Glorious Selfe in mystery.

Should all the Sparks in heaven, the Stars there dance
   A Galliard, Round about the Sun, and stay
His Servants (while on Easter morn his prance
   Is o're, which old wives prate of) O brave Play.
   Thy glorious Saints thus boss thee round, which stand
   Holding thy glorious Types out in their hand.

But can I thinck this Glory greate, its head
   Thrust in a pitchy cloude, should strangled ly
Or tucking up its beams should go to bed
   Within the Grave, darke me to glorify?
   This Mighty thought my hearts too streight for, though
   I hold it by the hand, and let not goe.

Then, my Blesst Lord, let not the Bondmaids type
   Take place in mee. But thy blesst Promisd Seed.
Distill thy Spirit through thy royall Pipe
   Into my Soule, and so my Spirits feed,
   Then them, and me still into praises right
   Into thy Cup where I to swim delight.

Though I desire so much, I can't o're doe.
   All that my Can contains, to nothing comes
When summed up, it onely Cyphers grows
   Unless thou set thy Figures to my Sums.
   Lord set thy Figure 'fore them, greate, or small.
   To make them something, and I'l give thee all.

12. Meditation. Ezek. 37.24.
David my Servant shall be their King

7.5 m 1695.

Dull, Dull indeed! What shall it e're be thus?
   And why? Are not thy Promises, my Lord,
Rich, Quick'ning things? How should my full Cheeks blush
   To finde mee thus? And those a lifeless Word?
   My Heart is heedless: unconcernd hereat:
   I finde my Spirits Spiritless, and flat.

Thou Courtst mine Eyes in Sparkling Colours bright,
   Most bright indeed, and soul enamoring,
With the most Shining Sun, whose beames did smite
   Me with delightfull Smiles to make mee spring.
   Embellisht knots of Love assault my minde
   Which still is Dull, as if this Sun ne're shin'de.

David in all his gallantry now comes,
   Bringing to tende thy Shrine, his Royall Glory,
Rich Prowess, Prudence, Victories, Sweet Songs,
   And Piety to Pensill out thy Story;
   To draw my Heart to thee in this brave shine
   Of typick Beams, most warm. But still I pine.

Shall not this Lovely Beauty, Lord, set out
   In Dazzling Shining Flashes 'fore mine Eye,
Enchant my heart, Love's golden mine, till't spout
   Out Streames of Love refin'd that on thee lie?
   Thy Glory's great: Thou Davids Kingdom shalt
   Enjoy for aye. I want and thats my fault.

Spare me, my Lord, spare me, I greatly pray,
   Let me thy Gold pass through thy Fire untill
Thy Fire refine, and take my filth away.
   That I may shine like Gold, and have my fill
   Of Love for thee; untill my Virginall
   Chime out in Changes sweet thy Praises shall.

Wipe off my Rust, Lord, with thy wisp me scoure,
   And make thy Beams pearch on my Strings their blaze.
My tunes Cloath with thy Shine, and Quavers poure
   My Cursing Strings on, loaded with thy Praise.
   My Fervent Love with Musick in her hand,
   Shall then attend thyselfe, and thy Command.

14. Meditation. Col. 2.3. In whom are hid all the Treasures of Wisdom, and Knowledge

3d.9m 1695.

Halfe Dead: and rotten at the Coare: my Lord!
 I am Consumptive: and my Wasted lungs
Scarce draw a Breath of aire: my Silver Coard
 Is loose. My buckles almost have no tongues.
 My Heart is Fistulate: I am a Shell.
 In Guilt and Filth I wallow, Sent and Smell.

Shall not that Wisdom horded up in thee
 (One key whereof is Sacerdotall Types)
Provide a Cure for all this griefe in mee
 And in the Court of Justice save from Stripes,
 And purge away all Filth and Guilt, and bring
 A Cure to my Consumption as a King?

Shall not that Wisdom horded in thee (which
 Prophetick Types enucleate) forth shine
With Light enough a Saving Light to fix
 On my Poore Taper? And a Flame Divine?
 Making my Soule thy Candle and its Flame
 Thy Light to guide mee, till I Glory gain?

Shall not that Wisdom horded in thee up
 (Which Kingly Types do shine upon in thee)
Mee with its Chrystall Cupping Glasses cup
 And draine ill Humours wholy out of mee?
 Ore come my Sin? And mee adorn with Grace
 And fit me for thy Service, and thy Face?

How do these Pointers type thee out most right
 As Graces Officine of Wisdom pure
The fingers Salves and Medicines so right
 That never faile, when usd, to worke a Cure?
 Oh! that it would my Wasted lungs recrute.
 And make my feeble Spirits upward shute.

How Glorious art thou, Lord? Cloathd with the Glory
   Of Prophets, Priests, and Kings? Nay all Types come
To lay their Glory on thee. (Brightsome Story).
     Their Rayes attend thee, as Sun Beams the Sun.
     And shall my Ulcer'd Soule have such reliefe?
     Such glorious Cure? Lord strengthen my beliefe.

Why dost not love, my Soule? or Love grow strong?
   These glorious Beams of Wisdom on thee shine.
Will not this Sunshine make thy branch green long,
     And flowrish as it doth to heaven climbe?
     Oh! chide thyselfe out of thy Lethargie,
     And unto Christ on Angells wings up fly.

Draw out thy Wisdom, Lord, and make mee just.
   Draw out thy Wisdom. Wisdoms Crown give mee.
With shining Holiness Candy my Crust:
     And make mee to thy Scepter bow the knee.
     Let thy rich Grace mee save from Sin, and Death:
     And I will tune thy Praise with holy Breath.

18. Meditation. Heb. 13.10. Wee have an Altar

Westfield 18.8m 1696.

A Bran, a Chaff, a very Barly yawn,
   An Husk, a Shell, a Nothing, nay yet Worse,
A Thistle, Bryer prickle, pricking Thorn
     A Lump of Lewdeness, Pouch of Sin, a purse
     Of Naughtiness, I am, yea what not Lord?
     And wilt thou be mine Altar? and my bord?

Mine Heart's a Park or Chase of sins: Mine Head
   'S a Bowling Alley. Sins play Ninehole here.
Phansy's a Green: sin Barly breaks in't led.
     Judgment's a pingle. Blindeman's Buff's plaid there.
     Sin playes at Coursey Parke within my Minde.
     My Wills a Walke in which it aires what's blinde.

Sure then I lack Atonement. Lord me help.
   Thy Shittim Wood ore laid With Wealthy brass
Was an Atoning altar, and sweet smelt:
   But if ore laid with pure pure gold it was
   It was an Incense Altar, all perfum'd
   With Odours, wherein Lord thou thus was bloom'd.

Did this ere during Wood when thus orespread
   With these erelasting Metalls altarwise
Type thy Eternall Plank of Godhead, Wed
   Unto our Mortall Chip, its sacrifice?
   Thy Deity mine Altar. Manhood thine.
   Mine Offring on't for all men's Sins, and mine?

This Golden Altar puts such weight into
   The sacrifices offer'd on't, that it
Ore weighs the Weight of all the sins that flow
   In thine Elect. This Wedge, and beetle split
   The knotty Logs of Vengeance too to shivers:
   And from their Guilt and shame them cleare delivers.

This Holy Altar by its Heavenly fire
   Refines our Offerings: casts out their dross
And sanctifies their Gold by its rich 'tire
   And all their steams with Holy Odours boss.
   Pillars of Frankincense and rich Perfume
   They 'tone Gods nosthrills with, off from this Loom.

Good News, Good Sirs, more good than comes within
   The Canopy of Angells. Heavens Hall
Allows no better: this atones for sin,
   My Glorious God, Whose Grace here thickest falls.
   May I my Barly yawn, Bran, Bryer Claw,
   Lay on't a Sacrifice? or Chaff or Straw?

Shall I my sin Pouch lay, on thy Gold Bench
   My Offering, Lord, to thee? I've such alone
But have no better. For my sins do drench
   My very best unto their very bone.
   And shall mine Offering by thine Altars fire
   Refin'd, and sanctifi'd to God aspire?

Amen, ev'n so be it. I now will climb
   The stares up to thine Altar, and on't lay
Myselfe, and services, even for its shrine.
   My sacrifice brought thee accept I pray.
   My Morn, and Evning Offerings I'le bring
   And on this Golden Altar Incense fling.

Lord let thy Diety mine Altar bee
   And make thy Manhood, on't my sacrifice.
For mine Atonement: make them both for mee
   My Altar t'sanctify my gifts likewise
   That so myselfe and service on't may bring
   Its worth along with them to thee my king.

The thoughts whereof, do make my tunes as fume,
   From off this Altar rise to thee Most High
And all their steams stufft with thy Altars blooms,
   My Sacrifice of Praise in Melody.
   Let thy bright Angells catch my tune, and sing't.
   That Equalls Davids Michtam which is in't.

Meditation 24. Joh. 1.14. ἐσκήνωσεν
ἐν ἡμῖν *Tabernacled amongst us*

25.10m 1697.

My Soul would gazing all amazed stand,
   To see the burning Sun, with'ts golden locks
(An hundred sixty six times more than th'land)
   Ly buttond up in a Tobacco box.
   But this bright Wonder, Lord, that fore us playes
   May make bright Angells gasterd, at it gaze.

That thou, my Lord, that hast the Heavens bright
   Pav'd with the Sun, and Moon, with Stars o're pinckt,
Thy Tabernacle, yet shouldst take delight
   To make my flesh thy Tent, and tent with in't.
   Wonders themselves do seem to faint away
   To finde the Heavens Filler housd in Clay.

Thy Godhead Cabbin'd in a Myrtle bowre,
    A Palm branch tent, an Olive Tabernacle,
A Pine bough Booth, An Osier House or tower
    A mortall bitt of Manhood, where the Staple
    Doth fixt, uniting of thy natures, hold,
    And hold out marvels more than can be told.

Thy Tabernacles floore Celestiall
    Doth Canopie the Whole World. Lord; and wilt
Thou tabernacle in a tent so small?
    Have Tent, and Tent cloath of a Humane Quilt?
    Thy Person make a bit of flesh of mee
    Thy Tabernacle, and its Canopee?

Wonders! my Lord, Thy Nature all With Mine
    Doth by the Feast of Booths Conjoynd appeare
Together in thy Person all Divine
    Stand House, and House holder. What Wonder's here?
    Thy Person infinite, without compare
    Cloaths made of a Carnation leafe doth ware.

What Glory to my nature doth thy Grace
    Confer, that it is made a Booth for thine
To tabernacle in? Wonders take place.
    Thou low dost step aloft to lift up mine.
    Septembers fifteenth day did type the Birth
    Of this thy tabernacle here on earth.

And through this leafy Tent the glory cleare
    Of thy Rich Godhead shineth very much:
The Crowds of Sacrifices which swarm here
    Shew forth thy Efficacy now is such
    Flowing in from thy natures thus united
    As Clears off Sin, and Victims all benighted.

But yet the Wonder grows: and groweth much,
    For thou wilt Tabernacles change with mee.
Not onely Nature, but my person tuch.
    Thou wilst mee thy, and thee, my tent to bee.
    Thou wilt, if I my heart will to thee rent,
    My Tabernacle make thy Tenement.

Thou'lt tent in mee, I dwell in thee shall here.
  For housing thou wilt pay mee rent in bliss:
And I shall pay thee rent of Reverent fear
    For Quarters in thy house. Rent mutuall is.
    Thy Tenent and thy Teniment I bee.
    Thou Landlord art and Tenent too to mee.

Lord lease thyselfe to mee out: make mee give
  A Leafe unto thy Lordship of myselfe.
Thy Tenent, and thy Teniment I'le live.
    And give and take Rent of Celestiall Wealth.
    I'le be thy Tabernacle: thou shalt bee
    My Tabernacle. Lord thus mutuall wee.

The Feast of Tabernacles makes me sing
  Out thy Theanthropy, my Lord, I'le spare
No Musick here. Sweet Songs of praises in
    The Tabernacles of the Righteous are.
    My Palmifer'd Hosannah Songs I'le raise
    On my Shoshannims blossoming thy praise.

34. Meditation. Rev. 1.5. Who loved us and washed away our Sins in his Blood

26.9m 1699.

Suppose this Earthy globe a Cocoe Nut
  Whose Shell most bright, and hard out challenge should
The richest Carbunckle in gold ring put
    How rich would proove the kirnell it should hold?
    But be it so, who then could breake this Shell,
    To pick the kirnell, walld within this Cell?

Should I, my Lord, call thee this nut, I should
  Debase thy Worth, and of thee basely stut.
Thou dost its worth as far excell as would
    Make it to thine worse than a worm eat nut.
    Were all the World a sparkling pearle, 't would bee
    Worse than a dot of Dung if weighd with thee.

What Elemented bit was that, thine eyes
  Before the Elements were moulded, ey'd?
And it Encabbineting Jewell wise
  Up in thy person, be'st nigh Deified?
  It lay as pearle in dust in this wide world,
  But thou it tookst, and in thy person firld.

To finde a Pearle in Oister Shells's not strange:
  For in such rugged bulwarks such abound.
But this Rich Gem in Humane Natures grange
  So bright could by none Eye but thine be found.
  Its mankind flowr'd, searst, kneaded up in Love
  To Manna in Gods moulding trough above.

This bit of Humane Flesh Divinizd in
  The Person of the Son of God; the Cell
Of Soule, and Blood, where Love Divine doth swim
  Through veans, through Arteries, Heart flesh, and fell,
  Doth with its Circkling Arms about entwinde
  A Portion of its kindred choice, Mankinde.

But these defild by Sin, Justice doth stave
  Off from the bliss Love them prepar'de, untill
She's satisfide, and sentence too she gave
  That thou should feel her vengeance and her will.
  Hence Love steps in, turns by the Conduit Cock:
  Her Veans full payment on the Counter drop.

Now Justice satisfi'de, Loves Milke white hand
  Them takes and brings unto her Ewer of blood
Doth make Free Grace her golden Wisp, and Sand
  With which she doth therein them Wash scoure, rub
  And Wrince them cleane untill their Beauty shows
  More pure, and white, than Lilly, Swan, or Rose.

What love, my Lord, dost thou lay out on thine
  When to the Court of Justice cald they're judg'd.
Thou with thy Blood and Life dost pay their fine
  Thy Life, for theirs, thy Blood for theirs must budge.
  Their Sin, Guilt, Curse upon thyselfe dost lay:
  Thy Grace, thy Justice, Life on them Convay.

Make such a Change, my Lord, with mee, I pray.
   I'le give thee then, my Heart, and Life to th'bargen.
Thy golden Scepter then my Soule shall sway
   Along my Path unto thy Palace garden.
   Wash off my filth, with thy rich blood, and I
   Will stud thy praise with thankfull melody.

*60a. Meditation. Joh. 6.51. I am the Living
Bread, that came down from Heaven*

16.2m 1704.

Count me not liquorish if my Soule do pine
   And long for Angells bread of Heavens wheate
Ground in thy Quorns, Searcde in the Laws Lawn fine
   And bakt in Heavens backhouse for our meate.
   Ist die of Famine, Lord, My Stomach's weak.
   And if I live, Manna must be my meate.

I'm sick; my sickness is mortality
   And Sin both Complicate (the worst of all).
No cure is found under the Chrystall Sky
   Save Manna, that from heaven down doth fall.
   My Queasy Stomach this alone doth Crave.
   Nought but a bit of manna can mee save.

This Bread came down from heaven in a Dew
   In which it bedded was, untill the Sun
Remoov'd its Cover lid: and did it shew
   Disht dayly food, while fourty years do run.
   For Isra'ls Camp to feast upon their fill
   Thy Emblem, Lord, in print by perfect Skill.

Thou in thy word as in a bed of Dewes
   Like Manna on thy Camp dost fall and light
Hid Manna, till the Sun Shine bright remooves
   The Rug, and doth display its beauty bright
   Like pearly Bdellium White and Cleare to set
   The Sight, and Appetite the same to get.

This is a Shining Glass, wherein thy face
  My Lord, as Bread of Life, is clearly seen.
The Bread of Life, and Life of lively Grace
    Of such as live upon't do flowrish Green.
    That makes their lives that on it live ascend
    In heav'nly rayes to heaven that have none end.

Refresh my Sight, Lord, with thy Manna's eye.
  Delight my tast within this sweet Honied Cake.
Enrich my Stomach with this Cake bread high.
    And with this Angells bread me recreate.
    Lord, make my Soule thy Manna's Golden Pot
    Within thine Arke: and never more forgot.

Here's food for ery day, and th'Seventh too:
  (Though't never fell upon the Seventh day
But on the first, and ery week day new)
    And now is on the Camp shour'd ery way.
    Yet where it is not rightly usd it turns
    To nauseous sent, and doth occasion worms.

It's first daye's Mess Disht up in Heavenly Dew.
  Lord feede mee all wayes with't: it will enable
Mee much to live up to thy praise anew.
    Angells delight, attending on this table.
    If on this Angell fare I'm fed, I shall
    Sing forth thy glory with bright Angells all.

150. Meditation. Cant. 7.3. Thy two breasts
are like two young Roes that are twins

6.7m 1719.

My Blessed Lord, how doth thy Beautious Spouse
  In Stately Stature rise in Comliness?
With her two breasts like two little Roes that browse
    Among the lillies in their Shining dress
    Like stately milke pailes ever full and flow
    With spirituall milke to make her babes to grow.

Celestiall Nectar Weathier far than Wine
   Wrought in the Spirits brew house and up tund
Within these Vessells which are trust up fine
   Likend to two pritty neate twin Roes that run'd
   Most pleasently by their dams sides like Cades
   And suckle with their milk Christs Spirituall Babes.

Lord put these nibbles then my mouth into
   And suckle me therewith I humbly pray,
Then with this milk thy Spirituall Babe I'st grow,
   And these two milke pails shall themselves display
   Like to these pritty twins in pairs round neate
   And shall sing forth thy praise over this meate.

FROM

Gods Determinations

The Preface

Infinity, when all things it beheld
In Nothing, and of Nothing all did build,
Upon what Base was fixt the Lath, wherein
He turn'd this Globe, and riggalld it so trim?
Who blew the Bellows of his Furnace Vast?
Or held the Mould wherein the world was Cast?
Who laid its Corner Stone? Or whose Command?
Where stand the Pillars upon which it stands?
Who Lac'de and Fillitted the earth so fine,
With Rivers like green Ribbons Smaragdine?
Who made the Sea's its Selvedge, and it locks
Like a Quilt Ball within a Silver Box?
Who Spread its Canopy? Or Curtains Spun?
Who in this Bowling Alley bowld the Sun?
Who made it always when it rises set
To go at once both down, and up to get?
Who th'Curtain rods made for this Tapistry?
Who hung the twinckling Lanthorns in the Sky?
Who? who did this? or who is he? Why, know

Its Onely Might Almighty this did doe.
His hand hath made this noble worke which Stands
His Glorious Handywork not made by hands.
Who spake all things from nothing; and with ease
Can speake all things to nothing, if he please.
Whose Little finger at his pleasure Can
Out mete ten thousand worlds with halfe a Span:
Whose Might Almighty can by half a looks
Root up the rocks and rock the hills by th'roots.
Can take this mighty World up in his hande,
And shake it like a Squitchen or a Wand.
Whose single Frown will make the Heavens shake
Like as an aspen leafe the Winde makes quake.
Oh! what a might is this Whose single frown
Doth shake the world as it would shake it down?
Which All from Nothing fet, from Nothing, All:
Hath All on Nothing set, lets Nothing fall.
Gave All to nothing Man indeed, whereby
Through nothing man all might him Glorify.
In Nothing then imbosst the brightest Gem
More pretious than all pretiousness in them.
But Nothing man did throw down all by Sin:
And darkened that lightsom Gem in him.
   That now his Brightest Diamond is grown
   Darker by far than any Coalpit Stone.

The Accusation of the Inward Man

You want Cleare Spectacles: your eyes are dim:
Turn inside out: and turn your Eyes within.
Your sins like motes in th'sun do swim: nay see
Your Mites are Molehills, Molehills Mountains bee.
Your Mountain Sins do magnitude transcend:
Whose number's numberless, and do want end.
The Understandings dark, and therefore Will
Account of Ill for Good, and Good for ill.
As to a Purblinde man men oft appeare
Like Walking Trees within the Hemisphere.
So in the judgment Carnall things Excell:

Pleasures and Profits beare away the Bell.
The Will is hereupon perverted so,
It laquyes after ill, doth good foregoe.
The Reasonable Soule doth much delight
A Pickpack t'ride o'th'Sensuall Appitite.
And hence the heart is hardened and toyes,
With Love, Delight, and Joy, yea Vanities.

  Make but a thorow search, and you may spy
Your soul a trudging hard, though secretly
Upon the feet of your Affections mute.
And hankering after all forbidden fruite.
Ask but yourselfe in secret laying neer
Thy head thereto: 'twill Whisper in thine eare
That it is tickled much, though secretly.
And greatly itches after Vilany.
'Twill fleere thee in thy face, and though it say,
It must not tell, it scorns to tell thee nay.
But Slack the rains, and Come a Loophole lower:
You'l finde it was but Pen-coop't up before.
Nay, muster up your thoughts, and take the Pole
Of what walk in the Entry of your Soule
Which if you do, you certainly will finde
With Robbers, Cut-throats, Theives its mostly linde.
And hundred Roagues you'l finde, ly gaming there.
For one true man, that in that path appears.
Your True man too's oft footsore, sildom is,
Sound Winde, and Limb: and still to add to this,
He's but a Traviller within that Way:
Whereas the rest there pitch their Tents, and stay.
Nay, nay, what thoughts Unclean? Lacivious?
Blasphemous? Murderous? and Malicious?
Tyranick? Wrathfull? Atheistick rise
Of Evills New, and Old, of e'ry Sise?
These bed, and board here, make the heart a sty
Of all Abominable Brothlery.
  Then is it pure? is this the fruite of Grace?
  If so, how do yee: You and I Embrace.

The Glory of and Grace in the Church set out

Come now behold
Within this Knot What Flowers do grow:
Spanglde like gold:
Whence Wreaths of all Perfumes do flow.
Most Curious Colours of all sorts you shall
With all Sweet Spirits sent. Yet thats not all.

Oh! Look, and finde
These Choicest Flowers most richly sweet
Are Disciplinde
With Artificiall Angells meet.
An heap of Pearls is precious: but they shall
When set by Art Excell: Yet that's not all.

Christ's Spirit showers
Down in his Word, and Sacraments
Upon these Flowers
The Clouds of Grace Divine Contents.
Such things of Wealthy Blessings on them fall
As make them sweetly thrive: Yet that's not all.

Yet still behold!
All flourish not at once. We see
While some Unfold
There blushing Leaves, some buds there bee.
Here's Faith, Hope, Charity in flower, which call
On yonders in the Bud. Yet that's not all.

But as they stand
Like Beauties reeching in perfume
A Divine Hand
Doth hand them up to Glories room:
Where Each in sweet'ned Songs all Praises shall
Sing all ore heaven for aye. And that's but all.

Upon a Spider Catching a Fly

Thou sorrow, venom Elfe.
  Is this thy play,
To spin a web out of thyselfe
  To Catch a Fly?
    For Why?

I saw a pettish wasp
  Fall foule therein.
Whom yet thy Whorle pins did not clasp
  Lest he should fling
    His sting.

But as affraid, remote
  Didst stand hereat
And with thy little fingers stroke
  And gently tap
    His back.

Thus gently him didst treate
  Lest he should pet,
And in a froppish, waspish heate
  Should greatly fret
    Thy net.

Whereas the silly Fly,
  Caught by its leg
Thou by the throate tookst hastily
  And 'hinde the head
    Bite Dead.

This goes to pot, that not
  Nature doth call.
Strive not above what strength hath got
  Lest in the brawle
    Thou fall.

This Frey seems thus to us.
   Hells Spider gets
His intrails spun to whip Cords thus
   And wove to nets
     And sets.

To tangle Adams race
   In's stratigems
To their Destructions, spoil'd, made base
   By venom things
     Damn'd Sins.

But mighty, Gracious Lord
   Communicate
Thy Grace to breake the Cord, afford
   Us Glorys Gate
     And State.

We'l Nightingaile sing like
   When pearcht on high
In Glories Cage, thy glory, bright,
   And thankfully,
     For joy.

Upon a Wasp Child with Cold

The Bare that breaths the Northern blast
Did numb, Torpedo like, a Wasp
Whose stiffend limbs encrampt, lay bathing
In Sol's warm breath and shine as saving,
Which with her hands she chafes and stands
Rubbing her Legs, Shanks, Thighs, and hands.
Her petty toes, and fingers ends
Nipt with this breath, she out extends
Unto the Sun, in greate desire
To warm her digits at that fire.
Doth hold her Temples in this state
Where pulse doth beate, and head doth ake.

Doth turn, and stretch her body small,
Doth Comb her velvet Capitall.
As if her little brain pan were
A Volume of Choice precepts cleare.
As if her sattin jacket hot
Contained Apothecaries Shop
Of Natures recepts, that prevails
To remedy all her said ailes,
As if her velvet helmet high
Did turret rationality.
She fans her wing up to the Winde
As if her Pettycoate were lin'de,
With reasons fleece, and hoises sails
And hu'ming flies in thankfull gails
Unto her dun Curld palace Hall
Her warm thanks offering for all.

Lord cleare my misted sight that I
May hence view thy Divinity.
Some sparkes whereof thou up dost hasp
Within this little downy Wasp
In whose small Corporation wee
A school and a schoolmaster see
Where we may learn, and easily finde
A nimble Spirit bravely minde
Her worke in e'ry limb: and lace
It up neate with a vitall grace,
Acting each part though ne'er so small
Here of this Fustian animall.
Till I enravisht Climb into
The Godhead on this Lather doe.
Where all my pipes inspir'de upraise
An Heavenly musick furrd with praise.

Huswifery

Make me, O Lord, thy Spining Wheele compleate.
    Thy Holy Worde my Distaff make for mee.
Make mine Affections thy Swift Flyers neate
    And make my Soule thy holy Spoole to bee.
    My Conversation make to be thy Reele
    And reele the yarn thereon spun of thy Wheele.

Make me thy Loome then, knit therein this Twine:
    And make thy Holy Spirit, Lord, winde quills:
Then weave the Web thyselfe. The yarn is fine.
    Thine Ordinances make my Fulling Mills.
    Then dy the same in Heavenly Colours Choice,
    All pinkt with Varnisht Flowers of Paradise.

Then cloath therewith mine Understanding, Will,
    Affections, Judgment, Conscience, Memory
My Words, and Actions, that their shine may fill
    My wayes with glory and thee glorify.
    Then mine apparell shall display before yee
    That I am Cloathd in Holy robes for glory.

The Ebb and Flow

When first thou on me Lord wrought'st thy Sweet Print,
    My heart was made thy tinder box.
    My 'ffections were thy tinder in't.
        Where fell thy Sparkes by drops.
Those holy Sparks of Heavenly Fire that came
Did ever catch and often out would flame.

But now my Heart is made thy Censar trim,
    Full of thy golden Altars fire,
    To offer up Sweet Incense in
        Unto thyselfe intire:
I finde my tinder scarce thy sparks can feel
That drop out from thy Holy flint and Steel.

Hence doubts out bud for feare thy fire in mee
   'S a mocking Ignis Fatuus
   Or lest thine Altars fire out bee,
     Its hid in ashes thus.
Yet when the bellows of thy Spirit blow
Away mine ashes, then thy fire doth glow.

Upon the Sweeping Flood
Aug: 13.14. 1683

Oh! that Id had a tear to've quencht that flame
   Which did dissolve the Heavens above
   Into those liquid drops that Came
     To drown our Carnall love.
Our cheeks were dry and eyes refusde to weep.
Tears bursting out ran down the skies darke Cheek.

Were th'Heavens sick? must wee their Doctors bee
   And physick them with pills, our sin?
   To make them purg and Vomit, see,
     And Excrements out fling?
We've griev'd them by such Physick that they shed
Their Excrements upon our lofty heads.

FRANCIS DANIEL PASTORIUS

(1651–1719)

In these Seven Languages I this my Book do own,
Friend, if thou find it, Send the same to Germantown;
Thy Recompense shall be the half of half a Crown:
But, tho' it be no more than half the half of this,
Pray! Be Content therewith, & think it not amiss.
Yea and if, when thou com'st, my Cash perhaps is gone,
(For Money is thus scarce, that often I have none)
A Cup of Drink may do: Or else, alas! thou must
Trust unto me a while, As I to Others Trust,
Who failing make me fail: A thing extreme unjust!
To which I have no lust; But must per Force, poor Dust.
    Freund, *Was du findest, wiedergieb,*
    Sonst hält man dich vor einen Dieb
      In diesem; und in jenem Leben
    Folgt anders nichts als Höllen-pein.
      Gott Selbst hat diß Gesetz gegeben
    Zu thun, wie man Gethan will seyn.
    Quod Tibi vis fieri, hoc facias Aliis.

A Token of Love and Gratitude

Just one and thirty years, or (says one, I know who,)
Eleven thousand and Three hundred Twenty two
Whole Days & Nights are past, since we arrived here
At Phi-la-del-phi-a, where ye three Sisters dear,
In Love together link'd, still arm in arm do hold
Each other, as they paint the Charities of old.
Should mine Arithmetick proceed, & multiply,
(Like God his Blessings does,) it would (Be pleas'd to try,
And pardon when ye find an overly mistake,)
Of Minuts, Seconds call'd, most thousand Millions make.
Thus long ye have been here! and ev'ry Moment he
(Or if this Web of Time in smaller Thrums can be

Divided,) has bestow'd some Benefits on you,
Brave husbands, Store of Goods, & hopeful Children too. &c.
Oh! that my slender Quill could further set in Ranks
His Graces to our Souls before your eyes, that Thanks
Might as of one heart rise to him the Holy One,
And like pure Incense yield sweet Savour at his Throne:
Where, with the Cherubims, and Spirits of Just Men,
Your Parents worship him, & that not now & then,
As we poor Mortals do, Confin'd below the Sky
To Faint & Weakness; but always, Incessantly.
John De la Val with them his Strength about this bends,
And all Eternity in Hallelu—Jahs spends.
Your Brother Mordecai, (I speak what I believe,)
And those your tender Babes, who left this Vale of Grief,
Of Sorrows & of Tears, to Heaven's Majesty
He his Te Deum sings, they their Hosanna cry.
There they expect, that ye and your Relations may
Depart in due Time, out of these Tents of Clay,
Into the Mansions, which the Lord prepar'd above,
For all his Followers, that live & die in Love,
Like Thomas Lloyd has done; whom God there does regard,
And in his Offspring here his Faithfulness Reward.
Now, notwithstanding he for you (his Daughters) longs
To mix your Melodies with his Celestial Songs;
Yet I say, Tarry ye! let me the first fall Sick,
Ascend & meet him in my last Climacterick,
Or LXIIIth year of age, I am in, and almost out.
I'm far from Flattering! and hope, ye read my mind,
Who can't, nor dare forget a Ship-Mate true & kind,
As he your Father was to me, (an Alien,)
My Lot being newly cast among such English men,
Whose Speech I thought were Welsh, their words a Canting
    Tune,
Alone with him I could in Latin then Commune:
Which Tongue he did pronounce right in our German way,
Hence presently we knew, what he or I would say.
Moreover, to the best of my Rememberance,
We never disagreed, nor were at Variance;
Because God's sacred Truth, (whereat we both did aim,)
To her indeared Friends is ev'ry where the same.

Therefore 'twas he that made my Passage short on Sea,
'Twas he & William Penn, that Caused me to stay
In this then uncouth land, & howling Wilderness,
Wherein I saw that I but little should possess,
And if I would Return home to my Father's house,
Perhaps great Riches & Preferments might espouse, &c.
How be't nought in the World could mine Affection quench
Towards Dear Penn, with whom I did converse in French.
The Vertues of these Two (and Three or Four beside,)
Have been the chiefest Charms, which forc'd me to abide.
And though these Persons, whom I mention with Respect,
(Whom God as Instruments, did graciously elect,
To be His Witnesses unto this faithless Age,)
Are at a distance now from our American Stage,
In which as Actors, or Spectators, we appear,
Their Memory Survives: To me they're very near.
I often wish I might their Patience so express
As I the want thereof ingenuously Confess.
Good Lord! what Injuries have your said Genitor
Of Villains, whilst he was Lieutenant-Governour!
It seem'd to me, he would his Master Equalize,
And suffer wretched Fools his Station to despise,
Especially George Keith, well nigh devour'd by Lice.
But honest Thomas Lloyd has laid his Body down
In Rest & Peace with God, & now does wear the Crown
Of Immortality, of Glory & of Life,
Laid up also for us, if lawfully we strive.

Fortunante Deo, Pietas Fert Denique Palmam.

Rachel Preston, Hannah Hill & Mary Norris

Your kindness wherewithal my last years Meeters met,
Does this new monument of ship-mate-ship beget,
Which, if it shall receive the selfsame Recompense,
May rise as high again, & shew a twelvemonth hence
Some Matters, as I hope, of greater Consequence,
Unless my Ink dry up, or my small Diligence.

Dear Friends, an other Year besides the thirty one,
(Whereof my former Sheet,) is now elaps'd and gone.
Sith that we landed here on Philadelphia's Shore
Our Duty then requires, to praise the Lord once more,
For all his Goodnesses, in the Plurality,
Which Ev'ry one of you enjoy'd as well as I:
This Second Paper shall enumerate but some,
In Grammars threefold Tense, Past, Present & to Come.
God's Mercies over Us have been before we were   1
Produced on the Stage of this Terrestrial Sphere,
He pour'd us out as Milk, within our Mother's Womb,
And least that this should be that First Stuff's* walking Tomb,
Did Crudle it like Chees, and when yet weak & fresh,
Fill up the tender skin with Sinews, Bones & Flesh.
Our Bodies thus prepared, He graciously would give
A never-dying Soul, thereby to move and live.
To move & live to Him, in Whom we live and move,
Oh! that we always might obedient Children prove,
Dread, love and worship God, the only Father, which
Beyond all Fathers is, most Bountiful and Rich.
'Tis He and He alone, that made us what we are,
And of His Handy-work did ever since take Care,
By Angels, Parents, Friends; Nay oft by wretched Foes,
Who, aiming at the Head, could scarcely hit our Toes.
So having been (poor things!) a Nine-month Closed in
A dark and narrow Vault, (Concluded under Sin,
Old Adam's Progeny,) were usher'd, that we should
As well our Genitors, as other men behold;
But presently we wept, quite overwhelm'd with Fears,
Forecasting, that we came into a Vale of Tears.
How be't they kiss'd, they buss'd, & dandled us so long,
Till with their Flatteries, & lulling Midwife's Song,
They Dun'd our Juicy Ears, And in our Nurse's Lap,
Outwearied by these Tunes, we took a Gentle Nap,
Soon wak'ned of our Trance, they laid us to the Breast,
The which of all the Sports, (me thinks,) has been the best;
For, when we grew some years, discerning sad from glad,
They sent us to the School, where we learn'd good & bad:

*Chaos.

More of the last than first—Had not our Parents skill
Surpass'd our Masters Wit, how Ill, alas! how Ill
Would things still be with us? Had God withheld his Light,
We were as blind as Moles; But Thanks to Him! our Sight
Increased with our Age: Wherefore I humbly bless
The Fountain of this Gift, the Sun of Righteousness;
Whose Rays, if well improv'd by us, so as they ought,
Will warm our fainting Hearts, and grant us what we sought,
When I from Franckenland, & you from Wales set forth,
The one out of the East, the Others of the North,*
In order to Exile ourselves towards the West,
And there to serve the Lord in Stillness, Peace & Rest.
He gave us our desires; For one, that rightly seeks,
Does never miss to find. A matter of eight weeks
Restrained in a ship, America by name,
Into America [Amo(a)rica:] we came:
A Countrey bitter-sweet, & pray! how can 't be less,
Consid'ring all the World does lie in wickedness?
And though perhaps some thought, that Penn-Silvania
Should be excepted, and dream'd of Utopia,
That Extramundane place (by Thomas Morus found,
Now with old Groenland lost,) where all are safe & sound;
Yet is it parcel of the odd and Cursed Ground.   Gen. 3:17.
What happ'nd by the way, is needless for to tell;
But this I dare not slip, that when the Lion fell
Upon my Back, and when next in a frightful Storm,
Once I myself did fall, there Crawling as a Worm,
Brave HONEST Thomas Lloyd has been the only Man,
That heal'd me by God's help, our great Physician,
Our Maker, Saviour & our Prophet, Priest and King,
Good Shepherd, Teacher, Guide: Our All and Ev'ry thing.
To Him the Holy One, we his Redeemed bow,
And Glory, Majesty, Renown and Praises owe,
For what He hitherto was pleased to bestow.
(On us poor Creatures, whose Cup did overflow,)
In two parts of this Globe, especially here,
Where we at present breathe, which Tense, tho' ne're   II
        so near,

*Francia Orientalis: Wallia Septentrionalis.

I hardly comprehend: It suddenly posts by,
E'en in an Instant, and the Twinkling of an Eye.
'Tis nothing but a Now, a Now that can not last;
Pronounce it with all haste, & with all haste it's past.
A Weaver's Shuttle is not half so Swift or fleet,
This momentary Jot has rather Wings than Feet:
It vanishes like Smoke, like Dust before the Wind,
And leaves, as sounding Brass, an Echoing Voice behind,
Which minds us, that it should be Carefully imploy'd,
So as the same has been by HONEST Thomas Lloyd,
My quondam real Friend, whom with this Epithet
I honour thankfully, and never shall forget
His many Courtesies, to my Departing hour,
Altho' my years should reach to other Sixty-four.
If you, his Daughters, & your Families, & I,
With mine do follow him, we may be sure to die
In Favour with the Lord, and Unity with Friends:
By three things he excell'd, Faith, Love & Patience.
And this (to wit the last,) adorned thus his life,
That I may truly say, she (it) was his Second Wife.
Concerning CHARITY, (the Center of my Trine,)
It did as clearly as his other Vertues shine:
He kindly deal'd with all, to ev'ry one did good,
Endearing chiefly God, and then the Brotherhood.
His Christian Belief was grounded on the Rock,
And so could easily endure the hardest Shock:
Plain-hearted he has been, profound & Orthodox,
Opposed by Geo. Keith's dull lowing of an Ox.*
A Bull of Bashan, who went willfully astray;
But honest Thomas Lloyd continued in the Way,
Christ Jesus, with streight Steps: If we walk on in them,
We shall undoubtedly get to Jerusalem,
The City of the Saints Solemnity above,
Built of the purest Gold, wall'd, pav'd & ciel'd with Love.
I say, we shall arrive, (and that is yet to come,)
Ere long in Paradise our long & lasting Home;   III
For, when what we call Time, (a thing at best but short,

*Vox Bovis, non Hominis.

And to be used as Paul the Brethren does exhort,)*
Will once be Swallow'd up, with Death, in Victory,
Those Tenses needs must cease to all Eternity.
ETERNITY, a word whereof I fain would speak,
Because I feel, it does a deep Impression make
Upon my Spirit; But as Augustin was out
In such like Mysteries, and proved too too stout,
Reproved by a Child, that tried to transfuse
The Waters of the Sea into his little Sluce.
So, if by Millions, yea by thousand Millions more,
Instead of Units, I shall Nine and Ninety Score
Fine Bales of Genoa all over Multiply,
'Twill but a Hair-breadth be as to ETERNITY.
The Stars, and Jacob's Seed, are without Number, and
He is a Shatter-pate, that Counts Grass, Drops & Sand:
A perfect Bedlam, ay! who with Simonides
Presumes to Chalk out God, & Everlastingness.
Let us be therefore wise, and thus retract the Days,
Which from our Cradle up in Idleness and Plays,
Or infinitely worse, have frequently been spent,
That for transacted Sins we seriously repent:
And take what heed we can, that in this running Time,
We nothing may mis-do, mis-think, mis-speak, mis-rime.
As to FUTURITY, none of us all can say,
That either you, or I, shall see an other Day;
For this good reason we Commit that unto Him,
Who rides, above all Times, upon the Cherubim.†
He sees the Pristine, and what henceforth must ensue,
Like present evermore: Gives unto Each his Due,
And they, who faithfully their Talents do imploy,
Shall be rewarded there with Crowns & boundless Joy.
Thus I am finishing my homely Lines, and Crave
Dear Shipmates, your Excuse, that I so boldly have
With Doggrels troubled you, Fare well, rememb'ring me,
Who am your loving & affectionate F. D. P.

———

*1. Cor. 7:29.
†2 Sam. 22:11 & Psalm 18:10.

As often as some where before my Feet
I with a fine, rare, and fair Object meet,
I shut my Outward Eyes,
And bid my Inward rise
To Him, who made, and does uphold that Thing
So that my heart (whilst I His praises sing,)
To the Creator cleaves
And that quaint Creature leaves.
Concluding thus: If this, which is but vain,
Appears to men so handsom, deft and clean,
How beautiful must he
Pure, Bright, and Glorious be
Whose wondrous works I see.

———

Delight in Books from Evening
Till mid-night when the Cocks do sing;
Till Morning when the day doth spring:
Till Sun-set when the Bell doth ring.
Delight in Books, for Books do bring
Poor men to learn most every thing;
The Art of true *Levelling*:
Yea even how to please the king.
Delight in Books, they're carrying
Us so far, that we know to fling
On waspish men (who taking wing
Surround us) that they cannot sting.
Ut ungant potius quam pungant.
Das sey aller Bücher Summ,
Glaub an Christum, u. Leb frumm.
          Ex Fide Vita.

———

When I solidly do ponder,
How *Thoughts wander*, I must wonder,
    And for Shame exclaim, and own,
    Mine are ranging up and down.
Now on Eagle's Wings ascending

Far above the Skies, there spending
　　Some good Minutes in a Song;
　　But, alas! this lasts not long.
Unawares they are departing,
And themselves (like Arrows,) darting
　　In the very Depth of Hell,
　　Where the Damned wail and yell.
Weari'd with this frightful Crying,
They in haste from thence are flying,
　　And as giddy-headed hurl'd
　　Fore- and back-ward in the World.
Thro' Great Britain, France and Holland,
Denmark, Moscovy, Spain, Polland,
　　Portugal and Italy,
　　Oft'ner yet thro' Germany.
Hence returning to Braganza,
To the Cape of Bon Speranza;
　　So, by way of Africa,
　　Home to Penn Silvania.
Here I bid them to be quiet,
They deny: however try it,
　　Go to bed, and sleep almost;
　　But soon starting, take the Post,
And afresh begin to travel,
Not regarding Mire nor Gravel,
　　River, Valley, Swamps nor hill,
　　Presently light where they will.
Tripping, traping still the faster
Like a Cur, that lost his Master,
　　To and fro, from place to place,
　　Stir their Stumps, and run a Race.
Some times in the Garden ramble
From the Tulip to the Bramble:
　　From the Rose and Eglantine
　　To the Nep or Columbine.
Then retiring leave these Flowers,
Sit a while in Shady Bowers,
　　With a Book to meditate,
　　And, as if it were, abate.
In a moment, loath to tarry,

Swiftly, as their feet can carry
 Their small Bodies, whip away
 In the Woods to seek a Stray.
Here they hith'r and thither straggle,
Gad, fig, frisk, stir, waver, waggle
 Course and roam, and rove about,
 Till there is no Coming out.
Justly I may call them Gropers,
Gypsies, Runnagates, Landlopers,
 Vagrants, Fugitives, and Rogues,
 That deserve the Stocks and Strokes.

Animus sine pondere velox.   *Horat.*

Epibaterium, Or a hearty Congratulation to William Penn

Chief Proprietary of the Province of Pennsilvania &c. Upon his third Arrival into the same

For which good Patriots these sev'ral years did long,
And which Occasions this his German's English Song,
Who'f old could talk with him but in the Gallic Tongue.
Ter Fortunatus, Felix, et Faustus ad Indos Tertius Adventus
 sit, Guiliellme, tuus!
Let Heroic Poets Tote of War and warlike Men,
My Reed (shrill Oaten-Straw!) does Welcome Wm. Penn,
A man of Love & Peace, abominating Strife,
To him its Welcome sounds, and to his dearest Wife,
And to his hopeful Son, his Daughter and all His,
With Cordial Wishes of God's everlasting Bliss.
The third time welcome Penn! Of good things (as we see
In Sacred History,) there have been often three.[1]

[1] I wittingly omit to speak of the holy & transcendent Three, who bear Record in Heaven & in Earth, 1 John 5, 7, 8 as also of the three Angels, whom Abraham entertained in the plains of Mamre, Gen. 18:2. Hebr. 12:2.

Neither do I quote, that three men of each Tribe were to describe the promised land, Josh. 18:4. nor that all the Males were three times in the year to appear before the Lord God, Exod. 23:17. nor that divers goodly persons,

Thrice Balaam's Ass would turn, & thrice the Prophet
    smites,[2]
And three times blesses he the blessed Israelites.[3]
Thrice every year the Jews must keep their Solemn Feasts,[4]
And Solomon the Wise thrice sacrifices Beasts.[5]
His Father David thrice (an exercised man,[6]
According to God's heart,) bows down to Jonathan.[7]
Elijah stretches him upon the Widow's Boy
No less than thrice, & thus death's Power does destroy.[8]
Thrice to his windows goes my Name Sake op'ning them
And ev'ry day prays thrice toward Jerusalem.[9]
Three times a Voice was heard, "Rise Peter, kill & eat,"[10]
Wild Beasts & creaping things make lawful Gospell-Meat.[11]
Paul's suff'rings threefold were, on this & th' other wise,[12]
For Satan's Buffeting he sighs to Heaven thrice.[13]
Thrice therefore Welcome Penn! (is my repeated cry,)
The third time to the land of thy Propriety!
Thy Province, into which these thirty one years past
My Lot, by Providence, most happily was cast.
Here in its Infancy thy Face I first did see
The one and twenti'th of the Sixth Month, Eighty three.   1683.

---

having many Sons, had but three Daughters, 1 Chron. 25:5. Job 1:2. Item what
I concerning this mystical Number might have allegorized out of Deut. 14:28,
29. Ezek. 14:14. Dan. 3:24. and 10:2. Matt. 13:33. Mark 9:5. Luke 10:36. &c. and
from Natural Philosophy, how all Elementary things consist of three, viz. Sal,
Sulphur and Mercurius. But only add the ancient Latin Proverb, in no more
than three words, Omne Trinum Perfectum; *i.e.* Of all Good things there
must be Three.

[2]Numb. 22:28, 32, 33.
[3]Numb. 24:10.
[4]Deut. 16:16.
[5]1 Kings 9:25.
[6]1 Sam. 24:5. 1 Kings 11:4. Acts 13:22.
[7]1 Sam. 20:41.
[8]1 Kings 17:21.
[9]Dan. 6:10, 13. Add Psal. 55:17.
[10]Acts 10:13, 16. and 11:7, 10.
[11]1 Cor. 10:25. Tit. 1:15. Matt. 15:11.
[12]2 Cor. 11:25. Acts ch. 14. & 16. & 27.
[13]2 Cor. 12:8.

When the Metropolis (which Brother-Love they call,)[14]
Three houses, & no more, could number up in all.
No Fulness then of Bread, no Idleness, no Pride,
Where into Belial since did many-ones misguide.[15]
There in thy Company I with my Soul's delight
At Intervals might sit till mid-time of the night.
Then (as the Chearing Sun) thou visitedst poor Caves,[16]
Pray! let us not forget those Emblems of our Graves.
But ever mindful of the Mercies of the Lord,
Thank Him for what He did so graciously afford,
In our first Meeting-Tent of Pine and Chest-nut boord.[17]
How be't thy Presence was withdrawing from us, ere
We understood what things in Pensilvania were
Of good or evil use, to follow, or t' avoid,
The wisest of us all was honest Thomas Lloid.[18]

[14]In Greek Philadelphia, Rom. 12:10. by reason of the Brotherly Affection & Kindness, which therein should abound, and not Philargyria, or Love of Money, as it is English'd, 1 Tim. 6:10 and Juxta Ovidium: crescit Amor Nummi. &c. Qu. Argenti Studium vestrâ dum regnat in Urbe, Curà Fraterno Nomen Amore trahit. Resp. Romulus, Abimeleck, Esau, Cain atq: Jehoram Fratres Frater habet; Gratia rara tamen.

[15]Ezech. 16:49.

> The Pit without a Bottom
> Brought forth these Sins of Sodom;
> Ye, who Commit the same,
> Are guilty of its Flame.

[16]The caves of that time were only holes digged in the Ground, Covered with Earth, a matter of 5. or 6. feet deep, 10. or 12. wide and about 20. long; whereof neither the Sides nor the Floors have been plank'd. Herein we lived more Contentedly than many nowadays in their painted & wainscotted Palaces, as I without the least hyperbole may call them in Comparison of the aforesaid Subterraneous Catatumbs or Dens. Vide Hebr. 11:38. I myself purchased one of the old Tho. Miller for 5£. then Currt. Silver Money of Pennsylvania in the midst of the Front-street at Philada., whenas the Servants, I had along with me, could have made a far better in less than two days, had they but known how to handle the spade.

[17]Our first Meeting-house in the said City was nothing else than a Lodge or Cottage, nailed together of Pine-boards, Imported from New-York, and sold a hundred foot at 10. Shill. And never the less the LORD appeared most powerfully in that Tabernacle of Shittim wood, (:See mine Onomastical Observations, Num. 1606). Glory be to His Name for ever and ever.

[18]This my well beloved Ship-mate has been no less Conspicuous for his Integrity & irreprovable Life, than for his singular Learning, Prudence &

Some lent their itching Ears to Kuster, Keith & Budd,
And miserably fell into the Ditch of Mud,
Where they may stick & stink; For as a sightless whelp,
So stark-blind Apostates do grin at profer'd help:
They spend their Mouths, & fain with vain words would
    ensnare,
Or if this will not do, scold, back-bite, bug-bear, scare;
Hereof, brave William Penn, me thinks, thou hadst thy share.
And yet the second time cam'st Safe to this thy Land,
Dogs, who at distance bark, bite not when near at hand.
Now I thought all was well, the Country full of Folks,
The City stately built, some houses 's tall as Oaks,
The Markets stall'd with Beef, whereof we nothing knew,
When (as aforesaid,) Hutts & Wigg-wams were so few.
However, feeble things we are below the Moon!
Change upon change, alas! befalls us very soon,
Till She with other Stars & Planets (which now meet
Above our heads,) will be the Pavement for our Feet.
Mean while away again, home to Great Britain thou
Downward th' Atlantic Sea must sail, ascend'st the Prow
Of that unlucky Ship; unlucky, why? Because
In her a harmless Lamb is carried to the Claws
Of Tygers, Bears and Wolves, who since they can't devour,
Shut him up in the Fleet, as form'rly in the Towr,
Old Baily's Bale-dock, and such Dungeons, apt to scour, &c.
Ay, sorry Turky quill! stop, stop, & say no more,
Make not afresh to bleed a newly healed Sore.
This World, thou knowst, has been most troublesom to the
    Best,
And so will always be: In Christ they find their Rest,[19]
The which suffices them. Job's Motto (:If God would
Ev'n slay, I'ld trust in Him,) remains their strongest Hold.[20]

---

great Knowledge in things Physical, Civil & divine, whereby (tho' Deputy
Governr. of this Province,) he was not puffed up at all, but of an affable, mild
& truly Christian Temper, Yet Zealous for the Truth, and undaunted in its de-
fense, his Charity still being greater than his Intellect, and his Love towards
GOD the greatest of all three.

[19] John 16:33. Hebr. 11:36. &c.
[20] Job 13:15.

They can Forget, Forgive & render good for Bad,[21]
Bless & Intreat when wrong'd; both sorrowful & glad.[22]
Rejoicing in the LORD, continually rejoice,[23]
Laugh at their Enemies, and at the cackling noise
Of their Persecutors, whom (scornful Brats!) God scorns,[24]
And in His fiery Wrath at last cuts off their horns.
For after he has try'd the Patience, Faith & Hope
Of His Espoused-Ones, and they do not Elope,
But firmly Cleave to Him, He Crowns & Comforts them
With Kisses of his Mouth: No Cross, No Diadem.[25]
God proves first, then approves; first wounds, then heals; first
    kills,
Then quickens by His WORD: first empties, and then fills,
With Pleasures, which none dare Compare to any thing:
Prais'd & extolled be the Name of Zion's King!
But why do I rehearse these Truths to thee dear Friend,
Who hast experienc'd them beyond what I intend
To mention in my Rime except that thread-bare Lie
(:Penn in America a Jesuite did Die?)
No sure! the self-same Man, whom Gazetteers have slain
So many Years agoe, lives still, or lives again:
Loves JESUS, and abhors the Insects of the Sect,
Wherewith black Loyol did this latter Age infect.
I say thou liv'st, dear Penn, Thanks be to GOD on high,
That to the Prince of Life thou art yet very nigh;
Yea nearer, I believe, than thou hast ever been,
Before this Province was by thee the third time seen.
The third time and the last, I question not, He will

[21]I Pet. 1:9. F. D. P. acer Eremi Penniaci Cultor, Te Colo Penne benè
        God Almighty pleas to Bless
        Penn, and Penn's brave Wilderness.
[22]I Cor. 4:13. 2 Cor. 6:10.
[23]Phil. 4:4.
[24]Psal. 2:4.
[25]Psal. 75:8, 10.2 Cant. 1:2. Hebr. 12:5. &c.
    W. P. Veritas Vincit, Prævalet. D. L. Diabolus Latrat.
        All Devilish Lyars delight in Lurking-holes.
    Vult Vertus Patere: Dolus Latere.
        Whenas Plaindealing Truth Will shine to both the Poles.
    Wahrheit: Wie der Palm-baum steht.
    Wann Dir Lügen untergeht.

Grant our Petition, and abundantly fulfill
The Number of thy Days, that when thou art to lay
Thy Body once aside, It undisturbed may
Sleep fast at Pennsberry; thy Soul Return & stay
With Him, from whom she came, as those do who are gone
Already, and their Task here faithfully have done,
Tho' younger than we both. In French now Je conclus,
Icy, et au Ciel Penn est le Bien-Venu!
Pour en avoir de Tout, il faut aussi un peu d'Allemand.

    Whereas, Loving and dearly Esteemed Friend, in thy Travails
in Holland and Germany thou hast heard & learned somewhat
of my Mother-tongue; I hereby make bold to subjoyn a few
lines in the same, as followeth:

Penn heißt auf Welsch ein Haubt, auf Nieder Teutsch ein
    Feder,
Die man zum schreiben braucht; das Haubt ersinn't entweder
Gut oder Bös, womit die Königin paar Geldt,
Durch Hülff der Feder Zwingt, die Gross und kleine Welt.
Nein, wanns hier Wünschens gält, so wolt ich, daß mein
    Feder
Ein solchen Nach-druck hätt, damit sich Ja Ein jeder
Als ein gehorsam Glied ergäbe Jesu Christ,
Der da das Eintzig Haubt der wahren Kirchen ist;
So wäre weder Heid, noch Jud; auch kein Papist.

————

If any honest Friend be pleased to walk into my poor Garden, I
heartily bid him welcome with this following Semi Distichon:

    Sit Pax Intranti, Cum Redeunte Salus!
      Mit Fried hinein; Mit Glück heraus!
      Vom Garten, Freünd, Geh' in das Haus,
    Und wünsche mir, Als ich wünsch dir. Dominus tecum
      Fare well.
Svaviter Accipitur Bonus; ast procul este Profani!
Die guten leüt sind hier willkomm: Ich liebe keinen der nicht
    fromm.

Janua nostra patet; dulces intretis Amici!
Qui malus es, longum iam tibi dico Vale. protervum.
     odi mendacem, non possum ferre procacem.

—

Nun Die nur ihr Hertzen und Augen erfreüen,
Hingegen die Hände zu brauchen sich scheüen,
Sothan'ger Gesellschafft mich nimmer wird reüen.
    Hic Argus esto, non Briareus.
        Vide, nec Invide.

—

Quisquis in hæc *furtim* reptas Viridaria nostra,
    Tangere fallaci Poma caveto manu;
Si non obsequeris, faxit DEUS omne quod opto,
    Cum malis nostris ut mala cuncta feras.

—

Friend, Coming in a friendly wise, From East, West, North or
        South,
Take here the Owner's own Advise, Put nothing in thy
        mouth;
But freely fill thy *Nose and Eyes* with all my Garden's Growth.
For, if thou imitate the Apes, And clandestinely steal my
        Grapes,
One wishes thee the Belly-Gripes, Another hundred
        Scaffold-Stripes, &c.
Therefore, Pray, Curb thine Appetite, And mind the next
        lines, I now write,
    viz. The best of Pilgrim's Shapes,
        Is that which never gapes;
But without any Bluster, Does buy a lusty Cluster.

—

Now, on those Terms, I give thee Leave to Enter,
And Penetrate, from both Ends, to the Center;
But do *not break, nor take* Stalks, Fruits, or Seed:
For thou and I are otherwise Agreed.
Such-like Contracts bind without Seal and hand,
A good Man's Word exceeds a bad ones Bond.

JOHN NORTON JR.

(1651–1716)

A Funeral Elogy

*Upon that Pattern and Patron of Virtue, the
truely pious, peerless & matchless Gentlewoman
Mrs. Anne Bradstreet,
right* Panaretes,
*Mirror of Her Age, Glory of her Sex, whose
Heaven-born-Soul leaving its earthly Shrine,
chose its native home, and was taken to its
Rest, upon 16th. Sept. 1672.*

Ask not why hearts turn Magazines of passions,
And why that grief is clad in sev'ral fashions;
Why She on progress goes, and doth not borrow
The smallest respite from th'extreams of sorrow,
Her misery is got to such an height,
As makes the earth groan to support its weight,
Such storms of woe, so strongly have beset her,
She hath no place for worse, nor hope for better;
Her comfort is, if any for her be,
That none can shew more cause of grief than she.
Ask not why some in mournfull black are clad;
The Sun is set, there needs must be a shade.
Ask not why every face a sadness shrowdes;
The setting Sun ore-cast us hath with Clouds.
Ask not why the great glory of the Skye
That gilds the starrs with heavenly Alchamy,
Which all the world doth lighten with his rayes,
The *Persian* God, the Monarch of the cayes;
Ask not the reason of his extasie,
Paleness of late, in midnoon Majesty,
Why that the palefac'd Empress of the night
Disrob'd her brother of his glorious light.
Did not the language of the starrs foretel
A mournfull Scœne when they with tears did swell?
Did not the glorious people of the Skye

Seem sensible of future misery?
Did not the lowring heavens seem to express
The worlds great lose, and their unhappiness?
Behold how tears flow from the learned hill,
How the bereaved Nine do daily fill
The bosome of the fleeting Air with groans,
And wofull Accents, which witness their moanes.
How doe the Goddesses of verse, the learned quire,
Lament their rival Quill, which all admire?
Could *Maro*'s Muse but hear her lively strain,
He would condemn his works to fire again.
Methinks I hear the Patron of the Spring,
The unshorn Diety abruptly sing.
Some doe for anguish weep, for anger I
That Ignorance should live, and Art should die.
Black, fatal, dismal, inauspicious day,
Unblest for ever by *Sol*'s precious Ray,
Be it the first of Miseries to all;
Or last of Life defam'd for Funeral.
When this day yearly comes, let every one,
Cast in their urne, the black and dismal stone.
Succeeding years as they their circuit goe,
Leap o're this day, as a sad time of woe.
Farewell my Muse, since thou hast left thy shrine,
I am unblest in one, but blest in nine.
Fair *Thespian* Ladyes, light your torches all,
Attend your glory to its Funeral,
To court her ashes with a learned tear,
A briny sacrifice, let not a smile appear.
Grave Matron, whoso seeks to blazon thee,
Needs not make use of witts false Heraldry;
Whoso should give thee all thy worth would swell
So high, as 'twould turn the world infidel.
Had he great *Maro*'s Muse, or *Tully*'s tongue,
Or raping numbers like the *Thracian* Song,
In crowning of her merits he would be
Sumptuously poor, low in Hyperbole.
To write is easie: but to write on thee,
Truth would be thought to forfeit modesty.
He'l seem a Poet that shall speak but true;

Hyperbole's in others, are thy due.
Like a most servile flatterer he will show
Though he write truth, and make the subject, You.
Virtue ne're dies, time will a Poet raise
Born under better Starrs, shall sing thy praise.
Praise her who list, yet he shall be a debtor
For Art ne're feign'd, nor Nature fram'd a better.
Her virtues were so great, that they do raise
A work to trouble fame, astonish praise.
When as her Name doth but salute the ear,
Men think that they perfections abstract hear.
Her breast was a brave Pallace, a *Broad-street*,
Where all heroick ample thoughts did meet,
Where nature such a Tenement had tane,
That others souls, to hers, dwelt in a lane.
Beneath her feet, pale envy bites her chain,
And poison Malice, whetts her sting in vain.
Let every Laurel, every Myrtel bough
Be stript for leaves t'adorn and load her brow.
Victorious wreathes, which 'cause they never fade
Wise elder times for Kings and Poets made.
Let not her happy memory e're lack
Its worth in Fames eternal Almanack,
Which none shall read, but straight their loss deplore,
And blame their Fates they were not born before.
Do not old men rejoyce their Fates did last;
And infants too, that theirs did make such hast,
In such a welcome time to bring them forth,
That they might be a witness to her worth.
Who undertakes this subject to commend
Shall nothing find so hard as how to end.

Finis & non.

Omnia Romanæ *sileant Miracula Gentis.*

SAMUEL SEWALL

(1652–1730)

WEDNESDAY
January 1. 1701.
A little before Break-a-day at Boston of Massachusetts

Once more! Our GOD, vouchsafe to Shine
Tame Thou the Rigour of our Clime.
Make haste with thy Impartial Light,
And terminate this long dark Night.

Let the transplanted *English* Vine
Spread further still: still call it Thine.
Prune it with Skill: for yield it can
More Fruit to Thee the Husbandman.

Give the poor *Indians* Eyes to see
The Light of Life: and set them free;
That they Religion may profess,
Denying all Ungodliness.

From hard'ned *Jews* the Vail remove,
Let them their Martyr'd JESUS love;
And Homage unto Him afford,
Because He is their Rightful LORD.

So false Religions shall decay,
And Darkness fly before bright Day:
So Men shall GOD in CHRIST adore;
And worship Idols vain, no more.

So *Asia*, and *Africa*,
Europa, with *America*;
All Four, in Consort join'd, shall Sing
New Songs of Praise to CHRIST our KING.

Upon the drying up that Ancient River, the River Merrimak

Long did *Euphrates* make us glad,
Such pleasant, steady Course he had:
Fight *White*, fight *Chesnut*, all was one,
In Peace profound our River Run
From his remote, and lofty Head,
Until he with the Ocean Wed.
Thousands of Years ran parallel,
View'd it throughout, and lik'd it well.
Herbs, Trees, Fowls, Fishes, Beasts, and Men,
Refresh'd were by this goodly Stream.
Dutiful *Salmon*, once a Year,
Still visited their Parent dear:
And royal *Sturgeon* saw it good
To Sport in the renowned Flood.
All sorts of *Geese*, and *Ducks*, and *Teal*,
In their Allotments fared well.
Many a *Moose*, and Thirsty *Dear*,
Drank to full Satisfaction here.
The *Fox*, the *Wolf*, the angry *Bear*,
Of Drink were not deny'd their share.
The Strangers, late Arrived here,
Were Entertain'd with Welcom chear;
The *Horse*, and *Ox*, at their own will,
Might taste, and drink, and drink their fill.
Thus *Merrymak* kept House secure,
And hop'd for Ages to endure;
Living in Love, and Union,
With every Tributary Son.
At length, an Ambushment was laid
Near *Powwow Hill*, when none afraid;
And unawares, at one Huge Sup,
Hydropick *Hampshire* Drunk it Up!
Look to thy self! *Wadchuset* Hill;
And Bold *Menadnuck*, Fear some Ill!
Envy'd *Earth* knows no certain Bound;
In HEAV'N alone, CONTENT is found.
January 15. 1719, 20.

BENJAMIN HARRIS

(c. 1655–c. 1720)

A

In *Adam's* Fall
We Sinned all.

B

Thy Life to Mend
This *Book* Attend.

C

The *Cat* doth play
And after slay.

D

A *Dog* will bite
A Thief at night.

E

An *Eagles* flight
Is out of sight.

F

The Idle *Fool*
Is whipt at School.

G

As runs the *Glass*
Mans life doth pass.

H

My *Book* and *Heart*
Shall never part.

J

Job feels the Rod
Yet blesses GOD.

K

Our *KING* the good
No man of blood.

L

The *Lion* bold
The *Lamb* doth hold.

M

The *Moon* gives light
In time of night.

N

Nightingales sing
In Time of Spring.

O

The *Royal Oak*
 it was the Tree
That sav'd His
 Royal Majestie.

P

Peter denies
His Lord and cries.

Q

Queen *Esther* comes
  in Royal State
To Save the JEWS
  from dismal Fate.

R

Rachol doth mourn
For her first born.

S

Samuel anoints
Whom God appoints.

T

Time cuts down all
Both great and small.

U

Uriah's beauteous Wife
Made *David* seek his Life.

W

Whales in the Sea
God's Voice obey.

X

Xerxes the great did die,
And so must you & I.

Y

Youth forward slips
Death soonest nips.

Z

Zacheus he
Did climb the Tree
His Lord to see.

JOHN DANFORTH

(1660–1730)

A few Lines to fill up a Vacant Page

Wo worth the Days! The Days I spent
I' th' Regions of Discontent;
Where I nought rightly understood,
But thought Good, Evil; Evil, Good;
Friends I deem'd Foes; Wrong I conceiv'd was done me;
I Swell'd & Rage'd; whole Heaven could not Atone me:
My Soul ('tis known) was not my Own, so far it had undone me.

Health, Fame, and Wealth were full of Stings;
Children, and Friends were no such Things;
My wholesome food was Poison'd all,
And Hony did but Swell my Gall;
God was no God, Christ was no Christ to me,
While thus I Drave in Discontentments Sea:
Thank this first Vice, that *Adam* e're lost Paradice, and me.

Thus being Lost, wrong Course I Steerd.
While neither Sun, nor Stars appear'd;
Instead of Heav'n's Land, I made Hell,
I knew't by its Sulphureous Smell:
Coming on Waters, strait my LORD spy'd I;
Avaunt, Foul Fiend! Avoid, fell Foe! Cry'd I;
So vilely I mistook, and therefore spake foul Blasphemy.

'Tis I, quoth He, Be not Afraid.
Which Words He had no sooner said,
But all my Discontents refil'd;
The Ruffling Winds, and Waves were still'd;
By what Time, Faith and Hope my Sailes could hoise,
I got safe and firm Anch'rage in a trice,
Within the very inmost Bays of blissfull Paradise.

COTTON MATHER

(1663–1728)

Go then, my DOVE, but now no longer *Mine*!
Leave *Earth*, & now in *Heavenly Glory* Shine.
Bright for thy Wisdom, Goodness, Beauty here;
Now *Brighter* in a more *Angelick Sphære*.
JESUS, with whom thy Soul did long to be,
Into His *Ark*, and Arms, has taken thee.
Dear *Friends* with whom thou didst so dearly Live,
Feel *Thy one Death* to *Them* a *Thousand* give.
Thy *Prayers* are done; thy *Alms* are spent; thy *Pains*
Are *Ended* now in *Endless* Joyes & Gains.
The *Torch* that gave my *House* its pleasant *Light*,
Extinguish'd leaves it in how *dark* a *Night*!
   I faint, till thy last words to mind I call;
Rich Words! HEAV'N, HEAV'N WILL MAKE AMENDS FOR ALL.

Gratitudinis Ergo

An Essay on the Memory of my Venerable Master; Ezekiel Cheever

Augusto perstringere Carmine Laudes,
Quas nulla Eloquii vis Celebrare queat.

You that are *Men*, & Thoughts of *Manhood* know,
Be Just now to the *Man* that made you so.
Martyr'd by *Scholars* the stabb'd *Cassian* dies,
And falls to cursed Lads a Sacrifice.
Not so my CHEEVER; Not by *Scholars* slain,
But Prais'd, and Lov'd, and wish'd to *Life* again.
A mighty *Tribe* of Well-instructed Youth
Tell what they owe to him, and Tell with Truth.
All the *Eight parts of Speech* he taught to them
They now Employ to *Trumpet* his Esteem.
They fill *Fames Trumpet*, and they spread a Fame
To last till the *Last Trumpet* drown the same.

225

Magister pleas'd them well, because 'twas *he*;
They saw that *Bonus* did with it agree.
While they said, *Amo*, they the Hint improve
Him for to make the Object of their *Love*.
No *Concord* so Inviolate they knew
As to pay Honours to their Master due.
With *Interjections* they break off at last,
But, *Ah*, is all they use, *Wo*, and, *Alas!*
We Learnt *Prosodia*, but with that Design
Our Masters Name should in our *Verses* shine.
Our Weeping *Ovid* but instructed us
To write upon *his* Death, *De Tristibus*.
Tully we read, but still with this Intent,
That in *his* praise we might be Eloquent.
Our Stately *Virgil* made us but Contrive
As our *Anchises* to keep *him* Alive,
When *Phœnix* to *Achilles* was assign'd
A *Master*, then we thought not *Homer* blind.
A *Phœnix*, which Oh! might his *Ashes* shew!
So rare a Thing we thought *our Master* too.
And if we made a *Theme*, 'twas with Regret
We might not on *his* Worth show all our Wit.

   Go on, ye Grateful Scholars, to proclame
To late Posterity your *Masters* Name.
Let it as many Languages declare
As on *Loretto*-Table do appear.

   Too much to be by any *one* exprest:
   I'll tell my share, and *you* shall tell the rest.
Ink is too vile a Liquor; *Liquid Gold*
Should fill the Pen, by which such things are told.
The book should *Amyanthus*-Paper be
All writ with *Gold*, from all corruption free.

   A Learned Master of the *Languages*
Which to Rich *Stores* of Learning are the *Keyes*;
He taught us first *Good Sense* to understand
And put the *Golden Keyes* into our Hand,
We but for him had been for Learning *Dumb*,
And had a sort of *Turkish Mutes* become.
Were *Grammar* quite Extinct, yet at his Brain
The *Candle* might have well been lit again.

If *Rhet'rick* had been stript of all her *Pride*
She from his *Wardrobe* might have been Supply'd.
Do but Name CHEEVER, and the *Echo* straight
Upon that Name, *Good Latin*, will Repeat.
A *Christian Terence*, Master of the *File*
That arms the Curious to Reform their *Style*.
Now *Rome* and *Athens* from their Ashes rise;
See their *Platonick Year* with vast surprise:
And in our *School* a *Miracle* is wrought;
For the *Dead Languages* to *Life* are brought.
   His *Work* he Lov'd: Oh! had we done the same!
Our *Play-dayes* still to him ungrateful came.
And yet so well our *Work* adjusted Lay,
We came to *Work*, as if we came to *Play*.
      Our *Lads* had been, but for his wondrous Cares,
      Boyes of my Lady *Mores* unquiet Pray'rs.
      Sure were it not for such informing *Schools*,
      Our *Lat'ran* too would soon be fill'd with *Owles*.
'Tis CORLET's pains, & CHEEVER's, we must own,
That thou, *New-England*, art not *Scythia* grown.
The *Isles* of *Silly* had o're-run this Day
      The *Continent* of our *America*.
Grammar he taught, which 'twas his work to do:
But he would *Hagar* have her place to know.
      The *Bible* is the Sacred *Grammar*, where
      The *Rules of speaking well*, contained are.
He taught us *Lilly*, and he *Gospel* taught;
And us poor Children to our *Saviour* brought.
Master of Sentences, he gave us more
Then we in our *Sententia* had before.
We Learn't Good Things in *Tullies Offices*;
But we from *him* Learn't Better things than these.
With *Cato's* he to us the *Higher* gave
Lessons of JESUS, that our Souls do save.
We Constru'd *Ovid's Metamorphosis*,
But on our selves charg'd, not a *Change* to miss.
Young *Austin* wept, when he saw *Dido* dead,
Tho' not a Tear for a *Lost Soul* he had:
Our Master would not let us be so vain,
But us from *Virgil* did to *David* train,

Textors Epistles would not *Cloathe* our Souls;
Pauls too we heard; we *went to School at Pauls.*

Syrs, Do you not Remember well the Times,
When us he warn'd against our *Youthful Crimes:*
What *Honey dropt* from our old *Nestors* mouth
When with his Counsels he Reform'd our Youth:
How much he did to make us *Wise* and *Good*;
And with what *Prayers*, his work he did conclude.
Concern'd, that when from him we *Learning* had,
It might not *Armed Wickedness* be made!
The *Sun* shall first the *Zodiac* forsake,
And *Stones* unto the *Stars* their Flight shall make:
First shall the *Summer* bring large drifts of *Snow*,
And beauteous Cherries in *December* grow;
E're of those Charges we Forgetful are
Which we, *O man of God*, from thee did hear.
    Such *Tutors* to the *Little Ones* would be
    Such that *in Flesh* we should *their Angels* see,
    Ezekiel should not be the Name of such;
    We'd *Agathangelus* not think too much,
Who Serv'd the *School*, the *Church* did not forget,
But Thought, and Pray'd, and often wept for it.
Mighty in Prayer: How did he wield thee, Pray'r!
Thou Reverst Thunder: CHRIST's-Sides-piercing Spear?
Soaring we saw the *Birds of Paradise*;
So Wing'd by Thee, for Flights beyond the Skies.
How oft we saw him tread the *Milky Way*,
Which to the Glorious *Throne of Mercy* lay!
    Come from the *Mount*, he shone with ancient Grace.
Awful the *Splendor* of his Aged Face
Cloath'd in the *Good Old Way*, his Garb did wage
A War with the Vain Fashions of the Age.
Fearful of nothing more than hateful *Sin*;
'Twas that from which he laboured all to win,
Zealous; And in *Truths Cause* ne'r known to trim;
No *Neuter Gender* there allow'd by him.
Stars but a *Thousand* did the Ancients know;
On later Globes they *Nineteen hundred* grow:
Now such a CHEEVER added to the Sphere;
Makes an Addition to the *Lustre* there.

Mean time *America* a *Wonder* saw;
A Youth in Age, forbid by *Natures* Law.
　You that in t'other Hemisphere do dwell,
Do of *Old Age* your dismal Stories tell.
You tell of *Snowy Heads* and *Rheumy Eyes*
And things that make a man himself despise.
You say, a *frozen Liquor* chills the Veins,
And scarce the *Shadow* of a *Man* remains.
Winter of Life, that *Sapless Age* you call,
And of all Maladies the *Hospital*:
The *Second Nonage* of the Soul; the *Brain*
Cover'd with Cloud; the *Body* all in pain.
To weak *Old Age*, you say, there must belong
A Trembling Palsey both of *Limb* and *Tongue*;
Dayes all Decrepit, and a Bending *Back*,
Propt by a *Staff*, in *Hands* that ever Shake.
　Nay, Syrs, our CHEEVER shall confute you all,
On whom there did none of these Mischefs fall.
He *Liv'd*, and to vast Age no Illness knew;
'Till *Time's Scythe* waiting for him Rusty grew.
He *Liv'd* and *Wrought*; His Labours were Immense;
But ne'er *Declin'd* to *Præter-perfect Tense*.
A *Blooming Youth* in him at *Ninety Four*
We saw; But, Oh! when such a sight before!
At Wondrous *Age* he did his *Youth* resume,
As when the *Eagle* mew's his Aged plume.
With Faculties of *Reason* still so bright
And at Good Services so Exquisite;
Sure our sound *Chiliast*, we wondring thought,
To the *First Resurrection* is not brought!
No, He for That was waiting at the Gate
In the *Pure Things* that fit a Candidate.
He in Good Actions did his Life Employ,
And to make others Good, he made his Joy.
Thus well-appris'd now of the *Life to Come*,
To *Live here* was to him a *Martyrdom*:
Our brave *Macrobius* Long'd to see the Day
Which others dread, of being *Call'd away*.
So, Ripe with Age, he does invite the Hook,
Which watchful does for its large Harvest look:

Death gently cut the *Stalk*, and kindly laid
Him, where our God His *Granary* has made.
   Who at *New-Haven* first began to Teach
Dying *Unshipwreck'd*, does *White-Haven* reach.
At that *Fair Haven* they all Storms forget;
He there his DAVENPORT with Love does meet.
   The *Luminous Robe*, the *Loss* whereof with *Shame*
Our Parents wept, when *Naked* they became;
Those Lovely *Spirits* wear it, and therein
Serve God with *Priestly Glory*, free from Sin.
   But in his *Paradisian Rest* above,
To *Us* does the Blest Shade retain his Love.
With *Rip'ned Thoughts* Above concern'd for Us,
We can't but hear him dart his Wishes, thus.
   "TUTORS, Be *Strict*; But yet be *Gentle* too:
Don't by fierce *Cruelties* fair *Hopes* undo.
Dream not, that they who are to Learning slow,
Will mend by Arguments in *Ferio*.
Who keeps the *Golden Fleece*, Oh, let him not
A *Dragon* be, tho' he *Three Tongues* have got.
Why can you not to Learning find the way,
But thro' the Province of *Severia*?
Twas *Moderatus*, who taught *Origen*;
A *Youth* which prov'd one of the Best of men.
The Lads with *Honour* first, and *Reason* Rule;
Blowes are but for the *Refractory Fool*.
But, Oh! First Teach them their Great God to fear;
That you like me, with Joy may meet them here."
             H' has said!—
Adieu, a little while, Dear Saint, Adieu;
Your *Scholar* won't be Long, Sir, after you.
In the mean time, with Gratitude I must
Engrave an EPITAPH upon your Dust.
'Tis true, *Excessive Merits* rarely safe:
Such an *Excess* forfeits an *Epitaph*.
But if Base men the Rules of Justice break,
The *Stones* (at least upon the *Tombs*) will speak.

Et Tumulum facite, et Tumulo superaddite carmen.
                    (Virg. in Daphn.)

EPITAPHIUM

EZEKIEL CHEEVERUS:
Ludimagister;
Primo Neo-portensis;
Deinde, Ipsuicensis;
Postea, Carolotenensis
Postremo, Bostonensis;
cuius
Doctrinam ac Virtutem
Nostri, si Sis Nov-Anglus,
Colis, si non Barbarus;
GRAMMATICUS,
a Quo, non pure tantum, sed et pie,
Loqui;
RHETORICUS,
a Quo non tantum Ornate dicere
coram Hominibus,
Sed et Orationes coram Deo fundere
Efficacissimas;
POETA
a Quo non tantum Carmina pangere
Sed et
Cælestes Hymnos, Odasq; Angelicas,
canere,
Didicerunt,
Qui discere voluerunt;
LUCERNA,
ad Quam accensa sunt,
Quis queat numerare,
Quot Ecclesiarum Lumina?
ET
Qui secum Corpus Theologiæ abstulit,
Peritissimus THEOLOGUS,
Corpus hic suum sibi minus Charum,
deposuit.
Vixit Annos, XCIV.
Docuit, Annos, LXX.
Obiit. A.D. M. DCC. VIII.
Et quod Mori potuit

HEIC

Expectat Exoptatq:

Primam Sanctorum Resurrectionem

ad

Immortalitatem.

Evuviis debetur. Honos Immortalitatem primam.

Singing at the Plow

My *Heart*, how very *Hard* its grown!
   Thicken'd and stiffen'd Clay:
Daily trod by the *Wicked One*;
   Of *Sin* the *Beaten Way*.
An *Heart*, wherein compacted *Weeds*
   Of *Diverse Lusts* abound;
No Entrance for the Heavenly *Seeds*,
   Falling on such a Ground!
O my Almighty SAVIOUR, come;
   Thy *Word*'s a wondrous *Plow*:
And let thy SPIRIT drive it home;
   This *Heart*, Oh! Break it so!
Lord, let my *Broken Heart* receive
   Thy Truth with Faith and Love:
May it a Just Reception give
   To what falls from Above.
Will my GOD *Plow upon a Rock!*
   Change thou the Soyl, my Lord!
My *Heart* once by thy *Plow-share* broke,
   Will Entertain thy Word.

The Songs of Harvest

Tis not the Till'd, Poor, Lifeless *Earth*
   Which gives me all my Store.
No: Tis my GOD! From *Him* comes forth
   All that has fill'd my Floor.

For what Iv'e gather'd from the Field
   Thee, Oh! my GOD I bless.
But, Oh! that I *Fruits* too may yield
   To Him who me does *dress*!

My Soul, with *Gladness* fill'd, and *Food*;
   Returns, what shall be made?
In this *Abundance serve* thy GOD,
   In Him for ever *glad.*

Now in *Obedience* all my Days
   Hard at my Work I'll keep;
Him I'l take pains to please and praise;
   Assur'd, *That I shall Reap.*

Yea, If I must thro' Sorrows go,
   And *Weeping Eyes* employ;
I'm sure, That they in *Tears* who *Sow*
   At length shall *Reap* with *Joy.*

But, Oh, What shall I *Reap* anon!
   What *Eyes* did ever see,
Or to what Man on Earth is known,
   What will the *Harvest* be!

My JESUS, My *Rewarder* Thou
   Wilt be; and more than so:
Thou my *Reward* wilt be. And now
   No Higher can I go.

SARAH KEMBLE KNIGHT

(1666–1727)

FROM

The Journal of Madam Knight

I ask thy Aid, O Potent Rum!
To Charm these wrangling Topers Dum.
Thou hast their Giddy Brains possest—
The man confounded with the Beast—
And I, poor I, can get no rest.
Intoxicate them with thy fumes:
O still their Tongues till morning comes!

———

Tho' Ill at ease, A stranger and alone,
All my fatigu's shall not extort a grone.
These Indigents have hunger with their ease;
Their best is wors behalfe then my disease.
Their Misirable hutt which Heat and Cold
Alternately without Repulse do hold;
Their Lodgings thyn and hard, their Indian fare,
The mean Apparel which the wretches wear,
And their ten thousand ills which can't be told,
Makes nature er'e 'tis midle age'd look old.
When I reflect, my late fatigues do seem
Only a notion or forgotten Dreem.

ROBERT HUNTER

(1666–1734)

Androboros: A Biographical Farce

The *Bees* so fam'd for Feats of War,
  And Arts of Peace, were once, of Sense
As void as other Insects are,
    'Till time and late Experience,
      The only Schoolmaster of Fools,
      Taught them the use of Laws and Rules.

In that wild state they were Assail'd
  By th' Wasps, oft routed and Opprest;
Not that their Hearts or Hands had fail'd,
    But that their Head was none o'th' best,
      The *Drone* being, by the Commons Voice,
      Chose for the Greatness of his Noise.

Thus ill they sped in every Battle;
  For tho' the Chief was in Request
At home, for's Fools Coat and his Rattle,
    Abroad he was the Common Jest.
      The *Wasps* in all Ingagements, held—
      His Folly more then half the Field.

Grown Wiser by repeated Woes,
  The Bees fit to change their Chief,
It was a *Humble Bee* they Chose,
    Whose Conduct brought them quick Relief;
      And ever since that Race has led 'em,
      The *Drones* are Drums, as Nature made 'em.

———

In the beginning God made Men,
   And all was well, but in the End
Men made their Gods, and Fondly pay'd 'em.
   The Worship due to him that made 'em,
And all was wrong; for they Increas'd,
   And Multiply'd like Man and Beast.
But none were bold in Reverence
   So much as *Phoebus*, God of sense
And Non-sense, Patron, as occasion
   Did serve, of Arts and Inspiration.
Once on a day as he was led
   About to give a Cast of's Trade,
Whether to Dance, or Sing, or Fiddle,
   Or as some say, to read a Riddle,
I know not; but what-e'er it was,
   His Vehicle was but an Ass,
And he none of the wisest neither;
   For when the Crowd had got together
To pay due Homage to their God,
   Strowing with Flow'rs the Path he rode,
And singing Paeans, the vain Beast
   Believ'd all this, to him Address't:
He Pranc'd, and Flung, and Frisk'd about,
   Scatt'ring much Dirt among the Rout,
And bray'd as if h' had got a Pack
   Of Dev'ls, and not God on's back.
The Crowd essay'd by gentle ways,
   To Curb his Pride, and smooth his Pace;
But all was talking to the Wind;
   For Zeal is deaf, when-e'er 'tis blind.
Finding all other Methods fail,
   They seiz'd him by the Ears and Tail,
And took the Idol from his back,
   With many a lusty Bang and Thwack.
They let him know, that *Phoebus* was
   The God, and he was but an Ass.

————

The Frogs, a Factious ficke Race,
With little Maners, and less Grace,
  Croak'd for a King so loud,
That all the Host of Heav'n sate mute
Nodding to *Jove* to grant their suit,
  And give 'em what they wou'd.

A King they had, of such a size
Who's Entry too, made such a Noise,
  That Ev'ry Neut and Frog
Affrighted, run to hide their heads;
Some in the Pool, some 'mongst the Reeds,
  Like Fools, 'Twas but a Log.

At last, one bolder than the rest,
Approach'd, and the new Prince Address't,
  No hurt from thence sustain'd,
He mock'd his former Fears, and swore
'Twas the best stick of Wood that o'er
  The Marshes ever Reign'd.

Then all the Croaking Crew drew near,
And in his shade from th' angry Air
  Were shelter'd safe, and eas'd,
Nay, more then that, they'd frisk and play
Upon his back a live long day,
  He Undisturb'd and pleas'd.

The Pertest Frog of all the Pack,
A Toad, some say, his hue was Black;
'Tis true; but that's no matter,
Upon the passive Monarch's head,
At times would Noxious Venom shed,
  And both his sides bespatter.

'Twas That same Frog, the Legends tell,
Burst when he only meant to swell,
  Soon after these Events.

Be that as 'twill, 'twas He that drew
That giddy Senseless Crowd to new
    Sedition and Complaints.

Give us a bustling King, *Dread Sir!*
They cry'd, a King that makes a stir;
    This is not to be mov'd.
Jove heard and gave 'm one, who's care
Was, that they should Obey and Fear,
    No matter how they Lov'd.

It was a *Stork*, who's Law-less Rage
Spar'd neither Sex, Degree nor Age,
    That came within his reach.
And that was great, for whilst his Claws
Ransack't the Deep, his Vulturs Jaws
    Could wander o'er the Beach.

Then they Implor'd the God to send
From heav'n a Plague, from Hell a Fiend,
    Or any but this Curse.
Peace, cry'd the Monarch of the Gods,
Ye Worms; Keep him you have, 'tis odds
    The Next may prove a Worse.

EBENEZER COOK

(c. 1667–c. 1733)

The Sot-Weed Factor;
or a Voyage to Maryland, &c.

Condemn'd by Fate to way-ward Curse,
Of Friends unkind, and empty Purse;
Plagues worse than fill'd *Pandora's* Box,
I took my leave of *Albion's* Rocks:
With heavy Heart, concern'd that I
Was forc'd my Native Soil to fly,
And the *Old World* must bid good-buy.
But Heav'n ordain'd it should be so,
And to repine is vain we know:
Freighted with Fools, from *Plymouth* sound,
To *Mary-Land* our Ship was bound,
Where we arriv'd in dreadful Pain,
Shock'd by the Terrours of the Main;
For full three Months, our wavering Boat,
Did thro' the surley Ocean float,
And furious Storms and threat'ning Blasts,
Both tore our Sails and sprung our Masts:
Wearied, yet pleas'd, we did escape
Such Ills, we anchor'd at the [a]*Cape*;
But weighing soon, we plough'd the *Bay*,
To [b]*Cove* it in [c]*Piscato-way*,
Intending there to open Store,
I put myself and Goods a-shore:
Where soon repair'd a numerous Crew,
In Shirts and Drawers of [d]*Scotch-cloth* Blue.
With neither Stockings, Hat, nor Shooe:

[a]By the *Cape*, is meant the *Capes of Virginia*, the first Land on the Coast of *Virginia* and *Mary-Land*.

[b]To *Cove* is to lie at Anchor safe in Harbour.

[c]The Bay of *Piscato-way*, the usual place where our Ships come to an Anchor in *Mary-Land*.

[d]The Planters generally wear Blue *Linnen*.

These *Sot-weed* Planters Crowd the Shoar,
In Hue as tawny as a Moor:
Figures so strange, no God design'd,
To be a part of Humane Kind:
But wanton Nature, void of Rest,
Moulded the brittle Clay in Jest.
At last a Fancy very odd
Took me, this was the Land of *Nod*;
Planted at first, when Vagrant *Cain*,
His Brother had unjustly slain:
Then conscious of the Crime he'd done,
From Vengeance dire, he hither run;
And in a Hut supinely dwelt,
The first in *Furs* and *Sot-weed* dealt.
And ever since his Time, the Place,
Has harbour'd a detested Race;
Who when they cou'd not live at Home,
For Refuge to these Worlds did roam;
In hopes by Flight they might prevent,
The Devil and his fell intent;
Obtain from Tripple Tree repreive,
And Heav'n and Hell alike deceive:
But e're their Manners I display,
I think it fit I open lay
My Entertainment by the way;
That Strangers well may be aware on,
What homely Diet they must fare on.
To touch that Shoar, where no good Sense is found,
But Conversation's lost, and Manners drown'd.
I crost unto the other side,
A River whose impetuous Tide,
The Savage Borders does divide;
In such a shining odd invention,
I scarce can give its due Dimention.
The *Indians* call this watry Waggon
[e]*Canoo*, a Vessel none can brag on;
Cut from a *Popular-Tree*, or *Pine*,
And fashion'd like a Trough for Swine:

[e]A *Canoo* is an *Indian* Boat, cut out of the body of a Popler-Tree.

In this most noble Fishing-Boat,
I boldly put myself a-float;
Standing Erect, with Legs stretch'd wide,
We paddled to the other side:
Where being Landed safe by hap,
As *Sol* fell into *Thetis* Lap.
A ravenous Gang bent on the stroul,
Of [f]Wolves for Prey, began to howl;
This put me in a pannick Fright,
Least I should be devoured quite:
But as I there a musing stood,
And quite benighted in a Wood,
A Female Voice pierc'd thro' my Ears,
Crying, *You Rogue drive home the Steers.*
I listen'd to th' attractive sound,
And straight a Herd of Cattel found
Drove by a Youth, and homewards bound:
Cheer'd with the sight, I straight thought fit,
To ask where I a Bed might get.
The surley Peasant bid me stay,
And ask'd from whom [g]I'de run away.
Surpriz'd at such a saucy Word,
I instantly lugg'd out my Sword;
Swearing I was no Fugitive,
But from *Great-Britain* did arrive,
In hopes I better there might Thrive.
To which he mildly made reply,
I beg your pardon, Sir, *that I*
Should talk to you Unmannerly;
But if you please to go with me,
To yonder House, you'll welcome be.
Encountering soon the smoaky Seat,
The Planter old did thus me greet:
"Whether you come from Goal or Colledge,
You're welcome to my certain Knowledge;
And if you please all Night to stay,
My Son shall put you in the way."

[f]Wolves are very numerous in *Mary-Land.*

[g]'Tis supposed by the Planters, that all unknown Persons are run away from some Master.

Which offer I most kindly took,
And for a Seat did round me look:
When presently amongst the rest,
He plac'd his unknown *English* Guest,
Who found them drinking for a whet,
A Cask of [h]Syder on the Fret,
Till Supper came upon the Table,
On which I fed whilst I was able.
So after hearty Entertainment,
Of Drink and Victuals without Payment;
For Planters Tables, you must know,
Are free for all that come and go.
While [i]Pon and Milk, with [j]Mush well stoar'd,
In wooden Dishes grac'd the Board;
With [k]Homine and Syder-pap,
(Which scarce a hungry Dog wou'd lap)
Well stuff'd with Fat, from Bacon fry'd,
Or with *Molossus* dulcify'd.
Then out our Landlord pulls a Pouch,
As greasy as the Leather Couch
On which he sat, and straight begun,
To load with Weed his *Indian* Gun;
In length, scarce longer than ones Finger,
Or that for which the Ladies linger.
His Pipe smoak'd out with aweful Grace,
With aspect grave and solemn pace;
The reverend Sire walks to a Chest,
Of all his Furniture the best,
Closely confin'd within a Room,
Which seldom felt the weight of Broom;
From thence he lugs a Cag of Rum,
And nodding to me, thus begun:
I find, says he, you don't much care,
For this our *Indian* Country Fare;

[h]Syder-pap is a sort of Food made of Syder and small Homine, like our Oatmeal.

[i]Pon is Bread made of *Indian-Corn*.

[j]Mush is a sort of Hasty-Pudding made with Water and *Indian* Flower.

[k]Homine is a Dish that is made of boiled *Indian* Wheat, eaten with Molossus, or Bacon-Fat.

But let me tell you, Friend of mine,
You may be glad of it in time,
Tho' now your Stomach is so fine;
And if within this Land you stay,
You'll find it true what I do say.
This said, the Rundlet up he threw,
And bending backwards strongly drew:
I pluck'd as stoutly for my part,
Altho' it made me sick at Heart,
And got so soon into my Head
I scarce cou'd find my way to Bed;
Where I was instantly convey'd
By one who pass'd for Chamber-Maid;
Tho' by her loose and sluttish Dress,
She rather seem'd a *Bedlam-Bess*:
Curious to know from whence she came,
I prest her to declare her Name.
She Blushing, seem'd to hide her Eyes,
And thus in Civil Terms replies;
In better Times, e'er to this Land,
I was unhappily Trapann'd;
Perchance as well I did appear,
As any Lord or Lady here,
Not then a Slave for twice two [l]Year.
My Cloaths were fashionably new,
Not were my Shifts of Linnen Blue;
But things are changed now at the Hoe,
I daily work, and Bare-foot go,
In weeding corn or feeding Swine,
I spend my melancholy Time.
Kidnap'd and Fool'd, I hither fled,
To shun a hated Nuptial [m]Bed,
And to my cost already find,
Worse Plagues than those I left behind.
Whate'er the Wanderer did profess,
Good-faith I cou'd not choose but guess

[l]Tis the Custom for Servants to be obliged for four Years to very servile Work; after which time they have their Freedom.

[m]These are the general Excuses made by *English* Women, which are sold, or sell themselves to *Mary-Land*.

The Cause which brought her to this place,
Was supping e'er the Priest said Grace.
Quick as my Thoughts, the Slave was fled,
(Her Candle left to shew my Bed)
Which made of Feathers soft and good,
Close in the [n]Chimney-corner stood;
I threw me down expecting Rest,
To be in golden Slumbers blest:
But soon a noise disturb'd my quiet,
And plagu'd me with nocturnal Riot;
A Puss which in the ashes lay,
With grunting Pig began a Fray;
And prudent Dog, that Feuds might cease,
Most strongly bark'd to keep the Peace.
This Quarrel scarcely was decided,
By stick that ready lay provided;
But *Reynard* arch and cunning Loon,
Broke into my Appartment soon;
In hot pursuit of Ducks and Geese,
With fell intent the same to seize:
Their Cackling Plaints with strange surprize,
Chac'd Sleeps thick Vapours from my Eyes:
Raging I jump'd upon the Floar,
And like a Drunken Saylor Swore;
With Sword I fiercly laid about,
And soon dispers'd the Feather'd Rout:
The Poultry out of Window flew,
And *Reynard* cautiously withdrew:
The Dogs who this Encounter heard,
Fiercly themselves to aid me rear'd,
And to the Place of Combat run,
Exactly as the Field was won.
Fretting and hot as roasting Capon,
And greasy as a Flitch of Bacon;
I to the Orchard did repair,
To Breathe the cool and open Air;
Expecting there the rising Day,
Extended on a Bank I lay;

[n]Beds stand in the Chimney-corner in this Country.

But Fortune here, that saucy Whore,
Disturb'd me worse and plagu'd me more,
Than she had done the night before.
Hoarse croaking [o]Frogs did 'bout me ring,
Such Peals the Dead to Life wou'd bring,
A Noise might move their Wooden King.
I stuff'd my Ears with Cotten white
For fear of being deaf out-right,
And curst the melancholy Night:
But soon my Vows I did recant,
And Hearing as a Blessing grant;
When a confounded Rattle-Snake,
With hissing made my Heart to ake:
Not knowing how to fly the Foe,
Or whether in the Dark to go;
By strange good Luck, I took a Tree,
Prepar'd by Fate to set me free;
Where riding on a Limb astride,
Night and the Branches did me hide,
And I the Devil and Snake defy'd.
Not yet from Plagues exempted quite,
The curst Muskitoes did me bite;
Till rising Morn' and blushing Day,
Drove both my Fears and Ills away;
And from Night's Errors set me free.
Discharg'd from hospitable Tree;
I did to Planters Booth repair,
And there at Breakfast nobly Fare,
On rashier broil'd of infant Bear:
I thought the Cub delicious Meat,
Which ne'er did ought but Chesnuts eat;
Nor was young Orsin's flesh the worse,
Because he suck'd a Pagan Nurse.
Our Breakfast done, my Landlord stout,
Handed a Glass of Rum about;
Pleas'd with the Treatment I did find,
I took my leave of Oast so kind;
Who to oblige me, did provide,

[o]Frogs are called *Virginea* Bells, and make, (both in that Country and *Mary-Land*) during the Night, a very hoarse ungrateful Noise.

His eldest Son to be my Guide,
And lent me Horses of his own,
A skittish Colt, and aged Rhoan,
The four-leg'd prop of his Wife *Joan*.
Steering our Barks in Trot or Pace,
We sail'd directly for a place
In *Mary-Land* of high renown,
Known by the Name of *Battle-Town*.
To view the Crowds did there resort,
Which Justice made, and Law their sport,
In that sagacious County Court:
Scarce had we enter'd on the way,
Which thro' thick Woods and Marshes lay;
But *Indians* strange did soon appear,
In hot persuit of wounded Deer;
No mortal Creature can express,
His wild fantastick Air and Dress;
His painted Skin in colours dy'd,
His sable Hair in Satchel ty'd,
Shew'd Savages not free from Pride:
His tawny Thighs, and Bosom bare,
Disdain'd a useless Coat to wear,
Scorn'd Summer's Heat, and Winters Air;
His manly Shoulders such as please,
Widows and Wives, were bath'd in Grease
Of Cub and Bear, whose supple Oil,
Prepar'd his Limbs 'gainst Heat or Toil.
Thus naked Pict in Battel faught,
Or undisguis'd his Mistress sought;
And knowing well his Ware was good,
Refus'd to screen it with a Hood;
His Visage dun, and chin that ne'er
Did Raizor feel or Scissers bear,
Or knew the Ornament of Hair,
Look'd sternly Grim, surpriz'd with Fear,
I spur'd my Horse, as he drew near:
But Rhoan who better knew than I,
The little Cause I had to fly;
Seem'd by his solemn steps and pace,
Resolv'd I shou'd the Specter face,

Nor faster mov'd, tho' spur'd and lick'd,
Than *Balaam's* Ass by Prophet kick'd
Kekicknitop[p] the Heathen cry'd:
How is it *Tom*, my Friend reply'd,
Judging from thence the Brute was civel,
I boldly fac'd the Courteous Devil;
And lugging out a Dram of Rum,
I gave his Tawny worship some:
Who in his language as I guess,
(My Guide informing me no less,)
Implored the [q]Devil, me to bless.
I thank'd him for his good Intent,
And forwards on my Journey went,
Discoursing as along I rode,
Whether this Race was framed by God
Or whether some Malignant pow'r,
Contriv'd them in an evil hour
And from his own Infernal Look,
Their Dusky form and Image took:
From hence we fell to Argument
Whence Peopled was this Continent.
My Friend suppos'd *Tartarians* wild,
Or *Chinese* from their Home exiled;
Wandering thro' Mountains hid with Snow,
And Rills did in the Vallies flow,
Far to the South of *Mexico*:
Broke thro' the Barrs which Nature cast,
And wide unbeaten Regions past,

[p]*Kekicknitop* is an *Indian* Expression, and signifies no more than this, *How do you do?*

[q]These *Indians* worship the Devil, and pray to him as we do to God Almighty. 'Tis suppos'd, That *America* was peopl'd from *Scythia* or *Tartaria*, which Borders on *China*, by reason the *Tartarians* and *Americans* very much agree in their Manners, Arms, and Government. Other Persons are of Opinion, that the *Chinese* first peopled the *West Indies*; imagining *China* and the Southern part of *America* to be contiguous. Others believe that the Phoenicians who were very skilful Mariners, first planted a Colony in the Isles of *America*, and supply'd the Persons left to inhabit there with Women and all other Necessaries; till either the Death or Shipwreck of the first Discovers, or some other Misfortune occasioned the loss of the Discovery, which had been purchased by the Peril of the first Adventurers.

Till near those Streams the humane deludge roll'd,
Which sparkling shin'd with glittering Sands of Gold,
And fetch [r] *Pizarro* from the [s] *Iberian* Shoar,
To Rob the Natives of their fatal Stoar.
I Smil'd to hear my young Logician,
Thus Reason like a Politician;
Who ne're by Fathers Pains and Earning
Had got at Mother *Cambridge* Learning;
Where Lubber youth just free from birch
Most stoutly drink to prop the Church;
Nor with [t] *Grey Groat* had taken Pains
To purge his Head and Cleanse his Reines:
And in obedience to the Colledge,
Had pleas'd himself with carnal Knowledge:
And tho' I lik'd the youngester's Wit,
I judg'd the Truth he had not hit;
And could not choose but smile to think
What they could do for Meat and Drink,
Who o'er so many Desarts ran,
With Brats and Wives in *Caravan*;
Unless perchance they'd got the Trick.
To eat no more than Porker sick;
Or could with well contented Maws,
Quarter like [u] Bears upon their Paws.
Thinking his Reasons to confute,
I gravely thus commenc'd Dispute,
And urg'd that tho' a *Chinese* Host,
Might penetrate this *Indian* Coast;
Yet this was certainly most true,
They never cou'd the Isles subdue;
For knowing not to steer a Boat,
They could not on the Ocean float,
Or plant their Sunburnt Colonies,

---

[r] *Pizarro* was the Person that conquer'd *Peru*; a Man of a most bloody Disposition, base, treacherous, covetous, and revengeful.

[s] *Spanish* Shoar.

[t] There is a very bad Custom in some Colledges, of giving the Students *A Groat ad purgandus Rhenes*, which is usually employ'd to the use of the Donor.

[u] Bears are said to live by sucking of their *Paws*, according to the Notion of some Learned Authors.

In Regions parted by the Seas:
I thence inferr'd [v]*Phoenicians* old,
Discover'd first with Vessels bold
These Western Shoars, and planted here,
Returning once or twice a Year,
With *Naval Stoars* and Lasses kind,
To comfort those were left behind;
Till by the Winds and Tempest toar,
From their intended Golden Shoar;
They suffer'd Ship-wreck, or were drown'd,
And lost the World so newly found.
But after long and learn'd Contention,
We could not finish our dissention;
And when that both had talk'd their fill,
We had the self same Notion still.
Thus Parson grave well read and Sage,
Does in dispute with Priest engage;
The one protests they are not Wise,
Who judge by [w]Sense and trust their Eyes;
And vows he'd burn for it at Stake,
That Man may God his Maker make;
The other smiles at his Religion,
And vows he's but a learned Widgeon:
And when they have empty'd all their stoar
From Books and Fathers, are not more
Convinc'd or wiser than before.
  Scarce had we finish'd serious Story,
But I espy'd the Town before me,
And roaring Planters on the ground,
Drinking of Healths in Circle round:
Dismounting Steed with friendly Guide,
Our Horses to a Tree we ty'd,
And forwards pass'd amongst the Rout,

---

[v]The *Phoenicians* were the best and boldest Saylors of Antiquity, and indeed the only *Persons*, in former Ages, who durst venture themselves on the Main Sea.

[w]The *Priests* argue, That our Senses in the point of *Transubstantiation* ought not to be believed, for tho' the Consecrated Bread has all the accidents of Bread, yet they affirm, 'tis the Body of Christ, and not Bread but Flesh and Bones.

To chuse convenient *Quarters* out:
But being none were to be found,
We sat like others on the ground
Carousing Punch in open Air
Till Cryer did the Court declare;
The planting Rabble being met,
Their Drunken Worships likewise set:
Cryer proclaims that Noise shou'd cease,
And streight the Lawyers broke the Peace:
Wrangling for Plaintiff and Defendant,
I thought they ne'er would make an end on't:
With nonsense, stuff and false quotations,
With brazen Lyes and Allegations;
And in the splitting of the Cause,
They us'd such Motions with their Paws,
As shew'd their Zeal was strongly bent,
In Blows to end the Argument.
A reverend Judge, who to the shame
Of all the Bench, cou'd write his [(x)]Name;
At Petty-fogger took offence,
And wonder'd at his Impudence.
My Neighbour *Dash* with scorn replies,
And in the Face of Justice flies:
The Bench in fury streight divide,
And Scribbles take, or Judges side;
The Jury, Lawyers, and their Clyents,
Contending, fight like earth-born Gyants:
But Sheriff wily lay perdue,
Hoping Indictments wou'd ensue,
And when——
A Hat or Wig fell in the way,
He seiz'd them for the *Queen* as stray:
The Court adjourn'd in usual manner,
In Battle Blood, and fractious Clamour:
I thought it proper to provide,
A Lodging for myself and Guide,
So to our Inn we march'd away,
Which at a little distance lay;

[(x)]In the County-Court of *Maryland*, very few of the Justices of the *Peace* can write or read.

Where all things were in such Confusion,
I thought the World at its conclusion:
A Herd of Planters on the ground,
O'er-whelm'd with Punch, dead drunk we found:
Others were fighting and contending,
Some burnt their Cloaths to save the mending.
A few whose Heads by frequent use,
Could better bare the potent Juice,
Gravely debated State Affairs.
Whilst I most nimbly trip'd up Stairs;
Leaving my Friend discoursing oddly,
And mixing things Prophane and Godly:
Just then beginning to be Drunk,
As from the Company I slunk,
To every Room and Nook I crept,
In hopes I might have somewhere slept;
But all the bedding was possest
By one or other drunken Guest:
But after looking long about,
I found an antient Corn-loft out,
Glad that I might in quiet sleep,
And there my bones unfractur'd keep.
I lay'd me down secure from Fray,
And soundly snoar'd till break of Day;
When waking fresh I sat upright,
And found my Shoes were vanish'd quite,
Hat, Wig, and Stockings, all were fled
From this extended *Indian* Bed:
Vext at the Loss of Goods and Chattel,
I swore I'd give the Rascal battel,
Who had abus'd me in this sort,
And Merchant Stranger made his Sport.
I furiously descended Ladder;
No Hare in *March* was ever madder:
In vain I search'd for my Apparel,
And did with Oast and Servants Quarrel;
For one whose Mind did much aspire
To [y]Mischief, threw them in the Fire;

[y]"Tis the Custom of the Planters, to throw their own, or any other Persons Hat, Wig, Shooes, or Stockings in the Fire.

Equipt with neither Hat nor Shooe,
I did my coming hither rue,
And doubtful thought what I should do:
Then looking round, I saw my Friend
Lie naked on a Tables end;
A Sight so dismal to behold,
One wou'd have judg'd him dead and cold;
When wringing of his bloody Nose,
By fighting got we may suppose;
I found him not so fast asleep,
Might give his Friends a cause to weep:
Rise [z] *Oronooko*, rise, said I,
And from this *Hell* and *Bedlam* fly.
My Guide starts up, and in amaze,
With blood-shot Eyes did round him gaze;
At length with many a sigh and groan,
He went in search of aged Rhoan;
But Rhoan, tho' seldom us'd to faulter,
Had fairly this time slipt his Halter;
And not content all Night to stay
Ty'd up from Fodder, ran away:
After my Guide to ketch him ran,
And so I lost both Horse and Man;
Which Disappointment, tho' so great,
Did only Mirth and Jests create:
Till one more Civil than the rest,
In Conversation for the best,
Observing that for want of Rhoan,
I should be left to walk alone;
Most readily did me intreat,
To take a Bottle at his Seat;
A Favour at that time so great,
I blest my kind propitious Fate;
And finding soon a fresh supply,
Of Cloaths from Stoar-house kept hard by,
I mounted streight on such a Steed,
Did rather curb, than whipping need;
And straining at the usual rate,

[z]Planters are usually call'd by the Name of Oronooko, from their Planting Oronooko-Tobacco.

With spur of Punch which lay in Pate,
E'er long we lighted at the Gate:
Where in an antient *Cedar* House,
Dwelt my new Friend, a [a]Cokerouse;
Whose Fabrick, tho' 'twas built of Wood,
Had many Springs and Winters stood;
When sturdy Oaks, and lofty Pines
Were level'd with [b]Musmelion Vines,
And Plants eradicated were,
By Hurricanes into the air;
There with good Punch and apple Juice,
We spent our Hours without abuse:
Till Midnight in her sable Vest,
Persuaded Gods and Men to rest;
And with a pleasing kind surprize,
Indulg'd soft Slumbers to my Eyes.
Fierce [c]*Æthon* courser of the Sun,
Had half his Race exactly run;
And breath'd on me a fiery Ray,
Darting hot Beams the following Day,
When snug in Blanket white I lay:
But Heat and [d]*Chinces* rais'd the Sinner,
Most opportunely to his Dinner;
Wild Fowl and Fish delicious Meats,
As good as *Neptune*'s Doxy eats,
Began our Hospitable Treat;
Fat Venson follow'd in the Rear,
And Turkies [e]wild Luxurious Chear:
But what the Feast did most commend,
Was hearty welcom from my Friend.
Thus having made a noble Feast,
And eat as well as pamper'd Priest,
Madera strong in flowing Bowls,
Fill'd with extream, delight our Souls;
Till wearied with a purple Flood,

[a]Cockerouse, is a Man of Quality.
[b]Musmilleon Vines are what we call Muskmilleon Plants.
[c]Æthon is one of the Poetical Horses of the Sun.
[d]Chinces are a sort of Vermin like our Bugs in England.
[e]Wild Turkies are very good Meat, and prodigiously large in Maryland.

Of generous Wine (the Giant's blood,
As Poets feign) away I made,
For some refreshing verdant Shade;
Where musing on my Rambles strange,
And Fortune which so oft did change;
In midst of various Contemplations
Of Fancies odd, and Meditations,
I slumber'd long——
Till hazy Night with noxious Dews,
Did Sleep's unwholsom Fetters lose:
With Vapours chil'd, and misty air,
To fire-side I did repair:
Near which a jolly Female Crew,
Were deep engag'd at *Lanctre-Looe*,
In Nightrails white, with dirty Mein,
Such Sights are scarce in *England* seen:
I thought them first some Witches bent,
On Black Designs in dire Convent.
Till one who with affected air,
Had nicely learn'd to Curse and Swear:
Cry'd Dealing's lost is but a Flam,
And vow'd by G—d she'd keep her *Pam*.
When dealing through the board had run,
They ask'd me kindly to make one;
Not staying often to be bid,
I sat me down as others did:
We scarce had play'd a Round about,
But that these *Indians* Froes fell out.
D—m you, says one, tho' now so brave,
I knew you late a Four-Years Slave;
What if for Planters Wife you go,
Nature design'd you for the Hoe.
Rot you replies the other streight,
The Captain kiss'd you for his Freight;
And if the Truth was known aright,
And how you walk'd the Streets by night,
You'd blush (if one cou'd blush) for shame,
Who from *Bridewell* or *Newgate* came.
From Words they fairly fell to Blows,
And being loath to interpose,

Or meddle in the Wars of Punk,
Away to Bed in hast I slunk.
Waking next day, with aking Head,
And Thirst, that made me quit my Bed;
I rigg'd myself, and soon got up,
To cool my Liver with a Cup
Of [f] *Succahana* fresh and clear,
Not half so good as *English* Beer;
Which ready stood in Kitchin Pail,
And was in fact but *Adam's* Ale;
For Planters Cellars you must know,
Seldom with good *October* flow,
But Perry Quince and Apple Juice,
Spout from the Tap like any Sluce;
Untill the Cask's grown low and stale,
They're forc'd again to [g] Goad and Pail:
The soathing drought scarce down my Throat,
Enough to put a Ship a float,
With Cockerouse as I was sitting,
I felt a Feaver Intermitting;
A fiery Pulse beat in my Veins,
From Cold I felt resembling Pains:
This cursed seasoning I remember,
Lasted from *March* to cold *December*;
Nor would it then its *Quarters* shift,
Until by *Cardus* turn'd a drift,
And had my Doctress wanted skill,
Or Kitchin Physick at her will,
My Father's Son had lost his Lands,
And never seen the *Goodwin-Sands*:
But thanks to Fortune and a Nurse
Whose Care depended on my Purse,
I saw myself in good Condition,
Without the help of a Physitian:
At length the shivering ill relieved,
Which long my Head and Heart had grieved;
I then began to think with Care,

[f] Succahana is Water.
[g] A *Goad* grows upon an *Indian* Vine, resembling a Bottle, when ripe it is hollow; this the Planters make use of to drink water out of.

How I might sell my *British* Ware,
That with my Freight I might comply,
Did on my Charter party lie:
To this intent, with Guide before,
I tript it to the Eastern Shoar;
While riding near a Sandy Bay,
I met a *Quaker, Yea* and *Nay*,
A Pious Conscientious Rogue,
As e'er woar Bonnet or a Brogue,
Who neither Swore nor kept his Word,
But cheated in the Fear of God;
And when his Debts he would not pay,
By Light within he ran away.
With this sly Zealot soon I struck
A Bargain for my *English* Truck,
Agreeing for ten thousand weight,
Of *Sot-weed* good and fit for freight,
Broad *Oronooko* bright and sound,
The growth and product of his ground;
In Cask that should contain compleat,
Five hundred of Tobacco neat.
The Contract thus betwixt us made,
Not well acquainted with the Trade,
My Goods I trusted to the Cheat,
Whose crop was then aboard the Fleet;
And going to receive my own,
I found the Bird was newly flown:
Cursing this execrable Slave,
This damn'd pretended Godly Knave;
On due Revenge and Justice bent,
I instantly to Counsel went,
Unto an ambodexter [h]*Quack*,
Who learnedly had got the knack
Of giving Glisters, making Pills,
Of filling Bonds, and forging Wills;
And with a stock of Impudence,
Supply'd his want of Wit and Sense;
With Looks demure, amazing People,

[h]This Fellow was an Apothecary, and turn'd an Attorney at Law.

No wiser than a Daw in Steeple;
My Anger flushing in my Face,
I stated the preceeding Case:
And of my Money was so lavish,
That he'd have poyson'd half the Parish,
And hang'd his Father on a Tree,
For such another tempting Fee,
Smiling, said he, the Cause is clear,
I'll manage him you need not fear;
The Case is judg'd, good Sir, but look
In *Galen*, No—in my Lord *Cook*,
I vow to God I was mistook:
I'll take out a Provincial Writ,
And Trounce him for his Knavish Wit;
Upon my Life we'll win the Cause,
With all the ease I cure the [i]*Yaws*:
Resolv'd to plague the holy Brother,
I set one Rogue to catch another;
To try the Cause then fully bent,
Up to [j]*Annapolis* I went,
A City Situate on a Plain,
Where scarce a House will keep out Rain;
The Buildings fram'd with Cyprus rare,
Resembles much our *Southwark* Fair:
But Stranger here will scarcely meet
With Market-place, Exchange, or Street;
And if the Truth I may report,
'Tis not so large as *Tottenham Court*.
St. *Mary's* once was in repute,
Now here the Judges try the Suit,
And Lawyers twice a Year dispute.
As oft the Bench most gravely meet,
Some to get Drunk, and some to eat
A swinging share of Country Treat.
But as for Justice right or wrong,
Not one amongst the numerous throng,
Knows what they mean, or has the Heart,
To give his Verdict on a Stranger's part:

[i]The *Yaws* is the *Pox*.
[j]The chief of Mary-land containing about twenty four Houses.

Now Court being call'd by beat of Drum,
The Judges left their Punch and Rum,
When Pettifogger Doctor draws,
His Paper forth, and opens Cause:
And least I shou'd the better get,
Brib'd *Quack* supprest his Knavish Wit.
So Maid upon the downy Field,
Pretends a Force, and Fights to yield:
The Byast Court without delay,
Adjudg'd my Debt in Country Pay;
In [k]Pipe staves, Corn, or Flesh of Boar,
Rare Cargo for the *English* Shoar:
Raging with Grief, full speed I ran,
To joyn the Fleet at [l]*Kicketan*;
Embarqu'd and waiting for a Wind,
I left this dreadful Curse behind.

    May Canniballs transported o'er the Sea
Prey on these Slaves, as they have done on me;
May never Merchant's, trading Sails explore
This Cruel, this Inhospitable Shoar;
But left abandon'd by the World to starve,
May they sustain the Fate they well deserve:
May they turn Savage, or as *Indians* Wild,
From Trade, Converse, and Happiness exil'd;
Recreant to Heaven, may they adore the Sun,
And into Pagan Superstitions run
For Vengence ripe——
May Wrath Divine then lay those Regions wast
Where no Man's [m]Faithful, nor a Woman Chast.

[k]There is a Law in this Country, the Plantiff may pay his Debt in Country pay, which consists in the produce of his Plantation.

[l]The homeward bound Fleet meets here.

[m]The Author does not intend by this, any of the *English* Gentlemen resident there.

LEWIS MORRIS II

(1671–1746)

The Mock Monarchy;
or, the Kingdom of Apes

In pious princes golden Days,
When men attempted honest ways
To gain a Reputation
Then publick Spirrit was itself,
Then men lov'd honnour more then pelf,
And Strove to raise the Nation.
They shunn'd the means of being great,
By vile meandring tricks of State,
Nor cringing for a feather.
The merchant lost his native Shore,
And went new regions to explore,
Exposed to winds and weather
Not lent his money votes to buy,
Or basely purchase Slavery,
For some two groats per cent.
The country Squire did then disdain
To bribe, or flatter, to obtain,
A Seat in Parliament.
The priests did then employ his tongue
To teach the Ignorant and young,
How to avoid perdition.
Would not foment intestine Jarrs
Or strive to cause destructive warrs
By his divine commission.
The Judges who disposed the laws,
Did Judge according to the cause
Before them in debate.
Not bend their genius to Support
A darling faction, or a court,
For reasons called of State.
Critticks may ask, and I cant tell
When 'twas those pious times befell,

Or that they ever were.
Whether the tale be true, or no;
If tis not, Sure it Should be so;
And that is pretty fair.
Be that as twill, Some happy Son
Of fortune, by design led on,
Or chanse, no matter which
Discover'd here a fertile Soile
In which whoever would but moile
Was certain to be rich.
No canting priest had here a place
Without a prigg, God gave his grase,
And health without Physician.
They had no lawers here to prate
And well they could preserve the State,
Without a Politician.
A paradise on earth twas called
For which divines, had often mauld
Without Success their brains,
To find the certain garden Spot,
That was our Grand sires happy lot,
But laught at for their paines
For they most certainly are right,
Who follow mother Natures light,
Which in each breast burnes clear.
They Safely Shun the Jugling feates
Of all the three Successful cheates
And danger need not fear,
And if to poets fertile brains,
We do not owe Elizian plaines
The case will then be cleare
That where we follow natures track
And have not Lawers priest or Quack
That paradise is there.
No sooner did the news get o'er
Of this vast, rich, prolifick Shore
Then numbers undertake,
At once to leave their native land
And waft themselves until this Strand
A monarchy to make.

The Earlyest are the darkest times
Discoverd, but by Poets chimes
On which the Mob depended.
They introdused a set of thieves
That Stol'd the farmers Swine and beeves
As from the Gods descended
But we that live in gospel tide,
Have records now, a surer guide
Than their poetick strain.
Nor need we rack our brains to find
The origins of our mankind,
Since that is but to plain
(From Danes, from Hollander, and Swede,
From Wales and from the north of Tweed
Our first Supply's came o'er,
From Franse a band of refugees,
And from fair Ireland rapperees,
Came crowding to this Shore.
A mungrell brood of canting Saints,
That filled all Europe with complaints
Came here to fix their Stakes
And such another whyning gang,
That rather chose to move than hang,
Came from the land of cakes.
The Germans send a numerous train,
And Some from England cross the main,
Who were none of the best
From the low country came a crue
Whose parents were the Lord knows who
The Jayles Supplyed the rest.)
Thus having ransact nations Store,
Of Bankrupts, pedlers, thieves, & poor,
To Stock our new Plantation,
Reason Suggested use of Law,
To keep this motley crowd in aw
As needfull in that Station.
This to Effect, a Governour
Was vested with an ample pow'r
To punnish and reward.
Out of this mob was chose some few,

That something more than others knew,
To be his aid and guard;
To Set him right if he went wrong,
And help him with their heads and tongue,
In giving of advise.
They were Yclep'd the councill board:
Each man a leather apron Lord:
For there was not much choice.
The Chieftain, brought a patch work train
Of Such as ne'r return'd gain;
But made our Gentry here.
A Scribe, that flagellation had
On tother Side, when here was made
Our minister primier,
Such of a Lawers chamber Swept
Or for to clean his bootes were kept
On tother Side the lake
When here, were metamorphos'd Streight
Into great ministers of State—
And all great Lawers make
A tooth drawer, there not worth a groat
Who run on tick or Stole a coat
Proves here a learn'd Phisician.
A fellow there that Starv'd by Sale
Of Strong waters, or beer or ale,
Makes here a Politician.
Even trulls, who ranged about the town
And there, would for a groate lye down,
And that without formallity,
No sooner touch these happy Shores,
But all the tribe of bawds and whores,
Do here, set up for Quality.
The chieftain too himself, its said,
However great was much afraid,
Of Some ill natured Score;
Which he put off from day to day,
Having not wherewithall to pay,
As being speciall poor.
But, he no sooner reached this Coast,
Where being master of the roast,

Dreaming on mines of ore.
Like to a chess man he became
A creature of diffrent name,
From what he had before.
And got beyond his masters reach,
Here, none was bold enough to preach
Against what he desired.
His will, was to his Councill Law;
Who never did refuse a Yea
When ever he requir'd:
And whether it was right, or wrong,
They never durst to wagg a tongue,
Against what he demanded:
But, like Spaniells Showing tricks
As master bid would leap o'er Sticks
Just as he commanded.
The State being setled to his mind,
And magistrates of Every kind,
Made of that rabble rout;
He soon began to think, that he
Could not less than a monarch be:
To put that past all doubt;
He gave himself new airs of State,
And awkwardly did ape the Great:
Would be forsooth a King.
And tho' he durst not own the name,
His conduct did to all Proclaim,
He would Exceed the thing
He had a crue of Scoundrell Spies,
Voucht all he said, with oaths and lyes,
And Sowre him very great.
Whereas twas plain, on tother Side,
Had he not played at seek and hide,
A Jayle had been his fate.
The Councell too, that harmless board!
In Immitation of their Lord,
Would need be Peeres, they Say
In absense of the thing, would be
As foolish, and as proud as he,
None else so big as they.

Thus, things roll'd on for many Years
And none so great as mock myne heers
In this fine Government:
Till commons, to compleat the farse,
Resolv'd they would not hang an arse,
But ask a Parliament.
In dolefull manner they complain
Of being rode with too Streight reign
And therefor do request
That Since they paid the bill of fare
They might admitted be, to Share
The pleasure of the feast.
And hop'd his Highness would consent
That they might have a parliament
And tast of Libertie
And if they could but breath free air,
To which their fathers Strangers were,
None would more gratefull be.
The Royall bounty did bestow
A favour which they know not how
To use in decent sort.
In after times twas plainly shewn,
And very fully in our own,
They prov'd ungratefull for't.
And tho' they little had to loose
But Iseland hose, and wooden Shoes
Within their plase of birth,
Yet, have grown rich, learn to dispise
The donours of their liberties,
And none more proud on Earth,
Tis known, they here a freedom have,
Their own Plantations never gave,
To any Brittain yet:
Yet, whosoe'r observes must see,
How ill they use that liberty
And how the Donours treat.
                    —but to leave that.
The Joyfull tidings soon came o'er,
And flew about from door to door,
How happy we were grown:

If now we crouch't to Lords or King,
Or bow to any Such like thing,
The fault would be our own.
The rabble rout did then prepare
To choose the men, who were to share
The ruling of this land:
And he that could Subscribe his name,
Or Just Subscratch it, twas the Same,
Was Said for one to Stand.
But those who understood them best,
With one consent did all protest,
No learning Should have quarter;
For if a man could write or read,
They all were in a mighty dread,
He would destroy their Charter.
And time which all things brings to light
Did soon discover who was right.
So, not to minse the matter,
A cobler first Stood up for choice,
And soon obtain'd the publick voice,
Because he much could chatter,
Next came a black smith with a din,
Enough to get five hundred in,
And for his anvills sake
Which was not lighter much than he,
With one consent they all agree,
Him Senator to make.
A Jayle bird next, Submissly beggs
With fawning voice and cringing leggs,
That he for one might be,
The poor man's case was fully known;
And most there, feared twould be their own
So chose to set him free.
A miller, and a weaver, came;
They both were known to publick fame;
And they were both Elected.
A Lawyer next step'd forth; the fop,
Held in his hand, an Inkhorn top;
For which he was rejected.
A peddler and a Carpenter,

They all resolved to preferre;
And them they would not loose
A taylor, and a cooper, then
Advanc'd; & taken they were in Hen
With one Huzzaa they choose
Tis needless to recount them all
On whome the publick choice did fall
Since they were such like men:
And had they been to vote anew,
In spite of all the knowing few,
They'd chose the same agen
Now things were fixed in their geers,
A house of commons, & of peeres,
Together with a thing
Who, tho' he had much pow'r to use
Did very much that pow'r abuse
In aping of a King.
Such as they were, they being met,
And every thing in order Set,
The chieftain to them Sayes,
For want he hither did not come,
Having Enough of that at home:
Therefore without delayes,
He hop'd they would enough provide
For him, and all the rest beside,
To make up their Support.
And, if Laws for their Government
They wanted, he would give consent
In very decent Sort.
This done they all on business go
The upper house, & that below,
As they reciev'd in charge
Their great debates, of piggs and fowl
What bigness Stallions ought to Strou'l?
If hogs Should run at large?
Concerning foxes Slaying Pullen,
Which made the good wives very Sullen;
And cattle that were stray'd.
Such things, took up most of their time,
And tis not worth a verse, rhyme,

To tell what each man said.
But, all their grand disputes were trash,
To that grand one of giving Cash,
Betwixt them and the Peeres
And spite of all the caution us'd
The terms each offer'd and refused
They fell to't by the Eares,
The Peeres to alter did pretend;
The commons, would not let them mend;
And that was very hard.
The Peeres Said, letters patent gave
To both, the only right they have,
By which they were not barr'd;
But had a voice in making Law,
And ought to See there was no flaw;
Which they could not deny.
The commons Said, of cash their owne
That any but themselves dispone,
They saw no reason why
The Peeres, upon the other Side,
That all the cash was theirs, deny'd
They paid a part no doubt:
And, that to make, or change a bill,
They'd equal right; and therefore, will
Not pass this one without.
Thus they held on a doubtfull fight,
And both pretending to be right,
Neither would quit the field;
Till arguments on both Sides failing,
They those declin'd, and fell to railing,
To make each other yield.
The Peeres did to the commons Say,
They upstarts were of Yesterday,
A vile mechanick race,
Who did reply, they should not huff
Since both were form'd of forreign Stuff
And differ'd not an ace.
The chieftain, knew not what to do;
Allow'd, what each Said, to be true;
But that, help'd not the matter;

For unlesse, they both agree
To pass the bill, he could not See,
But he might drink fair water.
He did confesse, they both were erring;
And ne'r a barrell better herring:
But, Still the matter lay.
And untill all their quarrells cease,
And they resolve to make a peace,
He must be without pay.
He did incline the peeres to favour;
But still, knew something had some savour,
Whate'r they thought about it
So, did resolve, the pense to have,
And take it, in the way they gave,
Rather than be without it,
The peeres might clamour loud, and prate,
About prerogative, and State,
And consequences dread:
But he, was no such ninny Oaf,
As nott to know, that half a loaf,
Was better than no bread,
He therefore Sumon'd all the heeres
That made up his mock house of peeres
And by broad hints he gave,
They soon found out, unless they Start
And from their resolutions part,
He other peeres would have.
One frown, convinced them ten times more
Than all the arguments before,
By those of ablest Skill.
As thunder Struck, they paus'd a while,
And after, with a fawning Smile,
Resolv'd to pass the bill.
Applause, the chieftaines conduct gain'd,
The commons, what they wish'd, obtain'd:
And, at a publick feast,
Where all were merry, blyth, and gay,
The Peeres (as they deserv'd) that day,
Were made the common Jest.
But, one there was, Stood not in aw,

And who, with Scorne this pleasure Saw
That gave the Thane a wiper;
And Said; our master sure should know
The fountain whense this mirth did flow,
Because he pay'd the piper.
This Thane recall'd, another came
His conduct proved much the Same
As his we had before,
And few Succeeding ones we find
But what were verry like inclin'd
To those in days of Yore
The men were changed, not the thing.
Each one affected to be King,
And rather something more.
The commons, who, too plainly Saw,
They kep't both Thane and peeres in aw,
Resolved to pull down,
The present form of motly dy,
That by a true onocracy
Themselves might rule alone.
None could pretend to greater meed,
Nor none more likely to Succeed,
In what they went upon.
They therefore do resolve N C
All other formes rejected be
And that Set up, or none,
They knew, the Thanes would make a Puff
And very Surly Seem, and Gruff
But that was all grimace
And notwithstanding their rough brow
To humble them, they well knew how,
In proper time and place.
Of Peeres, they something were affraid;
Believ'd they mean't wat e'r they Said;
But still they knew the men,
Who allwaies fawn'd when they were chid
And having leap'd when they were bid,
Was Sure they'd do't agen
They knew, the cash was in their hand;
That money doth all things command;

And they resolv'd to use it
And, as they understood the lay,
Knew, if they offer'd ready pay,
The Thanes wou'd ne'r refuse it,
And tho' they were obliged to give,
To make the publick Servants live,
And Government Support.
Yet, they resolv'd to let them know
They would not any thing bestow,
Unless they'd Something for't.
They left no Stone unturn'd to gain,
The power of ruling from the Thane
Now this, now that, desir'd
And tho' the Thanes most Surely Knew,
That by indulging them they grew
And dayly more requr'd
Yet, knowing remedies from home,
Tho' often ask'd do never come,
Would rarely make a stand.
Deeming, two birds, when in a bush
Their utmost value not a rush,
Compar'd to one in hand.
Tis needless ever long to dwell
On what too many know so well,
Or say, who is to blame,
The commons do the pow'r possesse,
And allwaies aim'd at nothing lesse.
The chieftain has the name.
The bending Peeres do Still remain,
Do still, their leaping pow'r retain
And nothing more they crave
And tis but Just, that any man
Who won't take freedom when he can
Should still remain a Slave.

BENJAMIN COLMAN

(1673–1747)

A Quarrel with Fortune

So have I seen a little silly Fly
Upon a blazing Taper dart and die.
The foolish Insect ravish'd with so bright
And fair a Glory, would devour the Light.
At first he wheels about the threatning Fire,
With a Career as fleet as his Desire:
This Ceremony past, he joins the same
In Hopes to be transform'd himself to Flame.
The fiery, circumambient Sparkles glow,
And vainly warn him of his Overthrow,
But resolute he'll to Destruction go.

    So mean-born Mortals, such as I, aspire,
And injure with unhallowed Desire,
The Glory we ought only to admire.

    We little think of the intense fierce Flame,
That Gold alone is Proof against the same;
And that such Trash as we like drossy Lead,
Consume before it, and it strikes us dead.

A Poem, on Elijahs Translation

*Occasion'd by the Death of the Reverend
and Learned, Mr. Samuel Willard*

I Sing the MAN, by Heav'ns peculiar Grace,
The *Prince of Prophets*, of the *Chosen Race*,
Rais'd and Accomplist for *degenerate Times*,
To Stem the *Ebb* with Faith & Zeal Sublime;
T' assert forsaken *Truth*, to *Check* the Rage
Of rampant Vice, and cure a Wicked *Age*.
Such *Times* need such a *Prophet*, & in his Death
Is quencht the *Light of Israel*, and their *Breath*.

Plain was the *Saint*, his Soul by Grace *refin'd*,
His *Girdle* mean, but much adorn'd his *Mind*:
In Face, as well as Mind, above the Toyes
Of this vain World, and all its sensual Joyes;
Simple in *Diet*, negligent of *Dress*,
Hairy and rough his Robe,[a] meet to express
One *Mortify'd* to things of Time and Sense,
To Truth & things Divine a Love Intense.

Jealous for *Israel*,[b] & the LORD OF HOSTS,
Disdain'd to see HIM Rival'd by a *Post*,
Mourn'd his *forsaken Covenant*, & Worship lost.
Courageous, dar'd Alone to stand the Shock,
Of num'rous *Priests* of *Baal*,[c] & to deride their *Stock*.
Fac'd feirce Tyrannous *Powers*, told their Crimes,
And shames deserv'd, the Judgments of their Times.
His & Truths *Triumphs* Glorious: Strange to say!
A debaucht Nation *Convert* in a Day,[d]
And sham'd, enrag'd *Impostures* fled away!
A wondrous *Saint*; Inspir'd, Imploy'd & Led
But Heav'nly Love; by many *Wonders* fed.[e]
The *Care* of Heav'n, the *Darling* of his GOD,
Signally *Sav'd*, cheer'd by his *Staff* and *Rod*.
Voracious *Ravens* yield Him up their Prey:
Glad *Angels* to his Succour wing away:
And Heav'n, to show its Empire more, commands
Hopeless Relief from famishing *Widows* hands.
He Pray'd,[f] the *Sealed Heav'ns* witheld their *Rain*:
He Pray'd, the op'ned Clouds discharge again.
Provokt, *He* askt;[g] *strange* blazing show'rs of *Flame*
Stream down, and *Sodoms Day* renewed came.
He struck the *Floods*,[h] the refluent Waves divide,
His *Mantles* Breath drove back the flowing Tyde.

[a] 2 Kings i. 8   St. Mat. iii. 4
[b] 1 Kings xix. 10
[c] xviii. 22, 27
[d] v. 39, 40
[e] xvii. 6, 9, 16 xix. 5, 7
[f] St. James v. 17
[g] 2 Kings i. 10   St. Luk ix. 54
[h] 2 Kings ii. 8

What aild thee, O astonisht Sea, to fly?
Jordan! from *Joshua*'s dayes thy Banks not dry!
Yet Greater Wonders view: He spake, the *Dead*[i]
In *Sin*, or *Grave*, lift up their fallen Head:
Witness the happy *Mother*, fully won
To Heaven as she receiv'd her raised *Son*:
Blest Work of *Grace*! the Mercy of the *Mean*
Illustrious, as the Saving *Change*, is Seen.
  Not less Miraculous the *Prophets Fasts*,
Labours and *Travels*[k] gloriously Surpast:
His Strength and Application, as his Trust
Noble and vast, Angelick and August:
In publick Toils consum'd, of Life profuse,
Exhausted in retired holy Muse,
On the deep things of God, & *Mysteries* Abstruse.
  Such Labours *Bounteous Heav'n* is wont to Crown
With Heav'nly *Visions*, Light & Joyes unknown.
So Heav'nly Glories dazled *Moses* Eyes,[l]
And Lab'ring *Paul*[m] was caught to *Paradise*.
No less *Elijah* to his *Saviour* dear,
No less his Cares & Toils, his Pray'rs & Tears;
Nor less wou'd Heav'n his suff'ring Soul to cheer.

  The GOD of *Israel* past before the *Cave*[n]
In Majesty, as 'erst the *Law* he gave,
And frightned Nature seem'd to seek a Grave.
Tempests and *Flames*, & *Earthquakes* marcht before,
Speaking the Terrors of Almighty Pow'r;
These usher'd in the *small still Voice* of Grace;
His Soul grew Calm, Serene the troubled Place:
Husht as the Winds were all his boist'rous Fears,
The Humble *Saint*, call'd forth by God, appears;
With Mantel *wrapt* about his face he stood,
Afraid to *hear*, nor wisht to *see* his GOD.
  Yet lest the *Hero* as his GOD we show,

[i] 1 Kings xvii. 22, 24
[k] 1 Kings xix. 8
[l] Exod. xxxiv. 6
[m] 2 Cor. xii. 4.
[n] 1 Kings xix. 11, 12, 13   Exod. xx. 18, 19

Or He‖ Elate with Visions, vain shou'd grow,
At times his *Passions* did the *Man* betray,
That Saints have *Sin*, & Prophets are but *Clay*.
Too *Tim'rous* midst his Triumphs;º left to *fly*
A *Womans* Rage and Threats, and wish to *die*.
*Desponding*ᴾ moan'd Christ of his Church bereft,
And not a single Saint in *Israel* left.
All to hide Pride from Man, to show how *Vain*�q
We are at *Best*, and undue Tho'ts restrain.

    GOD is the *Light*,ʳ in whom's no *Shade at all*,
To *Him* in prostrate Adorations fall.
Created Brightness ever has its Blots,
And even *Persia's Idol* has its *Spots*.

    Yet Admiration, Reverence and Love
Are due to Saints on Earth, or those Above.
Sure the *curst Spirit* that hates is born of Hell,
Nor is less *Monster* then foul *Jezebel*:
She Murd'rous sought his Blood.ˢ *Ahab* his Name
(*Dearer* than Life) with sland'rous lies defames:ᵗ
And both invet'rate *Hate*, & deadly *War* proclaim.
Yet Spite of *Envy*, Spite of *Malice* curst,
VERTUE shall live: see *bloated Fiend*, & burst!
See the *fair Name* Immortal in my *Verse*!
See the *Strew'd Glories* on the *Hero's Herse*!
A *Name imbalm'd* shall be the *Just* Mans lot,
While Vicious *Teeth* shall *gnash*, & *Names* shall *rot*.

    Return, *my Muse*, and Sing his faithful Care,
And noblest *Trust*, in happyᵘ *Bethels Chair*.
Hail, Venerable Seat! from *Jacobs* dayesʷ
Sacred to *Israels* GOD, and to his Praise!
Blest evermore with Visions! the Resort

‖2 Cor. xii. 7
º1 Kings xix. 3, 9   St. James v. 17
ᴾv. 14, 18
qPsal. xxxix. 5
ʳ1 John i. 5
ˢ1 Kings xix. 2
ᵗxviii. 17
ᵘ2 Kings ii. 2, 3
ʷGen. xxviii. 12, 17, 19

Of Holy Angels! Heav'ns Inferior Court!
Hail dreadful Place! th' *Eternals* blest Abode!
The Gate of Heav'n, and the House of GOD!
Blest place of Inspiration!—
   Here stood the Spacious *Colledge, Israels pride*:
And here th' Illustrious *Seer* did preside.
Stately the *Dome*, worthy the Beauteous *Train*,
Religion pure devoted to Maintain,
And to the Age to come the Laws Divine explain.
Richly *Endow'd* by every pious *Zeal*,
Studious of *Zions* Glory and her Weal:
Blest *Tribute*! dear to Heav'n: A pious *Aid*
Given to *Christ*, and liberally repaid
In richer Blessings to the *Church* and *State*;
So *He* returns us what we *Consecrate*.

   Hence *Israels Chiefs*, & hence her *Teachers* came;
Hence *Truth* & *Grace*, hence issu'd *Light* & *Flame*;
Hence Men Renown'd, & of Celebrious Fame.
Micaiah one: from foul *Illusion* free,
Faithful to God, and *Ahab* true to thee![x]
Kings trembled as he Spake and Homage paid,
Of *Truth* and the *Superior Man* afraid.
Elisha too, to greater *Glories* born,
Was hence: and high exalted is his *Horn*!

   These *beauteous Sons* were the blest *Prophets* pride,
Under *his Wing* they *bloom'd*, & flourisht by his Side:
Paid him a Reverence profound and true,
To Heav'ns Election, *Israels* Suffrage due.
   Them, as by Office bound, He did Inspect,
Taught heav'nly Truth, and Errors did correct:
Cherisht the Good, & form'd their Manners well,
But searcht out Vice, th' Infection to expel.
Meek and Majestick; Affable and Grave,
Lowly & Good; and all that's Great and Brave.
He Overaw'd and Charm'd: Base hearts he won,
And perfected where Goodness was begun.
   To *them* His *Lectures* on the Holy Law,

[x]1 Kings xxii. 8, 19, 28

Sublime they were, new *Mysteries* they saw:
Like Him with Heav'nly Light & Joyes Inspir'd,
Their ravisht Minds the *Sacred Deeps* admir'd.
They saw the promised MESSIAH's *dayes*,[y]
And the Glad *Schools* resounded with his Praise.
They Sang the *Baptist*[z] in their *Prophets Spirit*,
And blest the *Saint Elect* that shou'd Inherit.
They Sang of the * *Transfigur'd Saviours Rayes*,
What *Fav'rite Saints*, from Heav'n it self, to gaze,
On *Glories* yet Unknown; and *Talk* of High
Mysterious Truths; into which Angels Pry,
And pass in Transports *Immortality*.
They Sang his *High Ascent*, & *Gifts*[†] Ineffable,
The *Cloven Tongues of Fire* on *Pentecost* that *fell*,
And what *Great Type* shou'd all these Wonders *Figure* & *Foretell*.

   Thus *taught*, they waited long the *Great Event*,
Foresaw the Day, Amaz'd at the Portent:
Stupendous *Grace* and *Power* they view'd, Ador'd
The Sov'rain GOD, and Pry'd into his *Word*.

   And now the *Saint* had his *Last Visit* made,
His Solemn *Charge*, and final *Blessing* said.
His Weeping *Sons* receiv'd his last *Adieu*,
With eager Eyes their *Breath* departing View,
And following far behind to Jordans[||] *Brink they drew.*
Each Emulous to *Succeed*, but well prepar'd
To welcome Him whom Heav'n had *Heir* declar'd.

   ELISHA He![a] The Wisdom of the choice
Applauded with United Hearts and Voice.
Un-envy'd in the *Schools*, had long out-shone
In Gifts Divine, and *Rival* there was none.
   Glorious the *Seers* Fidelity was here,
And Heav'ns Good Conduct Splendid did appear.

[y]St. John viii. 56
[z]Mal. iv. 5   Mat. xvii. 12, 13   Luke i. 17
*St. Mat. xvii. 2, 3   Luke ix. 31
[†]Psalm lxviii. 18   Act. ii. 3, 4   *Designed to resemble the* Ascent *meditated on, and to represent the Poverty of* Number *and* Rhime *to express the* Unspeakable Gifts.
[||]2 Kings ii. 7
[a]1 xix. 16, 19

Nor *Blood*, nor *Name*, his upright Zeal retard,
Gods *Choice* & *Will* he simply did regard;
Whom Heav'n accomplishes it will reward.

The happy *Youth* cleav'd to his *Fathers* feet,
Ministring[b] to Him with a *Duty* meet;
From his *Oraculous* Lips askt Counsel Sage,
And had the Pray'rs and Blessings of his *Age*.

Yet there remain'd the last and *dy'ng Bequest*,
And the Wise *Son* had ready his Request.
"*Say, now at Parting*,[c] *what I shall bequeath!*
Trembling He fell the *Prophets* feet beneath,
Grieved to part, afraid to speak his Tho't,
Conscious how vast the Blessing was he so't:
With Mouth in dust he said,—"May I inherit
A *double Portion* of thy Blessed *Spirit*!
O might my last and highest *Wish* have place,
An *Em'nent Measure* of thy *Gifts* and *Grace*!"
Divine *Ambition*! to be *Wise* and *Good*!
So he his *Fame* and Interest understood.
Modest his Wish, He only askt *a part*,
And Heav'n gave *all*,[d] even an *Equal Heart*:
Obvious the Truth, from *Sacred Record* known,
None came so near *Elijah* as his wondrous *Son*.

'Twas at *high Noon*, the Day serene and fair,
Mountains of Lum'nous Clouds roll'd in the Air,
When on a sudden, from the *radiant* Skies,
Superior Light *flasht* in *Elisha's* Eyes:
The Heav'ns were *cleft*, & from th' *Imperial Throne*
A *Stream* of Glory, *daz'ling Splendor*, Shone:
Beams of ten Thousand *Suns* Shot round about,
The Sun and every blazon'd Cloud went out:
Bright Hosts of *Angels* lin'd the Heav'nly Way,
To guard the *Saint* up to Eternal Day.
Then down the *Steep Descent*, a *Chariot* Bright,

[b] 2 Kings iii. 11, 12
[c] 2 Kings ii. 9
[d] 1 Kings iii. 5, 9, 10, 12

And *Steeds of Fire*, swift as the Beams of Light.
Wing'd Seraphs ready stood, *bow'd low* to greet
The *Fav'rite Saint*, and *hand* him to his *Seat*.
  Enthron'd he Sat, *Transform'd* with Joyes his *Mein*,
Calm his *gay Soul*, and like his Face *Serene*.
His Eye and burning Wishes *to his* GOD,
Forward he bow'd, and on the *Triumph* rode.
*"Saluted, as he past the Heav'nly Croud,
With Shouts of Joy, and *Hallelujahs* laud.
Ten thousand thousand *Angel Trumpets* Sound,
And the vast Realms of Heav'n all eccho'd round."
They Sang of *Greater Triumphs*[c] yet to come,
Their next Descent to wait the SAVIOUR Home:
And the *glad Errand*[f] of the *Final Day*,
The *raised Dust* of Saints to bring away
In equal *Triumph*, and in like *Array*.
  Thus midst Inspir'd, Sublime, Prophetick *Songs*,
(Sweet Melody) the *Vision* past along.
The *Prince of Air* Accurst fled swift the *Light*,
And heav'nly *Sounds*, more grating than the *Sight*;
Blaspheem'd, & rag'd & gnasht in furious Spite.

  Elisha saw:[g] "*My Father*, loud he cry'd,
My Father! Israels Safety! and her *Pride!*
More wer't Thou our *Defence* and *Glory* far,
Than all our *Chariots* & strong Troops of War.
Thy Pray'rs & Pow'r with God did more secure
Our Tott'ring *State*, and *naked Coasts* immure,
Than all our Arms.——"

  He said: Nor *more* cou'd see: *Immense* the space!
The *Flying Glory* now had gain'd the Place
Of *Light* ne'er to be seen by *Mortal Eye*:[h]
Nor longer[i] *gaz'd* he on the *closing Skie*.

*Mr. *Standen*
[c]Acts i. 9, 10
[f]St. Mat. xxiv. 31
[g]2 Kings ii. 12
[h]1 Tim. vi. 16
[i]Acts i. 11

With Anguish seiz'd[k] his goodly *Robes he rent*,
Himself, the Church, & Schools did sore lament.
The *Prophets Bliss* cou'd not his *Tears* restrain,
He wept their *Loss*, in His Eternal *Gain*.
   Nor yet in Useless tears staid he to vent
His mighty Griefs, on Greater things Intent:
The *Mantle faln*[l] with Joy surprising spy'd,
Laid the *dear Pledge* close to his panting Side;
Sov'rain Receipt! his fainting heart reviv'd.
   By it *Install'd* in the blest *Prophets* Place!
With it *receiv'd* his *Spirit* and his *Grace*!
The Sacred *Banner* flying in his Hand,
Display'd his Empire, on the distant *Strand*;
Nature Obsequious, to his dread Command.
Triumphant-wise, the pensive *Conqu'ror* stood,
The precious *Relick* wav'd, and smote the flood:
"*Where is the* LORD,[m] *Elijahs* GOD?" He cry'd.
Th' Obedient Waves again in haste divide.
He pass'd the ravisht *Prophets* saw; confest
The Miracle of Grace, and thankful blest
Th' *Eternal* SPIRIT, and his Glorious *Rest*.[n]

   O'rejoy'd they run the *Saint Elect* to meet,
And *bow*[n] beneath the bright *Successors* feet.
They breathe their Pray'rs & Blessings in his Arms,
Cheer his sad Soul, & their own Passions charm
Their Hearts within 'em *glow*[o], their *Graces* burn;
Each speak Mysterious *Oracles* in their turn:
Inspir'd their Mind, *Transform'd*[p] their very Mein,
In Both *Superior Grace* and *Beauty* seen.
In Holiness and Truth sweet their *Accord*,
And Faith their *Consolation* did afford,
Elijahs more Illustrious *Second*[q] *Coming* with his LORD.

[k]2 Kings ii. 12
[l]v. 13
[m]v. 14
[n]v. 15
[o]St. Luke xxiv. 32
[p]Exod. xxxiv. 30
[q]St. Mark ix. 4

TOM LAW

(fl. 1720s)

Lovewell's Fight

1.

Of worthy Captain LOVEWELL, I purpose now to sing,
How valiantly he served his country and his King;
He and his valiant soldiers, did range the woods full wide,
And hardships they endured to quell the Indian's pride.

2.

'Twas nigh unto Pigwacket, on the eighth day of May,
They spied a rebel Indian soon after break of day;
He on a bank was walking, upon a neck of land,
Which leads into a pond as we're made to understand.

3.

Our men resolv'd to have him, and travell'd two miles round,
Until they met the Indian, who boldly stood his ground;
Then speaks up Captain LOVEWELL, "take you good heed,"
    says he,
"This rogue is to decoy us, I very plainly see.

4.

The Indians lie in ambush, in some place nigh at hand,
In order to surround us upon this neck of land;
Therefore we'll march in order, and each man leave his pack,
That we may briskly fight them when they make their attack."

5.

They came unto this Indian, who did them thus defy,
As soon as they came nigh him, two guns he did let fly,

Which wounded Captain LOVEWELL, and likewise one man
    more,
But when this rogue was running, they laid him in his gore.

6.

Then having scalp'd the Indian, they went back to the spot,
Where they had laid their packs down, but there they found
    them not,
For the Indians having spy'd them, when they them down
    did lay,
Did seize them for their plunder, and carry them away.

7.

These rebels lay in ambush, this very place hard by,
So that an English soldier did one of them espy,
And cried out, "here's an Indian," with that they started out,
As fiercely as old lions, and hideously did shout.

8.

With that our valiant English, all gave a loud huzza,
To shew the rebel Indians they fear'd them not a straw:
So now the fight began, and as fiercely as could be,
The Indians ran up to them, but soon were forced to flee.

9.

Then spake up Captain LOVEWELL, when first the fight began
"Fight on my valiant heroes! you see they fall like rain."
For as we are inform'd, the Indians were so thick,
A man could scarcly fire a gun and not some of them hit.

10.

Then did the rebels try their best our soldiers to surround,
But they could not accomplish it, because there was a pond,
To which our men retreated and covered all the rear,
The rogues were forc'd to flee them, altho' they skulked for
    fear.

11.

Two logs there were behind them that close together lay,
Without being discovered, they could not get away;
Therefore our valiant English, they travell'd in a row,
And at a handsome distance as they were wont to go.

12.

'Twas ten o'clock in the morning, when first the fight begun,
And fiercely did continue until the setting sun;
Excepting that the Indians some hours before 'twas night,
Drew off into the bushes and ceas'd a while to fight,

13.

But soon again returned, in fierce and furious mood,
Shouting as in the morning, but yet not half so loud;
For as we are informed, so thick and fast they fell,
Scarce twenty of their number, at night did get home well.

14.

And that our valiant English, till midnight there did stay,
To see whether the rebels would have another fray;
But they no more returning, they made off towards their
        home,
And brought away their wounded as far as they could come.

15.

Of all our valiant English, there were but thirty-four,
And of the rebel Indians, there were about fourscore.
And sixteen of our English did safely home return,
The rest were kill'd and wounded, for which we all must
        mourn.

16

Our worthy Captain LOVEWELL among them there did die,
They killed Lieut. ROBBINS, and wounded good young FRYE,
Who was our English Chaplain; he many Indians slew,
And some of them he scalp'd when bullets round him flew.

17.

Young FULLAM too I'll mention, because he fought so well,
Endeavouring to save a man, a sacrifice he fell;
But yet our valiant Englishmen in fight were ne'er dismay'd.
But still they kept their motion, and WYMAN's Captain made,

18.

Who shot the old chief PAUGUS, which did the foe defeat,
Then set his men in order, and brought off the retreat;
And braving many dangers and hardships in the way,
They safe arriv'd at Dunstable, the thirteenth day of May.

CHRISTOPHER WITT

(1675–1765)

From the Hymn-Book of Johannes Kelpius

Of the Wilderness of the Secret, or Private Virgin-Cross-Love

FIRST PART

1.

A True Friend came to see Johann in his Recesses;
In quiet Solitude, in lonesom wildernesses;
    For He was deadly Sick, & lonesom Day by day;
    For joy to see his frind he fainted quite away.

2.

The frind embraced him, with trying to relieve him,
Tho 'twas a pretty while before John could perceive him,
    Johannes, says the frind, I know what troubles thee,
    What makes thee sick, 'tis Love, which now thou canst
        not see.

3.

And since thou canst not now, as formerly enjoy her,
So will thou now in Grief, & floods of Tears Dispaier:
    Thou thinkst the first Love last, & from the former path,
    And that the Lord doth now chastise thee in his wrath.

4.

I Love, replyed John, & can't therefrom defend me.
This Life-consuming-fire; yet strive, with Doubt to mend me:
    Since my unworthyness, & my unfaithful wise,
    The Mountain of my Sins still comes before my Eyes.

5.

And Oh! how can I be so bold this Grace to do me?
That I do Love deserve, or yet encline unto me
   The High & Holy Mind such Favours me to do;
   Poluted as I am, should yet be gracious too?

6.

I, who the first love have most shamfully forsaken,
And in the trying times, the Right way had Mistaken,
   The Best of all my Works, with self-love chiefly mixt
   My then despised foe, has therefore now me fixt.

7.

Now lye I here ensnar'd, & in my Grief entangled;
My Soul doth wish with Job's, to be but only strangled:
   I Sinned have, & what shall I do unto thee,
   Preserver of Mankind, is there no Rest for me?

8.

So if, Reply'd the frind, as I have said, thou lovest,
And since experience thou want'st, thou sadly rovest,
   Thou know'st the hand not which thee secretly protects,
   Thou know'st the Mother not, who thee in love corrects.

9.

Since privisy thou Lov'st, to privet Grief thou'rt Bidden,
Since thou see'st not the Sun, Thou from thy self art hidden.
   Yet in similitudes I'll Paint thy self to thee.
   That thy distressed Soul somewhat refresh'd may be.

SECOND PART

10.

This Secret Love is like to sharp-Sword-pointed weapons,
Which Inward every where does wound thee, as now
      happens:

But when out of thy self, thy Lover thou shall wound,
Then will thy Body be, with Soul & Spirit found.

11.

The secret Jesus love is like one deeply wounded,
Whose Inward Bleeding flux, deep in the Heart is founded:
   Nothing can ease this Pain, & nought can give it Rest,
   Till it's into the Heart of it's Beloved prest.

12.

Think, said he, on the Stream, which by its silent flowing,
And stillness of its Ebb, its Depth there by is showing:
   So can the Ground of Love at once not well be seen,
   Untill the Sun's bright beams just over it has been.

13.

Consider precious Gold, how deep it lies infused
I'th Bowels of the Earth, & shall it once be used:
   So must it through the fire its greatest heat be born,
   Then may it after be as Crown and Septer worn.

14.

How sweet-wine must ferment, thou may'st thy self be
    thinking,
Before the fæces can be to the bottom sinking:
   How long it lies, stopt up, before it springs i'th Glass;
   Before it Nectar like, the Heart & Mind rejoyce.

15.

Think upon thy own Heart, the fountain of thy being
Its Motion may be felt, but ne'er was knowne by seeing:
   So will the Love without, be secret and unknown;
   But in the inward part her sev'nfold fire is blown.

16.

Think on all kind of Roots, how in the Earth they flowrish,
And therein seek thier food, the Plant & Seed to nourish,

So covered groweth Love, as all her fruits do show,
And is not hindered by Heat, Winter, Frost or Snow.

17.

Consider the Sun-flower, in Dark & Cloudy weather,
How faithfully she turns her face to her dear Lover;
　　Untill she's Pregnant grown, & bears like him a Seed:
　　Then Rests she, & does bow in gratitude her head.

18.

See the Senceable Plant, how if it be but touched,
It straitway sheds its Seed, altho in Pods 'tis couched:
　　It will by Heavens Dew be touched quite alone,
　　And only lookt upon but by the shining Sun.

19.

Consider Virgin Love, how Chast & Clean it gloweth:
How strong, yet Secret still, so that person knoweth;
　　No, not her Dear himself: She blush's to bashful face,
　　And Speechless quite she is when He doth her embrace.

20.

How grieveth she her self, when she cannot espie him?
Her Soul is fill'd with WO, because she is not by him:
　　She Grieves, she Longs, she Hopes, she fears, she frights,
　　　　she faints,
　　And yet her Only Dear, Unknown, does cause these plaints.

21.

Unworthy thinks she her, to be by Him beloved,
Whom in Esteem she holds, the best that ever moved:
　　The more she Him regards, the less she thinks of Her;
　　And her own Vertues she does never think on more.

22.

Her Stature's her delight, Her Life is in his living,
Her Love into his Love she only will be giving:

When He lives not content, Her Life does want its breath,
Thinks she He loves her not, She grieves her self to Death.

23.

Her only thinking is how shee may pleas him better,
And what she sees, & hears, must as his Echo meet her:
   How joys & springs she then! But when she does behold,
   And see herself alone, she thinks her self Befoul'd.

24.

This grieves her heartily, that shee's become so foolish,
And that by means of Love; her Hopes will now grow
    coolish:
   She now grows deadly sick, nought helps or strengthens
       her
   But only her Dear Love, if she could see him near.

25.

Think on a Mothers state, in what a privet manner,
E'en to her self unknown, her fruit she feedeth in her:
   Her Chast Heart needs will hide, when she is pregnant
       grown,
   She will in secret be, with Mothers Care alone.

26.

And to the latest hour, before she is Deliver'd,
She gives her Courage lost, & from all Hope is sever'd:
   She thinketh on no joy, but Trouble, fear, and Pain,
   But Anguish, Grief, & Plaint, is ov'r, and ov'r again.

27.

Think on the Lord himself, the Author of thy being,
How He near thirty years did keep from Vulgar seeing:
   His Converse was with God, not minded by the jews;
   Nor is it yet well known how he his time did use.

28.

Think on his Agony, the Scriptures only names it,
And self Experience the best of all explains it:
     How in his greatest need his father him forsook,
     To cast him down to Hell he this occasion took.

29.

He bids thee follow him, but not to go before him,
Here, on the Cross; & There, on his Right hand adore him.
     Yet forceth he no man, each one may will or no:
     Therefore make now thy Choice, whilst thou art here
          below.

30.

Why now so full of thoughts, wilt thou yet make election?
Johann I tell thee free, make thereof no Reflection;
     Thou hangst now on the Cross! take care & come not
          down;
     Upon the Jewish call, be faithful, winn the Crown.

31.

Give up thy self to God! He yet will bind thee faster
Than he has ever done, Think not of thy Disaster,
     Thy Sins & follies past, since God has giv'n thee Rest,
     And thinks on them no more, but only for thy best.

32.

I yet have something more I would have said unto thee,
But self-love not being Dead, it may some dammage do thee:
     I'll spare it at this time; In what thou hast be true,
     So will be, when I come, Thy Soule and Body new.

THIRD PART

33.

Thereon the Frind did leave Johannes much relieved,
Yet in his very Soul most sadly he was grieved:
 His frinds haste he could not a long while well digest,
 His chief hope cut i'th' midst, & there by lost the best.

34.

Yet fast brake forth, & said, So be then Inward turned
O Sword! O Love! in me, untill this House is stormed:
 Till Thine may raised, be instead of this my Old,
 Till Deifi'd my soul may therein thee behold.

35.

Come wound me more & more, by thy loves sacred power,
That I may find its strength, & working every hour:
 For killing of my strength, till through the Red-Sea Shore,
 I press to thee, therefore come, wound me more & more

36.

Shine down upon my Stream, that it in quiet stillness,
May Run both In, & Out, out of thy Boundless fullness:
 That I may see in Me, Thee with a Radiant Beam,
 To Stand thou still O Sun, & shine upon my Stream.

37.

Make me as Living Gold, after thou hast me urged,
From Worldly Vanities, & through the Cross me purged:
 The Test is wanting still, which therefore make me Cold,
 To say, melt farther forth, make me as living Gold.

38.

Make me as the New Wine! from many noble Berries,
Of Lamb like Vertues! & by still fermenting sceries;
 Till all the fæcis fall, and I a Guest of thine,
 May in thy Kingdom sit, make me as the New Wine.

39.

Make a new Heart in me, & only in thee living!
In Sacred Unity, & allways in thee moving!
   And that it might exalt in Salem, only thee
   For ever, so O Lord make a new Heart in me.

40.

So, Cover thou the Root begotten from thy fountain,
And sink it deeper down, when thou salt see it mounting:
   That covered it may 'bide, & bring its rip'ned fruit.
   In Drouth, & Wetness too, So cover thou the Root.

41.

Me, only thy Sun flower, let after thee be turning;
And in the pensive Night, & Darkness for thee mourning:
   Until thy form in me, thy Christus hath full pow'r
   Then stand I still in thee, I, only thy Sun flow'r.

42.

Me, thy senceable Plant, let no falce Love betide me,
No, ev'n thy Angels not! but only Thine let guide me:
   That may be but Thine Eternally, this grant!
   So am I full of fruit, I, thy Senceable Plant.

43.

The pure Virgin-love be brightly in me burning,
That when quite stript of All, to thee I may be turning:
   With Blushing I may feel thy Spirits draught above,
   That unknown may remain the pure Virgin-love.

44.

My only Lover, Thee, I have for me selected!
Know'st thou it or not, how the Love has me affected?
   But what? I ask in vain, for nought I trouble me
   Since I dare not behold my only Lover thee.

45.

Unworthy am I quite, how can I thus deceive me?
And yet methinks thou must at last in love receive Me:
    O! fye! this Selfish love! fye, Proudest Hellish might;
    Therefore I say with Grief, Unworthy am I quite.

46.

How like I my own wise! how love I my own living!
How can I with self-love my self be thus deceiving!
    When I lives not content the love is cold as Ice,
    And yet I think I love! So love I my own Wise.

47.

How finely do I think! but after my own measure;
And what I see & hear must Echo to my Pleasure:
    How joyful Spring I then? But then again I shrink,
    See Me, in Me belov'd! So finly do I think.

48.

I shall be scorn'd by fools, through this my selfish loving!
However I will still in Faith & Hope be Moving:
    I will with David cry Sleepst thou O God of Souls!
    Save Me from Me, that I be not the scorn of fools.

49.

As mother doth her fruit, so do thou Secret feed me
With Manna, me unknown, upon my Pilgram's journey:
    Guide me as thee it pleas; hold me as thee it suit;
    Lead me still by the Hand as Mother doth her fruit.

50.

O Center of my faith! let me remain so hidden
As thou hast done before, untill thy Day is bidden
    At Midnight on to break! I'll hold, as Jacob saith*
    Till thou hast Blessed me, O Center of my faith!

*Gen: 38.86

51.

The fiery Agony pierce through, Calcine and scoure
My Reins, my Heart & Mind! & tho thou me in th'hour
   Of greatest need forsak'st, I may thee Glorifie;
  And thereby still think on thy fiery Agony.

52.

Let me but follow thee, not strive to go before thee;
Let me Here on the Cross, There, on thy Right adore thee:
   Through Death & Hellish fear, through Kedrons blackest
        Sea,
  Into thy Glory, so let me but follow thee.

CONCLUTION

53.

But Thou Divinest Love! who thy self hast begun it,
(This work of Love in us) so strengthen us to Run it:
  Perfect it quite! & let us plainly see this is

(In this way of the Cross) the Love its Wilderness.

The Paradox and Seldom Contentment of the God loving Soul

*In answer to a Letter which was full of
Love, Comfort and Humility*

FIRST PART

1.

In Jesus loving frind! What love does thou inherit!
How glows, & burns thy Heart in true drift of the Spirit!
  In truth a Seraphim has thus thy Soul inflamed,
  And has with his bright Glance, & Beams upon thee
     gleamed.

2.

Thy tongue does really drop with Honey, sweet affected
And ev'ry syllable is with a kiss directed:

And that beloved pair, & Eyes do run with Wine,
With which, they droping, wet, & Moisten ev'ry line.

3.

Thy Spirit deals not in sharp, witty words subborned,
Neither sitst thou at the foot stool of the Learned:
    Thy Heart's only in love with Christ his thorny Crown:
    The Soul sees Jesus on as frind* before the Throne.

4.

There seek'st thou Help, & Means, & strength for Souls
    distressed;
This the Art to steal the Father's heart, most blessed:
    That He would yet his Grace to a poor Sinner lend,
    And him the Holy Ghost for lasting comfort send.

5.

This is Right well belov'd, This, this does strik exactly,
The Bolts of Heaven Door open to thee directly;
    To receive Grace for Grace, for thee & also Me;
    Thanks be for such kind love, to Love eternally.

SECOND PART

6.

Well who her not forsakes, that Once has tast her favour,
That so he might at last in full possession have her:
    But who her once has tast'd thirsts for her evermore,
    And waiteth Day & Night contented at her Door.

7.

Content, but without Rest, Content, but full desire;
Content, but wishing still, & longing to be by her:
    Now hopest thou she will yet once more gracious be,
    Then strikes a Thunder-clap and sadly frightens thee.

*Mediatour.

8.

So very seldom have the loving ones contentment.
They cannot conquer quite Surprise, fear, & Resentment:
  Since Conquest maks them Weak, & strength does make
        them fear,
  The best which they esteem it Nothingness, most dear.

9.

This thier greatest strength, here Life its growth does borrow,
Their chief delight & joy grows from the inmost sorrow:
  Yet Trouble only grows when Love does love admire,
  He sees his nothingness, who most does love desire.

10.

When strengthened by Love, then Weakness seems the
        dearest,[a]
When seeming quite forsook, then are they Her the nearest:[b]
  When treated like a Dog, shall have a Child his store[c]
  When they are silent quite, their Saviour speaks the more.[d]

11.

Like as the love does grow, so grows thier Discontentment,
Her deepest Wound doth make ith' Heart the sweet'st
        resentment:
  And when the grief's so great that Soul & Body faints,
  Then sings She first Love's praise in spite of all her plaints.

12.

Love is as strong as Death! for as this Kills & try's it,
So killeth she the Soul before she Deifies it:
  Therefore He loveth most, who his own doth hate,
  And all what e'er he hath, for love to love translate.

[a] 2 Cor. 12. 9, 10.
[b] Matt. 17. 26.
[c] Matt. 15. 26.
[d] Luke 7. 47.

13.

But Who loves most sincere can hardly think he loveth,
But thinks in his best acts he still in crossways moveth:
   His Love is much too Cold; his longing quite too weak,
   To tedious & to slow his tears doth run down his Cheeks.

14.

His wishing for the Love he thinks but self-election,
His brightest Vertues dark, & only imperfection:
   His heart enforced Oh! he deems as Lunacy,
   His talking of the Love but meer hypocricy.

15.

His most delightful speech is of his Sins directly,
But since Humility is there by seen perfectly:
   He's silent, highly griev'd, & to himself a sore,
   Thus hates he his own works & doings evermore.

THIRD PART

16.

My frind, I write not this to cause thee any grieving,
Since thou has Cut thy self in this thy heat of loving:
   In that thou hast too low demean'd thy self, & now
   Me Father cal'st, & fearest not to call me *Thou!*

17.

What! is not then the Thou a name of God most Holy!
By whom exchange of Light & Darkness none is folly:
   Since He is good & Light, but I am bad & good,
   It changes yet in me the Spir't with flesh and Blood.

18.

Therefore I should be *You*, & nothing of *thou* savour,
But since thy heart in me the good will only favour,
   Therefore it calls me *Thou*, I wish't to be alone.
   Without duality, with Love one only *One*.

19.

And when shall I this *One* Behold & well perceive him!
When shall I quite in *Him* be lost & never leave him!
　　When falls my little Spark into his Light intire!
　　When will my Spir't with Him be one pure flaming fire!

20.

Hold inn thou strong Desire! Thou thus thy self discovers.
Wilt thou fall in the Pit, from which thou counsil'st others?
　　May not one hence conclud & truly thereby dite,
　　Thou wouldst be hereby seen by him to whome thou
　　　　write?

21.

What does not Wit conclude? Bad be to them that thinks it,
True Love no Evil thinks, whereto this truly links it.
　　I Write in Innocence, & for thy Soul intend
　　And it most earnestly to God his love commend.

Of the Power of the New Virgin-Body,
Wherein the Lord himself dwelleth and Revealeth his Mysteries:
How it is to be obtained.

Done in a Pensive longing, in Febr: 1699.

1.

Alas how blind must be to Temporal things the Eye
Which shall the Glory see of the light Eternity!
　　In truth, shall thy Desire in Heaven still remain,
　　So must thou all what is of Temporals refrain.

2.

How Dumb must be the Mouth from Earthly things [　　]
Shall God divide thy Tongue by's Sprits fiery power:
　　Shall thy Hearts fire but come with Heav'nly flame to
　　　　burn,
　　So must it wholly from all other business turn.

3.

How leer must be the Soul from Thinking & from Willings
If that the Glory of the Lord her shall be filling!
   And shall the Lord at last himself to her reveal,
   So must she not in Spirit with Timely troubles deal.

4.

She must in Spirit & Day of God be Recollected,
Like unto John & Paul, from sences quite distracted:
   Forgetting their own selves, & ne'er a word in place,
   Then Views the Lord himself in her with open face.

5.

O Holy Day of God! break on in us for ever!
Chace out the Darksom Night, with all its Lights of Errour,
   Hunt out all gloomy Clouds, Thou Pow'rful Shining Sun!
   Erect also in us, for Thee, O God thy Throne!

6.

Command the Soul her Sea, her Passions to relinquish!
And let her anctious fire in Light of love extinguish!
   Prepare the Temple too, the holy Virgin-life!
   Of Wisdoms beauty full, the Lamb his Bride & Wife.

7.

Let Her sink perfectly into his groundless Essence!
Into her Mother's House, where She may have by presence:
   So draw her forth from Place, from Sence & time that she
   In Time, & evermore, thy pleasant Consort be
               Amen.

HENRY BROOKE

(1678–1736)

The New Metamorphosis,
or Fable of the Bald Eagle

The Argument

Michy, the Hero of my Rhyme
Sent to the Golden World, to trade,
All spent and gone, Returns in time,
With a Bald Eagle, to his Dad.
The Neighbo'rs big wth expectation,
In shoals attend the Rareeshow.

All You of the West, No'th, Eastward, or South,
Who Gape, for a Ballad, at eye ear and mouth,
Open all, to a tale told a thousand times o'er,
But never adorn'd with gay Dogrel before.

In Southwark, renown'd for those eminent Schools
Of faith and good pay the Kingsbench and the Rules,
A darksome old Shed, now on crutches for Age
Held the reverend head of Peltander the Sage.
Long time this old Sire in the liberal Arts
Of scraping and saving exerted his parts
And each night in good straw, threw himself and his care
On the fleabitten breast of Membrana the Fair.
With tumbling together and heaven knows what,
A thing on two legs, call'd a Son, was begot.
So taper and small that some Authors protest
He wrigled his way from his Mother's right breast
But whether 'twas so, or the commoner way
Or, as one, from Ear, it beho'ves not to say
For us 'tis enough that the day he came out
He dress'd leather, told money, got drunk and what not
As indeed was it fit that one born to such feats
Shou'd ignobly be swath'd or lose time at the teats?
Besides it agrees not with what we're adoing

To suffer our Hero be too long agrowing.
This Worthy hight Michy, a name so compleat
So fit, so fullmouth'd, so Heroick, and great,
That Pyrgopolinices, Bombardomachides
Orgoglio Pantagruel Roland Alcides
With all the tall Huffers that ever were written
To Michy compared are but names for a kitten
I'm amaz'd the dull writers neglected so long
A Name so well turn'd for Heroical Song;
But blest be the Muses it so was forgot,
And blest o'er and o'er that it falls to my lot;
Inspired, I scarce bear its impetuous sway,
And a Writer so help'd, what cannot he say.
And oh! had You seen, at a pun or a jeer
How he darted his tongue with an amorous leer,
Stretch'd his cheeks to a Cubit, and twinkled his eyes,
With me, you'd pronounce him as lovely, as Wise.—

Now so it fell out, by I know not what shifts
That Mich' gave his Daddy such hopes of his gifts
That all the gay gold he cou'd e'er rap or rend
With Michy to Sea for a venture he'll send
And having himself, with nineteen of his kin
To raise twenty good pounds pawn'd all to the skin;
And, withal, taken up, at unspeakable charge,
A Hopsellers coat of a sadcolourd serge,
With a gay Calimanco, the best you may swear
That Norwich cou'd boast, for 'twas made by the Mayor,
For a holyday vest; a special gray felt,
And ratling new breeks of an old weathers pelt,
A groat for the fob, woolen hose, russet shoen.
And dropping some tears for his gold, or his Son:
Brave Michy's cal'd in, he appear's, is made fine,
Scrapes a leg, goes abo'rd, and away for the Line,—

He's gone; he's return'd (for his errand is not,
Or at least, the most part, any part of the Plot)
He's ashoar, nobly mounted on that very beast
He bought by the pound; a notable jeast!
They that ask, may be told it some leagues to the West.

He realy
bought a lean
jade at 6s 4d
and had a
very hard
bargain.—

But Michy draws near, and now 'ery Friend
May expect his approach at Southwark townsend:
The Streets are all lined with the Bands, as 'tis said,
Not those of the City, the Orange, or Red;
But those of the Rules, the Mint, the Kingsbench,
Kent-Street, Pickle-herring; the devil a Wench
That cry's my fresh Oysters, brooms, matches, or dill,
But see jolly Mich had a hearty good will.
Away then, in shoals—when lo! as they wish'd,
He enters in pomp, with a Bird on his fist.
Ah Sirs! if you're Wise, take example this day,
Fit out the Young Urchins, and pack 'em to Sea:
See there what comes on't. Why Michy! why Sirrah!
I knew You the dirtiest rogue in the Burrough;
Oh [   ] how his Voyage has [   ]
How the Young Knave is chang'd? why H'as got a clean shirt
My Watty for farthings must trudge with a link,
Had I sent him to Sea—I know what I think;
Here! Michy returns so rich and so fat,
'Tis like he's too proud to take notice of Wat.
Who'd ha' thought twenty shillings so much cou'd ha' done?
Had I known't, I shou'd e'en ha' kept mine for my Son.
But bles'd be the loins that so richly were stow'd,
And happy the tripe that once held the dear load!
With joy my heart swels (like the Mother's) to think,—
When the bags are turn'd up, how the money will chink.
Oh Lud! what a glittering heap We shall see!
Alass my dear Watty! is none of't for thee?
Then the Bird, ay the bird, what a stately choice thing!
To be sure tis for no less a man than the King.—
But thereby hangs a tale—for that bird is the glory,
The flow'r, and the cream, and the Gem of my story;
Not hatch'd from an Egg, but in fashion so strange
That not Ovid himself hath so wondrous a change.
Then, while the Young Knight's by the Rabble's adored,
Let's withdraw from his joy's, and inquire of the Bird.—

Now Mich was arrived at Antigua, Jamaica
Barbado's, Bermude, or the Lands of Tobaco,
And had frugaly laid his twenty good pounds

In the best Oroonoke on American grounds;
His market soon made, and about to turn home,
He wash'd down his cares in all-sovereign Rum.
Night came, and 'twas time to retire to his lodging,
When lo! as Young Michy was thitherward trudg'ing
A Minion of Venus presents in his way,
And Michy was frail, and consented to stray;
But time and the place and the sum were agreed,
And my Gallant had all his affections cou'd need;
But his Mistress (poor heart) for demanding her pay,
Was dismis'd, with a kick, and my Spark slunk away.—
Enraged with her wrongs, and dissolving in tears;
To Venus her Goddes, she offered these prayr's.—

Oh thou! that from Cyprian Idalium, or Paphos,
Art charm'd by our sorrows, and haste: thee to save us!
Oh thou! to whose great and mysterious Rites
We devote all our thoughts our days, and our nights,
Thou! from whom thy inspired learn that speech of the Eye
That appoints where and when, tho' the husband be by;
To talk love upon fingers, to tread without noise,
Bribe hinges and locks that they blab not our joys;
In vain do'st thou teach, in vain do we serve,
Thy bounties are scorn'd, and thy Preistesses starve.
Young Michy tho' wanton voluptuous and strong,—
—But what need of telling a Goddes my wrong?
Thou knows't all my griefs, oh some succour dispense!
And teach the bold Atheist to know his offence.—
So may thy realms flourish, new votaries rise,
And thy Altars stil glow with the last Sacrifice.—
She said, she was heard—and the Goddess exprest
In Oracular wise how she lik'd her request:
A fierce Bird of prey shall the preyer chastise.
But hast thou to his store, understand, and rejoyce.—

Away, as comanded, my Damsel do's speed,
And finds Michy at work on a hogshead of Weed,
When, behold! he turn'd pale, and the Nymph drawing near,
To inquire of the cause of so sudden a fear,
What he pack'd for Tobaco, oh wondrous to speak!

Was converted to talons, plumes, quills, and a beak;
The Leaves, flesh and entrails and feathers were grown,
The stems and the fibres, beak talon and bone;
These scattering parts reunite in one frame,
And what, now, was a weed, a Bald Eagle became:
The like wonder was wrought in the hogshead unseen,
Which sprung up in a Cloud and left nothing within.—

No sooner 'twas done, but the birds took their flight;
Save that one staid behind to give som'thing to write.
For this was the Bird that we left long before,
Perch'd, on Michy's right hand, at his Daddy's own door;
Where, we now shou'd go on to relate what was done,
But You'l guess how a Miser, receiv'd such a Son.
Besides, we've perform'd what we first did intend,
The tale of the Eagle; which now's at an end.
Other times we shall tread in our Knights other paces,
And sing how he won a fair Widows good graces:
But sure we deserve many thanks, the mean time,
Who've enrich'd a dull Story with delicate Rhyme.

To my Bottle-friends

The Wine and Company are good,
Another flask, another hour;
Such juyce is Wits peculiar food:
And Wit's a Sociable Pow'r.—

Who's stealing off?—oh! let him go,
He's young enough to trust the Fair.
But we, who Love's delusions know,
Shall find it better to be here.—

Kind Bachus aids each Manly bliss;
Good humo'r, mirth, the song, the dance;
But what hath Love, beyond a kiss,
What, but a dozeing, drunken Trance?

Fond' hasty spark, when passion palls,
And Chloes charmes have lost their flow'r,
Will, one day, be the first that calls
Another flask, another hour.—

Fill then, and, wisely scorn the Boy:
What hath that Chit to do with Men?
At least, this interval enjoy
Til Beauty makes us Fools agen.—

Modern Politeness

1726

Young Dapper once had some pretence
To Mother Wit, and Common Sense;
And had he but apply'd those Parts
To Sciences, or useful Arts,
Religion, Med'cine, Law or Trade,
Lord, what a Figure had he made!
But all his Stars contriv'd in Spite
That he should only be Polite.
Only Polite, Whats that you'l say?
Observe him, and he'l show the way.
A Modish Suit, with Sword on Thigh,
A Wigg, and how to comb and tye;
To drink, to drab, to toast the Fair,
A brisk decisive tone and Air,
Are the first Rudiments: and these
Dapper acquir'd with so much Ease
As rather Nature seem'd than Art,
So sudden he commenc'd a Smart.
What follows next? to dance and sing;
Is that so difficult a Thing?
Not so to Dappers application,
Who boasts in each so good a fashion,   Memphis and
That He, who (as Epigram makes known) Demophilus
So Daphne danc'd, and Niobe,   in the
                                          Anthologia

As that a Stock, and this a Stone
Hardly so lifeless seem'd as he;
Nor t'other celebrated Head
Who sing the Rival Screech Owl dead.
(Tho' Fame hath blabb'd their worth's so long)
Excell'd his manner, or his Song.
Must the Proficient read and write?
For reading, tis not so polite,
It spoils the Features; and beware,
A thog'tfull, or Scholastic' Air:
But easy writing, Or to write*   *see
What any may with Ease indite   Wycherly
A flow of words dispos'd for Sound,
And Periods Numerous and Round:
The Subject trifling News and Chat,
Good sense apart, no matter what,
A dash of [   ] here and There,
Have such a Charm for modish Ear
As merits Dappers strictest Care:
And he (as Envy must confess)
Hath master'd with great Success.
So—but what Topicks for Discourse?
Oh Heaven's, how plenteous is the Sourse!
'Tis to have al the names by Rote
Of Lords and Commoners of Note,
To tell long Stories, wrong or right,
Of Robert's twain, the Peer and Knight.
Of Swifts inimitable Fancies;
And how his Highness bow's and dances.
On Church and Parsons to declame,
And call em by a filthy Name.
Praise Toland; sneer at Orthodox,   Hen Brooke
Creeds, Bubbles Mysteries and the Pox,   Anna Regina
Laugh at the City's awkard Pride,
And without Ear or Art decide
Betwixt Faustina and Cuzzone,
What gaming Ladies pledge for money,

What reigning Toasts in Order tell,
Who buys a Post, a Vote who sell.
Talk of the Play, the Opera, Park,
And what diversions there when Dark?
All these, and Twenty thousand more
Made but a part of Dappers Store.
How but a Part! pray whats the whole
Mark for he's reaching at the Goal.
His grand Ambition was in short,
To view the worst side of a Court.
He comes, he see's, and nobly fir'd,
Snatches the Palm so long desir'd,
Mounts the Professor's Chair, and thence,
With a becoming Negligence;
From Vulgar prejudice set free,
Ring's o'er the Changes on these Three,
Detraction, Bawdy, Blasphemy.
Oh! inexhaustible supply
Of wit, oh Fountain never dry!
Oh matchless Dapper! rising Name,
Consign'd to everduring Fame!
How surely did thy Stars contrive!
Thou'rt the Politest Thing alive.   Henry
                                                       Bowman

*An unwilling Farewel to Poesy**

And must we part?
Ah Yes, Dear Poesy! Farewell;
At last, I can of freedome tell:
At last, am I releas'd from thy bewitching Spel.
For Bu's'nes, a more gainful Art,
Content with a more reasonable dole,
Asks but my head & hand—but Thou! My head & heart:
Thou my tho'ghts, my inmost Soul;
Thou my wishes wou'd'st controll,
My hopes, my aim's, my time, my Whole.

*In imitation of Cowley.

What wou'd'st Thou with my tho'ghts? Or what
  My inmost Souls intended Lot?
What object for my wishes; or what part
Is there for hopes with thee? Unprofitable Art!
What wou'd'st thou with my Aims? What wou'd'st thou with
    my Time
But lavish All away in unavailing Rhyme.

  Then thus, I put thee from my heart & head;
My Mornings early Theme, my Ev'nings late delights,
The leisure of my Days, the quiet of my Nights;
    And take another in thy stead:
  Bu's'nes, a fitter Part'ner of my Bed
  Bu's'nes, a diligent, & frugal Spouse;
      Not, like thee, divine fair;
    But plain as Sabine Virgins were;
    Like them, renown'd for homely care:
      And of the richer House.
    Bu's'nes, that brings a mighty dow'r
    Of potent Gold whose mighty pow'r
    So foil'd Acrisius wakeful Care;
  Stop'd Atalanta in her swift Ca'reer:
    And urg'd three Goddesses to War.
  For thee, the Lovers whine, the Poets write,
  For thee, the Lawyers brawl, the Soldiers fight,
  The Statesman spies Abuses, by thy light;
The Moralists to Works, to Faith the Ministers invite.
  Thou art the Lover's Arbo'rs, Mistress, passion,
  The Poets Hero, Patron, Inspiration,
The Lawyers Love of Right, the Soldiers Reputation,
    The Statesmans Zeal to save the Nation;
    The Moralists philanthropy:
The Ministers pretended Calls & real Deity.
    All these to wealthy Bu's'nes wisely bow.
    But what hast Thou, Vain Phantasm! To bestow?
      A Silent grove, a purling Stream,
      A Kiss surprised, a joyous Dream,
      A Lock, a Fan, a Knot, A Toy,
      A Smile, a Step, a Lip, or Eye,

A Tale of Lesbia kind or coy,
　　Or blubber'd if her Sparrow dye,
A Gnat, a Grashopper, a Butterfly;
Or Issa's lamentable Tragedy:
These are the generous Themes thy Songs employ.
Or, if th' enchanting juyce inflame thy Rage;
Then the plump Clusters of the lusty Vine,
Good father Bachus, & thy Sparkling Wine,
　　Its dye, its flavor, & its Age;
The dress, & odor's of th' officious Page;
The Gravings, or Relievo: on the bowl;
Then clean welorder'd Treat, the Careless Soul;
In frantick Hymns, thy Vocal pow'rs engage:
Til e'ry L[   ] is turn'd to rage,
　　Thy sons fight o'er the Thracian Wars;
　　Hurl'd bowls with meeting botles tilt,
The precious stream is underserv'dly spilt;
The chearful song is drown'd in wild Uproar:
And heaps of cutting Paines spread the Floor.
Or do'st Thou boast thy famed Dramatic Rules?
What are thy Tragic & thy comic Tools,
　　But Ancient Madmen, Modern Fools?
　　Or if thy daring Pineons stretch
Epic's lofty heights, & that Immortal Man
Who from the flames of Troy undaunted ran:
Behold him dwindled to a timerous Slave:
　　A Superstitious sniveling Wretch,
　　And any thing but—Brave.

　　These are all thy boasted Store:
　　Which speak thee most emphatically Poor.
　　　　Yet these adorn'd with sparkling Wit,
　　　　And these in dancing Numbers writ,
　　　　(Joyn'd to the Witchcraft of thy Voice,
　　Thy Morals, and thy Figures happy choice)
　　The Wisdome of past Times to Us convey
　　In such an amiable, & potent way;
The Art of living teach in such a wanton Dress,
　　　　As They intended nothing less;
　　Give such agreable, & wholesome Food,

So gratifie the Sence, yet make us Good:
That did not hard Necessity controll
   The free Election of my Soul;
   I cou'd reject with just disdain
   Bus'ness, and her tawdry Train;
And take thee to my Arms, Dear Poesy! Again.

ROGER WOLCOTT

(1679–1767)

FROM

*Meditations on Man's First and Fallen Estate, and
the Wonderful Love of God Exhibited in a Redeemer*

Proverbs XVIII. 14.
A Wounded Spirit who can bear?

Money answers every thing,
But a Guilty Conscience Sting,
Whose Immortal Torments are
Quite Insupportable to bear,
Nor the Silver of *Peru*,
Nor the Wealth the *East* do shew,
Nor the softest Bed of Down,
Nor the Jewels of a Crown,
Can give unto the Mind a Power,
To bear its Twinges half an Hour.
When GOD's Iron Justice once
Seiseth on the Conscience,
And in fearful ample wise
Lays before the Sinners Eyes,
His Lifes Horrible Transgressions,
In their dreadful Aggravations;
And then for his greater aw,
In most ample forms doth draw
All the Curses of his Law;
Then the Worm begins to gnaw,
And altho' it every hour
Doth the very Soul Devour,
Yet it nothing doth Suffice;
Oh! this Worm that never Dies.
Oh! the Multitude of thought
Into which the Sinner's brought;
Looking up he sees GOD's Power
Through his Angry Face doth Lour;

And hath for his ruin Join'd
Ten Thousand Chariots in the Wind:
All prepar'd to Glorify,
The Strong Arm of the most high.
By Inflicting Punishments
Equal to his Vengeance.
Looking Down he amply seeth
Hell rowling in her Flames beneath;
Enlarg'd to take his Soul into
Its deep Caverns full of Wo:
Now the Sinners Apprehension
Stretcheth Large as Hells Dimensions,
And doth Comprehensively
Fathom out Eternity.
The most extream and Vexing Sense
Seiseth on the Conscience.
Fill'd with deepest Agony,
He maketh this Soliloquy.
View those Torments most extream,
See this torrid Liquid Stream,
In the which my Soul must fry
Ever, and yet never Dy.
When a Thousand Years are gone,
There's ten Thousand coming on:
And when these are over worn,
There's a Million to be born,
Yet they are not Comprehended,
For they Never shall be Ended.

Now Despair by Representing,
Eternity fill'd with Tormenting,
By Anticipation brings
All Eternal Sufferings,
Every Moment up at once
Into actual Sufferance,
Thus those Pains that are to come,
Ten Thousand Ages further down;
Every Moment must be born
Whilest Eternity is worn
Every Moment that doth come,

Such Torments brings; as if the sum
Of all God's anger now were pressing,
For all in which I liv'd transgressing.
Yet the next succeeding Hour,
Holdeth forth his Equal power;
And succeeding with it brings,
Up the sum of Sufferings.
Yet they are not Comprehended,
For they never shall be Ended.

For GOD Himself He is but One,
Without least Variation:
Just what He was; is, is to come
Always entirely the same.
Possessing his Eternity
Without succession instantly,
With whom the like proportion bears,
One Day as doth a Thousand Years.
He makes the Prison and the Chain,
He is the Author of my pain.
'Twas unto Him I made Offence;
Tis He that takes Recompence.
'Tis His design my Misery
Himself alone shall Glorify;
Therefore must some proportion bear
With Him, whose Glory they declare.
And so they shall, being Day and Night,
Unchangeable and Infinite.

These very Meditations are,
Quite Insupportable to bear:
The fire within my Conscience,
Is Grown so fervent and intense,
I cannot long its force endure,
But rather shall my End procure.
Griesly Death's pale Image lies,
On my Ghastly piercing Eyes.
My hands made for my lifes defence,
Are ready to do violence
Unto my life: And send me hence,

Unto that awful residence.
There to be fill'd with that Despair,
Of which the Incipiations are,
A Wounded Spirit none *can bear.*

    But, Oh! My Soul, think once again,
That there is for this burning Pain,
One only Medicine Soveraign.
CHRIST's Blood will fetch out all this Fire
If that God's SPIRIT be the Applyer.
Oh! Then my Soul when Grief abounds,
Shroud thy self within these Wounds:
And that thou there may'st be Secure,
Be Purified as He is Pure.

    And, Oh! my GOD, let me behold thy SON,
Impurpled in his Crucifixion,
With such an *eye of Faith* that may from thence
Derive from Him a Gracious Influence,
To cure my Sin and Wounded Conscience.
There, there alone is Healing to be had:
Oh! Let me have that Balm of *Gilead.*

FROM

A Brief Account of the Agency of the Honourable John Winthrop, Esq; in the Court of King Charles the Second

Anno Dom. 1662.
When he Obtained for the Colony of
Connecticut His Majesty's Gracious Charter.

The *English* Settlements when thus begun,
Were blest and prospered in their carrying on.
Churches Embody, Heaven they address,
For Preservation in the Wilderness.

The *Heathen* they Invite unto the Lord,
And teach them the good Knowledge of his word.
Heav'n heard their *Pray'rs* & their labour Crown'd,
With *Health* & *Peace* with all their Nei'bors round.

    Thus all Succeeded well until the Sun,
Had near one time his Annual Circle run,
When Great *Sasacus* rose in Impious Arms,
And fill'd the Land with Mischiefs and Alarms.

    But since I've mention'd Great *Sasacus* Name,
That Day so much a Terrour where it came:
Let me in Prosecuting of my Story,
Say something of his Pride and Kingdoms Glory.
Of the brave *Pequot* Nation he was Head,
And with such Conduct had their Armies led,
That by the Power of his Martial Bands,
He had Subjected all the Neigbouring Lands.
Upon the Vanquish'd he would Exercise
The most Inhumane Acts of Cruelties.
By which, and by his often Victories,
He grew so dreadful to his Enemies
That weaponless they fell before his Feet,
For Pardon and Protection to Intreat.

    Great was his Glory, greater still his Pride,
Much by himself and others Magnify'd.

    He hears the *English* in the *Eastern* Parts,
Are of such Stoutness and Resolved Hearts,
That they will do no Homage to the Throne
Of any Sov'reign Prince, except their own.
This suiteth not with his Ambitious Breast,
He'll have their Homage too amongst the rest.
And Such of them as fall within his Power,
He like an Hungry Lion doth Devour.

    He *Norton*, *Stone*, and *Oldham*, doth Surprise,
Then Murthers them and all their Companies;
Seiseth their Goods, and them for Presents sends,
At once to Comfort and Confirm his Friends.

Their Death's the *Massachusetts* doth Resent,
And *Endicott* is with an Army sent;
Who tho' he Wisely did the War Pursue,
And did what a brave General could do:
Yet he return'd again without Success,
And *Pequots* kept Insulting Ne'rtheless.
So Great a Work, and Mighty was it found
To fix Your *English* on that distant Ground.

Mean while the *English* of that Colony,
On whose account I'm here in Agency,
Entred the River and Possess'd the same,
Paying no Defference to his dreadful Name.

This high affront the Tyrant deep Resents,
And Vows to Ruinate their Settlements.
His Priests, his Captains, and Great Men of War.
He calleth to Consult on this Affair,
Who being met, the Case to them Relates,
And thus the Wretch on us Recriminates.

My Noble Captains and Wise Counsellers,
You know how that of Old our Ancestors,
By their known Liberties and Ancient Laws,
Were well allow'd to Marry many Squaws.

Their way of Worship was to Dance and Sing,
By the Religious rules of *Powawing*,
Their Gods always accepted their address,
And Crown'd their Arms with Glorious Success.
Then was the *Pequot* name Greatly Renown'd,
And terrible to Neighbouring Nations round.
These Rules and their Estate so prosperous,
They handed down unblemished to us:
And we have been as prosperous in our days,
In following their long approved ways.

But there's of men a most Audacious Brood,
Lately come hither from beyond the flood,
Who teach us other Doctrines to believe,
Than ever our Fore-fathers did receive.
These tell the *Indians* they have got no Eyes,
But as for they themselves are very Wise.

They Preach there is no other God but One,
Him whom your Fathers Worshipt, he is none.
Their way of Worship was a Cursed way,
They Serv'd the Devil in their Antick Play.
'Tis very like they now are all in Hell,
Where they in Fire & Brimstone Roar & Yell.
And you for following the steps they tread,
Are like enough so to be Punished.
Unless for what is past you soon Repent,
And turn you from those ways to full Intent.
You must not have so many handsome Wives,
That don't consist with Mortifyed lives.
And we allow no such Pluralities,
Therefore forsake them, pity not their Cryes.
The Sabbath you must keep, yea Fast and Pray,
And watch your *Wicked* hearts both *Night* & *Day*.
And when all this is done you must complain,
All stands for nothing till you'r Born again.

Now shall we all at once be rul'd by them,
And so our Fathers and our Gods Contemn?
Shall we at once forsake our pleasant Wives,
That so we may live Mortified lives?
Shall we yield them the Empire we command,
And humbly wait upon them Cap in hand?
Or shan't we rather curb them now betimes,
And make them feel the folly of their crimes?

Speak freely. On the Honour of a Prince,
I'll hear as freely and without Offence.

Then an old *Panime* rose to ease his breast,
And thus his deep resentments he Exprest;
Such Horrid words such sayings Blasphemous,
Comes from no Tongue but the most Impious.
All Nations yet have ever Honoured,
The sacred Name and Mem'ry of the dead.
No men till these dare ever yet despise,
And trample on Immortal Deities.
No Strangers yet; Till conquest gave them cause,
Dare once Prescribe to *Native* Princes Laws.
Which shews their Blasphemy and Insolence,
Is Great and doth Surpass all Presidents.
Our Laws, our Empire, and Religion too,
Are safely, *Sir*, deposited with you.
And you have kept them safely hitherto,
As 'tis your duty and your praise to do.
Suffer them not to keep Insulting thus,
Nor put such Impositions upon us.
But arm your Warriours, Let us try the odds,
'Twixt them and us, 'twixt theirs and our Gods.
For much I fear Impending Vengeance,
Will ruin us unless we drive them hence.

This said, One of his Chiefest Warriours rose,
And thus his Mind did to his Prince disclose;
If they are so Audacious while a few,
When grown a Multitude what will they Do?

Therefore 'tis my advice to Arm and Try,
The Quarrel with them in their Infancy.
Sure now if ever we may well Succeed,
Whilst Warlike *Sasacus* doth us Lead:
Whose very Name and Martial Policy,
Has always Gain'd us half the Victory.

To what he said they all agreed as one:
Now is the Trumpet of Defiance blown
War with the *English* Nation is Proclaim'd,
(Their *Priests* their *Martial* men greatly Enflam'd)

A Bloody Host is sent to *Say-Brook* Fort,
To Plunder, Kill, and cut the *English* short.
Where they Arriv'd and Diverse Murthered,
Then round the *English* Fort Beleaguered.

Another Army Cross the Land is sent,
With Fire and Sword to kill the Innocent.
At *Wethersfield* they lay an Ambuscade,
And a sad Slaughter of the People made.
Others they took and them in Captive Led,
Unto their Forts there to be Tortured.

Thus from our Peace most suddenly we are
Wrapt up in the Calamities of War.
So have I sometimes in the Summer seen,
The Sun ascending and the Skie serene.
Nor Wind nor Cloud in all the Hemisphere,
All things in such a perfect Calmness were.
At length a little Cloud doth up arise,
To which the nitrous sulphiry Vapour flys.
Soon a dark mantle over Heaven spread,
With which the Lamp of day was darkened.
And now the Clouds in tempest loud contend,
And rain and dreadful Lightning downward send.
With which such loud and mighty *Thunders* broke
As made Earth tremble & the Mountains smoke,
And the Convulsive world seem drawing on,
Apace to her own Dissolution
The awfulness of which amazing Sight,
Greatly did Earths Inhabitants affright.
Ev'n so those Halcyon days that were with us,
Were soon turn'd into Times Tempestuous.
Mischief on Mischief every day succeeds,
And Every Mischief Greater Mischief breeds
The Numerous Nations all the Country ore,
Who had appeared Friendly heretofore,
Seeing the *Pequots* had, the War begun,
And well Succeeded in their carrying on.
Calling to mind their former Victories,
The *English* Men grew Abject in their Eyes.

Some at the first the *Pequot* Armies joyn'd
And all the rest but of a Wavering mind.
Waiting but for an opportunity,
To Murther us by Force or Treachery.
No Confidence in any we repose,
Our seeming Friends we find our real Foes.
Fears never to behold the morning Light,
Encumbered our Natural rest each night.
Nor had we place of Refuge to Repair,
Only to the Most High in Heaven by Prayer,
To whom was offered up the Sacrifice,
Of Broken Hearts and Penitential Cryes.

A Council met at *Hartford* who Conclude,
We must Subdue the Foe, or be Subdued,
And that the Gangreen still would further stray,
'Till the Infected Limb be cut away.
And thereupon they Ordered and Decreed,
To raise our utmost Forces with all Speed.
This Resolution publisht and declar'd,
Ninety brave Combatants in Arms appear'd.
This was the Sum of all our Infantry,
Yet scarce a Tithe unto the Enemy.
But what they wanted in their Multitude,
'Twas hop'd their Resolution would make Good.

These were the Men, this was the little Band,
That durst the force of the new World withstand.
These were the men that by their *Swords made way*,
For Peace and Safety in *America*.
And these are those whose *Names fame hath Enrol'd*,
Fairly in brightest Characters of Gold.

The Army now drawn up. To be their Head
Our Valiant *Mason* was Commissioned.
(Whose Name is never mentioned by me,
Without a special Note of Dignity.)

The Leader March't them to the River side,
There to Embark his Army on the side;

Where lay our little Fleet to Wait upon
Our Army for their Transportation
(Going on board Oraculous *Hooker* said,
Fear not the Foe, they shall become your Bread.)

'Twas here that *Uncass* did the Army Meet,
With many stout *Mohegans* at his Feet.
He to the General goes, and doth Declare,
He came for our Assistance in the War.

He was that *Saggamore* whom great *Sasacus's* rage
Had hitherto kept under Vassalage.
But weary of his great Severity.
He now Revolts, and to the *English* fly.
With Chearful Air our Captain him Embraces,
And him and his Chief Men with Titles Graces;
But over them Preserv'd a Jealous Eye,
Lest all this might be done in Treachery.

Then down the *River* with their *Fleet* they stood
But stranding often on the Flats and Mud.
Uncass Impatient of such long delays,
Stood forth and freely to the General says,
Suffer me and my Men to go on shore,
We are not us'd to Shipping, Sails and Oar.
I'l Range the Woods to find the Enemy,
Where they in their close Ambushments may lie.
And unto you at *Say-Brook* will repair
And so attend your further Orders there.

Consented to, they Land Immediately,
And Marching down soon met the Enemy:
And Showers of Arrows on them he bestows,
Swifter than ever flew from *Parthian* Bows.

At length the *Pequots* left the Field and Fled,
There Leaving many of their Fellows Dead.

The News of this our Forces greatly Chears,
And turn'd to Confidence our Jealous Fears.

Coming to *Say-Brook*, *Uncass* on them Waits,
Whose good Success our Men Congratulates.

Here Captain *Underhill* with our Army join'd
And being favoured with a Lucky Wind,
All hast on Board, and soon forsake the Shoar;
With the rough Winds, both Sails & Tackle roar.
Their *Oaken* Oars, they in the Ocean steep,
And Cuff the foaming Billows of the Deep.
Swiftly thro' Tides & threatning Waves they scud,
Plowing the pavement of the briny Flood:
So fetch't about a Compass on the Sea,
And Landed in the *Narraghansetts*-Bay
And marching thro' that Country soon they met,
The *Narraghansett* Prince, proud *Ninegrett*.

To whom the *English* says, We Lead these Bands,
Arm'd in this manner thus into your Lands,
Without design to do you Injury,
But only to Invade the Enemy,
You who to the Expence of so much blood,
Have long time born their evil Neighbourhood,
Will bid us welcom; and will well Excuse,
That we this way have took our Rendezvouze.

Quoth *Ninegrett*, Your War I well approve,
And so your March Souldiers I always Love:
But sure *Sasacus* is quite unknown to you,
Else had you never hoped with so few,
One of his smallest Captains to Suppress,
Much less to storm him in his Fortresses.
Never believe it: In these Castles are,
Brave Captains and Couragious men of War.
All men have found it so that yet have try'd.
To whom the *English* thus in short reply'd;
Their Strength & Courage doth not us affright,
'Tis with such men we use and chuse to Fight.
Our Army Marching unto *Nayantick* goes,
Lying just in our Progress towards the Foes.

The news of this our march Fame doth transport,
With speed to great *Miaantinomohs* Court.
Nor had that pensive King forgot the Losses,
He had sustain'd thro' *Sasacus*'s Forces.
Chear'd with the news, his Captains all as one,
In humble manner do address the Throne,
And press the King to give them his Commission
To join the *English* in this Expedition.
To their request the chearful King assents,
And now they fill and form their Regiments,
To War: a *Co-hort* which came marching down
To us who lay Encamp'd before the Town.

Their Chiefs go to our General, and declare
What's their Intention and whose men they are.
We come, say they, with heart and hand to join,
With English men upon this brave design;
For *Pequots* pride allows them no Content
Within the sphere of their own Government:
Without Essays to wrong their Brethren
And ravish Freedom from the Sons of men,
Which makes this work most needful to be done,
To stop their measureless Ambition.
But sure the War that you intend to make
And manage thus must come from your mistake.
Can these Un-arrowed White men, such a few,
So much as hope the *Pequots* to Subdue?
Yes hope you may while fatal Ignorance,
Keeps back the knowledge of their Puissance.
But if you come to be Engaged once,
You'l Learn more wit by sad Experience.
But happy you: who thus your selves Expose,
To be the Prey and Triumph of your Foes.
Thrice happy you to be preserved thus,
From your Destruction and such Deaths by us:
And since our Numbers and our Feathers show,
Us men, as well & better men than you,
We hope it will offend not you nor yours,
The chiefest Post of Honour should be ours.

Mason Harrangues them with high *Compliment*,
And to confirm them he to them Consents.
Hold on bold Men, says he as you've began:
I'm Free and Easie, you shall take the Van.

And in this order Marching on they went
Towards the Enemy till the day was Spent.
And now Bright *Phœbus* had his Chariot driven,
Down from the Lofty Battlements of Heaven,
And weary put his tired steeds to rest,
Chearing himself on blushing *Thetis* breast.
But lest the horrid Darkness of the Night,
Should quite Eclipse the Glory of his light:
Fair *Cynthia* towering up did well Embrace,
Her Brothers light into her Orbed face.

The *Indians* still kept up their boasted flame,
Till near the Enemies Fortresses they came.

But as we always by Experience find,
Frost bitten Leaves will not abide the wind.
Hang Trembling on the limbs a while they may,
But when once *Boreas* roars they fly away,
To hide themselves in the deep Vales below,
And to his force leave the exposed bough.

So these who had so often to their harms,
Felt the great power of *Sasacus*'s Arms,
And now again just to Endure the same,
The dreadful sound of great *Sasacus*'s Name,
Seem'd every Moment to attack their Ears
And fill'd them with such heart amazing fears,
That suddenly they run and seek to hide,
Swifter than Leaves in the Autumnal Tide.
The *Narrhagansetts* quite the Service Clear,
But the *Mohegan* followed in the Rear.

Our Men perceives the Allies all are gone,
And scarce a Pilot left to lead them on:
Caused an *Alta*, and then from the Rear,

Summons's such *Indians* as were there.
At last after long waiting for the same,
Up Trusty *Uncass* and Stout *Wequash* came,
Of whom the General in strict Terms demands,
Where stands the *Fort*, & how their *Judgment* stands,
About the Enter-prise? And what's the Cause,
They left their Post against all Martial Laws?

To which we had this Answer from a Prince,
The Enemies Fort stands on yond Eminence;
Whose steep Ascent is now before your Eyes:
And for my Judgment in the enterprize,
Fain would my willing Heart hope for Success,
Fain would my eager Tongue such hopes express.
But Knowledge of the Foe such hope deny's,
And Sinks my Heart in deep Despondencies.
You cannot know the Danger of your case,
Not having yet beheld a *Pequots* Face.
But sad Experience hath Instructed me,
How Dreadful and Invincible they be,
What mighty Battles often have they won,
And cut down Armies like the Grass that's Mown.
And my Heart rues this day because I fear,
Those Lions will your Lambs in pieces tear.
When once they are Engag'd, 'tis hard to get,
A Dispensation from them to Retreat.

Sir, Be Advis'd before it be too late,
Trust not too far your Evil-boding Fate,
Great pity tis to lose so brave an Host;
And more that such a General should be lost.
Then steer another course: thrust not your selves
To certain ruin on these dangerous shelves:

Here stop't, and on the English fix'd his Eye,
With care Expecting what they would reply.
Brave *Mason* who had in his breast Enshrin'd,
A Prudent and Invulnerable mind;
Weighing the case & ground whereon they stood,
The Enemy how hard to be subdu'd:

How if the Field should by the Foe be won,
The *English* Settlements might be Undone.
His little Army now was left alone,
And all the *Allies* Hopes and Hearts were gone.
These and all other things that might Disswade,
From an Engagement having fully weigh'd:
But looking on his Chearful Soldiery,
True Sons of *Mars*, bred up in *Brittanny*,
Each firmly bent to Glorify his Name
By Dying bravely in the Bed of Fame,
In his New Countrys Just Defence, or else
To Extirpate these Murtherous Infidels;
This rais'd his Tho'ts his Vital Spirits Clear'd,
So that no Enemy on Earth he Fear'd.
And now resolv'd the City to Invade;
He to the tho'tful Prince this Answer made;

You say, My Men han't yet a *Pequot* seen;
'Tis true, yet they e're now in Wars have been,
Where mighty Captains & brave Men have shed,
Their Blood, while roaring Canons Ecchoed,
Yet they Undaunted Resolute go on
Where *dying springs* make *Sanguine Rivers* run.
Out-braving Danger mount the highest Wall,
Yea Play with Death it self without appal;
Nor turn the Back till they have won the Day,
And from the mighty torn the Spoils away;
And do you think that any *Pequots* face
Shall daunt us much, or alter much the case?
The Valour of our Foes we always prize,
As that which most our Triumph Glorifies.
Their Strength & Courage but allurements are,
To make us more Ambitious of the War.
Then don't Despair, but turn you back again
Encourag'd, & Confirm your Heartless Men,
And hinder them in their Intended Flight;
Only to see how *English* Men will Fight,
And let your Eyes themselves be Judges then
'Twixt Us & *Pequots*, which are better Men.

Down bow'd the Prince, down bow'd this trembling
   'Squire;
Greatly the Gen'rals Courage they Admire.
Back to the Rear, with speedy hast they went,
And call the Captains of their Regiment;
To whom the Prince doth in *short terms declare*,
English or Pequots must go hunt white Deer.
No Counsel can the General's wrath asswage,
Nor calm the fury of his Martial rage.
His men are all resolved to go on,
Unto the *Pequots* Ruin, or their own:
Then we our selves will stand in sight and see
The last Conclusion of this Tragedie.
Mean while the General his Oration makes,
And with his Army thus Expostulates;

There's such a Crisis now in Providence,
As scarce has been since time did first Commence,
Fate has determin'd that this very Day,
Shall try the Title of *America*:
And that these hands of ours shall be the hands,
That shall subdue or forfeit all these Lands.
If this days work by us be once well done,
America is for the *English* won:
But if we faint and fail in this design,
The numerous Nations will as one combine
Their Countries Forces and with Violence
Destroy the *English* and their Settlements.

Here we are Strangers, and if we are beat,
We have no Place for Safety or Retreat.
Therefore our Hands must be Preservatives,
Of our Religion, Liberties and Lives.
I urge not this as Motives from Despair,
To which I know you utter Strangers are.
Only to shew what great Advantages,
Attends your Valour urging the Success.
Mov'd with Despair the coward Fights & Storms,
But your brave Minds have more Angelick forms
Your high born Souls in Brighter orbs do move

And take in fair Ideas from Above.
Minding the Laurels that the Victor wears,
And great Example of your Ancestors.
I know you can't their Mighty acts forget,
And yet how often did they them repeat?
What did that ever famous Black Prince do,
At first at *Cressey*, after at *Poictou*?
Bravely he led the *English* Squadrons on,
Bravely they Fought till they had took King *John*.
Bravely he did his Fathers Message bear,
To save his Life and Honour in the War.
For in that Fight he rais'd the *English* Fame,
Above the *Grecian* or the *Roman* Name.
And with what Force and Martial Puissance
Did great King *Henry* claim the Crown of *France*
He like a Gamester play'd his tennis Balls,
Like Bolts of Thunder over *Paris* Walls.
How Lion-like he led his *British* Bands,
Tho' few in number through the *Gallick* Lands
To *Agin-Court*, then Fac'd his mighty Foe,
And gave his Multitude the Overthrow;
Where e're his Generals came they did Advance
The *English* Ensigns on the Towers of *France*:
Until that Nation rendered up to him
Their Heiress and Imperial Diadem.
And when of late King *Philip* did Attempt,
Quite to Subvert the *British* Government;
And for that end sent out his mighty Fleet,
Whom *Howards*, *Seymore*, & bold *Drake* did meet,
And meeting took or sunk into the main
The *wealth*, the *hope*, the *power* & *pride* of *Spain*.
By such Exploits, the *English* Glory went
Throughout from *Britain* to the *Orient*:
And there too soon 'twas bounded by the Seas
And limited from the *Antipodies*.
Nought of their *worth* in the *new world* was told,
Nor more could be expressed in the Old.
Then Fame it self dull and inactive grew
For want of other Business to Pursue.
But Fate which long hath Destinated you,

To prove the Stories of *th' old World i'th' New*,
Shipt you on Board & with full gales hath sent
You forth from *Britain* to this Continent;
And by this Foe gives Opportunity
Here to evince the *English* Bravery.
And give the World Assurance that we be,
Sons of those mighty Men of *Britannie*.
'Tis true, our Enemies are hard to tame,
The more the Danger is the more's the Fame,
But they are Strong, Immur'd, a Multitude:
The more's the Honour when they are Subdu'd.
But they are Valiant, us'd to overthrow,
What Glory 'tis to Conquer such a Foe?
Their very Name hath made our Allies run,
Oh how will this adorn the Field when won!

Leave the Success to *Him* whose boundless *Powers*
Will doubtless bless so just a War as ours.
Then let's not give the sence of Danger place,
But Storm the Enemies Fortress in the face.
So shall the Line of your high Praises run
The same in time and Circle with the Sun:
And Happy *Albion* shall for ever Glory,
Her distant Sons did here make good her Story.

No more he said, then thro' the Regiment
Was heard a softly Murmur of Consent.

CHARLES HANSFORD

(c. 1685–1761)

My Country's Worth

That most men have a great respect and love
To their own place of birth I need not prove—
Experience shows 'tis true; and the black brood
Of sunburnt Affrick makes the assertion good.
I oft with pleasure have observ'd how they
Their sultry country's worth strive to display
In broken language, how they praise their case
And happiness when in their native place.
Such tales and such descriptions, when I'd leisure,
I often have attended to with pleasure,
And many times with questions would assail
The sable lad to lengthen out his tale.
If, then, those wretched people so admire
Their native place and have so great desire
To reenjoy and visit it again—
Which, if by any means they might attain,
How would they dangers court and pains endure
If to their country they could get secure!
But, barr'd of that, some into madness fly,
Destroy themselves, and wretchedly they die.
Nor is this love to Affrick's race confin'd
But spreads itself (I think) through human kind.
A northern Tartar forc'd from thence would show
The warmest wishes for his ice and snow
Which in that climate doth so much abound
That they for months in caves live underground;
The snow so deep, the cold is so intense
Above ground, houses would be no defense.
For food their case must needs be very bad:
Horse-flesh and milk of mares by them are had
In much esteem. (A loathsome bill of fare—
Methinks t'would poison me did I live there!)

329

And yet those people love and like it well,
And praise (no doubt) the country where they dwell.

If, then, the torrid and the frozen zone
Are so esteem'd and loved by their own
Home-born inhabitants and natives, we,
Whom Providence hath plac'd in a degree
Of latitude so temperate and a clime
Where neither heat nor cold at any time
Rages to that excess, to that degree,
Where there it does, sure it is fit that we
Should thanks and praise to Providence return,
Who plac'd us where we neither freeze nor burn.
But yet I doubt (it may with truth be said)
Thanks of that kind are very seldom paid.

Here in Virginia everyone will grant
That we enjoy what other people want.
Climate alone is not the only favor:
Lands to produce, streams to transport, our labor.
Land carriage costs them dear that have no means
To move their goods by water. We have streams,
Plenty of bays, of rivers and of creeks
That any who for water carriage seeks
Will not be disappointed; for our streams
Doth much relieve the labor of our teams.
I formerly was very much delighted
To pore on maps and globes, 'til age benighted
And dimm'd my sight; yet never have I found
A continent where streams do so abound.
Let geographers show me where there lies
Four such fine rivers, whose beginnings rise
So near each other, yet unmix'd their streams:
Potomac, Rappahannock, York and James—
These are the four I mean. They are, 'tis true,
The largest of our rivers. Next in view
Appear five more, inclosed in the fork
That Rappahannock makes with pretty York.

Some friendly sea-nymph now assist my lay
That I those pretty rivers may display!

Four of the five in Gloucester County take
Their rise and straight for Mobjack Bay they make:
North River near Point Comfort ends its race;
Eastermost River next to him takes place;
Then Severn follows—boasts its British name;
This moves the pretty Ware to do the same;
Piankatank in sullen silence flows
And, mute, his Indian name will not expose.

Thus is Virginia water'd to one's wish—
Her streams affording various sorts of fish
Which to our people might great profit bring,
Increase our trade—an advantageous thing
Which the industrious Dutch would much improve,
And so should we if we our country love.
The greatest kindness to a country paid
Is to endeavor to increase its trade.

If this be true (which no one will deny),
I can't find out or tell the reason why
Such warm disputes and arguments should rise;
I say, my shallow thoughts cannot devise
Why our wise senators should disagree
Where plac'd our country's capitol should be.
To me it seems as if we did despise
Our ancestors' discretion; otherwise,
More deference to their prudence we should pay.
But be that as it will, yet, sure, we may
Believe they were not altogether blind
To leave those gaps their sons so quickly find.
There was a Carter then, as well as now,
Whose greatness, prudence, wisdom, did allow
His vast accomplishments as great as any,
Though even then Virginia had many
That were sagacious, thoughtful, prudent, wise—
As are their sons. A question here may rise
Why those great men none of those faults could see

Which now so visible appear to be.
They did, no doubt, use great deliberation:
It was no sudden, rash determination
That caused our senate to remove the station
Of the old State House. Where it first was plac'd,
And with the common gifts of nature grac'd,
Our ancient State House on James River stood—
A fair, convenient, navigable flood.
Jamestown then flourish'd; yet this hinders not
If a much better station may be got.
Middle Plantation is so plac'd that there
The profits of two rivers they do share.
For from each river there a creek doth flow
That almost cuts the tongue off and in two
That doth divide their streams—a thing so rare,
Scarce any place with this we can compare.

If any situation with it mates
'Tis the old city, Corinth, up the straits.
Indeed, two handsome bays that city grasp
And in their liquid arms do seem to clasp
That ancient town, but yet those bays extend
Not far into the land before they end.
(Not so our rivers; they their arms do stretch
Far in the land, commodities to fetch
From remote places and from distant parts
With much more ease than wagons, tumbrils, carts.)
And yet we find in ancient times this town
Had scarce her equal; her fame and renown
Was spread beyond the midland seas' extent.
It over a great part of Asia went;
For merchandise and traffic she sat queen;
Though now she's poor enough and low and mean,
We often read of rich Corinthian brass
(But few know now what that rich metal was).

'Tis certain any city's situation
Contributes much to trade or preservation.
There scarce a city in the world is known
That, being land-lock'd round, hath famous grown.

Constantinople, once Byzantium,
From Rome on Tiber did this city come.
Great Constantine that seat did so admire,
From Rome he mov'd the seat of the Empire.
He wisely saw the difference between
The Hellespont and Tiber's trifling stream.
The effect is plain: still old Byzantium stands
And half the world obeys her proud commands,
While ancient Rome is now reduced so,
Except her keys, small power she doth know.

Our ancestors in this their wisdom prov'd
When government from Jamestown they remov'd.
If navigation's wanting, traffic fails;
To strive with Nature little it avails.
Her favors to improve and nicely scan
Is all that is within the reach of Man.
Nature is to be follow'd, and not forc'd,
For, otherwise, our labor will be lost.

Of this our prudent ancestors took care,
And plac'd Virginia's capitol just where
Two friendly rivers did their aid afford,
Jointly to make the commerce safe and good.
To Williamsburg, an apt and well-chose seat,
Most capable of being soon made great,
James River's southern side doth thither send
Provisions plenty. Pretty York doth lend
Her helping hand and furnish many a dish
With many sorts of most delicious fish;
Delicate oysters, too, that's fresh and good
She plenty yields. Wholesome and pleasant food
Those from the Eastern Shore by water brings—
Wheat, oats and corn with many other things.
For commerce to our neighboring colonies
No place affords so great conveniences:
To Maryland, the Bay of Chesapeake
A passage gives to any who it seek;
If to North Carolina any's bound,
James River runneth pretty near their Sound.

To mention all conveniences attending
That well-chose place will scarce have any ending.

I know that some objections there are made
Which seem to clash with merchandise and trade.
They say that ships and vessels that are large
Cannot come near the town: they must discharge
Their burdens, and their freight they must take in
Some distance from the town—which charge had been
Much less or, rather, would be none at all,
Could ships come up close to the city wall.

All this is true, is very true; but yet
A great advantage may be made of it.
I have already said, trade makes a place
Greatly to flourish; those that do embrace
That way to gather wealth cannot succeed
If they no care take to nurse up a breed
Of seamen which may always ready be
To man their ships and send them out to sea.
England, reputed mistress of the seas,
Does always keep a nursery for these.
The trade to Newcastle for coals is still
A nursery for sea and always will
In peace or war. The colliers' fleet provides
For London coals, good store; that fleet, besides,
At the same time, are training up for sea
Hundreds of youths that, in due time, may be
Expert and gallant sailors to defend
England, whose safety doth so much depend
On walls of wood. If these should chance to fail,
England's undone—her bonnet she must veil.
Why should not we their wise example take,
And of our creeks some such advantage make?
And though by shorter trips our boys innure
The oar, to manage hardships to endure;
Small craft of all sorts on these creeks may go.
Ships to unload or load from thence would grow—
A good employment for our youth—and we,
By that means, train up many lads for sea.

Methinks 'tis easy to foresee the good
That would arise from such a useful brood.

Thus this objection hath its answer; yet
A second follows. It is, therefore, fit
To hear and to consider well the case
That so a prudent judgment we may pass.
'Tis much complained of by those that live
In frontier counties that they cannot give
Attendance on their lawsuits or complete
Other affairs, the distance is so great.
They say the seat of government should stand
Upon or near the center of the land,
That so the people may have equal shares
Of distance to negotiate affairs.
This is not practicable, for as soon
A garment may be made to fit the moon.
For I have known the County of New Kent
The utmost bounds our situations went.
Let those who thus complain but cast their eyes
On England's map and see how distant lies
London from Cumberland or from the Tweed.
'Tis true that distance remedy doth need
And finds it readily: judges are sent
To every shire and county with intent
To hear their causes, controversies try,
And justice to distribute equally.
This sure a great relief is to the poor
Thus to have justice brought unto their door.
Justice is sent, but London still remains
And riches draws from her beloved Thames.
Our capitol may stand where well 'tis plac'd,
And yet this grievance, too, may be redress'd.

But still my admiration will remain
To think our present Carter should maintain
A wrong opinion and quite counter run
To what our fathers have so wisely done!
I know great wits sometimes delight to show
How far bright parts and eloquence will go

To make bad arguments seem very right,
And to that end affirm that black is white.
A secret pleasure 'tis to try the strength
Of their great genius, and observe the length
An argument (though wrong) may be extended;
For maxims (though not true) may be defended.
Perhaps this was the case. At Carter's shove
Our capitol did shake, though not remove!
But let the motive be just what it will,
He then display'd great eloquence and skill.
That he his country's good has in pursuit,
His generous practice puts beyond dispute.
But men are men—all subject to mistakes—
And he perhaps as few as any makes!

I think that those objections mentioned
Are all of any weight that can be said.
The rest are very trifles and not worth
An answer. But now I hope our hearts are all compos'd,
And all our breaches by Dinwiddie clos'd.
May good and great Dinwiddie's able hand
Establish peace and concord in our land—
A land with many signal favors blest—
And may they by kind Heaven be increas'd!

After this long digression, now I come
Our country's love again to reassume
And mention motives which doth it advance,
Make it tenacious, and will it enhance.
For place alone without society
Will be but dull and joyless, languid, dry.
But if, with worthy men the soil is blest,
The measure's full; for that crowns all the rest.
Who can but love the place that hath brought forth
Such men of virtue, merit, honor, worth?
My countrymen (if I am not too fond)
For parts are by no people gone beyond.

The gentry of Virginia, I dare say,
For honor vie with all America.

Had I great Camden's skill, how freely I
Would celebrate our worthy gentry!
But I am no way equal to that task.
Such a performance certainly doth ask
For a more frequent use of conversation
Than could consist with my low place and station.
Tied down to labor, education wanting,
But yet my busy soul for knowledge panting,
Though struggling hard, I only just could peep
Above the vulgar, but with them must creep.
Neither my time nor means would suffer me
In polish'd conversation much to be,
'Tis true; I have in my declining age
Found courteous treatment from some wise and sage
And most accomplish'd men of the first rank
Whose goodness to me I am bound to thank
And gratefully acknowledge while I live.
'Tis all the tribute in my power to give.
Those men deserve, their worth should mentioned be,
And be display'd unto posterity,
That so their children may example take
And tread in the same path their fathers make.

Could I accomplish this, how gladly I
Would stretch my wit, and all my skill would try!
But, 'tis in vain. I, in my narrow view
Though there be many, yet can mention few,
And those by families (not single men—
That task's too great for my unskillful pen).

The Nelsons, Digges, Carters, Burwells, Pages,
The Grymes and the Robinsons engages
Respect, and reverence to those names be paid!
Blairs, Ludwells, Byrds in the same scale are laid.
Randolphs and Wallers, Harrisons likewise—
These all contend for honors, noble prize.
Willises, Wormeleys, Lewises do run
In honor's path, as loath to be outdone.
The Spotswoods, Berkeleys, Armisteads thither bend
Their steps and for the lovely prize contend.

I hope Virginia hath many more
To me unknown—might lengthen out the score.
As stars of the first magnitude these shine
And, in their several stations, do combine
The great support and ornament to be
Of Britain's first and ancient colony.

But here I fain would breathe a while and then
Pursue the worthy catalogue again.
Pleas'd with the toil—my country's worth to show—
I once again my narrative renew—
A field so spacious, it will sure be granted
That sooner words than matter will be wanted.

Sincere and brave, Harwood does fearless stand
And with sagacious Allen joins his hand.
Friends so united should not parted be!
A second Allen makes the number three—
All men of worth, though not of vast estates.
(But merit sure makes up what wealth abates.)
If worth deserves respect, then I am sure
Merit to Ambler will respect procure;
Nay, 'tis but just so good a man as he
Should by Viriginia much respected be.
Sweet-temper'd Norton hath experience had
How with the people's love his worth is paid.
Sheild when but young yet did I then foresee
A credit to his country he would be.
Let wary Jamison be mention'd here,
And manly Stephenson bring up the rear.

These worthy men Viriginia's credit raise,
Although ('tis like) by many different ways.
Men differ in the talents they possess,
Some having more and greater, others less.
Yet, all are useful if employ'd well,
And few there be but in some way excel.
'Tis true employments are not always suited
To every genius—this can't be disputed—
For, many times occasion don't allow

A man his great abilities to show.
For want of use and opportunity
Their talents are not known, but dormant lie.
Of this I many instances could give
Of worthy men who in Virginia live.
Though many might be mentioned, yet a few
I only shall present unto your view.

Had it been Carter Burwell's part or station
In arms to serve his king, defend a nation;
Had it been Burwell's lot in camp or field
The ranks to marshal, or a truncheon wield,
An army to command, or town to win—
This suited to his genius would have been.
I think his piercing eye, his gallant mien,
Doth very much resemble Prince Eugene.
Had war been his employment, doubtless he
A most accomplish'd general would be;
Or, were he to conduct a colony
To settle in some distant country,
His vigilance and foresight would be sure
The place to plant, and all his men secure.

May sweet and lovely Nat his father's merit,
His virtues and perfections all inherit;
May Burwell's, Grymes's virtues in him meet
And in his worthy heart erect their seat.
Sweet boy, though this I must not live to see,
Yet is it most sincerely wish'd by me.
When I am gone may well-deserved praise
Crown my dear little colonel's head with bays!

Had Harwood to a warlike life been bred,
What laurels might have crown'd his valiant head!
'Tis true the engine by which Sidney fell
Might kill a Harwood, or destroy Burwell;
Had virtue always with long life been bless'd,
How had great Sidney's glory been increas'd!
Titus, mankind's delight, soon left the stage,
And made his exit in the bloom of age.

There's some, again, whose genius seems design'd
For legislators and to keep mankind
Within the bounds of reason and justice.
This is a province that is very nice
And difficult, yet of the greatest use;
For men too often liberty abuse.
Bounds must be set to mankind, or else they
From justice and morality will stray.
'Tis difficult to make such laws, be sure
That vice be punish'd, liberty secure.
But yet Virginia yieldeth some of these
Whose penetrating judgment searches, sees
As far as human prudence will extend,
Good laws to make, and people's morals mend.

Within this class, the brothers Nelson shine
Like two rich diamonds in a golden mine.
Deep are their speculations; yet the spark
Will shine and luster even in the dark.
Their sweet behavior and their liberal hand
Do love and reverence from us all command.
Carter and Ludwell with these brothers suit;
And Waller's talents are beyond dispute;
Virginia ought to prize her flower de luce
Who is and hath been to her of great use.
The light in which Allen would best appear
Would be physician, statesman, engineer;
His country's interest he doth nicely scan,
And is a wise and a judicious man.

As merchandise and traffic much improve
A country's wealth, many there be that move
Within that circle and with industry
Themselves enrich, their country's wants supply—
A happy thing (no doubt) to any lands
Where public good and private join their hands.
Merchants of all sorts kindly should be us'd,
And just encouragement to none refus'd.
A government that so their laws contrive
Without dispute will flourish, grow, and thrive.

Virginia many worthy merchants yield:
Booth, Holt and Thurston, with the sprightly Sheild
Are all her natives. Doubtless many more
Unknown to me might lengthen out the score.

Thus far I have with pleasure gone; but now
A melancholy broods upon my brow.
For, oh, my country, it would not be right
Nor just for me only to show thy bright
And shining side! I fear thou hast a dark
And gloomy one. Attend thee! Do but hark!
The dice-box rattles; cards on tables flow.
I well remember, fifty years ago
This wretched practice scarcely then was known.
Then if a gentleman had lost a crown
At gleek or at backgammon, 'twere a wonder,
And rumbled through the neighborhood like thunder.
But many now do win and lose pistoles
By fifties—nay, by hundreds. In what shoals
Our gentry to the gaming tables run!
Scoundrels and sharpers—nay, the very scum
Of mankind—joins our gentry, wins their cash.
O countrymen! This surely would abash
Our sleeping sires! Should one of them arise,
How would it shock him! How would it surprise
An honorable shade to see his boy
His honor, time, and money thus employ!
How could he bear to hear that Sacred Name
From whose dread presence he so lately came
Profan'd and trifled with, their frauds to screen?
Methinks he'd wish his son had never been;
Methinks he'd wish for power to destroy
Such wretches and annihilate his boy!

Pardon such warm expressions from a father.
Who would not choose annihilation rather
Than into everlasting flames be press'd?
Oh, hideous thought! O gamesters, think the rest!

Horse racing and cockfighting do much harm
To some estates; 'tis like a spell or charm.
But would our gentry once be pleased to try
The experiment, they would most certainly
More satisfaction find in one pistole
Laid out in putting one poor boy to school
Than five or six expended in no worse
A way than making up a horse-race purse.
'Tis very true; I know some gentlemen
That secretly do this. Their pleasure, then,
Does far exceed the others; they receive
Comfort from this when trifles them will leave.

A gentleman is placed so that he
In his example cannot neuter be:
He's always doing good or doing harm.
And should not this a thinking man alarm?
If he lives ill, the vulgar will him trace;
They fancy his example theirs will grace.

Many are fond to imitate a man
That is above their class; their little span
Of knowledge they consult not. In the way
Their betters walk, they think they safely may.
Thus, both are wrong but may, perhaps, be lost,
And all God's goodness disappointed, cross'd.
For, sure, His goodness always should be prais'd
By those He hath above the vulgar rais'd.
'Tis most ungrateful not to bless that hand
By which we are plac'd above the crown to stand.

Contrariwise, when gentry do live well,
Their bright example is a kind of spell
Which does insensibly attract the crowd
To follow them in virtue's pleasant road.
In such a way, who would not take delight
To see gentry and commons both unite?
This would true honor to our gentry bring,
And happiness to all would flow and spring.
We find example is of greater force

Than the most famous clergyman's discourse.
None will deny the assertion to be true:
Example always precept will outdo.

I wish our gentry would consider this;
For, sure, much gaming most destructive is.
Honor it stabs; religion it disgraces;
It hurts our trade, and honesty defaces.
But, what is worse, it so much guilt does bring,
That many times distraction thence does spring.

But now Virginia's grand assembly's met
In solemn manner to consult and treat
Of their king's honor and their country's good.
So Rome's great senate, when that city stood
The world's great mistress, in their capitol
Sat to consult the interest of all
Their citizens both as to war and peace.
Their country's wealth and glory to increase,
Good laws to make, the useless to repeal,
Their country's interest and the public weal
Was still the mark at which those sages aim'd,
And yet, sometimes, their ends were not attain'd.

They bought and bred up slaves as we do now
And yet neglected (or they knew not how)
Those slaves to manage. Sometimes they rebell'd,
Which cost much sweat and blood ere they were quell'd.
The Roman legions they did often face
And sometimes rout them, and their masters chase.
For years together they resistance made
And many cities into ruins laid.
Those people found amongst them now and then
Some that were bold, courageous, able men—
Men that could form designs and act them, too,
With courage and discretion; they could view
Advantages and of them make the most.
The Romans often found this to their cost.
None so near ruin brought their capitol
As their own slaves and one-eyed Hannibal.

The Egyptians a much later instance show:
That nation scarce six hundred years ago
By their Circassian slaves were quite bereft
Of regal powers; for they had nothing left.
Their caliph kill'd, a slave usurp'd the throne;
Their slaves, the Mamelukes, made all their own.
Crown'd with success, they modell'd a new state;
In peace and war, the Mamelukes grew great.
Their caliphs (or successors) far extended
Their fame and grandeur; neither was it ended
In a short time. Their regal power lasted
Above two hundred years, till it was blasted
By Selimus, the son of Bajazett,
The Turkish chief—a warlike prince. But yet
They bravely did their monarchy defend,
Disputing every inch, from end to end.
Egypt hath ever since a province been
Unto the Turks, no regal power seen.
That ancient people, deemed once so wise,
Most other nations now contemn, despise.
Their hardships now are greater from the Turks
Than when they subject were to Mamelukes.
A melancholy scene! May Providence
Virginia still preserve, be her defense!

Our church hath taught us in her litany
To beg deliverance from conspiracy.
This was a gloomy view fifty years past;
May Heaven protect Virginia to the last!
Virginia's senate—here you stand alone.
Your Mother Country will admit of none
In her free air in slavery to be.
In England, all—both white and black—are free.
In other things her parliament's example
May you direct; in this, they are no sample.
They give you no direction how to ward
Off such a blow. Have, therefore, a regard
To your own safeties; ponder well the thing.
Neglect doth many times much danger bring.
I know you are wise; that wisdom then employ

In such a manner that you may enjoy
Safety and peace. They very precious are.
Likewise, of your posterity take care;
They, more than you, in this may be concern'd,
And yet the danger not so well discern'd.
'Tis true Great Britain (next to Heaven) would be
Our best support to succor us if we
Under this great calamity should fall.
But the wide ocean surely bars out all
Present assistance she to us could send.
Our neighbors are but weak to serve that end;
At the same time, Indians may them molest.
Nay, by a war Britain may be distress'd.
Oh, shocking thought! If we don't mend our ways,
Who knows how soon we may see wretched days?

Willing, though weak, I have in this essay
Done my endeavor truly to display
My country's worth in several respects
And not conceal'd some of her defects—
A theme deserving a much abler hand.
But, yet, I hope without offense I stand.
An innocent amusement was my end;
Offence to any I did not intend.
To flatter any was not in my view;
But all that here is said (I think) is true.
For, flattery I no occasion have;
No place I seek; no office do I crave.
Interest I cannot have and, sure, ambition
Suits very ill with my obscure condition.
'Tis true, the obscure man may honest be,
And have, and practice, great veracity.
If that be granted, I sit down contented;
'Tis in that light I would be represented.

Farewell, my country! May thy happiness,
Thy glory, goodness, virtue, still increase!

GEORGE BERKELEY

(1685–1753)

Verses on the Prospect of planting Arts and Learning in America

The Muse, disgusted at an Age and Clime,
   Barren of every glorious Theme,
In distant Lands now waits a better Time,
   Producing Subjects worthy Fame:

In happy Climes, where from the genial Sun
   And virgin Earth such Scenes ensue,
The Force of Art by Nature seems outdone,
   And fancied Beauties by the true:

In happy Climes the Seat of Innocence,
   Where Nature guides and Virtue rules,
Where Men shall not impose for Truth and Sense,
   The Pedantry of Courts and Schools:

There shall be sung another golden Age,
   The rise of Empire and of Arts,
The Good and Great inspiring epic Rage,
   The wisest Heads and noblest Hearts.

Not such as *Europe* breeds in her decay;
   Such as she bred when fresh and young,
When heavenly Flame did animate her Clay,
   By future Poets shall be sung.

Westward the Course of Empire takes its Way;
   The four first Acts already past,
A fifth shall close the Drama with the Day;
   Time's noblest Offspring is the last.

GEORGE SEAGOOD

(c. 1685–1724)

Mr. Blackmore's Expeditio Ultramontana

rendered into English Verse.
Inscrib'd to the Honourable the Governour

Let other Pens th' ungrateful News declare,
The dire Effects of *Northern* Civil War;
How furious Men by fatal Madness led,
Pull'd down devoted Vengeance on their Head.
Whilst we thy Care, O *Spotswood*, sing thy Toil,
Which bore thee far into a foreign Soil.
Urge thee to quit soft Ease and grateful Home,
O'er Mountains high and rapid Streams to roam;
And thro' thick Woods impervious to the Sun,
To poisonous Snakes and Monsters only known.
   Tell (Goddess Muse) for thy all pow'rful Art
Is only equal to the Godlike Part;
What lonesome Fields, and unfrequented Floods,
Spotswood did pass thro' dark and desert Woods;
Whilst he, intent upon *Virginia*'s Good,
O'er Hills and Dales the noble Task persu'd;
Up steepest Mountains in his Course did run,
Whose Tops were 'bove the Clouds, and Rivals to the Moon,
Contemn'd the Length and Danger of the Way.
So he might farther stretch his *Royal Master*'s Sway.
   Happy *Virginia*! wouldst thou prize thy Friend,
Who labour'd thus thy Borders to extend;
Encourag'd thee to Arts, train'd thee to Arms;
And guarded thee from more than foreign Harms:
Nor were his Thoughts to these alone confin'd,
But higher Cares imploy'd his Christian Mind.
For having read in God's Prophetic Page,
In after-times should come a glorious Age,
In which all Nations should agree as One;
Be all one Flock, of one Religion.
   "O Prospect sweet! he cries, hail happy Days!

When thus the Sun of Peace shall cast his rays?;
When his bless'd Influence shall the Globe controul,
And his Messias reign from Pole to Pole."
    Unwearied are his Pains, unshaken is his Mind,
To spread this Good to all of *Adam's* Kind:
In this, ambitious of eternal Fame,
T'advance his Sov'reigns and his Saviour's Name
That GEORGE's Fame may thro' the World be read,
And CHRIST's and *Britain*'s Cross in faithless Nations
        spread.
Now then, the Hero for his March prepares,
And t'wards the *Indian* Parts his Course he steers:
And thus begins to move by GOD's Command;
As once did *Joshua* to the Promis'd Land.
All Things and Places full of GOD appear,
And both his Goodness and his Power declare:
And all his Creatures his Commands fulfil
And act by his Express, or his permissive Will.
    This Expedition was design'd to trace
A Way to some yet undiscover'd Place;
And barb'rous savage Nations to subdue,
Which neither antient *Greece* or *Rome* e'er knew;
Or else *Virginia's* Borders to secure
And fix the Bounds of his deputed Power:
These, Day and Night, the Regent's Studies are.
And his *Virginia* is his constant Care.
    And now the Day was come, when his Command
To distant Climes led on a chosen Band;
All Things conspire to favour the Design,
And lucky Omens with their Wishes joyn.
    First then, he pass'd the antient Planters Seats,
Whilst each Plantation from his View retreats;
The winding Road thro' thickest Forest leads,
(Whose Trees tow'rds Heaven shoot up their lofty Heads)
And brings him to the Banks declining Side,
Where *Rapidanna* rowls his hasty Tyde;
Whose Current's fiercer than the *Tiber*'s was,
When he with headstrong Course his Bounds did pass,
O'erthrew the Rock where *Vesta*'s Temple stood,
And mixt the sacred Structure with the Mud.

Kind Nature dreading such Effects as these,
(Whose all-wise Author all Events foresees)
The like in future Ages to prevent,
Cut deep his Banks, and made a steep Ascent,
With rocky Cliffs his Waters did restrain,
Lest overcharg'd with sudden Snow or Rain,
He might o'erflow, and drown the Neighb'ring Plain.
    Crossing this Stream, he to *Germanna* came,
Which from new *German* Planters takes its Name,
Here taught to dig, by his auspicious Hand
They prov'd the teeming Pregnance of the Land;
For being search'd, the fertile Earth gave Signs
That her Womb swell'd with Gold and Silver Mines:
This Ground, if faithful, may in Time out-do
Potosi, *Mexico*, and fam'd *Peru*.
    When he from hence a hundred Miles had pass'd
T'wards *George*'s Hill a wishful Eye he cast;
This Mountain taller than the rest appears,
As to the Sky his stately Front he rears;
Which *Spotswood*, mindful of his Sov'reign's Fame,
Grac'd with the Title of his Royal Name,
As proud *Olympus* 'bove the Hills does rise,
And nearer views the Starry Pole and Skies;
So much thy Mountain upwards does aspire,
And o'er the Highest thrusts his Shoulders higher;
As Thou, Great *GEORGE*, the Monarchs dost surpass,
In vertuous Deeds familiar to thy Race.
    The steady *Spotswood* thither bends his Way,
Altho' thro' roughest pathless Woods it lay;
No Sign of Culture wears the desert Ground;
No Print of humane Footsteps to be found:
When streight the Sky is taken from his Sight,
And *Sylvan* Shades obstruct the Mid-day Light:
Yet on he goes, and does a Passage force;
Thro' Dens of Wolves and Bears he clears his Course.
Each Swamp is fill'd with Broods of horrid Snakes,
And savage Beasts lie lurking in the Brakes.
Unmov'd he hears the howling Wolfs shrill Voice,
And slights the roaring Bears more frightful Noise.
Here Snakes, like *Python*, of a monstrous Size,

With brandish'd Tongues dart out a spiteful Hiss;
With twirling Tails these Serpents coil'd, prepare,
(And with their Rattles beat the Alarm) for War;
And bid the wary Traveller retreat,
Or arm'd expect a deadly Foe to meet.
A Weapon on each Willow's to be found,
Which plenteous grow in Vale and swampy Ground;
One stroke of which the Monster's Blood will spill;
Whose mortal Venom with a Touch does kill.

    Yet arn't these Woods without their proper Grace;
The verdant Earth here shews a cheerful Face.
This fruitful Soil with richest Grass is crown'd,
And various Flow'rs adorn the gawdy Ground:
(Neglecting Order) Nature plants this Land,
And strews her Riches with a lavish Hand;
With Fruit her Bounty cloaths each well-deck'd Bush,
The luscious Cherries on the Branches blush.
Here silken Mulb'ries load the bending Boughs,
And there the cluster'd Grape luxuriant grows.
Here Currants, Peaches, Strawb'ries, Nature tends;
And other Dainties to the Hero lends.

    This, to the pleas'd Spectator, seems the Seat
Where rural *Ceres* makes her own Retreat;
Or else the Birth-place of the *Jolly God*,
Or where *Pomona* makes her chief Abode.

    These Things, as *Spotswood* and his Train admire,
Towards *Mount-George* their March conveys them nigher:
At length they reach the Bottom, and look up,
And nearer view its long-sought airy Top.
Spotswood had long pursu'd it with his Eye;
But as he follow'd, still it seem'd to fly:
His Haste was fruitless, like *Apollo's* Chace,
When *Daphne* shun'd the am'rous Gods embrace.

    Now they ascend and up that Mountain go,
Which looks with Scorn upon the World below.
Hard Labour! thus to climb so near the Skies;
But Strength and Honour, Courage fresh supplies:
Hopes of rare Sights, do strong Desires excite;
And so they gain the Mountains utmost Height.

Here are no Woods to intercept the Sight,
And form at Noon an antidated Night:
But freely now they breathe a purer Air,
The cloudless Sky is all serene and fair,
The Sun and Moon by Turns in Pomp appear.
    Here *Spotswood* stood, and looking from this Height,
The beauteous Landskip charm'd his ravish'd Sight,
Much pleas'd to see thro' Woods the Rivers stray,
And long the Vales in wanton Mazes play.
    The Hero smil'd, and thus express'd his Thought:
"Had th' antient Poets known this pleasant Spot,
They here had plac'd their great *Apollo's* Shrine,
Or else the Title of the tuneful *Nine*
Had always made it sacred and divine:
But since an higher Honour it does claim,
Forever let it bear the mighty *GEORGE*'s Name."
He spoke, then all their joint Assent declare
By joyful Shouts that rend the nitrous Air.
    Another Mountain meets their downward Sight;
Tho' lower far than this, yet next in height.
As there thou stoodst in Power, so next in Fame,
Let thine, O *Spotswood!* be its future Name.
Descending, many Fountains they descry,
That largest Rivers plenteously supply:
O'er Roots, o'er Rocks, a rapid Course they gain,
And in the Vales become a liquid Plain:
'Mongst verdant Trees, the Streams look bright and gay,
As in the Skies appears the *Milky Way*.
Here spangled Snakes, and Fish divert their Sight,
Which, as they swim, reflect a glitt'ring Light,
(Like Stars that twinkle in a frosty Night.)
Whose various Sorts and Numbers to rehearse,
Would tire the *Muse*, and pass the Bounds of Verse.
    But then, to paint the Joys this Prospect Breeds
From shady Groves, green Banks, and flow'ry Meads,
And all the Beauties that this Par'dice yields,
Be it *His* Task, who knows th' *Elysian* Fields.
After the Hero pass'd the gentle Flood
Thro' which directly went their mirey Road

Regardful of his Charge, he pausing stood:
He thought, and soon resolved without Delay,
Homewards to make his retrogressive Way,
Having for *GEORGE*, his King, Possession took,
And cut *his Name* in *Ultramontane* Rock.
Obeying then the Dictates of his Mind,
He streight return'd, and left this Scene behind;
When he, like *Hercules* in former Days,
Had made two Mountains, Pillars of his Praise.

JOSEPH BREINTNALL

(c. 1695–1746)

"A plain Description of one single Street in this City"

At *Delaware*'s broad Stream, the View begin,
Where jutting Wharfs, Food-freighted Boats take in.
Then with th' advancing Sun, direct your Eye;
Wide opes the Street, with firm Brick Buildings high:
Step, gently rising, o'er the Pebbly Way,
And see the Shops their tempting Wares display;
(Chief on the Right, screen'd from rude Winds and blest,
In Frost with Sunshine) Here, if Ails molest,
Plain surfac'd Flags, and smooth laid Bricks invite
Your tender Feet to Travel with Delight.
An Yew-Bow, Distance, from the Key built Strand,
Our Court-house fronts Cæsarea's Pine tree Land.
Thro' the arched Dome, and on each Side, the Street
Divided runs, remote again to meet:
Here Eastward stand the Traps to Obloquy,
And Petty Crimes, Stocks, Post and Pillory:
And (twice a Week) beyond, light Stalls are set
Loaded with Fruits and Fowls and *Jersey*'s Meat.
Westward, conjoin, the Shambles grace the Court;
Brick Piles their long extended Roof support.
Oft, West from these, the Country Wains are seen
To crowd each Hand, and leave a Breadth between:
Yet wide still (such is the City's Care)
To Right and Left, strong Bars a Passage spare,
South of the Mart a Meeting-house is rear'd,
Where by the Friends (so call'd) is Christ rever'd;
With Stone and Brick, the lasting Walls are made
High-rais'd the Roof, and Wide the Rafters spread.
Within a Voice of this, the Presbyters
Of like Materials, have erected theirs,
Thence, half a Furlong West, declining pace,
And see the Rock-built Prison's dreadful Face.
'Twixt, and beyond all those, near twice as far

As from a Sling a Stone might pass in Air,
The forging Shops of sooty Smiths are set,
And Wheelwrights Frames—with vacant Lots to let:
A Neighbourhood of Smoke, and piercing Dins,
From Trades, from Prison-Grates and Publick Inns.
But ev'n among this Noise, and Dirt, are plac'd
Some Buildings Fair, with peaceful Tenants grac'd,
Distant, more West, with unbuilt Grounds between,
The Furnace-House and Woods close up the Scene.
On th' other Side (left in my Verse disjoin'd,
But all one Picture in the Poet's Mind)
A comely Row of Tenements unite,
And set their various Goods and Works to Light;
Salesmen and Trades of decent Sorts are mixt,
(A lively place) some Tavern Signs betwixt:
Along their Doors, the clean hard Paving trends,
'Till at a plashy crossing Street it ends,
And thence, a short Arm's Throw, renew'd tends.
Mechanicks, here, in Iron, Brass, Wood and Horn,
Their narrow Shutters, with their Wares adorn.
'Mongst those, a few tall Structures proudly rise;
Th' adjacent Hutts look lessen'd at their Size.
Beyond, the Street is thinly wall'd, but fair,
With Gardens pale'd, and Orchards here and there
On either Side, those beauteous Prospects lie;
And some inclos'd with Hedges please the Eye.

The Rape of Fewel

A Cold-weather Poem

The bleak Norwest begins his dreaded Reign,
The Forest Chiefs his pow'rful Presence know,
And, bending, cast their faded Honours down;
A patch-work Veil Earth's mournful Face o'erspreads,
While the fierce Tyrant strips her Offspring bare.
    Close in their well-provided Hives the Bees,
And deep within-ground, or in porous Wood,

Th' industrious Emmets lie; and Men secure,
Warm hous'd, elude the Terrors waiting round;
All but wan Poverty's distressful Sons.
      Then 'tis that they, made desp'rate by their Wants,
And grievous Prospect of worse Penury,
Go shud'ring forth in early Hours and late,
Excluded from the Pleasure of Sol's Beams,
And Friendship of Mankind, whose Sight they fear
More than the piercing Winds they constant feel
At num'rous Inlets, wounding Trunk and Limbs.
      Their creaking Barrows oft their Fears encrease,
Loaden with interdicted Posts and Rails.
      And when a Splinter prominent appears,
(Predestinated to be torn away,
In Autumn's or in Winter's hoary Reign,
By frugal *Palatine*, or poor *Hibernian*,
Or *British* Convict; or a native born
Whom Rum and Strumpets have to Darkness doom'd,
Or who by Injuries unshunable
Has thus been driven to save a wretched Life,)
How does the wary Stroller look around
(Lest watching some pickthank Informer stand,
Or jealous Cowherd from his Pasture hears,)
And when with sudden Force he rives it off,
How loud he hems, the rending Crack to drown!
      What Fates attend on Crookedness and Age!
Not mortal Man alone may thus complain,
But Nature's Products, and the Architect's
Politest, and most nervous Labours too.
Bald antiquated Oaks, and Bark-shed Gums,
Mansions untenable, dismantled Barns,
Storm-shaken Fences, thin broad Rails oblique,
Distorted Posts, Gates clad with dismal Moss,
And rotten rooted Stumps; all bear the Marks
Of needy Thieves Perdition. On first Sight
They judge those odd Materials for their own;
But care not boldly in broad Day to seize,
Twilight or Moonshine suits the Execution.
      That these poor Wights, whose arbitrary Wills,
And griping Indigence thus drives them on,

To wrong their richer Neighbours, should be d——d,
Great Heaven forbid: Do they not act by Rules?
Tho' not indeed well ratified by Law;
There lies the Failure. Thus self-reasoning they.
    What if the op'lent Man from his full Table
Let fall the Crums and Offals to be trod on,
Or gather'd up by Dogs, and I observing
Softly collect those Morsels for my self,
Who's injur'd by't? So when a Tenement
Stands ticklish on an old decay'd Foundation,
And tott'ring Fences are beyond Repair,
I may determine that this House is dang'rous
And grown unfit for its great Owner's Use,
Whom to oblige I'll pull it piece-meal down,
And take it for my Pains, without disturbing
His Worship with the Bargain. And this Fence,
Were it remov'd a new one would be rais'd,
And Ground improv'd; what Lab'rer but my self
For so small Wages as th' old Stuff would do't?
Yet were I to propose it to the Landlord,
He would despise my Figure and Proposal,
And set me Terms injurious to us both,
Below his Character, too hard for mine;
Therefore as I'm acquainted with such Matters,
And best know how to judge, I'll judge alone;
The Work will please both Parties when 'tis done.
    But with what Sophistry can Rogues excuse,
How justify their Pillage, who make Breaches
In lonely Buildings and unwatch'd Enclosures,
Where neither Time nor Use have yet impair'd
The solid Timbers nor defac'd the Form?
    Thy Pasture, S——n, with sad Eyes I view:
Oft with thy Slaves and Team, in early Spring,
Thou dost repair and circumscribe the Whole,
And soon a verd'rous Crop begins to rise;
But e'er the Scythe is sharpen'd, 'tis too late,
For num'rous Kine have there a common Range;
One Entrance or a few, by Villains made,
Destroy thy Hopes. So lies neglected then,
The Cultivation. When cool Autumn comes,

Parts here and there, most easily remov'd,
Creep off the Ground, as if they could not bear
The Storms approaching, but in vilest Hovels
Chuse to be cramm'd.—
And as dire Winter boistrously alarms,
Each frighted Pannel follows to the Flames.
   So when great Rains a River's Waters raise,
Its Meadows Banks, where loosly crown'd or low,
Admit the Floods, and no bold Engineer
At hand to help, th' increasing Deluge wears
Breach into Breach, and levels all the Bounds.

To the Memory of Aquila Rose, Deceas'd

Oft', O ye Muses! to delightful Scenes,
Are you invok'd or courted on the Greens;
In soothing Verse, to lull the Lover's Pains,
Or sprightly Songs, to glad the blithy Swains:
O now assist! when Sighs and Tears implore,
To sing a Bard, whose Voice we hear no more.
   Albion his Birth, his Learning *Albion* gave;
To Manhood grown, he cross'd the stormy Wave,
More Arts, and Nature's wondrous Ways to find,
Illuminate, and fortify his Mind;
And to divert his Eyes from Cross Affairs:
For Love dissastrous fill'd his Breast with Cares.
In *Britain*, he would say, he once was bless'd,
And all the Joys of Love and Life possess'd:
But some strange Power who envy'd his Repose,
Chang'd his Enjoyments to combining Woes;
Forc'd him to quit his former peaceful Way,
And prove his Fortune o'er a foamy Sea.
"Dear native Land, he sadly said, farewel,
And those soft Shades where Love and *Silvia* dwell:
Blow swift ye Gales, and waft me from the Shore,
I fly from Love, and *Silvia* see no more."
   Long then the Wand'rer sail'd from Land to Land,
To servile Business of rough Seas constrain'd:

Yet not the less, where e'er their Vessel steer'd
Strangers admir'd him, as his Mates rever'd.
So 'tis, where Heaven exalted Sense bestows,
The limpid Mind thro' foul Obstructions glows:
Yet partial Fortune, or mysterious Fate
Debases wise Men, and to Fools gives State.
ROSE well some Post of Eminence could grace,
Who clad in Tar supplies a Sailor's Place.
Such was his Language, such his social Air,
As would th' unequal Destiny declare:
And while his Limbs to vulgar Service bend,
His brighter Thoughts to lofty Themes ascend.
Distinguish'd o're the common Crew he shone,
Unjustly ranked, or 'midst them all alone.
Bless'd in much Wit, and little Pride he strives
With adverse Fortune, as he further drives.
The *Iberian* Coast he saw, and swarthy *Moors*,
Etrurian Ports, and sweet *Sardinian* Shores;
Sardinia, where the Powers of Love reside,
Where sable Veils ten Thousand Beauties hide:
Yet not his Heart that charming Place confines,
A wider Search his active Soul designs:
He travels 'till our Western Tract he trode,
Which as he found a Home, here made his last Abode.
When thro' Fatigues by Land and Sea sustain'd,
His resting Point, our little Town he'd gain'd.
A few long Weeks by Sickness held, he lay,
Dark Hours to count, and slowly waste the Day:
Then gloomy Doubts, and pensive Thoughts arise,
And lonely thus, within himself he cries,
"Depriv'd of Health, and every bosom Friend,
When shall my Toils, my lengthening Sorrows end;
My own low Genius here forsakes me too,
And nothing for myself, myself can do:
But can the Muse by grievous Tempests tost,
Resume her Notes, and joyful Numbers boast!
O how shall she her soft Ideas bring,
And in strange Lands the Songs of Gladness sing!
When Sorrows draw black Curtains o're the Soul,
No gay Desires in our sad Bosoms roll:

But the Remembrance of the Joys I lost
On *Britain*'s happy Shore, afflicts me most.
O had I now those pleasing Volumes here,
Which in *Britannia* my Companions were;
They might indeed some tedious Thoughts divert,
Give some Refreshment to my drooping Heart:
But destitute of Books, of Health, and Friends,
As here my Wand'ring, here my Comfort ends."
   Thus wail'd he, yet while thus his Griefs complain'd,
His manly Soul to sink beneath disdain'd:
He rous'd anew his Reason to his Aid,
And charg'd his Spirits, not to fly dismay'd.
Now Hopes revive, and Health repairs her Seat,
Round flows the Blood, and equal Pulses beat:
His Name soon known, it led the Curious, where
They might his pleasing Conversation share.
Thus he, who late no friendly Pleasures knew,
Had daily now kind Visitants in View:
Each comes of Choice, and all his Friendship claim,
They courted him, and he delighted them:
Soft in Discourse, and easy of access,
Thankful his Mind, persuasive his address;
The learn'd approv'd his Wit, the unlearn'd admir'd,
And docile Youths to his Regard aspir'd.
O'erjoy'd to find himself so much caress'd,
His grateful Thoughts, he thus to them express'd,
"Tho' Agues late did chill, and Fevers burn,
Tho' Cares have Wrinkles in my Forehead worn,
I'll smiling bless, and mark the Day with white,
That brought such hospitable Friends to Light;
My native Brethren are in you supply'd,
And former Blessings now again preside."
   Then, lively, from his languid Bed he rose,
Free'd of his Pangs, and melancholy Woes,
Industrious Arts his active Hands could use;
He would the Bread of slothful Means refuse,
Them to his proper Livlihood he join'd,
Where leaden Speech unloads the lab'ring Mind,
And graven Words to distant Ages tell
What various Things in Times foregone befell:

As *Mercury* cuts thro' the yielding Sky,
So thro' the Work his nimble Fingers fly:
His novel Skill Spectators thronging drew,
Who haste the swift Compositer to view;
Not Men alone, but Maids of softer Air
And nicer Fancies, to the Room repair:
Pleas'd with such mild Impediments he frames,
As they Request, their dear enchanting Names,
To grace a Book, or feast a Lover's Eye,
Or tell Companions of their fancied Joy.
With Complaisance he still dismiss'd the Train,
None ever fought his Courtesy in vain:
Each transient fair one took her Name away,
But thee *Maria*—'Twas thy Doom to stay;
'Twas soon revers'd, the Work of his quick Hand,
Short did thy Name so gaily printed stand;
Both Hearts consent new Letters to compose,
And give to thine the pleasing Name of ROSE.

   Now here the Bard by his own Choice was ty'd,
(Renouncing further Rambling) to a Bride;
Albion for *Pennsylvania* he resigns,
And now no more at *Sylvia*'s Loss repines:
Those youthful Wounds, that bled so freely there,
Maria heals, more faithful, and as fair.
By this a Cure for former Ills was wrought,
But future to prevent employ'd his Thought:
Fix'd as he was far from his native Home,
Here to reside, and ne'er again to roam,
He counsels with himself what Means to use,
To live with Credit, and what Baits refuse:
First, Clerk to our Provincial Senate rais'd,
He found, besides the Stipend, he was prais'd.

   And now a greater Task he takes in Hand,
Which none but true Projectors understand.
What Pity 'tis they seldom live to taste
The Fruits of those pure Spirits that they waste!
For Works so hard and tedious, was it known
A Poet e'er did Poetry disown?
Or for a distant Livelihood give o'er
Those instant Pleasures that he felt before?

Yet so *Aquila* did—The rustic Toil,
To make firm Landings on a muddy Soil,
Erect a Ferry over *Schuylkil*'s Stream,
A Benefit to Thousands—Death to him!
　　Describe, O Muse, tho' in rough Lines the Place
Hard for the Pencil or the Pen to trace.
　　A short Hour's Walk from *Delaware* it lies
Due West, and which the City-Bounds comprise:
The Buildings yet reach but a Quarter Part,
But yet enough to bring a thronging Mart.
　　This Ferry-Spot t' improve, *Aquila* gain'd,
By Merit and polite Address obtain'd.
The Grantors saw, could such a Work be done
As he with Vigour by himself begun,
Both Town and Country must Advantage find
Their Commerce and their Int'rest closer join'd.
　　Now he, disguis'd, assumes the lab'ring Swain,
And looks as when he lately plough'd the Main.
Great Spirits thus can brook an humble Shew,
And unobserv'd beneath their Burthens grow:
Anon from their Obscurities to rise,
As Friends from Travels feed our wond'ring Eyes.
　　But passing great Fatigues, Expence and Geer,
The Scene alone shall bear Description here.
　　A Furlong from a Hill of Short Ascent,
A level Plain has on the Stream Extent,
Not many Feet above the Waters rais'd,
But firm the Ground, and for its Aspect prais'd;
The ebbing Tide presents the Sight with Ooze,
And then some Pleasure of the View we lose;
But worst of all to bear, and sad to see,
At Winter's End the Floods from Frost break free;
The River's mighty Length, and downward Course,
Gives to the roaring Ice resistless Force;
Away the Causeways, Boats and Piles are borne,
And bord'ring Trees press'd down, or rudely torn,
The House endanger'd, and one Story drown'd,
And scarce a Means of Safety to be found:
And sometimes too, in Seasons warm and gay,
Great sudden Rains their Violence display,

Sweep off the Soil, and bring a different Kind,
And Marks of Ruin ever leave behind.
    But neither breaking-Frost, or flooding Rains,
Destroy Projectors Hopes of Praise and Gains:
Nor ev'ry Year, do these their Pow'r exert;
Or what bold *Charon* could live here alert?
    Now (leaving to the last, the pleasing Part
That terrifies not, but delights the Heart.)
Look on the Stream as it pacifick flows,
Which largely bending, more the Prospect shows,
A Summer-Sight, none lovelier can be seen,
And on the Shore a varied Growth of Green:
The Poplars high, erect their stately Heads,
The tawny Water-Beech more widely spreads;
The Linden strong in Breadth and Height, is there,
With Mulberry Leaves—And Trees with Golden Hair,
These, of a smaller Stem, like Filberds seem,
But flatter-leaf'd, and always love the Stream.
Here grows the jagged Birch; and Elm, whose Leaves
With Sides ill-pair'd the observing Eye perceives;
Yet nobly tall and great, it yields a Shade
In which cool Arbours might be fitly made;
Such is the Linden, such the Beech above,
Each in itself contains a little Grove.
Here Hickeries, and Oaks, and Ashes rise,
All diff'ring, but much more in Use than Size;
And Walnuts, with their yellow bitter Dyes.
The fragrant Sassafras enjoys a Place;
And Crabs, whose Thorns their scented Blossoms grace:
Parsimmons vex the Ground, so thick they shoot,
But pleasant is their late autumnal Fruit.
Tedious to name the shrubby Kinds below,
That mingled for Defence, in Clusters grow.
Two Plants remain, with Flow'rs unlike, both fair,
And both deserve th' ingenious Florist's Care:
The wild *Althea*, red, and white, and cream,
And scarlet *Cardinal*, with dazzling Gleam:
These tempt the Humming-Bird, whose misty Wings
Support him as he sucks the Flow'r and sings;
Low is his Voice, and simple Notes but few;

And oft' his little Body's lost to View:
When he the Creeper's Blossom tries to drain,
The Blossom will his Beak and Tail distain;
But his gay-colour'd Plumage forms a Show
As mix'd and vivid as the Sky's fair Bow.

So great Variety no Tract can boast,
Of like Dimensions, as this narrow Coast.
The Botanist might here find Exercise;
And every curious Man regale his Eyes.
The Grass shines glist'ning of a lively Green;
And Northward hence the Quarry-Hill is seen,
Whose Top of late with verd'rous Pines is crown'd;
With Forest-Trees of various Kinds around.

And often here, the Clearness of the Stream
And cover'd Gravel-Banks, invite to swim:
But Anglers most their frequent Visits pay,
To toss Old-Wives, and Chubs, and Perch to Day;
And sometimes find the tasteful Trout their Prey.
Others with greater Pains their big Hooks bait;
But for the nobler Bite they seldom wait;
The Time to know their good Success adjourn,
And fail not by next Morning to return;
Then, hook'd, the weighty Rock-Fish draw to Shore
By Lines to Bushes ty'd, or those they moor.

How far th' Adventurer sped, now Muse relate,
Tho' loth we are to tell his early Fate.
He rais'd a Dwelling for himself and Friends,
And now his envy'd Labour almost ends:
He saw his Causeways firm above the Waves,
And nigh the Deeps, unless a Storm outbraves;
When Gusts unusual, strong with Wind and Rain,
Swell'd *Schuylkil*'s Waters o'er the humble Plain,
Sent hurrying all the Moveables afloat,
And drove afar, the needful'st Thing, the Boat.

'Twas then, that wading thro' the chilling Flood,
A cold ill Humour mingled with his Blood,
Convuls'd the Nerves, and shook the strugg'ling Frame,
Till overpower'd by *Febris* raging Flame;
Which freezing Juices into boiling turn'd,
Scalded the Veins, and sore the Vitals burn'd.

Alternately the Frost and Fire took Place,
His Joints enfeebl'd, and made pale his Face.
Then soon Defluxions thro' the Bowels rush,
Nor stay for Nature's kind digesting Push.
Physicians try'd their Skill, his Head reliev'd,
And his lost Appetite to Strength retriev'd:
But all was Flatt'ry—So the Lamp decays,
And near its Exit gives an ardent Blaze.
    Behind he left his Widow bath'd in Tears,
A Grief supportless to her tender Years:
Against her Breast their first-born Child inclines,
Its Father's Joy, and with its Mother pines:
To Health restor'd, if Heav'n so gracious prove,
He will deserve a Grandsire's Care and Love.
    Ah dearest *Rose*, Farewell, that Face of thine,
That pleasing Tongue, that Hand so near to mine!
How oft' were we to trace the pebbly Strand?
How toss the Fishes twinkling to the Land?
How gladsom on thy little Ocean sail?
And how at once do these fair Prospects fail?
    Deceitful *Schuylkil* thou no more shalt be
A pleasant River to my Friends and me:
Whenever I thy fatal Stream survey
My Blood forgets its Course, my Heart gives Way.
Last Night I dream'd along thy Banks I stray'd,
Where sate an Angler in the brinky Shade,
And sighing deep, in Words like these he pray'd:
"Ye Heavenly Muses with our Griefs complore
His early Fate, who calls on you no more:
Or have ye rais'd him to your Bow'rs above,
In blissful Union of harmonious Love?
There taught him Songs, immortal as your State,
Beyond the Reach of Envy and of Fate?
Once were ye pleas'd your Poet to inspire,
And warm his Bosom with your sacred Fire;
Whence Odes, and Hymns, and happiest Verse did flow,
To gladden and instruct the World below;
But now your Darling from our Eyes is ta'en,
And desolate we seek his Life in vain.
Shall we not weep so great a Loss to bear?

And will not you the Lamentation share?
Oh lend your Aid, as Men your Pow'rs adore,
To mourn his Death, whose Pen invokes no more.
To you 'tis giv'n to favour mortal Race,
While evil Dæmons watch for Man's Disgrace.
Good Works in dark Oblivion they conceal;
In florid Numbers you such Works reveal:
And when the Springs of human Wisdom fail,
Divine Inflations from your Founts prevail.
Ah leave us not all comfortless to moan;
Give us at least to sing the Bard that's gone."
So pray'd he pensive on that flatt'ring Coast
Where late he liv'd—to us forever lost.
  Ye *Rose*'s Friends, that in *Britannia* dwell,
Who knew his Worth, and best the Loss can tell:
As I transmit such mournful News to you,
Do you the tuneful sad Account pursue.
And ye bright Youths, that meet at *Bendall*'s Board,
An Elegy his hov'ring Shade afford:
Had one of you deceas'd, and he surviv'd,
His Memory by him had been reliv'd.
So true a Friend he was, his Learning such,
That much he lov'd, and would commend as much.
Too great this Talk to be perform'd by one
So near the Pole, and far from *Helicon*.
While Virtues like *Aquila*'s, in smooth Phrase,
Should shine applauded thro' the Length of Days.

JAMES KIRKPATRICK

(1696–1770)

The Nonpareil

Arabia's Bird, it's spicy Tomb and Nest,
It's glossy Plumage, and effulgent Crest,
Which, Fancy only seeing, Fame relates,
Not *Asia* breeds, but *Claudian's* Muse creates.
And while the Charms his brilliant Lines impart
Glow with his Fire, and vary with his Art;
The sweetly animated Form appears
To scorn his Term of twice five hundred Years;
But young to latest Time shall Age beguile,
And boast the Conflagration for it's Pyle.

   Whether our Parents, yet unfall'n, beheld
The Nonpareil in *Eden's* blissful Field;
Or if descending Nature since has wrought
A gay Production like the Poet's Thought,
The flaming Suns of *Florida* disclose
A painted Warbler on the living Boughs,
Claudian might deign to sing—then Ah! how hard
The fairer Bird shou'd gain the feebler Bard.
Yet while his real Glories fix the Sight;
While his sweet Notes the trembling Ear delight,
This Wonder of the Grove shall soon despise
The Gloss of Fable and melodious Lyes;
Shall best evince his Fame, by being shown,
And shame ev'n *Roman* Colours with his own,
If sparkling TOWNSHEND's Smiles my Theme rejoice,
While my low Strain's ennobled by my Choice.

   From no fantastic Birth the Bird assumes
His easy Flow of Shape, and gorgeous Plumes:
No spicy Nest, conspiring with the Sun,
Calcines the Old, to kindle up the Young;
But sweetest Flames suggest the dear Increase,

366

And fruitful Love renews the dazling Race.
Lo! from the azure Egg's elliptic Cell,
Amaz'd, to gradual Life the Embryos swell;
Yet while the callow Offspring safely dream,
Rock'd in the little Nest's involving Frame;
Or, 'midst the Orange-tree's seclusest Bow'rs,
Inhale the Odours of transpiring Flow'rs,
No Streak, no Plume, instructs the keenest Sight,
To hope the future Blaze and Breaks of Light.
Twelve following Signs the sleeker Plumes declare
A plain, but neat Inhabitant of Air,
Scarcely distinct amidst the flitting Throng,
And faint his Notes essay a feeble Song:
But when anew the circling Seasons shine,
As *Sol* to us, or we to *Sol* incline,
The glossy Feathers, varying to the Sight,
Attempt to part the diff'rent Rays of Light;
Yet, incompleat to form the perfect Scene,
The wav'ring Colours fix in central Green;
While a faint Yellow in the Front prevails,
Swells o'er the Breast, and tapers as it fails.

Thrice vernal Suns the fetter'd Glebe unty;
Soft Show'rs distill, and softer Breezes sigh,
When Nature's matchless Arts the Plume dispose,
And lo! the Bird with dazling Splendor glows!
Tho' less his richest Tints may here surprise,
By slow Advance familiar to the Eyes.
His chearful Music quavers thro' the Groves,
And with his Bloom his Melody improves.
Now haply first he melts with tender Fires,
And feels a Love his Lustre soon inspires;
For ah! what flying Prude cou'd Rigour show
To such a Chorister! and such a Beau!
The dusky Citron, that his Breast o'erspread,
From the bright Orange flames to deeper Red;
Tho' various oft the feasted Eyes behold
The pure Vermilion gleam with Streaks of *Gold.

*Chiefly in his moulting Season.

Round his bright Optics scarlet Circles rise,
And, elegant, inclose his jetty Eyes.
His Head and Neck, so late of verdant Hue,
From a fresh Surface beam a dazling Blue;
Whence a fair Cape of brightest Olive springs,
And slides adown his green, his glossy Wings;
His glossy Wings with mild Effulgence shine,
Frequent divided by a crimson Line;
The Feathers of his Tail the Verdure share,
Spread, as he ploughs the flowing Surge of Air.

What other nameless Shades the Songster grace!
What ample Glories! in how small a Space!
The flaming Redbird stimulates the Sight,
Martial his Garb, and resolute his Fight:
Tho' shrill, yet sweet, his whistling Trumpet flows,
And thrilling Echos swell the liquid Close:
While deep his downy Vesture seems to drink
The Tinctures of the *Lychnis* and the Pink.
Fair as the Bluebird skims the golden Scene,
While glancing Suns exalt his Hue serene,
Beyond the Hyacinth his Azure shows,
Or like a bright *Convolvulus* he glows.
The pretty Greenbird oft the Eye deceives,
His vivid Lustre blended with the Leaves;
And various Larks their glist'ning Pinions ope,
Or boast their Breasts resembling *Heliotrope*:
But Nonpareil excells in ev'ry Die,
This flying Prism, this Tulip of the Sky.
Nature, with some Reserve, to others kind,
To diff'rent Graces some Defect has join'd:
The crested Peacock spreads, with Beauty vain,
The eye-form'd Glories of his burnish'd Train,
Which, richly fring'd, the Nerves of Vision chear,
'Till shrill his Screams discordant pierce the Ear.
Fair arch-neck'd Swans, with fabled Dirge so sweet,
Shade in the Waters their ungraceful Feet:
While Parrot prates indeed, a tawdry Show,
Witty and fine as many a modern Beau:
But crawls uncouth, like Beau with Ails distrest,

Strange to that easy Air that crowns the rest.
To thee, without a Fine, her Favours flow,
Thine is the Shape and Song, the Mien and Show,
Clear from Defect, nor with a Blemish foul,
And sweet Proportion finishes the whole.
Catesby the Term of painted Finch conferr'd,
And *Carolinians* call'd him Rainbow-bird:
'Till curious DART, attentive to display
The early Wing, and nurse the Infant Lay;
As in the tuneful Room, with chearful Ease,
She cull'd their Food, or conquer'd their Disease,
The Bird's unequall'd Charms consider'd well,
And nam'd him, what he is, the Nonpareil;
Who Light's all-mingled Dyes distinct displays,
Shines on our Suns, and beautifies our Days.

But when the Days contract, the Region cools,
And Winter in his Turn, tho' gently, rules;
Conscious perhaps his Lustre might decay,
Beneath the Languors of a feebler Ray;
To sleepless Soils in hotter Climes he speeds,
And, cherish'd by the Sun, with him recedes.

Mean Time the Object of his yearly Vows
Emits no Radiance worthy such a Spouse:
Sullen and mute amidst the lattic'd Frame,
She hates Confinement, like a modern Dame.
A languid Yellowness her Breast assumes,
A dimly varying Green her other Plumes.
Thus *Juno*'s Bird his Partner might contemn,
And thus the varnish'd Cock his homely Hen;
The Summer Drake in Beauty far prevails,
And thro' the speechless World the gen'rous Males,
Of such excelling Form, or brighter Hue,
Might tempt us to suspect their Females woo;
But sighing Men by sad Experience find,
The total Sex reveng'd in Woman-kind.

Thus the ambitious Bard prefum'd to treat
The fair Descendent of the Good and Great;

Unrivall'd thro' the aromatic Shade,
The peerless Bird attends a peerless Maid,
Chearful from Innocence, with Freedom wise,
Of gayly beaming Wit, and sparkling Eyes,
Neglecting little Pride for gen'rous Ease,
Her noble Lineage her remotest Praise.
Ye steady Gales quick waft him o'er the Main!
Ye timely Show'rs provide him cordial Rain!
Still be his Galley fleet, his Cargo rare,
Who guards the pretty Creature to the Fair.
Fed by her Hand, and perch'd beside her Breast,
The fragrant Bird shall scorn a spicy Nest,
A chearful Captive chant his happy Days,
Fond to divert, and passionate to please.
Then, while th'officious Warbler You regard,
Pardon, accomplish'd Nymph, a ruder Bard;
Whose rustic Lays, that wrong his glitt'ring Theme,
Rush worthless to thy Sight, and snatch thy Name.

SUSANNA WRIGHT

(1697–1784)

Anna Boylens Letter to King Henry the 8th

From anxious Thoughts of every future Ill
From these lone Walls which Death & Terror fill,
To you great Sir! a loyal Wife from hence,
Writes to assert her injur'd Innocence.
To you, who on a Throne supremely great
Look down & guide the partial Hand of Fate,
Who rais'd your Subject to a royal Bride,
To the imperial Purples gaudy Pride
And glowing Gems around these Temples ty'd,
You glowing Gems your dazling Rays rebate
And fade thou purple, at thy wearers Fate,
To grandeur rais'd, to Misery cast down
And mourn my sad acquaintance with a Crown,
My Life & Fame must join the Sacrifice
The last alone all peaceful Thought denies,
Renews My Anguish & oe'rflows my Eyes.
For Life & Crown with Patience I forego,
There's no such Charm in filling Thrones below
My Name alone, 'tis Anna Boylens Name
With whose low Station & unspotted Fame
All innocent & happy Days I'd seen,
This harmless Name exalted to a Queen
Is handed infamous to future Times
Loaded with Falshoods, blacken'd o'er with Crimes
Your infant Daughter her sad Part must bear,
And with her Mother's Heart her Suff'ring share,
Poor lovely Offspring of a wretched Bed
What are thy hapless Mother's Crimes that shed
This baleful Influence on thy harmless Head?
Thy Father sternly casts thee from his knee,
Whilst each licentious Tongue that rails at me
Points o'er thy opening Years with Infamy,
All Hopes on Earth with Patience I forego

But thee—poor Child left in a World of Woe
May thy dear Life in smoother Channels run
Secure from Ills thy Mother could not shun
All this is Pain, but nothing of Surprise
This Fall I look'd for from my fatal Rise,
From that unhappy Day, my Person pleas'd your Eyes.
Such slight Foundations never lasting prove
Where Fancy only lights the Torch of Love,
I see another Fair assume My Place
Who's in your Eyes what Anna Boylen was,
Beware triumphant Beauty how you shine
Those Charms, those Vows & ardours all were mine.
Look on me & beware for as you see,
What I am now, that you shall surely be,
But since my Death & nothing less will do
To bring you to the Bliss you have in View,
May bounteous Heaven the mighty Sin forgive
And not repay, the Injuries I receive,
Yet think, o! think what Crimes will wound your Soul,
When your dim Eyes in search of Slumber rowl,
When Lamps burn blue & guilty Tapers fade,
As by your bridal Bed I glide a ghastly Shade,
While sanguine Streams from purple Fountains drain
And all around the gay Apartment stain,
From conscious Guilt will these Illusions rise,
And haunt your Steps & fill your watching Eyes,
For ever raising Tumults in your Breast,
But fear me not for I shall be at Rest.
But at that Day when the last Trumpets Sound,
Shall reach the dead, & break their Sleep profound,
Bones long sepulchred burst their narrow Rooms
And hostile Kings rise trembling from their Tombs,
When nor your Heart, nor mine can lie conceal'd
But ev'ry secret Sin shall stand reveal'd,
Stand full reveal'd that God & Man may see,
How Fate has err'd, & you have injur'd me,
When, but alas all Arguments are vain
To bring your royal wand'ring Heart again
What Innocence unaided & oppress'd
Could do, I've done but who can Pow'r resist.

I've but one Wish but one Request to make
Let not my Friends be Sufferers for my sake,
All Innocent, humane, & kindly good
May their dear Lives be ransom'd by my Blood,
For ev'ry one the Price I'd freely pay
So many Times could Life be drain'd away,
By what I once have been by what you are,
Happy & great,—by all your Joy & Care;
By all things sacred, all your Love forgive,
My Friends their harmless Crimes & let them live,
    Lo! on her bended Knees thus asks your Wife,
On terms, you see, she would not ask her Life,
With this I cease, to trouble your Repose,
A few short anxious Hours the stormy Scene will close.

On the Benefit of Labour

Adam from Paradise expell'd,
Was drove into a Locust Field,
Whose rich luxuriant Soils produce,
Nor Fruit, nor Plant, for human Use,
'Till clear'd by Toil, & till'd by Art
With Plenty chear'd his drooping Heart.—
—'Twas thus Relief our Father found
When sent to cultivate the Ground.
For God who knew what Man could bear,
Form'd not his Sentence too severe,
A Life of indolent Repose
Had been the Plan of greater Woes;
While tir'd with Ease too dearly bought,
He past the tedious Hours in Thought,
For Labour only causes Rest,
And calms the Tumults in the Breast.—
    More Leisure to revolve his Fate
Had added Sorrow to the Weight,
Of his unhappy fall'n State.—
While Memory drest the gaudy Scenes
Of Edens never fading Greens,

Of Trees that bloom without Decay,
Where Storms were silent—Zephyrs play,
And Flowers their rifling sweets bestow,
On all the gentle Winds that blow,
With ev'ry Charm that crown'd the Place
Design'd for Adam & his Race:
Our Sire too weak for such a Stroke,
Had sunk beneath the heavy Yoke,
Had on his Breast the Sentence try'd,
Let out his tortur'd Soul & dy'd.—
But kindly to suspend his Doom
For sake of Ages yet to come,
A Life of Action was decreed,
And Labour must produce him Bread;
His Hands the artful Web prepare
To screen him from inclement Air,
And equal Pains a Tent provide
To turn the beating Storm aside.—
—These necessary Toils & Cares
For present Wants & future Tears,
Joyn'd to the Curse, a Blessing grow,
And lessen or divert our Woe.
                                    —*Octobr. 1728 Ext.*

On the Death of a little Girl

—1735—

The little Bird at break of Day,
    That charm'd us with its Song,
And fondly hopp'd from Spray to Spray,
    The Musick to prolong,
As Ev'ning came, ill fated fell,
    Struck by a Hand unseen,
Resign'd that Breath which pleas'd so well
    And flutter'd on the Green.
The Lambs that wont to bleat & play,
    And bask in Sunshine Air,

That danc'd the fleeting Hours away,
    And knew not Want or Care,
When Night her sable Curtain spread,
    Fell to the Wolf a Prey,
And here & there dispers'd & dead,
    The scatter'd Fragments lay.
The Blossoms which to vernal Air,
    Their fragrant Leaves unfold,
And deck the spreading Branches fair
    With Purple, White & Gold.
Diffuse their Sweets & Charm the Eye,
    And promise future Store,
Nipp'd by a Frost untimely dye,
    And shed Perfumes no more.—
'Twas thus the Poppet ceas'd to breathe,
    The small Machine stood still,
The little Lungs no longer heave
    Or Motion follows Will.
No more that flattering Voice we hear,
    Soft as the Linets Song,
Each idle Hour to sooth & chear,
    Which slowly rolls along.
That sprightly Action's past & gone,
    With all its tempting Play,
Sprightly as Lambs that tread the Lawn
    Along a Summers Day.
The Dawn of Reason we admir'd,
    As op'ning Blossoms fair,
Now to the silent Grave retir'd,
    Its Organs moulder there.
Flowers on thy Breast & round thy Head,
    With thee their Sweets resign,
Nipp'd from their tender Stalks & dead,
    Their Fate resembles thine.
Just as their Charms allure the Eye,
    And fragrant Leaves unfold,
Clos'd in eternal Night they lie,
    To mix with common Mould.

Thy harmless Soul releas'd from Earth,
    A Cherub sings above,
Immortal in a second Birth,
    By thy Redeemer's Love.

My own Birth Day

—August 4th 1761

Few & evil have the Days of the Years of my Life been.—

Were few & Evil stil'd the Patriarchs Days,
    Extended to a Length of Years unknown
In this luxurious Age whose swift Decays,
    Allow to few so many as my own.
And what are they?—a Vision all the past,
    A Bubble on the Waters shining Face,
What yet remain 'till the first transient Blast
    Shall leave no more Remembrance of their Place.
Still few & evil, as the Days of old,
Are those allotted to the Race of Man,
    And three score Years in sounding Numbers told,
Where's the Amount?—a Shadow & a Span.—
    Look back through this long Tide of rolling Years
Since early Reason gave Reflection Birth,
    Recall each sad Occasion of thy Tears,
Then say can Happiness be found on Earth?
    Pass former Strokes—the recent only name!
A Brother whom no healing Art could save,
    In Life's full Prime unnerv'd his manly Frame
From wasting Pains took Refuge in the Grave.—
    A Sister who long causeless Anguish knew,
A tender Parent & a patient Wife,
    Calmly she bore the bitter Lot she drew,
And clos'd her Sorrows with her Close of Life.
    A darling Child, all lovely, all admir'd,
Snatch'd from our Arms in Youths engaging Bloom
    A Lazur turn'd e'er his short Date expir'd,
And laid a piteous Object in the Tomb.

Your Memory from my Breast shall never stray
Should years to Patriarchal Age extend,
   Thro' Glooms of Night, thro' social Hours of Day
The starting Tear stands ready to descend.—
But tho' I mourn, not without Hope I mourn,
   Dear kindred Shades! tho' all unknown your Place
Tho' to these Eyes you never must return,
   You're safe in the Infinitude of Space.—
One all disposing God who gave you Birth,
   That Life sustain'd which his good Pleasure gave,
Then cut you off from ev'ry Claim on Earth,
   Is the same guardian God beyond the Grave.
Tho' by impenetrable Darkness veil'd,
   Your separate State lies hid from mortal Sight,
The Saviour, Friend of Man, Messiah hail'd,
   Brought Life & Immortality to Light.
Rest then my Soul—in these Appointments rest,
   And down the Steep of Age pursue thy Way,
With humble Hope, & Faith unfailing blest,
   The mortal shall surpass the natal Day.

To Eliza Norris—at Fairhill

Since Adam, by our first fair Mother won
To share her fate, to taste, & be undone,
And that great law, whence no appeal must lie,
Pronounc'd a doom, that he should rule & die,
The partial race, rejoicing to fulfill
This pleasing dictate of almighty will
(With no superior virtue in their mind),
Assert their right to govern womankind.
But womankind call reason to their aid,
And question when or where that law was made,
That law divine (a plausible pretence)
Oft urg'd with none, & oft with little sense,
From wisdom's source no origin could draw,
That form'd the man to keep the sex in awe;
Say Reason governs all the mighty frame,

And Reason rules in every one the same,
No right has man his equal to control,
Since, all agree, there is no sex in soul;
Weak woman, thus in agreement grown strong,
Shakes off the yoke her parents wore too long;
But he, who arguments in vain had tried,
Hopes still for conquest from the yielding side,
Soft soothing flattery & persuasion tries,
And by a feign'd submission seeks to rise,
Steals, unperceiv'd, to the unguarded heart,
    And there reigns tyrant—

But you, whom no seducing tales can gain
To yield obedience, or to wear the chain,
But set a queen, & in your freedom reign
O'er your own thoughts, of your own heart secure,
You see what joys each erring sex allure,
Look round the most intelligent—how few
But passions sway, or childish joys pursue;
Then bless that choice which led your bloom of youth
From forms & shadows to enlight'ning truth,
Best found when leisure & retirement reign,
Far from the proud, the busy & the vain,
Where rural views soft gentle joys impart,
Enlarge the thought, & elevate the heart,
Each changing scene adorns gay Nature's face,
Ev'n winter wants not its peculiar grace,
Hoar frosts & dews, & pale & summer suns,
Paint each revolving season as it runs,
The showery bow delights your wond'ring eyes,
Its spacious arch, & variegated dyes,
You watch the transient colours as they fade,
Till, by degrees, they settle into shade,
Then calm reflect, so regular & fine,
Now seen no more, a fate will soon be mine,
When life's warm stream, chill'd by death's fey hand,
Within these veins a frozen current stands;
Tho' conscious of desert superior far,
Till then, my friend, the righteous claim forbear—
Indulge man in his darling vice of sway,

He only rules those who of choice obey;
When strip'd of power, & plac'd in equal light,
Angels shall judge who had the better right,
All you can do is but to let him see
That woman still shall sure his equal be,
By your example shake his ancient law,
And shine yourself, the finish'd piece you draw.

RICHARD LEWIS

(c. 1699–1734)

To Mr. Samuel Hastings, (Ship-wright of Philadelphia) on his launching the Maryland-Merchant, a large Ship built by him at Annapolis

Long since I bad the pleasing Muse adieu,
More profitable Studies to pursue;
But smit with Love of Art, I now again
Invoke the Goddess to inspire my Strain.
    Then do not *Hastings*, scorn these lowly Lays,
Tho' mean, design'd to celebrate thy Praise!
Accept this Off'ring of a grateful Heart!
And let Good-will excuse my want of Art.

    Thou wond'rous Architect! whose Palaces
Bear their Inhabitants o'er deepest Seas,
Where, while a longsome Voyage they pursue,
Surprizing Scenes of Wonder greet their View;
Attend! while I the slow Degrees disclose,
By which the Ship-wright to thy Skill arose.

    When *Adam*'s Offspring, in their first Abode
On the fam'd Borders of *Euphrates'* Flood,
Resolv'd t'explore the River's distant Side,
The vent'rous Youth their Floats unweildly guide,
And on these Ships they cross'd its foaming Tide.
Such cumb'rous Vessels, some nice Artists see
With Scorn, and of its Bark disrobe the Tree;
Whose fibrous Roots afford the rugged Twine,
With which their slight Canooe they closely join:
Pleas'd with this great Improvement of their Art,
To visit Shores more distant they depart;
But soon the Vessel strikes against a Rock,
And splits, unable to sustain the Shock:
The swimming Passengers the Shore regain,
Nor dare to venture on the liquid Plain;

380

'Till the devouring Fire affords them Aid,
And by its Force huge Trees are hollow made,
In which the watry Kingdom they pervade.

Here unimprov'd thy Art for Ages stood,
'Till the Supreme pour'd out his dreadful Flood,
T'entomb Mankind within one gen'ral Grave,
Except the Few his Mercy deign'd to save:
Then did thy God to bless thy Piety,
The Ship-wrights Art, O *Noah!* teach to Thee,
Thy wond'rous Ark, built by divine Command,
Rose slowly underneath thy forming Hand:
Finish'd at Length, the mighty Work appears,
The Labour of an Hundred rolling Years.
Within its Womb, the universal Race
Of Insects, Beasts, Birds, Men, obtain a Place,
Who in due Time should meet a second Birth,
And with their Offspring fill the future Earth:
The Rest were by the Deluge swept away,
While Angels o'er thy Ark their Wings display,
Their guiding Hands that Ship with Pleasure steer,
Which safely does its precious Cargo bear
O'er highest Hills in wild Disorder hurl'd,
On Seas which overwhelm'd the shatter'd World.

'Till God's Command fulfill'd, the Floods decay,
And lofty *Ararat* beholds the Day;
Upon whose cloudy Top the Vessel moors,
Which to instruct the Ship-wright Heav'n secures.
This the *Phœnicians* first with Wonder view;
And careful from its Form their Models drew,
Their heavy Ships around the neighb'ring Shores,
Creep slowly by the Help of num'rous Oars;
'Till *Dædalus*, Inventor of the Sails,
In Canvas Prisons bound the flying Gales:
And taught his Vessel by their Aid to fly
Swift as the Birds that range the spacious Sky:
These were the Wings from whence he gain'd his Fame,
These to remotest Climes convey'd his Name.

When proud *Sesostris* with resistless Sway
Made half the groaning World his Laws obey,
Brave *Jason*, Leader of the glorious Host,
Who greatly strove to gain their Freedom lost,
In the fam'd *Argo* did the Seas explore,
(A golden Ram, upon her Stern she bore,)
And leagu'd with num'rous Kings to break th' *Ægyptian*
     Pow'r.
Sesostris Doom the united Kings decree,
And soon regain'd their native Liberty.

Thus did a Ship preserve the Race of Man,
And by a Ship the *Greeks* their Freedom gain:
To Ships, we owe our Knowledge, and our Trade,
By them defend our own, and other Realms invade.
Without their Aid, *America* had been
To all, except its Natives, now unseen:
Her Trees whose stately Tops to Heaven aspire,
Had fall'n a Prey to Worms, or fed the Fire,
Which now with Pleasure shall forsake their Woods,
And fly to distant Lands o're deepest Floods,
From hence shall bear the Product of these Shores,
And make the Growth of foreign Climates ours:
In Ships of them compos'd, *Barbadoes* yields
To us the Product of her fertile Fields.
Iberias golden Fruit shall zest our Bowls,
And *Florence* send her Wine to chear our Souls.
To form our Cloaths shall *Britain* shear her Sheep,
And *Indian* Curtains screen us when we sleep.
What Nature has to *Maryland* deny'd,
She might by Ships from all the World provide.

Thus have I strove, my Friend, to sing the Praise
Of thy nice Art, which claims more lofty Lays.
In Thought thy finish'd Vessel oft I view'd
As on her growing Bulk I gazing stood;
But she out does the Image of my Mind,
Unthought of Beauties in her Form I find.
Of num'rous Hands the Toil of two long Years,
Whose Sickness oft has fill'd thy Heart with Cares:

How many Obstacles have clogg'd her Way,
But now thy Work shall find no more Delay;
For see 'tis done—Lo there the Fabrick stands
That shall convey thy Fame to distant Lands!
Where e'er urg'd on by winged Winds she flies,
To *Southern* Shores, or under *Northern* Skies;
Where grateful Odours flow from spicy Groves,
Or where around the Pole *Arcturus* moves:
Where e'er her prosp'rous Course this Ship shall bend;
So far, O *Hastings*, shall thy Fame extend!

Nor thou disdain to listen to my Song,
While pleas'd my Numbers I to thee prolong;
While I to thee some sacred Truths reveal,
Which from the Crowd profane the Gods conceal.

Not long ago thy Labours to survey,
To thy vast Building I pursu'd my Way;
Full orb'd the Moon roll'd o'er the æthereal Plain,
And Silence on the Earth began his Reign:
Deep-musing on her lofty Deck I stood,
And view'd, well-pleas'd, the gently moving Flood;
Whose smiling Surface the Resemblance bore
Of those tall Trees that grace the sandy Shore:
The floating Forest stretch'd its dusky Shade,
And nodding to thy Ship its Homage paid,
When to my ravish'd Eyes with vast Delight
The Muse appear'd,—quickly she clear'd my Sight,
And gave me to behold amidst the Floods,
Where lately I beheld the waving Woods,
A wond'rous Show;—A Triton first appears,
His sounding Shell alarm'd my list'ning Ears.
I am, he cries, sent to prepare the Way
For *Chesapeake*, great Ruler of the Bay:
He comes!—he comes!—ye Deities ascend
From all your Grotts!—Your Father's Words attend!

Fair *Severn* first appear'd to grace his Court,
Patuxent next did to her King resort;
Chester whose Stream o'er ouzy Islands strays;

Patapsco crown'd with Yews his Homage pays;
And *Sassafras*, whose Banks with graceful Pride
Behold their pleasing Prospects in his Tide:
Last *Susquahana*, vext to meet Delay,
O'er rugged Rocks rolls rapid on his Way,
Foaming with hast his Rule to obey.

The Father of the Floods began to speak,
And all attend the Words of *Chesapeake*.

Behold that stately Pile which greets our Eyes!
And shall in distant Lands with sweet Surprize
Be seen, while all her graceful Form admire,
And eager for her Builder's Name enquire.
How boldly regular she Charms the Sight!
Her Strength, her Symmetry, affords Delight;
What just Proportion shines in every Part!
A lovely Master-piece of curious Art!
How sweet those horizontal Lines appear!
From Keel to Wale how faultless and how fair;
Her grosser Part takes the eliptick Form,
Proof to the surging Sea and howling Storm;
Her Sweep how easy, and her lively Sheer!
Unbalasted her Course she safe shall steer!
Oh happy *Severn*, whose soft smiling Wave
The lovely Burden shortly shall receive!
But happier thou *Patuxent*, by whose Shores
To take her Freight the finish'd Vessel moors.
Her Freight, which shall be sent without Delay,
For all you Rivers must your Tribute pay:
Proud that the Produce of your Shores can be
Within her Bosom born upon the Sea.
My self shall wait on *Neptune*, and engage
Old *Ocean*'s God his Tempests to asswage,
To guide her safely thro' his vast Domain,
That she her Port in safety may attain.
And thou fair Moon, who rolling now on high
Dost with thy radiant Beams illume the Sky!
Thou who approaching near to some fix'd Star

Shalt to Mankind the *Longitude* declare,
Let him who first this stately Ship design'd,
In Recompence that long-sought Secret find;
So shall the grateful World proclaim his Name;
So shall my Bay exceed all Floods in Fame:
Since my fair Streams that happy Region lave,
Where the Inventor did his Birth receive.

But, Oh ye Floods, remark my sage Advice!
And bid the Dwellers on your Banks be wise;
Warn them—Oh warn them e're it be too late,
To save the Remnants of their small Estate!
Tell them, the Factors whom they now employ
In *Britain*'s Isle their Interest betray;
And when their Makers Ruin they have wrought,
They load each other with their mutual Fault:
In private, some false Brother they accuse,
In publick join to clear him from th' Abuse.
First moved by Envy, they his Faults detect,
Then basely sway'd by Fear, themselves they contradict.
To ruin *Maryland* they now unite
In montrous Leagues of amicable Spight.

Yet if my sons have Courage left to thrive,
If they their sinking Staple would revive;
Let strictest Bonds some Merchant's Faith secure,
Whom from their native Land they may procure;
For few, alas! are found to keep their Trust,
Unless their Int'rest binds them to be Just:
By him assisted, might they hope for Aid,
Nor need he learn the Mysteries of Trade:
An honest, plain Account of Sales to give,
And for his Care just Profits to receive.
But if this fails (because to my Regret
I see my Country deeply sunk in Debt)
Let such who have the Fortune to be Free,
Refuse to send their Crops across the Sea;
Let them in other Works employ their Hands,
Nor with Tobacco vex their fertil Lands;

'Till they've enjoy'd a Rest of one short Year,
Then Trade shall in a richer Dress appear,
And with a higher Price reward the Planter's Care.

Here ceas'd the watry Pow'r—his Train descend,
And the bright Vision vanish'd, from
                                        Your Friend

A Journey from Patapsco to Annapolis

Me vero primum dulces ante omnia Musæ
Quarum sacra fero ingenti percussus amore,
Accipiant; Cœliq; vias et Sydera *monstrent;—*
Sin has ne possim Naturæ accedere partis,
Frigidus obstiterit circum præcordia Sanguis
Rura *mihi, et* rigui *placeant in Vallibus* Amnes,
Flumina *amem,* Sylvasq; *inglorius.*
                                        —Virg. *Geor.* 2.

At length the wintry horrors disappear,
And APRIL views with smiles the infant year;
The grateful earth from frosty chains unbound,
Pours out its vernal treasures all around,
Her face bedeckt with grass, with leaves the trees are crown'd.
In this soft season, e'er the dawn of day,
I mount my horse, and lonely take my way,
From woody hills that shade Patapsko's head,
(In whose deep vales he makes his stony bed,
From whence he rushes with resistless force,
Tho' huge rough rocks retard his rapid course,)
Down to Annapolis, on that smooth stream
Which took from fair Anne-Arundel its name.
   And now the star that ushers in the day,
Begins to pale her ineffectual ray.
The moon with blunted horns now shines less bright,
Her fading face eclips'd with growing light;
The fleecy clouds with streaky lustre glow,
And day quits heav'n to view the earth below;
O'er yon tall trees the sun shews half his face,

And fires their floating foliage with his rays;
Now sheds aslant on earth his lightsome beams,
That trembling shine in many-colour'd streams:
Slow-rising from the marsh, the mist recedes,
The trees, emerging, rear their dewy heads;
Their dewy heads the sun with pleasure views,
And brightens into pearls the pendent dews.
    The beasts uprising quit their leafy beds,
And to the chearful sun erect their heads;
All joyful rise, except the filthy swine,
On obscene litter stretch'd they snore supine:
In vain the day awakes, sleep seals their eyes,
Till hunger breaks the bond and bids them rise.
    And now the sun with more exalted ray,
From cloudless skies distributes riper day;
Thro' sylvan scenes my journey I pursue,
Ten thousand beauties rising to my view;
Which kindle in my breast poetick flame,
And bid me my CREATOR's praise proclaim;
Tho' my low verse ill suits the noble theme.
    Here various flourets grace the teeming plains,
Adorn'd by nature's hand with beauteous stains;
First-born of spring here the pacone appears,
Whose golden root a silver blossom rears.
In spreading tufts see there the crowfoot blue,
On whose green leaves still shines a globous dew;
Behold the cinque-foil with its dazling dye
Of flaming yellow wounds the tender eye:
But there, enclos'd, the grassy wheat is seen,
To heal the aking sight with chearful green.
    Safe in yon cottage dwells the monarch-swain,
His subject-flocks, close-grazing, hide the plain;
For him they live,—and die t'uphold his reign.
Viands unbought his well till'd lands afford,
And smiling plenty waits upon his board;
Health shines with sprightly beams around his head,
And sleep with downy wings o'ershades his bed;
His sons robust his daily labours share,
Patient of toil, companions of his care;
And all their toils with sweet success are crown'd,

In graceful ranks these trees adorn the ground,
The peach, the plum, the apple here are found;
Delicious fruits—! which from their kernels rise,
So fruitful is the soil—so mild the skies.
The lowly quince yon sloping hill o'ershades;
Here lofty cherry-trees erect their heads;
High in the air each spiry summit waves,
Whose blooms thick-springing yield no space for leaves.
Evolving odours fill the ambient air,
The birds delighted to the grove repair:
On every tree behold a tuneful throng,
The vocal vallies echo to their song.
    But what is he, who perch'd above the rest
Pours out such various music from his breast!
His breast, whose plumes a chearful white display,
His quiv'ring wings are drest in sober grey.
Sure all the muses this their bird inspire!
And he, alone, is equal to the quire
Of warbling songsters who around him play,
While echo like he answers every lay.
The chirping lark now sings with sprightly note,
Responsive to her strain he shapes his throat:
Now the poor widow'd turtle wails her mate,
While in soft sounds he cooes to mourn his fate.
Oh sweet musician, thou dost far excel
The soothing song of pleasing Philomel!
Sweet is her song, but in few notes confin'd;
But thine, thou mimic of the feath'ry kind,
Runs thro' all notes!—thou only know'st them all,
At once the copy,—and the original.
    My ear thus charm'd, mine eye with pleasure sees,
Hov'ring about the flow'rs the industrious bees;
Like them in size the humming-bird I view,
Like them he sucks his food the hony-dew,
With nimble tongue, and beak of jetty hue,
He takes with rapid whirl his noisy flight,
His gemmy plumage strikes the gazers sight;
And as he moves his ever-flutt'ring wings,
Ten thousand colours he around him flings:
Now I behold the emrald's vivid green,

Now scarlet, now a purple dye is seen;
In brightest blue his breast he now arrays,
Then strait his plumes emit a golden blaze.
Thus whirring round he flies, and varying still,
He mocks the poet's and the painter's skill;
Who may forever strive with fruitless pains,
To catch and fix those beauteous changeful stains;
While scarlet now, and now the purple shines,
And gold to blue its transient gloss resigns;
Each quits, and quickly each resumes its place,
And ever varying dyes each other chase.
Smallest of Birds, what beauties shine in thee!
A living rainbow on thy breast I see.

   O had that *bard, in whose heart-pleasing lines
The phœnix in a blaze of glory shines,
Beheld those wonders which are shewn in thee,
That bird had lost its immortality!
Thou in his verse hadst stretch'd thy flutt'ring wing
Above all other birds,—their beauteous king.

   But now th' enclos'd plantation I forsake,
And onwards thro' the woods my journey take;
The level road the longsom way beguiles,
A blooming wilderness around me smiles:
Here hardy oak, there fragrant hick'ry grows,
Their bursting buds the tender leaves disclose;
The tender leaves in downy robes appear,
Trembling they seem to move with cautious fear,
Yet new to life, and strangers to the air.
Here stately pines unite their whisp'ring heads,
And with a solemn gloom embrown the glades.
See there a green savana opens wide,
Thro' which smooth streams in wanton mazes glide;
Thick-branching shrubs o'er-hang the silver streams
Which scarcely deign t' admit the solar beams.

   While with delight on this soft scene I gaze,
The cattle upward look, and cease to graze,
But into covert run thro' various ways.
And now the clouds in black assemblage rise,
And dreary darkness overspreads the skies,

  *Claudian.

Thro' which the sun strives to transmit his beams,
But sheds his sickly light in stragling streams.
Hush'd is the musick of the woodland quire,
Foreknowing of the storm, the birds retire
For shelter, and forsake the shrubby plains,
And a dumb horror thro' the forest reigns:
In that lone house which opens wide its door,
Safe—may I tarry till the storm is o'er.

Hark how the thunder rolls with solemn sound!
And see the forceful lightning darts a wound
On yon tall oak—! behold its top laid bare!
Its body rent, and scatter'd thro' the air,
The splinters fly!—now—now the winds arise,
From different quarters of the lowring skies;
Forth issuing fierce, the west and south engage,
The waving forest bends beneath their rage:
But where the winding valley checks their course,
They roar and ravage with redoubled force;
With circling sweep in dreadful whirlwinds move,
And from its roots tear up the gloomy grove;
Down-rushing fall the trees, and beat the ground,
In fragments fly the shatter'd limbs around;
Tremble the underwoods, the vales resound.

Follows with patt'ring noise the icy hail,
And rain fast falling floods the lowly vale.
Again the thunders roll, the lightnings fly,
And as they first disturb'd, now clear the sky;
For lo, the gust decreases by degrees,
The dying winds but sob amidst the trees;
With pleasing softness falls the silver rain,
Thro' which at first faint-gleaming o'er the plain,
The orb of light scarce darts a watry ray
To gild the drops that fall from ev'ry spray;
But soon the dusky Vapours are dispel'd,
And thro' the mist that late his face conceal'd,
Bursts the broad sun, triumphant in a blaze
Too keen for sight—yon cloud refracts his rays,
The mingling beams compose the ethereal bow,
How sweet, how soft its melting colours glow!
Gaily they shine, by heav'nly pencils laid,

Yet vanish swift;—how soon does beauty fade!
 The storm is past, my journey I renew,
And a new scene of pleasures greets my view:
Wash'd by the copious rain the gummy pine
Does chearful with unsully'd verdure shine;
The dogwood flowers assume a snowy white,
The maple blushing gratifies the sight:
The sassafras unfolds its fragrant bloom,
The vine affords an exquisite perfume;
These grateful scents wide-wafting the air,
The smelling sense with balmy odours cheer.
And now the birds sweet singing stretch their throats,
And in one choir unite their various notes,
Nor yet unpleasing is the turtles voice,
Tho' he complains while other birds rejoyce.
 These vernal joys, all restless thoughts controul,
And gently soothing calm the troubled soul.
 While such delights my senses entertain,
I scarce perceive that I have left the plain,
'Till now the summit of a mount I gain;
Low at whose sandy base the river glides,
Slow-rolling near their height his languid tides;
Shade above shade, the trees in rising ranks,
Cloath with eternal green his steepy banks:
The flood, well-pleas'd, reflects their verdant gleam
From the smooth mirror of his limpid stream.
 But see the hawk, who with acute survey,
Towring in air predestinates his prey
Amid the floods!—down-dropping from on high,
He strikes the fish, and bears him thro' the sky.
The stream disturb'd, no longer shews the scene
That lately stain'd its silver waves with green;
In spreading circles roll the troubled floods,
And to the shores bear off the pictur'd woods.
 Now looking round I view the outstretch'd land,
O'er which the sight exerts a wide command;
The fertile vallies, and the naked hills,
The cattle feeding near the chrystal rills;
The lawns wide op'ning to the sunny ray,
And mazy thickets that exclude the day.

A-while the eye is pleas'd these scenes to trace,
Then hurrying o'er the intermediate space,
Far-distant mountains drest in blue appear,
And all their woods are lost in empty air.

The sun near setting now arrays his head
In milder beams and lengthens ev'ry shade,
The rising clouds usurping on the day
A bright variety of dyes display;
About the wide horizon swift they fly,
And chase a change of colours round the sky:
And now I view but half the flaming sphere,
Now one faint glimmer shoots along the air,
And all his golden glories disappear.

Onwards the ev'ning moves in habit grey,
And for her sister night prepares the way.
The plumy people seek their secret nests,
To rest repair the ruminating beasts.
Now deepning shades confess th'approach of night,
Imperfect images elude the sight:
From earthly objects I remove mine eye,
And view with look erect the vaulted sky;
Where dimly-shining now the stars appear,
At first thin-scatt'ring thro' the misty air;
'Till night confirm'd, her jetty throne ascends,
On her the moon in clouded state attends,
But soon unveil'd her lovely face is seen
And stars unnumber'd wait around their queen;
Rang'd by their MAKER's hand in just array,
They march majestick thro' th' ethereal way.

Are these bright luminaries hung on high
Only to please with twinkling rays our eye?
Or may we rather count each star a sun,
Round which full peopled worlds their courses run?
Orb above orb harmoniously they steer
Their various voyages thro' seas of air.

Snatch me some angel to those high abodes,
The seats perhaps of saints and demigods;
Where such as bravely scorn'd the galling yoke
Of vulgar error, and her fetters broke;
Where patriots who to fix the publick good,

In fields of battle sacrific'd their blood;
Where pious priests who charity proclaim'd,
And poets whom a virtuous muse enflam'd;
Philosophers who strove to mend our hearts,
And such as polish'd life with useful arts,
Obtain a place; when by the hand of death
Touch'd, they retire from this poor speck of earth;
Their spirits freed from bodily alloy
Perceive a fore-taste of that endless joy,
Which from eternity hath been prepar'd,
To crown their labours with a vast reward.
While to these orbs my wandring thoughts aspire,
A falling meteor shoots his lambent fire;
Thrown from the heav'nly space he seeks the earth,
From whence he first deriv'd his humble birth.
    The mind advis'd by this instructive sight,
Descending sudden from th' aerial height,
Obliges me to view a different scene,
Of more importance to myself, tho' mean.
These distant objects I no more pursue,
But turning inward my reflective view,
My working fancy helps me to survey,
In the just picture of this April day,
My life o'erpast,—a course of thirty years
Blest with few joys, perplex'd with num'rous cares.
    In the dim twilight of our infancy,
Scarce can the eye surrounding objects see;
Then thoughtless childhood leads us pleas'd and gay,
In life's fair morning thro' a flowry way:
The youth in schools, inquisitive of good,
Science pursues thro' learning's mazy wood;
Whose lofty trees, he, to his grief perceives,
Are often bare of fruit, and only fill'd with leaves:
Thro' lonely wilds his tedious journey lies,
At last a brighter prospect cheers his eyes;
Now the gay fields of poetry he views,
And joyous, listens to the tuneful muse;
Now history affords him vast delight,
And opens lovely landschapes to his sight;
But ah too soon this scene of pleasure flies!

And o'er his head tempestuous troubles rise:
He hears the thunders roll, he feels the rains,
Before a friendly shelter he obtains;
And thence beholds with grief the furious storm,
The noon-tide beauties of his life deform:
He views the painted bow in distant skies;
Hence, in his heart some gleams of comfort rise:
He hopes the gust has almost spent its force,
And that he safely may pursue his course.
  Thus far my life does with the day agree,
Oh may its coming stage from storms be free!
While passing thro' the worlds most private way,
With pleasure I my MAKER's works survey;
Within my heart let peace a dwelling find,
Let my goodwill extend to all mankind:
Freed from necessity, and blest with health;
Give me content, let others toil for wealth:
In busy scenes of life let me exert
A careful hand, and wear an honest heart;
And suffer me my leisure hours to spend,
With chosen books, or a well natur'd friend.
Thus journeying on, as I advance in age,
May I look back with pleasure on my stage;
And as the setting sun withdrew his light
To rise on other worlds serene and bright,
Chearful may I resign my vital breath,
Nor anxious tremble at th' approach of death;
Which shall (I hope) but strip me of my clay,
And to a better world my soul convey.
  Thus musing I my silent moments spend,
'Till to the river's margin I descend,
From whence I may discern my journey's end:
Annapolis adorns its further shore,
To which the boat attends to bring me o'er.
And now the moving boat the floods divides,
While the stars tremble on the circling tides;
Pleas'd with the sight again I raise mine eye,
To the bright glories of the azure sky;
And fill'd with holy horror thus I cry.
  While I behold these wonders of thy hand;

The moon and stars that move at thy command,
Obedient thro' their circuit of the sky,
ALMIGHTY LORD! will thy dread majesty
Vouchsafe to view the wretched son of man,
Thy creature, who but yesterday began,
Thro' animated clay to draw his breath,
To-morrow doom'd a prey to ruthless death!
    TREMENDOUS GOD! may I not justly fear
That I, unworthy object of thy care,
Into this world from thy bright presence tost,
Am in the immensity of nature lost!
And that my notions of the world above,
Are but creations of my own self-love;
To feed my coward heart, afraid to die,
With fancied feasts of immortality!
    These thoughts, which thy amazing works suggest,
Oh glorious FATHER, rack my troubled breast.
    Yet, GRACIOUS GOD, reflecting that my frame
From thee deriv'd its animating flame;
And that whate'er I am, however mean,
By thy command I entred on this scene
Of life,—thy wretched creature of a day,
Condemn'd to travel thro' a tiresome way;
Upon whose banks, (perhaps to cheer my toil)
I see thin verdures rise, and daisies smile:
Poor comforts these, my pains t' alleviate;
While on my head tempestuous troubles beat.
And must I, when I quit this earthly scene,
Sink total into death, and never rise again!
    No sure,—these thoughts which in my bosome roll,
Must issue from a never-dying soul;
These active thoughts that penetrate the sky,
Excursive into dark futurity;
Which hope eternal happiness to gain,
Could never be bestow'd on man in vain.
    To thee, Oh FATHER, fill'd with fervent zeal,
And sunk in humble silence I appeal;
Take me my great CREATOR to thy care,
And gracious listen to my ardent prayer!
    SUPREME OF BEINGS, omnipresent power,

My great preserver from my natal-hour,
Fountain of wisdom, boundless Deity,
OMNISCIENT GOD, my wants are known to thee,
With mercy look on mine infirmity!
Whatever state thou shalt for me ordain,
Whether my lot in life be joy or pain;
Patient let me sustain thy wise decree,
And learn to know myself, and honour thee.

Food for Criticks

Hic sunt gelidi fontes, hic mollia prata, Lycori
Hic nemus, hic tecum toto consumerer ævo.

Virg.

Of ancient streams presume no more to tell,
The fam'd castalian or pierian well;
SKUYLKIL superior, must those springs confess,
As *Pensilvania* yields to *Rome* or *Greece*.
More limpid water can no fountain show,
A fairer bottom or a smoother brow.
A painted world its peaceful gleam contains
The heav'nly arch, the bord'ring groves and plains:
Here in mock silver Cynthia seems to roll,
And trusty pointers watch the frozen pole.
Here sages might observe the wandring stars,
And rudest swains commence astrologers.
Along the brink the lonely plover stalks,
And to his visionary fellow talks:
Amid the wave the vagrant blackbird sees,
And tries to perch upon the imag'd trees:
On flying clouds the simple bullocks gaze,
Or vainly reach to crop the shad'wy grass:
From neighb'ring hills the stately horse espies
Himself a feeding, and himself envies:
Hither persu'd by op'ning hounds, the hare
Blesses himself to see a forest near;
The waving shrubs he takes for real wood,

And boldly plunges in the yielding flood.
Here bending willows hem the border round,
There graceful trees the promontory crown,
Whose mingled tufts and outspread arms compose
A shade delightful to the lawrel'd brows.
Here mossy couches tempt to pleasing dreams
The love-sick soul; and ease the weary limbs.
No noxious snake disperses poison here,
Nor screams of night-bird rend the twilight air,
Excepting him, who when the groves are still,
Hums am'rous tunes, and whistles whip poor will;
To hear whose carol, elves in circles trip,
And lovers hearts within their bosoms leap;
Whose savage notes the troubled mind amuse,
Banish despair, and hold the falling dews.
    If to the west you turn your ravish'd eyes,
There shaggy hills prop up the bending skies,
And smoaky spires from lowly cots arise;
Tow'rds the northwest the distant mountains wear
In May a green, in June a whit'ning ear,
Or all alive with woolly flocks appear.
Beneath their feet a wide extended plain,
Or rich in cyder, or in swelling grain;
Does to the margin of the water stretch,
Bounded by meadows and a rushy beach.
The rest a motley mixture, hill and dale,
There open fields here mingled woods prevail:
Here lasting oaks, the hope of navies, stand,
There beauteous poplars hide th' unsightly strand:
In autumn there the full-ripe clusters blush
Around the walnut or the hawthorn bush.
Here fruitful orchards bend their aged boughs,
There sweats the reaper, her the peasant mows.
Each smiling month diversifies the view,
Ev'n hoary winter teems with something new:
A milkwhite fleece does then the lawns o'erspread,
The stream becomes a looking-glass indeed.
A polish'd surface spreads across the deep,
O'er which the youth with rapid vigour slip.

But now the groves the gayest liv'ries wear,
How pleas'd, could it be spring throughout the year!
And in these walks eternity be spent,
Atheists would then to immortality consent.
　The grateful shifting of the colour'd scene,
The rich embroid'ry of the level green;
The trees, and rusling of the branches there,
The silent whispers of the passing air;
Of falling cataracts the solemn roar,
By murmuring eccho sent from shore to shore,
Mix'd with the musick of the winged choir,
Awake the fancy and the poet's fire.
Here rural Maro might attend his sheep,
And the Mæonian with advantage sleep.
Hither ye bards for inspiration come,
Let ev'ry other fount but this be dumb.
Which way soe'er your airy genius leads,
Receive your model from these vocal shades:
Wou'd you in homely pastoral excel,
Take pattern from the merry piping quail;
Observe the bluebird for a roundelay,
The chatt'ring pie, or ever babling jay:
The plaintive dove the soft love verse can teach,
And mimick thrush to imitators preach.
In Pindar's strain the lark salutes the dawn;
The lyrick robin chirps the ev'ning on:
For poignant satyr mind the mavis well,
And hear the sparrow for a madrigal;
For every verse a pattern here you have,
From strains heroic down to humble stave.
Not Phœbus self, altho' the god of verse,
Could hit more fine, more entertaining airs;
Nor the fair maids who round the fountain sate,
Such artless heavenly music modulate.
Each thicket seems a paradise renew'd,
The soft vibrations fire the moving blood:
Each sense its part of sweet delusion shares,
The scenes bewitch the eye, the song the ears:
Pregnant with scent, each wind regales the smell,

Like cooling sheets th' enwrapping breezes feel.
During the dark, if poets eyes we trust,
These lawns are haunted by some swarthy ghost,
Some indian prince, who fond of former joys,
With bow and quiver thro' the shadow flies;
He can't in death his native groves forget,
But leaves elyzium for his ancient seat.
O happy stream! hadst thou in Grecia flow'd,
The bounteous blessing of some watry god
Thou'dst been; or had some Ovid sung thy rise
Distill'd perhaps from slighted virgins eyes.
Well is thy worth in indian story known,
Thy living lymph and fertile borders shown.
Thy shining roach and yellow bristly breme,
The pick'rel rav'nous monarch of the stream;
The pearch whose back a ring of colours shows;
The horned pout who courts the slimy ooze;
The eel serpentine, some of dubious race;
The tortoise with his golden spotted case;
The hairy musk-rat, whose perfume defies
The balmy odours of arabian spice;
Thy various flocks who shores alternate shun,
Drove by the fowler and the fatal gun.
  Young philadelphians know thy pleasures well,
Joys too extravagant perhaps to tell.
Hither oftimes th' ingenious youth repair,
When Sol returning warms the growing year:
Some take the fish with a delusive bait,
Or for the fowl beneath the arbors wait;
And arm'd with fire, endanger ev'ry shade,
Teaching ev'n unfledg'd innocence a dread.
To gratify a nice luxurious taste
How many pretty songsters breath their last:
Spite of his voice they fire the linnet down,
And make the widow'd dove renew his moan.
But some more humane seek the shady gloom,
Taste nature's bounty and admire her bloom:
In pensive thought revolve long vanish'd toil,
Or in soft song the pleasing hours beguile;

What Eden was, by every prospect told,
Strive to regain the temper of that age of gold;
No artful harms for simple brutes contrive,
But scorn to take a being they cannot give;
To leafy woods resort for health and ease,
Not to disturb their melody and peace.

THOMAS DALE

(1700–1750)

Prologue spoken to the Orphan

upon it's being play'd at Charlestown, on
Tuesday the 24th of Jan. 1734–5.

When first Columbus touch'd this distant Shore,
And vainly hop'd his Fears and Dangers o'er,
One boundless Wilderness in View appear'd!
No Champain Plains or rising Cities chear'd
His wearied Eye.—
Monsters unknown travers'd the hideous Waste,
And Men more Savage than the Beasts they chac'd.
But mark! how soon these gloomy Prospects clear,
And the new World's late horrors disappear.
The soil obedient to the industrious Swains,
With happy Harvests crowns their honest Pains,
And Peace and Plenty triumph o'er the Plains.
What various Products float on every Tide?
What numerous Navys in our Harbours ride?
Tillage and Trade conjoin their Friendly Aid,
T'enrich the thriving Boy and lovely Maid.
Hispania, it's true, her precious Mines engross'd;
And bore her shining Entrails to its Coast.
Britannia more humane supplys her wants,
The Brittish Sense and Brittish Beauty plants:
The Aged Sire beholds with sweet Surprize
In foreign Climes a numerous Offspring rize.
Sense, Virtue, worth and Honour stand confest,
In each brave Male, his prosp'rous hands have blest,
While the admiring Eye improv'd may trace
The Mother's Charms in each chast Virgins Face.
Hence we presume to usher in those Arts
Which oft have warm'd the best and bravest Hearts.
Faint our endeavours, rude are our Essays;

We strive to please, but can't pretend at praise;
Forgiving Smiles o'erpay the grateful Task;
They're all we hope and all we humbly ask.

Epilogue to the Orphan

Spoken after the Entertainment at CHARLESTOWN.

By various Arts we thus attempt to please,
And your Delight persue by different Ways;
Nor from our numerous Imports judge it fit
To banish Pleasure and prohibit Wit
But while from *Britain*'s wealthy Cities flow
Much for Necessity and much for Show,
From the old World in Miniature we shew
Her choicest Pleasures to regale the new.
For your Delight and Use has *Otway* wrote,
And pow'rful Music tunes her warbling Throat,
While other Objects entertain the Sight,
And we, you know, can die for your Delight.
Warm'd with th' Applause your Favour now bestows,
It may inspire the Merit you suppose;
If haply your continu'd Smiles produce
The *humble Fabrick* suited to the Use.
Then from the doubling Arch the Notes shall bound,
And Vaults responsive eccho to the sound:
Thence from their Graves pale Ghosts arising flow
Shall clear the injur'd and the guilty show.
From nobler Themes shall loftier Scenes appear,
And *Cato* urge what Senators may hear;
Or *Congreve*'s Drama shake the laughing Dome,
With Wit unmatch'd by *Athens* or by *Rome*.

The little Term that Heaven to Mortals spares,
Is daily clouded with prolonging Cares;
Nor *real* Virtue blames the pleasing strife,
To blend Amusement with the Shades of Life;
Wise, innocent, serene, she smiles at Ease,
Nor hanging Witches, nor Abjuring Plays.

"RALPHO COBBLE"

(fl. 1732)

To the Authr Gazitt

Sir,

what do you tell us of yr Larnin & exampels of our
Naboring colonees pish dont you no that Strangors
were alwase perferd here To All digintys And moly-
ments before any of Us Old Standerds Or our chil-
dren and sure some of us was as capuble of doing
Bisniss As Those I have seen perferred without
havin more Larnin.

Learning that Cobweb of the Brain,
Profane, erroneous, and vain,
A Trade of Knowledge, as replete
As others are with Fraud and Cheat.
An Art t' incumber Gifts and Wit,
And renders both for nothing fit.
A Cheat that Scholars put upon
Other Mens Reason and their own,
A Fort of Error to ensconce
Absurdity and Ignorance.
That renders all the Avenues
To Truth impervious and abstruse:
By making plain things in Debate
By Art perplext and intricate
For nothing goes for Sense or Light
That will not with old Rules jump write.
As if Rules were not in the Schools
Deriv'd from Truth, but Truth from Rules.
   This pagan heathenish Invention
   Is good for nothing but Contention,
For as in Sword or Buckler Fight,
All Blows do on the Target light
So when Men argue, the greatest part
O' th' Contest falls on Terms of Art,

> Until the fustian Stuff be spent
> And then they fall to th' Argument.

And there is an Answer for your *best Wrestler on the Green*. I hope my Cuntree Men will be wiser than to take your Advice for at your way of going to work I Shant be able to get a Prentice.

Your Sert.
Ralpho Cobble

If you dont print this I shall think you look upon your self above corresponden with a good honest Makanik.

JAMES STERLING

(1701–1763)

FROM

An Epistle to the Hon. Arthur Dobbs, Esq. in
Europe from a Clergyman in America

From Climes remote, but not to Thee unknown,
Whose Thoughts dilate beyond the polar Zone:
Whose Ken pervades whate'er the Sun surveys;
Accept, O DOBBS, these honorary Lays.
  While mighty Scenes thy vaster Soul engage,
To wake, to rouze, to warm a torpid Age:
The Fame and Pow'r of *Britain* to restore,
And bend her Sails on Earth's extremest Shore:
To join th' *Atlantic* and *Tartarian* Wave,
And tame the Skies where Artic Tempests rave:
Heav'n's Dispensations to diffuse below,
And bid divided Oceans interflow:
Anxious, *Messiah*'s Empire to extend,
And gen'rous Commerce with Discov'ry blend:
Apply thine Ear indulgent, nor refuse
The foreign Tribute of a wand'ring Muse.
  Hark! in wild Notes the tuneful Savage sings;
And for no vulgar Height prepares her Wings!
Lo, thro' th' uncultur'd Paradise she roves,
And first inchants *America*'s charm'd Groves!
She dares, (while Desarts hear th' heroic Lyre;
While in full Pomp thine Images inspire)
Like Nature's greater Works to raise her Song,
Irregularly bold, beneficently strong.
  Where *Sesquahanah** foams with rock-rais'd Sprey,
And swells lov'd *Chesapeak*'s capacious Bay:
Or where *Potowmac* with its placid Waves

---

  * *Sesquahanah* and *Potowmac* are the two noblest Rivers of *Maryland* and
Virginia, which after a Course of many hundred Miles fall into the great Bay
of *Chesapeak*.

Maria's Shores* and verdant Meadows laves;
Where *Europe*'s Monarchs scarce transfer their Name;
Thy Merits are convey'd by loudest Fame;
Amaz'd, All heard; All bless'd the great Design;
And Gratulations hail'd the Scheme Divine.

    The gen'ral Voice pierc'd thro' my shady Seats,
Where Speculation to her Grot retreats;
Where in my green Arcades o'er *Cestria*'s Stream,†
Of distant Friends in vacant Hours I dream.
Straight my Soul triumph'd in my Country's Good,
And Tears of Joy mix'd with the silent Flood;
Each lesser Thought thy brave Essay beguil'd;
My Heart exulted, and the Forest smil'd!

    That thine he fir'd our new World's Genius boasts,
While thy Name grows familiar to our Coasts;
This lulls, like Magic Songs, the barb'rous Ear,
And the fierce Tribes turn human, as they hear:
This bids enamour'd Nature bloom more gay,
Drest in wild Charms, and fair in loose Array:
Hence more luxuriant to poetic Eyes,
The wide *Savannahs* spread, and the tall Tulips rise.‡

    Fond Rumour hence delights repeating Hills,
Chants to the Dales, and entertains the Rills:
This in the Breeze refreshes *Cantia*'s Wood,
And warbles This thro' *Octarara*'s Flood.
Glad *Apalachia*§ clears her low'ring Brow:
Their nodding Heads the lofty Cedars bow:
While from a thousand Urns in spumy Show'rs
Her roaring Torrents *Niagara* pours.‖
Delug'd *Ontario*'s plausive Rocks rebound;
Proud Echo lengthens out the propagated Sound!

    Thy Praises to interior Seas are known,

---

* *Maryland.*

†The fine River *Chester*, dividing the Counties of *Kent* and *Queen Ann*, where the Author's Plantations are situated.

‡The largest and most beautiful Tree in *North-America*.

§The great Ridge of Mountains which extend from North to South, on the Back of our Colonies on the Continent.

‖The most celebrated Cataract in the World, down which the Waters of the Lake *Erie* are precipitated with many Circumstances of Horror into that of *Ontario*, or *Frontenac*.

Euxines and ampler *Caspians* of our own.*
These circumfus'd proclaim the gen'rous Man,
And *California* wafts thee to *Japan!*
  Ev'n now thy Name, on frighted Billows roll'd,
To hostile Shores by *Eurus'* Blast is told.
Lo, trembling *Gauls* the dire Report receive!
With Dread they listen, and with Guilt believe;
Predicting now our universal Sway,
Their notionary Empire shrinks away;
Louisiana's high Pretensions fail,†
And boastful Maps at once contract their Scale!
Fear multiplies *Britannia*'s naval Pow'rs,
And in thy Chart they see each *India* our's.
Desponding *Canada* now sighs around,
And *Mississippi* murmurs to the Sound.
A Fate, like *Louisburgh*'s, *Quebeck* fore-dates,‡
And hears brave *Pepp'rell* thund'ring on her Gates.§
  Thy bare Attempt has half their Pride supprest,
And pluck'd the Plume of Triumph from their Crest.
Confus'd *Rome*'s mission'd Janizaries stood,
While sudden Terrors damp'd their Lust of Blood.
(Whose Order *Jesus'* hallow'd Name defiles;
Deep-schem'd in Murder; principled in Wiles:)
Indian Allies thought Mercy touch'd their Breasts,
And wonder'd at Remorse in Christian Priests.
  Officious Fame will now no longer wait
Slow Explorators at thy purpos'd Strait.
Lo, with anticipating Haste she flies,
Thro' mediate Climes and occidental Skies,
O'ertakes the Sun, and bids both Poles resound

---

*The five mighty Lakes of many thousand Miles in Circumference, which communicate with each other, and lie to the West and North-west of our Settlements.

†So the *French* pompously name their new-arrogated Empire, which comprehends the most desirable Latitudes; and which they extend in their Maps to the South-Sea, excluding us from our prior Claim, and usurping in their public Declarations a Right to confine us to a narrow Slip on the Sea-Coast.

‡The Capital of the *French* Dominions in *Canada*.

§Well known, and renowned for reducing with his Countrymen of *New-England*, in Conjunction with the brave Admiral *Warren*, the strong and important Town of *Cape-Breton*.

With her inflated Trump thy Name renown'd.
New *Mexicoes* the Blast sonorous hear,
Which shakes their Pagods with foreboding Fear.
The wond'rous Change, by rev'rend Seers of old
To their primæval Ancestors foretold,
They hope at Hand; and with Impatience wait
The foreign Guests to mend their Minds and State:
Destin'd by purer Rites, and civil Arts,
To win Heav'n's Favor, and refine their Hearts;
While interdicted Altars smoke no more
With Captives sacrific'd and human Gore.

Each unfound Realm expectant now divines
The mighty Crisis by concurring Signs.
Whether their Heads the wreathing Plumes infold,
Or the spoil'd Beaver tolerates the Cold;
Whether beneath the torrid Line they glow,
Or freeze in Winters of relentless Snow.
Soon their swift Praws, or crouded Junks shall greet,
By thy propitious Care, our laden Fleet;
Bless the fair Strangers, spread their native Store,
And lure them to the hospitable Shore;
Their Treasures of barbaric Pride unfold,
The glossy Fur, Spice, Jewel, Balm, or Gold;
In rev'rence of superior Natures bend,
And high the sacred Calumet* extend;
Gaze on th' unoliv'd Skin and diff'rent Hue,
And the vast Ships with Admiration view;
Hear, as Instinct with Spirit, Cannons roar,
Fall prostrate, and the God inclos'd adore;
While silk-grass Flags, on masted Canes unfurl'd,
Salute the Benefactor of the World.

To Thee, who lov'st the Worth of ev'ry Clime,
All Men are Brethren, form'd with Souls sublime;
All Fellow-Citizens thro' peopled Earth;
Nor ask'st thou to what Soil they owe their Birth.
Perish, the local View; the narrow Breast,
That proves not Merit by its only Test!
When the rich Heart Virtues, like thine, adorn,

*The *Indian* Pipe of Peace.

The tawny Sons of *Ind* are *Britons* born.
These shall thy sympathizing Thoughts admire,
Their brave Ferocity, and Souls of Fire;
The Mien of Majesty, the stately Pace,
The Front erect, and Slave-disdaining Face;
Of varying Passions the quick genuine Start;
And honest Features op'ning to the Heart:
Gestures sincere: Words, that all Guile defy;
And Tongues untaught by Christian Fraud to lye:
Stature o'erlooking *Europe*'s Pigmy Breed;
And agile Limbs, that mate the Roe in speed:
While for their Country noble Ardors rise,
And burnish'd Freedom lightens from their Eyes!
    Soon shalt thou say:—"O *Britons*, what Disgrace
To injure these?—These, a fraternal Race!
What Jewels here inestimable shine;
Rude from rough Nature's adamantine Mine!
Such were our Ancestors; e'er *Cæsar*'s Sword
Impos'd the Yoke of a tyrannick Lord!
These by superior Skill in Murder's Trade,
O who, but Fiends incarnate, cou'd invade?
These who oppress; but Those, for Gold who yell;
Like *Cortez* imp'd by *Spain*, by *Rome*, by Hell?
Such, who, themselves dragging their Despot's Chain,
See alien Freedom with invidious Pain:
By Mufti-Feftas* with infernal Joy
Detach'd innoxious Kingdoms to destroy:
Rampant for Mines, who land; proceed to Shares;
Erect a Cross, and call the Country their's!
Christians; who like *Pizzaro*, or the Pest,
Massacre Millions, and inslave the Rest;
By Extirpation prove their Right supreme,
And swim to Empire thro' a purple Stream!
Who, pleas'd and wanton 'midst rackt Wretches Groans,
See golden Piles still rising from their Moans!
Vultures; who snuff refresh'd the Steam of Blood,
While salient Gore besmears their reeking Rood!
Egregious Chiefs; who pull indignant down

*The Pope's Bulls.

The native Idols, and advance their own!
The Head who polish, but the Heart pollute;
And file the Convert to a total Brute!
Who spoil their Morals to inlarge their Creed;
And leave them christen'd Cannibals indeed!

  "Happy *Peru*! ere *Spaniards* saw your Coast!
A *Charles* you got; but, O! an *Inca* loft!
By filial Subjects with aw'd Love addrest:
Their Legislator, Father, King, and Priest!
Direful Exchange! such Comfort *Rome* obtain'd;
When *Titus* perish'd, and *Domitian* reign'd!
Monstrous Transition! when ev'n Nature's Light
Sunk into Shades, o'ercast by Monkish Night!
When Inquest-Fire solder'd Religion's Flaws;
And Edicts superseded *Copac*'s Laws!

  "Yet to thy Sons opprest one Joy remains,
'Midst subterranean Darkness, Mines and Chains!
With Vengeance digging; from the shining Graves
They draw what makes their Masters greater Slaves;
And, taught their Bodies that their Souls survive,
Smiling renounce the Heav'n, where *Spaniards* live!

  "Blest Prince! once Patron of our great Design!
From whom descends *Britannia*'s regal Line!
Thou! for whom Mortals and Immortals strove;
If here thou shou'dst reign late, or soon above!
On whom, mature for the *supreme* Regard,
Justice confer'd an undelay'd Reward:
The Worth, it lent, from impious Realms remov'd;
And, scourging Earth, the Joys of Heav'n improv'd!
All-radiant; look from thy celestial Throne;
Social in Bliss with *Edward*'s glorious Son!
Teach us, Thou rais'd from Royal to Divine,
How we may only grieve and not repine.
O Thou, whose Form shall bless these Eyes no more,
Let us but weep, forbidden to adore.

  "If still thy *Britons*, late their *Fred'rick*'s Care,
Ought of thy Love 'midst Light eternal share:
If Heav'n averts its deprecated Ire;
O shed benign from Streams of Seraph Fire;
Shed Rays of Favor on our mourning Isle,

And still, unseen, with gracious Influence smile:
The State's slow Movements touch with regent Hand;
Retone its Springs, and animate our Land!
Soul of our honor'd Enterprize preside:
Our Hopes invig'rate; and our Councils guide!
    "Lo, we address Thee, wrapt in heav'nly Flames,
By those once tender, still endearing, Names:
By *Him*, to whom thou ow'dst thy mortal Part:
By *Her*, unrival'd in thy faithful Heart:
By *Those*, who still thy gentle Spirit move;
Pledges of national and nuptial Love!
Those, who receiv'd thy straining Eye's last Roll:
Her, who detain'd a while thy soaring Soul!
Lo, We address!—thy precious Reliques still
To guard from mental and external Ill!
Let the lov'd *Youth*, now to a Throne more near,
In Heav'n's due Time the Crown unsully'd wear!
On our bad World still some kind Thoughts imploy;
And from Pollution guard th' Imperial Boy!
Thro' Pleasure's Tears let grateful Millions see
Their *Fred'rick*'s living Image, worthy Thee!
While beams his Father's Goodness from his Face,
'Midst Sweetness smiling with maternal Grace!
    "And You, illustrious Prince, our Hopes repay:
Whom Aval Wisdom trains to future Sway!
Whose sequent Reign shall glorious Acts afford,
For future *Hides* or *Sallusts* to record.
O blooming *George*, in some yet distant Year,
When you the pond'rous Helm of Empire steer:
When Heav'n commits the Scepter to your Hand;
O with parental Virtues rule our Land!
Supremely with inherent Splendor blaze;
And vindicate hereditary Praise!
    "When public Spirit swells beneath your Sway,
And o'er new Oceans Commerce wings its Way:
Then let the Royal Clemency extend
The natal Rights of Mankind to defend:
Let new-known Worlds hail your protective Pow'r;
The Strong not grasp; the Greedy not devour:
Your Substitute let white-rob'd Justice stand;

And poize her Scales with uninclining Hand.
  "Your Navy's Triumph when new *Ophirs* hear,
And Southern Continents your Fame revere:
When your proud Capital thro' gazing Streets
Ambassadors in strange Procession greets:
When the vermilion'd and exotic Train
Draw Wonder's Eyes, and chronicle your Reign:
Let These, great Prince, find Favor in your Sight,
Nor ev'n their Tender of Alliance slight!
Thence fair-won Wealth your Glory shall support;
And moral Policy adorn your Court:
Thence Ministers shall fear no *French* Intrigues;
No foul Evasions, nor insidious Leagues.
Confed'rates These! no Stipend who require;
Who pawn not mercenary Faith for Hire:
Whose Truth not Oaths, nor written Treaties bind;
But gen'rous Sanctions, and a willing Mind.
These to your Equity shall Homage pay:
These uncompell'd more righteously obey;
And tho' their dearest Freedom they maintain,
The Tyrant's End without his Guilt you gain.
Convex'd o'er Earth while your Dominions run,
Pursue the Day, and tire th' unsetting Sun."

WILLIAM DAWSON

(1704–1752)

The Wager

A Tale.

Dare jura Maritis, Hor.

Two Sparks were earnest in Debate,
Touching Man's Life in marry'd State;
The One for Matrimony stood,
And preach'd in grave and solemn Mood,
By Head and Shoulders forcing, oddly,
To tagg each Sentence something Godly,
With many a learned Application
From *Genesis* to *Revelation*—
In Politick's he wisely shew'd,
What Honours *Sparta*'s Laws bestow'd
On those who marry'd in their Prime,
And never lost a teeming Time.
And how the ancient *Roman* Nation
Had the same Rules in Imitation;
And how their Senate oft decreed,
That Men should wed to mend the Breed:
How all those Heroes, whose Renown
Fame's Trump has handed to us down,
For Cities storm'd, and Kingdoms won,
Were each an honest Mother's Son.
How modern *Romans* do, indeed,
Neglect to mind a lawful Breed;
But diverse Practices pursue
Which their Fore-fathers never knew,
And set their whole Affections on
The Scarlet Whore of *Babylon*:
Which we, good *Protestants* o'th' Nation,
Are bound to think Abomination;
For which such mortal Hate they bear Us,
And Curse us bitterly like *Meroz*

413

Dick listen'd to his wise Quotations,
And heard him out with all his Patience,
At length he cry'd, *'Sblood* John (*bar swearing*)
This idle Talk is past all bearing.
You mention old *Lycurgus'* Laws,
And *Spartan* Rules and ancient Saws,
When all this foolish Prittle-prattle,
Is just like *rattle, Bladder, rattle*.
I say, that *Rome*'s a prudent City,
If you don't think so too, 'tis pity.
'Pray, if your Memory don't 'scape ye,
Know you a marry'd Man that's happy?
People may talk and make a Pother,
They're but Decoys for one another.
The *Fox* had ne'er Aversion shewn
To Tails—if he had had his own.
So they, that fall into the Gin,
Draw, like *Free-Masons*, others in.
Women, I own, were made for Men,
For their Diversion now and then:
But then, to cap your wisest Sentence,
Pleasure's attended by Repentance.
What we may once repent; a Wife
Makes us repent of *during Life*.
For whatsoever some pretend,
Wives are but Wives, to their Lives End.
And he that marries, to his Cost,
Will find his Labour not well lost.
As *France*'s King, of high Renown,
Went up the Hill—and so came down.
    John bless'd himself, and scratcht his Head,
And looking very wisely, said,
Methinks I smell, in this Discourse,
Free-thinking rank—or something worse.
Don't you think Marriage is a serious
Type of a Tye abstruse, mysterious?
Surely the Text you understand ill,
Else Women you would better handle.
Diversion, quotha why, we find
Women for graver Ends design'd:

To be our Help-meets in our Need,
When real Friends are Friends indeed,
To share a Part of our Distress,
And, by that Share, to make it less.
To clean our Houses, milk our Kine.
And mind when Boars gallant our Swine;
To drudge about domestick Bus'ness,
And scold at Servants for Remissness:
Are not these Things of mighty Weight,
To ease us, in the marry'd State?
Besides an hundred Things of Course,
That might my Argument enforce,
To strive an hundred Ways t' oblige us,
Which I'll abridge, as being tedious,
Since all the Joys that Life affords,
Are comprehended in few Words;
For don't the Rituals plainly say,
To love, to honour and obey?

    You have it there indeed, says *Dick*,
Obedience is the usual Trick.
They promise it before the Priest,
But saying that, they mean it least:
Or else they take so little Notice,
That what they promise soon forgot is;
For other Thoughts so crowd the Head
They neither mind what's done or said,
Obedience soon has lost its Force,
And only seems a Word of Course,
And notwithstanding Vows or Oaths
They doff it with their Wedding-Cloaths.

    But since the Rituals, you maintain,
Appear so positive and plain,
I'll venture with you, if you dare,
A Wager you shall own is fair,
That low Obedience is more common,
And oft'ner found, in Man than Woman.
And thus the Matter we'll decide,
A Cart and Horses we'll provide,
Hampers of Eggs shall be the Load,
Thus furnish'd out, we'll take the Road,

At each Plantation make a Stand,
To know who bears the upper Hand.
Where e'er the Wife usurps the Throne,
An Egg we'll leave them and be gone:
But if the Woman does obey,
Submitting to her Husband's Sway,
If all his Orders have full Force,
We'll give this Miracle an Horse.
Yet all I'm worth I will engage here,
To half its Value, on this Wager,
That all our Eggs are gone in Course,
Before one Husband gets a Horse.

   So said so done—the Wager's laid,
Preliminary Earnest paid,
They both consult the Men of Law
Authentic Covenants to draw,
And then the hopeful Tour begin,
Both pleas'd—for both were sure to win.

   From that fair Town* where rising Day
Does first thy House of Law survey,
Where Learning's Seat behold th'Extreams
Of *Western* Lights departing Beams,
As if contriv'd to let us see
Both one and t'other's Destiny,
Our Travellers jog'd easy on,
Nor left a House uncall'd-upon,
Both where *James*-River's *Northern* Shore
Shrinks from its foamy Current's Roar,
And where *York* River's angry Tide
Impetuous beats its *Southern* Side;
But still where e'er they did advance
Dick seem'd to stand the fairest Chance:
The gentle Husband, at each House,
Gave Way to his superior Spouse,
The Wife took all the Rule upon her,
Just to preserve her Sex's Honour.
The Widow's Houses pass'd no Trial,

---

* *Williamsburgh* in *Virginia*: The Court-House stands at the East End of the
City, and the College at the West End. The Towns of *Hampton*, *York*,
Williamsburgh and *James-Town*, all lie between *James-River* and *York-River*.

Their's was the Sway without Denial.
And Widow'rs came with Honour off,
Whose Cases could admit no Proof,
Elsewhere th' Event was still the same,
The Man obey'd the ruling Dame.
And still those Tyrants were the proudest,
Who oft'nest bred, or scolded loudest.
    Dick now, whose rip'ning Hopes to win,
Had rais'd him to a merry Pin,
Cry'd out, Ay, ay, it will be so,
When Cocks are trod, the Hens may Crow.
O the delicious blissful Joys
Of Pride, Impertinence and Noise!
I'll tell thee what, my Friend—I know,
A Man whose Wife is—but so, so;
And tho' she oft adorns his Scull
With the fine Feathers of a Bull,
And many a Time has fork'd his Crown,
By Night, by Day, up Stairs and down,
And tho' her Actions plainly shew it,
Yet dares not he be thought to know it:
Not that he fears or minds the Shame
Attendant on a Cuckold's Name,
Nor for the Credit of his Wife,
But for the Quiet of his Life:
For if a Wife's a Vixen Scold,
Imperious, termagant, and bold,
Whilst she conceals herself, and none
Know, or will speak of, what sh' has done,
How will she grow more fierce and stout,
When all her Treachery breaks out,
And hearing on't from Time to Time,
She grows more harden'd in her Crime?—
But let us on—we soon shall know
Which Way the Wager is to go.
    The Story says, that thus they travel'd
Till luckless *John* was sorely gravel'd;
Of Hope and Patience quite bereft,
And only one poor Egg was left:
When Fortune wary of her Spleen

Contriv'd to shew a diff'rent Scene,
And prove that *Dick*, how e'er elate,
Was not above the Reach of Fate:
For near that Spring which hands us down
King *Totapotamoy*'s Renown,
Arriving at a Planter's Door,
They ask'd, as they'd done oft before,
Whose House was that? With surly Phiz,
The Planter answer'd, It was his:
But, Sir, says *Dick, Sans Complement,*
Our Question otherwise was meant,
We want to know who rules the House,
Whether yourself, or else your Spouse?
Walk in, the Planter cry'd, we'll try
Who's Master here, my Wife or I.

This Planter had a Hick'ry Stick,
Well-season'd, drubbing proof, and thick,
Oft and on many Causes try'd
To dress and tan his Dearest's Hide,
Whether she lay too long in Bed,
Or left uncomb'd her Daughter's Head;
Or if she fail'd to sweep the House,
Or night and morn to milk the Cows;
Sometimes, for thirst, his Limbs would fail,
And lo! no Gourd was in the Pail!
Sometimes his Beef was over boil'd,
At other Times his Coleworts spoil'd;
Or if she fail'd in her Allegiance.
The Hick'ry taught her due Obedience:
As you may see on Muster-Days,
When * *Nicholas* does his Cudgel raise,
And when his Looks the Soldier quails
Who awkward in his Duty fails:
Thus were this Pain in diff'rent Taking,
Imperious he, for Fear she quaking:
He order'd her to wipe his Shoes,
She lowly stoop'd, nor durst refuse;
He sent her to the Spring, she went

---

*Late Adjutant-General.

Nor shew'd the smallest Discontent;
He gave her many Orders more
Which I for Brevity pass o'er,
Until he shew'd to *Dick*'s Disaster,
That He was Sov'reign, Lord, and Master.
   Dick give the Wager now for lost,
And *John* had kindly thank'd his Host,
Bidding him choose among the Team
Which Horse the best for him should seem;
The Planter look'd on all around,
And chose the Horse he likeliest found;
When as his Wife with angry Voice
Cry'd out, You've made a silly Choice:
Where are your Eyes? What, Can't you see?
You'd better far be rul'd by me.
And make your Choice of that Grey Mare,
I'm sure you'll find no better there.
   The Planter straight the Grey Mare views,
And handles her as Jockeys use;
Adzooks cries he, you're in the Right,
This Grey is better than that White,
So I'll e'en take the Mare away—
Dick interrupting, bid him stay;
My Case was desperate I own,
But now the Table's turn'd, I've won;
You see here, *John*, how Woman rules,
We Men have ever been their Tools:
The surly, and the complaisant,
The sly, the witty, and gallant,
Spight of their Haughtiness or Funning,
Must yield, or to their Pow'r or Cunning.
   Then to the Planter turning round,
I'm glad the Mare's the better found;
But 'tis not worth your While to fret, or
Fume, tho' th' Grey Mare proves the better:
'Tis ev'ry honest Husband's Case,
And will be so, and always was:
My Luck has prov'd me not mistaken,
And with this Egg—I've sav'd my Bacon.

On the Corruptions of the Stage

Long did the Stage with nervous Sense delight,
Exalt the ravish'd Soul, and charm the Sight;
Whilst *Shakespear*, *Row*, and all those Sons of Fame,
(Our greatest Glory, and our greatest Shame)
With lofty Buskin, or facetious Lay,
Held o'er the captive Mind despotic Sway.
With noble Ardor then they trod the Scene,
We came, we saw, we gaz'd ourselves to Men.

At length from *Latian* Shores, infectious Clime!
Came the soft Cadence and inervate Chime.
Amphion-like, those modern Sons of Art
Could chain the Sense and captivate the Heart.
Oh wond'rous Skill! but mark the *Syren* Rocks;
He Blocks to Men, they Men transform'd to Blocks.

Next *Harlequin*, ingenious Antique, came;
The same his Magic, and his Sourse the same.
With Kick facetious, or with witty Grin,
He rais'd our Laughter—but expos'd our Brain.
In vain *Mercutio* jests, poor *Juliet* mourns in vain.
Phogh! who can bear th' intolerable Strain!
Where strong and manly Sense disturbs our Ease,
And Passions, too affecting e'er to please.
To burning Houses, Monsters, and Grimace,
To flying Bottles, Wands, and waving Seas,
To cheated Cuckolds, and the bold * *Rogere*,
Illustrious Hero! pendent in the Air;
To these we fly, and leave those Sons of Spleen,
The Fools of Sense, to doat on *Shakespear*'s Scene.

*A French *Player at the Old House*.

Macheath at last arose with vent'rous Wing,
And laugh'd away the Brethren of the String.
But whilst he cures the Head-Ake's trifling Pain,
With raging Frenzy he infects the Brain.
To awkard Imitations next we came,
The nauseous Snuffs of true poetick Flame.
From foreign Trifling and unmanly Tone,
We turn to downright Nonsense of our own.

To a Friend,
Who recommended a Wife to him

I own, the Match, you recommend,
    Is far above my mean Desert;
I own, you've acted like a Friend,
    A hearty, kind, and gen'rous Part.

But Marriage, Sir,'s a serious Case;
    Maturest Thought should chuse a Wife;
Tho' some aver, the wisest Way's
    To think upon it all one's Life.

To a Lady,
on a Screen of Her Working

A NEW CREATION charms the ravish'd Sight;
Delightful Harmony of Shade and Light!
ART vies with NATURE in a doubtful Strife,
The finish'd Copy, which and which the Life.
The Blooming Flow'rs the painted Bow excel;
The gay Delusion courts, and cheats the Smell.
What Beauty does ANEMONE disclose!
What flushing Glories the CARNATION shews!
The TULIP here displays her motley Pride;
The PIONY there in richest *Crimson* dy'd.
The HYACINTH, tho' rais'd by *Phœbus*' Pow'r,

Derives from Female Skill a fairer Flow'r.
The POPPY with lethargic Force opprest,
Her *Scarlet* Head reclines upon her Breast;
So *Henley*'s drooping Hearers sink to Rest.
Incircling Beams the SUN-FLOW'R'S Orb surround;
With flaming Gold RENUNCULA is crown'd.
Array'd in Snowy Tresses LILLIES shine,
Pure as Her Mind that form'd the neat Design.
The ROSE here buds, there opens ev'ry Grace;
So modest Blushes stain the Virgin Face.
Here we admire the NIGHT-SHADE'S darker Blue;
The twining WOOD-BIND there of various Hue.
Here Silver Blooms of Golden ORANGE blow;
STOCK-GILLY-FLOWERS there, and JONQUILS glow,
And Leaves of chearful GREEN the Ground bestrew;
Refreshing *Green*, from Age preserve those Eyes,
By which You flourish in immortal Dies.

JOHN ADAMS

(1705–1740)

Melancholly discrib'd and dispell'd

Muse, sing the Man, whose overclouded Head,
Is with a Mist of rising Shades o'er-spread;
Whose Fancy, wild, a thousand Evils forms,
And shakes and shudders at imagin'd Storms:
Whose Mind in endless Whirls is toss'd around,
Whose quivering Feet scarce touch the solid Ground.
Look deep into the Caverns of his Mind,
And, there, ten thousand monstrous Shapes you'l find;
Gloomy as Night, and airy as the Wind.
Deep drench'd in Melancholly's baleful Streams,
Quick up his Brain ascend eternal Streams;
And his dull Life flows heavily in Dreams.

Give me the Man, whose easy cheerful Soul
Can stand secure when heaving Billows roll;
Whose House, forever built upon a Rock,
Can bear the furious Wind's tremendous Shock:
Whose Faith, in JESUS' Sacrifice immur'd,
Stands firm and everlastingly secur'd.
While up to Heav'n he lifts his longing Eyes,
He views fair Streaks of Glory paint the Skies;
He sees the Blush of everlasting Day
Bear on his Soul, in Scenes forever gay:
The warbling Seraphs, with their tuneful Strains
Of heavenly Musick, charm away his Pains;
Nought fears he from the grizly Face of Death,
Divinely pleas'd, he ebbs away his Breath.
When all the Scenes of Life flow swift away,
And his frail Body hastens to decay,
Swift up the Skies his Wings the Saint convey.

But there, oh there! what sacred Prospects rise,
And spread a Heav'n of Glories o'er his Eyes!

There JESUS, thou th' incarnate GOD dost sit,
Confess'd in all thy God-like Robes of State;
High o'er thy blazing Throne, thy beamy Light
Flashes with quick Succession on his Sight.
Thy Wounds no more in sanguine Riv'lets flow,
Thy Purple Stains shine whiter than the Snow;
And from their Sources Beams of Glory grow.
Thy Eyes, which burn like Lamps of purest Fire,
Thy Eyes, which mildly shine with kind Desire,
With everlasting Smiles of Grace are fill'd;
Grace, which the raging Pow'r of Satan quell'd;
Which broke my Soul from all its servile Chains,
And fix'd my Feet on *Zion*'s wid'ning Plains.
But, oh! what big, what high transporting Joys,
Feels the blest Man amidst the vast Applause,
Of Angels shouting in a general Song;
While mingling Musick breathes its Way along?

Rouze up, my Soul, let Heav'n thy Vigour raise,
Where JESUS Flames with everlasting Rays.
JESUS can all thy daring Foes repell,
And speak Confusion to the Pow'rs of Hell.
Thy feeble Loins with Strength renew'd can bind,
And make thy trembling Feet outstrip the Wind;
Like the rent Cloud, can scatter wide thy Fears,
And bear away th' o'er-pressing Load of Cares:
Can lift a gracious Glance thro' Horrors Gloom,
And lighten Heaven into thy darkned Room.
Come JESUS, quickly come with smoaking Wheels,
And drag the conquer'd Devils at thy Heels;
More rapid than the driving Blasts of Wind,
Or, when inspir'd with Terror, springs the Hind.
Ye louring Clouds, when will ye break away,
And, on my darken'd Mind, let in the welcome Day?
He comes, He comes; I see, I feel the GOD,
See! where his fiery Coursers scour the Road:
Nor now I'll fear, tho' armed Hosts unite,
And raging Devils push their eager Spight;
The Breath of CHRIST their harmless Fury blows,
As Whirlwinds sport away the new-fall'n Snows.

ARCHIBALD HOME

(c. 1705–1744)

An Elegy
On the much to be lamented Death of
George Fraser of Elizabeth Town

Jersey! Lament in briny tears,
Your Dawty's gane to his Forebears;
Wae worth him! Death has clos'd the Sheers
           And clipd his Thread:
Just in the Prime of a' his Years
           George Frazers dead.

Sure Heav'n beheld our Courses thrawn,
And him in Anger has withdrawn;
This Tide o' Grief, poor Parson Vaughn
           Can never stem it:
Nor mair the blythsome day shall dawn,
           On thee, George Emmott!

Well skill'd he was in Physick's Art;
And cheaply wad his Drugs impart;
Oh! How he did himself exert,
           This to converse on
And had sik kittle Terms b' heart
           They poz'd the Parson.

The Wide sawt seas he oft had crost,
And kent the Towns on ilka Coast;
Wad shaw us where his Bark was lost
           Withouten grieving
His like alas we canna boast;
           Among the Living.

Sae ruddy was his Face & blooming,
That when his Head he pat the Room in,

425

Ye'd true that Summer was a coming,
                    The Melted Snaw,
Before his sat the Gait a Sooming,
                    Just like a Thaw.

Wha wast that gae us halesome Cheer,
And Waughts o'Syder and o Beer.
Wha wast that lernt our Bairns to Swear
                    Or they could read?
George Frazer did; What need ye Speer?
                    But now he's dead.

When passing thro' Elizabeth Town,
Wi' Hunger ready for to swoon,
His Table, ay weel spred at noon,
                    Was sure relief
A South of Fare his Boord did crown
                    Baith Broth & Beeff.

He was a deadly fae to starting
And when at night they talk'd o'parting
A Pint at least, but oft a Quart in,
                    George Frazer yet would;
O Death! Why didst thou throw thy Dart in
                    To hurt Will: Chetwood!

But what mais things upo' my Mind,
He has nae left a Bairn behind;
His wooing Tangerlow unkind
                    Wad never hear it
Oh now! That she should be sae blind
                    To a'his Merit.

To ithers too he had made Proffers,
To Share wi' them his weel pang'd Coffers,
Shame fa them! They refus'd his offers
                    In troth Miss ____
When you and ____ play'd the Scoffers
                    Ye shaw'd your Folly.

Weel since from weeping us he's riv'n
Just at the Age of Forty Seven,
May to his Hands the Staff be given
    Which he on Earth,
Refus'd, and Constable in Heav'n
    Be George's Birth!

The Ear-Ring

Ovid has sweetly sung how mighty Jove
On Earth pursued in various shapes his Love
Took any Form wore whatsoever dress
So'st pleas'd the Nymph, and promised him success.
 When Brisk Agenors Daughter fir'd his soul,
The wanton God put on the milk white Bull
Far from his sire to Crete's delightful shore
Safe thro' the flood the Dame triumphant bore.
 In the Swan's soft and snowy Plumage drest,
He flew to Leda's soft and Snowy Breast;
Surprized Laconia saw two Lovely Boys,
Hatch'd from an Egg, the product of their Joys.
 In Thebes enamour'd of a wedded Fair
The God assum'd the absent Husband's air;
Array'd in all her lov'd Amphytrions Charms,
He revell'd in deceiv'd Alemena's Arms.
 A Slave to Grecian Danaes bright Eyes
He meditates a new, a sure Disguise;
The God who made her knew the fair ones mind
To sordid love of Wealth too much inclind
Perceived the Daughter Coy the Father nice,
To raise his Passion, and inhance her Price
To a dazling Show'r of all commanding Gold
Transform'd the gen'rous Lover now behold
Pour down abundant from his Heav'n of Love.
 To me, your suppliant, Gracious Jove! Impart
This blest, this wond'rous commutative art;
Give me this Happy Pendant's shape to wear,
To dangle in my charming Flavia's Ear

There whispering in tender plaints my Flame,
Help to adorn the bright the matchless Dame
O'er paid my Suff'rings, if the Fair bestows
One pitying sigh on her adorer's Woes.

Black-Joke: A Song

The various ills that have happen'd to Man
Have taken their rise, Since this World began
        From a black Joke &c

What I have asserted the Bible shall prove
And demonstrate our miseries sprung from the Love
        Of a Coal black Joke &c

Our Paradice Dad ne'er had eaten the Sweet,
If that Sly Devil Eve had not tempted him to't
        With her coal black Joke &c

He tasted the Pippen, he mounted his Bride
He damn'd his whole race, and drove on till he dy'd
        At her coal black Joke &c

His sons too as the Story goes
From dearest of Friends, became fiercest of Foes
        For a black Joke &c

The Youngest was slain, and the murdering Spark
Was branded by G-d, and sent of with the Mark
        Of a coal black Joke &c

The wanton young Daughters of old Father Lot
Perceiving no Male, but their Sire, to be got
        For their Black Jokes &c

So ply'd him with Bumpers, that he e'er the morn
Forgetting their Kindred with each had a turn
        At her coal black Joke &c

The strongest man in Israel
A Prey to the mercyless Philistines fell
                    For a black Joke &c

The treacherous Dalilah tickled his Lust
And his Secret obtain'd as the Price of a Thrust
                    At her coal black Joke &c

When Jael led Sisera into her Tent,
She concluded the General stiffly was bent
                    On a black Joke &c

But he fell a Sleep, and the Jade drove a Nail,
In his Temples because that he drove not his Tail
                    In her coal black Joke &c

King David, the man after G-ds own Heart
From praying and praising would often depart
                    For a black Joke &c

It chanc'd he saw naked Uriah's Fine Wife
And the Husband, poor Cuckold, was rob'd of his Life
                    For her Coal black Joke &c

Desunt Catera

On killing a Book-Worm

Vermine accurst, how couldst thou thus abuse
This Precious product of the Noblest Muse?
I gave thee ample range o'er ev'ry Shelf,
This Sacred Fruit reserving for my self;
Eve thus in Eden broke tho' Gods betrest,
And damn'd Mankind to gratify her Taste,
Nor dos't thou perish, tho thy Blood is spilt,
While thus the Muse perpetuates thy guilt
Like his thy Crime, like his thy Thirst of Fame,
Who burnt a Temple, to preserve a Name.

JOSEPH GREEN

(1706–1780)

To Mr. B occasioned by his Verse, to Mr. Smibert on seeing his Pictures

Unhappy Bard! sprung in such Gothic Times
As yield no friendly muse, t'extol your Rhymes.
Hard is the Task you singly undergo
To praise the Painter and the Poet too.
But much I fear you raise a short liv'd *Fame*,
Which lives but on the Pen from whence it came.
Boast on, and take what fleeting Life can give,
For when you cease to write, you cease to live.
If you to future Ages would be known
Make this Advice I freely give—your own.
　　Go to the Painter—for your Picture sit;
　　His art will long survive the Poets Wit.

The Poet's Lamentation for the Loss of his Cat, which he us'd to call his Muse

Felis quædam Delicium erat cuiusdam Adolescentis.
Æsop

Opress'd with grief, in heavy strains I mourn
The partner of my studies from me torn:
How shall I sing? what numbers shall I chuse?
For in my fav'rite *cat* I've lost my muse.
No more I feel my mind with raptures fir'd,
I want those airs that *Puss* so oft inspir'd;
No crowding thoughts my ready fancy fill,
Nor words run fluent from my easy quill:
Yet shall my verse deplore her cruel fate,
And celebrate the virutes of my cat.

In acts obscene she never took delight;
No catterwawls disturb'd our sleep by night;
Chaste as a virgin, free from every strain,
And neighb'ring cats mew'd for her love in vain.

She never thirsted for the chickens blood;
Her teeth she only us'd to chew her food:
Harmless as satires which her master writes,
A foe to scratching, and unus'd to bites.

She in the study was my constant mate;
There we together many evenings sat.
Whene'er I felt my tow'ring fancy fail,
I strok'd her head, her ears, her back, and tail;
And, as I strok'd, improv'd my dying song
From the sweet notes of her melodious tongue;
Her purrs and mews so evenly kept time,
She purr'd in metre and she mew'd in rhime.
But when my dullness has too stuborn prov'd,
Nor could by *Puss*'s musick be remov'd,
Oft to the well-known volumes have I gone,
And stole a line from Pope or Addison.

Oftimes, when lost amidst poetic heat,
She leaping on my knee has took her seat;
There saw the throes that rack'd my lab'ring brain,
And lick'd and claw'd me to myself again.

Then, friends, indulge my grief, and let me mourn;
My cat is gone, ah! never to return.
Now in my study all the tedious night,
Alone I sit, and unassisted write:
Look often round (O greatest cause of pain)
And view the num'rous labours of my brain;
Those quires of words array'd in pompous rhime,
Which brav'd the jaws of all-devouring time,
Now undefended, and unwatch'd by cats,
Are doom'd a victim to the teeth of rats.

On Mr. B—s's singing an Hymn of his own composing

at Sea, on a Voyage from Boston to an Interview with the Indians in New England

In *David*'s psalms, an oversight,
  Byles found one morning at his tea:
Alas! why did not *David* write
  A proper psalm to sing at sea?

Thus ruminating, on his seat,
  Ambitious thoughts at length prevail'd;
The bard determin'd to compleat
  The part in which the prophet fail'd.

A while he paus'd, and strok'd his muse;
  Then, taking up his tuneful pen,
Wrote a few stanzas for the use
  Of his sea-faring bretheren.

The task perform'd, the bard content,
  (Well chosen was each flowing word)
On a short voyage himself he went,
  To hear it read and sung on board.

What extasies of joy appear!
  What pleasure and unknown delights
Thrill the vain poet's soul to hear
  Others repeat the things he writes.

Most aged Christians do aver
  (Their credit sure we may rely on)
In former times, that after prayer,
  They us'd to sing a song of *Zion*.

Our modern parson having pray'd,
  (Unless loud fame our faith beguiles)
Sat down, took out his book and say'd,
  Let's sing a song of *Mather Byles*.

As soon as he began to read,
    Their heads th' assembly downward hung;
Yet he with boldness did proceed,
    And thus he read, and thus they sung.

THE HYMN

With vast amazement we survey
    The wonders of the deep:
Where mack'rel swim, and porpoise play,
    And crabs and lobsters creep.

Fish of all kinds inhabit there,
    And throng the dark abode;
There haddock, hake and flounders are,
    And eels, and perch, and cod.

From raging winds and tempests free,
    So smooth, that, as you pass,
The shining surface seems to be
    A piece of *Bristol* glass.

But when the winds tempestuous rise,
    And foaming billows swell,
The vessel mounts above the skies,
    Then lower sinks than hell.

Our brains the tott'ring motion feel,
    And quickly we become
Giddy as new-dropt calves, and reel
    Like *Indians* drunk with rum.

What praises then are due, that we
    Thus far are safely got;
*Amarriscoggin tribe to see,
    And tribe of **Penobscot*!

*The Names of two of the *Indian* Tribes.

To the Author of the Poetry in the last Weekly Journal

Illustrious Bard! (whoe'er thou art,)
Whom *Hymen's* Joys have made so pert;
That 'cause the *Hony-moon* is gone,
And Nuptial Troubles not come on;
Eager, the *Wonder* should be known,
In am'rous Strains have told the *Town*;
How happy 'tis to have a WIFE,
Rather than live a single Life:
And what fine Things you've been a doing,
Since you for *Marriage* chang'd your *Wooing*:
And made young Fellows Mouths to water;
Impatient to be coming after.
The Country *Proverb* you han't follow'd;
But *whilst you're in the Winds have bellow'd.*
The *Latin* too I think *a propos*;
That tell us, *Finis coronat opus.*
But since what's done you can't recant:
(Tho' oft, it's like, you will repent:)
Before you string your *Lyre* again;
(Unless 'tis to divert your Pain;)
If you'l accept a *Friend's* Advice;
(Th' *old Saying's* good, if 'tis not nice;)
First *with her eat a Peck of Salt*:
And then if you can find no Fault;
And She should prove not *Slut* nor *Scold*;
Nor with your *Head* should make too bold;
(Either with *Horns*, or with a *Stick*;)
Or play some other Female Trick;
To make you turn your am'rous Tone,
And often with your self alone:
If you can find me such another,
I'll recommend her to a Brother.

A True Impartial Account of the Celebration of the Prince of Orange's Nuptials at Portsmouth

June 3d: 1734

The Chief, to whose extended sway
Two provinces obedience pay,
As soon as he receiv'd the News
Of Brittain's Princess takeing Spouse,
A Messenger, with Orders, sent
Unto his other Government,
To Keepe a day with pomp & State
To drink and eke illuminate;
As soon as the August Command
Which he had sent, should come to hand,
Council was summon'd in a trice
To judge of an affaire so nice,
No disobedient factious Blades
But Grave substantial, solid Heads,
Submissive, resolute and stable
Wise, just, discerning, honourable
Who always will and always did
Dare boldly do—as they ware bid,
Here there Arose a small debate
About the Charges and all that,
But they Resolved to wave dispute
Belcher Commands & they must do't
All things in readiness were Got
A Drum a Pistol and what not,
For though a Great Gun Goes off Louder
A Pistol takes but little powder,
Nay if they could have made it do
They wou'd have had a Trumpet too,
But in it's stead, were forc'd to Chuse
The horn which Posts in rideing use,
To tell the people, by their Blowing
When they are comeing & when Goeing,
And thus Equip'd, they went away
To Tavern, to conclude the day,

But haveing on their hatts first ty'd
Ribbons of Various Colours dy'd,
Green, Yellow, Purple, red & Blue
All of an Exact Orange Hue,
Hatts none made fine, and Hung; instead
Of wooden Pine, on wooden head,
Three Candles and a Lamp of Tin
Plac'd in the Chamber, they ware in,
Adorn'd the windows, broke by stone
Which Boys unluckily had thrown—
Pipes & Tobacco they ware strow'd
And limejuice punch in Plenty flow'd,
In the first place they drank the King
Then beat the Drum; like any thing,
Next came the Quene, the Prince, His Grace
The duke, and all the Royall Race,
The Prince of Orange, and then—Pounce,
The Pistole went off all at once,
Next in a Brimer, one Cries here
We'll drink our Noble Governour,
The Health Quick round the board was bourn
And streight the post loud blue his horn,
An Instrument, to most mens thinking
Most fit to show, whose Health was drinking,
Thus they Carous'd it, without Stopping
With beating Drum & Pistol popping,
At length they laid aside their pipes
Complaining sorely of the Gripes,
Both one and all which made 'em think
Their paine was owing to their drink.
Punch, as Philosophy maintains,
Has a Sure effect on the Brains;
And, as Experience can tell ye
Some Peoples Brains are in the Belly,
Hence when drink Gripes, 'tis a sad Omen
The Brains are lodg'd in the abdomen,
And this most certainly may pass
For Good Proof in the present Case,
Then haveing pass'd thro' Bloodless Fray
About what each man Ought to pay,

They settle'd with the help of Host
Who should pay least, & who pay most,
Concludeing thus the joyfull Night
Some went to sleep, others to fight.

Inscription under Revd. Jn. Checkley's Picture

John! had thy Sickness snatch'd thee from our Sight,
And sent thee to the Realms of endless Night;
Posterity, perhaps, would ne'er have known
Thy Eye, thy Beard, thy Cowl & shaven Crown.
But now, Thy Face, by Smiberts matchless Hand,
Of Imortality secured shall stand.
When Nature into Ruin shall be hurl'd,
And the last Conflagration burn the World;
Then shall this Piece survive the gen'ral Evil,
For Flames, you know, will ne'er consume the Devil.

———

A fig for your learning, I tell you the Town
To make the church larger, must pull the school down.
Unluckily spoken—replied Master Birch,
Then Learning I fear stops the growth of the Church.

The Disappointed Cooper

*N.B. The subject is the Rev Mr W C, late of Boston who
married for his second wife a Maide with red hair much
younger than himself. He was a zealous supporter of some
itinerant preachers who were called "New Lights."*

A Cooper there was, he work'd at his trade
Old barrells he mended, and new one's he made,
So stiff in his way, he had Will for his Name,
Yet he liv'd a long while in good credit and fame.

But his credit Will lost—Lost how? do you ask?
Why he put an old bung in a new red-oak Cask.

He long dealt in mending—nor dealt he in Vain,
For the pence tumbled in, and rewarded his pain,
Till riches increasing—he at length grew so bold,
He was all for New Work and despised the old.

But his credit Will lost—Lost how? do you ask?
Why he put an old bung in a new red-oak Cask.

He now was resolv'd with all possible care
And contrivance—a mighty hugh Barrell to rear;
Not like other barrells so paultry and weak,
But the biggest and strongest that ever was seen.

But his credit Will lost—Lost how? do ye ask?
Why he put an old bung in a new red-oak Cask.

So he muster'd all hands—George,* Gilbert† and James‡
And Daniel,§ and Andrew‖ were call'd by their names,
And Bound¶ to assist in this great undertaking,
For they'd have a barrell, all of their own making.

But his credit Will lost—Lost how? do ye ask?
Why he put an old bung in a new red-oak Cask.

Then to it they went, and the stave they upreared,
And as well as they could the Heading prepar'd,
Then trust the long Hoops to put over all,
For they knew without Hooping, the barrell must fall.

But his credit Will lost—Lost how? do ye ask?
Why he put an old bung in a new red-oak Cask.

*Whitefield.
†Tennent.
‡Davenport.
§Rogers.
‖Croswell.
¶Bound the Baptist.

With driver and addze they go merrily round,
And dub-dub a dub, the barrell does sound,
So the New Work, the Great Work, the Good Work goes on;
Will swore it should equal the Heidelburg Tun.*

    But his credit Will lost—Lost how? do ye ask?
    Why he put an old bung in a new red-oak Cask.

Now Will on surveying his tools and his stuff,
Perceiv'd he had not got Heading enough;
So he call'd for More-head,† for do what he will,
He knew without More-head the Work must stand still.

    But his credit Will lost—Lost how? do ye ask?
    Why he put an old bung in a new red-oak Cask.

The Cask was now try'd but it leak'd at each head
The joints were so open it would scarcely hold bread.
This abated Will's pride, so he took the hoops off
Lest neigh'bring Coopers should at the Work scoff.

    But his credit Will lost—Lost how? do ye ask?
    Why he put an old bung in a new red-oak Cask.

But Will he espy'd on a careful survey
A Stave of sound Ash-ly‡ light in his Way,
So he took it—'twill make the Cask tight with a jerk
And 'twill honour the Staves to be put in the Work.

    But his credit Will lost—Lost how? do ye ask?
    Why he put an old bung in a new red-oak Cask.

This Stave was so sound, and infallibly right,
That Will could not bend it, with all main and might;

---

*The legendary "largest barrel" in the world.
†Morehead the Irish Minister.
‡Reverend Mr. Ashely in a sermon at Mr. Cooper's Meeting House discovered a dislike to itinerant preachers which disgusted Mr. C and he attacked Mr. Ashely in a pamphlet not much to Mr. Cs credit.

So vex'd to the heart, he fell beating on,
But sure he had better, have let it alone.

> For his credit Will lost—Lost how? do ye ask?
> Why he put an old bung in a new red-oak Cask.

And thus with the powerful stroke of his giving,
He started the Hoops with his furious driving:
The barrell no longer with Hoops being bound—
Down fell the whole Work all flat to the ground.

> For his credit Will lost—Lost how? do ye ask?
> Why he put an old bung in a new red-oak Cask.

All you Coopers beware of this Coopers fate,
Be advis'd and take Warning before 'tis too late,
Lest it fare with you all, as with him it has far'd:
So in driving be careful you drive not too hard.

> But his credit Will lost—Lost how? do ye ask?
> Why he put an old bung in a new red-oak Cask.

———

> Hail! *D—p—t* of wondrous fame
> Why so long before you came?
> All our hopes began to fail
> When we heard, you took a Sail;
> But maugre all their Boats and LAWs,
> You have found out a saving clause,
> And got to *Boston* free from harm,
> Except, by chance, a broken Arm.
> We, greet your Rev'rence, on your coming
> Being convinc'd, 'tis not a dunning,
> Let *White—d* come and drain our Purses
> And *Cross—l* load us with his Curses,
> Let *Ten—t* sentence Foes to Hell
> And *Bu—l* strip himself to yell,

You open, *Sir*, a chearful Spring
And teach us, young and old to Sing
For all are ours, *Cephas* and *Paul*
And young *Apollos*, whom they call.
Then let us sing, *Hei derry down*
As we walk about the Town
'Tis but a Fable, *Sir* we hate them.
Cantant Cicadæ per Æstatem
But, granting this, from Winters cold
You may be shelter'd at *Southold*,
Let *Boston* be your Summer-Seat
No danger of the raging Heat,
Itinerants, you need not fear
While *White—d*'s Name is held so dear,
Let *Hartford*, know here *Leges nuper*,
Editæ placent, et, insuper,
Now, all are ours, *Cephas* and *Paul*
And young *Apollos* with you all
Then let us sing, *Hei derre down*
Here we may sing from Town to Town.
Laymen, stir up your talent Gifts
For want of Learning use your Fists.
Artificers, your Weapons ply,
Coblers this Proverb is a lie,
'Tis carnal Reason, all a Sham
Ne Sutor, ultra Crepidam.
Sisters, no longer mind old *Paul*,
To teach, we know you have a Call
For all are ours, *Paul* and *Cephas*
Apollos young, *per Magnum fas*,
Then let us sing, *Hei derry day.*
And we will sing while that we may
And while we sing, eke we will Dance
Honi soit qui Mal y pence.
We hope to see old *Halcyon* Days
They'r now begun as *Cross—l* says,
Reason, no more shall show her Head,
Let Order, sleep among the Dead,
Blessed Confusion Now takes Place
A happy prelude to true Grace.

We shortly hope to see good Works
All left with *Pagans*, or to *Turks*,
Abominable in their Nature
And must be left sooner or later.
Here what the ancient Record saith
All must be Sin that is not Faith,
And to this Truth we all consent
We can be good and not repent.
For *Cephas*, *Paul* and young *Apollos*
Are stirred up to come and call us
Then let us sing, *Hei derry dum*,
The famous DAVEN—T is come
Opposers, call him not crack-Brain'd
Who has so long in Triumph reign'd,
Si talis, qualis, sit non Compos
We should be glad to get Sense from us.
With *Babel*'s Prince we'll graze; at least
We shortly hope to be all Beast,
And then no fear of moral Evil
Leave that to mongrel Beast and De—l.
Blockheads, once call'd, now show your Faces
Pregnant with Nonsense, ripe with Graces
Now is the Time to rise to light
You need but favour the New-Light.
Assurance be your constant Guest
If carnal Preachers give no rest,
'Till you like *Lot* are hous'd in Zoar
And thus our *Sodom* is no more
For *Paul*, *Apollos*, *Cephas* too
Are all our own. No more adieu,
Sing on dear *Sir*, and as you sing
We'll join the Chorus *derre ding*.

BENJAMIN FRANKLIN

(1706–1790)

Drinking Song

To the Abbé de la Roche, at Auteuil

Singer.

Fair Venus calls, her voice obey,
In beauty's arms spend night and day.
The joys of love, all joys excel,
And loving's certainly doing well.

Chorus.

Oh! no!
Not so!
For honest souls know,
Friends and a bottle still bear the bell.

Singer.

Then let us get money, like bees lay up honey;
We'll build us new hives, and store each cell.
The sight of our treasure shall yield us great pleasure;
We'll count it, and chink it, and jingle it well.

Chorus.

Oh! no!
Not so!
For honest souls know,
Friends and a bottle still bear the bell.

Singer.

If this does not fit ye, let's govern the city,
In power is pleasure no tongue can tell;
By crowds tho' you're teas'd, your pride shall be pleas'd,
And this can make Lucifer happy in hell!

Chorus.

Oh! no!
Not so!
For honest souls know,
Friends and a bottle still bear the bell.

Singer.

Then toss off your glasses, and scorn the dull asses,
Who, missing the kernel, still gnaw the shell;
What's love, rule, or riches? wise Solomon teaches,
They're vanity, vanity, vanity, still.

Chorus.

That's true;
He knew;
He'd tried them all through;
Friends and a bottle still bore the bell.

I Sing My Plain Country Joan

Poor Richard's Description of his Country Wife Joan.

A SONG—TUNE, *The Hounds are all out.*

I.

Of their *Chloes* and *Phyllises* Poets may prate,
    I will sing my plain COUNTRY JOAN;
Twice twelve Years my Wife, still the Joy of my Life:
    Bless'd Day that I made her my own,
                        My dear Friends.
Bless'd Day that I made her my own.

2.

Not a Word of her Shape, or her Face, or her Eyes,
    Of Flames or of Darts shall you hear;
Though I BEAUTY admire, 'tis VIRTUE I prize,
    Which fades not in seventy Years.

3.

In Health a Companion delightful and gay,
    Still easy, engaging, and free;
In Sickness no less than the faithfullest Nurse,
    As tender as tender can be.

4.

In Peace and good Order my Houshold she guides,
    Right careful to save what I gain;
Yet chearfully spends, and smiles on the Friends
    I've the Pleasure to entertain.

5.

Am I laden with Care, she takes off a large Share,
    That the Burden ne'er makes me to reel;
Does good Fortune arrive, the Joy of my Wife
    Quite doubles the Pleasure I feel.

6.

She defends my good Name, even when I'm to blame,
    Friend firmer to Man ne'er was given:
Her compassionate Breast feels for all the distress'd,
    Which draws down the Blessings of Heaven.

7.

In Raptures the giddy Rake talks of his Fair,
    Enjoyment will make him despise.
I speak my cool Sense, which long Exper'ence
    And Acquaintance has chang'd in no Wise.

8.

The Best have some Faults, and so has My JOAN,
    But then they're exceedingly small,
And, now I'm us'd to 'em, they're so like my own,
    I scarcely can feel them at all.

9.

Was the fairest young Princess, with Millions in Purse,
   To be had in Exchange for My JOAN,
She could not be a better Wife, might be a worse,
   So I'll stick to My JUGGY alone.

Three Precepts

Precept I.

In Things of moment, on thy self depend,
Nor trust too far thy Servant or thy Friend:
With private Views, thy Friend may promise fair,
And Servants very seldom prove sincere.

Precept II.

What can be done, with Care perform to Day,
Dangers unthought-of will attend Delay;
Your distant Prospects all precarious are,
And Fortune is as fickle as she's fair.

Precept III.

Nor trivial Loss, nor trivial Gain despise;
Molehills, if often heap'd, to Mountains rise:
Weigh every small Expence, and nothing waste,
Farthings long sav'd, amount to Pounds at last.

MATHER BYLES

(1707–1790)

Hymn to Christ for our Regeneration and Resurrection

I.

To Thee, my LORD, I lift the Song,
  Awake, my tuneful Pow'rs:
In constant Praise my grateful Tongue
  Shall fill my foll'wing Hours.

II.

Guilty, condemn'd, undone I stood;
  I bid my GOD depart:
He took my Sins, and paid his Blood,
  And turn'd this wand'ring Heart.

III.

Death, the grim Tyrant, seiz'd my Frame,
  Vile, loathsome and accurst:
His Breath renews the vital Flame,
  And Glories change the Dust.

IV.

Now, SAVIOUR, shall thy Praise commence;
  My Soul by Thee brought Home,
And ev'ry Member, ev'ry Sense,
  Recover'd from the Tomb.

V.

To Thee my Reason I submit,
  My Love, my Mem'ry, LORD,
My Eyes to read, my Hands to write,
  My Lips to preach thy Word.

To Pictorio, on the Sight of his Pictures

Ages our Land a barbarous Desart stood,
And savage Nations howl'd in ev'ry Wood;
No laurel'd Art o'er the rude Region smil'd,
Nor bless'd Religion dawn'd amidst the Wild;
Dulness and Tyranny confederate reign'd,
And Ignorance her gloomy State maintain'd.

    An hundred Journies now the Earth has run,
In annual Circles, round the central Sun,
Since the first Ship the unpolish'd Letters bore
Thro' the wide Ocean to the barb'rous Shore.
Then Infant-Science made it's early Proof,
Honest, sincere, tho' unadorn'd, and rough;
Still thro' a Cloud the rugged Stranger shone,
Politeness, and the softer Arts unknown:
No heavenly Pencil the free Stroke could give,
Nor the warm Canvass felt its Colours live.
No moving Rhet'rick rais'd the ravish'd Soul,
Flourish'd in Flames, or heard it's Thunder roll;
Rough horrid Verse, harsh, grated thro' the Ear,
And jarring Discords tore the tortur'd Air;
Solid, and grave, and plain the Country stood,
Inelegant, and rigorously good.

    Each Year, succeeding, the rude Rust devours,
And softer Arts lead on the following Hours;
The tuneful Nine begin to touch the Lyre,
And flowing Pencils light the living Fire;
In the fair Page new Beauties learn to shine,
The Thoughts to brighten, and the Style refine,
Till the great Year the finish'd Period brought;
PICTORIO painted, and MÆCENAS wrote.

    Thy Fame, PICTORIO, shall the Muse rehearse,
And sing her Sister-Art in softer Verse:
'Tis your's, great Master, in just Lines to trace
The rising Prospect, or the lovely Face.
In the fair Round to swell the glowing Cheek,

Give Thought to Shades, and teach the Paints to speak.
Touch'd by thy Hand, how *Sylvia*'s Charms engage!
And *Flavia*'s Features smile thro' ev'ry Age.
In *Clio*'s Face, th' attentive Gazer spies
Minerva's reasoning Brow, and azure Eyes,
Thy Blush, *Belinda*, future Hearts shall warm,
And *Celia* shine in *Citherea*'s Form.
In hoary Majesty, see CATO here;
Fix'd strong in Thought, there NEWTON's Lines appear;
Here in full Beauty blooms the charming Maid;
Here *Roman* Ruins nod their awful Head;
Here gloting Monks their am'rous Rights debate,
The *Italian* Master sits in easy State,
VANDIKE and RUBENS show their rival Forms,
And CÆSAR flashes in the Blaze of Arms.

But cease, fond Muse, nor the rude Lays prolong,
A thousand Wonders must remain unsung;
Crowds of new Beings lift their wond'ring Heads,
In conscious Forms, and animated Shades.
What Sounds can speak, to ev'ry Figure just,
The breathing Statue, and the living Bust?
Landskips how gay! arise in ev'ry Light,
And fresh Creations rush upon the Sight;
Thro' fairy Scenes the roving Fancy strays,
Lost in the endless, visionary Maze.

Still, wondrous Artist, let thy Pencil flow,
Still, warm with Life, thy blended Colours glow,
Raise the ripe Blush, bid the quick Eye-balls roll
And call forth every Passion of the Soul.
Let thy soft Shades in mimick Figures play,
Steal on the Heart, and catch the Mind away.
Yet *Painter*, on the kindred Muse attend,
The Poet ever proves the Painter's Friend.
In the same Studies Nature we pursue,
I the Description touch, the Picture you;
The same gay Scenes our beauteous Works adorn,
The purple Ev'ning, or the flamy Morn:
Now, with bold Hand, we strike the strong Design;

Mature in Thought, now soften every Line;
Now, unrestrain'd, in freer Airs surprize,
And sudden, at our Word, new World's arise.
In gen'rous Passion let our Breasts conspire,
As is the Fancy's, be the Friendship's Fire;
Alike our Labour, and alike our Flame:
'Tis thine to raise the Shape; 'tis mine to fix the Name.

The Conflagration

In some calm Midnight, when no whisp'ring Breeze
Waves the tall Woods, or curls th' undimpled Seas,
Lull'd on their oazy Beds, the Rivers seem
Softly to murmur in a pleasing Dream;
The shaded Fields confess a still Repose,
And on each Hand the dewy Mountains drowse:
Mean time the Moon, fair Empress of the Night!
In solemn Silence sheds her silver Light,
While twinkling Stars their glimm'ring Beauties shew,
And wink perpetual o'er the heav'nly blue:
Sleep nodding, consecrates the Deep serene,
And spreads her brooding Wings o'er all the dusky Scene:
Thro' the fine Æther moves no single Breath;
But all is hush as in the Arms of Death.

At once, Great GOD! thy dire Command is giv'n,
That the last Tempest shake the Frame of Heav'n.
Strait thick'ning Clouds in gloomy Volumes rise,
Gather on Heaps, and blacken in the Skies;
Sublime through Heav'n, redoubling Thunders roll,
And gleamy Lightnings flash from Pole to Pole.
Old Ocean with presaging Horror rores,
And rousing Earthquakes rumble round the Shores;
Ten thousand Terrors o'er the Globe are hurl'd,
And gen'ral Dread alarms a guilty World.

But Oh! what Glory breaks the scatt'ring Glooms?
Lo! down the op'ning Skies, he comes! he comes!
The Judge descending Flames along the Air;
And shouting Myriads pour around his Car:
Each ravish'd Seraph labours in his Praise,
And Saints, alternate, catch th' immortal Lays;
Here in melodious Strains blest Voices sing,
Here warbling Tubes, and here the vocal String,
Here from sweet Trumpets silver Accents rise
And the shril Clangour echo's round the Skies.

And now, O Earth! thy final Doom attend,
In awful Silence meet thy fiery End.
Lo! rising radiant from his burning Throne,
The God-Head, thund'ring, calls the Ruins on.
"*Curst Earth polluted with the Prophets Blood,*
Thou, the vile Murd'rer of the Son of GOD,
Full ripe for Vengeance, Vengeance be thy due,
Perish in Flames, refine, and rise anew."
Thus as he speaks, all Nature owns the GOD,
Quiver the Plains, the lofty Mountains nod,
The hollow winding Caverns echo round,
And Earth, and Sea, and Air, and Heav'n resound.

Now ratt'ling on, tremendous Thunder rolls,
And loudly crashing, shakes the distant Poles.
O'er the thick Clouds, amazing Lightnings glare,
Flames flash at Flames, and vibrate through the Air.
Roaring Vulcanoes murmur for their Prey,
And from their Mouth curls the Black Smoke away.
Deep groans the Earth, at its approaching Doom,
While in slow Pomp the mighty Burnings come.
As when dark Clouds rise slowly from the Main,
Then, in swift Sluices, deluge all the Plain,
Descending headlong down the Mountains sides,
A thousand Torrents roll their foamy Tides,
The rushing Rivers rapid roar around,
And all the Shores return the dashing sound:
Thus awful, slow, the fiery Deluge low'rs,
Thus rushes down, and thus resounding rores.

But O! what Sounds are able to convey
The wild Confusions of the dreadful Day!
Eternal Mountains totter on their Base,
And strong Convulsions work the Valley's Face.
Fierce Hurricanes on founding Pinions soar,
Rush o'er the Land, on the toss'd Billows rore,
And dreadful in resistless Eddies driv'n,
Shake all the chrystal Battlements of Heav'n.
See the wild Winds, big blust'ring in the Air,
Drive thro' the Forests, down the Mountains tare,
Sweep o'er the Vallies in their rapid Course,
And Nature bends beneath th' impetuous Force.
Storms rush at Storms, at Tempests Tempests rore,
Dash Waves on Waves, and thunder to the Shore.
Columns of Smoke on heavy Wings ascend,
And dancing Sparkles fly before the Wind.
Devouring Flames, wide-waving, rore aloud,
And melted Mountains form a fiery Flood:
Then, all at once, immense, the Fires arise,
A bright Destruction wraps the crackling Skies:
While all the Elements to melt conspire,
And the World blazes in the final Fire.

Yet shall ye, Flames, the wasting Globe refine,
And bid the Skies with purer Splendour shine;
The Earth, which the prolifick Fires consume,
To Beauty burns, and withers into Bloom;
Improving in the fertile Flame it lies,
Fades into Form, and into Vigour dies:
Fresh-dawning Glories blush amidst the Blaze,
And Nature all renews her flow'ry Face.
With endless Charms the everlasting Year
Rolls round the Seasons in a full Career;
Spring, ever blooming, bids the Fields rejoyce,
And warbling Birds try their melodious Voice;
Where-e'er she treads, Lillies unbidden blow,
Quick Tulips rise, and sudden Roses glow:
Her Pencil paints a thousand beauteous Scenes,
Where Blossoms bud amid immortal Greens,
Each Stream, in Mazes, murmurs as it flows,

And floating Forests gently bend their Boughs.
Thou, *Autumn*, too, sitt'st in the fragrant Shade,
While the ripe Fruits blush all around thy Head:
And lavish Nature, with luxuriant Hands,
All the soft Months, in gay Confusion, blends.

  The holy Nation here transported roves
Beneath the spreading Honours of the Groves,
And pleas'd, attend, descending down the Hills,
The murm'ring Musick of the running Rills.
Anthems divine by ev'ry Harp are play'd,
And the soft Musick warbles thro' the Shade.

  Hither, my Lyre, thy soft Assistance bring,
And let sweet Accents leap from String to String;
Join the bright Chorus of the future Skies,
While all around loud *Hallelujah's* rise,
And to the tuneful Lays the echoing Vault replies.

  This blessed Hope, my ravish'd Mind inspires,
And through my Bosom flash the sacred Fires:
No more my Heart it's growing Joy contains,
But driving Transports rush along my Veins;
I feel a Paradise within my Breast,
And seem already of a Heav'n possess'd.

JANE COLMAN TURELL

(1708–1735)

To my Muse, December 29. 1725

Come Gentle *Muse*, and once more lend thine aid,
O bring thy Succour to a humble Maid!
How often dost thou liberally dispense
To our dull Breast thy quick'ning Influence!
By thee inspir'd, I'll chearful tune my Voice,
And Love and sacred Friendship make my Choice.
In my pleas'd Bosom you can freely pour,
A greater Treasure than *Joves Golden Shower*.
Come now, *fair Muse*, and fill my empty Mind,
With rich Idea's, great and unconfin'd.
Instruct me in those secret Arts that lie
Unseen to all but to a *Poet's* Eye.
O let me burn with *Sappho's* noble Fire,
But not like her for faithless Man expire.
And let me rival great *Orinda's* Fame,
Or like sweet *Philomela's* be my Name.
Go lead the way, my Muse, nor must you stop,
'Till we have gain'd *Parnassus* shady Top:
'Till I have view'd those fragrant soft Retreats,
Those Fields of Bliss, the Muses sacred Seats.
I'll then devote thee to fair *Virtues* Fame,
And so be worthy of a *Poet's* name.

An Invitation into the Country

in Imitation of Horace, *left only in a rough Copy*

From the soft Shades, and from the balmy Sweets
Of *Medford*'s flow'ry Vales, and green Retreats,
Your absent *Delia* to her *Father* sends
And prays to see him 'ere the Summer ends.

Now while the Earth's with beauteous Verdure dy'd,
And *Flora* paints the Meads in all her Pride;
While laden Trees *Pomonia*'s Bounty own,
And *Ceres* Treasures do the Fields adorn.
From the thick Smokes, and noisy *Town*, O come,
And in these Plains a while forget your Home.

Tho' my small Incomes never can afford,
Like wealthy *Celsus* to regale a Lord;
No Ivory Tables groan beneath the Weight
Of sumptuous Dishes, serv'd in massy Plate:
The Forest ne'r was search'd for Food for me,
Nor from my Hounds the timerous Hare does flee:
No leaden Thunder strikes the Fowl in Air,
Nor from my Shaft the winged Death do fear:
With silken Nets I ne're the Lake despoil,
Nor with my Bait the larger Fish beguile.
No luscious Sweet-Meats, by my Servants plac'd
In curious Order, 'ere my Table grac'd:
To please the Taste, no rich *Burgundian* Wine,
In chrystal Glasses on my Side-board shine;
The luscious Sweets of fair *Canaries* Isle
Ne'r fill'd my Casks, nor in my Flaggons smile:
No Wine, but what does from my Apples flow,
My frugal House on any can bestow:
Except when *Cæsar*'s Birth-day does return,
And joyful Fires throughout the Village burn;
Then moderate each takes his chearful Glass,
And our good Wishes to *Augustus* pass.

But tho' rich Dainties never spread my Board,
Nor my cool Vaults *Calabrian* Wines afford;
Yet what is neat and wholesome I can spread,
My good fat Bacon, and our homely Bread,
With which my healthful Family is fed.
Milk from the Cow, and Butter newly churn'd,
And new fresh Cheese, with Curds and Cream just turn'd.
For a Desert upon my Table's seen
The Golden Apple, and the Melon green;
The blushing Peech and glossy Plumb there lies,
And with the *Mandrake* tempt your Hands and Eyes.

This I can give, and if you'l here repair,
To slake your Thirst a Cask of *Autumn Beer*,
Reserv'd on purpose for your drinking here.

Under the Spreading Elms our Limbs we'll lay,
While fragrant *Zephires* round our Temples play.
Retir'd from Courts, and Crouds, secure we'll set,
And freely feed upon our Country Treat.
No noisy Faction here shall dare intrude,
Or once disturb our peaceful Solitude.

No stately Beds my humble Roofs adorn
Of costly Purple, by carv'd *Panthers* born.
Nor can I boast *Arabia*'s rich Perfumes,
Diffusing Odours thro' out stately Rooms.
For me no fair *Egyptian* plies the Loam,
But my fine Linnen all is made at Home.
Tho' I no Down or *Tapestry* can spread,
A clean soft *Pillow* shall support your Head,
Fill'd with the Wool from off my tender Sheep,
On which with Ease and Safety you may sleep.
The *Nightingale* shall lull You to your Rest,
And all be calm and still as is your Breast.

————

Phoebus has thrice his Yearly Circuit run,
The Winter's over, and the Summer's done;
Since that *bright Day* on which our hands were join'd,
And to *Philander* I my All resign'd.

Thrice in my Womb I've found the pleasing Strife,
In the first Struggles of my Infants Life:
But O how soon by Heaven I'm call'd to mourn,
While from my Womb a *lifeless Babe* is torn?
Born to the Grave 'ere it had seen the Light,
Or with one Smile had cheer'd my longing Sight.

Again in Travail-Pains my Nerves are wreck'd,
My Eye-balls start, my Heart-strings almost crack'd;
Now I forget my Pains, and now I press
Philander's Image to my panting Breast.
Ten Days I hold him in my joyful Arms,
And feast my Eyes upon his Infant Charms.
But then the King of Terrors does advance
To pierce it's Bosom with his Iron Lance.
It's Soul releas'd, upward it takes it's Flight,
Oh never more below to bless my Sight!
Farewell sweet *Babes* I hope to meet above,
And there with you Sing the Redeemer's Love.

And now O gracious Saviour lend thine Ear,
To this my earnest Cry and humble Prayer,
That when the Hour arrives with painful Throws,
Which shall my Burden to the World disclose;
I may Deliverance have, and joy to see
A living Child, to Dedicate to Thee.

MARY HIRST PEPPERELL

(1708–1789)

A Lamentation &c. On the Death of a Child

A Pritty BIRD did lately please my sight,
Ravish'd my Heart, and fill'd me with delight.
And as it grew, at once my joy and pride,
Belov'd by all that e're its Beauty spy'd,
I fondly call'd it mine, nor could I bear
A thought of loosing what I held so dear:
For it had just began with warbling strain
To raise my Pleasure, and to sooth my pain:
Its artless Notes, and lisping Melody,
Made in my Ears a tuneful Harmony.
Thus while I heard, and lov'd its charming Tongue,
For the sweet Singer's sake admir'd the Song:
Alass, when I least dreamt of its decay,
The pleasant Bird by Death was snatch'd away.
Snatch'd, did I say, no, I recall the Word,
'Twas sent for home by its most rightful LORD;
To whose bless'd Will, I must and do resign,
Since LORD, Thou tak'st but what was doubly thine.
'Twas thine bless'd LORD, thy Goodness lent it me;
'Twas doubly thine, because giv'n back to Thee.
Then go sweet BIRD, mount up, and sing on high,
Whilst winged Seraphs bear thee thro' the Sky.
There clad with Glory and with Joy sereen,
On Boughs Immortal ever fresh and green
Chant forth high Praises, with the lovely Train
Of spotless Doves, for whom the Lamb was slain,
Touch *David*'s Harp with wonder and surprize,
While our's neglected, on the Willows lies.
Hosanna's sound on each exalted String,
There join the Cherubim and Seraphim,
In endless Songs of Triumph to this KING.

JOHN SECCOMB

(1708–1793)

Father Abbey's Will

Cambridge, Decemb. 1731.

Some time since died here Mr. *Matth. A——y*, in a very advanc'd Age, he had for a great Number of Years served the College here, in Quality of a Bed maker and Sweeper, Having left no Child, his Wife inherits his whole Estate which he bequeathed to her by his last Will and Testament as follow,

1.

To my dear Wife,
My Joy and Life,
I freely now do give her
My whole Estate,
With all my Plate
Being just about to leave her.

2.

A Tub of Soap,
A long Cart Rope,
A Frying Pan & Kettle,
An Ashes Pail,
A threshing Flail,
An iron Wedge & Beetle.

3.

Two painted Chairs,
Nine Warden Pairs,
A large old dripping Platter,
The Bed of Hay
On which I lay,
An old Sauce Pan for Butter.

4.

A little Mugg,
A Two Quart Jugg,
A Bottle full of Brandy,
A Looking Glass
To see your Face
You'l find it very handy.

5.

A Musket true
As ever flew,
A pound of Shot and Wallett
A Leather Sash
My Calabash
My Powder Horn & Bullet.

6.

An old Sword Blade,
A Garden Spade
A Ho, a Rake, a Ladder,
A wooden Cann,
A Close Stool Pan,
A Clyster Pipe and Bladder.

7.

A greazy Hat,
My old Ram Cat,
A yard & half of Linnen,
A Pot of Grease,
A woollen Fleece,
In order for your spinning.

8.

A small Tooth Comb,
An ashen Broom,
A Candlestick & Hatchet,

A Coverlid
Strip'd down with Red,
A Bagg of Rags to patch it.

9.

A ragged Mat,
A Tub of Fat,
A Book put out by *Bunnian*,
Another Book
By *Robin Rook*,
A Skain or two of Spun yarn.

10.

An old black Muff,
Some Garden Stuff,
A Quantity of Burrage,
Some Devil's Weed
And Burdock Seed
To season well your Porridge.

11.

A Chafing Dish
With one Salt Fish,
If I am not mistaken,
A Leg of Pork,
A broken Fork
And half a Flitch of Bacon.

12.

A spinning Wheel,
One Peck of Meal,
A Knife without a handle,
A rusty Lamp,
Two Quarts of Samp,
And half a Tallow Candle.

13.

My Pouch and Pipes,
Two Oxen Tripes,
An oaken Dish well carved,
My little Dog,
And spotted Hog,
With two young Pigs just starv'd.

14.

This is my Store
I have no more,
I heartily do give it,
My Years are spun
My Days are done,
And so I think to leave it.

Proposal to Mistress Abbey

Our Sweeper having lately buryed his Spouse, and accidentally hearing the Death and Will of his deceas'd *Cambridge Brother*, has conceiv'd a violent Passion for the Relict. As Love softens the Mind, and disposes to Poetry, he has eas'd himself in the following Strains, which he transmits to the charming Widow, as the first Essay of his Courtship.

1.

Mistress *A——y*,
To you I fly,
You only can relieve me,
To you I turn, for you I burn,
If you will but believe me.

2.

Then gentle Dame
Admit my Flame,
And grant me my Petition,
If you deny
Alas! I die
In pitiful Condition.

3.

Before the News
Of your poor Spouse
Had reach'd us at *New Haven*,
My dear Wife dy'd
Who was my Bride
In *Anno* Eighty seven.

4.

Thus being free
Let's both agree
To join our Hands for I do
Boldly aver
A Widower
Is fittest for a Widow.

5.

You may be sure
'Tis not your Dower
I make this flowing Verse on;
In these smooth lays
I only praise
The glories of your Person.

6.

For the whole that
Was left by *Mat.*
Fortune to me has granted

In equal Store,
Nay I've too more,
What *Matthew* always wanted:

7.

No Teeth, 'tis true
You have to shew,
The young think Teeth inviting,
But silly Youths!
I love those Mouths
Where there's no fear of biting.

8.

A leaky Eye
That's never dry
These woful Times is fitting,
A wrinkled Face
Adds solemn Grace
To Folks devout at Meeting.

9.

Thus to go on
I would Pen down
Your Charms from Head to Foot
Set all your Glory
In Verse before ye
But I've no Mind to do't.

10.

Then hast away
And make no stay,
For soon as you come hither,
We'll eat and sleep,
Make Beds and sweep,
And talk and smoke together.

II.

But if, my Dear,
I must move there
Towards *Cambridge* streight I'll set me
To towze the Hay
On which you lay,
If Madam you will let me.

ANON.

The Convert to Tobacco

A Tale.
(From a MS.)

Disce Tubo genitos haurire et reddere Fumos.

Hail RALEIGH! Venerable Shade,
Accept this Tribute humbly paid,
Great Patron of the Sailing Crew,
Who gav'st us Weed to smoke and chew,
Kindly accept these Honours due.
To Thee we owe our Country's Wealth,
And smirking Glee, and lusty Health.
From Ashes white as driven Snow,
Tobacco Clouds, 'tis what we owe,
In Fragrant Wreaths ascend the Sky
To Thee, the Smoaker's Deity.

   Immortal Weed! all-healing Plant!
Possessing Thee we nothing want.
Assistant Chief to Country Vicar,
Next to his Concordance and Liquor;
If Text obscure perplex his Brain,
He scratches, thinks, but all in vain,
Till lighted Pipe's prevailing Ray,
Like Phœbus, drives the Fog away.

   Concomitant of Cambro Briton,
(If I a Rhime, for that cou'd hit on)
Content with thee, he'll bare-foot trudge it,
His Hose and Shoes fast bound in Budget;
Bleak blow the Winds, thick fall the Snows,
With thee he warms his dripping Nose,
And scrubs, and puffs, and on he goes.

   With Thee, dear Partner of his Ale,
The Justice grave prolongs his Tale;
And fast asleep does wisely prate us,
Whilst sober Whiff fills each HIATUS.

With thee—but hark'ee, says a Friend,
TOM, will thy Preface never end?
We want the Tale, you promis'd us;
The Tale d'ye want?—then take it thus:
 BUXOMA was a Banker's Widow,
Frolick and free as good Queen Dido;
For now twelve Months were past and gone;
Since Spouse lay cover'd with a Stone.
At first, indeed, for Fashion Sake,
She must not rest a-sleep, or wake;
The wretched'st Woman sure alive,
The best of Husbands to survive.
O had she dy'd (but 'twas too late!)
To save her Dearee from his Fate.
Poor ten per Cent! his Hour was come,
E'er he had half made up his Plumb.
You'd swear she'd learnt to mourn at School;
She sigh'd by Note, and wept by Rule.
The Neighbours saw't; and who but she
For conjugal Sincerity!
 But now the Farce was o'er, she saw
'Twas time the Vizard to withdraw.
The Sable Weeds, are thrown aside,
No more she wrung her Hands and cry'd;
But gay at all Assemblies shone,
And—who was blest that lay alone?
The Charms of Forty Thousand Pound
Drew from each Quartet all around;
The Templer spruce, and formal Citt,
The Man of War, and Man of Wit.
The last indeed despair'd to win her,
Yet still pursu'd her for a Dinner.
For Madam's Gate, or she's belie'd,
Stood ever hospitably wide.
Good Beef and Mutton grac'd her Table,
And who eat most she judg'd most able.
The Cloth remov'd, the Board was spread,
With Choice of Wine, both White and Red.
Pipes and Tobacco next appear,
And Tapers bright bring up the Rear.

Now by the by, Sir, you must know,
Our Widow whilom made a Vow,
Tho' Age and Ugliness o'ertook her,
Never to wed with filthy Smoaker:
And therefore slyly laid a Plot
To try who smoakt, and who did not.

   Unhappy State of human kind!
To future Evils ever blind!
The gilded Pill we rashly swallow,
Nor heed what Bitterness may follow.
This to make out and eke my Tale,
Our Lovers smoak'd it one and all,
Unthinking of th' impending Doom,
And spicy Whiffs perfum'd the Room;
When strait the Widow, SANS excuse,
Their Offers bluntly did refuse.

   Thus had she packt off Lovers plenty,
Some say a Dozen, others Twenty;
And now began to fear, I trow,
Lest she were hamper'd in her Vow.
When lo! a Swain of Irish Race
With Back of Steel, and Front of Brass,
Resolv'd BUXOMA to assail,
And wisely, that he might not fail,
Struck in with Mistress ABIGAIL.
Now ABIGAILS, the learned say,
To Lady's Hearts can pave the way;
The Jade, unable to resist
Five Pieces clapt in Lilly Fist,
Betray'd (a Mercenary Whore!)
The Vow I told you of before,
And MAC succeeds in his Amour.
He wou'd not smoke, to save his Life,
Prais'd the good Taste of PAULO's Wife;
"Tobacco, Fogh! he cou'd not bear it,
Filthy Concomitant of Claret."

   Our Widow chuckled here to find
At last a Lover to her Mind;
And strait an honest Parson got

To tye the Matrimonial Knot.
Here, to be short, the Wedding-day
Was eat, and drank, and danc'd away;
The wishing Guests the Stocking threw,
Jested a while, and then with drew.
When loud the Groom began to roar,
And bang his Slipper 'gainst the Floor,
—Here bring a Pipe—A Pipe! she cry'd!—
"Nay, do not fret, good angry Bride,
For I must smoak, or else—my Dear,"
(Then whisper'd something in her Ear)
"Tis true by Heaven! my former Spouse
Lov'd to see Pipes come into th' House."
With wistful Eye, poor Madam view'd
Her Dear Deceiver, thought him rude;
Yet Silent lay, in sad Suspence,
Waiting the happy Consequence.
Which, Authors say, she did not miss;
The Pipe was out, an eager Kiss
Preluded to th' ensuing Bliss.
He smoak'd a Second, and a Third,
Nay, and a Fourth too ('tis aver'd,)
And still the well experienc'd Dame
Found the yet wish'd Effect the Same.
Some have affirm'd, he was so stout
To take a Fifth e'er he gave out.
What yet again, the Devil's in thee.
NAT! Fetch the Pound of SLY's Virginia,
All the new Pipes, and a fresh Light,
Your Master says he'll smoak all Night.

"POOR JULIAN"

Poor Julleyoun's Warnings to Children and Servants

To shun the ways of Sin, and those particularly which hath brought him to his doleful End.

Poor *Julleyoun* now doth cry aloud,
To all this numerous thronging croud,
To hear his doleful dying cries,
To learn from him now to be wise.

O how aloud he doth proclaim,
His Sin, his Sorrow and his Shame,
And Warns the vast Assembly here,
With trembling and with shocking Fear.

To Cry aloud that they may'nt come,
To his deserved doleful Doom.
O can't you hear the Sinner speak,
Enough to make your Hearts to break.

Of what the Lord hath done for him,
Who now is dying for his Sin.
O can't you hear him say I came
From darksome Shades of Death and Rome;

Into a Land of Gospel Light,
Where *Jesus* Gospel shines so bright,
But now behold and hear him groan,
For the Transgressions he hath done.

And take his Warnings in your way,
And hear him now you beg and pray,
To fly the Guilt which he's pursu'd,
To the Sheding of his Neighbour's Blood.

See how he doth confess and say,
My dearest Life I've Sinn'd away,
By my attrocious ways of Sin,
Which all my Days I have liv'd in.

Be warn'd you disobedient ones,
Both Children, Servants, and all Sons
Of sinful *Adam* here on Earth,
Lest you should Die the second Death.

Beware of Lying, Stealing too,
And joining with a wicked Crew,
Who will the Sabbath Day Prophane,
The sacred Name of GOD blaspheme.

Bad Company besure to shun,
And join not with the Wicked one,
Who seeks and lurks for Prey and Blood,
Who by all means must be withstood.

All Drunkenness and Profaneness fly,
And every evil way discry,
Adultery, Fornication too
Abhored let it be by you.

But O the Murder I have done,
To the poor faultless dying Man,
Who dying at my Feet fell down,
An awful Victim on the Ground.

O my vile Rage when at one thrust,
I sent his Body to the Dust,
His Soul I know not where its gone.
But now I beg as for mine own,

I may find Mercy when from this Tree,
I launch into Eternity.
O now behold and see me here,
A dying Sinner full of Fear.

And take you Warning all by me,
Least this your dreadful Portion be.
O let the amazing doleful Sight,
Perswade you all with greatest might.

To shun the Sins for which I Die,
And now pass to Eternity.
O did you know but what I felt,
For my Transgressions and my Guilt.

O! O how quick my Moments pass,
The trembling Sands haste in my Glass.
O an amazing thing it is,
To stand upon the great Abyss,

Of the Eternal Flames of Hell,
Where such vile Sinners sure must dwell,
Unless the great Redeemer come,
To save us from our doleful Doom.

And now Farewell my dearest Friends,
For Times with me have now its ends,
Until the last great Trump shall sound,
When Rising from the lonesom Ground,
In *Jesus* I do Hope to Rise,
In Peace and Joy to my Surprise.

Advice from the Dead to the Living

or, a Solemn Warning to the World.
Occasioned by the untimely Death of poor Julian,
Who was Executed on Boston Neck, on Thursday
the 22 d. of March, 1733. for the Murder of Mr. John
Rogers of Pembrake, the 12 th of September, 1732.

Very proper to be Read by all Persons, but especially
young People, and Servants of all Sorts.

This Day take warning young and old,
By a sad Sight we here behold,
Of one whom Vengeance in his Chase
Hath taken in his sinful Race.

Here we behold amidst the Throng,
Condemned *Julian* guarded strong,
To Gallows bound with heavy Heart,
To suffer as his just Desert.

Where we for Warning may observe
What cruel Murder doth deserve,
Also the sad procuring Cause
Why Sinners die amidst their Days.

Here now we have a lively View,
Of *Cain*'s vile Action fresh and new,
That old Revenge is by Permit
Prevailing in our Natures yet.

Revenge is sweet, we often hear,
How bitter now doth it appear?
It leads to Ruine, Death and Fate,
And bitter Mourning when too late.

We often hear Men to complain,
Their Punishment like guilty *Cain*,
Which justly falleth to their Share,
Is great, and more than they can bear!

The Prisoner owns the bloody Act,
And faith the Sentence on his Fact,
Was pass'd on him impartially,
And therefore doth deserve to die.

By his Account he first was sold,
When he was not quite three Years old;
And by his Master in his Youth,
Instructed in the Ways of Truth.

Was also taught to Write and Read,
And learn'd his Catechise and Creed,
And what was proper (as he saith)
Relating to the Christian Faith.

His pious Master did with care,
By Counsels warn him to beware
Of wicked Courses, that would tend
To his Destruction in the End.

When Twenty Years were gone and past,
By his Account he took at last
To Drinking and ill Company,
Which prov'd his fatal Destany,

No timely Warnings would he hear,
From kind Reproofs he turn'd his Ear,
Provoked God for to depart,
And leave him to an harden'd Heart.

Since he despis'd the Ways of Truth,
And good Instruction in his Youth,
God then withdrew restraining Grace,
And let him run his wicked Race.

From Sin to Sin advancing thus,
By sad Degrees from bad to worse,
He did at length commit the Crime,
For which he dies before his Time.

He prays his sad untimely Fall,
May be a Warning unto all,
That they no such like Steps do tread,
Nor lead such Life as he has led.

That Children and all Servants they
Would in their Stations all obey,
Parents and Masters every one,
And not to do as he has done.

Obey them with a willing Mind,
Be always honest, just and kind,
And pray to God to give them Grace,
To do their Duty in their Place.

He thanks good Preachers heartily,
For all their Helps of Piety,
Which to his Soul they did extend,
To fit him for his latter End.

So here we leave his pitious Case,
In tender Arms of sov'reign Grace,
Altho' his Crimes are great and sore,
Grace can abound and pardon more.

Now may the Congregation hear,
This awful Voice, and stand in fear,
And being timely warn'd thereby,
May do no more so wickedly.

JUPITER HAMMON

(1711–c. 1806)

An Address to Miss Phillis Wheatly, Ethiopian Poetess, in Boston

who came from Africa at eight years of age, and soon became acquainted with the gospel of Jesus Christ

Miss Wheatly, pray give me leave to express as follows:

1.

O Come you pious youth! adore   Eccles. xii. 1.
   The wisdom of thy God,
In bringing thee from distant shore,
   To learn his holy word.

2.

Thou mightst been left behind,   Psal. cxxxvi. 1, 2, 3.
   Amidst a dark abode;
God's tender mercy still combin'd,
   Thou hast the holy word.

3.

Fair wisdom's ways are paths of peace,   Psal. i. 1, 2, 3.
   And they that walk therein,   Prov. iii. 7.
Shall reap the joys that never cease,
   And Christ shall be their king.

4.

God's tender mercy brought thee here,
   Tost o'er the raging main;   Psal. ciii. 1, 2, 3, 4.
In Christian faith thou hast a share,
   Worth all the gold of Spain.

5.

While thousands tossed by the sea,
   And others settled down,   Death.
God's tender mercy set thee free,
   From dangers still unknown.

6.

That thou a pattern still might be,
   To youth of Boston town,   2 Cor. v. 10.
The blessed Jesus set thee free,
   From every sinful wound.

7.

The blessed Jesus, who came down,
   Unvail'd his sacred face,   Rom. v. 21.
To cleanse the soul of every wound,
   And give repenting grace.

8.

That we poor sinners may obtain
   The pardon of our sin;   Psal. xxxiv. 6, 7, 8.
Dear blessed Jesus now constrain,
   And bring us flocking in.

9.

Come you, Phillis, now aspire,
   And seek the living God,   Matth. vii. 7, 8.
So step by step thou mayst go higher,
   Till perfect in the word.

10.

While thousands mov'd to distant shore,
   And others left behind,   Psal. lxxxix. 1.
The blessed Jesus still adore,
   Implant this in thy mind.

11.

Thou hast left the heathen shore,
   Thro' mercy of the Lord;   Psal. xxxiv. 1, 2, 3.
Among the heathen live no more,
   Come magnify thy God.

12.

I pray the living God may be,
   The shepherd of thy soul;   Psal. lxxx. 1, 2, 3.
His tender mercies still are free,
   His mysteries to unfold.

13.

Thou, Phillis, when thou hunger hast,
   Or pantest for thy God;   Psal. xlii. 1, 2, 3.
Jesus Christ is thy relief,
   Thou hast the holy word.

14.

The bounteous mercies of the Lord
   Are hid beyond the sky,   Psal. xvi. 10, 11.
And holy souls that love his word,
   Shall taste them when they die.

15.

These bounteous mercies are from God,
   The merits of his Son;   Psal. xxxiv. 15.
The humble soul that loves his word,
   He chooses for his own.

16.

Come, dear Phillis, be advis'd,
   To drink Samaria's flood;   John iv. 13, 14.
There nothing is that shall suffice,
   But Christ's redeming blood.

17.

While thousands muse with earthly toys,
    And range about the street,   Matth. vi. 33.
Dear Phillis, seek for heaven's joys,
    Where we do hope to meet.

18.

When God shall send his summons down,
    And number saints together,   Psal. cxvi. 15.
Blest angels chant, (triumphant sound)
    Come live with me for ever.

19.

The humble soul shall fly to God,
    And leave the things of time,   Mat. v. 3, 8.
Start forth as 'twere at the first word,
    To taste things more divine.

20.

Behold! the soul shall wast away,
    Whene'er we come to die,   Cor. xv. 51, 52, 53.
And leave its cottage made of clay,
    In twinkling of an eye.

21.

Now glory be to the Most High,
    United praises given,   Psal. cl. 6.
By all on earth, incessantly,
    And all the host of heav'n.

JOHN OSBORN

(1713–1753)

A Whaling Song

When spring returns with western gales,
   And gentle breezes sweep
The ruffling seas, we spread our sails
   To plough the watry deep.

For killing northern whales prepar'd,
   Our nimble boats on board,
With craft and rum (our chief regard)
   And good provision stor'd.

Cape-Cod, our dearest, native land,
   We leave astern, and lose
Its sinking cliffs and less'ning sands,
   While Zephyr gently blows.

Bold, hardy men, with blooming age,
   Our sandy shores produce;
With monstrous fish they dare engage
   And dang'rous callings choose.

Now tow'rds the early dawning East
   We speed our course away,
With eager minds, and joyful hearts,
   To meet the rising day.

Then as we turn our wond'ring eyes,
   We view one constant show;
Above, around, the circl'ing skies;
   The rolling seas below.

When eastward, clear of *Newfoundland*,
    We stem the frozen pole,
We see the icy islands stand,
    The northern billows roll.

As to the North we make our way,
    Surprising scenes we find;
We lengthen out the tedious day,
    And leave the night behind.

Now see the northern regions, where
    Eternal winter reigns;
One day and night fills up the year,
    And endless cold maintains.

We view the monsters of the deep,
    Great whales in num'rous swarms;
And creatures there, that play and leap,
    Of strange, unusual forms.

When in our station we are plac'd,
    And whales around us play;
We launch our boats into the main,
    And swiftly chase our prey.

In haste we ply our nimble oars,
    For an assault design'd;
The sea beneath us foams and roars,
    And leaves a wake behind.

A mighty whale we rush upon,
    And in our irons throw:
She sinks her monstrous body down
    Among the waves below.

And when she rises out again,
    We soon renew the fight;
Thrust our sharp lancets in amain,
    And all her rage excite.

Enrag'd, she makes a mighty bound;
   Thick foams the whiten'd sea;
The waves in circles rise around,
   And wid'ning roll away.

She thrashes with her tail around,
   And blows her red'ning breath;
She breaks the air, a deaf'ning sound,
   While ocean groans beneath.

From num'rous wounds, with crimson flood
   She stains the frothy seas,
And gasps, and blows her latest blood,
   While quiv'ring life decays.

With joyful hearts we see her die,
   And on the surface lay;
While all with eager haste apply,
   To save our deathful prey.

THOMAS CRADOCK

(1718–1770)

Hymn for Ascension

1

He springs, he rises from the ground
   He cleaves the yielding sky.
Then Earth, the heavens with joy resound,
   That Savior mounts on high.

2

O Wondrous proof of power divine
   The God, the God ascends;
With what a lustre does he shine,
   And what a train attends.

3

The cherubim & seraphim
   Crowd thick his azure way;
And hark in one continued hymn
   Their duteous homage pay.

4

Hear this ye nations and adore;
   The Era is begun,
When time and death—their ravage o'er—
   Lie vanquished by the Son.

5

Again he'll in the clouds appear;
   When—all-tremendous thought—
For what we've live & acted here,
   Shall be to judgement brought.

6

The wicked in the depths of hell,
    To wail eternal woe;
The righteous with their Lord to dwell,
    Where joys immortal flow.

FROM

Maryland Eclogues in Imitation of Virgil's

Split-Text
Eclogue 1st.

Argument

Crape, a Virginian Clergyman, being turn'd out
of his Living for Misdemeanours, comes to the
House of Split-text in Maryland, where Split-text's
happy Situation & Crape's Misfortune naturally
beget the following Dialogue.

Crape, Split-text

Crape:

Beneath the Shade of these wide-spreading Trees,
Dear Split-text. You can smoke your Chunk at Ease;
I hapless Wretch! must bid such joys Adieu;
Strip't of my Credit, & my Income too;
Must leave my Glebe, which all my Bacon fed,
(Bacon, my rich repast so often made)
While you, while chearful, Plenty round you dwells,
Can talk with D——y, how Tobacco sells.

Split-text:

Yes, Brother Crape—a gen'rous Chief bestow'd
On me these Blessings—all to him I ow'd.
For which I'll ne'er forget, each Sabbath-Day,
With hearty Zeal for my good Lord to pray:
He made me Parson here; & bids me fill
My Pipe & Bowl, as often as I will.

Crape:

I envy not your Bliss, but wonder much
Their Hate for Pray'rs & Parsons here is such!
Poor I am forc'd on this lank jade to ride,
Which often alate with hunger lik'd to 've died:
But yesterday she tumbled in the Dirt,
And 'gainst a *white oak* Stump my Forehead hurt,
Fool! that I was!—I might have known my Fate;
But Man is conscious of his Faults too late;
My Vestry told me oft, they'd bear no more,
And now at length have turn'd me out of Door.
—But say how you have all this Favour got?

Split-text:

Assurance & Good Luck:—what will they not?
A— by Birth, I came a School to teach;
But little thought (God knows) I e'er should preach;
I found the Parsons here such Clods of Clay,
That soon to my Ambition I gave Way:
Why might not I, I said, harangue as well
As W——n or Wh——r or D-ll?
For we resemble those at Home no more,
Than Saints of Modern Days do Saints of yore.

Crape:

And pray, what made you to this Country come?

Split-text:

Faith! Poverty—I shou'd have starv'd at Home.
Soon as the Down 'gan on my Chin t'appear;
I quite grew weary of my country Fare.
Oatmeal & Water was too thin a Diet,
To keep my grumbling Guts in peace & Quiet;
So Fear of Starving, Hope of living better,
Made me have Heart enough to cross the Water.

Crape:

I was surpris'd, that tho' you liv'd so well,
Your Carcase was so lank, your Phiz so pale;
The Cause is plain—your native, hungry Food

So gain'd th' Ascendant o'er your youthful Blood,
You look, as, if no meat cou'd do you good.

Split-text:
Twas Time then to some other place to roam,
And seek for better Fare than was at home;
Here then I came—but soon went back again,
The Bishop's Blessing, & my Lord's to gain
Soon both I got—I saw that noble Peer,
For whom our Church puts up each week a Pray'r.
He bad me come, he bad me preach & pray,
And, if the Planters wou'd not, make 'em pay.

Crape:
O happy Brother; happy is Thy Plight;
Happy in all that can thy Soul delight;
Sure of the Forties, Whate'er Loss betide
The Planter's Toil; since they must be supply'd.
O happy Brother—By this purling Rill
These shady *Locusts*, & that pleasant Hill,
What dost thou not enjoy?—the fanning Breeze
Comes sweetly breathing on thee thru the trees;
That busy Swarm with lulling sound compose
Thy wearied Soul to gentle, soft Repose;
Thy *Negros*, chanting forth their rustick Loves,
The melancholy Musick of the Doves;
The feather'd Choir, which, while they skim along
The liquid Plain, regale thee with a Song;
All, all conspire to heighten ev'ry Bliss,
And make thee taste sincerest Happiness.

Split-text:
Planters Tobacco shall forget to smoke,
Hogs to love Mast and Peaches, Frogs to croak,
The Indians range, where flows the princely *Thames*,
And Duchess live nigh *Potomack's* Streams,
'Ere from my Heart that smiling Mien I lose
With which the gen'rous Lord his Gifts bestows.

Crape:

But I alass! no more my Glebe must view,
But to my once-lov'd Dwelling bid Adieu,
Go preach the Gospel in some *Indian's* Ear,
Who'll mind my Preaching, like your *Planters* here?
And must a Stranger—*Parson* rule the roost,
And Glean the Harvest I so stupid lost?
What has my Guzzling & my Folly done?
Go, *Planters*, go, your *quondam* Parson shun;
No more shall I with you rant, drink & smoke;
Toast baudy Healths, or crack a smutty joak;
No more in Bumbo, or in Cyder swill;
Faith! all's o'er now—I may go where I will.

Split-text:

To night howe'er with me you'll foul a Plate;
A juicy fat Gammon & a Chick we'll get;
Wine I have none; Good Bumbo & small Beer,
Clean, tho' coarse Linnen, will be all your Fare.
This year of Cyder I but made one Stoup,
One Night the *Planters* came & drank it up,
Walk in—the Chimney's Smoke's more plainly seen;
And Giant Shadows cross the dewy Green;
In louder Musick sing the marshy Frogs;
—Sambo, go, pen the Turkies, feed the Hogs.

CHARLES WOODMASON

(c. 1720–c. 1777)

To Benjamin Franklin Esq; of Philadelphia, on his Experiments and Discoveries of Electricity

Let others muse on sublunary things,
The rise of empires and the fall of kings;
Thine is the praise, with bolder flight to soar,
And airy regions, yet untrack'd, explore;
To dictate science with imperial nod,
And save not ruin by an *iron rod*.*

 If for thy birth, when latest times draw night,
As now for *Homer*'s, rival cities vie;
This spot perhaps unmov'd may hear the strife,
Content to claim the vigour of thy life;
To shew thy tomb, like *Virgil*'s shewn before,
With laurel, proof to lightning, cover'd o'er.

 Happy that here we boast the guardian friend,
Where most the hostile elements contend:
This hour tremendous thunders strike my ear,
Keen light'nings dart, and threat'ning clouds appear:
Now fly the negroes from the impending storm!
The air how cold! this moment mild and warm.
Now down it pours! the tempest shakes the skies,
On flashes flashes, clouds on clouds arise;
The noxious rattle snake with fear deprest,
Now creeps for safety to his poisonous nest;
Bears, foxes, lynxes, seek the thickest brake,
Wolves, tygers, panthers in their caverns quake:
Now allegators diving quit the strand,
And birds unknown, in flocks repair to land;
Small riv'lets swell to streams, and streams to floods,
Loud whirlwinds rush impetuous thro' the woods,
Huge oaks midst foaming torrents fiercely burn,

---

*By the application of a rod of iron, or a wire, the effect of thunder and lightning is prevented.

And tall pines blasted from their roots are torn:
The bolt descends and harrows up the ground,
And stones and sand are widely scatter'd round;
How near the welkin breaks! now nearer still!
But now askance, it drives o'er yonder hill;
The rain abates, the gloomy clouds retreat,
And all is light, serenity and heat:
The change how sudden! but how frequent too!
The change, at length, without one fear I view:
Sedate, composed, I hear the tempest roll,
Which once with terror shook my boding soul!
No fire I fear my dwelling shou'd invade,
No bolt transfix me, in the dreadful shade;
No falling steeple trembles from on high,
No shivered organs now in fragments fly*,
The guardian point erected high in air,
Nature disarms, and teaches storms to spare.
So through the sultry deep unmov'd I sail,
When the wave whitens with a boding gale;
A fire ball strikes the mast a silent blow,
Then thunder speaks—no further shalt thou go;
Quick it descends the wire, around the shrouds,
Which checks the fury of the flaming clouds.
With hallow'd wands strange circles once were made,
To gull an ign'rant crowd, the jugglers trade;
Within the line no blue infernal fire,
Could pierce, but hence, malignant powers, retire;
What these pretended, *Franklin*, thou hast wrought,
And truth is own'd what once was fiction thought;
Within thy magic circle calm I sit,
Nor friends nor business in confusion quit;
What e'er explosions dreadful break around,
Or fiery meteors sweep the cracking ground.
    O friend, at once to science, and to man,
Persue each noble and each gen'rous plan;
With all the bliss beneficence obtains,
Be thine whate'er from gratitude it gains,

*The steeple and organ of *St. Philip's Church* at *Charles Town* have been twice damaged by lightning.

Be thine those honours that are virtue's meed,
Whate'er to genius wisdom has decreed!
    Accept this off'ring of an humble mind,
By sickness weaken'd—long to cares confin'd:
Tho' yet untasted the *Pierian* spring,
In lonely woods she thus attempts to sing,
Where seldom muse before e'er tun'd a lay,
Where yet the graces slowly find ther way:
Wild as the fragrant shrubs and blooming flow'rs
Which nature scatters round o'er artless bow'rs.
More soft and sweet will be her future strain,
Should this rude note thy approbation gain.

Cooper River, S. Carolina,
Sept. 20, 1753

JAMES GRAINGER

(c. 1721–1766)

The Sugar-Cane

BOOK IV.

Genius of Africk! whether thou bestrid'st
The castled elephant; or at the source,
(While howls the desert fearfully around,)
Of thine own Niger, sadly thou reclin'st
Thy temples shaded by the tremulous palm,
Or quick papaw, whose top is necklac'd round
With numerous rows of party-colour'd fruit:
Or hear'st thou rather from the rocky banks
Of Rio Grandê, or black Sanaga?
Where dauntless thou the headlong torrent brav'st
In search of gold, to brede thy wooly locks,
Or with bright ringlets ornament thine ears,
Thine arms, and ankles: O attend my song.
A muse that pities thy distressful state;
Who sees, with grief, thy sons in fetters bound;
Who wishes freedom to the race of man;
Thy nod assenting craves: dread Genius, come!

    Yet vain thy presence, vain thy favouring nod;
Unless once more the muses, that erewhile
Upheld me fainting in my past career,
Through Caribbe's cane-isles; kind condescend
To guide my footsteps, through parch'd Libya's wilds;
And bind my sun-burnt brow with other bays,
Than ever deck'd the Sylvan bard before.

    Say, will my Melvil, from the public care,
Withdraw one moment, to the muses shrine?
Who smit with thy fair fame, industrious cull
An Indian wreath to mingle with thy bays,
And deck the hero, and the scholar's brow!

Wilt thou, whose mildness smooths the face of war,
Who round the victor-blade the myrtle twin'st,
And mak'st subjection loyal and sincere;
O wilt thou gracious hear the unartful strain,
Whose mild instructions teach, no trivial theme,
What care the jetty African requires?
Yes, thou wilt deign to hear; a man thou art
Who deem'st nought foreign that belongs to man.

    In mind, and aptitude for useful toil,
The negroes differ: muse that difference sing.

    Whether to wield the hoe, or guide the plane;
Or for domestic uses thou intend'st
The sunny Libyan: from what clime they spring,
It not imports; if strength and youth be theirs.

    Yet those from Congo's wide-extended plains,
Through which the long Zaire winds with chrystal stream,
Where lavish Nature sends indulgent forth
Fruits of high flavour, and spontaneous seeds
Of bland nutritious quality, ill bear
The toilsome field; but boast a docile mind,
And happiness of features. These, with care,
Be taught each nice mechanic art: or train'd
To houshold offices: their ductile souls
Will all thy care, and all thy gold repay.

    But, if the labours of the field demand
Thy chief attention; and the ambrosial cane
Thou long'st to see, with spiry frequence, shade
Many an acre: planter, chuse the slave,
Who sails from barren climes; where art alone,
Offspring of rude necessity, compells
The sturdy native, or to plant the soil,
Or stem vast rivers for his daily food.

    Such are the children of the Golden Coast;
Such the Papaws, of negroes far the best:
And such the numerous tribes, that skirt the shore,
From rapid Volta to the distant Rey.

But, planter, from what coast soe'er they sail,
Buy not the old: they ever sullen prove;
With heart-felt anguish, they lament their home;
They will not, cannot work; they never learn
Thy native language; they are prone to ails;
And oft by suicide their being end.—

Must thou from Africk reinforce thy gang?—
Let health and youth their every sinew firm;
Clear roll their ample eye; their tongue be red,
Broad swell their chest; their shoulders wide expand;
Not prominent their belly; clean and strong
Their thighs and legs, in just proportion rise.
Such soon will brave the fervours of the clime;
And free from ails, that kill thy negroe-train,
A useful servitude will long support.

Yet, if thine own, thy childrens life, be dear;
Buy not a Cormantee, tho' healthy, young.
Of breed too generous for the servile field;
They, born to freedom in their native land,
Chuse death before dishonourable bonds:
Or, fir'd with vengeance, at the midnight hour,
Sudden they seize thine unsuspecting watch,
And thine own poinard bury in thy breast.

At home, the men, in many a sylvan realm,
Their rank tobacco, charm of sauntering minds,
From clayey tubes inhale; or, vacant, beat
For prey the forest; or, in war's dread ranks,
Their country's foes affront: while, in the field,
Their wives plant rice, or yams, or lofty maize,
Fell hunger to repel. Be these thy choice:
They, hardy, with the labours of the Cane
Soon grow familiar; while unusual toil,
And new severities their husbands kill.

The slaves from Minnah are of stubborn breed:
But, when the bill, or hammer, they affect;

They soon perfection reach. But fly, with care,
The Moco-nation; they themselves destroy.

Worms lurk in all: yet, pronest they to worms,
Who from Mundingo sail. When therefore such
Thou buy'st for sturdy and laborious they,
Straight let some learned leach strong medicines give,
Till food and climate both familiar grow.
Thus, tho' from rise to set, in Phœbus' eye,
They toil, unceasing; yet, at night, they'll sleep,
Lap'd in Elysium; and, each day, at dawn,
Spring from their couch, as blythsome as the sun.

One precept more, it much imports to know.—
The Blacks, who drink the Quanza's lucid stream,
Fed by ten thousand springs, are prone to bloat,
Whether at home or in these ocean-isles:
And tho' nice art the water may subdue,
Yet many die; and few, for many a year,
Just strength attain to labour for their lord.

Would'st thou secure thine Ethiop from those ails,
Which change of climate, change of waters breed,
And food unusual? let Machaon draw
From each some blood, as age and sex require;
And well with vervain, well with sempre-vive,
Unload their bowels.—These, in every hedge,
Spontaneous grow.—Nor will it not conduce
To give what chemists, in mysterious phrase,
Term the white eagle; deadly foe to worms.
But chief do thou, my friend, with hearty food,
Yet easy of digestion, likest that
Which they at home regal'd on; renovate
Their sea-worn appetites. Let gentle work,
Or rather playful excercise, amuse
The novel gang: and far be angry words;
Far ponderous chains; and far disheartning blows.—
From fruits restrain their eagerness; yet if
The acajou, haply, in thy garden bloom,

With cherries,* or of white or purple hue,
Thrice wholesome fruit in this relaxing clime!
Safely thou may'st their appetite indulge.
Their arid skins will plump, their features shine:
No rheums, no dysenteric ails torment:
The thirsty hydrops flies.—'Tis even averr'd,
(Ah, did experience sanctify the fact;
How many Lybians now would dig the soil,
Who pine in hourly agonies away!)
This pleasing fruit, if turtle join its aid,
Removes that worst of ails, disgrace of art,
The loathsome leprosy's infectious bane.

There are, the muse hath oft abhorrent seen,
Who swallow dirt; (so the chlorotic fair
Oft chalk prefer to the most poignant cates:)
Such, dropsy bloats, and to sure death consigns;
Unless restrain'd from this unwholesome food,
By soothing words, by menaces, by blows:
Nor yet will threats, or blows, or soothing words,
Perfect their cure; unless thou, Pæan, deign'st
By medicine's power their cravings to subdue.

To easy labour first inure thy slaves;
Extremes are dangerous. With industrious search,
Let them fit grassy provender collect
For thy keen stomach'd herds.—But when the earth

*The tree which produces this wholesome fruit is tall, shady, and of quick
growth. Its Indian name is *Acajou*; hence corruptly called *Cashew* by the En-
glish. The fruit has no resemblance to a cherry, either in shape or size; and bears,
at its lower extremity, a nut (which the Spaniards name *Anacardo*, and physi-
cians *Anacardium*) that resembles a large kidney-bean. Its kernel is as grateful
as an almond, and more easy of disgestion. Between its rhinds is contained a
highly caustic oil; which, being held to a candle, emits bright salient sparkles,
in which the American fortune-tellers pretended they saw spirits who gave an-
swers to whatever questions were put to them by their ignorant followers. This
oil is used as a cosmetic by the ladies, to remove freckles and sun-burning; but
the pain they necessarily suffer makes its use not very frequent. This tree also
produces a gum not inferior to Gum-Arabic; and its bark is an approved as-
tringent. The juice of the cherry stains exceedingly. The long citron, or amber-
coloured, is the best. The cashew-nuts, when unripe, are of a green colour;
but, ripe, they assume that of a pale olive. This tree bears fruit but once a year.

Hath made her annual progress round the sun,
What time the conch* or bell resounds, they may
All to the Cane-ground, with thy gang, repair.

   Nor, Negroe, at thy destiny repine,
Tho' doom'd to toil from dawn to setting sun.
How far more pleasant is thy rural task,
Than theirs who sweat, sequester'd from the day,
In dark tartarean caves, sunk far beneath
The earth's dark surface; where sulphureous flames,
Oft from their vapoury prisons bursting wild,
To dire explosion give the cavern'd deep,
And in dread ruin all its inmates whelm?—
Nor fateful only is the bursting flame;
The exhalations of the deep-dug mine,
Tho' slow, shake from thier wings as sure a death.
With what intense severity of pain
Hath the afflicted muse, in Scotia, seen
The miners rack'd, who toil for fatal lead?
What cramps, what palsies shake their feeble limbs,
Who, on the margin of the rocky Drave,†
Trace silver's fluent ore? Yet white men these!

   How far more happy ye, than those poor slaves,
Who, whilom, under native, gracious chiefs,
Incas and emperors, long time enjoy'd
Mild government, with every sweet of life,
In blissful climates? See them dragg'd in chains,
By proud insulting tyrants, to the mines
Which once they call'd their own, and then despis'd!
See, in the mineral bosom of their land,
How hard they toil! how soon their youthful limbs
Feel the decrepitude of age! how soon
Their teeth desert their sockets! and how soon
Shaking paralysis unstrings their frame!
Yet scarce, even then, are they allow'd to view

---

*Plantations that have no bells, assemble their Negroes by sounding a conch-shell.
†A river in Hungary, on whose banks are found mines of quicksilver.

The glorious God of day, of whom they beg,
With earnest hourly supplications, death;
Yet death slow comes, to torture them the more!

    With these compar'd, ye sons of Afric, say,
How far more happy is your lot? Bland health,
Of ardent eye, and limb robust, attends
Your custom'd labour; and, should sickness seize,
With what solicitude are ye not nurs'd!—
Ye Negroes, then, your pleasing task pursue;
And, by your toil, deserve your master's care.

    When first your Blacks are novel to the hoe;
Study their humours: Some, soft-soothing words;
Some, presents; and some, menaces subdue;
And some I've known, so stubborn is their kind,
Whom blows, alas! could win alone to toil.

    Yet, planter, let humanity prevail.—
Perhaps thy Negroe, in his native land,
Possest large fertile plains, and slaves, and herds:
Perhaps, whene'er he deign'd to walk abroad,
The richest silks, from where the Indus rolls,
His limbs invested in their gorgeous pleats:
Perhaps he wails his wife, his children, left
To struggle with adversity: Perhaps
Fortune, in battle for his country fought,
Gave him a captive to his deadliest foe:
Perhaps, incautious, in his native fields,
(On pleasurable scenes his mind intent)
All as he wandered; from the neighbouring grove,
Fell ambush dragg'd him to the hated main.—
Were they even sold for crimes; ye polish'd, say!
Ye, to whom Learning opes her amplest page!
Ye, whom the knowledge of a living God
Should lead to virtue! Are ye free from crimes?
Ah pity, then, these uninstructed swains;
And still let mercy soften the decrees
Of rigid justice, with her lenient hand.

Oh, did the tender muse possess the power,
Which monarchs have, and monarchs oft abuse:
'Twould be the fond ambition of her soul,
To quell tyrannic sway; knock off the chains
Of heart-debasing slavery; give to man,
Of every colour and of every clime,
Freedom, which stamps him image of his God.
Then laws, Oppression's scourge, fair Virtue's prop,
Offspring of Wisdom! Should impartial reign,
To knit the whole in well-accorded strife:
Servants, not slaves; of choice, and not compell'd;
The Blacks should cultivate the Cane-land isles.

Say, shall the muse the various ills recount,
Which Negroe-nations feel? Shall she describe
The worm that subtly winds into their flesh,
All as they bathe them in their native streams?
There, with fell increment, it soon attains
A direful length of harm. Yet, if due skill,
And proper circumspection are employed,
It may be won its volumes to wind round
A leaden cyclinder: But, O, beware,
No rashness practise; else 'twill surely snap,
And suddenly, retreating, dire produce
An annual lameness to the tortured Moor.

Nor only is the dragon worm to dread:
Fell, winged insects,* which the visual ray
Scarcely discerns, their sable feet and hands
Oft penetrate; and, in the fleshy nest,

*These, by the English, are called *Chigoes* or *Chigres*. They chiefly perforate the toes, and sometimes the fingers; occasioning an itching, which some people think not unpleasing, and are at pains to get, by going to the copper-holes, or mill-round, where chigres most abound. They lay their nits in a bag, about the size of a small pea, and are partly contained therein themselves. This the Negroes extract without bursting, by means of a needle, and filling up the place with a little snuff; it soon heals, if the person has a good constitution. One species of them is supposed to be poisonous; but, I believe, unjustly. When they bury themselves near a tendon, especially if the person is in a bad habit of body, they occasion troublesome sores. The South-Americans call them *Miguas*.

Myriads of young produce; which soon destroy
The parts they breed in; if assiduous care,
With art, extract not the prolific foe.

    Or, shall she sing, and not debase her lay,
The pest peculiar to the Æthiop-kind,
The yaw's infectious bane?—The infected far
In huts, to leeward, lodge; or near the main.
With heartning food, with turtle, and with conchs;
The flowers of sulphur, and hard niccars* burnt,
The lurking evil from the blood expel,
And throw it on the surface: There in spots
Which cause no pain, and scanty ichor yield,
It chiefly breaks about the arms and hips,
A virulent contagion!—When no more
Round knobby spots deform, but the disease
Seems at a pause: then let the learned leach
Give, in due dose, live-silver from the mine;
Till copious spitting the whole taint exhaust.—
Nor thou repine, tho' half-way round the sun,
This globe, her annual progress shall absolve;
Ere, clear'd, thy slave from all infection shine.
Nor then be confident; successive crops
Of defœdations oft will spot the skin:
These thou, with turpentine and guaiac pods,
Reduc'd by coction to a wholesome draught,
Total remove, and give the blood its balm.

    Say, as this malady but once infests
The sons of Guinea, might not skill ingraft
(Thus, the small-pox are happily convey'd;)
This ailment early to thy Negro-train?

    Yet, of the ills which torture Libya's sons,
Worms tyrannize the worst. They, Proteus-like,
Each symptom of each malady assume;

*The botanical name of this medicinal shrub is *Guilandina*. The fruit resembles marbles, though not so round. Their shell is hard and smooth, and contains a farinaceous nut, of admirable use in seminal weaknesses. They are also given to throw out the yaws.

And, under every mask, the assassins kill.
Now, in the guise of horrid spasms, they writhe
The tortured body, and all sense o'er-power.
Sometimes, like Mania, with her head downcast,
They cause the wretch in solitude to pine;
Or frantic, bursting from the strongest chains,
To frown with look terrific, not his own.
Sometimes like Ague, with a shivering mien,
The teeth gnash fearful, and the blood runs chill:
Anon the ferment maddens in the veins,
And a false vigour animates the frame.
Again, the dropsy's bloated mask they steal;
Or, "melt with minings of the hectic fire."

    Say, to such various mimic forms of death;
What remedies shall puzzled art oppose?—
Thanks to the Almighty, in each path-way hedge,
Rank cow-itch* grows, whose sharp unnumber'd stings,
Sheath'd in Melasses, from their dens expell,
Fell dens of death, the reptile lurking foe.—
A powerful vermifuge, in skilful hands,
The worm-grass proves; yet, even in hands of skill,
Sudden, I've known it dim the visual ray
For a whole day and night. There are who use
(And sage Experience justifies the use)
The mineral product of the Cornish mine;†

*This extraordinary vine should not be permitted to grow in a Cane-piece; for Negroes have been known to fire the Canes, to save themselves from the torture which attends working in grounds where it has abounded. Mixed with melasses, it is a safe and excellent vermifuge. Its seeds, which resemble blackish small beans, are purgative. Its flower is purple; and its pods, on which the stinging brown *Setæ* are found, are as large as a full-grown English field-pea.

†Tin-filings are a better vermifuge than tin in powder. The western parts of Britain, and the neighbouring isles, have been famous for this useful metal from the remotest antiquity; for we find from Strabo, that the Phænicians made frequent voyages to those parts (which they called *Cassiterides* from Κασσιτερον stannum) in quest of that commodity, which turned out so beneficial to them, that a pilot of that nation stranded his vessel, rather than show a Roman ship, that watched him, the way to those mines. For this public spirited action he was amply rewarded, says that accurate writer, upon his return to his country. The Romans, however, soon made themselves masters of the secret, and shared with them in the profit of that merchandize.

Which in old times, ere Britain laws enjoyed,
The polish'd Tyrians, monarchs of the main,
In their swift ships convey'd to foreign realms:
The sun by day, by night the northern star,
Their course conducted.—Mighty commerce, hail!
By thee the sons of Attic's sterile land,
A scanty number, laws impos'd on Greece:
Nor aw'd they Greece alone; vast Asia's King,
Tho' girt by rich arm'd myriads, at their frown
Felt his heart wither on his farthest throne.
Perennial source of population thou!
While scanty peasants plough the flowery plains
Of purple Enna; from the Belgian fens,
What swarms of useful citizens spring up,
Hatch'd by thy fostering wing. Ah where is flown
That dauntless free-born spirit, which of old,
Taught them to shake off the tyrannic yoke
Of Spains insulting King; on whose wide realms,
The sun still shone with undiminished beam?
Parent of wealth! in vain, coy nature hoards
Her gold and diamonds; toil, thy firm compeer,
And industry of unremitting nerve,
Scale the cleft mountain, the loud torrent brave,
Plunge to the center, and thro' Nature's wiles,
(Led on by skill of penetrative soul)
Her following close, her secret treasures find,
To pour them plenteous on the laughing world.
On thee Sylvanus, thee each rural god,
On thee chief Ceres, with unfailing love
And fond distinction, emulously gaze.
In vain hath nature pour'd vast seas between
Far-distant kingdoms; endless storms in vain
With double night brood o'er them; thou dost throw,
O'er far-divided nature's realms, a chain
To bind in sweet society mankind.
By thee white Albion, once a barbarous clime,
Grew fam'd for arms, for wisdom, and for laws;
By thee she holds the balance of the world,
Acknowledg'd now sole empress of the main.
Coy though thou art, and mutable of love,

There may'st thou ever fix thy wandering steps;
While Eurus rules the wide atlantic foam!
By thee, thy favourite, great Columbus found
That world, where now thy praises I rehearse
To the resounding main and palmy shore;
And Lusitania's chiefs those realms explor'd,
Whence negroes spring, the subject of my song.

    Nor pine the Blacks, alone, with real ills,
That baffle oft the wisest rules of art:
They likewise feel imaginary woes;
Woes no less deadly. Luckless he who owns
The slave, who thinks himself bewitch'd; and whom,
In wrath, a conjurer's snake-mark'd* staff hath struck!
They mope, love silence, every friend avoid;
They inly pine; all aliment reject;
Or insufficient for nutrition take:
Their features droop; a sickly yellowish hue
Their skin deforms; their strength and beauty fly.
Then comes the feverish fiend, with firy eyes,
Whom drowth, convulsions, and whom death surround,
Fatal attendants! if some subtle slave
(Such, Obia-men are stil'd) do not engage,
To save the wretch by antidote or spell.

    In magic spells, in Obia, all the sons
Of sable Africk trust:—Ye, sacred nine!
(For ye each hidden preparation know)
Transpierce the gloom, which ignorance and fraud
Have render'd awful; tell the laughing world
Of what these wonder-working charms are made.

*The negroe-conjurers, or Obia-men, as they are called, carry about them a staff, which is marked with frogs, snakes, &c. The blacks imagine that its blow, if not mortal, will at least occasion long and troublesome disorders. A belief in magic is inseparable from human nature, but those nations are most addicted thereto, among whom learning, and of course, philosophy have least obtained. As in all other countries, so in Guinea, the conjurers, as they have more understanding, so are they almost always more wicked than the common herd of their deluded countrymen; and as the negroe-magicians can do mischief, so they can also do good on a plantation, provided they are kept by the white people in proper subordination.

Fern root cut small, and tied with many a knot;
Old teeth extracted from a white man's skull;
A lizard's skeleton; a serpent's head:
These mix'd with salt, and water from the spring,
Are in a phial pour'd; o'er these the leach
Mutters strange jargon, and wild circles forms.

Of this possest, each negroe deems himself
Secure from poison; for to poison they
Are infamously prone: and arm'd with this,
Their sable country dæmons they defy,
Who fearful haunt them at the midnight hour,
To work them mischief. This, diseases fly;
Diseases follow: such its wonderous power!
This o'er the threshold of their cottage hung,
No thieves break in; or, if they dare to steal,
Their feet in blotches, which admit no cure,
Burst loathsome out: but should its owner filch,
As slaves were ever of the pilfering kind,
This from detection screens;—so conjurers swear.

'Till morning dawn, and Lucifer withdraw
His beamy chariot; let not the loud bell
Call forth thy negroes from their rushy couch:
And ere the sun with mid-day fervour glow,
When every broom-bush* opes her yellow flower;
Let thy black labourers from their toil desist:
Nor till the broom her every petal lock,
Let the loud bell recall them to the hoe.
But when the jalap her bright tint displays,
When the solanum† fills her cup with dew,

---

*This small plant, which grows in every pasture, may, with propriety, be termed an American clock; for it begins every forenoon at eleven to open its yellow flowers, which about one are fully expanded, and at two closed. The jalap, or marvel of Peru, unfolds its petals between five and six in the evening, which shut again as soon as night comes on, to open again in the cool of the morning. This plant is called four o'clock by the natives, and bears either a yellow or purple-coloured flower.

†So some authors name the fire-weed, which grows every where, and is the *datura* of Linnæus; whose virtues Dr. Stork, at Vienna, has greatly extolled in

And crickets, snakes, and lizards 'gin their coil;
Let them find shelter in their cane-thatch'd huts:
Or, if constrain'd unusual hours to toil,
(For even the best must sometimes urge their gang)
With double nutriment reward their pains.

Howe'er insensate some may deem their slaves,
Nor 'bove the bestial rank; far other thoughts
The muse, soft daughter of humanity!
Will ever entertain.—The Ethiop knows,
The Ethiop feels, when treated like a man;
Nor grudges, should necessity compell,
By day, by night, to labour for his lord.

Not less inhuman, than unthrifty those;
Who, half the year's rotation round the sun,
Deny subsistence to their labouring slaves.
But would'st thou see thy negroe-train encrease,
Free from disorders; and thine acres clad
With groves of sugar: every week dispense
Or English beans, or Carolinian rice;
Iërne's beef, or Pensilvanian flour;
Newfoundland cod, or herrings from the main
That howls tempestuous round the Scotian isles!

Yet some there are so lazily inclin'd,
And so neglectful of their food, that thou,
Would'st thou preserve them from the jaws of death;
Daily, their wholesome viands must prepare:
With these let all the young, and childless old,
And all the morbid share;—so heaven will bless,
With manifold encrease, thy costly care.

Suffice not this; to every slave assign
Some mountain-ground: or, if waste broken land
To thee belong, that broken land divide.
This let them cultivate, one day, each week;

a late publication. It bears a white monopetalous flower, which opens always
about sun-set.

And there raise yams, and there cassada's root:
From a good dæmon's staff cassada* sprang,
Tradition says, and Caribbees believe;
Which into three the white-rob'd genius broke,
And bade them plant, their hunger to repel.
There let angola's† bloomy bush supply,
For many a year, with wholesome pulse their board.
There let the bonavist,‡ his fringed pods
Throw liberal o'er the prop; while ochra§ bears
Aloft his slimy pulp, and help disdains.
There let potatos‖ mantle o'er the ground;
Sweet as the cane-juice is the root they bear.

*To an antient Carribean, bemoaning the savage uncomfortable life of his countrymen, a deity clad in white apparel appeared, and told him, he would have come sooner to have taught him the ways of civil life, had he been addressed before. He then showed him sharp-cutting stones to fell trees and build houses; and bade him cover them with the palm leaves. Then he broke his staff in three; which, being planted, soon after produced cassada. See Ogilvy's America.

†This is called *Pidgeon-pea*, and grows on a sturdy shrub, that will last for years. It is justly reckoned among the most wholesome legumens. The juice of the leaves, dropt into the eye, will remove incipient films. The botanic name is *Cytisus.*

‡This is the Spanish name of a plant, which produces an excellent bean. It is a parasitical plant. There are five sorts of bonavist, the green, the white, the moon-shine, the small or common; and, lastly, the black and red. The flowers of all are white and papilionaceous; except the last, whose blossoms are purple. They commonly bear in six weeks. Their pulse is wholesome, though somewhat flatulent; especially those from the black and red. The pods are flattish, two or three inches long; and contain from three to five seeds in partitional cells.

§Or *Ockro.* This shrub, which will last for years, produces a not less agreeable, than wholesome pod. It bears all the year round. Being of a slimy and balsamic nature, it becomes a truly medicinal aliment in dysenteric complaints. It is of the *Malva* species. It rises to about four or five feet high, bearing, on and near the summit, many yellow flowers; succeeded by green, conic, fleshy pods, channelled into several grooves. There are as many cells filled with small round seeds, as there are channels.

‖I cannot positively say, whether these vines are of Indian original or not; but as in their fructification, they differ from potatos at home, they probably are not European. They are sweet. There are four kinds, the red, the white, the long, and round: The juice of each may be made into a pleasant cool drink; and, being distilled, yield an excellent spirit.

There too let eddas* spring in order meet,
With Indian cale,† and foodful calaloo‡:
While mint, thyme, balm, and Europe's coyer herbs,
Shoot gladsome forth, nor reprobate the clime.

   This tract secure, with hedges or of limes,
Or bushy citrons, or the shapely tree§
That glows at once with aromatic blooms,
And golden fruit mature. To these be join'd,
In comely neighbourhood, the cotton shrub;
In this delicious clime the cotton bursts
On rocky soils.—The coffee also plant;
White as the skin of Albion's lovely fair,
Are the thick snowy fragrant blooms it boasts:
Nor wilt thou, cocô, thy rich pods refuse;
Tho' years, and heat, and moisture they require,
Ere the stone grind them to the food of health.
Of thee, perhaps, and of thy various sorts,
And that kind sheltering tree, thy mother nam'd,‖
With crimson flowerets prodigally grac'd;
In future times, the enraptur'd muse may sing:
If public favour crown her present lay.

   But let some antient, faithful slave erect
His sheltered mansion near; and with his dog,
His loaded gun, and cutlass, guard the whole:
Else negro-fugitives, who skulk 'mid rocks

*The French call this plant *Tayove*. It produces eatable roots every four months, for one year only.

†This green, which is a native of the New World, equals any of the greens in the Old.

‡Another species of Indian pot-herb, no less wholesome than the preceding. These, with mezamby, and the Jamaica prickle-weed, yield to no esculent plants in Europe. This is an Indian name.

§The orange tree.

‖Those who plant cacao-walks, sometimes screen them by a hardier tree, which the Spaniards aptly term *Madre de Cacao*. They may be planted fifteen or twenty feet distant, though some advise to plant them much nearer, and perhaps wisely; for it is an easy matter to thin them, when they are past the danger of being destroyed by dry weather, *&c.*

And shrubby wilds, in bands will soon destroy
Thy labourer's honest wealth; their loss and yours.

Perhaps, of Indian gardens I could sing,
Beyond what bloom'd on blest Phæacia's isle,
Or eastern climes admir'd in days of yore:
How Europe's foodful, culinary plants;
How gay Pomona's ruby-tinctured births;
And gawdy Flora's various-vested train;
Might be instructed to unlearn their clime,
And by due discipline adopt the sun.
The muse might tell what culture will entice
The ripened melon, to perfume each month;
And with the anana load the fragrant board.
The muse might tell, what trees will best exclude
("Insuperable height of airiest shade")
With their vast umbrage the noon's fervent ray.
Thee, verdant mammey,* first, her song should praise:
Thee, the first natives of these Ocean-isles,
Fell anthropophagi, still sacred held;
And from thy large high-flavour'd fruit abstain'd,
With pious awe; for thine high-flavoured fruit,
The airy phantoms of their friends deceas'd
Joy'd to regale on.—Such their simple creed.
The tamarind† likewise should adorn her theme,

*This is a lofty, shady, and beautiful tree. Its fruit is as large as the largest
melon, and of an exquisite smell, greatly superior to it in point of taste. Within
the fruit are contained one or two large stones, which when distilled, give to
spirits a ratafia flavour, and therefore the French call them *Les apricots de St.
Domingue*: accordingly, the *l'eau des noiaux*, one of the best West-Indian cor-
dials, is made from them. The fruit, eaten raw, is of an aperient quality; and
made into sweet-meats, *&c.* is truly exquisite. This tree, contrary to most oth-
ers in the New World, shoots up to a pyramidal figure: the leaves are uncom-
monly green; and it produces fruit, but once a year. The name is Indian. The
English commonly call it *Mammey-sapota*. There are two species of it, the
sweet, and the tart. The botanical name is *Achras*.

†This large, shady, and beautiful tree grows fast even in the driest soils, and
lasts long; and yet its wood is hard, and very fit for mechanical uses. The leaves
are smaller than those of senna, and pennated: they taste sourish, as does the
pulp, which is contained in pods four or five inches long. They bear once a
year. An excellent vinegar may be made from the fruit; but the Creoles chiefly
preserve it with sugar, as the Spaniards with salt. A pleasant syrup may be

With whose tart fruit the sweltering fever loves
To quench his thirst, whose breezy umbrage soon
Shades the pleas'd planter, shades his children long.
Nor, lofty cassia,* should she not recount
Thy woodland honours! See, what yellow flowers
Dance in the gale, and scent the ambient air;
While thy long pods, full-fraught with nectared sweets,
Relieve the bowels from their lagging load.
Nor chirimoia, though these torrid isles
Boast not thy fruit, to which the anana yields
In taste and flavour, wilt thou coy refuse
Thy fragrant shade to beautify the scene.
But, chief of palms, and pride of Indian-groves,
Thee, fair palmeto,† should her song resound:
What swelling columns, form'd by Jones or Wren,
Or great Palladio, may with thee compare?
Not nice-proportion'd, but of size immense,
Swells the wild fig-tree, and should claim her lay:
For, from its numerous bearded twigs proceed

---

made from it. The name is, in Arabic, *Tamara*. The Antients were not ac-
quainted therewith; for the Arabians first introduced tamarinds into physic; it
is a native of the East as well as of the West-Indies and South-America, where
different provinces call it by different names. Its cathartic qualities are well
known. It is good in sea-sickness. The botanical name is *Tamarindus*.

*Both this tree and its mild purgative pulp are sufficiently known.

†This being the most beautiful of palms, nay, perhaps, superior to any other
known tree in the world, has with propriety obtained the name of *Royal*. The
botanical name is *Palma Maxima*. It will shoot up perpendicularly to an hun-
dred feet and more. The stem is perfectly circular; only towards the root, and
immediately under the branches at top, it bulges out. The bark is smooth, and
of an ash-brown colour, except at the top where it is green. It grows very fast,
and the seed from whence it springs is not bigger than an acorn. In this, as in
all the palm-genus, what the natives call *Cabbage* is found; but it resembles in
taste an almond, and is in fact the pith of the upper, or greenish part of the
stem. But it would be the most unpardonable luxury to cut down so lovely a
tree, for so mean a gratification; especially as the wild, or mountain cabbage
tree, sufficiently supplies the table with that esculent. I never ride past the
charming vista of royal palms on the Cayon-estate of Daniel Mathew, Esq; in
St. Christopher, without being put in mind of the pillars of the Temple of the
Sun at Palmyra. This tree grows on the tops of hills, as well as in valleys; its
hard cortical part makes very durable laths for houses. There is a smaller
species not quite so beautiful.

A filial train, stupendous as their sire,
In quick succession; and, o'er many a rood,
Extend their uncouth limbs; which not the bolt
Of heaven can scathe; nor yet the all-wasting rage
Of Typhon, or of hurricane, destroy.
Nor should, tho' small, the anata* not be sung:
Thy purple dye, the silk and cotton fleece
Delighted drink; thy purple dye the tribes
Of Northern-Ind, a fierce and wily race,
Carouse, assembled; and with it they paint
Their manly make in many a horrid form,
To add new terrors to the face of war.
The muse might teach to twine the verdant arch,
And the cool alcove's lofty roof adorn,
With ponderous granadillas,† and the fruit
Call'd water-lemon; grateful to the taste:
Nor should she not pursue the mountain-streams,
But pleas'd decoy them from their shady haunts,
In rills, to visit every tree and herb;
Or fall o'er fern-clad cliffs, with foaming rage;
Or in huge basons float, a fair expanse;
Or, bound in chains of artificial force,
Arise thro' sculptured stone, or breathing brass.—
But I'm in haste to furl my wind-worn sails,
And anchor my tir'd vessel on the shore.

---

*Or *Anotto*, or *Arnotta*; thence corruptly called *Indian Otter*, by the English. The tree is about the size of an ordinary apple-tree. The French call it *Rocou*; and send the farina home as a paint, &c. for which purpose the tree is cultivated by them in their islands. The flower is pentapetalous, of a bluish and spoon-like appearance. The yellow filaments are tipped with purplish apices. The style proves the rudiment of the succeeding pod, which is of a conic shape, an inch and a half long. This is divided into many cells, which contain a great number of small seeds, covered with a red farina.

†This is the Spanish name, and is a species of the *passiflora*, or passion-flower, called by Linnæus *Musa*. The seeds and pulp, through which the seeds are dispersed, are cooling, and grateful to the palate. This, as well as the water-lemon, bell-apple, or honeysuckle, as it is named, being parasitical plants, are easily formed into cooling arbors, than which nothing can be more grateful in warm climates. Both fruits are wholesome. The granadilla is commonly eat with sugar, on account of its tartness, and yet the pulp is viscid. Plumier calls it *Granadilla, latefolia, fructu maliformi*. It grows best in shady places. The unripe fruit makes an excellent pickle.

It much imports to build thy Negroe-huts,
Or on the sounding margin of the main,
Or on some dry hill's gently-sloping sides,
In streets, at distance due.—When near the beach,
Let frequent coco cast its wavy shade;
'Tis Neptune's tree; and, nourish'd by the spray,
Soon round the bending stem's aerial height,
Clusters of mighty nuts, with milk and fruit
Delicious fraught, hang clattering in the sky.
There let the bay-grape,* too, its crooked limbs
Project enormous; of impurpled hue
Its frequent clusters glow. And there, if thou
Would'st make the sand yield salutary food,
Let Indian millet† rear its corny reed,
Like arm'd battalions in array of war.
But, round the upland huts, bananas plant;
A wholesome nutriment bananas yield,
And sun-burnt labour loves its breezy shade.
Their graceful screen let kindred plantanes join,
And with their broad vans shiver in the breeze;
So flames design'd, or by imprudence caught,
Shall spread no ruin to the neighbouring roof.

Yet nor the founding margin of the main,
Nor gently sloping side of breezy hill,
Nor streets, at distance due, imbower'd in trees;

*Or sea-side grape, as it is more commonly called. This is a large, crooked, and shady tree, (the leaves being broad, thick, and almost circular;) and succeeds best in sandy places. It bears large clusters of grapes once a year; which, when ripe, are not disagreeable. The stones, seeds, or *acini*, contained in them, are large in proportion; and, being reduced to a powder, are an excellent astringent. The bark of the tree has the same property. The grapes, steept in water and fermented with sugar, make an agreeable wine.

†Or maise. This is commonly called *Guinea-corn*, to distinguish it from the great or Indian-corn, that grows in the southern parts of North-America. It soon shoots up to a great height, often twenty feet high, and will ratoon like the other; but its blades are not so nourishing to horses as those of the great corn, although its seeds are more so, and rather more agreeable to the taste. The Indians, Negroes, and poor white people, make many (not unsavoury) dishes with them. It is also called *Turkey wheat*. The turpentine tree will also grow in the sand, and is most useful upon a plantation.

Will half the health, or half the pleasure yield,
Unless some pitying naiad deign to lave,
With an unceasing stream, thy thirsty bounds.

On festal days; or when their work is done;
Permit thy slaves to lead the choral dance,
To the wild banshaw's* melancholy sound.
Responsive to the sound, head feet and frame
Move aukwardly harmonious; hand in hand
Now lock'd, the gay troop circularly wheels,
And frisks and capers with intemperate joy.
Halts the vast circle, all clap hands and sing;
While those distinguish'd for their heels and air,
Bound in the center, and fantastic twine.
Meanwhile some stripling, from the choral ring,
Trips forth; and, not ungallantly, bestows
On her who nimblest hath the greensward beat,
And whose flush'd beauties have inthrall'd his soul,
A silver token of his fond applause.
Anon they form in ranks; nor inexpert
A thousand tuneful intricacies weave,
Shaking their sable limbs; and oft a kiss
Steal from their partners; who, with neck reclin'd,
And semblant scorn, resent the ravish'd bliss.
But let not thou the drum their mirth inspire;
Nor vinous spirits: else, to madness fir'd,
(What will not bacchanalian frenzy dare?)
Fell acts of blood, and vengeance they pursue.

Compel by threats, or win by soothing arts,
Thy slaves to wed their fellow slaves at home;
So shall they not their vigorous prime destroy,
By distant journeys, at untimely hours,
When muffled midnight decks her raven-hair
With the white plumage of the prickly vine.†

*This is a sort of rude guitar, invented by the Negroes. It produces a wild
pleasing melancholy sound.

†This beautiful white rosaceous flower is as large as the crown of one's hat,
and only blows at midnight. The plant, which is prickly and attaches itself
firmly to the sides of houses, trees, &c. produces a fruit, which some call

Would'st thou from countless ails preserve thy gang;
To every Negroe, as the candle-weed*
Expands his blossoms to the cloudy sky,
And moist Aquarius melts in daily showers;
A woolly vestment give, (this Wiltshire weaves)
Warm to repel chill Night's unwholesome dews:
While strong coarse linen, from the Scotian loom,
Wards off the fervours of the burning day.

The truly great, tho' from a hostile clime,
The sacred Nine embalm; then, Muses, chant,
In grateful numbers, Gallic Lewis' praise:
For private murder quell'd; for laurel'd arts,
Invented, cherish'd in his native realm;
For rapine punish'd; for grim famine fed;
For sly chicane expell'd the wrangling bar;
And rightful Themis seated on her throne:
But, chief, for those mild laws his wisdom fram'd,
To guard the Æthiop from tyrannic sway!

Did such, in these green isles which Albion claims,
Did such obtain; the muse, at midnight-hour,
This last brain-racking study had not ply'd:
But, sunk in slumbers of immortal bliss,
To bards had listned on a fancied Thames!

All hail, old father Thames! tho' not from far
Thy springing waters roll; nor countless streams,
Of name conspicuous, swell thy watery store;
Tho' thou, no Plata,† to the sea devolve
Vast humid offerings; thou art king of streams:

Wythe Apple, and others with more propriety, *Mountain-strawberry*. But
though it resembles the large Chili-strawberry in looks and size; yet being in-
elegant of taste, it is seldom eaten. The botanical name is *Cereus scandens mi-
nor*. The rind of the fruit is here and there studded with tufts of small sharp
prickles.

*This shrub, which produces a yellow flower somewhat resembling a narcis-
sus, makes a beautiful hedge, and blows about November. It grows wild every
where. It is said to be diuretic, but this I do not know from experience.

†One of the largest rivers of South America.

Delighted Commerce broods upon thy wave;
And every quarter of this sea-girt globe
To thee due tribute pays; but chief the world
By great Columbus found, where now the muse
Beholds, transported, slow vast fleecy clouds,
Alps pil'd on Alps romantically high,
Which charm the sight with many a pleasing form.
The moon, in virgin-glory, gilds the pole,
And tips yon tamarinds, tips yon Cane-crown'd vale,
With fluent silver; while unnumbered stars
Gild the vast concave with their lively beams.
The main, a moving burnish'd mirror, shines;
No noise is heard, save when the distant surge
With drouzy murmurings breaks upon the shore!—

Ah me, what thunders roll! the sky's on fire!
Now sudden darkness muffles up the pole!
Heavens! what wild scenes, before the affrighted sense,
Imperfect swim!—See! in that flaming scroll,
Which Time unfolds, the future germs bud forth,
Of mighty empires! independent realms!—
And must Britannia, Neptune's favourite queen,
Protect'ress of true science, freedom, arts;
Must she, ah! must she, to her offspring crouch?
Ah, must my Thames, old Ocean's favourite son,
Resign his trident to barbaric streams;
His banks neglected, and his waves unsought,
No bards to sing them, and no fleets to grace?—
Again the fleecy clouds amuse the eye,
And sparkling stars the vast horizon gild—
She shall not crouch; if Wisdom guide the helm,
Wisdom that bade loud Fame, with justest praise,
Record her triumphs! bade the lacquaying winds
Transport, to every quarter of the globe,
Her winged navies! bade the scepter'd sons
Of earth acknowledge her pre-eminence!—
She shall not crouch; if these Cane ocean-isles,
Isles which on Britain for their all depend,
And must for ever; still indulgent share

Her fostering smile: and other isles be given,
From vanquish'd foes.—And, see, another race!
A golden æra dazzles my fond sight!
That other race, that long'd-for æra, hail!
THE BRITISH GEORGE NOW REIGNS, THE PATRIOT KING!
BRITAIN SHALL EVER TRIUMPH O'ER THE MAIN.

SAMUEL DAVIES

(1723–1761)

Of Him, and thro' Him, and to Him
are all Things. ROM. 11. ult.

I.

What IS great *God*! and what IS NOT,
Should BE, and NOT BE, to thy Praise:
Then, if my Non-Existence should but raise,
Thy Glory, I'm content thy Hand should blot
Me from the Rank of Being, and conclude my Days.
'Tis owing to thy Glory that I AM,
And fit I should NOT BE, if that might raise thy Name.
Should I relapse to Nothing, scarce
Would it appear a Blank in thy vast Universe.

II.

Thou art th' eternal Source and Spring
Of Being and of Possibility:
Thy wise omnific Hand can bring
Non-Entity TO BE:
Then with a Sov'reign Nod Thou can'st remand
The vast Productions of thy Hand,
To dreary Nothing whence they came,—
And be it so, if that might glorify thy Name!

III.

Ah! what are Worlds compar'd with Thee,
Great everlasting ALL!
But Atoms hov'ring in the Air,
Bubbles and Vanity,
That at thy great Command appear,
And at thy Word to nothing fall,
Whose Pleasure gives them Leave TO BE.

Thou viewest, independent, from on high,
A Sparrow or a Hero die,
Atoms or Systems moulder into Dust,
And now a World, and now a Bubble burst.*

IV.

Yet since Thy Hand did build my Frame
With Pow'r and Skill Divine,
And in my Life Thy glorious Name
Does more illustrious shine;
O! let me still exist,—But to Thy Praise,
That out of Nothing did me raise.

"While o'er our guilty Land, O Lord"

An Hymn

I

While o'er our guilty Land, O Lord,
We view the Terrors of thy Sword;
While Heav'n her fruitful Showers denies,
And Nature round us fades and dies.

II

While Clouds of Vengeance o'er our Head,
Seem thickning, and pronounce us dead;
Oh! whither shall the Helpless fly?
To whom but Thee direct their Cry?

---

*Mr. *Pope*, in his *Essay on Man*, expresses this Thought with inimitable Sublimity.
— *"Who sees with equal Eye, as God of all,*
A Hero perish, or a Sparrow fall;
Atoms or Systems into Ruin hurl'd,
And now a Bubble burst, and now a World."

III

The helpless Sinner's Cries and Tears,
Are grown familiar to thine Ears:
Oft has thy Mercy sent Relief,
When all was Fear and hopeless Grief.

IV

On Thee, our guardian God, we call;
Before thy Throne of Grace we fall:
Oh! is there no Deliv'rance there?
Or must we perish in Despair?

V

See we repent, we weep, we mourn;
To our *forsaken* God we turn;
O spare our guilty Country; spare
Thy Church which thou has planted here!

VI

Revive our withering Fields with Rain;
Let Peace compose our Land again:
Silence the horrid Noise of War;
O spare a guilty People; spare!

VII

We plead thy Grace, indulgent God;
We plead thy Son's attoning Blood;
We plead thy gracious Promises;
Nor are these unavailing Pleas.

VIII

These Pleas by Faith urg'd at thy Throne,
Have brought Ten Thousand Blessings down
On guilty Lands in helpless Woe;
Let them prevail to save us too.

"While various Rumours spread abroad"

An Hymn

I

While various Rumours spread abroad,
    And hold our Souls in dread Suspence,
We fly to Thee, our Country's God;
    Our Refuge is thy Providence.

II

This Wilderness so long untill'd,
    An hideous Waste of barren Ground,
Thy Care has made a fruitful Field,
    With Peace and Plenty richly crown'd.

III

Thy Gospel spreads an heavenly Day,
    Throughout this once benighted Land,
A Land once wild with Beasts of Prey,
    By impious Heathen Rites profan'd.

IV

Thy Gospel, like a heavenly Vine,
    Its Branches did begin to spread;
Refresh'd our Souls with sacred Wine,
    And screen'd the Fainting with its Shade.

V

And shall these Blessings now remove?
    Shall Peace and Plenty fly away?
The Land thy Care did thus improve,
    Wilt thou give up, a helpless Prey?

VI

O! must we bid our God adieu?
    And must thy Gospel take its Flight?
Oh! shall our Children never view,
    The Beamings of that heavenly Light?

VII

Forbid it Lord! with Arms of Faith,
    We'll hold Thee fast, and thou shalt stay:
We'll cry while we have Life or Breath,
    "*Our God, do not depart away!*"

VIII

If broken Hearts and weeping Eyes,
Can find Acceptance at thy Throne;
Lo, here they are; this Sacrifice,
Thou wilt accept thro' Christ thy Son.

The Invitations of the Gospel

(*Annext to a Sermon on Rev. XXII. 17. April 9, 1753.*)

1.

To-day the living streams of grace
Flow to refresh the thirsty soul:
Pardon and life and boundlese bliss
In plenteous rivers round us roll.

2.

Ho! ye that pine away and die,
Come, and your raging thirst allay:
Come all that will; here's rich supply;
A fountain that shall ne'er decay.

3.

"Come ALL," the blessed *Jesus* cries,
"Freely my blessings I will give:"
The spirit echo's back the voice,
And bids us freely drink and live.

4.

The saints below, that do but taste,
And saints above, who drink at will,
Cry jointly, "Thirsty sinners! haste,
And drink, the spring's exhaustless still."

5.

Let all that hear the joyful sound,
To spread it thro' the world unite;
From house to house proclaim it round,
Each man his fellow-man invite.

6.

Like thirsty flocks, come let us go;
Come every colour,* every age:
And while the living waters flow,
Let all their parching thirst assuage.

Self-Dedication at the Table of the Lord

Long Metre.
A Sacramental Hymn.

I.

LORD, I am thine, entirely thine,
Purchas'd and sav'd by Blood Divine,
With full Consent thine I would be,
And own thy sov'reign Right in me.

*Whites and Negroes.

II.

Here, LORD, my Flesh, my Soul, my All
I yield to Thee beyond Recal;
Accept thine own so long withheld,
Accept what I so freely yield!

III.

Grant one poor Sinner more a Place
Among the Children of thy Grace;
A wretched Sinner lost to GOD,
But ransom'd by EMANUEL's Blood.

IV.

Thine would I live, thine would I die,
Be thine thro' all Eternity:
The Vow is past beyond Repeal,
Now will I set a solemn Seal.

V.

Be Thou the Witness of my Vow,
Angels and Men attest it too,
That to thy Board I now repair,
And seal the sacred Contract there.

VI.

Here at that Cross, where flows the Blood
That bought my guilty Soul for GOD,
Thee my new Master now I call,
And consecrate to Thee my All;

VII.

Do Thou assist a feeble Worm
The great Engagement to perform:
Thy Grace can full Assistance lend,
And on that Grace I dare depend.

A.L.M.

(fl. 1744)

A College Room

I Stroll'd one day into a room,
When honest *Bob* was not at home;
But as his key was in the door,
I sat me down for half an hour;
When round the room I cast my eyes,
A medley of such objects rise,
That straightway to employ my time,
I thus describ'd them all in rhyme.
  A table first, which, made of oak,
Had one leg short, another broke;
As much of it as well could stand,
Was fill'd with papers, pen, and sand;
While various *books* confus'dly lie,
Scotch songs, with deep *philosophy*.
A *Prior* here, and *Euclid* there,
A *Rochester*, and *book of prayer*;
Here *Tillotson* with *French romances*,
And pious *South* with *country dances*;
Foul pipes and mugs together lay,
With box of best *Virginia*.
The newest method for the fiddle,
A violin broke in the middle,
With great variety of prints,
Of copper-plates, and metzotints;
Here *Phaeton* from heaven was hurl'd,
And here the wonders of the world;
The *Cartoons* mix'd with *Arateens*,
With heads of *British* kings and queens;
Joan with her consort Punchanello,
With *Vernon*'s siege of *Porto-Bello*;
Here *Drake* that glorious English tar,
With *Ormond* and the *Russian* Czar:
A cat without a tail or ear,

Lay sleeping by a mug of beer;
Along with her upon the hearth,
Lay *Pope*'s new *Dunciad* & *Garth*.
Which did not dread the harmless fire,
Which just was going to expire;
Upon the floor was careless thrown,
A dirty shirt, and tatter'd gown;
An *Homer* never meant to look on,
A wooden desk to set a book on;
Two globes, 'twas difficult to find,
Which was for heaven or earth design'd.
A pair of Bellows, and a broom,
And a bureau adorn'd his room;
In bottle neck was fix'd a candle,
An earthen jug without an handle,
A grate, I could not help admiring,
Was ne'er design'd to make a fire in,
So much decay'd, & full of holes,
It would not hold a pan of coals.
Upon a little table stood
A *China* bason full of blood;
A tweezer-case, a dirty towel,
A pitcher of hot water-grewel;
A glass which some unlucky stroke
Had in a dozen pieces broke;
A chest half full of right *bohea*,
With proper furniture for tea,
Had not the cups and saucers been
Some blue and white, some red and green,
Some large enough to hold a gill,
While others scarce a spoon would fill;
Here lay a female's fan and gloves,
The trophies of his former loves;
To *Chloe* lay an open letter,
To which he own'd himself her debtor,
But could not her requests fulfil,
He had not yet receiv'd his bill:
Upon the window stood a bowl,
With relicks of a roasted fowl,
A College plate with dirty dishes,

A powder-horn & net for fishes;
A rusty gun without a lock,
A racket and a shuttle-cock,
With oil and combs & powd'ring block;
A canister and pair of shoes,
A pistol ne'er design'd to use,
A coffee-mill and perfum'd ball,
A champer-pot—and that was all.

THOMAS CLEMSON

(fl. 1746)

Philadelphia, August 7. 1746.

From Thomas Clemson ran away,
One Evening on a Saturday,
The Six and Twentieth Day of July,
If that I am informed truly;
A Man, one Joseph Willard call'd,
His Hair is brown, he is not bald;
His Visage long, and wou'd you know
His Colour, it is swarthy too;
His Hat, it is of an antient Date,
Which keeps the Weather from his Pate;
A yellow Jacket, old and torn,
His wretched Carcase doth adorn;
A Homespun Shirt, and look below,
You'll find his Trowsers made of Tow,
And also coarse; and for his Shoes,
He did the same this six Months use;
They ragged are: He with him took
(If that you will be pleas'd to look)
A Handsaw, made of London Steel,
And stamped with White, near to the Heel;
A Broad-ax, of an ugly Shape,
A Justice made it, near to the Gap;
And other Clothes, perhaps may have,
That he may better play the Knave.
By Calling, he pretends to be
A Person used to the Sea,
A Millwright, Carpenter, and all
The Crafts which you to Mind can call.
If you shou'd happen for to be
By Chance drawn into his Company,
You'll find him lye at such a Rate,
You can't conceive it in your Pate.
His Birth Bucks County did adorn,

To all his Friends he is a Scorn;
His Father left him an Estate
Enough, with Care, to make him great;
He wasted it, and then he went
To Lancaster, with Intent
His ragged Fortune to repair,
And soon was made a Servant there.
If you'll expect to have a Fee
For taking up this Man for me,
Full TWENTY SHILLINGS I will give,
And truly pay it, as I live;
Provided, that you will not fail
To cast him in the nearest Goal,
And send me Word, you need not doubt,
I'll quickly lug the Money out:
In Christine Hundred, there you may
Soon find me out, on any Day;
I at John Heath's doth make my Home,
It will please me, if you hither come;
Pray use your Skill, to help your Friend,
And I'll conclude, and make an End.

"CAROLINA, A YOUNG LADY"

On her Father having desired her
to forbid all young Men the House

When filial Words describe a Daughter's Grief,
The Heart parental, ought to plead Relief;
Ease all the Pain, alleviate all the Woe,
And stem the Source from whence the Sorrows flow:
But then, if Reason join the Daughter's Side,
The Father sure will walk by Reason's Guide;
Divest his Thoughts of that false Prejudice,
That *every Woman* must be giv'n to Vice.
    SOCIETY you know's a Bliss design'd
To form the Manners and instruct the Mind;
By mutual Converse mutual Wants supply,
To teach us how to live and to die;
By free-born Thoughts to form a Judgment clear,
Know right from wrong, and what is bad to fear:
And must I then the *social Bliss* forego?
'Cause *Woman's frail*, or Woman *may* be so?
Must I obey? Decree too hard I find,
Must Woman live a-part from all Mankind?
Freedom and *Virtue* bless'd Product of our Isle,
Grow on one Stalk, and flourish in one Soil;
Freedom and *Virtue* wither *in one* Hour,
There is no Virtue when not in our Power.
    Believe me, Father, what knows most Restraint,
To that the Passions are more strongly bent;
Forbidden Fruit first *ruin'd* Mother EVE,
Forbidden Things *We* mostly long to have:
Think you Vice banish'd from the Monkish State?
Or Virtue guarded by the Convent Grate?
No Vows in Convents, Lust can there aswage,
For Fires conceal'd flame with a fiercer Rage.
    Forgive, *dear Sire*, if an Offence it be,
For *British* Fair to sue for LIBERTY:
Britannia's Fair, unspotted in your Fame,
Forgive, if I assume in *Britain*'s Name.

JOSEPH DUMBLETON

(fl. 1744–1749)

A Rhapsody on Rum

Nec prius est extincta sitis, quam vita, Bibendo.
OVID. MET.

Great Spirit, hail!—confusion's angry sire;
And like thy parent *Bacchus*, born of fire:
The jail's decoy, the greedy merchant's lure;
Disease of money, but reflection's cure.
　In thy pursuit our fields are left forlorn,
While giant weeds oppress the pigmy corn:
Thou throw'st a gloom before the planter's eyes;
The plow grows idle, and Tobacco dies.
　At thine approach our houshold staff retires;
And we, distress'd, retreat to kindly fires:
Our skins we burn, and yet our limbs are cold;
We kiss the dust, like penitents of old.
Who would not think, but what they do repent,
That sit in ashes, and whose cloaths are rent?
While yawning roofs unnumber'd vents display,
That let in sullen winds as well as smiling day:
On native earth to these expos'd we lie,
And, be but thou to our assistance nigh,
Dare all the malice of a weeping sky.
　If to the matron's head thy fumes arise,
She drops her spindle, and her wheel defies;
Thou interposing, she regards no more
The oath she to her God, and to her husband swore;
Than brutes more stupid, more than tygers wild,
The giddy wretch forgets her sucking child:
As deaf as rocks, it's piteous cries she hears,
And largely feeds it with the bread of tears.
We owe, great DRAM! the trembling hand to thee,
The headstrong purpose, and the feeble knee;
The loss of senses, the disfigur'd nose;
The hit of bruises, and the miss of cloaths.

To thee we offer dear invalu'd fame,
And barter credit for immortal shame.
    The passive tongue, as influenc'd by thy strength,
Is mute, or runs a most unseemly length.
While caution dies in each delirious fit,
And bleeding prudence in attempts to wit.
    Diseases still attend thy courtly train;
Asthmatic lungs, that breath with anxious pain;
And pale consumptions hover in thy view,
Those of the purse, and of the vitals too;
Repining gout, that head and breast alarms,
The legs confines, and captivates the arms;
The flaming entrails, nose of *Tyrian* dye;
The cheek of lillies, and the ferret's eye;
Afflictive dreams, that terrify by night;
Fallacious hearing, and imperfect sight;
And vapours, fiends, that from thy bosom stray,
Which thou dost raise, and thou the best canst lay.
    Fom thee a thousand flut'ring whims escape
Like hasty births, that ne'er have perfect shape.
Thine ideots seem in gay delusion fair;
But born in flame, they soon expire in air.

WILLIAM LIVINGSTON

(1723–1790)

Philosophic Solitude

or, The Choice of a Rural Life

Let ardent heroes seek renown in arms,
Pant after fame, and rush to war's alarms;
To shining palaces, let fools resort,
And dunces cringe to be esteem'd at court:
Mine be the pleasures of a *rural* life,
From noise remote, and ignorant of strife;
Far from the painted Belle, and white-glov'd Beau,
The lawless masquerade, and midnight show,
From ladies, lap dogs, courtiers, garters, stars,
Fops, fiddlers, tyrants, emperors, and czars.

Full in the center of some shady grove,
By nature form'd for solitude and love;
On banks array'd with ever-blooming flow'rs,
Near beauteous landskips, or by rosiate bow'rs;
My neat, but simple mansion I would raise,
Unlike the sumptuous domes of modern days;
Devoid of pomp, with rural plainess form'd,
With savage game, and glossy shells adorn'd.

No costly furniture shou'd grace my hall;
But curling vines ascend against the wall,
Whose pliant branches shou'd luxuriant twine,
While purple clusters swell'd with future wine:
To slake my thirst a liquid lapse distil
From craggy rocks, and spread a limpid rill.
Along my mansion spiry firrs should grow,
And gloomy yews extend the shady row;
The cedars flourish, and the poplars rise
Sublimely tall, and shoot into the skies:

Among the leaves refreshing Zephyrs play,
And crowding trees exclude the noon-tide ray;
Whereon the birds their downy nests shou'd form,
Securely shelter'd from the batt'ring storm;
And to melodious notes their choir apply,
Soon as *Aurora* blush'd along the sky:
While all around th' enchanting music rings,
And ev'ry vocal grove responsive sings.

Me to sequester'd scenes, ye muses guide,
Where nature wantons in her virgin-pride;
To mossy banks edg'd round with op'ning flow'rs,
Elysian fields, and amaranthin bow'rs,
T' ambrosial founts, and sleep-inspiring rills,
To herbag'd vales, gay lawns, and sunny hills.

Welcome ye shades! all hail, ye vernal blooms!
Ye bow'ry thickets, and prophetic glooms!
Ye forests hail! ye solitary woods!
Love-whisp'ring groves, and silver-streaming floods!
Ye meads, that aromatic sweets exhale!
Ye birds, and all ye sylvan beauties hail!
Oh how I long with you to spend my days,
Invoke the muse, and try the rural lays!

No trumpets there with martial clangor sound,
No prostrate heroes strew the crimson'd ground;
No groves of lances glitter in the air,
Nor thund'ring drums provoke the sanguine war:
But white-rob'd peace, and universal love
Smile in the field, and brighten every grove.
There all the beauties of the circling year,
In native ornamental pride appear.
Gay rosy-bosom'd SPRING, and *April* show'rs
Wake from the womb of earth the rising flow'rs:
In deeper verdure SUMMER cloaths the plain,
And AUTUMN bends beneath the golden grain;
The trees weep amber, and the whispering gales
Breeze o'er the lawn, or murmur thro' the vales.
The flow'ry tribes in gay confusion bloom,

Profuse of sweets, and fragrant with perfume.
On blossoms blossoms, fruits on fruits arise,
And varied prospects glad the wandring eyes.
In these fair Seats I'd pass the joyous day
Where meadows flourish and where fields look gay;
From bliss to bliss with endless pleasure rove,
Seek crystal streams, or haunt the vernal grove,
Woods, fountains, lakes, the fertile fields, or shades,
Aërial mountains, or subjacent glades.

There from the polish'd fetters of the great,
Triumphal piles, and gilded rooms of state;
Prime ministers, and sycophantic knaves,
Illustrious villains, and illustrious slaves!
From all the vain formality of fools,
And odious task of arbitrary rules,
The ruffling cares which the vex'd soul annoy,
The wealth the rich possess, but not enjoy,
The visionary bliss the world can lend,
Th' insidious foe, and false designing friend,
The seven-fold fury of *Xantippe*'s Soul,
And S*****'s rage that burns without controul;
I'd live retir'd, contented, and serene,
Forgot, unknown, unenvied, and unseen.

Yet not a real hermitage I'd chuse,
Nor wish to live from all the world recluse;
But with a friend sometimes unbend the soul
In social converse, o'er the sprightly bowl.
With chearful W****, serene and wisely gay,
I'd often pass the dancing hours away:
He skill'd alike to profit and to please,
Politely talks with unaffected ease;
Sage in debate, and faithful to his trust,
Mature in science, and severely just;
Of soul diffusive, vast and unconfin'd,
Breathing benevolence to all mankind;
Cautious to censure, ready to commend,
A firm unshaken, uncorrupted friend:
In early youth fair wisdom's paths be trod,

In early youth a minister of God:
Each pupil lov'd him when at *Yale* he shone,
And ev'ry bleeding bosom weeps him gone.
Dear *A***** too, should grace my rural Seat,
Forever welcome to the green retreat.
Heav'n for the cause of righteousness design'd
His florid genius, and capacious mind:
Oft' have I heard, amidst th' adoring throng,
Celestial truths devolving from his tongue;
High o'er the list'ning audience seen him stand,
Divinely speak, and graceful stretch his hand:
With such becoming grace and pompous sound,
With long-rob'd senators encircled round,
Before the roman bar, while *Rome* was free,
Nor bow'd to *Cæsar*'s throne the servile knee,
Immortal *Tully* plead the patriot cause,
While ev'ry tongue resounded his applause.
Next round my board should candid *S**** appear,
Of manners gentle, and a friend sincere,
Averse to discord, party-rage, and strife
He sails serenely down the stream of life.
With these *three friends*, beneath a spreading shade,
Where silver fountains murmur thro' the glade;
Or in cool grotts, perfum'd with native flow'rs,
In harmless mirth I'd spend the circling hours;
Or gravely talk, or innocently sing,
Or in harmonious concert strike the trembling string.

                              *   *   *

     By love directed, I wou'd chuse a wife,
T' improve my bliss, and ease the load of life.
Hail *Wedlock!* hail, inviolable tye!
Perpetual fountain of domestic joy!
Love, friendship, honour, truth, and pure delight
Harmonious mingle in the nuptial rite.
In *Eden* first the holy state began,
When perfect innocence distinguish'd man;
The human pair th' Almighty Pontiff led,
Gay as the morning to the bridal bed;
A dread solemnity th' espousals grac'd,

Angels the *Witnesses*, and GOD the PRIEST!
All earth exulted on the nuptial hour,
And voluntary roses deck'd the bow'r;
The joyous birds on ev'ry blossom'd spray,
Sung *Hymeneans* to th' important day,
While *Philomela* swell'd the spousal song,
And Paradise with gratulation rung.

Relate, inspiring muse! where shall I find
A blooming virgin with an angel-mind?
Unblemish'd as the white-rob'd virgin-quire
That fed, O *Rome!* thy consecrated fire?
By reason aw'd, ambitious to be good,
Averse to vice, and zealous for her God?
Relate, in what blest region can I find
Such bright perfections in a female mind?
What *Phœnix*-woman breathes the vital air,
So greatly good, and so divinely fair?
Sure not the gay and fashionable train,
Licentious, proud, immoral and profane;
Who spend their golden hours in antic-dress,
Malicious whispers, and inglorious ease.—

Lo! round the board a shining train appears
In rosy beauty, and in prime of years!
This hates a flounce, and *this* a flounce approves,
This shews the trophies of her former loves;
Polly avers that *Sylvia* drest in green,
When last at Church the gaudy Nymph was seen,
Cloe condemns her optics, and will lay
'Twas azure sattin inter-streak'd with grey;
Lucy invested with judicial pow'r
Awards 'twas neither—and the strife is o'er.
Then parrots, lap-dogs, monkeys, squirrels, beaux,
Fans, ribbands, tuckers, patches, furbeloes,
In quick succession thro' their fancies run,
And dance incessant on the flippant tongue.
And when fatigu'd with every other sport,
The belles prepare to grace the sacred court,
They marshal all their forces in array,

To kill with glances, and destroy in play.
Two skillful *maids* with reverential fear
In wanton wreaths collect their silken hair;
Two paint their cheeks, and round their temples pour
The fragrant unguent, and th'ambrosial show'r;
One pulls the shape-creating stays, and one
Encircles round their waist the golden zone:
Not with more toil t'improve immortal charms,
Strove *Juno, Venus,* and the *Queen* of *Arms,*
When *Priam*'s Son adjudg'd the golden prize,
To the resistless Beauty of the skies.
At length equipp'd in love's enticing arms,
With all that glitters, and with all that charms,
Th' ideal goddesses to church repair,
Peep thro' the fan, and mutter o'er a pray'r,
Or listen to the organ's pompous sound,
Or eye the gilded images around;
Or, deeply studied in coquettish rules,
Aim wily glances at unthinking fools;
Or shew the lilly hand with graceful air,
Or wound the fopling with a lock of hair.
And when the hated discipline is o'er,
And *Misses* tortur'd with *Repent,* no more,
They mount the pictur'd coach, and to the play,
The celebrated Idols hie away.

Not so the *Lass* that shou'd my joys improve,
With solid friendship, and connubial love:
A native bloom with intermingled white
Should set her features in a pleasing light;
Like *Helen* flushing with unrival'd charms,
When raptur'd *Paris* darted in her arms.
But what alas! avails a ruby cheek,
A downy bosom, or a snowy neck!
Charms ill supply the want of innocence,
Nor beauty forms intrinsic excellence:
But in her breast let moral beauties shine,
Supernal grace and purity divine:
Sublime her reason, and her native wit
Unstain'd with pedantry, and low conceit:

Her fancy lively, and her judgment free
From female prejudice and bigotry:
Averse to idle pomp, and outward show,
The flatt'ring coxcomb, and fantastic beau.
The fop's impertinence she should despise,
Tho' *sorely wounded by her radiant eyes*;
But pay due rev'rence to th' exalted mind
By learning polish'd, and by wit refin'd,
Who all her virtues, without guile commends,
And all her faults as freely reprehends.
Soft *Hymen*'s rites her passions should approve,
And in her bosom glow the flames of love:
To me her soul by sacred friendship turn,
And I for her with equal friendship burn:
In ev'ry stage of life afford relief,
Partake my joys, and sympathize my grief:
Unshaken walk in vertue's peaceful road,
Nor bribe her reason to pursue the mode;
Mild as the saint whose errors are forgiv'n,
Calm as a vestal, and compos'd as heav'n.
This be the partner, this the lovely wife
That should embellish, and prolong my life;
A nymph! who might a second fall inspire,
And fill a glowing *Cherub* with desire!
With her I'd spend the pleasurable day,
While fleeting minutes gayly danc'd away:
With her I'd walk delighted o'er the green,
Thro' ev'ry blooming mead, and rural scene,
Or sit in open fields damask'd with flow'rs,
Or where cool shades imbrown the noon-tide bow'rs
Imparadis'd within my eager arms,
I'd reign the happy monarch of her charms.
Oft on her panting bosom would I lay,
And in dissolving raptures melt away;
Then lull'd by nightingales to balmy rest,
My blooming fair shou'd slumber at my breast.

And when decrepid age (frail mortal's doom!)
Should bend my wither'd body to the tomb,
No warbling *Syrens* shou'd retard my flight

To heav'nly mansions of unclouded light.
Tho' Death, with his imperial horrors crown'd,
Terrific grinn'd, and formidably frown'd,
Offences pardon'd, and remitted sin
Shou'd form a calm serenity within:
Blessing my *natal* and my *mortal* hour,
(My soul committed to th' eternal pow'r)
Inexorable Death shou'd smile, for I
Who *knew* to LIVE, wou'd never *fear* to DIE.

Proclamation

By *John Burgoyne* and *Burgoyne John*, Esquire,
And grac'd with titles still *more* higher,
For I'm Lieutenant-General too,
Of *George*'s troops both *red* and *blue*
On this extensive Continent,
And of Queen *Charlotte*'s regiment
Of light dragoons the Colonel;
And Governor eke of Castle *Will*
And furthermore, when I am there,
In House of Commons I appear
(Hoping e're long to be a Peer)
Being member of that virtuous band
Who always vote at *North*'s command;
Directing too the fleets and troops
From *Canada* as thick as hops:
And all my titles to display,
I'll end with thrice et cætera.

The troops consign'd to my command
Like *Hercules* to purge the land,
Intend to act in combination
With th' other forces of the nation,
Displaying wide thro' every quarter
What Briton's justice would be after.
It is not difficult to shew it,
And every mother's son must know it,

That what she meant at first to gain
By requisitions and chicane,
She's now determin'd to acquire
By *kingly reason, sword* and *fire*.
I can appeal to all your senses,
Your judgments, feelings, tastes and fancies;
Your ears and eyes have heard and seen
How causeless this revolt has been;
And what a dust your leaders kick up;
In this rebellious civil hick-up,
And how upon this curs'd foundation
Was rear'd the system of vexation
Over a stubborn generation.
But now inspir'd with patriot love
I come th' oppression to remove;
To free you from the heavy clogg
Of every tyrant-demagogue,
Who for the most romantic story
Claps into limbo loyal Tory,
All hurly burly, hot and hasty,
Without a writ to hold him fast by;
Nor suffers any living creature
(Led by the dictates of his nature)
To fight in *green* for Britain's cause,
Or aid us to restore her laws:
In short, the vilest generation
Which in vindictive indignation
Almighty vengeance ever hurl'd
From this, to the infernal world.
A Tory cannot move his tongue
But whip, in prison he is flung,
His goods and chattels made a prey
By those vile mushrooms of a day,
He's tortur'd too, and scratch'd and bit,
And plung'd into a dreary pit;
Where he must suffer sharper doom,
Than e're was hatch'd by Church of Rome.
These things are done by rogues, who dare
Profess to breathe in Freedom's air.
To petticoats alike and breeches

Their cruel domination stretches,
For the sole crime, or sole suspicion
(What worse is done by th' inquisition?)
Of still adhering to the Crown,
Their tyrants striving to kick down,
Who by perverting law and reason
Allegiance construe into treason.
Religion too is often made
A stalking horse to drive the trade,
And warring churches dare implore
Protection from th' Almighty pow'r;
They fast and pray: In Providence
Profess to place their confidence;
And vainly think the Lord of all
Regards our squabbles on this ball;
Which would appear as droll in Britain
As any whim that one could hit on:
Men's consciences are set at naught,
Nor reason valued at a groat;
And they that will not swear and fight
Must sell their all, and say *good night.*

By such important views there prest to,
I issue this my manifesto.
I, the great knight of *De la Mancha,*
Without 'Squire *Carleton* my *Sancho,*
Will tear you limb from limb assunder
With cannon, blunderbuss and thunder;
And spoil your feath'ring and your *tarring;*
And cage you up for pickl'd herring.
In front of troops as spruce as beaux,
And ready to lay on their blows,
I'll spread destruction far and near,
And when I cannot kill, I'll spare,
Inviting by these presents all,
Both old and young and great and small,
And rich and poor and Whig and Tory,
In cellar deep or lofty story;
Where'er my troops at my command
Shall swarm like locusts o'er the land,

(And they shall march from the North Pole,
As far at least as Pensicole.)
So break off their communications,
That I can save their habitations;
For finding that *Sir William*'s plunders
Prove in the event apparent blunders,
It is my full determination
To check all kinds of depredation;
But when I've got you in my pow'r,
Favour'd is he, I *last devour.*

From him who loves a quiet life,
And keeps at home to kiss his wife,
And drink success to King Pigmalion,
And calls all congresses Rabscallion,
With *neutral* stomach eats his supper
Nor deems the contest worth a copper,
I will not defalcate a groat,
Nor force his wife to cut his throat;
But with his doxy, he may stay,
And live to fight another day;
Drink all the cyder he has made
And have to boot, a green cockade.
But as I like a good *Sir Loin*,
And *mutton chop*, whene'er I dine,
And my poor troops have long kept Lent,
Not for religion, but for want,
Whoe'er secretes cow, bull or ox,
Or shall presume to hide his flocks;
Or with felonious hand eloign
Pig, duck, or gosling from *Burgoyne*;
Or dare to pull the bridges down,
My boys to puzzle or to drown;
Or smuggle hay, or plow or harrow,
Cart, horses, waggons, or wheel-barrow;
Or 'thwart the path lay straw or switch,
As folks are wont to stop a witch,
I'll hang him as the Jews did *Haman*;
And smoke his carcass for a gammon.

I'll pay in COIN for what I eat,
Or *Continental counterfeit*;
But what's more likely still, I shall
(So fare my troops) not pay at all.

With the most Christian spirit fir'd,
And by true soldiership inspired,
I speak as men do in a passion
To give my speech the more impression,
If any should so hardened be
As to expect impunity,
Because *procul a fulmine*,
I will let loose the dogs of Hell,
Ten thousand Indians, who shall yell,
And foam and tear, and grin and roar,
And drench their maukesins in gore;
To these I'll give full scope and play
From *Ticonderog* to *Florida*;
They'll scalp your heads, and kick your shins,
And rip your guts, and flay your skins,
And of your ears be nimble croppers,
And make your thumbs tobacco stoppers.

If after all these loving warnings,
My wishes and my bowels yearnings,
You shall remain as deaf as adder,
Or grow with hostile rage the madder,
I swear by *George* and by *St. Paul*
I will exterminate you all,
Subscribed with my manual sign
To test these presents, JOHN BURGOYNE.

SAMSON OCCOM

(1723–1792)

The Sufferings of Christ

Throughout the Saviour's Life we trace,
Nothing but Shame and deep Disgrace,
    No period else is seen;
Till he a spotless Victim fell,
Tasting in Soul a painful Hell,
    Caus'd by the Creature's Sin.

On the cold Ground methinks I see
My Jesus kneel, and pray for me;
    For this I him adore;
Siez'd with a chilly sweat throughout,
Blood-drops did force their Passage out
    Through ev'ry open'd Pore.

A pricking Thorn his Temples bore;
His Back with Lashes all was tore,
    Till one the Bones might see;
Mocking, they push'd him here and there,
Marking his Way with Blood and Tear,
    Press'd by the heavy Tree.

Thus up the Hill he painful came,
Round him they mock, and make their Game,
    At length his Cross they rear:
And can you see the mighty God,
Cry out beneath sin's heavy Load,
    Without one thankful Tear?

Thus vailed in Humanity,
He dies in Anguish on the Tree;
    What Tongue his Grief can tell?

The shudd'ring Rocks their Heads recline,
The mourning Sun refuse to shine,
   When the Creator fell.

Shout, Brethren, shout in songs divine,
He drank the Gall, to give us Wine,
   To quench our parching Thirst;
Seraphs advance your Voices higher;
Bride of the Lamb, unite the Choir,
   And Laud thy precious Christ.

A Morning Hymn

1

Now the shades of night are gone,
Now the morning light is come;
Lord, we would be thine to-day,
Drive the shades of sin away.

2

Make our souls as noon-day clear,
Banish ev'ry doubt and fear;
In thy vineyard, Lord, to-day,
We would labour, we would pray.

3

Keep our haughty passions bound;
Rising up and sitting down,
Going out and coming in,
Keep us safe from ev'ry sin.

4

When our work of life is past,
O receive us then at last;
Labour then will all be o'er,
Night of sin will be no more.

A Son's Farewell

1

I hear the Gospel's joyful sound,
  An organ I shall be,
For to sound forth redeeming love,
  And sinner's misery.

2

Honor'd parents, fare you well,
  My Jesus doth me call,
I leave you here with God until
  I meet you once for all.

3

My due affections I'll forsake,
  My parents and their house,
And to the wilderness betake,
  To pay the Lord my vows.

4

Then I'll forsake my chiefest mates
  That nature could afford,
And wear the shield into the field,
  To wait upon the Lord.

5

Then thro' the wilderness I'll run,
  Preaching the gospel free;
O be not anxious for your son,
  The Lord will comfort me.

6

And if thro' preaching I shall gain
  True subjects to my Lord,
'Twill more than recompence my pain,
  To see them love the Lord.

7

My soul doth wish mount Zion well,
    Whate'er becomes of me;
There my best friends and kindred dwell,
    And there I long to be.

The Slow Traveller

1

Oh! happy soul how fast you go,
    And leave me here behind;
Don't stop for me, for now I see
    The Lord is just and kind.

2

Go on, go on, my soul says go,
    And I'll come after you;
Tho' I'm behind, yet I can find,
    I'll sing hosanna too.

3

God give you strength that you may run,
    And keep your footsteps right;
Tho' fast you go, and I so slow,
    You are not out of sight.

4

When you get to the worlds above,
    And all their glories see;
When you get home your work is done,
    Then look you out for me.

5

For I will come fast as I can,
   A long the way I'll steer;
Lord give me strength, I shall at length,
   Be one amongst you there.

6

There altogether we shall be,
   Together we will sing;
Together we will praise our God
   And everlasting King.

ANON.

A Description of a Winter's Morning

The bleak North-west with nipping rigour reigns,
Congeals the Ponds, and crusts the Fields and Plains;
The Sun (in Mists arising) faintly sees
Each Cottage tipt with Snow—the leafless Trees,
Silver'd with Frost—the Fowler, for his Prey,
With stealing steps, explores the roughen'd Way;
The Milk-Maid he, resembling Daphne, spies,
With freshen'd Vigour in her Cheeks and Eyes:
Now curling Smoak from Cottages ascends,
And kindled Fire his failing Heat amends:
The tender Gentry, tim'rous of the Cold,
Cling to their Nests—th' athletick Swain, more bold,
To the near Farm, or distant Market hies,
His Limbs infolded with defensive Prize;
With sturdy Strides he tramples o'er the Mound,
And beats with Iron Hoof, the clatt'ring Ground;
The Houshold Maid industriously prepares
To regulate her necessary Cares;
While th' idle Landlord, or the sottish 'Squire,
Sluggs in the Bed, or hovers o'er the Fire.

ANON.

The Petition

Artful Painter, by this Plan
Draw a Female if you can.
Paint her Features bold and gay,
Casting Modesty away;
Let her Air the Mode express,
And fantastick be her Dress;
Cock her up a little Hat
Of various Colours, this and that;
Make her Cap the Fashion new,
An Inch of Gauze or Lace will do;
Cut her Hair the shortest Dock;
Nicely braid her Forehead Lock;
Put her on a Negligee,
A short Sack or Sheperdee
Ruffled up to keep her warm,
Eight or Ten upon an Arm;
Let her Hoop extending wide
Shew her Garters and her Pride.
Her Stockings must be pure and white,
For they are seldom out of Sight,
Let her have a high heel'd Shoe,
And a glittering Buckle too;
Other Trifles that you find,
Make quite Careless as her Mind.
Thus equipp'd she's charming Ware
For the Races or the Fair.

WILLIAM SMITH

(1727–1803)

The Mock Bird and Red Bird

A Fable

Cantando tu illum?
Vis ergo inter nos quid possit uterque vicissim
Experiamur.   VIRG.

Some Birds, (it is no News to tell)
Can sing, and in their Songs excel,
Then, need we any Wonder make,
If, sometimes, we should hear them speak?
    The *Mock Bird*, on a Time, 'tis said,
Thus the sweet *Red Bird* did upbraid:
"Ah, simple Bird! With one poor Note!
One, and no more! to swell thy Throat;
One, and no more! canst thou repeat.
To charm the Woods, or chear thy Mate.
One, and no more! poor Bird, whilst I
Abound in sweet Variety.
Nor is't thy Voice, thy Voice alone,
Thou Simpleton! that I bemoan,
Methinks, your Colour looks as mean,
All of one Hue! all red, in grain!ᵃ
Your Topping's something like, 'tis true.
But that too's red! all red! poor you."

    The *Red Bird* heard the taunting Strain,
And answer'd, without Pride or Pain,
"Poor me! thou proud ambitious Bird,
Thyself may better claim that Word.
They're poor, who never are content,
But still t'usurp from others bent,
Poor is the Lilly that's so fair?
Or red Rose? which embalms the Air?
I wish not to grow proud and vain,ᵇ
By picking Plumes of various Stain,

550

Nor would feign'd Song, by Rapine raise,
Content with my own native Lays.
My Voice, thou Mocker, 'tis well known,
Such as it is,—it is my own;
And let us leave it to fair Votes,
As sweet as yours, with all your Notes.
But your small Eyes can only see
The beauties in yourself that be:
And there, as little as they are,
They magnify,—and so prefer."

   The *Mock Bird* cry'd— "Ha! my small Eyes—
But Eyes are not to win the Prize.
The Question is of Voice and Colour,
And not whose gogle Eyes are fuller.
Hark, have you Ears?"—each Stain it try'd,
And swell'd with Musick, and with Pride.
Then would have spoke again,—but, choak'd
With Spite and Spleen—it rather croak'd,
"Ah! my Throat's hoarse"—it scarce could utter—
And yet seem'd something more to mutter.
Then, taking Flight, its Weakness found,
And flutt'ring, fell upon the Ground.

   The *Red Bird* not insulting stood,
But wing'd and warbl'd thro' the Wood.

   The MORAL to be learn'd from hence,
Is pretty plain—let's have the Sense
Simplicity of Life and Heart
To love, and scorn delusive Art:
Never, thro' Spite, which swells and bloats,
T' enflame our Breasts, or strain our Throats:
To shun all foolish Ostentation;
And be contented with our Station.

---

  [a] [b]There is some little variety of Colour in the *Red Bird*, tho', by what the *Mocking Bird* says, we might think there was none at all; but it is not in Taunts and Scoffs that we are to expect Truth. The *Red Bird* seems little careful to answer that Taunt, as taking no Pride in Colours.

The Cherry-Tree and Peach-Tree

An American Fable

Trees once could speak, some Authors say,
And now, 'tis talk'd, that 'tother Day,
A *Cherry-Tree*, in vernal Pride,
A *Peach*, hard by, did thus deride.
  "Ha! Neighbor *Peach* methinks, you look
Like one with some Disaster struck;
I doubt that this last Winter's Frost,
Has shewn its Rigour to your Cost.
The Birds, wont to frequent, so fond,
Your early Sweets, now fly, beyond.
No Blossom's there, scarce, ev'n a Leaf,
Your very Life's no more than safe.
Well! Nothing's stable here below,
Blossoms and Flow'rs are but a Show.
One Year, perhaps, it may go well,
And how the next, 'tis hard to tell:
But y'are more fit to moralize,
And, if less fair, should be more wise."
  The *Peach*,—"I find y'have learn'd to taunt,
So nigh to Houses since you haunt;
Tis not for nothing in that Corner
You stand so close, as an Adorner.
But, surely, 'tis a bad World, when
Trees shew such Pride,—leave that to Men:
Or leave it to the gentler Sex,
Their lovely Bosoms to perplex:
If their own Charms are not enough,
Let them be vain of Silk-Worm Stuff;
Vain of the Glittering of a Gem,
For Brightness not to match with them.
Excuse the Fair-ones, what is said,
For them, for Man, Pride was not made.
Leave it to Turky-Cocks and Pea-Cocks,
And May-poles drest with Garlands, Gay-stocks.
There is a Pride, that gives a Grace,

That's suitable to human Race;
Which it becomes them to defend,
From their Original, and End.—
Yet, even that to attemper's just,
Both great,—both mean,—the Heav'ns & Dust.
The Orient Form, here, humbly dwells
In Clay—so Pearls in vulgar Shells.
So some fair Saphire, in a Shrine
Of meaner Wood,—like yours or mine.
But as for us, and our Array,—"
   The *Cherry* interrupts—"Hey-day;
Who learn'd you to make Similes?
They're too ambitious for us Trees.
Our language should be clear and plain,
And shew directly what we mean:
And not pretend to so much Knowledge,
As if we grew beside a Colledge.—
'Thad been as fit, and not amiss,
In your Harangue, t'have touch'd on this.
To Men, but still their Pardon craving,
To learn from Scant the Art of Saving.
And, if, this Year, some Fruits are few'r.
Give less to Hogs, and more to Poor.
But when Things are beyond our Sphere,
'Tis not our Part to interfere
In such high Matters,—let them be,
Now, say, what you've to say to me:"
   "To you I say wh'are so bedeck'd,
You look too lofty to be check'd.
Short's the Duration of the Spring,
Beauty is but a fading Thing.
E'er long a sudden stormy Gust,
May lay your Honour's in the Dust.
The Birds, your Boughs that now salute,
Will be the first to peck your Fruit.
If I now look but wan and bare,
Shall Winters still be so severe.
You on your present Form presume,
I live in Hopes of future Bloom."—

The MORAL—learn it from the *Peach*,
And *Cherry*—both of them may teach:—
And some may hear—but as we treat them,
Many there are who'd rather eat them.—

The Birds of different Feather

An American Fable

When fair Intention has been slighted,
And kind Address but ill requited;
The gentler Style, essay'd vain,
Demands a somewhat different Strain.
   In solemn Notes, the *Turtle Dove*,
Perform'd his Music in the Grove,
Whilst all the Warblers of the Wood,
Of sweetest Voice, Attention shew'd.
   Not far off a malicious *Crow*,
The gentle *Dove*'s invet'rate Foe,
To his Tribe, and Associate kind,
That perch'd around, explain'd his Mind.
   "I swear I hate those dismal Strains,
They're perfect Discord to my Brains.
Perhaps he thinks our Hearts to move?
Shall ever *Crows* such Warblers love?
Shall we forget our ancient Few'd,
Our hatred against all his Blood?
Now raise th' whole Posse of the Air;
If possible, our War to share.
Our Kindred certainly will aid,
And other Allies will accede,
Demean him thro' the feather'd Race,
Impute t' him every Thing that's base.
And what you say, say oft and long,
That renders an Impeachment strong.
As for the Music of his Notes,
I hope that we have likewise Throats.
And when our Consorts he provokes,
If he has Cooings, we have Croaks:

And, more, to fortify our Cause,
Have we not Beaks? Have we not Claws?"
   The Birds which Rage and Rapine love,
By a hoarse Cry seem'd to approve.
A *Red Bird*, who th' Harangue o'er-heard,
Provok'd, thus his Dissent prefer'd.
"Thou, who, with thy associate Race,
Are Foes to Harmony and Peace;
No Birds wh' are good, from thee expect
Aught, but of Enmity th' Effect.
The bad Birds may improve their Parts,
From the incendiary Arts;
And learn, from thy presuming Pride,
To ravage and defame beside.
'Tis well known, that your Meaning such is,
And that as well as Croaks y'have Clutches.
Against the *Dove*, 'gainst all that's Good,
Your base Conspiracy's avow'd.
Who-e'er was by his Song annoy'd?
Not thus his gentle Notes employ'd.
But Malice tunes thy hobbling Song,
And both the Notes and Sense are wrong.
While you bear such a Mind unblest,
Your Punishment is in your Breast.
Can'st thou not change? Say, can a *Crow*
It's Colour quit, and candid grow?
In the same Forest, whilst the Range,
The same Air breath'd,—Canst thou not change?"
   Here paus'd the *Red Bird*, as to weigh
What he intended yet to say;
Perhaps, in doubt, if to advance; or
Wait for a While th' Opponent's Answer.
Mean Time, the *Crow*, "Thou senseless Ninny,
Who'd think such prating had been in ye,
Have you been learning in some Cage,
Or College to become so sage?
No doubt, you for a Champion suit,
And y'are an Orator to boot,
But prithee, *Red Pate*, now, go on,
Our Colour,—that you was upon.

I can't pretend with you to scold,
The *Red Bird* cry'd, I'm not so bold.
Nor is it that your Colour's bad,
Some lovely Birds are darkly clad.
'Tis not your Feather that's the Flaw,
But the black Malice in your Maw.
From that 'tis you'd do well to vary,
But y'are not to be alter'd,—are ye?
Not thou.—Time, Virtue may complain,
Sense, Echo, th' Air, the Grove, in vain.
Can Obstinacy have the Force
To make Wrong Right, by a long Course?
Some Birds, who oft false Notes renew,
'Tis said, at length conceit them true.
The Mind, long set on base Intent,
Can it recover from its bent?
The Tree of crooked growth, 'tis late
To think again to set it strait,
Perhaps a *Panther* may be tam'd,
And wicked Spite, grown old, reclaim'd."

   "Confound your Similies," the Crow
Exclaim'd, and seem'd with Rage to glow.
Flutt'ring he shook his Head, and peck'd,
And croak's more hoarse for being check'd,
"Will none, he cry'd, here, take my Part,
And tear yon little Wretch's Heart?"
A rustling *Buz* to War did cry:—
An *Eagle* darted from on high:—
"Be gone, he said, base Crew, be gone;—
Thou little noble Bird, come on;
Come on my Pinions,—Thou shalt be
Secure: for, now, to thee, to thee
To raise upon my Wings 'tis giv'n,
And thus I bear thee up to Heav'n."

   'Tis said the *Crow* was struck with Dread,
As th' *Eagle* brush'd just o'er his Head,
And, since, on any, the least Fright,
Enquires, is that an *Eagle*'s Flight?

   The Moral—Something, on that Head,
It seems, must still of Course be said.

The various Birds, of different Note,
According to their Natures, vote.
All kinds are in the human Brood,
Strange Mixture of what's bad and good!
Passion provok'd may, sometimes do ill,
Malice perpetually is cruel.
Who cherish it, indulge a Cancer,
Contaminating by its Rancour.
In vain, soft Music is addrest,
While that *Tarant'la* stings the Breast.
'Twere good, in Time, then, to restrain,
What is productive of such Bane.
At least, let those of sound Complexion,
Beware of such a base Infection;
Nor, to promote a vile Intrigue,
Become Partakers in its Plague:
And such a Wickedness not new is,
That some are fond to spread their Lues.
The gentle Birds may still suppose,
To meet with Enmity from *Crows*;
Yet, let them not the Air upbraid,
The *Red Bird* found an *Eagle*'s Aid.

HANNAH GRIFFITTS

(1727–1817)

The female Patriots

Address'd to the Daughters of Liberty in America

Since the Men from a Party, or fear of a Frown,
Are kept by a Sugar-Plumb, quietly down.
Supinely asleep, & depriv'd of their Sight
Are strip'd of their Freedom, & rob'd of their Right.
If the Sons (so degenerate) the Blessing despise,
Let the Daughters of Liberty, nobly arise,
And tho' we've no Voice, but a negative here.
The use of the *Taxables, let us forebear,
(Then Merchants import till your Stores are all full
May the Buyers be few & your Traffick be dull.)
Stand firmly resolved & bid Grenville to see
That rather than Freedom, we'll part with our Tea
And well as we love the dear Draught when a dry,
As American Patriots,—our Taste we deny,
Sylvania's gay Meadows, can richly afford,
To pamper our Fancy, or furnish our Board,
And Paper sufficient (at home) still we have,
To assure the Wise-acre, we will not sign Slave.
When this Homespun shall fail, to remonstrate our Grief
We can speak with the Tongue or scratch on a Leaf.
　Refuse all their Colours, tho richest of Dye,
The juice of a Berry—our Paint can supply,
To humour our Fancy—& as for our Houses,
They'll do without painting as well as our Spouses,
While to keep out the Cold of a keen winter Morn
We can screen the Northwest, with a well polish'd Horn,
And trust me a Woman by honest Invention
Might give this State Doctor a Dose of Prevention.
Join mutual in this, & but small as it seems
We may Jostle a Grenville & puzzle his Schemes

*Tea—Paper—Glass—& Paints.—

558

But a motive more worthy our patriot Pen,
Thus acting—we point out their Duty to Men,
And should the bound Pensioners, tell us to hush
We can throw back the Satire by biding them blush.

To Sophronia

*In answer to some Lines she directed
to be wrote on my Fan. 1769*

I've neither Reserve or aversion to Man,
  (I assure you Sophronia in jingle)
But to keep my dear Liberty, long as I can,
  Is the Reason I chuse to live single,
My Sense, or the Want of it—free you may jest
  And censure, dispise, or impeach,
But the Happiness center'd within my own Breast,
  Is luckily out of your reach.
The Men, (as a Friend) I prefer, I esteem,
  And love them as well as I ought
But to fix all my Happiness, solely in Him
  Was never my Wish or my Thought,
The cowardly Nymph, you so often reprove,
  Is not frighted by *Giants like these,
Leave me to enjoy the sweet Freedom I love
  And go marry—as soon as you please.

The Cits Return from the
Wilderness to the City

1770

Hail! once again, dear natal Seats
Ye plodding Cits, & slipp'ry Streets,
Better, a gentle fall, from you,
Than live excluded of the View,

---

*The satyrical Sneers thrown on the single Life.—

Retir'd amidst the dismal Shades,
And Cows—& Chicks, & chattering Maids,
Who criticise with publick wonder,
Their undesigning Neighbour's blunder,
Blunders, in Cities, pass along,
Unnotic'd, with the blundering Throng,
But here, each little Slip is thrown
In public View—except their own.
Ye criticising Dames adieu,
And fellow Cits—all hail to you!
The very Dust—on which you tread
I value—nearly with your Head,
Pardon the odd Compare, nor grumble
For should my hurrying gain a tumble,
I need not long deploring stand,
While Men are plenty, helps at hand.
But let us guard, midst all our blunder
To keep our brittle Heads asunder,
For should they strike, this frosty Weather,
'Twill silence all their Wit forever,
The very Smoak, your Chimnies lend
Are pleasing Prospects to your Friend,
But oh! the hurrying Crowds that beat
The broken Pavement of each Street,
Are Sights more fair than all the Plains
That dress the Songsters rural Strains,
Let them, to mount Parnassus climb,
And with their Fiction swell their Rhyme,
Ye dear Realities of Life,
The happy Husband & his Wife,
The weeping Widower in his Sable
(Who eyes his second at the Table)
E'er for the first—his Tears are spent
If those kind drops were ever lent,—
And all the rest—who humbly wait
Their entrance to this blessed State,
I truly Joy, with you to meet
Tho' at the Risk of Head & Feet.

Wrote on the last Day of February 1775

Beware of the Ides of March

Had Caesar took this useful Hint
   E're to the senate House he enter'd,
Longer he might have liv'd to think
   Nor midst his cruel Murd'rers ventur'd.
Ladies this wiser Caution take,
   Trust not your Tea to *Marcus Brutus,
Our Draught he'll spoil our China break,
   And raise a Storm that will not suit us.
Then for the Sake of Freedom's Name
   (Since British Wisdom scorns repealing)
Come sacrifise to Patriot Fame,
   And give up Tea by way of healing.
This done within ourselves retreat
   The industrious Arts of Life to follow
Let the proud Nabobs storm & fret,
   They cannot force our Throats to swallow.
Tho' now the boistrous Surges rowl,
   Of wicked North's tempestuous Ocean,
Leave him for Justice to controul
   And strive to calm our own Commotion.
With us each prudent Caution meet,
   Against this blustering Son of Thunder,
And let our firm Resolve, defeat
   His Lordship's ministerial Blunder.—

Upon reading a Book entituled Common Sense

January. 1776

The Vizard drop'd, see Subtilty prevail,
Thro' ev'ry Page of this fallacious Tale,
Sylvania let it not unanswer'd pass,
But heed the well guess'd Snake beneath the Grass,
A deeper Wound at Freedom, ne'er was made,

*Marcus Brutus was one of Caesars Murderers.

Than by this Oliverian is display'd.
Orders confounded,—Dignities thrown down,
Charters degraded equal with the Crown,
The impartial Press, most partially maintain'd
Freedom infring'd, & Conscience is restrain'd,
The moderate Man is held to publick View,
"The Friend of Tyranny & Foe to you,"
Deny'd the common Right to represent
Forbid to give his Reasons for Dissent,
Whilst base Informers—(Own'd a publick Pest)
Are round the Land encourag'd & caress'd
Our Representatives,—the Peoples Choice
Are held contemptuous by this daring Voice
Persons are seiz'd & Posts monopoliz'd
And all our Form of Government despis'd,—
—Then from this "Specimen of Rule" beware,
Behold the Serpent & avoid his Snare.
'Tis not in Names, our present Danger lyes
Sixty as well as one can tyrannize,
Ah! then awake Sylvania & beware,
The fatal Danger of this subtle Snare,
Hold fast your own, your charter'd Rights maintain
Nor let them weave the Snare into the Chain,
And whilst firm Union stands the British Foes,
Let not the native Hand your Date of Freedom close.—

On reading a few Paragraphs in the Crisis

April 1777

Paine, tho' thy Tongue may now run glibber,
Warm'd with thy independent Glow,
Thou art indeed, the boldest Fibber,
I ever knew or wish to know.
Here Page & Page,* ev'n num'rous Pages,
Are void of Breeding, Sense or Truth,
I hope thou dont receive thy Wages,

*citing the Pages.

As Tutor to our rising Youth.
Of female Manners never scribble,
Nor with thy Rudeness wound our Ear,
How e'er thy trimming Pen may quibble,
The Delicate—is not thy Sphere;
And now to prove how false thy Stories
By Facts,—which wont admit a Doubt
Know there are conscientious Tories
And one poor Whig at least without
Wilt thou permit the Muse to mention,
A Whisper circulated round,
"Let Howe encrease the Scribblers Pension
No more will Paine a Whig be found."—
For not from Principle, but Lucre,
He gains his Bread from out the Fire,
Let Court & Congress, both stand neuter,
And the poor Creature must expire.

MARY NELSON

(fl. 1769)

Forty Shillings Reward

Last Wednesday morn, at break of day,
From Philadelphia run away,
An Irish man, nam'd John M'Keoghn,
To fraud and imposition prone;
About five feet five inches high,
Can curse and swear as well as lie;
How old he is I can't engage,
But forty-five is near his age;
He came (as all reports agree)
From Belfast town in sixty-three,
On board the Culloden, a ship
Commanded by M'Lean that trip;
Speaks like a Scotchman, very broad,
Is round shoulder'd, and meagre jaw'd;
Has thick short hair, of sandy hue,
Breeches and hose of maz'reen blue;
Of lightish cloth an outside vest,
In which he commonly is dress'd;
Inside of which two more I've seen,
One flannel, th' other coarse nankeen.
He stole, and from my house convey'd,
A man's blue coat, of broadcloth made;
A grey great coat, of bearskin stuff,
(Nor had the villain yet enough;)
Some chintz (the ground was Pompadour)
I lately purchas'd in a store,
Besides a pair of blue ribb'd hose,
Which he has on as I suppose.
He oft in conversation chatters,
Of scripture and religious matters,
And fain would to the world impart,
That virtue lodges in his heart;
But take the rogue from stem to stern,

The hypocrite you'll soon discern,
And find (tho' his deportment's civil)
A saint without, within a devil.
Whoe'er secures said John M'Keoghn,
(Provided I should get my own)
Shall have from me, in cash paid down,
Five Dollar-Bills, and Half-a-Crown.

Water-street, Jan. 10, 1769

MERCY OTIS WARREN

(1728–1814)

A Thought on the Inestimable Blessing of Reason

occasioned by its privation to a friend
of very superior talents and virtues
1770.

What is it moves within my soul,
And as the needle to the pole
Directs me to the final cause
The central point of nature's laws?
'Tis reason, Lord, which thou hast given
A ray divine, let down from Heaven,
A spark struck from effulgent light,
Transcendant, clear,—divinely bright,
Thou hast bestow'd lest man should grope
In endless darkness, void of hope.
　　Creative being!—who reason gave
And by whose aid the powers we have
To think, to judge, to will, to know,
From whom these reasoning powers flow,
Thy name be ever magnified
That thus to Angels we're allied,
Distinguish'd thus in the great chain
Nor left the least in thy domain.
　　Yet should'st thou but a moment frown,
Or wink this boasted reason down
'Twould level proud imperious man
With the least worm in nature's plan.
Then humbly will I thee implore,
Whom worlds of rationals adore,
That thou this taper should preserve
From reason's laws let me ne'er swerve,
But calmly, mistress of my mind
A friend to virtue and mankind.
Oh! gently lead me on to peace
May years the heavenly gleam increase,

Nor waste beneath the frown of age,
As I tread down time's narrow stage,
But brighter burn as life decays
More fit to join the heavenly lays.
And when the tenement shall fall
When broken down this feeble wall
Then may the glad, enlighten'd soul
Freed from these clogs, this dull controul
Expand her wings, shake off her load
And rise to glorify her God.

To Mr. ———

*Alluding to a Conversation which favoured the Opinion of
Fatalism; that human Action, whether good or evil, springs
from the Principle of self Love, void of any real
Benevolence, when traced up to its Source.*

Though short, far short, my pen of the sublime,
Fate urges on, and bids me write in rhyme;
I hope my friend the effort will excuse,
Nor blame the heart, but chide the niggard muse.

Is it a wild enthusiastic flame,
That swells the bosom panting after fame;
Dilates the mind, while every sail's unfurl'd,
To catch the plaudits of a gazing world?
Is there no permanent, no steady pole,
To point us on, and guide the wandering soul?
Does prejudice and passion rule mankind?
Are there no springs that actuate the mind,
Whose deep meanders have a nobler source,
Than vain self love, to guide their winding course?

The gen'rous ardour, still'd benevolence,
Is it all art, to gratify the sense?
Or give imagination further scope?
That airy queen, who guides the helm of hope,
Holds a false mirror to the dazzled sight;

A dim perspective, a delusive light,
That swells the bubbles of life's shorten'd span,
While wisdom laughs at the deluded man,
Wrap'd in ecstatics, by imagin'd fame,
When the next moment may blot out his name.

Can't the wise precepts of a Plato's school,
Or a divine—a still more perfect rule,
Arouse, exalt, and animate the soul
Self to renounce, and rise above control
Of narrow passions, that the man debase,
And from his breast his maker's image rase;
Or are the fetters that enslave the mind
Of such a strong and adamantine kind,
So firmly lock'd, and so securely riv'd,
The more we strive, the more we're still deceiv'd;
Are truth and friendship no where to be found,
And patriot virtue nothing but a sound?
Then may a Cæsar equal honours claim,
With gen'rous Brutus' celebrated name:
For the poor tribute of a short applause,
One stabb'd a tyrant, trampling on the laws;
While the proud despot mark'd his baneful way,
With virtue's tears, and triumph'd o'er his prey.

Cæsar enslav'd, and Brutus would have freed,
Self, the sole point in which they're both agreed.

Self love, that stimulus to nobler aims,
Bade Nero light the capital in flames;
Bade Borgia act a most infernal part,
Or Scipio to triumph o'er his heart;
Bids —— betray his native land,
And his base brother lend his perjur'd hand,
While freedom weeps, and heav'n forbears to shed
Its awful vengeance on the guilty head.

If such is life, and fancy throws the bowl,
And appetite and caprice rule the whole;
If virtuous friendship has no solid base,

But false deception holds the sacred place;
Then from thy mem'ry rase out every line,
Nor recollect a sentiment of mine,
But dark oblivion's sable veil draw o'er,
And I'll forbear to interrupt thee more.

For if vice boasts her origin the same
With social joy and patriotic flame,
Then I must wish to bid the world farewel,
Turn Anchoret, and choose some lonely cell,
Beneath some peaceful hermitage reclin'd,
To weep the misery of all mankind,
'Till days and years, till time shall cease to roll,
And truth eternal strike the wondering soul.

LUCY TERRY

(c. 1730–1821)

Bars Fight

August 'twas the twenty-fifth,
Seventeen hundred forty-six;
The Indians did in ambush lay,
Some very valiant men to slay,
The names of whom I'll not leave out.
Samuel Allen like a hero fout.
And though he was so brave and bold,
His face no more shall we behold.
Eleazer Hawks was killed outright,
Before he had time to fight,—
Before he did the Indians see,
Was shot and killed immediately.
Oliver Amsden he was slain,
Which caused his friends much grief and pain.
Simeon Amsden they found dead,
Not many rods distant from his head.
Adonijah Gillett we do hear
Did lose his life which was so dear.
John Sadler fled across the water,
And thus escaped the dreadful slaughter.
Eunice Allen see the Indians coming,
And hopes to save herself by running,
And had not her petticoats stopped her,
The awful creatures had not catched her,
Nor tommy hawked her on her head,
And left her on the ground for dead.
Young Samuel Allen, Oh lack-a-day!
Was taken and carried to Canada.

NED BOTWOOD

(c. 1730–1759)

Hot Stuff

(*Tune, Lilies of France*)

Come, each death-doing dog who dare venture his neck,
Come follow the Hero that goes to Quebec;
Jump aboard of the transports, and loose every sail,
Pay your debts at the tavern by giving leg-bail;
And ye that love fighting, shall soon have enough:
Wolf commands us, my boys, we will give them Hot Stuff.

　　Up the River St. Lawrence our troops shall advance;
To the Grenadier's March we will teach them to dance:
Cape-Breton we have taken, and next we will try
At their capital, to give them another black eye.
Vaudreuil, 'tis in vain ye pretend to look gruff,
Those are coming who know how to give you Hot Stuff.

　　With powder in his periwig, and snuff in his nose,
Monsieur will run down our descent to oppose;
And the Indians will come; but the light infantry
Will soon oblige them to betake to a tree.
From such rascals as these may we fear a rebuff?
Advance, Grenadiers, and let fly your Hot Stuff.

　　When the forty-seventh regiment is dashing ashore,
While bullets are whistling and cannons do roar,
Says Montcalm, Those are Shirley's, I know the lappells;
You lie, says Ned Botwood, we belong to Lascelles:
Tho' our cloathing is changed, yet we scorn a powder puff,
So at you, ye B——s, here's give you Hot Stuff.

　　With Monckton and Townshend, those brave Brigadiers,
I think we shall soon knock the town 'bout their ears;
And when we have done with the mortars and guns,
If you please, madam Abbess,—a word with your Nuns;
Each soldier shall enter the Convent in buff,
And then, never fear us,—we will give them Hot Stuff.

HENRY TIMBERLAKE

(1730–1765)

A Translation of the War-Song

Caw waw noo dee, &c.

Where'er the earth's enlighten'd by the sun,
Moon shines by night, grass grows, or waters run,
Be't known that we are going, like men, afar,
In hostile fields to wage destructive war;
Like men we go, to meet our country's foes,
Who, woman-like, shall fly our dreaded blows;
Yes, as a woman, who beholds a snake,
In gaudy horror, glisten thro' the brake,
Starts trembling back, and stares with wild surprize,
Or pale thro' fear, unconscious, panting, flies.
*Just so these foes, more tim'rous than the hind,
Shall leave their arms and only cloaths behind;
Pinch'd by each blast, by ev'ry thicket torn,
Run back to their own nation, now its scorn:
Or in the winter, when the barren wood
Denies their gnawing entrails nature's food,
Let them sit down, from friends and country far,
And wish, with tears, they ne'er had come to war.

†We'll leave our clubs, dew'd with their country show'rs,
And, if they dare to bring them back to our's,
Their painted scalps shall be a step to fame,
And grace our own and glorious country's name.
Or if we warriors spare the yielding foe,

*As the Indians fight naked, the vanquished are constrained to endure the rigours of the weather in their flight, and live upon roots and fruit, as they throw down their arms to accelerate their flight thro' the woods.

†It is the custom of the Indians, to leave a club, something of the form of a cricket-bat, but with their warlike exploits engraved on it, in their enemy's country, and the enemy accepts the defiance, by bringing this back to their country.

Torments at home the wretch must undergo*.
But when we go, who knows which shall return,
When growing dangers rise with each new morn?
Farewel, ye little ones, ye tender wives,
For you alone we would conserve our lives!
But cease to mourn, 'tis unavailing pain,
If not fore-doom'd, we soon shall meet again.
But, O ye friends! in case your comrades fall,
Think that on you our deaths for vengeance call;
With uprais'd tommahawkes pursue our blood,
And stain, with hostile streams, the conscious wood,
That pointing enemies may never tell
The boasted place where we, their victims, fell†.

*The prisoners of war are generally tortured by the women, at the party's
return, to revenge the death of those that have perished by the wretch's coun-
trymen. This savage custom has been so much mitigated of late, that the
prisoners were only compelled to marry, and then generally allowed all the
privileges of the natives. This lenity, however, has been a detriment to the na-
tion; for many of these returning to their countrymen, have made them ac-
quainted with the country-passes, weakness, and haunts of the Cherokees;
besides that it gave the enemy greater courage to fight against them.

†Their custom is generally to engrave their victory on some neighbouring
tree, or set up some token of it near the field of battle; to this their enemies are
here supposed to point to, as boasting their victory over them, and the slaugh-
ter that they made.

BENJAMIN BANNEKER

(1731–1806)

The Puzzle of the Hare and Hound

Question for Hopkins
   When fleecy skies have Cloth'd the ground
   With a white mantle all around
   Then with a grey hound Snowy fair
   In milk white fields we Cours'd a Hare
   Just in the midst of a Champaign
   We set her up, away she ran,
   The Hound I think was from her then
   Just thirty leaps or three times ten
   Oh it was pleasant for to see
   How the Hare did run so timorously
   But yet so very Swift that I
   Did think she did not run but Fly
   When the Dog was almost at her heels
   She quickly turn'd, and down the fields
   She ran again with full Career
   And 'gain she turn'd to the place she were
   At every turn she gain'd of ground
   As many yards as the greyhound
   Could leap at thrice, and She did make,
   Just Six, if I do not mistake
   Four times She Leap'd for the Dogs three
   But two of the Dogs leaps did agree
   With three of hers, nor pray declare
   How many leaps he took to Catch the Hare.

574

Just Seventy two I did Suppose,
An Answer false from thence arose,
I Doubled the Sum of Seventy two,
But still I found that would not do,
I mix'd the Numbers of them both,
Which Shew'd so plain that I'll make Oath,
Eight hundred leaps the Dog to make,
And Sixty four, the Hare to take.

4 :   72   :   : 48
        48
       576
      288
     4)3456
       864   ans.

THOMAS GODFREY JR.

(1736–1763)

Verses Occasioned by a Young Lady's asking the Author, What was a Cure for Love?

1758

From me, my Dear, O seek not to receive
What e'en deep-read Experience cannot give.
We may, indeed, from the Physician's skill
Some Med'cine find to cure the body's ill.
But who e'er found the physic for the soul,
Or made th' affections bend to his controul?
When thro' the blaze of passion objects show
How dark 's the shade! how bright the colours glow!
All the rous'd soul with transport's overcome,
And the mind's surly Monitor is dumb.

    In vain the sages turn their volumes o'er,
And on the musty page incessant pore,
Still mighty LOVE triumphant rules the heart,
Baffles their labour, and eludes their art.

    Say what is science, what is reason's force
To stop the passions wild ungovern'd course?
Reason, 'tis true, may point the rocky shore,
And shew the danger, but can serve no more,
From wave to wave the wretched wreck is tost,
And reason 's in th' impetuous torrent lost.

    In vain we strive, when urg'd by cold neglect,
By various means our freedom to effect,
Tho' like the bee from sweet to sweet we rove,
And search for ease in the vast round of Love,
Tho' in each Nymph we meet a kind return,
Still in the firstfond hopeless flame we burn,
That dear idea still our thoughts employs,

And blest variety itself e'en cloys.
So exiles banish'd from their native home
Are met with pity wheresoe'er they come,
Yet still their native soil employs their care,
And death were ease to lay their ashes there.

*Epistle to a Friend; from Fort Henry

Dated August 10, 1758

From where his lofty head TALHEO rears,
And o'er the wild in majesty appears,
What shall I write that *——* won't disdain,
Or worth, from Thee one moment's space to gain?
The Muse, in vain, I court the lovely maid,
Views with contempt the rude unpolish'd shade,
Nor only this, she flies fierce war's alarms,
And seeks where peace invites with softer charms;
Where the gay landscapes strike the travellers eyes,
And woods and lawns in beauteous order rise;
Where the glad Swain sings on th' enamel'd green,
And views unaw'd by fears the pleasing scene.
Here no enchanting prospects yield delight,
But darksome forests intercept the sight;
Here fill'd with dread the trembling peasants go,
And start with terror at each nodding bough,
Nor as they trace the gloomy way along
Dare ask the influence of a chearing song.

If in this wild a pleasing spot we meet,
In happier times some humble swain's retreat;
Where once with joy he saw the grateful soil
Yield a luxuriant harvest to his toil,

*Wrote, when the Author was a Lieutenant in the Pennsylvania Forces, and, garrisoned at Fort HENRY. This little piece is the more valuable, as it contains a striking picture, and perhaps the only one, of this kind, that will be preserved, of the deep distress that overwhelmed our Frontier Settlements, when every field was stained with the blood of its Owners, by the merciless hands of unfeeling Savages.

(Blest with content, enjoy'd his solitude,
And knew his pleasures, tho' of manners rude);
The lonely prospect strikes a secret dread,
While round the ravag'd Cott we silent tread,
Whose Owner fell beneath the savage hand,
Or roves a captive on some hostile land,
While the rich fields, with Ceres' blessings stor'd,
Grieve for their slaughter'd, or their absent lord.

Yet, would I now attempt, some sprightly strain,
And strive to wake your breast to mirth again,
Yet, would I call you from your Delia's urn,
But *Britain's* Genius bids her sons to mourn;
She shews the fatal field, all drench'd in gore,
And in sad accents cries, my *Howe's* no more!
Then let again the briny torrents flow,
Oh! teach your breast a nobler kind of woe!
To mourn *her* faded beauties now forbear,
And give the gallant Chief a *British* tear.

*A Dithyrambic on Wine

I.

Come! let Mirth our hours employ,
The jolly God inspires;
The rosy juice our bosom fires,
And tunes our souls to joy.
See, great *Bacchus* now descending,
Gay, with blushing honours crown'd;

---

*The DITHYRAMBIC demands a greater boldness than any other poetical composition, and is indeed the only one in which a lyric irregularity may be happily indulged.

                                        Francis's HORACE.

As our Poet appears so warm on his subject, it may not be amiss to remark here, that *he never drank any Wine*, and that his *bumpers* are all *ideal*, which may serve, perhaps, as a refutation of that noted adage, that *a water drinker can never be a good Dithyrambic Poet.*

Sprightly *Mirth* and *Love* attending,
 Around him wait,
 In smiling state—
 Let *Echo* resound,
 Let *Echo* resound
 The joyful news all around.

II.

Fond Mortals come, if love perplex,
In *Wine* relief you'll find;
Who'd whine for womens giddy sex
More fickle than the wind?
If beauty's bloom thy fancy warms,
Here, see her shine,
Cloath'd in superior charms;
More lovely than the blushing morn,
When first the op'ning day
Bedecks the thorn,
And makes the meadows gay.
Here see her in her crystal shrine;
See and adore; confess her all divine,
The Queen of Love and Joy.
Heed not thy Chloe's scorn—
 This sparkling glass,
 With winning grace,
Shall ever meet thy fond embrace,
And never, never, never cloy,
 No never, never cloy.

III.

Here, POET! see, *Castalia's* spring—
Come, give me a bumper, I'll mount to the skies,
Another, another— 'Tis done! I arise;
 On fancy's wing,
 I mount, I sing,
 And now, sublime,
Parnassus' lofty top I climb—
But hark! what sounds are these I hear,
Soft as the dream of her in love,

Or *Zephyr's* whisp'ring thro' the Grove?
And now, more solemn far than fun'ral woe,
The heavy numbers flow!
  And now again,
  The varied strain,
Grown louder and bolder, strikes quick on the ear,
And thrills thro' ev'ry vein.

IV.

'Tis *Pindar's* song!
His softer notes the fanning gales
Waft across the spicy vales,
  While, thro' the air,
  Loud whirlwinds bear
The harsher notes along.
  Inspir'd by *Wine*,
He leaves the lazy croud below,
Who never dar'd to peep abroad,
And, mounting to his native sky,
For ever there shall shine.
  No more I'll plod
  The beaten road;
Like him inspir'd, like him I'll mount on high;
  Like his my strain shall flow.

V.

Haste, ye Mortals! leave your sorrow;
Let pleasure crown to day—to morrow
  Yield to fate.
Join the universal chorus,
  Bacchus reigns,
   Ever great;
  Bacchus reigns
   Ever glorious—
Hark! the joyful groves rebound,
Sporting breezes catch the sound,
And tell to hill and dale around—
  "*Bacchus* reigns"—
  While far away,
The busy *Echoes* die away.—

ANNIS BOUDINOT STOCKTON

(1736–1801)

A Satire on the fashionable pompoons worn
by the Ladies in the year 1753. by a Gentleman;
Answered by a young Lady of sixteen

How dull the age when ladies must express—
Each darling wish in emblematic dress—
See how the wheels in various colours roll
Speaking the wish of every female soul
Oh let a windmill decorate the hair
A windmill proper emblemn of the fair
As every blast of wind impells the vane
So every blast of folly whirls their brain.—

Answered by a young Lady of sixteen

Forbear unkind ungenerous muse forbear
To brand with folly the whole race of fair
Thousands whose minds each manly grace improve
Soften'd by smiles by elegance and love
Might well in spite of satires keenest hate
Redeem them from an undistinguish'd fate.—
Sure all the poets laurels now must fade
Or some dread blight must blast the cyprian shade
Or jaundic'd eye must tinge each verdant scene
That we fall victims to the scribbling vein.—
But what the fabl'd Lion said is true
And if apply'd May serve for us and you
Were we but *writers we'd* reform the age
And make your queus adorn some Ingling page
For metaphors a bubble should suffice
Whose consequence the softest breath destroys
—Oh then behave like men offend no more
Cherish our virtues, and our faults pass o'er
Rous'd be your talents in your countries cause

Fight for her intrests liberty and laws
And let the sex whom nature made your care
Claim you as gaurds to banish all their fear

A Sarcasm against the ladies in a newspaper; An impromptu answer

A Sarcasm against the ladies in a newspaper

Woman are books in which we often spy
Some bloted lines and sometimes lines awry
And tho perhaps some strait ones intervene
In all of them erata may be seen
If it be so I wish my wife were
An almanack—to change her every year

An impromptu answer

"Woman are books"—in this I do agree
But men there are that cant read A B C
And more who have not genius to discern
The beauties of those books they attempt to learn
For these an almanack may always hold
As much of Science as *they* can unfold.—
But thank our stars, our Critics are not *these*
The men of sense and taste we always please
Who know to choose and then to prize their books
Nor leave the strait lines for to search for crooks
And from these books their noblest pleasures flow
Altho perfections never found below
With them into a world of error thrown
And our eratas place against their own

Compos'd in a dancing room

December 69

Tho you have stop'd the muses tongue
And broke her lute her harp unstrung
By frowning on her lay
Yet the deep Sigh assumes the strain
Of plaintive notes to sooth my pain
And find it self a way.—
It prompts the much acknowledg'd truth
That State nor place nor age nor youth
Can all our wishes crown
The sighing heart in deepest shades
Proves to the mind that grief invades
The Cottage and the throne.—
Nor can the chearful mein declare
The bosom free from pining care
While blasted Joys recur
And like the canker in the bud
Preys ruthless on the vital flood
Till health is known no more
For me I try in vain the art
Of Musics power to heal the heart
The mazy dance in vain
The lighted room the graceful fair
With all the various movements here
Is only change of pain.—
I sigh because my mentors gone
And wit and elegance have flown
And attic ease and fire
I look among the powder'd beaux
And Say t'were vain to think that those
Could Chearfulness inspire.—
But candour breathes the enlivning thought
And tells me that I surely ought
To think you may approve—
Tho youth and bloom will soon recede
My truth may in your bosom plead
And you not cease to love.—

A Poetical Epistle, addressed by a Lady of New-Jersey, to her Niece, upon her Marriage, in this City

Well! my lov'd Niece, I hear the bustle's o'er,
The wedding cake and visits are no more;
The gay ones buzzing round some other bride,
While you with grave ones grace the fire's side.
Now with your usual sweetness deign to hear,
What from a heart most friendly flows sincere:
Nor do I fear a supercilious Smile—
To pay with gay contempt the muse's toil.
For be assur'd, I never will presume,
Superior sense or judgment to assume;
But barely that which long experience brings,
To men and women, those capricious things,
Nor do I once forget how very sage
Th'advice of Aunts has been in ev'ry age:
On matrimonial themes they all debate—
Wiseacres too who never try'd the state.
And 'twould, I own, appear as truly vain
For me, but to suppose I could attain
New light, upon a subject worn out quite;
And which both Aunts and Authors deem so trite.
But all the nuptial virtues in the class
Of spirit meek, and prudence, I shall pass;
Good nature—sense—of these you've ample store,
And Oeconomicks you have learnt before.
But there are lurking evils that do prove
Under the name of trifles—death to love.—
And from these trifles, all the jarring springs,
And trust me, child, they're formidable things.
First then—with rev'rence treat in ev'ry place,
The chosen patron of your future days;
For when you shew him but the least neglect,
Yourself you rifle of your due respect.—
But never let your fondness for him rise,
In words or actions to the prying eyes
Of witnesses—who claim a right to sneer
At all the honey'd words, "My life,—my love,—my dear."

Nor from your husband should you e'er require
Those epithets, which little minds admire—
Such short restraints will constantly maintain
That pow'r which fondness strives to reach in vain.
And give new joy to the returning hour,
When sweet retirement bars the op'ning door.
Nor do nor say, before the man you love,—
What in its nature must offensive prove;
However closely drawn the mystic ties,
Yet men have always microscopic eyes;
And easily advert to former time,
When nice reserve made females all divine.
"Would she to Damon or Alexis say,
A thing so rude? and am I less than they?"

Whene'er your husband means to stay at home,
Whate'er th'occasion—dont consent to roam;
For home's a solitary place to one
Who loves his wife, and finds her always gone.
At least consult the temper of his mind,
If vex'd abroad, he finds himself inclin'd
From public business to relax awhile;
How pleasing then the solace of a smile—
A soft companion to relieve his care,
His joy to heighten—or his grief to share?

Unbend his thoughts and from the world retire,
Within his sacred home and round his chearful fire;
Nor let him know you've made a sacrifice,
He'll find it out himself: And then he'll prize
Your kind endeavours to promote his ease,
And make the study of your life to please.

Another rule you'll find of equal weight,
When jars subside, never recriminate;
And when the cloud is breaking from his brow,
Repeat not *what* he said—nor *when* nor *how*.
If he's tenacious, gently give him way—
And tho' 'tis night, if he should say, 'tis day—
Dispute it not—but pass it with a smile;
He'll recollect himself—and pay your toil—
And shew he views it in a proper light;
And no Confusion seek—to do you right:

Just in his humour meet him—no debate,
And let it be your pleasure to forget.
His friends with kindness always entertain,
And tho' by chance he brings them, ne'er complain;
Whate'er's provided for himself and you,
With neatness serv'd, will surely please them too.
Nor e'er restrict him, when he would invite
His friends in form, to spend a day or night:
Some ladies think the trouble is so great,
That all such motions cause a high debate;
And madam pouts and says, I would not mind
How much to company you were inclin'd,
If I had things to entertain genteel;
And could but make my table look as well
As Mrs. A. and Mrs. B. can do;
I'd be as fond of company as you.—
And oft a richer service bribes the feast,
Than suits his purse, and makes himself a jest:
And tho' the good man gains his point at last,
It damps convivial mirth, and poisons the repast.
But you, my dear—if you would wish to shine,
Must always say, *your* friends are also *mine*:
The house is your's, and I will do the best,
To give a chearful welcome to each guest.

   Nor are those maxims difficult to cope
When stimulated by so fair a hope,
To reach the summit of domestic bliss;
And crown each day with ever smiling peace.

   Now if these lines one caution should contain,
To gain that end, my labour's not in vain;
And be assur'd, my dear, while life endures
With every tender sentiment, I'm your's.

To Miss Mary Stockton

*an epistle upon some gentleman refusing to admit
ladies of their circle into the parlour till supper where
they met for conversation and business once a week
lest the Ladies should hinder by their chit chat the
purpose of their meeting*

Could I envy Maria I certainly shou'd
A circle so elegant learned and good
For I'm mightily pleas'd with the good natur'd Jarr
That subsists between spirits so fine and so rare
T'will serve like the steel from the flint to extract
The fire of wit and like lenses refract
And with pleasure I view the cause of our sex
In the hands of Amanda whose genius reflects
A splendor on those who are call'd feminine
At least in her rays like luna we'll shine
And had I but talents to emulate her
Id be an auxil-ry in literary war—
For these men are so saucy because they can boast
Of Conjugating verbs as we can make toast
Or declining of nouns in number and case
And boldly can look father Euclid in face
And pretend they are masters of all the deep parts
Of *theology law* of *physics* and arts
They despise us poor females, and say that our sphere
Must move in the kitchen or heaven knows where
The nursery the pantry the dairy is made
The theatre on which our worth is display'd.
Tis true worthy *sirs* and if rightly I deem
Without the plumb pudding your science would seem
Like chips in the porridge—the fruit of our care
Inspired more genius than helicon air.—
—But hark-ee Maria a word in your ear
Ill whisper so low that the men shall not hear
And tell you the reason the *why* and the what
That they ever reproach us with silly chit chat
And say that we always their counsels impede
But to make me believe it they'll never succeed

Tis only for envy they banish us quite
And refuse to make us free masons for spite
For they know that your minds as bright as your eyes
Can give life to dull maxims and sages make wise
That without the least study you off hand can hit
The spirit and strength of their masculine wit
By quick apprehension you soon penetrate
The opaque that surrounds them and conquer your fate
An eclipse of this kind these lordlings do fear
For amidst Constellations dark bodies appear

Sensibility, an ode

Sweet Sensibility Celestial power
Raise in my heart thy altar and thy throne
Nor punish me with one unfeeling hour
But temper all my soul, and mark me for thy own
Give me to feel the tender trembling tear
Glide down my cheek at sight of human woe
And when I cant relieve the pang severe
The melting sigh of sympathy to know
To stretch the hand to sorrows tutor'd child
To wipe the tear from off the orphans eye
To turn from error by instruction mild
And snatch from vice the offspring of the sky
By thee inspir'd oh may I never dare
To join the herd in scandals groveling vale
Repeat the whisper in my neighbours ear
And give a sanction to the slanderous tale
But let me feel the sisters mothers heart
When e'er I view my species go astray
Nor with the pride of virtue plant a dart
To fright returning prodigals away.—
And may I too participate each Joy
That mixes with the cup of human life
Nor by the stoics frown the balm alloy
The balm that sweetens all this mortal strife
May sprightly wit and true benevolence

Give relish to each good which heaven bestows
May cheerfulness with smiling innocence
Increase the charms that o'er creation glows
Nor to these only do thy laws extend
For love and friendship claim an ample part
Ah now I feel them with my being blend
And with my Anna's image fill my heart

JOHN SINGLETON

(fl. c. 1750–1767)

FROM

A General Description of
the West-Indian Islands

FROM

Book III:
A hurricane.—A negro burial

But now the wand'ring muse, returning, points
Where the neat capital convenient lies,
Extending thro' the vales its ample bounds.
And, not content with circumscription, spreads
O'er two contiguous hills its mansions fair.
This beauteous spot a noble harbour boasts,
Where cautious mariners may safely moor
Their sea-beat barks, and smile at threat'ning storms,
What time the Dog-star reigns, and blazing fierce,
Autumnal Phœbus in th'equator shines;
Whilst the pale moon, full orb'd, encircled round
With hazy ring far distant from her sphere,
Starless, rides up th'orient path of Heav'n.
Then eastern winds no longer fan the sky,
But from th'unwholesome south hot breezes float
On wings contagious, and pollute th' air;
Or a dead calm ensues, or whissling gales
O'er the smooth surface of the ocean creep,
Scarce wrinkling as they pass the glassy plain;
Then the light scuds from diff'rent quarters fly,
And low'ring clouds the darksome day obscure;
Fierce meteors blaze, and fiery vapours stream,
Thro' the thick concave of the gloomy night;
The livid lightnings flash, and balls of fire
Shoot o'er the singed surface of the earth;
Then heaving surges lash the sounding beach,
And south-west blasts, by currents strong oppos'd,

Drive the resisting waves with hollow noise
Upon the roaring strand, like thunder heard
Far off in distant clouds rumbling and hoarse;
Surge follows surge, the whit'ning breakers dash
Their hoary heads against the senseless rocks,
And in their rear, waves riding over waves,
Burst in a deluge on the trembling shore.
Then it behoves the skilful mariner
Careful to watch, and ride with tackle tough,
Lest he lament in vain his costly bark
Bulg'd on remorseless rocks, or useless plung'd
Fast in a bed of sand, a doleful sight!
When the loud tempest bellows thro' the deep,
And the dread hurricane affrights the ear
Of peaceful night, alarming nature's sons,
Yet some, incautious, oft their lab'ring barks
Neglect, forgetful of their freighted charge,
Whilst they to pleasure sacrifice the time,
Or, with riotous debauch o'erwhelm'd,
In dangerous stews intoxicated snore.
Others, more wise, prepare to ride the storm,
Or to th'approaching gale, with cautious hand,
Distrustfully extend the tim'rous sail,
And rather busk far off the raging deep,
Than trust their cordage to the restless winds,
Which now let loose, from out their caverns vast
Impetuous rush, and harrow up the deep.
From either pole the grumbling thunder rolls,
From ev'ry cloud the forked lightnings flash,
The dreadful storm from ev'ry quarter howls,
And the distracted deep runs mountains high;
Waves dash on waves, opposing foam to foam,
Th'insolent billows to the clouds ascend;
Wild rout and uproar thro' th' horizon reign,
The Heav'ns themselves, descending, seem to rush
From out their lofty spheres, and falling, mix
Celestial waters with the ocean brine.
Now, for a moment, all the weilkin burns,
And one terrific blaze th'expanse inflames;
Ear-deaf'ning claps of thunder rend the air,

Kindling on high the elemental war,
Till with th' astounding crash all æther shakes:
Havock let loose, strews earth and seas around
With devastation wild; grim visag'd death
In various shapes appears, nor heeds the call
Of drowning wretches, who, with tearful eye,
And out-stretch'd arms, grasping their last, in vain
Implore a rescue from the wat'ry grave.
Here one awhile, undaunted, bold and strong,
Buffets the waves, and struggles with the storm;
Tho' well instructed in the swimmer's art,
In vain both hand and foot he stoutly plies,
Or, with the skilful stroke, plays on the wave,
Regardless of the furious dangers round;
Till weary grown, all spiritless and faint,
His languid limbs their wonted aid refuse:
Deep down beneath the wat'ry flood he sinks
O'erwhelm'd, soon he returns, aghast and pale,
Then eager strives, and on the surface toils;
Anon he cries aloud with mournful voice,
To earth, to seas, and man, with ceaseless tears,
But cries in vain, amidst the general wreck,
Nor earth, nor seas, nor man regard his pray'rs.
Here shatter'd barks lie tossing up and down,
Nor can their lacerated sides repel
The wasteful vengeance of the surly blasts;
For now the storm, increasing loud and high,
Renders the skilful pilot's art but vain;
Frantic confusion trammels up command,
From ev'ry quarter of the compass rage
The roaring winds, waging relentless war:
Heav'n, earth, and seas, the wild disorder aid,
Encreasing still the air-engender'd fray.
Here the stout prow the raging billows rides,
Once taught to humble to the rudder's beck,
But now, repugnant to command, she veers
With ev'ry blast, and drives before the storm.
Tremendous surges o'er the gilded poop
Impetuous sweep, and shatter all within:
The watchful mariner each danger views,

Trembling, aghast! nor can his skill direct
Aright what to command, or what forbid.
Th' inhospitable shore, with horror struck,
He dreads; and hears, or thinks he hears, appall'd,
The boist'rous surges bellowing on the rocks
With unavailing rage; too true, alas!
His boding fears inform! The billows break
With desp'rate force! the shore approaches nigh!
Whilst the huge-gathering surf impetuous rolls,
And the devoted bark high on the strand
Impels with ruinous shock, the dreary wreck
The rueful mariners forsake, quit the sad sight,
And wander thro' the storm-drench'd night forlorn.
Some vessels, with stout timber'd sides, awhile
The pityless storm's impetuous rage sustain,
But doom'd, alas! to still severer fate,
Scudding before two adverse winds they fly,
Or o'er the tops of heaving mountains dance;
Sometimes they seem the height of Heav'n to rise,
Dreading the hollow dismal vales below,
As Ach'ron deep, dark as infernal Styx:
Sometimes, by wild outrageous blasts impell'd,
Deep down the wat'ry precipice they rush
With headlong speed, and from the gloomy pit,
The Heav'ns obscur'd behold, the blust'ring storm
Lab'ring they 'bide, and all at random roam,
Till, from two hollow seas rising, they meet,
And, with the surge, dash on each others bow
With force impetuous, and tremendous crash:
As when two bulls in furious combat meet,
And with ferocious ire their frontlets drive
Against each other in the bloody strife;
So these, in dang'rous fray encount'ring sore,
Engage, unwilling, and with dreadful force,
High o'er the waves uprear their fractur'd bows.
This plunges down, beneath the surface urg'd,
And found'ring sinks, with all her wretched crew.
That, too, had met the same distressful fate,
Had not cool prudence, in the pilot's breast
Unshaken, bore him thro' the dismal scene.

Now to the coast her shatter'd stem he plies,
Rather than perish in the raging deep;
Aghast the shore he seeks, and on the beach
Drives her devoted hull; then, with his crew,
Last quits the fatal scene, and from the sea
Turns his dejected eye, aiding the winds
With loud complaints and ceaseless piteous moan;
Whilst the new horrors of the land he views,
Sorely, with perils imminent beset,
For not less vex'd the ruinous earth appears.
O'er nature's face the desolation spreads,
The mountains from their firm foundations shake,
And rolling o'er their heads loud thunders crash;
The vallies tremble, whilst the frightful gust
With fatal blast destroys the hopeful field.
High over head, from sable clouds surcharg'd,
The streaming rains descend, and the huge floods
In wide extended sheets of waters rise,
O'er land dispreading vast extensive seas;
The furious whirl-winds gather in the vales,
And with destructive force uprend the earth;
Whilst torrents in collected bodies rush
With course impetuous from the mountains height
Down the steep slopes, and deluge all the plain.
Rocks, stumps and stones, and bulky trees they whirl
Adown their channels vast, with rumbling noise;
As once they say the furious gushing flood
Bore headlong with it from adjacent hills
The solid earth (sage* men, for truth renown'd,
This tale relate) then in main ocean fix'd
In firm foundation fast, and, for a while,
To antient Neptune a new island gave.
Mean while the blust'ring winds rage furious on;
High over head the spacious roof they bear
Of some gay lofty mansion; whirling it plays,
Like a light feather in a summer's breeze:

*The honorable George Wyke, Esq; president of Montserrat when I was in
that island, informed me, that a huge piece of land was carried by the floods
into the sea, at the mouth of Old Road river; that it remained there some time,
and that he himself had been on it, and fishing round it.

Dwellings entire, from strong foundations torn,
Are hurl'd from hill-tops to the neighb'ring plain;
The heads of huge enormous mills they send
To distance far, on hill or drenched vale;
Cattle, o'erborne, rush to the raging main,
And trees uptorn in rattling whirl-winds spin;
Earth to the deep her dreadful horrors sends,
And the mad deep worse horrors back returns;
Earth, air, and all the elements contend,
Till in the end, the howling tempest spent,
Ruin subsides, and all is hush'd around.
  Renewing filial and parental griefs,
Then frequent toll'd the doleful deep-mouth'd bell,
Foretelling the slow funeral's approach.
Distressful scene for melting hearts to view!
The wife, disconsolate, her widow'd bed
Bedew'd with tears forsakes; frantic she runs,
Lamenting, to her lord's new-open'd grave,
And, in a storm of passion, plunges in,
Eager to share his fate, and be interr'd
Alive with the dear object of her love.
Or else the lover, prostrate on the turf
Where all his joy's entomb'd, distracted raves;
Whilst the big tear bursts from his turgid eye,
And many an intervening sob breaks in,
Stopping th' impetuous torrent of his grief,
That vents its piteous moan, by turns, in vows,
In pray'rs, and passionate appeals to Heav'n.
  Ah me! how diff'rently th' untutored slave,
To no philosophy indebted, views
The obsequies of his departed friend,
And with his calm deportment puts to shame
The boasted reason of the polish'd world:
A moment dries his manly eye, untaught
To melt at death, the necessary end
Of all terrestrial things. His creed (the voice
Of nature) keeps him firm, nay, gives him joy,
When he considers (so the sages teach
Of Afric's sun-burnt realms) that the freed soul,
Soon as it leaves its mortal coil behind,

Transported to some distant world, is wrapt
In bliss eternal. There the man begins,
With organs more refin'd, to live again,
And taste such sweets as were deny'd him here,
The sweets of liberty. Oh glorious name!
Oh pow'rful soother of the suff'ring heart!
That with thy spark divine can'st animate
Unletter'd slaves to stretch their simple thoughts
In search of thee, beyond this gloomy vale
Of painful life, where all their piteous hours
Drag heavily along in constant toil,
In stripes, in tears, in hunger, or in chains:
These are the ills which they rejoice to fly,
Unless, by partial chance, their lot is cast
Beneath some kind indulgent master's sway,
Whose hand, like their good genius, feeds their wants,
And with protection shields their helpless state.
    But see what strange procession hither winds,
With long continued stream, through yonder wood!
Like gentle waves hundreds of sable heads
Float onwards; still they move, and still they seem
With unexhausted flow to keep their course.
    In calm succession thus th' unruffl'd main
Rolls on its peaceful waters to the shore,
With easy swell, wave gliding over wave,
Till the spectator can no longer count
Their breaks incessant, but the numbers past
Are in succeeding numbers quickly lost.
Behold the white-rob'd train in form advance
To yonder new-made grave: Six ugly hags,
Their visage seam'd with honorary scars,
In wild contorsive postures lead the van;
High o'er their palsied heads, rattling, they wave
Their noisy instruments; whilst to the sound
In dance progressive their shrunk shanks keep time.
With more composure the succeeding ranks,
Chanting their fun'ral song in chorus full,
Precede the mournful bier, by friendly hands
Supported: Sudden stops the flowing line;
The puzzled bearers of the restive corps

Stand for a while, fast rooted to the ground,
Depriv'd of motion, or, perhaps, impell'd
This way, or that, unable to proceed
In course direct, until the troubled dead
Has to some friend imparted his request;
That gratify'd, again the fun'ral moves:
When at the grave arriv'd the solemn rites
Begin; the slave's cold reliques gently laid
Within their earthy bed, some veteran
Among the sable Archimages,* pours
Her mercenary panegyric forth,
In all the jargon of mysterious speech;
And, to compose the spirit of the dead,
Sprinkles his fav'rite liquor on the grave.
This done, the mourners form a spacious ring,
When sudden clangours, blended with shrill notes,
Pour'd forth from many a piercing pipe, surprize
The deafen'd ear. Nor Corybantian brass,
Nor rattling sistrum, ever rung a peal
So frantic, when th' Idæan dactyli
At their intoxicated feasts ran wild,
Dizzily weaving the fantastic dance,
And with extended throats proclaiming high
Their goddess Rhea, thro' the giddy croud.
Thus do these sooty children of the sun,
"Unused to the melting mood," perform
Their fun'ral obsequies, and joyous chaunt
In concert full, the requiem of the dead;
Wheeling in many a mazy round, they fill
The jocund dance, and take a last farewell
Of their departed friend, without a tear.

* *Archimages*] i.e. chief magicians among the Obeah negroes.—The word is often used by Spencer.

FRANCIS HOPKINSON

(1737–1791)

1.

My gen'rous heart disdains
The slave of Love to be,
I scorn his servile chains
And boast my liberty.
  This whining
  And pining
And wasting with care
Are not to my taste, be she ever so fair.

2.

Shall a girl's capricious frown
Sink my noble spirits down?
Shall a face of white and red
Make me droop my silly head?
Shall I set me down and sigh
For an eye-brow or an eye?
For a braided lock of hair
Curse my fortune and despair?
 My gen'rous heart disdains, &c.

3.

Still uncertain is to-morrow,
Not quite certain is to-day—
Shall I waste my time in sorrow?
Shall I languish life away?
All because a cruel maid
Hath not Love with Love repaid.
 My gen'rous heart disdains, &c.

An Epitaph for an Infant

Sleep on, sweet babe! no dreams annoy thy rest,
Thy spirit flew unsullied from thy breast:
Sleep on, sweet innocent! nor shalt thou dread
The passing storm that thunders o'er thy head:
Thro' the bright regions of yon azure sky,
A winged seraph, now she soars on high;
Or, on the bosom of a cloud reclin'd,
She rides triumphant on the rapid wind;
Or from its source pursues the radiant day;
Or on a sun-beam, smoothly glides away;
Or mounts aerial, to her blest abode,
And sings, inspir'd, the praises of her *God*:
Unveiled, thence, to her extensive eye,
Nature, and Nature's Laws, expanded lie:
Death, in one moment, taught this infant more
Than years or ages ever taught before.

The Battle of the Kegs

Gallants attend and hear a friend,
   Trill forth harmonious ditty,
Strange things I'll tell which late befel
   In Philadelphia city.

'Twas early day, as poets say,
   Just when the sun was rising,
A soldier stood on a log of wood,
   And saw a thing surprising.

As in amaze he stood to gaze,
   The truth can't be denied, sir,
He spied a score of kegs or more
   Come floating down the tide, sir.

A sailor too in jerkin blue,
    This strange appearance viewing,
First damn'd his eyes, in great surprise,
    Then said some mischief's brewing.

These kegs, I'm told, the rebels bold,
    Pack'd up like pickling herring;
And they're come down t' attack the town,
    In this new way of ferrying.

The soldier flew, the sailor too,
    And scar'd almost to death, sir,
Wore out their shoes, to spread the news,
    And ran till out of breath, sir.

Now up and down throughout the town,
    Most frantic scenes were acted;
And some ran here, and others there,
    Like men almost distracted.

Some fire cry'd, which some denied,
    But said the earth had quaked;
And girls and boys, with hideous noise,
    Ran thro' the streets half naked.

Sir William he, snug as a flea,
    Lay all this time a snoring,
Nor dream'd of harm as he lay warm,
    In bed with Mrs. L——g.

Now in a fright, he starts upright,
    Awak'd by such a clatter;
He rubs both eyes, and boldly cries,
    For God's sake, what's the matter?

At his bed-side he then espy'd,
    Sir Erskine at command, sir,
Upon one foot, he had one boot,
    And th' other in his hand, sir.

"Arise, arise, sir Erskine cries,
 The rebels—more's the pity,
Without a boat are all afloat,
 And rang'd before the city.

The motly crew, in vessels new,
 With Satan for their guide, sir.
Pack'd up in bags, or wooden kegs,
 Come driving down the tide, sir.

Therefore prepare for bloody war,
 These kegs must all be routed,
Or surely we despised shall be,
 And British courage doubted."

The royal band, now ready stand
 All rang'd in dread array, sir,
With stomach stout to see it out,
 And make a bloody day, sir.

The cannons roar from shore to shore,
 The small arms make a rattle;
Since wars began I'm sure no man
 E'er saw so strange a battle.

The rebel dales, the rebel vales,
 With rebel trees surrounded;
The distant wood, the hills and floods,
 With rebel echos sounded.

The fish below swam to and fro,
 Attack'd from ev'ry quarter;
Why sure, thought they, the devil's to pay,
 'Mongst folks above the water.

The kegs, 'tis said, tho' strongly made,
 Of rebel staves and hoops, sir,
Could not oppose their powerful foes,
 The conqu'ring British troops, sir.

From morn to night these men of might
   Display'd amazing courage;
And when the sun was fairly down,
   Retir'd to sup their porrage.

An hundred men with each a pen,
   Or more upon my word, sir.
It is most true would be too few,
   Their valour to record, sir.

Such feats did they perform that day,
   Against these wick'd kegs, sir,
That years to come, if they get home,
   They'll make their boasts and brags, sir.

N. B. This ballad was occasioned by a real incident. Certain machines, in the form of kegs, charg'd with gun powder, were sent down the river to annoy the British shipping then at Philadelphia. The danger of these machines being discovered, the British manned the wharfs and shipping, and discharged their small arms and cannons at every thing they saw floating in the river during the ebb tide.

A Camp Ballad

Make room, oh! ye kingdoms in hist'ry renowned
Whose arms have in battle with glory been crown'd,
Make room for America, another great nation,
Arises to claim in your council a station.

Her sons fought for freedom, and by their own brav'ry
Have rescued themselves from the shackles of slav'ry.
America's free, and tho' Britain abhor'd it,
Yet fame a new volume prepares to record it.

Fair freedom in Briton her throne had erected,
But her sons growing venal, and she disrespected;
The goddess offended forsook the base nation,
And fix'd on our mountains a more honour'd station.

With glory immortal she here sits enthron'd,
Nor fears the vain vengeance of Britain disown'd,
Whilst Washington guards her with heroes surrounded,
Her foes shall with shameful defeat be confounded.

To arms then, to arms, 'tis fair freedom invites us;
The trumpet shrill sounding to battle excites us;
The banners of virtue unfurl'd, shall wave o'er us,
Our hero lead on, and the foe fly before us.

On Heav'n and Washington placing reliance,
We'll meet the bold Britton, and bid him defiance:
Our cause we'll support, for 'tis just and 'tis glorious
When men fight for freedom they must be victorious.

JONATHAN ODELL

(1737–1818)

The Word of Congress

Tartaream intendit vocem.—
VIRGIL

The word of Congress, like a round of beef,
To hungry Satire gives a sure relief;
No trifling tid-bits to delude the pen,
But solid victuals, cut and come again.
Whitfield 'tis said, this simile was thine;
Unapt for thy discourse, it suits with mine.
   O P——n, I should think it joy supreme
To win thy kind attention to my theme,
To cheer thy heart with native humour fraught,
And steal thee from the painful task of thought:
Oft has thy lib'ral, thy capacious mind,
Griev'd for the wicked, sorrow'd for the blind,
Deplor'd past errors, present ills bemoan'd,
And anxious for the future deeply groan'd.
Were it not best to quit these gloomy views,
And join the sportfull sallies of the muse;
Smile at those evils we must both endure,
And laugh at follies, which we cannot cure:
Come friend, and let us mock, till mirth be stir'd
In every vein, the many colour'd word.
   Oh! 'tis a word of pow'r, of prime account,
I've seen it like the daring Osprey mount;
I've seen it like a dirty reptile creep,
Rush into flame, or plunge into the deep;
I've heard it like a hungry lion roar,
Who tears the prey, and bathes himself in gore—
I've felt it softer than the vernal rain
Mildly descending on the grassy plain—
I've heard it pious as a saint in pray'r—
I've heard it like an angry trooper swear—
I've known it suit itself to every plan—

I've known it lie to God and lie to man.
Have you not read the marvellous escapes,
Of Proteus shifting to a thousand shapes;
Have you not seen the wonders of the stage,
When pantomime delights a trifling age;
Such and more various, such and more absurd,
Charles Thompson witness of the changeful word,
He'll sign to any thing no matter what—
At truth alone his pen would make a blot.

There dwelt in Norriton's sequester'd bow'rs,
A mortal blest with mathematic pow'rs,
To whom was David Rittenhouse unknown,
Fair science saw, and mark'd him for her own.
His eye creation to its bounds would trace,
His mind, the regions of unbounded space:
Whilst thus he soar'd above the starry spheres,
The word of Congress sounded in his ears;
He listen'd to the voice with strange delight,
And swift descended from his dazling height,
Then mixing eager with seditious tools,
Vice-President elect of rogues and fools;
His hopes resign'd of philosophic fame,
A paltry statesman Rittenhouse became.

A saint of old, as learned monks have said,
Preach'd to the fish—the fish his voice obey'd—
The same good man conven'd the grunting herd,
Who bow'd obedient to his pow'rful word—
Such energy had truth in days of yore,
Falsehood and nonsense in our days have more.
Duffield avows them to be all in all,
And mounts or quits the pulpit at their call—
In vain new light displays her heav'nly shine,
In vain attract him oracles divine;
Chaplain of Congress give him to become,
Light may be dark and oracles be dumb—
It pleas'd Saint Anthony to preach to brutes,
To preach to Devils best with Duffield suits.

Tim Matlack once had credit and esteem—
His follies made them vanish as a dream—
By all his sober friends abandon'd quite,

Game-cocks and negroes were his whole delight.
Vagrant, and poor, his reputations slurr'd,
He hasten'd to obey the factious word:
Who now so active in the cause as Tim—
Tho' death to honour, it was life to him—
Restor'd to consequence tho' not to grace,
Behold him fill the secretary's place—
His pen can write you paragraphs by scores,
His valour kick two Quakers out of doors,
Tim for their champion let the People dub,
Yet virtue still must hold him for a scrub.

    Kerr, and Carmichael, schismatics obscure,
Who deem that all things to the pure are pure,
Hag-rid by Congress, by sedition spur'd,
Desert the bible to proclaim the word;
Such force attends the fascinating sound,
Murder is sainted, perjury renown'd.

    Spencer and Caldwell, evangelic pair,
This a smooth serpent, that a furious bear;
With equal zeal but different cast of head,
Prepar'd the doctrine of the word to spread.
One on the thunder of his tongue relied,
The other wisely to his pen applied.
Figures and tropes rough Spencer chose to pour,
Arabian figures suited Caldwell more;
The first was bold in treasonable talk,
The second took the commissary's walk;
Both were detested, as they both deserv'd,
But whilst the penman throve, the spokesman starv'd:
Spencer a martyr falls to rage and rum,
Whilst Caldwell snug retires with half a plumb.

    Tucker from want, and dirt, and darkness sprung,
Of formal face, and Oliverian tongue,
'Scap'd from the gallows, gain'd the mob's esteem,
But no promotion could from fraud redeem;
No rank his heart to honesty could fix,
Still graceless he pursued his native tricks:
Now rose against him the tumultuous din,
The dev'l himself can sometimes rail at sin;
Too much a knave for knaves thenselves to bear,

Abhorr'd by all men Tucker quits the chair.
 Paschal, who never right from wrong could tell,
Who never yet could read, or write, or spell,
From last, from awl, from cutting knife is torn,
Whilst tanners weep, and half-shod soldiers mourn.
He's now a Justice—Wherefore should we grudge—
When Cong reigns King, a Cobler may be Judge.
 These are poor characters—Rise Satire, rise
And seize on villains of superior size:
Let censure reach to Shippen and to Yates,
Or dignify the verse with Green and Gates;
Expose the meanness of the P——'s to view,
Or strike at Willing, Hamilton, and Chew,
Macdougal, Maxwell, Muhlenberg attack,
Or Baylor clad in white, or Knox in black,
Or blast Poughkeepsie's Lord, who soils a name—
That never but in him was doom'd to shame;
Or vengeful draw the weapon from the sheath
And plunge it in the murd'rous breast of Heath.
The blust'rer, the poltroon, the vile, the weak,
Who fight for Congress, or in Congress speak,
Or to its edicts cowardly submit,
Alike should undergo the lash of wit.
 Come Mifflin, let me post thee on the page—
As thou with Britain, war with thee I wage.
Fierce Mifflin foremost in the ranks was found—
Ask you the cause?—He owed ten thousand pound.
Great thanks to Congress, and its doughty word,
He cancell'd debts by flourishing his sword—
Not that he cares for Congress, or its voice,
Broils are his int'rest—tumult is his choice—
But that he wants the necessary skill
A pliant people to inflame at will;
But that his genius yields to Roberdeau
In every art of managing the low;
Confusion would in aid of justice rise,
Revenge the widow's groans, the orphan's cries,
The robbers of their ill-got treasure rob,
And give Joe Reed a victim to the mob.
 Gates I have nam'd, but have not yet forsook—

Step forward Gates, and tremble at my look.
Can'st thou, most harden'd tho' thou art, sustain
The glance of anger mingled with disdain.
I've seen thy father—has thy pride forgot—
Mean was his office—very mean his lot—
A gracious Master overlook'd thy birth
And rais'd thee far above the dregs of earth.
Each act of favour how hast thou return'd,
How all the laws of sacred honour spurn'd,
What vile ingratitude thy soul has shown,
Is fit for devils to relate alone.
Go hide, abandon'd monster, hide thy head—
Go fly, if fly thou can'st, from inward dread—
Call cliffs, call mountains on thee to descend—
But rocks nor hills from terror shall defend—
In hell seek refuge,—even there thou'lt find
A fiercer hell hot-burning in thy mind.

  Where, where is Sinclair? Takes he to his heels?
Blows aim'd at Gates by instinct Sinclair feels.
He too fought nobly in his country's cause;
He too the sword against his Sov'reign draws—
Like Gates entangled in rebellion's snare,
He too like him should tremble, and despair.
What comfort can they hope, what peace deserve,
Who forfeit virtue, and from duty swerve?
Avenging furies shall their steps pursue
Till chas'd from earth they join th' infernal crew.

  Schuyler, whose meanness in the prime of life,
Allow'd old Bradstreet to pollute his wife,
Who still, regardless of the filthy blot,
Owns all the bastards, which the letcher got—
In age, and equally to honour's grief,
From a tame cuckold grows a rebel chief.—
O may no saucy cannons round him roar,
No rude court-martials vex his quiet more—
His days awhile good destiny secure,
Tho' stinking, great, and wealthy, tho' impure.
Yes, let him live, kind fate, but live abhorr'd
Till justice fastens to his neck the cord.

  Amidst ten thousand eminently base

Thou Sullivan assume the highest place,
Sailor, and farmer,—barrister of vogue;
Each state was thine, and thou in each a rogue—
Ambition came, and swallow'd in a trice,
Like Aaron's rod, the reptile fry of vice—
One giant passion then his soul possess'd,
And dreams of lawless sway disturb'd his rest.
He gave each wild imagination scope,
And flew to Congress on the wings of hope.

Behold him there, but still behold him curst—
He sat in Congress, but he sat not first—
What could the fever of his mind compose?
Make him a Gen'ral—Gen'ral straight he grows.
Head of a shirtless, shoeless gang he strides,
While folly stares, and laughter shakes his sides.

And must I sing the wonders of his might?
What are they? Rout, captivity, and flight.—
Rhode-Island saw him to her forts advance,
Assisted by the ships of faithless France—
Rhode-Island saw him shamefully retreat,
In imitation of the Gallic fleet.
His banners last on Susquehanna wav'd,
Where lucky to excess, his scalp he sav'd.

All these, and more, whose praise must be deferr'd,
Seditious rose, when Congress gave the word.
Of various principles, from various soils,
Smit with desire of change, or love of broils.
As when an ass with hideous clamour brays,
Unnumber'd asses loud their voices raise—
As when a restless ram the fence o'erleaps,
Flocks leave their grazing, and pursue in heaps:
So at one noisy, turbulent command,
Contagion seiz'd, and uproar fill'd the land—
All rush'd like frighten'd sheep to join the cause,
Or in sonorous cadence bray'd applause.

Come heav'n born Truth, and analyze a word
To all things human and divine preferr'd.
Guide of the will, and ruler of the heart—
Why not examine each component part?
Impress'd so deeply, and diffus'd so wide,

It ought the test of reason to abide—
Serene, and beautiful its outward face,
Within all wisdom, sanctity, and grace,
Impartial it should be, and void of faults—
It should—but truth from this account revolts.
    Far other portrait the prevailing word
From truth's unerring pencil has incurr'd.
Bid her describe the Congress, straight she draws
An hydra-headed form, with harpies claws,
Lo! numerous mouths hiss, chatter, bark, or croak;
Here one like Cacus belches fire, and smoak,
The second like a monkey grins, and chats,
A third squalls horrible like angry cats;
Here you've the growls, and snarlings of a dog,
And there the beastly gruntings of a hog,
Others affect the puritanic tone,
The whine, the cant, the snuffle, and the groan;
In candour's accents falsehoods some disguise,
Whilst others vomit forth essential lies—
All sounds delusive, all disgustful notes,
Pour like a torrent from their brazen throats,
To fill with rage the poor distracted croud,
Whilst discord claps her hands, and shouts aloud.
    This harsh account should Charity distrust,
Yet sad experience will pronounce it just.
Whoe'er the word of Congress shall peruse,
In every piece will see it change its views—
Now swell with duty to the King elate,
Now melt with kindness to the parent state,
Then back to treason suddenly revolve,
And join in Suffolk's infamous resolve.
Trace it through all the windings of the press,
Vote or appeal, petition or address,
Trace it in every act, in every speech,
Too sure you'll find duplicity in each—
Mark now its soothing, now its threat'ning strain,
Mark its hypocrisy, deceit, chicane,
From the soft breathings of the new-form'd hoard,
To that fell hour when Independence roar'd,
Forc'd you'll acknowledge, since creation's dawn,

Earth never yet produc'd so vile a spawn.
   But still in Britain many disbelieve—
I own 'tis hard such baseness to conceive—
Who, that beheld these foul impostors rave,
When law confirm'd the rights, which treaties gave,
Heard them foretell Religion's general wreck,
From Romish faith establish'd in Quebec,
Who that observ'd all this could once opine,
That Saints like these with popery should join—
Imagination must it not surpass,
That Congress should proceed in pomp to mass—
Yet that they did authentic proofs can show,
Myriads the frontless fact, nay millions know.
   Here gentle reader, we'll go back a space,
Two famous missions of the world to trace—
Saint —— with a priest in either hand,
Devoutly travell'd to Canadian land—
For those, who should rebel, a copious store
Of absolutions our Apostles bore—
In faith it prov'd a memorable job—
Its gracious sounds avail'd not with the mob—
Like Paul at Lystra, it provok'd the stones,
And scarce the factious preachers sav'd their bones.
   McWhorter, Spencer, with the same designs,
A brace of flaming pestilent divines,
To Carolina went by Cong's decree,
From oaths the fetter'd populace to free—
Ridiculous attempt, unhallow'd work,
Plain sense abhor'd the miserable quirk—
The wretched bigots were dismiss'd with jeers,
But kept ('twas more than they deserv'd) their ears.
   Not so discourag'd, the prolific word
To more successful artifice recurr'd—
Swarms of deceivers, practic'd in the trade,
Were sent abroad to gull, cajole, persuade,
Scoff with the scoffer, with the pious pray,
Drink with the drunkard, frolick with the gay.
All things to all with varied skill become,
And bribe with paper, or inflame with rum.
Others apart in some obscure recess,

The studied lie for publication dress—
Prepare the vague report, fallacious tale,
Invent fresh calumnies, revive the stale—
Pervert all records sacred and profane—
And chief among them stands the Villain Payne.

This scribbling imp, 'tis said, from London came,
That seat of glory, intermix'd with shame—
Imperial city, Queen of arts enroll'd,
But full of vice as Sodom was of old—
Once with the deathless name of Barnard grac'd,
By Wilkes, and Ball, and Sawbridge now defac'd.

Our hireling author having chang'd his soil,
True son of Grubstreet, here renew'd his toil—
What cannot ceaseless impudence produce—
Old —— knows its value, and its use.
He caught at Payne, reliev'd his wretched plight,
And gave him notes, and set him down to write—
Fire from the Doctor's hints the miscreant took,
Discarded truth, and soon compos'd a book,
A pamphlet, which without the least pretence
To reason, bore the name of Common Sense.

No matter what you call this doggerel stuff;
Bad as it was, it pleas'd, and that's enough—
The work like wildfire thro' the country ran,
And folly bow'd the knee to ——'s plan.—
Sense, reason, judgment were abash'd and fled,
And Congress reign'd triumphant in their stead.
O hapless land! O people void of brains,
My heart bleeds for you, tho' my soul disdains.

Deep schemes ensued, to all appearance vague,
But fitted to disseminate the plague.—
From the back woods half savages came down,
And awkward troops paraded every town—
Committees and conventions met by scores,
Justice was banish'd, law turn'd out of doors.—
Disorder seem'd to overset the land,
They, who appear'd to rule, the tumult fan'd,
But cunning stood behind with sure controul,
And in one centre caus'd to meet the whole.
By what contrivance this effect was gain'd,

How the new states were finish'd, and sustain'd,
All, all should be held up to public scorn,
An useful lesson to the child unborn.
    But this would open an immense career—
And into port 'twere prudent now to steer.
Much have we labour'd in tempestuous seas—
'Tis time to give the shatter'd vessel ease,
Yet once refitted, we'll again display
Satire's red ensign on the watry way.
Again encounter the rebellious flag,
And from the staff the stripes of Faction drag.
These pirates hovering on the coast disperse,
And chace them with the flowing sail of verse.
    O grace of every virtue, meek eyed maid,
Sweet modesty in purple robes array'd,
Think me not vain of these enervate lines,
These feeble colourings, and faint designs.—
To bring some stouter champion on the scene,
Is all I meditate, is all I mean.
I but endeavour to amuse the foe,
'Till Genius rise, and deal the fatal blow;
But Genius, careless of his charge, sits still,
And lets the monster Congress rage at will—
Lifts not the terror of his pond'rous lance,
Arrests not those, who sell the land to France.
Tilts not with bitter Wayne, with boist'rous Lee,
But leaves the task to weakness, and to me.
    Thus, 'till some favour'd mortal raise his voice,
I must go on—'tis duty, and not choice.—
Sister of Wisdom, Goddess of the Song,
Protect the meanest of the tuneful throng—
And when the feather'd weapon I prepare,
Once more to lay the villains bosom bare,
Let inspiration from th' ethereal height
Shed on my soul her vivifying light—
Poetic ardour, strength of thought infuse,
The life, the spirit of a glowing muse—
Ask I too much—then grant me for a time
Some deleterious pow'rs of acrid rhyme:
Some ars'nic verse, to poison with the pen,
These rats, who nestle in the Lion's den.

THOMAS PAINE

(1737–1809)

Liberty Tree

A new Song

Tune, *The Gods of the Greeks.*

I.

In a chariot of light from the regions of day,
    The Goddess of Liberty came;
Ten thousand celestials directed the way,
    And hither conducted the dame.
A fair budding branch from the gardens above,
    Where millions with millions agree,
She brought in her hand, as a pledge of her love,
    And the plant she named, *Liberty Tree.*

II.

The celestial exotic struck deep in the ground,
    Like a native it flourish'd and bore.
The fame of its fruit drew the nations around,
    To seek out this peaceable shore.
Unmindful of names or distinctions they came,
    For freemen like brothers agree,
With one spirit endued, they one friendship pursued,
    And their temple was *Liberty tree.*

III.

Beneath this fair tree, like the patriarchs of old,
    Their bread in contentment they eat,
Unvex'd with the troubles of silver and gold,
    The cares of the grand and the great.
With timber and tar they Old England supply'd,
    And supported her power on the sea;
Her battles they fought, without getting a groat,
    For the honour of *Liberty tree.*

IV.

But hear, O ye swains, ('tis a tale most profane,)
   How all the tyrannical powers,
King, Commons, and Lords, are uniting amain,
   To cut down this guardian of ours;
From the east to the west, blow the trumpet to arms,
   Thro' the land let the sound of it flee,
Let the far and the near,—all unite with a cheer,
   In defence of our *Liberty tree*.

YANKEE DOODLE

Yankee Doodle, or
(as now christened by the Saints of New England)
The Lexington March

NB *the words to be sung through the Nose*
and in the West Country Drawl and Dialect

Brother Ephraim sold his Cow
   And bought him a Commission
And then he went to Canada
   To Fight for the Nation.
But when Ephraim he came home
   He prov'd an arrant Coward,
He wou'd'n't fight the Frenchmen there
   For fear of being devour'd.

(2)

Sheep's Head and Vinegar
   Butter Milk and Tansy
Boston is a Yankee Town
   Sing Hey Doodle Dandy,
First we'll take a Pinch of Snuff
   And then a drink of Water
And then we'll say How do you do
   And that's a Yanky's Supper.

(3)

Aminadab is just come Home,
   His Eyes all greas'd with Bacon
And all the news that he cou'd tell
   Is Cape Breton is taken,
Stand up Jonathan
   Figure in by Neighbour
Vathen stand a little off
   And make the Room some wider.

(4)

Christmas is a coming Boys,
   We'll go to Mother Chase's,
And there we'll get a Sugar Dram
   Sweetn'd with Melasses,
Heigh ho for our Cape Cod,
   Heigh ho Nantasket,
Do not let the Boston wags
   Feel your Oyster Basket.

(5)

Punkin Pye is very good
   And so is Apple Lantern;
Had you been whipp'd as oft as I,
   You'd not have been so wanton.
Uncle is a Yankee Man
   'Ifaith he pays us all of
And he has got a Fiddle
   As big as Daddy's Hog's Trough.

(6)

Seth's Mother went to Lynn,
   To buy a pair of Breeches;
The first time Vathen put them on
   He tore out all the Stitches.
Dolly-Bushel let a Fart
   Jenny Jones she found it;
Ambrose carried it to Mill
   Where Doctor Warren ground it.

(7)

Our Jemima's lost her Mare,
   And can't tell where to find her;
But she'll come trotting by and by
   And bring her Tail behind her.
Two and two may go to Bed,
   Two and two together;
And if there is not room enough,
   Lie one a top o'to'ther.

The Yankey's return from Camp

Father and I went down to camp,
   Along with Captain Gooding,
There we see the men and boys.
   As thick as hasty pudding.

Chorus.
Yankey doodle keep it up,
   Yankey doodle, dandy,
Mind the music and the step,
   And with the girls be handy.

And there we see a thousand men,
   As rich as 'Squire David;
And what they wasted every day,
   I wish it could be saved.

      Yankey doodle, &c.

The 'lasses they eat every day,
   Would keep a house a winter:
They have as much that I'll be bound
   They eat it when they're a mind to.

      Yankey doodle, &c.

And there we see a swamping gun,
   Large as a log of maple,
Upon a ducid little cart,
   A load for father's cattle.

      Yankey doodle, &c.

And every time they shoot it off,
   It takes a horn of powder—
It makes a noise like father's gun,
   Only a nation louder.

      Yankey doodle, &c.

I went as nigh to one myself,
   As 'Siah's underpining;
And father went as nigh again,
   I tho't the deuce was in him.

      Yankey doodle, &c.

Cousin Simon grew so bold,
   I tho't he would have cock'd it:
It scar'd me so, I shrink'd it off,
   And hung by father's pocket.

      Yankey doodle, &c.

And captain Davis had a gun,
   He kind of clapt his hand on't,
And stuck a crooked stabbing iron
   Upon the little end on't.

      Yankey doodle, &c.

And there I see a pumpkin shell
   As big as mother's bason,
And ev'ery time they touch'd it off,
   They scamper'd like the nation.

      Yankey doodle, &c.

I see a little barrel too,
   The heads were made of leather,
They knock'd upon't with little clubs,
   And call'd the folks together.

      Yankey doodle, &c.

And there was captain Washington,
   And gentlefolks about him,
They say he's grown so tarnal proud,
   He will not ride without 'em.

Yankey doodle, &c.

He got him on his meeting clothes,
    Upon a slapping stallion,
He set the world along in rows,
    In hundreds and in millions.

Yankey doodle, &c.

The flaming ribbons in their hats,
    They look'd so taring fine, ah,
I wanted pockily to get
    To give to my Jemimah.

Yankey doodle, &c.

I see another snarl of men
    A digging graves, they told me,
So tarnal long, so tarnal deep,
    They 'tended they should hold me.

Yankey doodle, &c.

It scar'd me so, I hook'd it off,
    Nor stop'd, as I remember,
Nor turn'd about 'till I got home,
    Lock'd up in mother's chamber.

Yankey doodle, &c.

ELIZABETH GRAEME
FERGUSSON

(1737–1801)

To Doctor Fothergill

As Happiness must ever be our Aim,
By various Paths, we still pursue the same
We long for Pleasure & for Ease we sigh
And strain the Cords that draw the Object nigh.
Tho' Taste & Whim do oft, too oft prevail
And Arts refin'd pervert not trim the Scale,
Where Heav'n & Nature kindly meant to weigh,
With moral Rectitude each well spent Day,
While mild Humility that soft-ey'd Maid,
Views virtuous Actions, as if half afraid,
The very Thought, her Pupils could excell
Might stain the Lustre of their doing well
Internal Peace from different Causes flow,
Too deep the Subject to attempt to shew,
Howe'er Mankind thro' different Mediums see,
In this one Point I think they all agree,
To draw, sweet Health, a pleasing Stream from thee.
As Soul & Body's for a Time confin'd,
'Till Heav'n permits the Knot to be disjoin'd;
Its but vain boasting, then, to talk of Bliss,
While this fine Frame feels—there is aught amiss.
The Stoics Tongue won't own the Force of Pain,
Too proud to yield, too Stubborn to complain,
From his first Maxims won't in Word depart,
And Doubly suffers for his Pride of Heart,
Tho' this great Evil can't be quite redrest,
It's vastly soften'd in a Patient Breast,
Who prays of Heav'n to calm their gloomy Fears
And trust their Pray'rs will reach th'Almightys Ears.
In certain Herbs & Plants there lays a Power
To lull the Anguish of the painful Hour,
In Gums & Fossils was this Pow'r conceal'd,

'Till Chance, & Skill, & Time, this Pow'r reveal'd.
Deep Secrets yet may Nature have in Store,
But bless the present—humbly hope for more.
Most true her Bounties have been oft abus'd
And oft thro' Ignorance her Aid's misus'd.
For venal Gold, her Poisons dealt around,
And added Anguish to the aching Wound.
In ev'ry Age, in every Clime this wrong
Has damp'd th' Eulogy of Friendships Song,
Yet low Pretenders to each nobler Art
Serve but as Steps to mount the better Part.
Who rais'd, exalted, to a higher Sphere,
Not only heal, but drop the gen'rous Tear,
Their Heads may dictate, but their Hearts will feel
And mourn those Woes beyond their Pow'r to heal,
The Good & Modest, all unite in this
The bold Assumer thinks he ne'er can miss.
O Britain bless'd, for many Favours sent
Allow'd in Fame, by Europes in joint Consent,
To boast the Knowledge of the healing Tribe,
Where Skill with Virtue has been closely tied,
In Painting, Sculpture, & poetic Fire,
Your neighb'ring Nations may with Truth aspire
To struggle for the Laurel or the Palm;
Yet ev'n here you're far from proving Calm,
Let Naples boast the Pow'r of forming Stone,
Like Life born Features—this be all her own;
Let art drawn Pencils every Beauty trace,
And glowing Colours animate the Face
But Englands Sons more useful in their Skill
Can stop the Progress of destructive Ill,
The fine Anatomist can point the Way;
And find the Source where every Evil lay.
As some nice Florist marks the falling Show'r
That gives fresh Vigour to the drooping Flow'r,
Thro' ev'ry Tube or Channel views the Course
Where gently moving, or with active Force,
Thus Harvey trac'd the Bloods meand'ring Stream
And saw thro' Natures fine wrought complex Scheme:
Untwin'd the Clue that veil'd the purple Tide

Explor'd those Views, no longer doom'd to hide,
Nor dy'd with him this Science so profound,
While Hunter lives it falls not to the Ground;
The nice Contexture of the human Frame
But adds fresh Honour to his growing Fame.
Impartial Justice only waits the dead,
Then selfish Envy bends her drooping Head,
And all Mankind unite to praise those gone
Which living is with such reluctance done.
May Months & Years, in gentle Peace roll round,
Before that Justice to a Name is found;
Which to his Merit & his Skill they owe
My heart can dictate my Pen cant shew,
The first among Physicians may he shine.
As Friend as Brother I have shar'd his Time
Alone & Pensive & opprest with Pain
The starting Tear sometimes could scarce refrain.
Tho' England's Pleasures open to me lay
Pain barr'd my Entrance & forbad the Way.—
But Joy unmix'd is not our Fate below,
Still dash'd & sully'd from the Cup of Woe,
Lest I should cry from here, I can't depart
And Dissipation had usurp'd my Heart.
But let not here my Obligations end
But add to Favours of your grateful Friend;
Let me intreat Advice in distant Climes
Where Boreas blusters, & where Phoebus shines,
I wish to lead a calm & tranquil Life
Distant from Bustle & a noisy Strife
Action & Exercise the World admire,
And call that best their Souls do most desire
No rich dress'd Viands shall my Health confound
Nor in strain'd Passions be my Senses drown'd
Nor very early would I meet the Dawn
While Dew drops glitter on the verdant Lawn;
A moon light Walk indulge me on the Green,
Or when the Sun makes ev'ry Shadow seen
In Forms gigantick, let me stroll along,
To hear the Mock-bird chaunt his rural Song
But when rough Winter with his Iron Hand,

Collects round crackling Fires a social Band;
I sit by that dear Pair unknown to you
Whose Souls can feel for Virtue all thats due
Let me remain nor rove abroad nor stray
Where Snows & Frosts point out the slipp'ry way.
The Book, the Work, the Pen can all employ
The vacant Moment to some peaceful Joy.
My Mentor too, shall join our little round,
And much we'll talk & think of british Ground,
More temp'rate Climes you & your Friends enjoy
No suns that scorch, nor Cold your Frames destroy,
    May ev'ry Pleasure to your Lot be join'd
You know the greatest of a virtuous Mind,
"As those we love, decay, we dye in Part
String after String is sever'd from the Heart,
'Till loosen'd Life at last but breathing Clay,
Without one Pang is glad to fall away.
Unhappy he who latest feels the Blow,
Whose Eyes have wept o'er ev'ry Friend laid low,
Dragg'd ling'ring on from partial Death to Death,
Still dying all he can resigns his Breath."

Londo. Pall Mall July 3rd. 1765.

ROBERT BOLLING

(1738–1775)

Neanthe

an heroitragicomic Tale

Provai un Tratto a scrivere elegante
In Prosa e'n Versi e fecine parecchi
Et ebbi Voglia anch'io dèsser Gigante
Ma Messer Cintio mi tirò gli Orecchi
E disse
Arte non è da te cantar d' Achille
A un Pastor poveretto tuo pari
Convien far versi da Boschi e da Ville.
IL BERNI

At Pungoteague a Planter erst
In lucrative Pursuits immersed,
Abstaind from nothing, like Expence,
And held Enjoyment Want of Sense.
But such is Man's frail Nature (let
The Pulpitier, til weary, fret)
That, fence out Pleasure e'er so well,
She will besiege our Citadel,
And, Spite of the Resistance made,
Take by Surrender, or Scalade.
At first we laugh, in Time we weep
Great Caesar once she lull'd to Sleep.
He made Defence, till out of Breath;
Then gave his Rapier to the Sheath.
But what of Caesar? Argus found,
At Pleasure's Voice, his Brain whirl round:
His hundred Eyelids closed at last,
Your Pair of Peepers ne'er so fast.
Ah! Pleasure is invincible,
Let Vertue mutter what she will.
Her conquered Subjects, loyal Souls,
With Ease th' engaging Pow'r controls.
We ne'er forsake her: she, when old,

Expels us weeping from her fold
And virtue conquers but, we find,
That Refuse, Pleasure leaves behind.
Ah! Pleasure is invincible;
Let Virtue mutter, what she will!
Why then against her keep the Field?
God can but damn us; tho we yield.

   The honest Man of Pungoteague
With his Maid Servant made a League,
In Substance, that, if in her Bed
She gave to him her Maidenhead,
In Consequence of which good Deed
The quondam Virgin chanced to breed;
He wou'd, t'eschew what might betide,
The kind Assistant make his Bride.
She from her Contract wou'd not flinch:
He scorn'd to be behind an Inch.
The Coupler blest their Tie, one Morn,
Neanthe fair the next was born,
A chopping Lass, as e'er struck Sight,
That cauterwaul'd from Morn to Night.
The Parents, good, industrious Folk,
In Diligence maintaind th' old Stroke:
And (tho they boasted but that Child)
For Opulence still running wild,
By Dint of rigid Industry,
Still more by close Economy—
(Their Drink Persimon Beer, their Food
Crabs, Oysters by the Bay bestowd)
They scraped together an Estate,
That gave them with their Neighbours Weight
And to Neanthe, as a Match,
The just Repute of no small Catch.

   With that th'old People, satisfied,
No more, as erst, themselves denied
What Pleasure yellowboys afford;
Content not to decrease their Hoard.
Grown hospitable, all around
They heard their just Applause resound
And own'd, tho not unblest before,

Their Happiness now ten Times more.
   Mean Time apace Neanthe grew
And Crouds of warm Adorers drew.
Their Excellence you soon shall read
But stay; the Lady's must precede.
   None on the Shoals, like her, cou'd nab
Or, brought to Table, scoop a Crab:
The Cockle none detect, like her,
Or daintier Cockle-Broth prefer:
The bloated Oyster none so well
Extort from the reluctant Shell:
None such delicious Scollops make
Or Drums, in Cream, or Sheepsheads bake
(Things—O most exquisite of Test!)
None like her, what she cook'd digest.
   Possess'd of every native Grace,
Round as a Dumpling was her face.
No Turkey's Egg was freckled so:
No Brick's Complexion had her Glow.
Her Hair, whose Color rivall'd Jett,
(With her own Bear's Oil dripping wet)
So matted hung her Face upon,
That, as to Forehead, she had none.
Her Nose was short and thick: you'd swear,
Some short Potato stationd there.
Black Eyebrows, like the Drays rough Mane,
Close Guard upon her Eyes maintain.
Their Lashes, of the same dark Hue,
Seem'd a thick Bush, those Eyes peep'd thro,
Eyes, large as Peas, and fiery red;
Enough to strike a Lover dead.
Her Mouth, from Ear to Ear display'd,
Discovered every Tooth, she had:
And they were polish'd, white and strong,
As Juniper's, and quite as long.
Upon her Lip a reverend Beard,
That claimd the Barber's Aid, appear'd. . . . .
A vast Profusion! but her Chin
A noble Tuft was smother'd in.
That Chin upon two Sacks reclind,

That went and came as she took Wind. . . . .
Sweet Sacks, that on her Belly laid,
Like two fat Twins, upon a Bed.
That Bed projected oer two Knees,
Sustain'd by two such Buttresses,
As were the very Type of Strength. . . . .
Their Thickness greater than their Length.
Three Yards about and four feet high
Was that terrene: Divinity,
Who struck, with Rapture and Surprize,
Whoe'er upon her laid his Eyes,
And made him think, that Shirly House,
One Day perhaps, might get a Spouse.
   One Quality Neanthe had,
Which almost ran her Lovers mad.
A most divine and powerful Scent
She scattered round, where e'er she went,
Which, smelt by them, gave such keen Twitches,
They scarce contain them in their Breeches.
Pulsation rapid, Breathing thick,
Complexion flaming, Glances quick—
Who ne'er observed the Case before
Thought, the poor Lovers at Death's Door.
   Tho' to relieve, when they complaind,
She, like some moving Gable End,
Would kindly waddle where they chose,
Behind th'impervious Hedge's Rows,
Or under close-wove myrtle Branches,
She Scarcely cou'd compose her Haunches,
Display the Wonders of the Peake
And hasten the—*Moment critique*;
Ere th' Odors did forme curious guide,
By whom their Pleasures were descried.
No Junction did the Blowze refuse
But that, allow'd by nuptial Noose.
She wou'd do any thing, but wed;
"If she did that, God strike her dead."
Yet, so intent, so feazy hot
Were certain Youths to tie the Knot
(Tho freely they such Solace had)

That half a Score ran almost mad.
And two, more furious than the Rest,
Abundantly their friends distress'd.
Euphenor, Dolon, Lads of Worth,
In different Regions had their Birth.
Anancock first heard Dolon squeak:
Euphenor was of Matsapreak.
The Sire of Dolon rich was grown
By selling +Bullfrogs to the Town
(Where certain merry Blades of Taste
Grew fat upon the sweet Repast)
Euphenor's was as rich, or more,
By plundering Wrecks, on the Sea Shore.
Thus blest by Fortune in Descent,
In Bloom of Youth and opulent,
They, without Respite of their Pains,
Aspired to give Neanthe Chains.

That Emulation in each Mind
An ancient Friendship had disjoind.
Tho whilom for their Fondness known
(As Thomas now and Harrison)
None greater cou'd attract the View;
They now, in cold Distrust, pursue
Their Object with mysterious Face. . . . .
Each strives t'impede the other's Chace.
Yet not upon such Terms they stood
As Conversation to preclude.

Dolon, an arch designing Knave,
Accosted thus his Fellow-Slave.
Euphenor, far as I can see,
The contest lies 'tween you and me.
Tho soft Devoirs here others urge;
They will but dabble in the Gurge.
Conceiving such to be the Case,
And bent to penetrate the Maze
I did old Scarborough, hoary sage,
To cast a figure late engage.

+This (so far as relates to Frogeating) is no Fiction. The Author has some
Acquaintance with a few Members of the Anancock Club of Frogeaters: very
worthy Gentlemen qui scavaient vivre.

You know the Man, at least, have heard
Thro Accomack how he was feard.
How th' Indian Warriors by Device
He used to send to Paradise,
Inducing them by Crouds to flock,
For Passport, to the dire Tomauk,
And taking, for their Road, a Ditch,
Which with their Bodies he made rich.
How, in the Night-time, he wou'd ride
By Light, infernal Slaves supplied.
And all that List of wonderous Things,
Loquacious Fame about him sings:
Which prove, that Superstition's Fools
Have always been Imposture's Tools.

   I to the Warlock wise applied,
Upon the Case his Art he tried:
At Length he said, with some Alarm,
May Heaven forefend unthought of Harm!
He shook his Locks and, with a Sigh,
Revealed a Secret of the Sky
Whence to discern, without Disguise,
For whom the Gods allot the Prize.

   Suppose the Moon (behold it there)
An Emblem of Neanthe fair.
Euph. That Emblem's good, for every Maid
And Matron too: but, as you said. . . . .
Dol. As we that Map of Joy pursue;
So we must move this Emblem too.
In such a Fashion, as may bear
Relation to our Love-Affair.
For tis a Mode, well known of old,
Whoe'er a charm wou'd well unfold
(To quell a foe, or Mistress win)
He must, in Emblem, act the Scene.
To send the first across the Styx,
He, with a Pin, his Image pricks.
To make the last her Thighs relax,
He ravishes the Maid in Wax.
So here, t'unfold what Fate designs,
We th' Emblem move, which yonder shines.

Against that Sister of the Sun
Present the Muzzle of your Gun.
If thence a greater Flame arise
Than from between my shaggy Thighs
(In Turn when I prepare to blaze
Against her with my rival Rays)
Neanthe's yours I will agree;
Mine, otherwise, the Fate decree.

 Euphenor smiles, the Firelock takes,
Presents and fierce Explosion makes.
The Zephyrs soon disperse the Smoke;
Yet much he chuckles at the Joke.

 Now Dolon rais'd his Buttocks bare. . . .
Good Heaven what a Sight was there!
Aloft he turnd a villous Tail:
That Buttock was not born to fail.
The Cunning Dolon from his Pocket
With Caution drew a huge Sky-Rocket,
Applied it . . . . fah! . . No Matter where. . . .
In Blaze his nether Parts appear;
Not more the fair Charroon's, I trow,
Tho good t'emblaze all Buffalo,
The vivid Nucleus mounts on high,
A thousand Stars around it fly,
Behind it leaves a fiery Trace:
The bashful Phoebe hides her Face.
Euph. Gadzooks! whence cou'd that Flame derive? . . . .
From Dolon's Guts, and *he* survive!
Foregad, I shall forswear my Sight,
Confused by Darkness and by Light.

 And is she lost (for whom I prove
The keenest Stings of dubious Love)
And such Perdition brought to bear
By that Volcano, smoking there!
So strange a Case . . . . What, Friend, a *Match*!
And—Sir—the Use? . . . . that Fire to catch?
Wherefore that Implement in Hand?
T' abuse my Faith? I understand!
Abominable, shameless Cheat,
Whom Ill chastise for the fine Feat:

Whom, as behoves, I'll soundly teach
(If you must strive to over-reach)
To do't by less preposterous Farce!
Now take that Foottack on your A
Dull Clodpoll (answerd Dolon strait)
I'll make you soon repent, too late,
This Treatment and the Breech of Faith,
You now support with so much Wrath.
Ramscalian, Drazel, draffy Dog,
I'll give you such a Catalogue
Of lusty Wherrets, you shall count,
Till Doomsday, ere you reach th' Amount.
    Few Words suffice, for Time and Hour,
Where Anger adds the Will to Power.
    What Time the rory Lady stole
From the cold Arms of her old Soul,
And, just departing on his Race,
Apollo smiled in Thetis Face,
Behold the Heroes, in their Buffs,
At fierce Exchange of cursed Cuffs.
Less frequent fall (when Vulcans nine
To make some great Sheet-anchor join)
The short, thick Strokes, than fell their Blows.
The Blood gush'd smoking from each Nose:
Their Cheeks were puff'd, their Eyes bloodshot,
Their Bodies pommell'd: still they fought;
'Til, sickened of that Storm of Blows,
As by Consent, the Wights enclose.
Close, Breast to Breast, they tug and strain
To cast each other on the Plain:
Advantage give, that ta'en, they sway,
(By sudden Yerk) another Way
With all their Weight. Each well employs
His flexile Powers to keep due Poise.
Their Muscles swell, contract, relax
Like Lizards, talent in their Backs,
Their Backs, their Bellies, Arms & Thighs,
As new Positions still arise.
Such Prospect erst inspired those Dreams
Of Bistnoo, with a hundred Limbs.

Their Bodies seemd as glued: the Rest
As Members to some wretched Beast,
Convulsion-wrung: until, at last,
Cross-buttock'd, Dolon down was cast.
Euphenor, at full Length allonged,
An Elbow in his Stomach plunged,
Held stiff, t'uphold his Weight in Fall,
And then, in Thumps, his Rage gave all.

The other, prostrate on his Back,
To aid himself was nothing slack.
Tho worsed by various rugged Knocks,
And most by th' Elbows worst of Shocks
(His Strength each Moment failing fast)
He still persisted to the last.

You English wou'd abhor that Plight,
Who strain no Tackling, gouge, nor bite.
Unknown to Britain are our Modes
Of Fight, or, if she knows, explodes.
Upright, her Bruisers ply their Fists
And all is Peace, when one desists.

Tho we from Britons are descended;
Hibernians have our Manners mended.
When our good Planters fisticuff,
They never think, they hurt enough:
A toute Outrance they Combat wage;
Submissions scarce their Wrath assuage.

While on the Swerd Euphenor prest,
At all Advantage, Dolon's Breast
And levell'd at him some Awhapes
Enough to dislocate his Chaps,
A Hand was seized, by him beneath,
And clench'd the Thumb between his Teeth.
A worse Manoevre Dolon makes
(Which, but to name, a Lady shakes)
He reachd his Hand below to seize
Euphenor's latin Witnesses
And took such Gripe, the piercing Pain
Had well nigh turnd Euphenor's Brain.

His Eyes in Anguish rolld, his Face,
With Sweat bedewd, wore vile Grimace.

He had with Speed the Fray declind,
But Wrath the warmer stung his Mind,
That Rage a quick Revenge supplies
And bids him gouge poor Dolon's Eyes.
His Finger round his Eyeballs play,
Half from their Sockets thrust away.
(The Bard hath heard, from who well knew,
Twill blazing stars, by daylight, shew)
In fine, such mutual Anguish grows,
Each, by Consent, his Hold foregoes.
    No sooner loos'd, again on Feet,
Th' Antagonists in Fury meet.
Brave Dolon, tho his Wind is spent,
Has Valor in it's full Extent.
(Dear Rascow, never be too bold)
His Locks inextricable Hold
Afford to both Euphenor's Hands,
Who now, at Will, his Head commands.
Before he used the Pow'r, he had,
He press'd his Foe to beat Chamade.
But Dolon held Submission base
And felt the Tempest in his Face. . . .
The Vigor of Euphenor's Knee,
Uprais'd in horrid Battery. . .
'Til every feature there was gone
And a black Puddle left alone.
When he no light cou'd longer see,
But groping, seized that fatal Knee;
By __ __ all Impression of his Strength,
He threw Euphenor at full length.
He quickly prest him, with his Weight;
But that Advantage came too late.
In greater Rage Euphenor rose
And gave his Rival no Repose
From Stamping, Kicking, 'til, obscene!
He saw him retch and, mixd with Green,
And white disgorge red Gore . . . . the Spilth
Laid all the Turf around in Filth.
He stood confounded: prudent Fear
of Murder rein'd his wild Career.

That Fear, like Colier's, came too late;
Friend Dolon had received his Fate.
Cold on the Turf his Body laid,
His Spirit trod th' Elysian Shade.

So far 'twas with Euphenor well;
But, ah! the Muse has much to tell.

While JUSTICE undertakes to rule,
Let none, with Justice, play the Fool.

Take Life, *who will* (unless indeed
Th' Attorney general be well fee'd:
And, to decide the Culprit's Doom,
From Surry, the *venire* come.)
Take Life, *who will*; the Vixen rears
Her gorgon Crest and in his Ears
Resounds a Tune, few Men in France,
Or Spain, or Britain, love to dance.
She's so sagacious, active, rude,
'Tis hard to 'scape her, in her Mood.
Yet sometimes (Let, who like it, praise)
She has, I think, unseemly Ways.
When Folks in Concert from her steer;
Why will the Meddler interfere?

Euphenor to Lob's Pound soon got,
In so much just Renown, capot.
Behold, and drop one piteous Tear
He spurns, Favonius up in Air. . . .
Euphenor . . . who aspired to join
And, from Neanthe, raise a Line
Of little Pagods, which had been
Adored, transported to Cochin.

Th' above (let others be prolix)
Are but a Sketch of Madam's Tricks!
I cou'd a thousand Tales adduce
Of her Exploits, when she breaks loose—
The Gallows, groaning with a Load
Of Gleeners, on the public Road:
And other mighty pretty Tales;
But, with the Will, my Paper fails.

Ah cou'd I, in harmonious Verse,
(Extorting Tears around), rehearse

Neanthe's Anguish; wretched Maid!
When Fame pronounced her Dolon dead.
　　And is he gone: Said Echo, gone.
Ah poor Neanthe, thou'rt undone!
Ah what a Gap, unfilled, is left,
Since Dolon is of Life bereft. . . .
O horrid Chasm, tremendous Void!
Why were those Buttocks misemploy'd
That single Time? None, I can tell,
Else-how have managed half so well.
Ah, had he farted less; he might
(For all his Bargain) have got by't.
He might his Wishes have possess'd,
And I, *with him*, had lived most blest.
But live *without him*! I, as soon,
With virgin Lymph cou'd wet the Moon.
　　This friendly Cable (one lay there)
Can, and shall, cure my just Despair.
First let me view th'abhor'd Remains
Of him, who slew the Pink of Swains,
Enjoy the shocking Spectacle,
He now affords, and then fulfil
This only Business left for me,
Ah Heaven! in such Extremity.
She viewd the gloomy Trunk enchain'd:
His hanging Head, e'en then, complaind.
　　And cou'dst thou then, o barbarous Man,
She cried (and pointed with a Fan,
That, once, of Paper, now, might pass,
Diaphanous thro Greese, for Glass)
And cou'dst thou, with such brutal Spight,
Destroy my Soul's supreme Delight. . . .
Him, who cou'd only (while you'd strain
Your trembling Nerves and fag in vain)
Appease, when Passion fired my Soul,
The Tempest, and it's Rage control!
　　Ah cou'd I live; twou'd be to think
How thou dost grin and smell thee stink!
It cannot be; Death I must brave:
Some Cellar will afford a Grave.

These ample Charms will moulder there,
While thou dost stink, in open Air.
Adieu, sweet myrtle Shade, where erst
My Dolon gave me Rapture first!
Adieu the Thicket, with all Might
Where Dolon gave me dear Delight,
When, by that Murderer, we were watched
And (as *those* were *by Vulcan*) catchd!
Adieu the Porch, where Rapture last
My Dolon gave, in too much Haste!
Adieu the World, so lov'd of yore,
Where Rapture I shall taste no more!

   She turnd and in Distraction went
To give Effect to dire Intent.
Upon an Oak (seen by the Muse)
Her Maid en fixd a running Noose,
And . . . but the Muse, as for the Rest . . .
Is dubious, it shou'd be suppress'd.

   The piteous Virgin turnd aside
Nor knows how poor Neanthe died.

   She thinks, in general, that a Fair,
In all those Horrors of Despair,
Might likely the Design complete:
The Muse, for her Part, made Retreat.
She heard indeed, the Sire and Mother,
About her Exit, made sad Pother:
That much they sorrowd, and (to show it)
T' expand her Fame, employ'd a Poet:
And that the Product of his Brains,
Appear'd to be the following Strains.

   A NYMPH at Pungoteague was seen
Of such an Air, of such a Mien,
Of so much Beauty, so much Wit;
Twere hard to find the like of it.
Wheneer she oped her lovely Eyes,
The Wife of Jove look'd from the Skies.
Whene'er she danced upon the Green,
The World beheld the Paphian Queen.
Wheneer she sang, a Syren's Throat
Attuned it's most Melodious Note.

Where'er she gravely spoke, Men hung
Amazed upon Minerva's Tongue.
Whene'er to Mirth she lowr'd her Tone,
They blest the Wit of Maia's Son.
In short, that Maid was such a Maid,
As never Greece, but once, displayd
And *then* (forsooth, because to Troy
She made Excursion, with a Boy,
And on Scamander chose to dwell)
The Grecians raved, like Devils in Hell.
    To make this lovely Maid a Wife
No Wonder then, there rose great Strife.
Tis Beauty's Privilege t'enchant
The Eyes and make the Bosom pant.
Who Pleasure, for their Sight, procure,
It's Opposite, in Breast, endure.
    Two blooming Youths, as e'er broke Bread,
Had got the Maggot in their Head,
And much their Hearts went pit a pat. . . .
This Dolon call'd, Euphenor that.
They went to Blows, poor Dolon fell,
Whom fair Neanthe loved too well.
For Him Neanthe pleased had died:
Without Delay, she went and tied
A Knot, around that driven Snow
(Thro which Arabia used to blow
Its sweetest Gales) and gave to Death
The sweetest Soul, that e'er drew Breath.
Ah let her Fate your Pity move:
Ah spare! ah spare the Crime of Love!
So sung the Bard and he sung well.
The Muse has nothing more to tell.

Occlusion

or final Poem if ever my Compositions be published

To please Mankind enough I've writ
But never have succeeded yet
I therefore bid a Dieu to Verse
For who wou'd toil and rack his Brain
For pleasing Rhymes and but to gain
From every one who reads a Curse!
The Man who does sure
Is mad beyond Sequeira's Art to cure.

A pert a lively Brat at Schole
Old Clarke woud cry This Boy's no Fool
And in our annual Lays to Bess
(Such Lays I ween were never known
But in her royal Praise alone)
Because my Lines had equal Pace
My Rhymes were aptly paird
Th' old Man wou'd say—the Whelp was born a Bard
Thence thence the tuneful Rage began
What warmd the Scholeboy warms the Man
Roxana Celia Delia heard
How horribly the Chimes I rung
How heartily their Charms I sung
In Troth the Maids plain Prose preferr'd
And what was meant as Praise
They swore was Slander in such wretched Lays.

I tho't my Verses very good
And wondered Maids cou'd be rude
So vain fantastical precise
To Satire then I gave my Song
The Devil to pay there was ere long
My dear Self-love began to rise
But what nigh run me made
Th' Illnature pleased my Verse they swore was bad.

God's curse, as Miller says, I said,
I wish I ne'er had writ or read.

Such Miracles, such Beauties lost!
God's curse again!—but tis Man's Way
To shade th' enlivening solar Ray
From rising Flowers;—but not the Frost.
Again my skill Ill try;
And then I warbled forth in Elegy.
A Maid, expiring in her Bloom,
A worth unequalled in the Tomb.
Torn from the tenderest Lover's Breast,
I thought, e'en Hearts of Ice or Snow
Had warmed, to sympathetic glow;
But they, O Heaven! were London's Jest!
I then began, with shame,
Then first, to fear the Bard might be to blame.

In that for full Eclaircissement
On Blood and Wounds to work I went.
A War an Indian War God knows
Is no such easy Thing to write
But (Food by Day Repose by Night
Neglected) it received a Close.
But the first Friend I met
Condemn'd it kindly to the Cabinet:

From Rhyme twas always vastly hard
By counsil to reclaim a Bard.
Th' atrocious Theme (said Pride) tho new,
Revolts the Soul . . . those spouting veins,
Those roasted Reeds and scattered Brains
(Not the Bards Dulness) make Men spew.
I next gave a Repast,
Which none digested, very few woud taste
Ye Gods, ye Gods, what Fate is mine!
Why Burke gains Glory from the nine
And must I judge in the same Class
With Paisly, Davis, Randolph, Grymes,
And Exposed to Laughter for my Rhymes,
And, tho no Knave, confirmed an Ass!
Thanks to my worthy Friend;
Here ends my Poem, here my Follies end.

NATHANIEL EVANS

(1742–1767)

To Benjamin Franklin, Esq: L.L.D.

Occasioned by hearing him play on the Harmonica

In grateful wonder lost, long had we view'd
Each gen'rous act thy patriot-soul pursu'd;
Our Little State resounds thy just applause,
And, pleas'd, from thee new fame and honour draws;
In thee those various virtues are combin'd,
That form the true pre-eminence of mind.

What wonder struck us when we did survey
The lambent lightnings innocently play,
And down thy *rods beheld the dreaded fire
In a swift flame descend—and then expire;
While the red thunders, roaring loud around,
Burst the black clouds, and harmless smite the ground.

Blest use of art! apply'd to serve mankind,
The noble province of the sapient mind!
For this the soul's best faculties were giv'n,
To trace great nature's laws from earth to heav'n!

Yet not these themes alone thy thoughts command,
Each softer *science* owns thy fostering hand;
Aided by thee, Urania's heav'nly art,
With finer raptures charms the feeling heart;
Th' *Harmonica* shall join the sacred choir,
Fresh transports kindle, and new joys inspire—

Hark! the soft warblings, sounding smooth and clear,
Strike with celestial ravishment the ear,

---

*Alluding to his noble discovery of the use of Pointed Rods of metal for saving houses from damage by lightning.

Conveying inward, as they sweetly roll,
A tide of melting music to the soul;
And sure if aught of mortal-moving strain,
Can touch with joy the high angelic train,
'Tis this enchanting instrument of thine,
Which speaks in accents more than half divine!

JOSEPH STANSBURY

(1742–1809)

Verses to the Tories

Come, ye brave, by Fortune wounded
More than by the vaunting Foe,
Chear your hearts, ne'er be confounded;
Trials all must undergo.
Tho' without Rhyme or Reason
Hurried back thro' Wilds unknown,
Virtue's smiles can make a Prison
Far more charming than a Throne.
Think not, tho' wretched, poor, or naked,
Your breast alone the Load sustains:
Sympathizing Hearts partake it—
Britain's Monarch shares your Pains.
This Night of Pride and Folly over,
A dawn of Hope will soon appear.
In its light you shall discover
Your triumphant day is near.

The United States

Now this War at length is o'er;
Let us think of it no more.
Every Party Lie or Name,
Cancel as our mutual Shame.
Bid each wound of Faction close,
Blushing we were ever Foes.

Now restor'd to Peace again,
Active Commerce ploughs the Main;
All the arts of Civil Life
Swift succeed to Martial Strife;
Britain now allows their claim,
Rising Empire, Wealth, and Fame.

To Cordelia

Believe me, Love, this vagrant life
   O'er Nova Scotia's wilds to roam,
While far from children, friends, or wife,
   Or place that I can call a home
Delights not me;—another way
My treasures, pleasures, wishes lay.

In piercing, wet, and wintry skies,
   Where man would seem in vain to toil
I see, where'er I turn my eyes,
   Luxuriant pasture, trees and soil.
Uncharm'd I see:—another way
My fondest hopes and wishes lay.

Oh could I through the future see
   Enough to form a settled plan,
To feed my infant train and thee
   And fill the rank and style of man:
I'd cheerful be the livelong day;
Since all my wishes point that way.

But when I see a sordid shed
   Of birchen bark, procured with care,
Design'd to shield the aged head
   Which British mercy placed there—
'Tis too, too much: I cannot stay,
But turn with streaming eyes away.

Oh! how your heart would bleed to view
   Six pretty prattlers like your own,
Expos'd to every wind that blew;
   Condemn'd in such a hut to moan.
Could this be borne, Cordelia, say?
Contented in your cottage stay.

'Tis true, that in this climate rude,
   The mind resolv'd may happy be;
And may, with toil and solitude,

Live independent and be free.
So the lone hermit yields to slow decay:
Unfriended lives—unheeded glides away.

If so far humbled that no pride remains,
    But moot indifference which way flows the stream;
Resign'd to penury, its cares and pains;
    And hope has left you like a painted dream;
Then here, Cordelia, bend your pensive way,
And close the evening of Life's wretched day.

WILLIAM BILLINGS

(1746–1800)

Chester

Let tyrants shake their iron rod,
And Slav'ry clank her galling chains,
We fear them not we trust in God,
New-england's God forever reigns.

2

Howe and Burgoyne and Clinton too,
With Prescot and Cornwallis join'd,
Together plot our Overthrow
In one Infernal league combin'd.

3

When God inspir'd us for the fight,
Their ranks were broke, their lines were forc'd,
Their Ships were Shatter'd in our sight,
Or swiftly driven from our Coast.

4

The Foe comes on with haughty Stride,
Our troops advance with martial noise,
Their Vet'rans flee before our Youth,
And Gen'rals yield to beardless Boys.

5

What grateful Off'ring shall we bring?
What shall we render to the Lord?
Loud Halleluiahs let us Sing,
And praise his name on ev'ry Chord.

JOHN ANDRE

Cow-Chace

Canto I

ELIZABETH-TOWN, *August 1, 1780*

To drive the kine one summer's morn,
   The TANNER took his way;
The Calf shall rue that is unborn
   The jumbling of that day.

And *Wayne* descending Steers shall know,
   And tauntingly deride,
And call to mind in ev'ry Low
   The tanning of his hide.

Yet *Bergen* Cows still ruminate
   Unconscious in the stall,
What mighty means were used to get
   And lose them after all.

For many heroes bold and brave
   From *New-Bridge* and *Tapaan*,
And those that drink *Passaick*'s wave,
   And those that eat soupaan,

And sons of distant *Delaware*,
   And still remoter *Shannon*,
And Major *Lee* with horses rare,
   And *Proctor* with his cannon.

All wond'rous proud in arms they came,
   What Hero could refuse
To tread the rugged path to fame
   Who had a pair of shoes?

At six the host, with sweating buff,
    Arriv'd at Freedom's Pole,
When *Wayne*, who thought he'd time enough,
    Thus speechified the whole:

O ye whom glory doth unite,
    Who freedom's cause espouse,
Whether the wing that's doom'd to fight,
    Or that to drive the Cows.

Ere yet you tempt your further way,
    Or into action come,
Hear, soldiers, what I have to say,
    And take a pint of rum;

Intemp'rate valour then will string
    Each nervous arm the better,
So all the land shall IO sing,
    And read the Gen'ral's letter.

Know that some paltry Refugees,
    Whom I've a mind to fight,
Are playing H-ll amongst the trees
    That grow on yonder height.

Their fort and block-houses we'll level,
    And deal a horrid slaughter;
We'll drive the scoundrels to the devil,
    And ravish wife and daughter.

I, under cover of th' attack,
    Whilst you are all at blows,
From *English Neighb'rood* and *Tinack*
    Will drive away the Cows:

For well you know the latter is
    The serious operation,
And fighting with the Refugees
    Is only demonstration.

His daring words from all the crowd
    Such great applause did gain,
That every man declar'd aloud
    For serious work with *Wayne*.

Then from the cask of rum once more
    They took a heady gill,
When one and all they loudly swore
    They'd fight upon the hill.

But here—the Muse has not a strain
    Befitting such great deeds,—
Huzza, they cried, Huzza for *Wayne*,
    And shouting——did their *needs*.

Canto II

Near his meridian pomp the sun
    Had journey'd from the hor'zon,
When fierce the dusky tribe mov'd on
    Of heroes drunk as poison.

The sounds confus'd the boasting oaths
    Re-echoed through the wood,
Some vow'd to sleep in dead Men's cloathes,
    And some to swim in blood.

At *Irvine*'s nod 'twas fine to see
    The left prepare to fight,
The while the drovers, *Wayne* and *Lee*,
    Drew off upon the right.

Which *Irvine* 'twas, Fame don't relate,
    Nor can the Muse assist her,
Whether 'twas he that cocks a hat,
    Or he that gives a clyster.

For greatly one was signaliz'd
    That fought at *Chesnut-Hill*,

And *Canada* immortaliz'd,
   The Vender of the Pill.

Yet the attendance upon *Proctor*
   They both might have to boast of;
For there was business for the Doctor,
   And hats to be disposed of.

Let none uncandidly infer,
   That *Stirling* wanted spunk,
The self-made Peer had sure been there,
   But that the Peer was drunk.

But turn we to the *Hudson*'s banks,
   Where stood the modest train,
With purpose firm, tho' slender ranks,
   Nor car'd a pin for *Wayne*.

For them the unrelenting hand
   Of Rebel fury drove,
And tore from ev'ry genial band,
   Of friendship and of love.

And some within a dungeon's gloom,
   By mock tribunals laid,
Had waited long a cruel doom,
   Impending o'er their heads.

Here one bewails a brother's fate,
   There one a sire demands,
Cut off alas! before their date
   By ignominious hands.

And silver'd grandsires here appear'd,
   In deep distress serene,
Of reverend manners that declared
   The better days they'd seen.

Oh curs'd Rebellion, these are thine,
   Thine are these tales of woe,

Shall at thy dire insatiate shrine
    Blood never cease to flow?

And now the foe began to lead
    His forces to th'attack;
Balls whistling unto balls succeed,
    And make the block-house crack.

No shot could pass, if you will take
    The Gen'ral's word for true;
But 'tis a d—ble mistake,
    For ev'ry shot went through.

The firmer as the Rebels press'd
    The loyal heroes stand;
Virtue had nerv'd each honest breast,
    And industry each hand.

"In Valour's phrenzy*, *Hamilton*
    Rode like a soldier big,
And Secretary *Harrison*,
    With pen stuck in his wig.

"But least their Chieftain *Washington*
    Should mourn them in the mumps,†
The fate of *Withrington* to shun,
    They fought behind the stumps."

But ah, *Thadæus Posset*, why
    Should thy poor soul elope,
And why should *Titus Hooper* die,
    Ah die—without a rope!

Apostate *Murphy*, thou to whom
    Fair *Shela* ne'er was cruel,

---

*Vide Lee's Trial.

†A disorder prevalent in the Rebel lines. "The merit of these lines, which is doubtless very great, can only be felt by true connoisseurs conversant in ancient song."

In death, shalt hear her mourn thy doom,
  Auch would you die my jewel?

Thee *Nathan Pumpkin* I lament,
  Of melancholy fate,
The Grey Goose stolen as he went,
  In his heart's blood was wet.

Now as the fight was further fought,
  And balls began to thicken,
The fray assum'd the Gen'ral's thought,
  The colour of a licking.

Yet undismay'd the Chiefs command,
  And to redeem the day,
Cry, SOLDIERS CHARGE! they hear, they stand,
  They turn and run away.

Canto III

Not all delights the bloody spear,
  Or horrid din of battle,
There are, I'm sure, who'd like to hear
  A word about the cattle.

The Chief whom we beheld of late,
  Near *Schralenberg* haranguing,
At *Yan Van Poop*'s unconscious sat
  Of *Irvine*'s hearty banging,

Whilst valiant *Lee*, with courage wild,
  Most bravely did oppose
The tears of woman and of child,
  Who begg'd he'd leave the cows.

But *Wayne*, of sympathizing heart,
  Required a relief
Not all the blessings could impart
  Of battle or of beef;

For now a prey to female charms,
   His soul took more delight in
A lovely HAMADRYAD'S* arms,
   Than cow-driving or fighting:

A nymph, the REFUGEES had drove
   Far from her native tree,
Just happen'd to be on the move,
   When up came *Wayne* and *Lee*.

She in mad *Anthony*'s fierce eye
   The hero saw pourtray'd,
And all in tears she took him by
   ——The bridle of his jade;

Hear, said the nymph, O great commander!
   No human lamentations;
The trees you see them cutting yonder
   Are all my near relation's,

And I, forlorn! implore thine aid
   To free the sacred grove;
So shall thy prowess be repaid
   With an immortal's love.

Now some, to prove she was a goddess,
   Said this enchanting Fair
Had late retired from the *Bodies*†
   In all the pomp of war;

That drums and merry fifes had play'd
   To honour her retreat,
And *Cunningham* himself convey'd
   The lady thro' the street.

*A Deity of the Woods.

†A cant appellation given amongst the soldiery to the corps that has the honour to guard his Majesty's person.

Great *Wayne*, by soft compassion sway'd,
    To no enquiry stoops,
But takes the fair afflicted maid
    Right into *Yan Van Poop*'s.

So *Roman Anthony*, they say,
    Disgrac'd th'imperial banner,
And for a gipsy lost a day,
    Like *Anthony* the TANNER.

The HAMADRYAD had but half
    Receiv'd redress from *Wayne*,
When drums and colours, cow and calf,
    Came down the road amain.

All in a cloud of dust were seen
    The sheep, the horse, the goat,
The gentle heifer, ass obscene,
    The yearling and the shoat;

And pack-horses with fowls came by,
    Befeather'd on each side,
Like PEGASUS, the horse that I
    And other poets ride.

Sublime upon his stirrups rose
    The mighty *Lee* behind,
And drove the terror-smitten cows,
    Like chaff before the wind.

But sudden see the woods above
    Pour down another corps,
All helter skelter in a drove,
    Like that I sung before.

Irvine and terror in the van
    Came flying all abroad,
And cannon, colours, horse and man,
    Ran tumbling to the road.

Still as he fled, 'twas *Irvine*'s cry,
   And his example too,
"Run on, my merry men all"—For why?
   The shot will not go thro'!*

As when two kennels in the street,
   Swell'd with a recent rain,
In gushing streams together meet,
   And seek the neighbouring drain.

So met these dung-born tribes in one,
   As swift in their career,
And so to *Newbridge* they ran on,—
   But all the cows got clear.

Poor Parson *Caldwell*, all in wonder,
   Saw the returning train,
And mourn'd to *Wayne* the lack of plunder,
   For them to steal again:

For 'twas his right to seize the spoil and
   To share with each commander,
As he had done at *Staten-Island*
   With frost-bit *Alexander*.†

In his dismay the frantic priest
   Began to grow prophetic,
You had swore, to see his lab'ring breast,
   He'd taken an emetic.

I view a future day, said he,
   Brighter than this day dark is,
And you shall see what you shall see,
   Ha! ha! one pretty Marquis;

*Five Refugees ('tis true) were found
   Stiff on the block-house floor,
But then 'tis thought the shot went round,
   And in at the back door.
†Lord Stirling.

And he shall come to *Paulus-Hook*,
    And great atchievements think on,
And make a bow and take a look,
    Like SATAN over *Lincoln*.

And all the land around shall glory
    To see the *Frenchman* caper,
And pretty *Susan** tell the story
    In the next *Chatham* paper.

This solemn prophecy, of course,
    Gave all much consolation,
Except to *Wayne*, who lost his horse
    Upon the great occasion.

His horse that carried all his prog,
    His military speeches,
His corn-stalk whisky for his grog,
    Blue stockings and brown breeches.

And now, I've clos'd my epic strain,
    I tremble as I shew it,
Lest this same warrio-drover, *Wayne*,
    Should ever catch the poet.

*Miss Livingston.

JOHN TRUMBULL

(1750–1831)

FROM

The Progress of Dulness

FROM *Part Third*:
The Progress of Coquetry,
or, The Adventures of Miss Harriet Simper

"Come hither, *Harriet*, pretty Miss,
Come hither; give your aunt a kiss.
What, blushing? fye, hold up your head.
Full six years old, and yet afraid!
With such a form, an air, a grace,
You're not asham'd to shew your face!
Look like a Lady—bold—my Child—
   Why, Ma'am, your *Harriet* will be spoil'd.
What pity 'tis, a girl so sprightly
Should hang her head so unpolitely?
And sure there's nothing worth a rush in
That odd, unnatural trick of blushing;
It marks one ungenteelly bred,
And shows she's mischief in her head.
I've heard *Dick Hairbrain* prove from *Paul*,
Eve never blush'd before the fall.
'Tis said indeed, in later days,
It gain'd our grandmothers some praise;
Perhaps it suited well enough
With hoop and fardingale and ruff;
But this politer generation
Hold ruffs and blushes out of fashion.

   And what can mean that gown so odd?
You ought to dress her in the mode,
To teach her how to make a figure;
Or she'll be awkward when she's bigger,
And look as queer as *Joan of Nokes*,
And never rig like other folks;

657

Her cloaths will trail, all fashion lost,
As if she hung them on a post,
And sit as awkwardly as *Eve*'s
First peagreen petticoat of leaves.
    And what can mean your simple whim here
To keep her poring on her primmer?
'Tis quite enough for girls to know,
If she can read a billet-doux,
Or write a line you'd understand
Without an alphabet o'th' hand.
Why needs she learn to write, or spell?
A pothook-scrawl is just as well;
It ranks her with the better sort,
For 'tis the reigning mode at court.
And why should girls be learn'd or wise?
Books only serve to spoil their eyes.
The studious eye but faintly twinkles,
And reading paves the way to wrinkles.
In vain may learning fill the head full:
'Tis Beauty that's the one thing needful;
Beauty, our sex's sole pretence,
The best receipt for female sense,
The charm, that turns all words to witty,
And makes the silliest speeches pretty.
Ev'n folly borrows killing graces
From ruby lips and roseate faces.
Give airs and beauty to your daughter,
And sense and wit will follow after."
    Thus round the infant Miss in state
The council of the Ladies meet,
And gay in modern style and fashion
Prescribe their rules of education.
The Mother, once herself a toast,
Prays for her child the self-same post;
The Father hates the toil and pother,
And leaves his daughters to their mother;
A proper hand their youth to guide,
And o'er their studies to preside;
From whom her faults, that never vary,
May come by right hereditary,

Follies be multiplied with quickness,
And whims keep up the family likeness.
    Ye Parents, shall those forms so fair,
The Graces might be proud to wear,
The charms those speaking eyes display,
Where passion sits in ev'ry ray,
Th' expressive glance, the air refin'd,
That sweet vivacity of mind,
Be doom'd for life to folly's sway,
By trifles lur'd, to fops a prey,
Blank all the pow'rs that nature gave,
To dress and tinsel-show the slave!
Say, can ye think that charms so bright,
Were giv'n alone to please the sight,
Or like the moon, that forms so fine
Were made for nothing but to shine?
With lips of rose and cheeks of cherry,
Out go the works of statuary?
And gain the prize of show, as victors
O'er busts and effigies and pictures?
Can female Sense no trophies raise?
Are dress and beauty all their praise?
And does no lover hope to find
An angel in his charmer's mind?
First from the dust our sex began:
But woman was refin'd from man;
Receiv'd again, with softer air,
The great Creator's forming care.
And shall it no attention claim
Their beauteous infant souls to frame?
Shall half your precepts tend the while
Fair nature's lovely work to spoil,
The native innocence deface,
The glowing blush, the modest grace,
On follies fix their young desire,
To trifles bid their souls aspire,
Fill their gay heads with whims of fashion,
And slight all other cultivation,
Let ev'ry useless barren weed
Of foolish fancy run to seed,

And make their minds the receptacle
Of ev'ry thing that's false and fickle,
Where gay Caprice with wanton air,
And Vanity keep constant fair,
Where ribbands, laces, patches, puffs,
Caps, jewels, ruffles, tippets, muffs,
With gaudy whims of vain parade,
Croud each apartment of the head,
Where stands display'd with costly pains
The toyshop of Coquettish brains,
And high-crown'd caps hang out the sign,
And beaus, as customers throng in;
Whence Sense is banish'd in disgrace,
Where Wisdom dares not shew her face,
Where calm Reflection cannot live,
Nor thought sublime an hour survive;
Where the light head and vacant brain
Spoil all ideas they contain,
As th' airpump kills in half a minute
Each living thing you put within it.
    It must be so; by antient rule
The Fair are nurst in Folly's school,
And all their education done
Is none at all, or worse than none;
Whence still proceed in maid or wife,
The follies and the ills of life.
Learning is call'd our mental diet,
That serves the hungry mind to quiet,
That gives the genius fresh supplies,
Till souls grow up to common size:
But here, despising sense refin'd,
Gay trifles feed the youthful mind.
Chamæleons thus, whose colours airy
As often as Coquettes can vary,
Despise all dishes rich and rare,
And diet wholly on the air;
Think fogs blest eating nothing finer,
And can on whirlwinds make a dinner;
And thronging all to feast together,
Fare daintily in blustring weather.

Here to the Fair alone remain
Long years of action spent in vain;
In numbers little skill it shows
To cast the sum of all she knows.
Perhaps she learns (what can she less?)
The arts of dancing and of dress.
But dress and dancing are to women,
Their education's mint and cummin;
These lighter graces should be taught,
And weightier matters not forgot.
For there, where only these are shown,
The soul will fix on these alone.
Then most the fineries of dress
Her thoughts, her wish and time possess;
She values only to be gay,
And works to rig herself for play;
Weaves scores of caps with diff'rent spires,
And all varieties of wires;
Gay ruffles varying just as flow'd
The tides and ebbings of the mode;
Bright flow'rs, and topknots waving high,
That float, like streamers in the sky;
Work'd catgut handkerchiefs, whose flaws
Display the neck, as well as gauze;
Or network aprons somewhat thinnish,
That cost but six weeks time to finish,
And yet so neat, as you must own
You could not buy for half a crown—
Perhaps in youth (for country-fashions
Prescrib'd that mode of educations)
She wastes long months in still more tawdry,
And useless labours of embroid'ry;
With toil weaves up for chairs together,
Six bottoms quite as good as leather;
A set of curtains tap'stry work,
The figures frowning like the Turk;
A tentstitch picture, work of folly,
With portraits wrought of *Dick* and *Polly*;
A coat of arms, that mark'd her house,
Three owls rampant, the crest a goose:

Or shews in waxwork Goodman *Adam*,
And Serpent gay, gallanting Madam,
A woeful mimickry of *Eden*,
With fruit, that needs not be forbidden:
All useless works, that fill for Beauties
Of time and sense their vast vacuities;
Of sense, which reading might bestow,
And time, whose worth they never know.

Now to some pop'lous city sent,
She comes back prouder than she went;
Few months in vain parade she spares,
Nor learns, but apes, politer airs;
So formal acts, with such a set air,
That country-manners far were better.
This springs from want of just discerning,
As pedantry from want of learning;
And proves this maxim true to sight,
The half-genteel are least polite.

Yet still that active spark, the mind
Employment constantly will find,
And when on trifles most 'tis bent,
Is always found most diligent;
For, weighty works men shew most sloth in,
But labour hard at *Doing Nothing*,
A trade, that needs no deep concern,
Or long apprenticeship to learn,
To which mankind at first apply
As naturally as to cry,
Till at the last their latest groan
Proclaims their idleness is done.
Good sense, like fruits, is rais'd by toil;
But follies sprout in ev'ry soil,
And where no tillage finds a place,
They grow, like tares, the more apace,
Nor culture, pains, nor planting need,
As moss and mushrooms have no seed.

Thus *Harriet*, rising on the stage,
Learns all the arts, that please the age,
And studies well, as fits her station,
The trade and politics of fashion:

A judge of modes, in silks and sattens,
From tassels down to clogs and pattens;
A genius, that can calculate
When modes of dress are out of date,
Cast the nativity with ease
Of gowns, and sacks and negligees,
And tell, exact to half a minute,
What's out of fashion and what's in it;
And scanning all with curious eye
Minutest faults in dresses spy;
(So in nice points of sight, a flea
Sees atoms better far than we,)
A Patriot too, she greatly labours,
To spread her arts among her neighbours,
Holds correspondencies to learn
What facts the female world concern,
To gain authentic state-reports
Of varied modes in distant courts,
The present state and swift decays
Of tuckers, handkerchiefs and stays,
The colour'd silk that Beauties wraps,
And all the rise and fall of caps,
Then shines, a pattern to the fair,
Of mein, address and modish air,
Of ev'ry new, affected grace,
That plays the eye, or decks the face,
The artful smile, that beauty warms,
And all th' hypocrisy of charms.

On sunday see the haughty Maid
In all the glare of dress aray'd,
Deck'd in her most fantastic gown,
Because a stranger's come to town.
Heedless at church she spends the day
For homelier folks may serve to pray,
And for devotion those may go,
Who can have nothing else to do.
Beauties at church must spend their care in
Far other work, than pious hearing;
They've Beaus to conquer, Belles to rival;
To make them serious were uncivil.

For, like the preacher, they each sunday
Must do their whole week's work in one day.

   As tho' they meant to take by blows
Th' opposing galleries of Beaus,
To church the female Squadron move,
All arm'd with weapons used in love.
Like colour'd ensigns gay and fair,
High caps rise floating in the air;
Bright silk its varied radiance flings,
And streamers wave in kissing-strings;
Their darts and arrows are not seen,
But lovers tell us what they mean;
Each bears th' artill'ry of her charms,
Like training bands at viewing arms.

   So once, in fear of Indian beating,
Our grandsires bore their guns to meeting,
Each man equipp'd on sunday morn,
With psalm-book, shot and powder-horn;
And look'd in form, as all must grant,
Like th' antient, true church militant;
Or fierce, like modern deep Divines,
Who fight with quills, like porcupines.

   Or let us turn the style and see
Our Belles assembled o'er their tea;
Where folly sweetens ev'ry theme,
And scandal serves for sugar'd cream.

   "And did you hear the news? (they cry)
The court wear caps full three feet high,
Built gay with wire, and at the end on't,
Red tassels streaming like a pendant:
Well sure, it must be vastly pretty;
'Tis all the fashion in the city.
And were you at the ball last night?
Well *Chloe* look'd like any fright;
Her day is over for a toast;
She'd now do best to act a ghost.
You saw our *Fanny*, envy must own
She figures, since she came from *Boston*,
Good company improves one's air—
I think the troops were station'd there.

Poor *Cælia* ventur'd to the place;
The small-pox quite has spoil'd her face.
A sad affair, we all confest:
But providence knows what is best.
Poor *Dolly* too, that writ the letter
Of love to *Dick*; but *Dick* knew better;
A secret that; you'll not disclose it:
There's not a person living knows it.
Sylvia shone out, no peacock finer;
I wonder what the fops see in her.
Perhaps 'tis true, what *Harry* maintains,
She mends on *intimate acquaintance*."

    Hail British Lands! to whom belongs
Untroubled privilege of tongues,
Blest gift of freedom, priz'd as rare
By all, but dearest to the fair;
From grandmothers of loud renown,
Thro' long succession handed down,
Thence with affection kind and hearty,
Bequeath'd unlessen'd to poster'ty!
And all ye Pow'rs of slander, hail,
Who teach to censure and to rail!
By you, kind aids to prying eyes,
Minutest faults the fair one spies,
And specks in rival toasts can mind,
Which no one else could ever find;
By shrewdest hints and doubtful guesses,
Tears reputations all in pieces;
Points out what smiles to sin advance,
Finds assignations in a glance;
And shews how rival toasts (you'll think)
Break all commandments with a wink.

    So Priests drive poets to the lurch
By fulminations of the church,
Mark in our titlepage our crimes,
Find heresies in double rhymes,
Charge tropes with damnable opinion,
And prove a metaphor *Arminian*,
Peep for our doctrines, as at windows,
And pick out creeds of innuendoes.

And now the conversation sporting
From scandal turns to trying fortune.
Their future luck the fair foresee
In dreams, in cards, but most in tea.
Each finds of love some future trophy
In settlings left of tea, or coffee:
There fate displays its book, she believes,
And Lovers swim in form of tea-leaves;
Where oblong stalks she takes for Beaus,
And squares of leaves for billet-doux,
Gay balls in parboil'd fragments rise,
And specks for kisses greet her eyes.

So Roman Augurs wont to pry
In victims hearts for prophecy,
Sought from the future world advices,
By lights and lungs of sacrifices,
And read with eyes more sharp than wizards,
The book of fate in pigeon's gizzards;
Could tell what chief would be survivor,
From aspects of an oxes liver,
And cast what luck would fall in fights,
By trine and quartile of its lights.

Yet that we fairly may proceed,
We own that Ladies sometimes read,
And grieve *that* reading is confin'd
To books that poison all the mind;
The bluster of romance, that fills
The head brimfull of purling rills,
Inspires with dreams the witless maiden
On flow'ry vales, and fields Arcadian,
And swells the mind with haughty fancies,
And am'rous follies of romances,
With whims that in no place exist,
But author's heads and woman's breast.

For while she reads romance, the Fair one
Fails not to think herself the Heroine;
For ev'ry glance, or smile, or grace,
She finds resemblance in her face,
Thinks while the fancied beauties strike,
Two peas were never more alike,

Expects the world to fall before her,
And ev'ry fop she meets adore her.
   Thus *Harriet* reads, and reading really
Believes herself a young *Pamela*,
The high-wrought whim, the tender strain
Elate her mind and turn her brain:
Before her glass, with smiling grace,
She views the wonders of her face;
There stands in admiration moveless,
And hopes a *Grandison*, or *Lovelace*.
   Then shines She forth, and round her hovers
The powder'd swarm of bowing Lovers;
By flames of love attracted thither,
Fops, scholars, dunces, cits, together.
No lamp expos'd in nightly skies
E'er gather'd such a swarm of flies;
Or flame in tube electric draws
Such thronging multitudes of straws.
(For I shall still take similes
From *fire electric* when I please.)
   With vast confusion swells the sound,
When all the Coxcombs flutter round.
What undulation wide of bows!
What gentle oaths and am'rous vows!
What doubl' entendres all so smart!
What sighs hot-piping from the heart!
What jealous leers! what angry brawls
To gain the Lady's hand at balls!
What billet-doux, brimful of flame!
Acrostics lined with *Harriet*'s name!
What compliments o'erstrain'd with telling
Sad lies of *Venus* and of *Hellen*!
What wits half-crack'd with common places
On angels, goddesses and graces!
On fires of love what witty puns!
What similes of stars and suns!
What cringing, dancing, ogling, sighing,
What languishing for love, and dying!
   For Lovers of all things that breathe
Are most expos'd to sudden death,

And many a swain much fam'd in rhymes
Hath died some hundred thousand times:
Yet tho' love oft their breath may stifle,
'Tis sung it hurts them but a trifle.
The swain revives by equal wonder,
As snakes will join when cut asunder,
And often murther'd still survives;
No cat hath half so many lives.

FROM
M'Fingal

FROM
Canto Third

The Liberty Pole

Now arm'd with ministerial ire,
Fierce sallied forth our loyal 'Squire,
And on his striding steps attends,
His desp'rate clan of Tory friends;
When sudden met his angry eye,
A pole, ascending thro' the sky,
Which num'rous throngs of Whiggish race
Were raising in the market-place;
Not higher school-boys kites aspire,
Or royal mast or country spire,
Like spears at Brobdignagian tilting,
Or Satan's walking-staff in Milton;
And on its top the flag unfurl'd,
Waved triumph o'er the prostrate world,
Inscribed with inconsistent types
Of liberty and thirteen stripes.
Beneath, the croud without delay,
The dedication-rites essay,
And gladly pay in antient fashion,
The ceremonies of libation;
While briskly to each patriot lip

Walks eager round th' inspiring flip:
Delicious draught, whose pow'rs inherit
The quintessence of public spirit!
Which whoso tastes, perceives his mind
To nobler politics refined,
Or rouz'd for martial controversy,
As from transforming cups of Circe;
Or warm'd with Homer's nectar'd liquor,
That fill'd the veins of gods with ichor.
At hand for new supplies in store,
The tavern opes its friendly door,
Whence to and fro the waiters run,
Like bucket-men at fires in town.
Then with three shouts that tore the sky,
'Tis consecrate to Liberty;
To guard it from th' attacks of Tories,
A grand committee cull'd of four is,
Who foremost on the patriot spot,
Had brought the flip and paid the shot.
    By this, M'Fingal with his train,
Advanc'd upon th' adjacent plain,
And fierce with loyal rage possess'd,
Pour'd forth the zeal, that fired his breast.
"What madbrain'd rebel gave commission,
To raise this Maypole of sedition!
Like Babel rear'd by bawling throngs,
With like confusion too of tongues,
To point at heav'n and summon down,
The thunders of the British crown?
Say will this paltry pole secure
Your forfeit heads from Gage's pow'r?
Attack'd by heroes brave and crafty,
Is this to stand your ark of safety?
Or driv'n by Scottish laird and laddie,
Think ye to rest beneath its shadow?
When bombs, like fiery serpents, fly
And balls move hissing thro' the sky,
With this vile pole, devote to freedom,
Save like the Jewish pole in Edom,
Or like the brazen snake of Moses,

Cure your crackt skulls and batter'd noses?
Ye dupes to ev'ry factious rogue,
Or tavernprating demagogue,
Whose tongue but rings, with sound more full,
On th' empty drumhead of his skull,
Behold you know not what noisy fools
Use you, worse simpletons, for tools?
For Liberty in your own by-sense
Is but for crimes a patent licence;
To break of law th' Egyptian yoke,
And throw the world in common stock,
Reduce all grievances and ills
To Magna Charta of your wills,
Establish cheats and frauds and nonsense,
Fram'd by the model of your conscience,
Cry justice down, as out of fashion
And fix its scale of depreciation,
Defy all creditors to trouble ye,
And pass new years of Jewish jubilee;
Drive judges out, like Aaron's calves,
By jurisdictions of white staves,
And make the bar and bench and steeple,
Submit t' our sov'reign Lord, the People;
Assure each knave his whole assets,
By gen'ral amnesty of debts;
By plunder rise to pow'r and glory,
And brand all property as tory;
Expose all wares to lawful seizures
Of mobbers and monopolizers;
Break heads and windows and the peace,
For your own int'rest and increase;
Dispute and pray and fight and groan,
For public good, and mean your own;
Prevent the laws, by fierce attacks,
From quitting scores upon your backs,
Lay your old dread, the gallows, low,
And seize the stocks your antient foe;
And turn them, as convenient engines
To wreak your patriotic vengeance;
While all, your claims who understand,

Confess they're in the owner's hand:
And when by clamours and confusions,
Your freedom's grown a public nuisance,
Cry, Liberty, with pow'rful yearning,
As he does, fire, whose house is burning,
Tho' he already has much more,
Than he can find occasion for.
While ev'ry dunce, that turns the plains
Tho' bankrupt in estate and brains,
By this new light transform'd to traitor,
Forsakes his plow to turn dictator,
Starts an haranguing chief of Whigs,
And drags you by the ears, like pigs.
All bluster arm'd with factious licence,
Transform'd at once to politicians;
Each leather-apron'd clown grown wise,
Presents his forward face t' advise,
And tatter'd legislators meet
From ev'ry workshop thro' the street;
His goose the tailor finds new use in,
To patch and turn the constitution;
The blacksmith comes with sledge and grate,
To ironbind the wheels of state;
The quack forbears his patient's souse,
To purge the Council and the House,
The tinker quits his molds and doxies,
To cast assembly-men at proxies.
From dunghills deep of sable hue,
Your dirtbred patriots spring to view,
To wealth and pow'r and pension rise,
Like new-wing'd maggots chang'd to flies;
And fluttring round in proud parade,
Strut in the robe, or gay cocade.
See *Arnold quits for ways more certain,

*Arnold's perjuries at the time of his pretended bankruptcy, which was the first rise of his fortune, and his curious law suit against a brother-skipper, who had charged him with having caught the above-mentioned disease, by his connection with a certain African princess in the West-Indies, with its humorous issue, are matters, not I believe so generally known, as the other circumstances of his public and private character.

His bankrupt perj'ries for his fortune,
Brews rum no longer in his store,
Jockey and skipper now no more;
Forsakes his warehouses and docks,
And writs of slander for the pox,
And purg'd by patriotism from shame,
Grows Gen'ral of the foremost name.

*Hiatus

For in this ferment of the stream,
The dregs have work'd up to the brim,
And by the rule of topsyturvys,
The skum stands swelling on the surface.
You've caus'd your pyramid t'ascend
And set it on the little end;
Like Hudibras, your empire's made,
Whose crupper had o'ertop'd his head;
You've push'd and turn'd the whole world up-
Side down and got yourselves a-top:
While all the great ones of your state,
Are crush'd beneath the pop'lar weight,
Nor can you boast this present hour,
The shadow of the form of pow'r.
For what's your Congress, or its end?
A power t' advise and recommend;
To call for troops, adjust your quotas,
And yet no soul is bound to notice;
To pawn your faith to th' utmost limit,
But cannot bind you to redeem it,
And when in want no more in them lies,
Than begging of your State-Assemblies;
Can utter oracles of dread,
Like friar Bacon's brazen head,
But should a faction e'er dispute 'em,
Has ne'er an arm to execute 'em.
As tho' you chose supreme dictators,
And put them under conservators;

*M'Fingal having here inserted the names and characters of several great men, whom the public have not yet fully detected, it is thought proper to omit sundry paragraphs of his speech, in the present edition.

You've but pursued the selfsame way,
With Shakespeare's Trinclo in the play,
"You shall be viceroys here,'tis true,
But we'll be viceroys over you."
What wild confusion hence must ensue,
Tho' common danger yet cements you;
So some wreck'd vessel, all in shatters,
Is held up by surrounding waters,
But stranded, when the pressure ceases,
Falls by its rottenness to pieces.
And fall it must—if wars were ended,
You'll ne'er have sense enough to mend it;
But creeping on with low intrigues
Like vermin of an hundred legs,
Will find as short a life assign'd,
As all things else of reptile kind.
Your Commonwealth's a common harlot,
The property of ev'ry varlet,
Which now in taste and full employ,
All sorts admire, as all enjoy;
But soon a batter'd strumpet grown,
You'll curse and drum her out of town.
Such is the government you chose,
For this you bade the world be foes,
For this so mark'd for dissolution,
You scorn the British constitution,
That constitution, form'd by sages,
The wonder of all modern ages:
Which owns no failure in reality,
Except corruption and venality;
And only proves the adage just,
That best things spoil'd corrupt to worst.
So man supreme in mortal station,
And mighty lord of this creation,
When once his corse is dead as herring,
Becomes the most offensive carrion,
And sooner breeds the plague, 'tis found,
Than all beasts rotting 'bove the ground.
Yet for this gov'rnment, to dismay us,
You've call'd up anarchy from chaos,

With all the followers of her school,
Uproar and rage and wild misrule;
For whom this rout of Whigs distracted
And ravings dire of ev'ry crack'd head;
These new-cast legislative engines
Of county-musters and conventions,
Committees vile of correspondence,
And mobs, whose tricks have almost undone's;
While reason fails to check your course,
And loyalty's kick'd out of doors,
And folly, like inviting landlord,
Hoists on your poles her royal standard.
While the king's friends in doleful dumps,
Have worn their courage to the stumps,
And leaving George in sad disaster,
Most sinfully deny their master.
What furies raged when you in sea,
In shape of Indians drown'd the tea,
When your gay sparks, fatigued to watch it,
Assumed the moggison and hatchet,
With wampom'd blankets hid their laces,
And like their sweethearts, primed their faces:
While not a redcoat dar'd oppose,
And scarce a Tory show'd his nose,
While Hutchinson for sure retreat,
Manouvred to his country seat,
And thence affrighted in the suds,
Stole off bareheaded thro' the woods!
Have you not rous'd your mobs to join,
And make Mandamus-men resign,
Call'd forth each duffil-dress'd curmudgeon,
With dirty trowsers and white bludgeon,
Forc'd all our Councils thro' the land,
To yield their necks to your command;
While paleness marks their late disgraces
Thro' all their rueful length of faces?
Have you not caused as woful work,
In loyal city of New-York,
When all the rabble well cockaded,
In triumph thro' the streets paraded;

And mobb'd the Tories, scared their spouses,
And ransack'd all the custom-houses,
Made such a tumult, bluster, jarring,
That mid the clash of tempests warring,
Smith's weathercock with veers forlorn,
Could hardly tell which way to turn;
Burnt effigies of th' higher powers,
Contriv'd in planetary hours,
As witches with clay-images,
Destroy or torture whom they please;
Till fired with rage, th' ungrateful club
Spared not your best friend, Belzebub,
O'erlook'd his favours and forgot
The rev'rence due his cloven foot,
And in the selfsame furnace frying,
Burn'd him and North and Bute and Tryon?
Did you not in as vile and shallow way,
Fright our poor Philadelphian, Galloway,
Your Congress when the daring ribald
Belied, berated and bescribbled?
What ropes and halters did you send,
Terrific emblems of his end,
Till least he'd hang in more than effigy,
Fled in a fog the trembling refugee?
Now rising in progression fatal,
Have you not ventur'd to give battle?
When treason chaced our heroes troubled,
With rusty gun and leathern doublet,
Turn'd all stonewalls and groves and bushes,
To batt'ries arm'd with blunderbusses,
And with deep wounds that fate portend,
Gaul'd many a reg'lar's latter end,
Drove them to Boston, as in jail,
Confined without mainprize or bail.
Were not these deeds enough betimes,
To heap the measure of your crimes,
But in this loyal town and dwelling,
You raise these ensigns of rebellion?
'Tis done; fair Mercy shuts her door;
And Vengeance now shall sleep no more;

Rise then, my friends, in terror rise,
And wipe this scandal from the skies!
You'll see their Dagon, tho' well jointed,
Will sink before the Lord's anointed,
And like old Jericho's proud wall,
Before our ram's horns prostrate fall."

   This said, our 'Squire, yet undismay'd,
Call'd forth the Constable to aid,
And bade him read in nearer station,
The riot-act and proclamation;
Who now advancing tow'rd the ring,
Began, "Our sov'reign Lord the King"—
When thousand clam'rous tongues he hears,
And clubs and stones assail his ears;
To fly was vain, to fight was idle,
By foes encompass'd in the middle;
In stratagem his aid he found,
And fell right craftily to ground;
Then crept to seek an hiding place,
'Twas all he could, beneath a brace;
Where soon the conq'ring crew espied him,
And where he lurk'd, they caught and tied him.

   At once with resolution fatal,
Both Whigs and Tories rush'd to battle;
Instead of weapons, either band
Seiz'd on such arms, as came to hand.
And as fam'd *Ovid paints th' adventures
Of wrangling Lapithæ and Centaurs,
Who at their feast, by Bacchus led,
Threw bottles at each other's head,
And these arms failing in their scuffles,
Attack'd with handirons, tongs and shovels:
So clubs and billets, staves and stones
Met fierce, encount'ring ev'ry sconce,
And cover'd o'er with knobs and pains
Each void receptacle for brains;
Their clamours rend the hills around,
And earth rebellows with the sound;

*Ovid's Metamorphoses, Book 12.

And many a groan increas'd the din
From broken nose and batter'd shin.
M'Fingal rising at the word,
Drew forth his old militia sword;
Thrice cried, "King George," as erst in distress
Romancing heroes did their mistress,
And brandishing the blade in air,
Struck terror thro' th' opposing war.
The Whigs, unsafe within the wind
Of such commotion shrunk behind.
With whirling steel around address'd,
Fierce thro' their thickest throng he press'd,
(Who roll'd on either side in arch,
Like Red-sea waves in Israel's march)
And like a meteor rushing through,
Struck on their pole a vengeful blow.
Around, the Whigs, of clubs and stones
Discharg'd whole vollies in platoons,
That o'er in whistling terror fly,
But not a foe dares venture nigh.
And now perhaps with conquest crown'd,
Our 'Squire had fell'd their pole to ground;
Had not some Pow'r, a Whig at heart,
Descended down and took their part;
(Whether 'twere Pallas, Mars or Iris,
'Tis scarce worth while to make enquiries)
Who at the nick of time alarming,
Assumed the graver form of Chairman;
Address'd a Whig, in ev'ry scene
The stoutest wrestler on the green,
And pointed where the spade was found,
Late used to fix their pole in ground,
And urg'd with equal arms and might
To dare our 'Squire to single fight.*
The Whig thus arm'd, untaught to yield,
Advanc'd tremendous to the field;
Nor did M'Fingal shun the foe,

*The learned reader will readily observe the allusions in this scene to the single combats of Paris and Menelaus in Homer, Æneas and Turnus in Virgil, and Michael and Satan in Milton.

But stood to brave the desp'rate blow;
While all the party gaz'd suspended,
To see the deadly combat ended.
And Jove in equal balance weigh'd
The sword against the brandish'd spade,
He weigh'd; but lighter than a dream,
The sword flew up and kick'd the beam.
Our 'Squire on tiptoe rising fair,
Lifts high a noble stroke in air,
Which hung not, but like dreadful engines
Descended on the foe in vengeance.
But ah, in danger with dishonor
The sword perfidious fails its owner;
That sword, which oft had stood its ground
By huge trainbands encompass'd round,
Or on the bench, with blade right loyal,
Had won the day at many a trial,
Of stones and clubs had brav'd th' alarms,
Shrunk from these new Vulcanian arms.
The spade so temper'd from the sledge,
Nor keen nor solid harm'd its edge,
Now met it from his arm of might
Descending with steep force to smite;
The blade snapp'd short—and from his hand
With rust embrown'd the glitt'ring sand.
Swift turn'd M'Fingal at the view,
And call'd for aid th' attendant crew,
In vain; the Tories all had run,
When scarce the fight was well begun;
Their setting wigs he saw decreas'd
Far in th' horizon tow'rd the west.
Amaz'd he view'd the shameful sight,
And saw no refuge but in flight:
But age unweildy check'd his pace,
Tho' fear had wing'd his flying race;
For not a trifling prize at stake;
No less than great M'Fingal's back.
With legs and arms he work'd his course,
Like rider that outgoes his horse,
And labour'd hard to get away, as

Old Satan * struggling on thro' chaos:
Till looking back he spied in rear
The spade-arm'd chief advanc'd too near.
Then stopp'd and seiz'd a stone that lay,
An antient land-mark near the way;
Nor shall we, as old Bards have done,
Affirm it weigh'd an hundred ton:
But such a stone as at a shift
A modern might suffice to lift,
Since men, to credit their enigmas,
Are dwindled down to dwarfs and pigmies,
And giants exiled with their cronies,
To Brobdingnags and Patagonias.
But while our hero turn'd him round,
And stoop'd to raise it from the ground,
The deadly spade discharg'd a blow
Tremendous on his rear below:
His bent knee fail'd, and void of strength,
Stretch'd on the ground his manly length;
Like antient oak o'erturn'd he lay,
Or tow'rs to tempests fall'n a prey,
And more things else—but all men know 'em,
If slightly vers'd in Epic Poem.
At once the crew, at this sad crisis,
Fall on and bind him ere he rises,
And with loud shouts and joyful soul
Conduct him pris'ner to the pole.

*In Milton.

ANN ELIZA BLEECKER

(1752–1783)

Written in the Retreat from Burgoyne

Was it for this, with thee a pleasing load,
I sadly wander'd thro' the hostile wood;
When I thought fortune's spite could do no more,
To see thee perish on a foreign shore?
    Oh my lov'd babe! my treasure's left behind,
Ne'er sunk a cloud of grief upon my mind;
Rich in my children—on my arms I bore
My living treasures from the scalper's pow'r:
When I sat down to rest beneath some shade,
On the soft grass how innocent she play'd,
While her sweet sister, from the fragrant wild,
Collects the flow'rs to please my precious child;
Unconscious of her danger, laughing roves,
Nor dreads the painted savage in the groves.
    Soon as the spires of *Albany* appear'd,
With fallacies my rising grief I cheer'd;
"Resign'd I bear," said I, "heaven's just reproof,
Content to dwell beneath a stranger's roof;
Content my babes should eat dependent bread,
Or by the labour of my hands be fed:
What tho' my houses, lands, and goods are gone,
My babes remain—these I can call my own."
But soon my lov'd *Abella* hung her head,
From her soft cheek the bright carnation fled;
Her smooth transparent skin too plainly shew'd
How fierce thro' every vein the fever glow'd.
—In bitter anguish o'er her limbs I hung,
I wept and sigh'd, but sorrow chain'd my tongue;
At length her languid eyes clos'd from the day,
The idol of my soul was torn away;
Her spirit fled and left me ghastly clay!
    Then—then my soul rejected all relief,
Comfort I wish'd not for, I lov'd my grief:

"Hear, my *Abella!*" cried I, "hear me mourn,
For one short moment, oh! my child return;
Let my complaint detain thee from the skies,
Though troops of angels urge thee on to rise."
All night I mourn'd—and when the rising day
Gilt her sad chest with his benignest ray,
My friends press round me with officious care,
Bid me suppress my sighs, nor drop a tear;
Of resignation talk'd—passions subdu'd,
Of souls serene and christian fortitude;
Bade me be calm, nor murmur at my loss,
But unrepining bear each heavy cross.
　　"Go!" cried I raging, "stoick bosoms go!
Whose hearts vibrate not to the sound of woe;
Go from the sweet society of men,
Seek some unfeeling tyger's savage den,
There calm—alone—of resignation preach,
My Christ's examples better precepts teach."
Where the cold limbs of gentle *Laz'rus* lay
I find him weeping o'er the humid clay;
His spirit groan'd, while the beholders said
(With gushing eyes) "see how he lov'd the dead!"
And when his thoughts on great *Jerus'lem* turn'd,
Oh! how pathetic o'er her fall he mourn'd!
And sad *Gethsemene*'s nocturnal shade
The anguish of my weeping Lord survey'd:
Yes, 'tis my boast to harbour in my breast
The sensibilities by God exprest;
Nor shall the mollifying hand of time,
Which wipes off common sorrows, cancel mine.

On Reading Dryden's Virgil

Now cease *these* tears, lay gentle *Virgil* by,
Let *recent* sorrows dim the pausing eye:
Shall *Æneas* for lost *Creusa* mourn,
And tears be wanting on *Abella's* urn?
Like him I lost my fair one in my flight

From cruel foes—and in the dead of night.
Shall *he* lament the fall of *Illian's tow'rs*,
And *we* not mourn the sudden ruin of *our's*?
See *York* on fire—while borne by winds each flame
Projects its glowing sheet o'er half the main:
Th' affrighted savage, yelling with amaze,
From *Allegany* sees the rolling blaze.
Far from these scenes of horror, in the shade
I saw my *aged parent* safe convey'd;
Then sadly follow'd to the friendly land,
With my *surviving infant* by the hand.
No cumb'rous houshold gods had I indeed
To load my shoulders, and my flight impede;
The hero's idols sav'd by *him* remain;
My gods took care of *me*—not *I* of *them*!
The Trojan saw *Anchises* breathe his last,
When all domestic dangers he had pass'd:
So my lov'd *parent*, after she had fled,
Lamented, perish'd on a stranger's bed.
—*He* held his way o'er the Cerulian Main,
But *I* return'd to hostile fields again.

Return to Tomhanick

Hail, happy shades! tho' clad with heavy snows,
At sight of you with joy my bosom glows;
Ye arching *pines*, that bow with every breeze,
Ye *poplars*, *elms*, all hail my well-known trees!
And now my peaceful *mansion* strikes my eye,
And now the tinkling *rivulet* I spy;
My *little garden* Flora hast thou kept,
And watch'd my *pinks* and *lilies* while I wept?
Or has the grubbing *swine*, by furies led,
Th' inclosure broke, and on my flowrets fed?

   Ah me! that spot with blooms so lately grac'd,
With storms and driving snows is now defac'd;
Sharp icicles from ev'ry bush depend,

And frosts all dazzling o'er the beds extend:
Yet soon fair *Spring* shall give another scene,
And yellow *cowslips* gild the level green;
My little *orchard* sprouting at each bough,
Fragrant with clust'ring blossoms deep shall glow:
Ah! then 'tis sweet the *tufted grass* to tread,
But sweeter slumb'ring in the balmy shade;
The rapid *humming bird*, with ruby breast,
Seeks the parterre with early *blue bells* drest,
Drinks deep the *honeysuckle dew*, or drives
The lab'ring bee to her domestic hives:
Then shines the *lupin* bright with morning gems,
And sleepy *poppies* nod upon their stems;
The humble *violet* and the dulcet *rose*,
The stately *lily* then, and *tulip* blows.

    Farewell my *Plutarch!* farewell pen and Muse!
Nature exults—shall I her call refuse?
Apollo fervid glitters in my face,
And threatens with his beam each feeble grace:
Yet still around the lovely plants I toil,
And draw obnoxious herbage from the soil;
Or with the lime-twigs *little birds* surprise,
Or angle for the *trout* of many dyes.

    But when the vernal breezes pass away,
And loftier *Phœbus* darts a fiercer ray,
The spiky corn then rattles all around,
And dashing cascades give a pleasing sound;
Shrill sings the locust with prolonged note,
The cricket chirps familiar in each cot,
The village children, rambling o'er yon hill,
With berries all their painted baskets fill,
They rob the sqirrels little walnut store,
And climb the half exhausted tree for more;
Or else to fields of maize nocturnal hie,
Where hid, th' elusive water-melons lie;
Sportive, they make incisions in the rind,
The riper from the immature to find;
Then load their tender shoulders with the prey,
And laughing bear the bulky fruit away.

TIMOTHY DWIGHT

(1752–1817)

FROM

The Triumph of Infidelity

Enough, the Bible is by wits arraign'd,
Genteel men doubt it, smart men say it's feign'd,
Onward my powder'd beaux and boobies throng,
As puppies float the kennel's stream along.
But their defects to varnish, and, in spite
Of pride and dignity, resolv'd to write,
I seiz'd the work myself. Straight, in a cloud
Of night involv'd, to Scotia's realms I rode.
There, in the cobwebs of a college room,
I found my best Amanuensis, Hume,
And bosom'd in his breast. On dreams afloat,
The youth soar'd high, and, as I prompted, wrote.
Sublimest nonsense there I taught mankind,
Pure, genuine dross, from gold seven times refin'd.
From realm to realm the strains exalted rung,
And thus the sage, and thus his teacher, sung.
All things roll on, by fix'd eternal laws;
Yet no effect depends upon a cause:
Hence every law was made by Chance divine,
Parent most fit of order, and design!
Earth was not made, but happen'd: Yet, on earth,
All beings happen, by most stated birth;
Each thing miraculous; yet strange to tell,
Not God himself can shew a miracle.

    Mean time, lest these great things, the vulgar mind,
With learning vast, and deep research, should blind,
Lest dull to read, and duller still when known,
My favorite scheme should mould, and sleep, alone;
To* France I posted, on the wings of air,

---

*Satan seems guilty of an anachronism here, Voltaire being the eldest writer of the two.   SCRIBLERUS.

And fir'd the labors of the gay Voltaire.
He, light and gay, o'er learning's surface flew,
And prov'd all things at option, false or true.
The gospel's truths he saw were airy dreams,
The shades of nonsense, and the whims of whims.
Before his face no Jew could tell what past;
Or know the right from left, the first from last;
Conjecture where his native Salem stood,
Or find, if Jordan had a bank, or flood.
The Greeks, and Romans, never truth descried;
But always (when they proved the gospel) lied.
He, he alone, the blest retreat had smelt,
The * Well, where long with frogs, the goddess dwelt;
In China dug, at Chihohamti's† call,
And curb'd with bricks, the refuse of his wall.
There, mid a realm of cheat, a world of lies,
Where alter'd nature wears one great disguise,
Where shrunk, mishapen bodies mock the eye,
And shrivell'd souls the power of thought deny,
Mid idiot Mandarins, and baby Kings,
And dwarf Philosophers, in leading-strings,
Mid senseless votaries of less senseless Fo,‡
Wretches who nothing even seem'd to know,
Bonzes, with souls more naked than their skin,
All brute without, and more than brute within,
From Europe's rougher sons the goddess shrunk,
Tripp'd in her iron shoes, and sail'd her junk.
Nice, pretty, wondrous stories there she told,
Of empires, forty thousand ages old,
Of Tohi, born with rainbows round his nose,—

---

*It appears, by the testimony of all the antient historians, that truth originally lived in a well; but Voltaire was the first geographer, who discovered where it was dug——Lord Kaims's sketches of the weakness of man; article Voltaire.

†The Emperor, who burnt all the ancient records of his country, and built the great wall to defend it from the Tartars. Quere—In which instance did he do his countrymen the most good; if the books, he burnt, were like those written by them afterwards?

‡Fo, principal Idol of the Chinese.

Lao's long day—Ginseng* alchymic dose—
Stories, at which all Behmen's dreams awake,
Start into truth, and sense and virtue speak;
To which, all, lisping children e'er began
With, "At a time," or "Once there was a man,"
Is reason, truth, and fact; and sanctioned clear
With heaven's own voice, or proof of eye and ear.
He† too reveal'd, that candour bade mankind
Believe my haughty rival weak, and blind;
That all things wrong a ruling God denied;
Or a satanic imp that God implied
An imp, per chance of power and skill possest,
But not with justice, truth, or goodness blest.
Doctrines divine! would men their force receive,
And live to Satan's glory, as believe.

  Nor these alone: from every class of man,
I gain'd new aids to build the darling plan.
But chief his favorite class, his priests, I won,
To undermine his cause, and prop my own.
Here Jesuitic art its frauds combin'd
To draw ten thousand cobwebs o'er the mind.
In poisoned toils the flutterer to inclose,
And fix, with venom'd fangs, eternal woes.
On sceptic dross they stamp'd heavens image bright,
And nam'd their will a wisp, immortal light,
Thro' moors, and fens, the sightless wanderer led,
'Till down he plung'd, ingulph'd among the dead.
To life,‡ Socinus here his millions drew,

---

*A plant, to which the Chinese ascribe all virtues of food and medicine, and proved by European scrutiny to be just as remote from them, as the date of the Chinese empire from 40,000 years. In the same manner, all Chinese extraordinaries, except a few mechanical ones, when examined, descend to plain dock and plaintain. Yet, when swallowed by Voltaire, they will help to expel gripes of conscience, as a decoction of Ginseng will those of the flatulent cholic, full as well as warm water.

GARTH'S alphabetical prophecies, article Ginseng.

†See Voltaire's Candide, the great purpose of which is to prove, what whichever is, is *not* right.

‡Great men, if closely examined, will generally be found strongly to resemble each other. Thus Milton, Homer and Ossian were blind. Thus this great man exceedingly resembled Milton. There was however one or two trifling circumstances of difference. Milton, for instance, was stone-blind in his bodly

In ways, the art of Heaven conceal'd from view,
Undeified the world's almighty trust,
And lower'd eternity's great* sire to dust.
He taught, O first of men! the Son of God,
Who hung the globe, and stretch'd the heavens abroad,
Spoke into life the sun's supernal fire,
And mov'd to harmony the flaming choir,
Who in his hand immensity infolds,
And angels, worlds, and suns, and heavens, upholds,
Is—what? a worm, on far creation's limb,
A minim, in intelligence extreme.
O wondrous gospel, where such doctrines rise!
Discoveries wondrous of most wondrous eyes!
From him, a darling race descended fair,
Even to this day my first and chiefest care,
When pertest Priestly† calls mankind, to see
His own corruptions of christianity.

FROM
Greenfield Hill

PART II.
THE FLOURISHING VILLAGE

The Argument.

*View of the Village invested with the pleasing appearances
of Spring—Recollection of the Winter—Pleasures of Winter
—Of Nature and humble life—March—Original subject*

---

eyes, but had clear and intuitive moral optics. In Socinus the case was exactly
reversed. Milton also rose in his moral conceptions, with no unhappy imita-
tion of the scriptural sublimity: Socinus, on the contrary, anticlimaxed the
scriptural system down to nothing.   SCRIBLERUS.

*Isai. ix. 6.

†A celebrated philosopher of the present day, who has carried chemical com-
position to a higher perfection than any other man living; for he has advanced
so far, as to form a whole system of divinity out of fixed air.   SCRIBLERUS.

resumed—Freedom of the Villagers from manorial evils—
Address to Competence, reciting its pleasures, charitable ef-
fects, virtues attendant upon it, and its utility to the public
—Contrasted by European artificial society—Further ef-
fects of Competence on Society, particularly in improving
the People at large—African appears—State of Negro slav-
ery in Connecticut—Effects of Slavery on the African, from
his childhood through life—Slavery generally character-
ized—West-Indies Slavery—True cause of the calamities
of the West-Indies—Church—Effects of the Sabbath—
Academic School—School-master—House of Sloth—
Female Worthy—Inferior Schools—Female Visit—What is
not, and what is, a social female visit—Pleasure of living
in an improving state of society, contrasted by the dullness
of stagnated society—Emigrations to the Western Country
—Conclusion.

Fair Verna! loveliest village of the west;
Of every joy, and every charm, possess'd;
How pleas'd amid thy varied walks I rove,
Sweet, cheerful walks of innocence, and love,
And o'er thy smiling prospects cast my eyes,
And see the seats of peace, and pleasure, rise,
And hear the voice of Industry resound,
And mark the smile of Competence, around!
Hail, happy village! O'er thy cheerful lawns,
With earliest beauty, spring delighted dawns;
The northward sun begins his vernal smile;
The spring-bird carols o'er the cressy rill:
The shower, that patters in the ruffled stream,
The ploughboy's voice, that chides the lingering team,
The bee, industrious, with his busy song,
The woodman's axe, the distant groves among,
The waggon, rattling down the rugged steep,
The light wind, lulling every care to sleep,
All these, with mingled music, from below,
Deceive intruding sorrow, as I go.

How pleas'd, fond Recollection, with a smile,
Surveys the varied round of wintery toil!
How pleas'd, amid the flowers, that scent the plain,

Recalls the vanish'd frost, and sleeted rain;
The chilling damp, the ice-endangering street,
And treacherous earth that slump'd beneath the feet.

Yet even stern winter's glooms could joy inspire:
Then social circles grac'd the nutwood fire;
The axe resounded, at the sunny door;
The swain, industrious, trimm'd his flaxen store;
Or thresh'd, with vigorous flail, the bounding wheat,
His poultry round him pilfering for their meat;
Or slid his firewood on the creaking snow;
Or bore his produce to the main below;
Or o'er his rich returns exulting laugh'd;
Or pledg'd the healthful orchard's sparkling draught:
While, on his board, for friends and neighbours spread,
The turkey smoak'd, his busy housewife fed;
And Hospitality look'd smiling round,
And Leisure told his tale, with gleeful sound.

Then too, the rough road hid beneath the sleigh,
The distant friend despis'd a length of way,
And join'd the warm embrace, and mingling smile,
And told of all his bliss, and all his toil;
And, many a month elaps'd, was pleas'd to view
How well the houshold far'd, the children grew;
While tales of sympathy deceiv'd the hour,
And Sleep, amus'd, resign'd, his wonted power.

Yes! let the proud despise, the rich deride,
These humble joys, to Competence allied:
To me, they bloom, all fragrant to my heart,
Nor ask the pomp of wealth, nor gloss of art.
And as a bird, in prison long confin'd,
Springs from his open'd cage, and mounts the wind,
Thro' fields of flowers, and fragrance, gaily flies,
Or re-assumes his birth-right, in the skies:
Unprison'd thus from artificial joys,
Where pomp fatigues, and fussful fashion cloys,
The soul, reviving, loves to wander free
Thro' native scenes of sweet simplicity;

Thro' Peace' low vale, where Pleasure lingers long,
And every songster tunes his sweetest song,
And Zephyr hastes, to breathe his first perfume,
And Autumn stays, to drop his latest bloom:
'Till grown mature, and gathering strength to roam,
She lifts her lengthen'd wings, and seeks her home.

But now the wintery glooms are vanish'd all;
The lingering drift behind the shady wall;
The dark-brown spots, that patch'd the snowy field;
The surly frost, that every bud conceal'd;
The russet veil, the way with slime o'erspread,
And all the saddening scenes of March are fled.

Sweet-smiling village! loveliest of the hills!
How green thy groves! How pure thy glassy rills!
With what new joy, I walk thy verdant streets!
How often pause, to breathe thy gale of sweets;
To mark thy well-built walls! thy budding fields!
And every charm, that rural nature yields;
And every joy, to Competence allied,
And every good, that Virtue gains from Pride!

No griping landlord here alarms the door,
To halve, for rent, the poor man's little store.
No haughty owner drives the humble swain
To some far refuge from his dread domain;
Nor wastes, upon his robe of useless pride,
The wealth, which shivering thousands want beside;
Nor in one palace sinks a hundred cots;
Nor in one manor drowns a thousand lots;
Nor, on one table, spread for death and pain,
Devours what would a village well sustain.

O Competence, thou bless'd by Heaven's decree,
How well exchang'd is empty pride for thee!
Oft to thy cot my feet delighted turn,
To meet thy chearful smile, at peep of morn;
To join thy toils, that bid the earth look gay;
To mark thy sports, that hail the eve of May;

To see thy ruddy children, at thy board,
And share thy temperate meal, and frugal hoard;
And every joy, by winning prattlers giv'n,
And every earnest of a future Heaven.

There the poor wanderer finds a table spread,
The fireside welcome, and the peaceful bed.
The needy neighbour, oft by wealth denied,
There finds the little aids of life supplied;
The horse, that bears to mill the hard-earn'd grain;
The day's work given, to reap the ripen'd plain;
The useful team, to house the precious food,
And all the offices of real good.

There too, divine Religion is a guest,
And all the Virtues join the daily feast.
Kind Hospitality attends the door,
To welcome in the stranger and the poor;
Sweet Chastity, still blushing as she goes;
And Patience smiling at her train of woes;
And meek-eyed Innocence, and Truth refin'd,
And Fortitude, of bold, but gentle mind.

Thou pay'st the tax, the rich man will not pay;
Thou feed'st the poor, the rich man drives away.
Thy sons, for freedom, hazard limbs, and life,
While pride applauds, but shuns the manly strife:
Thou prop'st religion's cause, the world around,
And shew'st thy faith in works, and not in sound.

Say, child of passion! while, with idiot stare,
Thou seest proud grandeur wheel her sunny car;
While kings, and nobles, roll bespangled by,
And the tall palace lessens in the sky;
Say, while with pomp thy giddy brain runs round,
What joys, like these, in splendour can be found?
Ah, yonder turn thy wealth-inchanted eyes,
Where that poor, friendless wretch expiring lies!
Hear his sad partner shriek, beside his bed,
And call down curses on her landlord's head,

Who drove, from yon small cot, her houshold sweet,
To pine with want, and perish in the street.
See the pale tradesman toil, the livelong day,
To deck imperious lords, who never pay!
Who waste, at dice, their boundless breadth of soil,
But grudge the scanty meed of honest toil.
See hounds and horses riot on the store,
By HEAVEN created for the hapless poor!
See half a realm one tyrant scarce sustain,
While meagre thousands round him glean the plain!
See, for his mistress' robe, a village sold,
Whose matrons shrink from nakedness and cold!
See too the Farmer prowl around the shed,
To rob the starving houshold of their bread;
And seize, with cruel fangs, the helpless swain,
While wives, and daughters, plead, and weep, in vain;
Or yield to infamy themselves, to save
Their fire from prison, famine, and the grave.

There too foul luxury taints the putrid mind,
And slavery there imbrutes the reasoning kind:
There humble worth, in damps of deep despair,
Is bound by poverty's eternal bar:
No motives bright the etherial aim impart,
Nor one fair ray of hope allures the heart.

But, O sweet Competence! how chang'd the scene,
Where thy soft footsteps lightly print the green!
Where Freedom walks erect, with manly port,
And all the blessings to his side resort,
In every hamlet, Learning builds her schools,
And beggars, children gain her arts, and rules;
And mild Simplicity o'er manners reigns,
And blameless morals Purity sustains.

From thee the rich enjoyments round me spring,
Where every farmer reigns a little king;
Where all to comfort, none to danger, rise;
Where pride finds few, but nature all supplies;
Where peace and sweet civility are seen,

And meek good-neighbourhood endears the green.
Here every class (if classes those we call,
Where one extended class embraces all,
All mingling, as the rainbow's beauty blends,
Unknown where every hue begins or ends)
Each following, each, with uninvidious strife,
Wears every feature of improving life.
Each gains from other comeliness of dress,
And learns, with gentle mein to win and bless,
With welcome mild the stranger to receive,
And with plain, pleasing decency to live.
Refinement hence even humblest life improves;
Not the loose fair, that form and frippery loves;
But she, whose mansion is the gentle mind,
In thought, and action, virtuously refin'd.
Hence, wives and husbands act a lovelier part,
More just the conduct, and more kind the heart;
Hence brother, sister, parent, child, and friend,
The harmony of life more sweetly blend;
Hence labour brightens every rural scene;
Hence cheerful plenty lives along the green;
Still Prudence eyes her hoard, with watchful care,
And robes of thrift and neatness, all things wear.

But hark! what voice so gaily fills the wind?
Of care oblivious, whose that laughing mind?
'Tis yon poor black, who ceases now his song,
And whistling, drives the cumbrous wain along.
He never, dragg'd, with groans, the galling chain;
Nor hung, suspended, on th' infernal crane;
No dim, white spots deform his face, or hand,
Memorials hellish of the marking brand!
No seams of pincers, scars of scalding oil;
No waste of famine, and no wear of toil.
But kindly fed, and clad, and treated, he
Slides on, thro' life, with more than common glee.
For here mild manners good to all impart,
And stamp with infamy th' unfeeling heart;
Here law, from vengeful rage, the slave defends,
And here the gospel peace on earth extends.

He toils, 'tis true; but shares his master's toil;
With him, he feeds the herd, and trims the soil;
Helps to sustain the house, with clothes, and food,
And takes his portion of the common good:
Lost liberty his sole, peculiar ill,
And fix'd submission to another's will.
Ill, ah, how great! without that cheering sun,
The world is chang'd to one wide, frigid zone;
The mind, a chill'd exotic, cannot grow,
Nor leaf with vigour, nor with promise blow;
Pale, sickly, shrunk, it strives in vain to rise,
Scarce lives, while living, and untimely dies.

See fresh to life the Afric infant spring,
And plume its powers, and spread its little wing!
Firm is it's frame, and vigorous is its mind,
Too young to think, and yet to misery blind.
But soon he sees himself to slavery born;
Soon meets the voice of power, the eye of scorn;
Sighs for the blessings of his peers, in vain;
Condition'd as a brute, tho' form'd a man.
Around he casts his fond, instinctive eyes,
And sees no good, to fill his wishes, rise:
(No motive warms, with animating beam,
Nor praise, nor property, nor kind esteem,
Bless'd independence, on his native ground,
Nor sweet equality with those around;)
Himself, and his, another's shrinks to find,
Levell'd below the lot of human kind.
Thus, shut from honour's paths, he turns to shame,
And filches the small good, he cannot claim.
To sour, and stupid, sinks his active mind;
Finds joys in drink, he cannot elsewhere find;
Rule disobeys; of half his labour cheats;
In some safe cot, the pilfer'd turkey eats;
Rides hard, by night, the steed, his art purloins;
Serene from conscience' bar himself essoins;
Sees from himself his sole redress must flow,
And makes revenge the balsam of his woe.

Thus slavery's blast bids sense and virtue die;
Thus lower'd to dust the sons of Afric lie.
Hence sages grave, to lunar systems given,
Shall ask, why two-legg'd brutes were made by HEAVEN;
HOME seek, what pair first peopled Afric's vales,
And nice MONBODDO calculate their tails.

O thou chief curse, since curses here began;
First guilt, first woe, first infamy of man;
Thou spot of hell, deep smirch'd on human kind,
The uncur'd gangrene of the reasoning mind;
Alike in church, in state, and houshold all,
Supreme memorial of the world's dread fall;
O slavery! laurel of the Infernal mind,
Proud Satan's triumph over lost mankind!

See the fell Spirit mount his sooty car!
While Hell's black trump proclaims the finish'd war;
Her choicest fiends his wheels exulting draw,
And scream the fall of GOD's most holy law.
In dread procession see the pomp begin,
Sad pomp of woe, of madness, and of sin!
Grav'd on the chariot, all earth's ages roll,
And all her climes, and realms, to either pole.
Fierce in the flash of arms, see Europe spread!
Her jails, and gibbets, fleets, and hosts, display'd!
Awe-struck, see silken Asia silent bow!
And feeble Afric writhe in blood below!
Before, peace, freedom, virtue, bliss, move on,
The spoils, the treasures, of a world undone;
Behind, earth's bedlam millions clank the chain,
Hymn their disgrace, and celebrate their pain;
Kings, nobles, priests, dread senate! lead the van,
And shout "Te-Deum!" o'er defeated man.

Oft, wing'd by thought, I seek those Indian isles,
Where endless spring, with endless summer smiles,
Where fruits of gold untir'd Vertumnus pours,
And Flora dances o'er undying flowers.
There, as I walk thro' fields, as Eden gay,

And breathe the incense of immortal May,
Ceaseless I hear the smacking whip resound;
Hark! that shrill scream! that groan of death-bed sound!
See those throng'd wretches pant along the plain,
Tug the hard hoe, and sigh in hopeless pain!
Yon mother, loaded with her sucking child,
Her rags with frequent spots of blood defil'd,
Drags slowly fainting on; the fiend is nigh;
Rings the shrill cowskin; roars the tyger-cry;
In pangs, th' unfriended suppliant crawls along,
And shrieks the prayer of agonizing wrong.

Why glows yon oven with a sevenfold fire?
Crisp'd in the flames, behold a man expire!
Lo! by that vampyre's hand, yon infant dies,
It's brains dash'd out, beneath it's father's eyes.
Why shrinks yon slave, with horror, from his meat?
Heavens! 'tis his flesh, the wretch is whipp'd to eat.
Why streams the life-blood from that female's throat?
She sprinkled gravy on a guest's new coat!

.   .   .

Why croud those quivering blacks yon dock around?
Those screams announce; that cowskin's shrilling sound.
See, that poor victim hanging from the crane,
While loaded weights his limbs to torture strain;
At each keen stroke, far spouts the bursting gore,
And shrieks, and dying groans, fill all the shore.
Around, in throngs, his brother-victims wait,
And feel, in every stroke, their coming fate;
While each, with palsied hands, and shuddering fears,
The cause, the rule, and price, of torment bears.

Hark, hark, from morn to night, the realm around,
The cracking whip, keen taunt, and shriek, resound!
O'ercast are all the splendors of the spring;
Sweets court in vain; in vain the warblers sing;
Illusious all! 'tis Tartarus round me spreads
His dismal screams, and melancholy shades.
The damned, sure, here clank th' eternal chain,
And waste with grief, or agonize with pain.

A Tartarus new! inversion strange of hell!
Guilt wreaks the vengeance, and the guiltless feel.
The heart, not form'd of flint, here all things rend;
Each fair a fury, and each man a fiend;
From childhood, train'd to every baleful ill,
And their first sport, to torture, and to kill.

    Ask not, why earthquakes rock that fateful land;
Fires waste the city; ocean whelms the strand;
Why the fierce whirlwind, with electric sway,
Springs from the storm, and fastens on his prey,
Shakes heaven, rends earth, upheaves the cumbrous wave,
And with destruction's besom fills the grave:
Why dark disease roams swift her nightly round,
Knocks at each door, and wakes the gasping sound.
Ask, shuddering ask, why, earth-embosom'd sleep
The unbroken fountains of the angry deep:
Why, bound, and furnac'd, by the globe's strong frame,
In sullen quiet, waits the final flame:
Why surge not, o'er yon isles it's spouting fires,
'Till all their living world in dust expires.
Crimes sound their ruin's moral cause aloud,
And all heaven, sighing, rings with cries of brother's blood.

    Beside yon church, that beams a modest ray,
With tidy neatness reputably gay,
When, mild and fair, as Eden's seventh-day light,
In silver silence, shines the Sabbath bright,
In neat attire, the village housholds come,
And learn the path-way to the eternal home.
Hail solemn ordinance! worthy of the SKIES;
Whence thousand richest blessings daily rise;
Peace, order, cleanliness, and manners sweet,
A sober mind, to rule submission meet,
Enlarging knowledge, life from guilt refin'd,
And love to God, and friendship to mankind.
In the clear splendour of thy vernal morn,
New-quicken'd man to light, and life, is born;
The desert of the mind with virtue blooms;
It's flowers unfold, it's fruits exhale perfumes;

Proud guilt dissolves, beneath the searching ray,
And low debasement, trembling, creeps away;
Vice bites the dust; foul Error seeks her den;
And God, descending, dwells anew with men.
Where yonder humbler spire salutes the eye,
It's vane slow turning in the liquid sky,
Where, in light gambols, healthy striplings sport,
Ambitious learning builds her outer court;
A grave preceptor, there, her usher stands,
And rules, without a rod, her little bands.
Some half-grown sprigs of learning grac'd his brow:
Little he knew, though much he wish'd to know,
Inchanted hung o'er Virgil's honey'd lay,
And smil'd, to see desipient Horace play;
Glean'd scraps of Greek; and, curious, trac'd afar,
Through Pope's clear glass, the bright Mæonian star.
Yet oft his students at his wisdom star'd,
For many a student to his side repair'd,
Surpriz'd, they heard him Dilworth's knots untie,
And tell, what lands beyond the Atlantic lie.

Many his faults; his virtues small, and few;
Some little good he did, or strove to do;
Laborious still, he taught the early mind,
And urg'd to manners meek, and thoughts refin'd;
Truth he impress'd, and every virtue prais'd;
While infant eyes, in wondering silence, gaz'd;
The worth of time would, day by day, unfold,
And tell them, every hour was made of gold.
Brown Industry he lov'd; and oft declar'd
How hardy Sloth, in life's sad evening, far'd;
Through grave examples, with sage meaning, ran,
Whist was each form, and thus the tale began.

"Beside yon lonely tree, whose branches bare
Rise white, and murmur to the passing air,
There, where the twining briars the yard enclose,
The house of Sloth stands hush'd in long repose."

"In a late round of solitary care,
My feet instinct to rove, they knew not where,
I thither came. With yellow blossoms gay,
The tall rank weed begirt the tangled way:
Curious to view, I forc'd a path between,
And climb'd the broken stile, and gaz'd the scene."

"O'er an old well, the curb half-fallen spread,
Whose boards, end-loose, a mournful creaking made;
Poiz'd on a leaning post, and ill-sustain'd,
In ruin sad, a mouldering swepe remain'd;
Useless, the crooked pole still dangling hung,
And, tied with thrumbs, a broken bucket swung."

"A half-made wall around the garden lay,
Mended, in gaps, with brushwood in decay.
No culture through the woven briars was seen,
Save a few sickly plants of faded green:
The starv'd potatoe hung it's blasted seeds,
And fennel struggled to o'ertop the weeds.
There gaz'd a ragged sheep, with wild surprise,
And too lean geese upturn'd their slanting eyes."

"The cottage gap'd, with many a dismal yawn,
Where, rent to burn, the covering boards were gone;
Or, by one nail, where others endwise hung,
The sky look'd thro', and winds portentous rung.
In waves, the yielding roof appear'd to run,
And half the chimney-top was fallen down."

"The ancient cellar-door, of structure rude,
With tatter'd garments calk'd, half open stood.
There, as I peep'd, I saw the ruin'd bin;
The sills were broke; the wall had crumbled in;
A few, long-emptied casks lay mouldering round,
And wasted ashes sprinkled o'er the ground;
While, a sad sharer in the houshold ill,
A half-starv'd rat crawl'd out, and bade farewell."

"One window dim, a loop-hole to the sight,
Shed round the room a pale, penurious light;
Here rags gay-colour'd eked the broken glass;
There panes of wood supplied the vacant space."

"As, pondering deep, I gaz'd, with gritty roar,
The hinges creak'd, and open stood the door.
Two little boys, half-naked from the waist,
With staring wonder, ey'd me, as I pass'd.
The smile of Pity blended with her tear—
Ah me! how rarely Comfort visits here!"

"On a lean hammoc, once with feathers fill'd,
His limbs by dirty tatters ill conceal'd,
Tho' now the sun had rounded half the day,
Stretch'd at full length, the lounger snoring lay:
While his sad wife, beside her dresser stood,
And wash'd her hungry houshold's meagre food,
His aged sire, whose beard, and flowing hair,
Wav'd silvery, o'er his antiquated chair,
Rose from his seat; and, as he watch'd my eye,
Deep from his bosom heav'd a mournful sigh—
'Stranger, he cried, once better days I knew;'
And, trembling, shed the venerable dew.
I wish'd a kind reply; but wish'd in vain;
No words came timely to relieve my pain:
To the poor parent, and her infants dear,
Two mites I gave, besprinkled with a tear;
And, fix'd again to see the wretched shed,
Withdrew in silence, clos'd the door, and fled."

"Yet this so lazy man I've often seen
Hurrying, and bustling, round the busy green;
The loudest prater, in a blacksmith's shop;
The wisest statesman, o'er a drunken cup;
(His sharp-bon'd horse, the street that nightly fed,
Tied, many an hour, in yonder tavern-shed)
In every gambling, racing match, abroad:
But a rare hearer, in the house of God."

"Such, such, my children, is the dismal cot,
Where drowsy Sloth receives her wretched lot:
But O how different is the charming cell,
Where Industry and Virtue love to dwell!"

"Beyond that hillock, topp'd with scatter'd trees,
That meet, with freshest green, the hastening breeze,
There, where the glassy brook reflects the day,
Nor weeds, nor sedges, choke its crystal way,
Where budding willows feel the earliest spring,
And wonted red-breasts safely nest, and sing,
A female Worthy lives; and all the poor
Can point the way to her sequester'd door."

"She, unseduc'd by dress and idle shew,
The forms, and rules, of fashion never knew;
Nor glittering in the ball, her form display'd;
Nor yet can tell a diamond, from a spade.
Far other objects claim'd her steady care;
The morning chapter, and the nightly prayer;
The frequent visit to the poor man's shed;
The wakeful nursing, at the sick man's bed;
Each day, to rise, before the early sun;
Each day, to see her daily duty done;
To cheer the partner of her houshold cares,
And mould her children, from their earliest years.

"Small is her house; but fill'd with stores of good;
Good, earn'd with toil, and with delight bestow'd.
In the clean cellar, rang'd in order neat,
Gay-smiling Plenty boasts her casks of meat,
Points, to small eyes, the bins where apples glow,
And marks her cyder-butts, in stately row.
Her granary, fill'd with harvest's various pride,
Still sees the poor man's bushel laid aside;
Here swells the flaxen, there the fleecy store,
And the long wood-pile mocks the winter's power:
White are the swine; the poultry plump and large;
For every creature thrives, beneath her charge."

"Plenteous, and plain, the furniture is seen;
All form'd for use, and all as silver clean.
On the clean dresser, pewter shines arow;
The clean-scower'd bowls are trimly set below;
While the wash'd coverlet, and linen white,
Assure the traveller a refreshing night."

"Oft have I seen, and oft still hope to see,
This friend, this parent to the poor and me,
Tho' bent with years, and toil, and care, and woe,
Age lightly silver'd on her furrow'd brow,
Her frame still useful, and her mind still young,
Her judgment vigorous, and her memory strong,
Serene her spirits, and her temper sweet,
And pleas'd the youthful circle still to meet,
Cheerful, the long-accustom'd task pursue,
Prevent the rust of age, and life renew;
To church, still pleas'd, and able still, to come,
And shame the lounging youth, who sleep at home."

"Such as her toils, has been the bright reward;
For Heaven will always toils like these regard.
Safe, on her love, her truth and wisdom tried,
Her husband's heart, thro' lengthened life, relied;
From little, daily saw his wealth increase,
His neighbours love him, and his houshold bless;
In peace and plenty liv'd, and died resign'd,
And, dying, left six thousand pounds behind.
Her children, train'd to usefulness alone,
Still love the hand, which led them kindly on,
With pious duty, own her wise behest,
And, every day, rise up, and call her bless'd."

"More would ye know, of each poor hind enquire,
Who sees no sun go down upon his hire;
A cheerful witness, bid each neighbour come;
Ask each sad wanderer, where he finds a home;
His tribute even the vilest wretch will give,
And praise the useful life, he will not live."

"Oft have the prattlers, GOD to me has giv'n,
The flock, I hope, and strive, to train for Heaven,
With little footsteps, sought her mansion dear,
To meet the welcome, given with heart sincere;
And cheer'd with all, that early minds can move,
The smiles of gentleness, and acts of love,
At home, in lisping tales, her worth display'd,
And pour'd their infant blessings on her head."

"Ye kings, of pomp, ye nobles proud of blood,
Heroes of arms, of science sages proud!
Read, blush, and weep, to see, with all your store,
Fame, genius, knowledge, bravery, wealth, and power,
Crown'd, laurell'd, worshipp'd, gods beneath the sun,
Far less of real good enjoy'd, or done."

Such lessons, pleas'd, he taught. The precepts new
Oft the young train to early wisdom drew;
And, when his influence willing minds confess'd,
The children lov'd him, and the parents bless'd;
But, when by soft indulgence led astray,
His pupil's hearts had learn'd the idle way,
Tho' constant, kind, and hard, his toils had been,
For all those toils, small thanks had he, I ween.

Behold yon humbler mansion lift its head!
Where infant minds to science door are led.
As now, by kind indulgence loos'd to play,
From place to place, from sport to sport, they stray,
How light their gambols frolic o'er the green!
How their shrill voices cheer the rural scene!
Sweet harmless elves! in Freedom's houshold born,
Enjoy the raptures of your transient morn;
And let no hour of anxious manhood see
Your minds less innocent, or bless'd, or free!

See too, in every hamlet, round me rise
A central school-house, dress'd in modest guise!
Where every child for useful life prepares,
To business moulded, ere he knows its cares;

In worth matures, to independence grows,
And twines the civic garland o'er his brows.

Mark, how invited by the vernal sky,
Yon cheerful group of females passes by!
Whose hearts, attun'd to social joy, prepare
A friendly visit to some neighbouring fair.
How neatness glistens from the lovely train!
Bright charm! which pomp to rival tries in vain.

Ye Muses! dames of dignified renown,
Rever'd alike in country, and in town,
Your bard the mysteries of a visit show;
For sure your Ladyships those mysteries know:
What is it then, obliging Sisters! say,
The debt of social visiting to pay?

'Tis not to toil before the idol pier;
To shine the first in fashion's lunar sphere;
By sad engagements forc'd, abroad to roam,
And dread to find the expecting fair, at home!
To stop at thirty doors, in half a day,
Drop the gilt card, and proudly roll away;
To alight, and yield the hand, with nice parade;
Up stairs to rustle in the stiff brocade;
Swim thro' the drawing room, with studied air;
Catch the pink'd beau, and shade the rival fair;
To sit, to curb, to toss, with bridled mien,
Mince the scant speech, and lose a glance between;
Unfurl the fan, display the snowy arm,
And ope, with each new motion, some new charm:
Or sit, in silent solitude, to spy
Each little failing, with malignant eye;
Or chatter, with incessancy of tongue,
Careless, if kind, or cruel, right, or wrong;
To trill of us, and ours, of mine, and me,
Our house, our coach, our friends, our family,
While all th' excluded circle sit in pain,
And glance their cool contempt, or keen disdain:
T' inhale, from proud Nanking, a sip of tea,

And wave a curtsey trim, and flirt away:
Or waste, at cards, peace, temper, health and life,
Begin with sullenness, and end in strife,
Lose the rich feast, by friendly converse given,
And backward turn from happiness, and heaven.

It is, in decent habit, plain and neat,
To spend a few choice hours, in converse sweet;
Careless of forms, to act th' unstudied part,
To mix in friendship, and to blend the heart;
To choose those happy themes, which all must feel,
The moral duties, and the houshold weal,
The tale of sympathy, the kind design,
Where rich affections soften, and refine;
T' amuse, to be amus'd, to bless, be bless'd,
And tune to harmony the common breast;
To cheer, with mild good-humour's sprightly ray,
And smooth life's passage, o'er its thorny way;
To circle round the hospitable board,
And taste each good, our generous climes afford;
To court a quick return, with accents kind,
And leave, at parting, some regret behind.

Such, here, the social intercourse is found;
So slides the year, in smooth enjoyment, round.

Thrice bless'd the life, in this glad region spent,
In peace, in competence, and still content;
Where bright, and brighter, all things daily smile,
And rare and scanty, flow the streams of ill;
Where undecaying youth sits blooming round,
And Spring looks lovely on the happy ground;
Improvement glows, along life's cheerful way,
And with soft lustre makes the passage gay.
Thus oft, on yonder Sound, when evening gales
Breath'd o'er th' expanse, and gently fill'd the sails,
The world was still, the heavens were dress'd in smiles,
And the clear moon-beam tipp'd the distant isles,
On the blue plain a lucid image gave,
And capp'd, with silver light, each little wave;

The silent splendour, floating at our side,
Mov'd as we mov'd, and wanton'd on the tide;
While shadowy points, and havens, met the eye,
And the faint-glimmering landmark told us home was nigh.

Ah, dire reverse! in yonder eastern clime,
Where heavy drags the sluggish car of time;
The world unalter'd by the change of years,
Age after age, the same dull aspect wears;
On the bold mind the weight of system spread,
Resistless lies, a cumbrous load of lead;
One beaten course, the wheels politic keep,
And slaves of custom, lose their woes in sleep;
Stagnant is social life; no bright design,
Quickens the sloth, or checks the sad decline.
The friend of man casts round a wishful eye,
And hopes, in vain, improving scenes to spy;
Slow o'er his head, the dragging moments roll,
And damp each cheerful purpose of the soul.

Thus the bewilder'd traveller, forc'd to roam
Through a lone forest, leaves his friends, and home;
Dun evening hangs the sky; the woods around
Join their dun umbrage o'er the russet ground;
At every step, new gloom inshrouds the skies;
His path grows doubtful, and his fears arise:
No woodland songstress soothes his mournful way;
No taper gilds the gloom with cheering ray;
On the cold earth he laps his head forlorn,
And watching, looks, and looks, to spy the lingering morn.

And when new regions prompt their feet to roam,
And fix, in untrod fields, another home,
No dreary realms our happy race explore,
Nor mourn their exile from their native shore.
For there no endless frosts the glebe deform,
Nor blows, with icy breath, perpetual storm:
No wrathful suns, with sickly splendour glare,
Nor moors, impoison'd, taint the balmy air,
But medial climates change the healthful year;

Pure streamlets wind, and gales of Eden cheer;
In misty pomp the sky-topp'd mountains stand,
And with green bosom humbler hills expand:
With flowery brilliance smiles the woodland glade;
Full teems the soil, and fragrant twines the shade.
There cheaper fields the numerous houshold charm,
And the glad sire gives every son a farm;
In falling forests, Labour's axe resounds;
Opes the new field; and wind the fence's bounds;
The green wheat sparkles; nods the towering corn;
And meads, and pastures, lessening wastes adorn.
Where howl'd the forest, herds unnumber'd low;
The fleecy wanderers fear no prowling foe;
The village springs; the humble school aspires;
And the church brightens in the morning fires!
Young Freedom wantons; Art exalts her head;
And infant Science prattles through the shade.
There changing neighbours learn their manners mild;
And toil and prudence dress th' improving wild:
The savage shrinks, nor dares the bliss annoy;
And the glad traveller wonders at the joy.

All hail, thou western world! by heaven design'd
Th' example bright, to renovate mankind.
Soon shall thy sons across the mainland roam;
And claim, on far Pacific shores, their home;
Their rule, religion, manners, arts, convey,
And spread their freedom to the Asian sea.
Where erst six thousand suns have roll'd the year
O'er plains of slaughter, and o'er wilds of fear,
Towns, cities, fanes, shall lift their towery pride;
The village bloom, on every streamlets side;
Proud Commerce, mole the western surges lave;
The long, white spire lie imag'd on the wave;
O'er morn's pellucid main expand their sails,
And the starr'd ensign court Korean gales.
Then nobler thoughts shall savage trains inform;
Then barbarous passions cease the heart to storm:
No more the captive circling flames devour;
Through the war path the Indian creep no more;

No midnight scout the slumbering village fire;
Nor the scalp'd infant stain his gasping sire:
But peace, and truth, illume the twilight mind,
The gospel's sunshine, and the purpose kind.
Where marshes teem'd with death, shall meads unfold;
Untrodden cliffs resign their stores of gold;
The dance refin'd on Albion's margin move,
And her lone bowers rehearse the tale of love.
Where slept perennial night, shall science rise,
And new-born Oxfords cheer the evening skies;
Miltonic strains the Mexic hills prolong,
And Louis murmurs to Sicilian song.

Then to new climes the bliss shall trace its way,
And Tartar desarts hail the rising day;
From the long torpor startled China wake;
Her chains of misery rous'd Peruvia break;
Man link to man; with bosom bosom twine;
And one great bond the house of Adam join;
The sacred promise full completion know,
And peace, and piety, the world o'erflow.

FROM

The Psalms of David

Psalm LXXXVIII. *Second Part.* Long Metre.

Death not the end of our being.

Ver. 10, 11, 12. Paraphrased.

See Bishop Horne on these verses.

I.

Shall man, O God of light, and life,
Forever moulder in the grave?
Can'st thou forget thy glorious work,
Thy promise, and thy power, to save?

2.

In death's obscure, oblivious realms
No truths are taught, nor wonders shown;
No mercy beams to warn the heart;
Thy name unsung, thy grace unknown.

3.

No lips proclaim redeeming love,
With praise and transport in the sound;
The gospel's glory never shines,
And hope and peace are never found.

4.

But in those silent realms of night
Shall peace and hope no more arise?
No future morning light the tomb,
Nor day-star gild the darksome skies?

5.

Shall spring the faded world revive?
Shall waning moons their light return?
Again shall setting suns ascend,
And the lost day anew be born?

6.

Shall life revisit dying worms,
And spread the joyful insect's wing?
And Oh shall man awake no more,
To see thy face, thy name to sing?

7.

Cease, cease, ye vain, desponding fears:
When Christ, our Lord, from darkness sprang,
Death, the last for, was captive led,
And heaven with praise and wonder rang.

8.

Him, the first fruits, his chosen sons
Shall follow from the vanquish'd grave;
He mounts his throne, the King of Kings,
His church to quicken, and to save.

9.

Faith sees the bright, eternal doors
Unfold, to make his children way;
They shall be cloth'd with endless life,
And shine in everlasting day.

10.

The trump shall sound; the dust awake;
From the cold tomb the slumberers spring;
Through heaven with joy their myriads rise,
And hail their Saviour, and their King.

Psalm LXXXVIII. *Third Part.* Long Metre.

Life the only accepted time.

1.

While life prolongs its precious light,
Mercy is found, and peace is given;
But soon, ah soon! approaching night
Shall blot out every hope of heaven.

2.

While God invites, how bless'd the day!
How sweet the gospel's charming sound!
"Come sinners, haste, oh haste away,
While yet a pardoning God he's found."

3.

"Soon, borne on time's most rapid wing,
Shall death command you to the grave,

Before his bar your spirits bring,
And none be found to hear, or save."

4.

"In that lone land of deep despair,
No Sabbath's heavenly light shall rise;
No God regard your bitter prayer,
Nor Saviour call you to the skies."

5.

No wonders to the dead are shown,
(The wonders of redeeming love;)
No voice his glorious truth makes known,
Nor sings the bliss of climes above.

6.

Silence, and solitude, and gloom,
In these forgetful realms appear,
Deep sorrows fill the dismal tomb,
And hope shall never enter there.

Psalm CXXXVII. *Short Metre. Third Part.*

Love to the Church.

1.

I love thy kingdom, Lord,
  The house of thine abode,
The church, our blest Redeemer sav'd
  With his own precious blood.

2.

I love thy Church, O God!
  Her walls before thee stand,
Dear as the apple of thine eye,
  And graven on thy hand.

3.

If e'er to bless thy sons
   My voice, or hands, deny,
These hands let useful skill forsake,
   This voice in silence die.

4.

If e'er my heart forget
   Her welfare, or her woe,
Let every joy this heart forsake,
   And every grief o'erflow.

5.

For her my tears shall fall;
   For her my prayers ascend;
To her my cares and toils be given,
   'Till toils and cares shall end.

6.

Beyond my highest joy
   I prize her heavenly ways,
Her sweet communion, solemn vows,
   Her hymns of love and praise.

7.

Jesus, thou Friend divine,
   Our Saviour, and our King,
Thy hand from every snare and foe
   Shall great deliverance bring.

8.

Sure as thy truth shall last,
   To Zion shall be given
The brightest glories, earth can yield,
   And brighter bliss of heaven.

ANON.

The Philadelphiad

Country Clown

Just from the plough observe the country clown,
His first fond visit to the splended town,
Round all he gazes rudely with delight,
No foolish object 'scapes his wheeling sight:
The lofty spires that seem to touch the skies,
He views with wonder and with wild surprize;
Each shop and store where childrens toys are sold,
He fancies magazines of countless gold,
The stalls and signs with pleasure he surveys;
Still disconcerted by surrounding drays,
And crouds and fops, and noise, and "*here's the news!*"
And thus he judges as the whole he views.
"La! what a pow'r o' shining whokes are here!
'Tis surely Sunday—all in dress appear;
A charming place for frolicks this indeed,
No corn to hoe, nor fields of wheat to weed,
I swear now, *Jonathan*, the town's delightful,
The country nasty, stupid, dull and frightful,
And O whot kliver girls—so fine a sight!—
Our country hoydens is to these a fright,
There's *Sall* & *Suk* that shines the village toast,
Compar'd with these they'r negars at the most."
  Poor simple soul! go tend the village team,
Keep from the city and secure thy fame.
Beneath these cloths the tempting female wears,
Lurk baneful cunning and delusive snares,
And sweeter far the buxom country maid,
Whom pride and prejudice hath ne'er betray'd;
She healthful drinks the rosy-pinion'd gale,
Fresh from the blossom or the grassy dale;
Nor knows the arts the city wantons use,
Who follow fashion and the mode pursues.

Think not the toys which fondly you behold,
Because they glitter, made of solid gold;
And learn this lesson—*seek content at home*;
'Tis in the mind and not the clime we roam.

Quaker

The ambling *Quaker* glides along the street,
With *thee* and *thou*, and *friend* and *neighbour* sweet,
Rogue in her eye, religion in her look,
With even pace that wanton ways rebuke—
Just *Penseroso* with *L'legroe's* heart,
A sad *Melpomene* in *Thalia's* part.
Tho' seeming heedless of the passing throng,
She quaintly eyes them as she moves along,
Admires each spark and pants for every swain,
Wishes them *friends* or that they dress'd as *plain*;
For daddy never could endure a man
Whose coat was cut to fashion's modish plan;
He vows such fools are perfect frights to see;
And for a wife!—they'll not find one in me;
But *Simeon Steady* must make me a bride—
O La! to have the statue by my side!—
I swear *aunt Rachel* that I'd rather die
A maid at sixty than beside him lie,—
Tho' daddy says he has a world of sense,
And knows completely how to make the pence
—But then to see his coat without a collar,
His buckles just th'size of half a dollar,
His smooth lank hair cut formal round his neck,
His broad brimm'd hat that half-way shade his back,
His shirt's so plain, his cravat smooth and long,
And then, what stupid nonsense from his tongue!
No, let me die and never be a wife
Before I should with *Simeon* spend my life.
Such is the *Quaker's* self-denying ways,
They outward blame what most they inward praise,
Think it a sin that man should dress a-mode,
As if a coat or hat offended God.

Reason the matter and debate it o'er,
He's still tenacious as he was before,
A perfect bigot wedded to his notion,
Who proves that silence is the best devotion;
But contradict him in his steady ways?
"*Friend* thee is wrong", or "knows thee what thee says?"
Yet there are some whose views are unconfin'd,
Who scorn the bigot principle of mind,
Who see religion in its proper view,
Knows what is prejudice and what is true,
Pursues the road which reason says is best,
And thinks the Roman with the Quaker blest.

The Universal Motive

"'Tis from high life high characters we trace,
A judge in lawn is twice a judge in lace;"
A county member shines with double glare,
When he to sessions drives his new gilt chair;
Then plodding fools will take him by the hand,
The chair, like magic, friendship can command,
The self-same man on foot may trudge along,
Unknown to all the *friendly knowing* throng.
A worthy cobler long might beat the stone,
Before his trade could make his merits known;
But let some god, as fable sings of old,
Descend a show'r of man-betwitching gold—
Then he is equal both in sense and breeding,
(For money cancels ev'ry want of reading.)
To M-rr-s, H-p-k-ns, Maevius and the rest,
Of tip-top folks that here are thought the best.
   Hail! sacred drug! thou cure for ev'ry pain,
To foolish man both antidote and bane;
Life-giving nostrum, death-dispensing rod,
That works such wonders not inspir'd by God,
The selfish motive for each nobler deed,
That guards the worthless while the virtuous bleed
Brib'd by thy pow'r the virgin sells her *all*,
The desp'rate heart for murder hears thy call,

For you the merchant tempts th'dangrou's deep
For you the miser robs himself of sleep,
For you mechanics ply the forming tool,
For you the knowing knave will act the fool,
For you the lawyer proves that black is white,
For you the judge will say that wrong is right,
For you the coward fights with courage fell,
For you the general will his army sell,*
For you the clergy (heav'nly sons below)
Will cure our sins and heal each mental woe,
For you the world, with unremitting toil,
Builds tow'ring hopes on Fortune's faithless spoil;
And men may call their actions what they will,
But gold's *their motive universal* still.

Bagnio

Turn we to view the Bagnio's horrid scene,
Tho' modest virtue lifts her veil between;
Where tender sympathy should touch the heart,
And soft benevolence distend its part,
The tender tear should glisten in the eye,
For injur'd innocence demands the sigh;
The social throb should faulter in the breast
To see the relicks of the fair distress'd,
No wanton heart should triumph o'er the maid
Whom some low villain roguishly betray'd,
But ev'ry aid humanity dilate,
To mourn or mend the wand'ring females fate.
Now see the youth by facination led,
Court the low raptures of the harlot bed,
His sad dark vigils nightly here to keep,
Where dire compunction robs the wretch of sleep;
Delusive joys betray his tender heart,
Ensnar'd, bewilder'd by the wanton's art;
The leg half-naked and the breast quite bare,
With all the studied ornament of hair,
The garments loose to raise the warm desire,

*A glaring instance is recent to the Americans.

And touch the passions with a keener fire,
Her syren voice that captivates the ear,
With tempting gestures and inviting leer:
These move his heart and youthful mind employ,
'Till sated pleasure proves 'tis baneful joy.
    Here lurks the bully, (horror in his face)
The shame of nature and his own disgrace;
A beastly pander duteous to the call,
A slave, a pimp, a tool, a knave to all.
    Next see the matron's well-dissembled looks,
With pious prejudice for heav'nly books,
A nun-procuress; devotee quite sad;
With good monitions but with actions bad,
Prone to deceive and watchful to beguile,
To trap th'unwary female with her smile,
Or specious presents seeming fair and kind,
She ready makes to win the thoughtless mind,
Talks in one breath of minister and wh-r-,
Of young debauchers and of famisht poor,
Quotes scripture scraps to shew her orthodox,
Next tells that *Sall* and *Suk* has not the p—.

The Emigrant

    See the lone emigrant just come on shore,
Far from relations which he'll see no more,
Far from his native country where he spent
The playful moments youthful pleasure lent;
Thrown here unfriended, fortune to appease,
Or endless vain cur'osity to please:
His father, mother, brother, sister dear,
Dropt at his parting many a tender tear,
And sobb'd and wish'd th'adventurer to stay,
Nor brave the dangers of the raging sea.
But all their kind monitions were in vain,
For fate decreed the youth to cross the main.
    Some rustic relics of paternal care,
His mindful mother ready does prepare;
The woolly garments, shirts & stockings strong,

The crock of butter and the old neat's tongue,
The new laid eggs and cheese ne'er cut before,
With bread and spirits to complete his store.
Then to the beach his com'rades true conveys,
This for his wealth, and that his safety prays,
Each in his turn sincerely shakes his hand,
And wish him safely to his destin'd land.

Scarce had the prow its canvass pinions spread
When dizzy sickness seiz'd his giddy head,
Dim grows the land, the surging billows roar,
'Twas then alas! he wish'd himself on shore;
Sadly he gaz'd and took his last adieu,
Its charms but rising as it sunk to view.

Unhappy Europe! thus thy children stray
To shun thy tyrants of remorseless sway,
Down from the knavish minister of state
To kindred lackeys that around him wait,
All, all combine to hurt the needy poor,
"To spurn imploring famine from the door."

Miss Kitty Cut-a-dash;
Or the Arch-street Flirt

Observe that foot, how nice the shoe it fits,
Her waist how slender, how her gown it sits,
How bold she walks, what fierceness in her air,
And how the croud submissively do stare,
And hail her goddess of the beaut'ous throng
But cease good folks, your high opinion's wrong.
First at her toilette *Kitty* spends the morn,
To curl and patch, and face & neck adorn;
She studies fashions with religious care,
And scoffs religion with a scornful air,
Thinks that the ways to heaven are laid with gauze,
And that religion has no modern laws:
When full equipt she rambles through the town,
Or with her aunt some character runs down,
Or with an air important through the shops,
She cheapens fans and talks with ruffled fops:

The young apprentice knows her tricks full well,
For tossing goods without the hopes to sell
And spruce young milliners do often curse
Her wanton taste and coin-unsulli'd purse:
Sweethearts by dozens in her train appears,
Altho' the nymph is falling into years;
They come like seasons and like seasons go,
This one forgets her, that one answers *no*:
And all despise and seek some happier dame,
Less fond of dress and more unknown to fame,
The babbling slut* will loudly whisper round
That maids of stricter virtue can be found.

*Common fame.

ANNE HECHT

(fl. 1780s)

Advice to Mrs. Mowat

Dear Hetty—
    Since the single state
    You've left to choose yourself a mate,
    Since metamorphosed to a wife,
    And bliss or woe insured for life,
    A friendly muse the way should show
    To gain the bliss and miss the woe.
    But first of all I must suppose
    You've with mature reflection chose.
    And thus premised I think you may
    Here find to married bliss the way.
    Small is the province of a wife
    And narrow is her sphere in life,
    Within that sphere to walk aright
    Should be her principal delight.
    To grace the home with prudent care
    And properly to spend and spare,
    To make her husband bless the day
    He gave his liberty away,
    To train the tender infants mind,
    These are the tasks to wives assigned.
    Then never think domestic care
    Beneath the notice of the fair.
    But matters every day inspect
    That naught be wasted by neglect.
    Be frugal (plenty round you seen)
    And always keep the golden mean.
    Let decent neatness round you shine
    Be always clean but seldom fine.
    If once fair decency be fled
    Love soon deserts the genial bed.
    Not nice your house, though neat and clean
    In all things there's a proper mean.

Some of our sex mistake in this;
Too anxious some—some too remiss.
The early days of married life
Are oft o'er cast with childish strife
Then let it be your chiefest care
To keep that hour bright and fair
Then is the time, by gentlest art
To fix his empire in your heart.
For should it by neglect expire
No art again can light the fire.
To charm his reason dress your mind
Till love shall be with friendship joined.
Raised on that basis t'will endure
From time and death itself secure.
Be sure you ne'er for power contend
Or try with tears to gain your end
Sometimes the tears that dim your eyes
From pride and obstancy arise.
Heaven gave to man unquestioned sway
Then Heaven and man at once obey.
Let sullen looks your brow ne'er cloud
Be always cheerful, never loud.
Let trifles never discompose
Your temper, features or repose.
Abroad for happiness ne'er roam
True happiness resides at home.
Still make your partner easy there
Man finds abroad sufficient care.
If every thing at home be right
He'll always enter with delight.
Your presence he'll prefer to all,
That cheats the world does pleasure call
With cheerful chat his cares beguile
And always greet him with a smile
Never with woe his thoughts engage
Nor ever meet his rage with rage
With all our sex's softening art
Recall lost reason to his heart.
Thus calm the tempest in his breast
And sweetly soothe his soul to rest.

Be sure you ne'er arraign his sense,
Few husbands pardon that offence,
T'will discord raise, disgust it breeds
And hatred certainly succeeds.
Then shun O shun that hated shelf
Still think him wiser than yourself.
And if you otherwise believe
Ne'er let him such a thought perceive.
When cares invade your partners heart
Bear you a sympathetic part.
[   ]
From morn till noon, from noon till night
To see him pleased your chief delight.
And now, methinks, I hear you cry;
Shall she presume—Oh vanity!
To lay down rules for wedded life
Who never was herself a wife
I've done nor longer will presume
To tresspass on time that's not your own.

PHILIP FRENEAU

(1752–1832)

American Liberty, A Poem

Sit mihi fas audita loqui.
VIRG.

Jove fix'd it certain, that whatever day
Makes Man a slave, takes half his worth away.
POPE.

ARGUMENT.

Present Situation of Affairs in North-America—Address to the Deity—Unhappy Situation of New-England, in particular—The first Emigrations of the Colonists from Europe—Cruelties of the Indian Natives—All our Hopes of future Safety depend secondarily on our present Resolution and Activity—Impossible for British Soldiers to join heartily for the Purpose of enslaving us—Present happy Unanimity among the Colonies—The Baseness of pensioned Writers against their native Country—General Gage's late Proclamation—The Odium consequent upon his Undertaking his present Office—Character of a weak Monarch—Popery established in Canada—General Washington—The Honourable Continental Congress—Hancock—Adams—Invitation to Foreigners to retire hither from their respective Slavish Regions—Bravery of the New-England Forces in the late Engagements—The determined Resolution of the Colonies to be free—The future Happiness of America if she surmounts the present Difficulties.

Once more Bellona, forc'd upon the stage,
Inspires new fury, and awakes her rage,
From North to South her thun'dring trumpet spreads
Tumults, and war and death, and daring deeds,
What breast but kindles at the martial sound?
What heart but bleeds to feel it's country's wound?
For thee, blest freedom, to protect thy sway,
We rush undaunted to the bloody fray,
For thee, each province arms its vig'rous host,
Content to die, e'er freedom shall be lost.

Kind watchful power, on whose supreme command
The fate of monarchs, empires, worlds depend,
Grant, in a cause thy wisdom must approve,
Undaunted valour kindled from above,
Let not our souls descend to dastard fear,
Be valour, prudence both united here,
Now as of old thy mighty arm display,
Relieve the opprest, and saving power convey,
'Tis done, and see th'omnipotent befriends,
The sword of Gideon, and of God descends.
　　Ah, see with grief fair Massachusetts plains,
The seat of war, and death's terrific scenes,
Where darling peace with smiling aspect stood,
Lo! the grim Soldier stalks in quest of blood:
What madness heaven, has made Britannia frown?
Who plans our schemes to pull Columbia* down,
See Boston groan beneath the strong blockade,
Her freedom vanish'd, and destroy'd her trade,
Injur'd, opprest, no tyrant could exceed,
The cruel vengeance of so base a deed.
　　New Albion's sons† whom honest freedom moves
(My heart admires them, and my verse approves)
Tir'd of oppression in a Stuart's reign,
A Popish faction, ministerial train;
Bravely resolv'd to leave their native shore
And some new world they knew not where explore,
Far in the West, beyond where Poets said,
The Sun retir'd, and Cynthia went to bed,
Few then had seen the scarce discover'd Bourne,
From whence like death yet fewer did return:
Dire truths from thence the wand'ring sailor brought
Enlarg'd by terror, and the power of thought,
With all the forms that pict'ring fancy gives,
With all the dread that in idea lives,
Fierce Cannibals that fought the blood of man,

---

　　*Columbia, America sometimes so called, from Columbus the first dis-
coverer.
　　†New Albion, properly New England, but is often applied to all British
America.

Vast cruel tribes that through the desart ran,
Giants whose height transcends the tow'ring oak,
Brutes with whose screams the trembling forest shook
All these and more they held no cause of fear,
Since nought but slavery, dreadful could appear.
    Ah see the day, distressful to the view,
Wives, husbands, fathers, bid a long adieu,
    Dear native land, how heav'd the heavy sigh,
When thy last mountains vanish'd on the eye,
Then their frail barks, just enter'd on the sea,
Pursu'd the long uncomfortable way:
But pitying heav'n the just design surveys,
Sends prosp'rous gales, and wafts them o'er the seas.
    Behold the shore; no rising cities there,
To hail them welcome from the sea appear,
In the wild woods the exil'd host were spread,
The heavens their covering, and the earth their bed:
What expectations but a life of woe?
Unnumber'd Myriads of the savage foe,
Whose brutal fury rais'd, at once might sweep
The adventurers all to death's destructive sleep;
Yet 'midst this scene of horror and despair,
Stout industry began his office here,
Made forests bend beneath his sturdy stroke,
Made oxen groan beneath the sweaty yoke,
Till half the desart smil'd and look'd as gay
As northern gardens in the bloom of May.
    But ah, review the sorrows interwove,
How the fierce native with the stranger strove;—
So heaven's bright lamp the all-reviving sun,
Just as his flaming journey is begun,
Mists, fogs and vapours, sprung from damps of night,
Mount up and strive to dim the approach of light;
But he in triumph darts his piercing ray,
Scatters their forces and pursues his way.
Oft when the husband did his labour leave
To meet his little family at eve,
Stretchd in their blood he saw each well known face,
His dear companion and his youthful race;
Perhaps the scalp with barbarous fury torn,

The visage mangled, and the babe unborn
Ripp'd from its dark abode, to view the sun,
Ere nature finish'd half she had begun.
    And should we now when spread thro' ev'ry shore,
Submit to that our fathers shunn'd before?
Should we, just heaven, our blood and labour spent,
Be slaves and minions to a parliament?
Perish the thought, nor may one wretch remain,
Who dares not fight and in our cause be slain;
The cause of freedom daunts the hireling foe,
And gives each Sampson's strength toward the blow,
And each, like him, whom fear nor force confines,
Destroys a thousand modern Philistines.
    Who fights to take our liberty away,
Dead-hearted fights and falls an easy prey;
The cause, the cause, most cruel to enslave,
Disheartens thousands, and unmans the brave:
Who could have thought that Britons bore a heart,
Or British troops to act so base a part?
Britons of old renown'd, can they descend,
T' enslave their brethren in a foreign land?
What oath, what oath, inform us if you can,
Binds them to act below the worth of man?
Can they whom half the world admires, can they
Be advocates for vile despotic sway?
Shall they to every shore and clime renown'd
Enforce those acts that tyranny did found?
"Yet sure if this be their resolv'd design,
Conquer they shall where'er the sun doth shine;
No expedition prov'd unhappy yet,
Can we Havanna's bloody siege forget,
Where British cannon the strong fortress tore,
And wing'd whole legions to its infernal shore
Or does the voice of fame so soon forego
Gibraltar's action, and the vanquish'd foe,
Where art and nature both at once combin'd
To baffle all our hardy troops design'd?—
Yet there Britannia's arms successful sped,
While haughty Spaniards trembled, felt and fled."
    So say the pension'd tools of slavery,

So say our traitors, but so say not I—
(Tories or traitors, call them which you choose,
Tories are rogues, and traitors imps broke lose)
But know ye few, the scandal of our land,
On whom returns the blood that we expend.
Those troops whose feats are told on every shore,
Here lose their spirit and are brave no more;
When armies fight to gain some cruel cause,
Establish tyrants or destructive laws.
True courage scorns to inspire the hateful crew,
Recall past fame, or spur them on to new;
Dark boding thoughts the heavy soul possess,
And ancient valour turns to cowardice.
  Dark was the prospect, gloomy was the scene,
When traitors join'd to break our union chain:
But soon by heaven inspir'd arose the cry,
Freedom or death, unite, unite or die.
Now far and wide a manly spirit reigns,
From Canada to Georgia's sun burnt plains;
Few now insult with falshoods, shameless pen,
Monsters from Tophet driv'n in shapes of men:
Few pension'd scribblers left the daring head,
Some have turn'd lunatics and some have fled—
Some late converted, scarce their pensions hold,
And from mere force disdain the charms of gold.
  What deep offence has fir'd a monarch's rage,
What moonstruck madness seiz'd the brain of Gage?
Laughs not the soul, when an imprison'd few,
Affect to pardon those they can't subdue?
Tho' twice repuls'd and hemm'd up to their stations,
Yet issue pardons, oaths and proclamations,
As if at sea some desperate madman crew
Should threat the tempest with what they could do,
And like proud Xerxes lash the angry waves,
At the same instant that they find their graves.
  But not the pomps and favours of a crown,
A nations anger, or a statesman frown,
Could draw the virtuous man from virtue's way,
To chain by force what treach'ry can't betray,
Virtue disdains to own tyrannic laws,

Takes part with freedom, and assumes its cause,
No part had she, her fiercest forces own,
To bring so far this heavy vengeance on;
She stood with Romans while their hearts were true,
And so she shall, Americans with you.

    Should heaven in wrath decree some nations fall,
Whose crimes from thence for sacred vengeance call,
A monarch first of vulgar soul should rise,
A sure fore-runner of its obsequies,
Whose heart should glow with not one gen'rous thought
Born to oppress, to propagate, and rot,
Whose lengthen'd reign no deed of worth should grace
None trusted but a servile pensioned race;
Too dull to know what saving course to take,
That heaven in time its purpose might forsake,
Too obstinately will'd to bow his ear
To groaning thousands or petitions hear,
Dare break all oaths that bind the just like fate,
Oaths, that th'Arch-Devil would blush to violate,
And foe to truth both oaths and honour fell,
To establish principles, the growth of hell,
Stile those who aim to be his truest friends,
Traitors, insidious rebels, madmen, fiends,
Hoodwink'd and blind, deceived by secret foes,
Whose fathers once with exil'd tyrants rose,
Bless'd with as little sense as God e'er gave,
Slave to wrong schemes, dupe to a noble knave.
So odd a monarch heaven in wrath would plan,
And such would be the fury of a man.

    See far and wide o'er long Canadia's plains,
Old popish fraud and superstition reigns;
The scarlet whore long hath heaven withstood,
Who cries for murder and who thirsts for blood,
Establish'd there, marks down each destined name,
And plants the stake impatient for the flame,
With sanguinary soul her trade begins,
To doom her foes to hell or pardon sins;
Her crafty priests their impious rites maintain,
And crucify their Saviour once again;
Defend his rights, who scatt'ring lies abroad,

With shameless front usurps the seat of God:
Those are, we fear, who his vile cause assert,
But half reform'd and papists at the heart.
  Bear me some power as far as winds can blow,
As ships can travel, or as waves can flow,
To some lone isle beyond the southern pole,
Or lands round which pacific waters roll,
There should oblivion stop the heaving sigh,
There should I live at least with liberty,
But honour checks my speed and bids me stay,
To try the fortune of the well fought day,
Resentment for my country's fate I bear,
And mix with thousands for the willing war;
See Washington New Albion's freedom owns,
And moves to war with half Virginia's sons,
Bold in the fight, whose actions might have aw'd,
A Roman Hero, or a Grecian God,
He, he, as first, his gallant troops shall lead
Undaunted man a second Diomede,
As when he fought at wild Ohio's flood,
When savage thousands issu'd from the wood,
When Braddock's fall disgrac'd the mighty day,
And Death himself stood weeping o'er his prey,
When doubting vict'ry chang'd from side to side,
And Indian soil with Indian blood was dy'd,
When the last charge repuls'd th'invenom'd foe,
And lightnings lit them to the shades below.
  See where from various distant climes unites,
A generous council to protect our rights,
Fix'd on a base too stedfast to be mov'd,
Loving their country, by their country lov'd,
Great guardians of our freedom, we pursue
Each patriot measure as inspir'd by you;
Columbia, nor shall fame deny it owes
Past safety to the counsel you propose,
And if they do not keep Columbia free,
What will alas! become of Liberty?
Great souls grow bolder in their country's cause,
Detest enslavers, and despise their laws,
O Congress fam'd, accept this humbly lay,

The little tribute that the muse can pay,
On you depends Columbia's future fate
A free asylum or a wretched state,
Fall'n on disastrous times we push our plea,
Heard or not heard, and struggle to be free,
Born to contend, our lives we place at stake,
And grow immortal by the stand we make,
　　O you, who far from liberty detain'd,
Wear out existence in some slavish land,
Fly thence from tyrants, and their flatt'ring throng,
And bring the fiery freeborn soul along,
Neptune for you shall smooth the hoary deep,
And awe the wild tumultuous waves to sleep;
Here vernal woods, and flow'ry meadows blow,
Luxuriant harvests in rich plenty grow,
Commerce extends as far as waves can roll
And freedom, God-like freedom crowns the whole.
　　And you brave men who scorn the dread of death,
Resolv'd to conquer to the latest breath,
Soldiers in act, and heroes in renown
Warm in the cause of Boston's hapless town,
Still guard each pass, like ancient Romans, you
At once are soldiers, and are farmers too;
Still arm impatient for the vengeful blow,
And rush intrepid on the yielding foe;
As when of late midst clouds of fire and smoke,
Whole squadrons fell, or to the center shook,
When even the bravest to your arms gave way,
And death exulting, ey'd the unhappy fray,
Behold, your WARREN bleeds, who both inspir'd,
To noble deeds, and by his actions sir'd
What pity heaven!—but you who yet remain
Affect his spirit as you lov'd the man:
Once more, and yet once more for freedom strive,
To be a slave what wretch would dare to live?
We too to the last drop our blood will drain,
And not till then shall hated slavery reign,
When every effort, every hope is o'er,
And lost Columbia swells our breasts no more.
　　O if that day, which heaven avert must come,

And fathers, husbands, children meet their doom
Let one brave onset yet that doom preceed,
To shew the world America can bleed,
One thund'ring raise the midnight cry,
And one last flame send Boston to the sky.
    But cease, foreboding Muse, nor strive to see
Dark times deriv'd by fatal destiny;
If ever Heaven befriended the distrest,
If ever valour succour'd those opprest,
America rejoice, thy standard rear,
Let the loud trumpet animate to war:
Thy guardian Genius haste thee on thy way,
To strike whole hosts with terror and dismay.
    Happy some land, which all for freedom gave,
Happier the men whom their own virtues save;
Thrice happy we who long attacks have stood,
And swam to Liberty thro' seas of blood;
The time shall come when strangers rule no more,
Nor cruel mandates vex from Britain's shore;
When Commerce shall extend her short'ned wing,
And her free freights from every climate bring.
When mighty towns shall flourish free and great,
Vast their dominion, opulent their state;
When one vast cultivated region teems,
From ocean's edge to Mississippi streams;
While each enjoys his vineyard's peaceful shade,
And even the meanest has no cause to dread;
Such is the life our foes with envy see,
Such is the godlike glory to be free.

Libera nos, Domine—Deliver us, O Lord

Written 1775

From a junto that labour for absolute power,
Whose schemes disappointed have made them look sowr,
From the lords of the council, who fight against freedom,
Who still follow on where the devil shall lead 'em.

From the group at St. James's, that slight our Petitions,
And fools that are waiting for further submissions—
From a nation whose manners are rough and abrupt,
From scoundrels and rascals whom gold can corrupt.

From pirates sent out by command of the king
To murder and plunder, but never to swing.
From *Wallace* and *Greaves*, and *Vipers* and *Roses**,
Whom, if heaven pleases, we'll give bloody noses.

From the valiant Dunmore, with his crew of banditti,
Who plunder Virginians at Williamsburg city,
From hot-headed Montague, mighty to swear,
The little fat man with his pretty white hair.

From bishops in Britain, who butchers are grown,
From slaves that would die for a smile from the throne,
From assemblies that vote against Congress proceedings,
(Who now see the fruit of their stupid misleadings).

From Tryon the mighty, who flies from our city,
And, swell'd with importance, disdains the committee;
(But since he is pleas'd to proclaim us his foes,
What the devil care we where the devil he goes).

From the scoundrel, lord *North*, who would bind us in chains,
From a dunce of a king who was born without brains,
The utmost extent of whose sense is to see
That reigning and making of buttons agree.

*Captains and Ships of the British navy then employed on our coasts.

From an island that bullies, and hectors, and swears,
I send up to heaven my wishes and prayers
That we, disunited, may freemen be still,
And Britain go on——to be damn'd, if she will.

Female Frailty

Written November 1775.

DAMON—LUCINDA—THYRSIS.

Damon.

In vain you talk of shady bowers
When frosts, my fair one, chill the plain
And nights are cold, and long the hours
That damp the ardour of the swain,
Who, parting from his social fire,
All comfort doth forego,
And here and there, and every where,
Pursues the invading foe.

But we must sleep on frosts and snows,
No season hinders our campaign,
Hard as the oaks, we dare oppose
The autumnal or the wint'ry reign:
Alike to us the winds that blow
In summer's season gay,
Or those that rave on Hudson's cave,
And drift his ice away.

Winter and *death* may change the scene,
The ball may pierce, the cold may kill,
And dire misfortunes intervene,
But Freedom shall be potent still
To drive these Britons from our shore,
Who, cruel and unkind,
With slavish chain shall strive, in vain,
Our freeborn hearts to bind.

*

Lucinda.

They chide me, and tell me I must not complain
To part a few days with my favourite swain—
He is gone to the battle, and leaves me to mourn,
And, say what you please, he will never return.

When he left me, he kiss'd me, and said, "My sweet dear,
In less than a month I again will be here."—
With anguish and sorrow my bosom did burn,
And I wept, being sure he would never return.

I said, My dear creature, I beg you would stay—
But he, with his soldiers, went strutting away!
Then why should I longer my sorrows adjourn?—
You may call me a fool if he ever return.

Thyrsis.

Sweetest of the virgin train,
You must seek another swain,
Damon will not come again—
    All his toils are over!
As you lov'd him to excess,
Your loss is great, I must confess;
But, madam, yield not to distress—
    I will be your lover.

Lucinda.

Not all the swains the world can show
Can from this bosom drive this woe,
Or bid another passion glow
    Where Damon has possession.
Not all the gifts that wealth can bring,
Not all the airs that you can sing,
Nor all the musick of that string
    Can banish his impression.

Thyrsis.

Marriage and *Death* forever prove
Destructive to the flames of love,
With equal strength they both combine

Hearts once united to disjoin;
Hence mutual loves so soon remit,
Hence die the fires that Cupid lit.

Female tears and April snow
Sudden come and sudden go—
Since his head is levell'd low
Cease the memory of your woe.
Never yet was reason found
So distracted with love's wound
As to be in sorrow drown'd
For a lover under ground.

Lucinda.
What a picture have I seen!—
What can all these visions mean!—
Winter groves and empty halls,
Coffins wrapt in velvet palls,
Monuments and funerals;
Forms terrific to the sight,
Weeping phantoms clad in white,
Streams that ever seem'd to freeze
Planted round with cypress trees
Ever drooping—never green—
What a vision have I seen!—

One I saw of angel kind,
From the dregs of life refin'd,
All in beams of light array'd,
And thus the gentle spirit said—
"Fair Lucinda, come to me:
What has grief to do with thee?
O forsake that joyless shore,
Shrouded all with darkness o'er—
Could you but a moment stray
In the meadows where I play,
You would beg to come away—
Come away! and speed thy flight,
All with me is endless light."

Thyrsis.

You have not yet forgot your glooms,
The heavy heart, the downcast eye,
The cheek that no gay smile assumes,
    The breast that heaves a sigh.

Lucinda.

Had you the secret cause to grieve
That in this breast doth lie,
Instead of wishing to relieve,
You would be just as I.

Thyrsis.

What secret cause have you to grieve—
A lover gone away?—
If one was able to deceive,
Perhaps another may.

Lucinda.

My lover has not me deceiv'd,
A part he would disdain—
But he is gone—and I am griev'd—
    He'll never come again—
    He'll never come again!

Thyrsis.

The turtle on yon' wither'd bough,
That lately mourn'd her murder'd mate,
Has found another comrade now—
Such changes all await!
Again her drooping plume is drest,
Again she's willing to be blest,
And takes her lover to her nest.

If nature has decreed it so
With all above, and all below,
Let us, like them, forget our woe,
    And not be kill'd with sorrow.
If I should quit your arms to-night
And chance to die before 'twas light,
I would advise you—and you might
    Love again to-morrow.

Lucinda.

The turtle on yon' wither'd tree!
That turtle never felt like me—
Her grief is but a moment's date;
Another day another mate—
Besides, observe, the feather'd race
Hold a new lover no disgrace—
How would the world my guilt display!
What would censorious *Chloe* say—
Would say—while laughing folly hears—
"She made a conquest by her tears."

Thyrsis.

My Polly—once the pride of all
That shepherd lads their charmers call—
Too early parted with her bloom,
And sleeps in yonder furzy tomb—!
    Her fate has set me free—
Fair as the day, and sweet as May,
    But what is that to me!
    Since all must bow to death's arrest,
    No love deceas'd shall rack my breast—
    Come, then, Lucinda, and be blest.

Lucinda.

My Damon O!—can I forget
The day you left these longing eyes
O'er northern lakes to wander far
To colder climes, and darker skies!—
There, shrouded in his wastes of snow,
The *Briton* guards the icy shore,
And there my Damon wanders now—
The swain that shall return no more!

Thyrsis.

Weep, weep no more, my lovely lass—
The pang is o'er that fix'd his doom—
They too shall to destruction pass,
Nor find a triumph in a tomb.—
Ah! dry these tears—enough are shed—

They too shall have their hour of woe;
Fled is their fame—their honours fled—
For WASHINGTON shall lay them low.

Lucinda.

If you had once a soldier's guise,
The splendid coat, the sprightly air,
You might seem charming in these eyes,
   Nor would I quite despair.

There's something in your face, I find
Recalling Damon to my mind—
He's dead—but I must be resign'd!

His handsome shape, his manly face,
His youthful step in you I trace—
All, all I wish for, but the *lace.*

Thyrsis.

For you I would forego my ease,
And traverse lakes, or ravage seas,
And dress in lace, or what you please.

This enchanting month of May,
So bright, so bloomy, and so gay,
Claims our nuptials on this day.

For her vernal triumphs, we
Tune the harp to symphony—
Conquest has attended me!

Brightest season for the mind,
Vigorous, free, and unconfin'd,
Golden age of human kind.

Still at variance with thy charms
Death's eternal empire stands.
Hymen, come—while rapture warms,
And give Lucinda to my arms.

Stanzas Occasioned by
the Ruins of a Country Inn

unroofed and blown down in a Storm

Where now these mingled ruins ly
    A temple once to Bacchus rose,
Beneath whose roof, aspiring high,
    Full many a guest forgot his woes;

No more this dome, by tempests torn,
    Affords a social safe retreat;
But ravens here, with eye forlorn,
    And clustering batts henceforth shall meet.

The Priestess of this ruin'd shrine,
    Unable to survive the stroke,
Presents no more the ruddy wine,
    Her glasses gone, her china broke.

The friendly Host, whose social hand
    Accosted strangers at the door,
Has left at length his wonted stand,
    And greets the weary guest no more.

Old creeping time, that brings decay,
    Might yet have spar'd these mouldering walls,
Alike beneath whose potent sway
    A *temple* or a *tavern* falls.

Is this the place where mirth and joy,
    Coy nymphs and sprightly lads were found?
Alas! no more the nymphs are coy,
    No more the flowing bowls go round.

Is this the place where festive song
    Deceiv'd the wint'ry hours away?
No more the swains the tune prolong,
    No more the maidens join the lays.

Is this the place where Chloe slept
   In downy beds of blue and green?
Dame Nature here no vigils kept,
   No cold unfeeling guards were seen.

'Tis gone!—and Chloe tempts no more,
   Deep, unrelenting silence reigns;
Of all that pleas'd, that charm'd before,
   The tott'ring chimney scarce remains!

Ye tyrant winds! whose ruffian blast
   From locks and hinges rent the door,
And all the roof to ruin cast,
   The roof that shelter'd us before,

Your wrath appeas'd, I pray be kind
   If Mopsus should the dome renew;
That we again may quaff his wine,
   Again collect our jovial crew.

The Dying Indian

or Last Words of Shalum

March, 1784.
Debemur morti nos, nostraque.

"On yonder lake I spread the sail no more!
 Vigour, and youth, and active days are past—
 Relentless demons urge me to that shore
 On whose black forests all the dead are cast:
 Ye solemn train, prepare the funeral song,
 For I must go to shades below,
 Where all is strange, and all is new;
 Companion to the airy throng,
    What solitary streams,
    In dull and dreary dreams,
  All melancholy, must I rove along!

To what strange lands must Shalum take his way!
Groves of the dead departed mortals trace;
No deer along these gloomy forests stray,
No huntsmen there take pleasure in the chace,
But all are empty unsubstantial shades,
That ramble through those visionary glades;
   No spongy fruits from verdant trees depend,
     But sickly orchards there
     Do fruits as sickly bear,
And apples a consumptive visage shew,
And wither'd hangs the hurtle-berry blue,
   Ah me! what mischiefs on the dead attend.

Wandering a stranger to the shores below,
Where shall I brook or real fountain find?
Lazy and sad deluding waters flow—
Such is the picture in my boding mind!
     Fine tales, indeed, they tell
     Of shades and purling rills,
     Where our dead fathers dwell
     Beyond the western hills,
But when did ghost return his state to shew;
Or who can promise half the tale is true?

I too must be a fleeting ghost—no more—
None, none but shadows to those mansions go;
I leave my woods, I leave the Huron shore,
     For emptier groves below!
     Ye charming solitudes,
     Ye tall ascending woods,
Ye glassy lakes and prattling streams,
     Whose aspect still was sweet,
     Whether the sun did greet,
Or the pale moon embrac'd you with his beams—
     Adieu to all!
To all that charm'd me where I stray'd,
The winding stream, the dark sequester'd shade;
     Adieu all triumphs here!
   Adieu the mountain's lofty swell,
   Adieu, thou little verdant hill,

And seas, and stars, and skies—farewell,
    For some remoter sphere!

Perplex'd with doubts, and tortur'd with despair,
Why so dejected at this hopeless sleep?
Nature at least these ruins may repair,
When death's long dream is o'er, and she forgets to weep;
Some real world once more may be assign'd,
Some new born mansion for the immortal mind!—
Farewell, sweet lake; farewell surrounding woods,
To other groves through midnight glooms I stray,
Beyond the mountains, and beyond the floods,
    Beyond the Huron bay!
Prepare the hollow tomb, and place me low,
My trusty bow, and arrows by my side,
The cheerful bottle, and the ven'son store;
For long the journey is that I must go,
Without a partner, and without a guide."

He spoke, and bid the attending mourners weep;
Then clos'd his eyes, and sunk to endless sleep.

The Wild Honey Suckle

Fair flower, that dost so comely grow,
Hid in this silent dull retreat,
Untouch'd thy honey'd blossoms blow,
Unseen thy little branches greet:
    No roving foot shall find thee here,
    No busy hand provoke a tear.

By Nature's self in white array'd,
She bade thee shun the vulgar eye,
And planted here the guardian shade,
And sent soft waters murmuring by;
    Thus quietly thy summer goes,
    Thy days declining to repose.

Smit with these charms, that must decay,
I grieve to see thy future doom;
They died—nor were those flowers less gay,
(The flowers that did in Eden bloom)
    Unpitying frosts, and Autumn's power
    Shall leave no vestige of this flower.

From morning suns and evening dews
At first, thy little being came:
If nothing once, you nothing lose,
For when you die you are the same;
    The space between is but an hour,
    The mere idea of a flower.

The Indian Student

or, Force of Nature

Rura mihi et requi placeant in vallibus amnes;
Flumina amem, sylvasque inglorius.—
                VIRG. GEORG. II. V. 483.

From Susquehanna's utmost springs
Where savage tribes pursue their game,
His blanket tied with yellow strings,
A shepherd of the forest came.

Not long before, a wandering priest
Express'd his wish, with visage sad—
"Ah, why (he cry'd) in Satan's waste,
Ah, why detain so fine a lad?

In Yanky land there stands a town
Where learning may be purchas'd low—
Exchange his blanket for a gown,
And let the lad to college go."—

From long debate the Council rose,
And viewing *Shalum's* tricks with joy,

To *Havard hall*,* o'er wastes of snows,
They sent the copper-colour'd boy.

One generous chief a bow supply'd,
This gave a shaft, and that a skin;
The feathers, in vermillion dy'd,
Himself did from a turkey win:

Thus dress'd so gay, he took his way
O'er barren hills, alone, alone!
His guide a star, he wander'd far,
His pillow every night a stone.

At last he came, with leg so lame,
Where learned men talk heathen Greek,
And Hebrew lore is gabbled o'er,
To please the Muses, twice a week.

Awhile he writ, awhile he read,
Awhile he learn'd the grammar rules—
An Indian savage so well bred
Great credit promis'd to their schools.

Some thought he would in *law* excel,
Some said in *physic* he would shine;
And one that knew him, passing well,
Beheld, in him, a sound divine.

But those of more discerning eye
Even then could other prospects show,
And saw him lay his *Virgil* by
To wander with his dearer *bow*.

The tedious hours of study spent,
The heavy-moulded lecture done,
He to the woods a hunting went,
But sigh'd to see the setting sun.

*Harvard College, at Cambridge in Massachusetts.

No mystic wonders fir'd his mind;
He fought to gain no learn'd degree,
But only sense enough to find
The squirrel in the hollow tree.

The shady bank, the purling stream,
The woody wild his heart possess'd,
The dewy lawn, his morning dream
In Fancy's gayest colours dress'd.

"And why (he cry'd) did I forsake
My native wood for gloomy walls;
The silver stream, the limpid lake
For musty books and college halls.

A little could my wants supply—
Can wealth and honour give me more;
Or, will the sylvan god deny
The humble treat he gave before?

Let Seraphs reach the bright abode,
And heaven's sublimest mansions see—
I only bow to NATURE'S GOD—
The Land of Shades will do for me.

These dreadful secrets of the sky
Alarm my soul with chilling fear—
Do planets in their orbits fly,
And is the earth, indeed, a sphere?

Let planets still their aims pursue,
And comets round creation run—
In HIM my faithful friend I view,
The image of my God—the Sun.

Where Nature's ancient forests grow,
And mingled laurel never fades,
My heart is fix'd;—and I must go
To die among my native shades."

He spoke, and to the western springs,
(His gown discharg'd, his money spent)
His blanket tied with yellow strings,
The shepherd of the forest went.

Returning to the rural reign
The Indians welcom'd him with joy;
The council took him home again,
And bless'd the copper-colour'd boy.

Lines occasioned by a Visit
to an old Indian Burying Ground

In spite of all the learn'd have said
I still my old opinion keep;
The *posture* that *we* give the dead
Points out the soul's eternal sleep.

Not so the ancients of these lands;—
The Indian, when from life releas'd,
Again is *seated* with his friends,
And shares again the joyous feast.

His imag'd birds, and painted bowl,
And ven'son, for a journey drest,
Bespeak the *nature* of the soul,
Activity, that wants no rest.

His bow for action ready bent,
And arrows, with a head of bone,
Can only mean that life is spent,
And not the finer essence gone.

Thou, stranger, that shalt come this way,
No fraud upon the dead commit,
Yet, mark the swelling turf, and say,
They do not *lie*, but here they *sit*.

Here, still a lofty rock remains,
On which the curious eye may trace
(Now wasted half by wearing rains)
The fancies of a ruder race.

Here, still an aged elm aspires,
Beneath whose far projecting shade
(And which the shepherd still admires)
The children of the forest play'd.

There oft a restless Indian queen,
(Pale Marian with her braided hair)
And many a barbarous form is seen
To chide the man that lingers there.

By midnight moons, o'er moistening dews,
In vestments for the chace array'd,
The hunter still the deer pursues,
The hunter and the deer—a shade.

And long shall timorous Fancy see
The painted chief, and pointed spear,
And *reason's self* shall bow the knee
To shadows and delusions here.

The Country Printer

I.

(*Description of his Village.*)
Beside a stream, that never yet ran dry,
There stands a TOWN, not high advanced in fame;
Tho' few its buildings rais'd to please the eye,
Still this proud title it may fairly claim;
A *Tavern* (its first requisite) is there,
A *mill*, a *black-smith's shop, a place of prayer.*

Nay, more—a little market-house is seen
And iron hooks, where beef was never hung,
Nor pork, nor bacon, poultry fat or lean,
Pig's head, or sausage link, or bullock's tongue.
Look when you will, you see the vacant bench
No butcher seated there, no country wench.

Great aims were his, who first contriv'd this town;
A market he would have—but, humbled now,
Sighing, we see its fabric mouldering down,
That only serves, at night, to pen the cow:
And hence, by way of jest, it may be said
That beef is there, tho' never beef that's dead.

Abreast the inn—a tree before the door,
A Printing-Office lifts its humble head
Where busy *Type* old journals doth explore
For news that is thro' all the village read;
Who, year from year, (so cruel is his lot)
Is author, pressman, devil—and what not?

Fame says he is an odd and curious wight,
Fond to distraction of this native place;
In sense, not very dull nor very bright,
Yet shews some marks of humour in his face,
One who can pen an anecdote, complete,
Or plague the parson with the mackled sheet.

Three times a week, by nimble geldings drawn
A stage arrives; but scarcely deigns to stop,
Unless the driver, far in liquor gone,
Has made some business for the black-smith-shop;
Then comes this printer's harvest-time of news,
Welcome alike from Christians, Turks, or Jews.

Each passenger he eyes with curious glance,
And, if his phiz be mark'd of courteous kind,
To conversation, straight, he makes advance,

Hoping, from thence, some paragraph to find,
Some odd adventure, something new and rare,
To set the town a-gape, and make it stare.

II.

All is not *Truth* ('tis said) that travellers tell—
So much the better for this man of news;
For hence the country round, that know him well,
Will, if he prints some lies, his lies excuse.
Earthquakes, and battles, shipwrecks, myriads slain—
If false or true—alike to him are gain.

But if this motley tribe say nothing new,
Then many a lazy, longing look is cast
To watch the weary post-boy travelling through,
On horse's rump his budget buckled fast;
With letters, safe in leathern prison pent,
And, wet from press, full many a packet sent.

Not Argus with his fifty pair of eyes
Look'd sharper for his prey than honest TYPE
Explores each package, of alluring size,
Prepar'd to seize them with a nimble gripe,
Did not the post-boy watch his goods, and swear
That village TYPE shall only have his share.

Ask you what *matter* fills his various page?
A mere *farrago* 'tis, of mingled things;
Whate'er is done on madam TERRA's stage
He to the knowledge of his townsmen brings:
One while, he tells of monarchs run away;
And now, of witches drown'd in Buzzard's bay.

Some miracles he makes, and some he steals;
Half Nature's works are giants in his eyes:
Much, very much, in wonderment he deals,—
New Hampshire apples grown to pumpkin size,
Pumpkins almost as large as country inns,
And ladies bearing, each,—three lovely twins.

He, births and deaths with cold indifference views;
A paragraph from him is all they claim:
And here the rural squire, amongst the news
Sees the fair record of some lordling's fame;
All that was good, minutely brought to light,
All that was ill,—conceal'd from vulgar sight!

III.

The Office.

Source of the wisdom of the country round!
Again I turn to that poor lonely *shed*
Where many an author all his fame has found,
And wretched *proofs* by candle-light are read,
Inverted letters, left the page to grace,
Colons derang'd, and *commas* out of place.

Beneath this roof the Muses chose their home;—
Sad was their choice, less bookish ladies say.
Since from the blessed bour they deign'd to come
One single cob-web was not brush'd away:—
Fate early had pronounc'd this building's doom,
Ne'er to be vex'd with boonder, brush, or broom.

Here, full in view, the ink-bespangled press
Gives to the world its children, with a groan,
Some born to live a month—a day—some less;
Some, why they live at all, not clearly known,
All that are born must die—Type well knows that—
The *Almanack's* his longest-living brat.

Here lie the types, in curious order rang'd
Ready alike to imprint your prose or verse;
Ready to speak (their order only chang'd)
Creek-Indian lingo, Dutch, or Highland erse;
These types have printed Erskine's *Gospel Treat*,
Tom Durfey's songs, and Bunyan's works, complete.

But faded are their charms—their beauty fled!
No more their work your nicer eyes admire;
Hence, from this press no *courtly* stuff is read;
But almanacks, and ballads for the Squire,
Dull paragraphs, in homely language dress'd,
The pedlar's bill, and sermons by request.

Here, doom'd the fortune of the press to try,
From year to year poor TYPE his trade pursues—
With anxious care and circumspective eye
He dresses out his little sheet of news;
Now laughing at the world, now looking grave,
At once the Muse's midwife—and her slave.

In by-past years, perplext with vast designs,
In cities fair he strove to gain a seat;
But, wandering to a wood of many pines,
In solitude he found his best retreat,
When sick of towns, and sorrowful at heart,
He to those deserts brought his favorite art.

IV.

Thou, who art plac'd in some more favour'd spot,
Where spires ascend, and ships from every clime
Discharge their freights—despise not thou the lot
Of humble TYPE, who here has pass'd his prime;
At *case* and *press* has labour'd many a day,
But now, in years, is verging to decay.

He, in his time, the patriot of his town,
With press and pen attack'd the royal side,
Did what he could to pull their Lion down,
Clipp'd at his beard, and twitch'd his *sacred* hide,
Mimick'd his roarings, trod upon his toes,
Pelted young *whelps*, and tweak'd the old one's nose.

Rous'd by his page, at church or court-house read,
From depths of woods the willing rustics ran,
Now by a priest, and now some deacon led

With clubs and spits to guard the rights of man;
Lads from the spade, the pick-ax, or the plough
Marching afar, to fight *Burgoyne* or *Howe*.

Where are they now?—the Village asks with grief,
What were their toils, their conquests, or their gains?—
Perhaps, they near some State-House beg relief,
Perhaps, they sleep on Saratoga's plains;
Doom'd not to live, their country to reproach
For seven-years' pay transferr'd to Mammon's coach.

Ye *Guardians* of your country and her laws!
Since to the pen and press so much we owe
Still bid them favour freedom's sacred cause,
From this pure source, let streams unsullied flow;
Hence, a new order grows on reason's plan,
And turns the fierce barbarian into—man.

Child of the earth, of rude materials fram'd,
Man, always found a tyrant or a slave,
Fond to be honour'd, valued, rich, or fam'd
Roves o'er the earth, and subjugates the wave:
Despots and kings this restless race may share,—
But knowledge only makes them worth *your* care!

To Sir Toby,

a Sugar-Planter in the interior parts of Jamaica

If there exists a HELL—the case is clear—
Sir Toby's slaves enjoy that portion here:
Here are no blazing brimstone lakes—'tis true,
But kindled RUM full often burns as blue,*
In which some fiend (whom NATURE must detest)
Steeps TOBY's name, and brands poor CUDJOE's breast.
      Here, whips on whips excite a thousand fears,
And mingled howlings vibrate on my ears:

*This passage has a reference to the custom of branding the slaves in the is-
lands, as a mark of property.—

Here Nature's plagues abound, of all degrees,
Snakes, scorpions, despots, lizards, centipees—
No art, no care escapes the busy lash,
All have their dues, and all are paid in cash:
The lengthy cart-whip guards this tyrant's reign,
And cracks like pistols from the fields of CANE.
    Ye POWERS that form'd these wretched tribes, relate,
What had they done, to merit such a fate?
Why were they brought from EBOE's sultry waste
To see the plenty which they must not taste—
Food, which they cannot buy, and dare not steal,
Yams and potatoes!—many a scanty meal!
One, with a jibbet wakes his negro's fears,
One, to the wind-mill nails him by the ears;
One keeps his slave in dismal dens, unfed,
One puts the wretch in pickle, ere he's dead;
This, from a tree suspends him by the thumbs,
That, from his table grudges even the crumbs!
    O'er yon' rough hills a tribe of females go,
Each with her gourd, her infant, and her hoe,
Scorch'd by a sun, that has no mercy here,
Driven by a devil, that men call Overseer:
In chains twelve wretches to their labour haste,
Twice twelve I see with iron collars grac'd:—
Are these the joys that flow from vast domains!
Is wealth thus got, Sir Toby, worth your pains—
Who would that wealth, on terms like these, possess,
Where all we see is pregnant with distress;
ANGOLA's natives scourg'd by hireling hands,
And toil's hard earnings shipp'd to foreign lands?
    Talk not of blossoms and your endless spring—
No joys, no smiles, such scenes of misery bring!
Though Nature here has every blessing spread,
Poor is the labourer—and how meanly fed!
Here, Stygian paintings all their shades renew,
Pictures of woe, that VIRGIL's pencil drew:
Here, surly Charons make their annual trip,
And souls arrive in every Guinea ship
To find what hells this western world affords,
Plutonian scourges, and Tartarian lords;—

Where they who pine, and languish to be free
Must climb the tall cliffs of the LIGUANEE,
Beyond the clouds in sculking haste repair,
And hardly safe from brother butchers there!*

To Mr. Blanchard

*The celebrated Æronaut: on his ascent in a Balloon,
from the jail-yard in Philadelphia: 1793.*

By Science taught, on silken wings
Beyond our grovelling race you rise,
And, soaring from terrestrial things,
Explore a passage to the skies—
O, could I thus exalted sail,
And rise, with you, beyond the JAIL!

Ah! when you rose, impell'd by fear
Each bosom heav'd a thousand sighs;
To you each female lent a tear,
And held the 'kerchief to her eyes:
All hearts still follow'd, as you flew,
All eyes admir'd a sight so new.

Whoe'er shall thus presume to fly,
While downward with disdain they look
Shall own this journey, through the sky,
The *dearest* jaunt they ever took;
And choose, next time, without reproach,
A humbler seat in INSKEEP'S coach.

The birds, that cleave the expanse of air,
Admiring, view your globe full-blown,
And, chattering round the painted car,
Complain your flight out-does their own:
Beyond their track you proudly swim,
Nor fear the loss of life or limb.

*Alluding to the independent Negroes in the Blue-Mountains; who, for a
stipulated reward deliver up every fugitive that falls into their hands.

How vast the height, how grand the scene
That your enraptured eye surveys,
When, towering in your gay machine,
You leave the astonish'd world to gaze,
And, wandering in the ætherial blue,
Our eyes, in vain, your course pursue.

The ORB OF DAY, how dazzling bright!
In paler radiance gleams the MOON,
And TERRA, whence you took your flight,
Appears to you—a meer balloon:
Its noisy crew no longer heard,
Towns, cities, forests, disappear'd.

Yet, travelling through the azure road,
Soar not too high for human ken;
Reflect, our humble safe abode
Is all that Nature meant for men:
Take in your sails before you freeze,
And sink again among the trees.

The Republican Genius of Europe

Emperors and kings! in vain you strive
    Your torments to conceal—
The age is come that shakes your thrones,
Tramples in dust despotic crowns,
    And bids the sceptre fail,

In western worlds the flame began:
    From thence to France it flew—
Through Europe, now, it takes its way,
Beams an insufferable day,
    And lays all tyrants low.

GENIUS of France! pursue the chace
    Till REASON'S laws restore
Man to be MAN, in every clime;—
That BEING, active, great, sublime
    Debas'd in dust no more.

In dreadful pomp he takes his way
O'er ruin'd crowns, demolish'd thrones—
Pale tyrants shrink before his blaze—
Round him terrific lightnings play—
With eyes of fire, he looks them through,
Crushes the vile despotic crew,
    And Pride in ruin lays.

On a Honey Bee, Drinking from a Glass of Wine, and Drowned Therein

Thou, born to sip the lake or spring,
Or quaff the waters of the stream,
Why hither come on vagrant wing?—
Does Bacchus tempting seem—
Did he, for you, this glass prepare?—
Will I admit you to a share?

Did storms harrass or foes perplex,
Did wasps or king-birds bring dismay—
Did wars distress, or labours vex,
Or did you miss your way?—
A better seat you could not take
Than on the margin of this lake.

Welcome!—I hail you to my glass:
All welcome, here, you find;
Here, let the cloud of trouble pass,
Here, be all care resigned.—
This fluid never fails to please,
And drown the griefs of men or bees.

What forced you here, we cannot know,
And you will scarcely tell—
But cheery we would have you go
And bid a glad farewell:
On lighter wings we bid you fly,
Your dart will now all foes defy.

Yet take not, oh! too deep a drink,
And in this ocean die;
Here bigger bees than you might sink,
Even bees full six feet high.
Like Pharaoh, then, you would be said
To perish in a sea of red.

Do as you please, your will is mine;
Enjoy it without fear—
And your grave will be this glass of wine,
Your epitaph—a tear—
Go, take your seat in Charon's boat,
We'll tell the hive, you died afloat.

DAVID HUMPHREYS

(1752–1818)

Mount Vernon: An Ode

By broad Potowmack's azure tide,
Where Vernon's mount, in sylvan pride,
   Displays its beauties far,
Great Washington, to peaceful shades,
Where no unhallow'd wish invades,
   Retir'd from fields of war.

Angels might see, with joy, the sage,
Who taught the battle where to rage,
   Or quench'd its spreading flame,
On works of peace employ that hand,
Which wav'd the blade of high command,
   And hew'd the path to fame.

Let others sing his deeds in arms,
A nation sav'd, and conquest's charms:
   Posterity shall hear,
'Twas mine, return'd from Europe's courts,
To share his thoughts, partake his sports,
   And sooth his partial ear.

To thee, my friend, these lays belong:
Thy happy seat inspires my song,
   With gay, perennial blooms,
With fruitage fair, and cool retreats,
Whose bow'ry wilderness of sweets
   The ambient air perfumes.

Here spring its earliest buds displays,
Here latest on the leafless sprays,
   The plumy people sing;
The vernal show'r, the rip'ning year,
Th' autumnal store, the winter drear,
   For thee new pleasures bring.

Here lapp'd in philosophic ease,
Within thy walks, beneath thy trees,
   Amidst thine ample farms,
No vulgar converse heroes hold,
But past or future scenes unfold,
   Or dwell on nature's charms.

What wond'rous era have we seen,
Plac'd on this isthmus, half between
   A rude and polish'd state!
We saw the war tempestuous rise,
In arms a world, in blood the skies,
   In doubt an empire's fate.

The storm is calm'd, seren'd the heav'n,
And mildly o'er the climes of ev'n
   Expands th' imperial day:
"O God, the source of light supreme,
Shed on our dusky morn a gleam,
   To guide our doubtful way!

Restrain, dread pow'r, our land from crimes!
What seeks, tho' blest beyond all times,
   So querulous an age?
What means to freedom such disgust,
Of change, of anarchy the lust,
   The fickleness and rage?"

So spake his country's friend, with sighs,
To find that country still despise
   The legacy he gave—
And half he fear'd his toils were vain,
And much that man would court a chain,
   And live through vice a slave.

A transient gloom o'ercast his mind:
Yet, still on providence reclin'd,
   The patriot fond believ'd,
That pow'r benign too much had done,
To leave an empire's task begun,
   Imperfectly achiev'd.

Thus buoy'd with hope, with virtue blest,
Of ev'ry human bliss possest,
   He meets the happier hours;
His skies assume a lovelier blue,
His prospects brighter rise to view,
   And fairer bloom his flow'rs.

The Genius of America

A song.—Tune, the watry god, &c.

Where spirits dwell and shad'wy forms,
On Andes' cliffs mid black'ning storms,
   With livid lightnings curl'd:
The awful genius of our clime,
In thunder rais'd his voice sublime,
   And hush'd the list'ning world.

"In lonely waves and wastes of earth,
A mighty empire claims its birth,
   And heav'n asserts the claim;
The sails that hang in yon dim sky,
Proclaim the promis'd era nigh,
   Which wakes a world to fame.

Hail ye first bounding barks that roam,
Blue-tumbling billows topp'd with foam,
   Which keel ne'er plough'd before!
Here suns perform their useless round,
Here rove the naked tribes embrown'd,
   Who feed on living gore.

To midnight orgies, off'ring dire,
The human sacrifice on fire,
   A heav'nly light succeeds—
But, lo! what horrors intervene,
The toils severe, the carnag'd scene,
   And more than mortal deeds!

Ye FATHERS, spread your fame afar,
'Tis yours to still the sounds of war,
   And bid the slaughter cease;
The peopling hamlets wide extend,
The harvests spring, the spires ascend,
   Mid grateful songs of peace.

Shall steed to steed, and man to man,
With discord thund'ring in the van,
   Again destroy the bliss?
Enough my mystic words reveal,
The rest the shades of night conceal,
   In fate's profound abyss."

The Monkey, Who Shaved Himself and His Friends

A fable.—Addressed to the hon.—— ——

A Man who own'd a barber's shop
At York, and shav'd full many a fop,
A monkey kept for their amusement;
He made no other kind of use on't—
This monkey took great observation,
Was wonderful at imitation,
And all he saw the barber do,
He mimick'd strait, and did it too.

   It chanc'd in shop, the dog and cat,
While friseur din'd, demurely sat,
Jacko found nought to play the knave in,
So thought he'd try his hand at shaving.
Around the shop in haste he rushes,
And gets the razors, soap, and brushes;
Now puss he fix'd (no muscle miss stirs)
And lather'd well her beard and whiskers,
Then gave a gash, as he began—
The cat cried waugh! and off she ran.

Next towser's beard he tried his skill in,
Tho' towser seem'd somewhat unwilling:
As badly here again succeeding,
The dog runs howling round and bleeding.

Nor yet was tir'd our roguish elf,
He'd seen the barber shave himself;
So by the glass, upon the table,
He rubs with soap his visage sable,
Then with left-hand hold smooth his jaw,—
The razor, in his dexter paw;
Around he flourishes and slashes,
Till all his face is seam'd with gashes.
His cheeks dispatch'd—his visage thin
He cock'd, to shave beneath his chin;
Drew razor swift as he could pull it,
And cut, from ear to ear, his gullet.

MORAL
Who cannot write, yet handle pens,
Are apt to hurt themselves and friends.
Tho' others use them well, yet fools
Should never meddle with edge tools.

ST. GEORGE TUCKER

(1752–1827)

A Dream on Bridecake

Dear girls, since you the task impose
Of scribbling rhyme, or humbler prose,
Whene'er the bridecake fills the brain
With emblematic dreams of pain,
Or pleasure to be had hereafter,
Or, whatso'er can move your laughter,
The swain to you devoted ever
Will every try his best endeavor,
To tell you in his doggerel strain,
What fancies visited his brain.

   Brimful of claret wine and perry,
You know I went to bed quite merry,
But, as I soon grew wonderous sick,
I wished my carcass at Old Nick.
At length, I sunk into a nap,
With head reclined in fancy's lap;
She rubbed my temples, chaffed my brain,
And then displayed this scene of pain.

   Methought, the claret I'd been drinking
So far from giving aid to thinking,
Had muddled my idea-box,
And clapped my body in the stocks.
Beneath a beach's spreading shade
At lubber's length my limbs were laid;
My tongue alone had power to move,
To rest in vain might wish to rove:
Just then, my Flora passing by
This pretty object chanced to spy;
The wanton saw my hapless case,
And clapped me in a warm embrace;
Her balmy lips to mine she pressed,
And leaned her bosom on my breast,
Her fingers everywhere were gadding,

And set my soul a madding;
Whilst I, in vain, resistance made,
Still on my back supinely laid.
She whispered something in my ear
Which I could not distinctly hear:
Then cried, "Pray when will you be sober?"
"My dear," said I, "not till October.
My nerves I find are all unstrung
Except the one that rules my tongue;
Their wonted tones so wholly lost
I shan't recover till a frost."
Away the wanton baggage flew
Laughing like any one of you
And left me in that sordid plight,
To mourn the follies of the night.

Sept. 19, 1777

A Second Dream on Bridecake

Well—sure no mortal e'er was cursed
With dreams like mine—for they're the worst
That ever visited a sinner,
E'en after fat turtle dinner,
And six good bottles to defend him
From evils that might else attend him.
    Methought, I turned a mighty rover
Resolved new countries to discover,
And having travelled all around
The globe, a desert isle I found,
Where witches with their train resort
To amuse themselves with magic sport.
    As soon as I set foot on land,
And, in an instant—think how shocking,
Turned me into a white silk stocking,
Then wrapped me up among a dozen
Which she was carrying to a cousin.
Thru' various stores and shops I past,

But got to Williamsburg at last,
Where Flora, to the country gadding
Resolved to buy me for a wedding:
My fate I thought was much improved,
For Flora was the maid I loved;
But, little dreamed of pains in store,
Such as ne'er mortal felt before.
The wedding day at length was come,
The girls retired to a room,
Where first they dizzen out the bride,
That done—they for themselves provide.
My Flora laid me on the bed
Whilst she was dressing out her head;
And little thinking who was near,
She laid her snowy bosom bare,
Then wiped her ivory neck and breast,
And then proceeded with the rest.

But now, began the dreadful part,
Which plunged a dagger in my heart;
She thrust her hand into my throat,
And quickly turned me, inside out;
Then raised her pretty little foot,
And finding that my mouth would suit,
She drew me quickly on her heel,
Which made my very vitals feel.
But, here methinks I shall disclose
The beauty of her foot and toes;
Her foot and toes were alabaster
And whiter, far, than Paris plaster;
Of mother-pearl I thought her nails
Or else, the silverfish's scales.
She tried to draw me on her leg,
I stuck, and would compassion beg,
But, as, alas, I could not speak,
She forced me on without a squeak.
Her polished knee I next embraced,
And there I stuck until the last;
For tho' she wished to draw me higher,
Yet, troth, I would not venture nigher.
Then to my grief, and great surprise

She with her garter bound my eyes.
Good heaven, was ever such a case?
Was ever man in such a place?
My Flora tripped about, but where
She went, her stocking still was there;
I still embraced her leg and knee,
But yet no object could I see,
Until she went to bed at night,
When she restored me to my sight;
But then, with wonder and surprise,
Poor I, like Milton, lost my eyes;
And thus to utter darkness hurled,
I wished myself in the other world.

Sept. 20, 1777

GEORGE OGILVIE

(c. 1753–1801)

FROM

Carolina; or, The Planter

Having, with searching eye, remark'd ere while,
Nature's wild landscape in each varying soil;
We sing what toils these varying soils demand,
Work of the mind, or labour of the hand;
To be by Ceres, or Pomona paid;
By joyous Bacchus, or th'Athenian maid;
With Grain nutricious, th'orchards mellow load,
The bleeding clusters of the social god,
The melting Olive, or what bids the loom
Contend with Flora in her vernal bloom.

Say! do our pupils daring thoughts invade,
Yonder tall forest's venerable shade,
Where swelling tides o'er spacious valleys stray,
Hid from our almost vertic Phœbus' ray;
Where, whilst the lofty boughs her beams oppose,
Safe in the gloom, the Sylvan herds repose:
No huntsman there asserts his bloody claim,
But turns reluctant from the shelter'd game.

Close as the Macedonian phalanx stood
On Issus plain, within yon aged wood
So close the trees—whilst round each ample root
Thorns, Reeds, and Vines, in wild luxuriance shoot;
Nor only these obstruct th'invader's way,
Through the drear forest countless serpents stray;
Whose mingled hiss, and fascinating eyes,
Bid unknown fears in boldest bosoms rise.
As o'er the rest his scaly bulk he rears,
Like the Arch-fiend amongst his hellish peers,
Proud of his venom'd tusks, and rustling train,
Threat'ning, or instant death, or tort'ring pain;

Shaking the cymbols of a score of years,
The *Rattle* first assails your startled ears.
Next see the *Black Snake*, whose undaunted soul,
Dares e'en the Rattle's deathful rage control;
Scorning his safety to the shade to owe,
Darts from the covert to attack his foe.
In vain you grasp his throat t'escape from harm,
His twisting wreaths unnerve your palsy'd arm;
Alike in vain you trust to flight—behind
He quick pursues as flies the timid hind—
But should some weapon haply arm your hand,
Tho' but a vine branch, or more slender wand,
One well-aim'd stroke secures your safe retreat,
Uncoils and lays him gasping at your feet;
Then press his tumid head with active heel,
Else soon the foe returning strength shall feel;
Tho' now with gaping jaws he crawls along,
And impotently darts his forked tongue.
More dang'rous far, the Moccazine, nor sounds
The notes of war, nor quits the shelter'd bounds;
But coil'd in many a squalid fold, beneath
Some rotting log, prepares insiduous death,
And at th'unguarded wand'rer darting flies,
Who scarcely feels the wound before he dies.

   A thousand snakes of meaner note around,
Wreath on the trees, or glide along the ground;
Myriads of insects, bread in putrid air,
With stings invenom'd, drive you to despair;
From ev'ry pore your vital fluid drain,
At ev'ry pore infuse a racking bane.
And hark! from dark recesses of the wood,
How fierce the language of the *rav'nous brood!*
Loud screams the *Wild-cat*, *Wolves* yet louder howl,
And shaggy *Bears*, like distant thunder growl;
Whilst *Cat-o-mountains*, with discordant roar,
Join the harsh grunting of the tusked boar.
Till circling danger ev'ry sense subdues
But fear, which to bewilder'd thought renews
The fabl'd phantoms of our childish age,

And demons in the shape of monsters rage.
From ev'ry hollow tree Medusa shakes,
Her visage horrid with surrounding snakes;
And Fate, tremendous with all mortal ills;
Or instant snatches, or by piece-meal kills;
With yellow jaundice, shiv'ring ague dwells,
Wild fever raves, or bloated dropsy swells;
Or through the brain quick shoots the solar ray,
Or slow consumption lingers in decay.

If still your ardent thirst for wealth invites,
There to raise altars to Agrarian rites;
Attend the Muse, preparing to relate
What cares, what toil, the bold attempt await.

First, of your destin'd field the *outlines* mark,
Not groping devious thro' the woodland dark;
But let the compass to the pole-star true,
Direct your progress, and assist your view;
As, from where higher land the swamp confines,
You seek the river with two par'llel lines,
Then let a third its winding course pursue,
Till intersected by the other two:
But where the sportive stream meand'ring makes
Projecting points, peninsulated necks,
Throw from your juster plan such scraps away,
Whose narrow bounds would not th'expence repay.
Should you command the wreathing mound t'explore,
Each frequent winding of the sedgy shore.
Lastly, as nature points, direct the drain
Where springy uplands skirt the marshy plain.

Thus mark'd the limits of a spacious field,
The gleaming ax your vig'rous lab'rers wield;
Beneath repeated strokes the Cypress groans;
The falling Oak his timeless fate bemoans;
In his vast bulk the Tupelo trusts in vain,
The tranchent steel divides his spungy grain,
Yet sever'd from the root that gave them birth,
His tow'ring honours still disdain the earth,

And aged vines, that neighb'ring trees uphold,
In screw-like wreaths his quiv'ring boughs infold,
Whilst streams of seeming anguish bathe his sides,
As limb from limb the woodman's arm divides.
Thus when some stag, t'escape pursuing hounds,
O'er lawns and downs with rapid fleetness bounds,
Stop'd by a hedge impervious in his way,
A while he rests, and holds the chase at bay,
Till, prompted by despair, he vainly tries,
With his last effort, o'er its tops to rise;
But springs, alas, too short—entangling thorns
Hold him suspended by his branchy horns;
Adown his cheeks so rolls the silent tear,
Whilst famish'd hounds his living members tear.

    Nor should the grove yet undistinguish'd feel
The heedless fury of the woodman's steel,
But let his hatchet all its force confine
To form an avenue along each line,
In which no tree, however priz'd, you save;
E'en reeds and vines must meet one common grave,
When all-consuming fire vast piles shall seize
Of limbs dissever'd, heap'd on parent trees.

    This task accomplish'd, round your field you frame
A trench, two cubits wide, its depth the same,
By which a two-fold service is supply'd,
Th'ejected earth repels each *common* tide;
Whilst in the trench your future ramparts find,
A firmer base by strong ingraftment join'd.
As when some gard'ner bids a savage root
Bend with a mellower load of alien fruit,
Clasp'd in th'embraces of the wounded rhind,
The stranger bud's adoptively combin'd.

    Hence twice twelve feet, on either side, you delve
A ditch, full six feet deep, its wideness twelve—
And scarce, ere now, have you begun to prove
How hard the task, to subjugate the grove.

What tho' huge trees, laid prostrate by your hand,
Tow'ring in smoke, have darkn'd half the land!
Still their tenacious roots their rights defend
And wide and deep these nether limbs extend;
In vain the hoe, in vain the spade is try'd,
In vain the mattock, would those roots divide;
The ax alone, with many a painful stroke,
Unspurs the cypress, and *unprongs* the oak;
And slow the ditches parts, with endless toil,
The rooty fragments from th'adhesive soil.
The roots, high-pil'd, await consuming fires;
The mould to swell the rising bank retires;
Where youths and females to receive it stand,
And form the sloping dike with plastic hand.
But lo! ere half the needful depth you gain,
Quick gushing streams o'erflow th'unfinished drain!
No more your lab'rers see their strokes to aim;
Chills shake their limbs, and cramps distort their frame;
Unless some sluice, or floodgates, valves allow
The waters, to their parent stream to flow;
Till rising tides, by Cynthia backwards roll'd,
With outward weight th'obedient gates refold.

Soon as the shelving ditch, and sloping mound,
On ev'ry side the leaguer'd grove surround,
To fell the destin'd wood your lab'rers throng,
Whose fate might thus be told in pagan song.
The brandish'd axe the weeping Dryad sees,
And flies reluctant from her falling trees;
Whilst raging Vulcan, with unequal pace,
Pursues the Sylvan Nymph of Nereus' race.

Now on the rivers oozy brink she stands,
Now clasps in woe, now suppliant lifts her hands;
Or frantic, from disorder'd ringlets tears
Her faded garlands, mix'd with auburn hairs.
Now to the Nereids of the flood she cries,
Now to Diana lifts her tearful eyes.
"Bright virgin Goddess! sister nymphs!" she said,
"Hear and protect a heav'n-descended maid,

Whose fate impending, impious men conspire,
Leagu'd with the unrelenting God of fire!
If e'er within my cool retreats you lay,
And bath'd inobvious to the God of day,
Lend! lend your aid, to save that lov'd abode
From hands profane, and th'all-consuming God!"
The suppliant nymph, the huntress Goddess hears,
Then seek united, the Cerûlean plain,
To court his aid whose trident shakes the main.

   Nor long in vain the queen of night implores;
With ready waves he swept his western shores.
Exulting Nereids in the front appear,
And stormy Eurus blusters in the rear,
Whilst whelming billows lead their monarch's way,
And far beyond their wonted limits stray;
Seeking the flaming wood with foaming rage,
Impatient with the Lemnean God t'engage;
Who safe behind the clay-built rampart stands,
In bold defiance of the wat'ry bands.
In vain each nymph, with lab'ring sinews, strove
To pour her urn, and quench the crackling grove;
In vain the Tritons heave their frothy waves;
Th'unshaken mound their bootless fury braves;
Defended by the wariour maid unseen,
Victorious Liber, and the Ear-crown'd Queen;
Who view the op'ning scene with fav'ring eyes,
Whence future tribute to their Fanes shall rise.
Great Jove himself th'immortal strife beholds,
And thus th'unerring rolls of fate unfolds.

   "Know! Queen of Night, and Brother of the main,
Ye war," he said, "against these walls in vain:
For now the Fates and pow'rful gods agree
To guard that work of human industry.
But learn, ye heav'nly pow'rs, nymphs of the flood,
And you, fair Dryad of yon flaming wood,
A time shall come, nor far remov'd by fate,
When trembling sacrilege shall feel your hate.
A pitying ear from him who rules the wind,

Your story'd wrongs, sad Sylvan Maid, shall find.
Mov'd by your tale, he opes his caverns dire,
Whence rushing blasts t'avenge your cause conspire.
His aid the wave-compelling Monarch joins,
And Cynthia's orb with ruddy vengeance shines.
I see the waves like snow-crown'd mountains rise,
Whose whit'ning summits emulate the skies,
As erst the giant sons of Terra strove
To shake the adamantine throne of Jove!"

Nor yet, tho' pow'rful banks the tides repel,
And Sol's bright rays the chilling damps exhale,
Scarce half subdu'd by man, doth the rude soil,
With plenteous crops, repay the planter's toil.
From massy roots luxuriant scions rise,
Beneath whose shade the gift of Ceres dies:
And oft betwixt, in pools, the waters lie,
When bursting clouds obscure the azure sky.
Or else those roots an equal flow withstand,
When parching heats the rivers aid demand,
Till frequent drains divide the level'd fields,
And the last stump to painful labour yields.

PHILLIS WHEATLEY

(c. 1753–1784)

To Mæcenas

Mæcenas, you, beneath the myrtle shade,
Read o'er what poets sung, and shepherds play'd.
What felt those poets but you feel the same?
Does not your soul possess the sacred flame?
Their noble strains your equal genius shares
In softer language, and diviner airs.

   While *Homer* paints lo! circumfus'd in air,
Celestial Gods in mortal forms appear;
Swift as they move hear each recess rebound,
Heav'n quakes, earth trembles, and the shores resound.
Great Sire of verse, before my mortal eyes,
The lightnings blaze across the vaulted skies,
And, as the thunder shakes the heav'nly plains,
A deep-felt horror thrills through all my veins.
When gentler strains demand thy graceful song,
The length'ning line moves languishing along.
When great *Patroclus* courts *Achilles'* aid,
The grateful tribute of my tears is paid;
Prone on the shore he feels the pangs of love,
And stern *Pelides* tend'rest passions move.

   Great *Maro's* strain in heav'nly numbers flows,
The *Nine* inspire, and all the bosom glows.
O could I rival thine and *Virgil's* page,
Or claim the *Muses* with the *Mantuan* Sage;
Soon the same beauties should my mind adorn,
And the same ardors in my soul should burn:
Then should my song in bolder notes arise,
And all my numbers pleasingly surprize;
But here I sit, and mourn a grov'ling mind
That fain would mount and ride upon the wind.

Not you, my friend, these plaintive strains become,
Not you, whose bosom is the *Muses* home;
When they from tow'ring *Helicon* retire,
They fan in you the bright immortal fire,
But I less happy, cannot raise the song,
The fault'ring music dies upon my tongue.

The happier *Terence** all the choir inspir'd,
His soul replenish'd, and his bosom fir'd;
But say, ye *Muses*, why this partial grace,
To one alone of *Afric*'s sable race;
From age to age transmitting thus his name
With the first glory in the rolls of fame?

Thy virtues, great *Mæcenas!* shall be sung
In praise of him, from whom those virtues sprung:
While blooming wreaths around thy temples spread,
I'll snatch a laurel from thine honour'd head,
While you indulgent smile upon the deed.

As long as *Thames* in streams majestic flows,
Or *Naiads* in their oozy beds repose,
While *Phœbus* reigns above the starry train,
While bright *Aurora* purples o'er the main,
So long, great Sir, the muse thy praise shall sing,
So long thy praise shall make *Parnassus* ring:
Then grant, *Mæcenas*, thy paternal rays,
Hear me propitious, and defend my lays.

To the University of Cambridge, in New-England

While an intrinsic ardor prompts to write,
The muses promise to assist my pen;
'Twas not long since I left my native shore
The land of errors, and *Egyptian* gloom:
Father of mercy, 'twas thy gracious hand
Brought me in safety from those dark abodes.

---

*He was an *African* by birth.

Students, to you 'tis giv'n to scan the heights
Above, to traverse the ethereal space,
And mark the systems of revolving worlds.
Still more, ye sons of science ye receive
The blissful news by messengers from heav'n,
How *Jesus*' blood for your redemption flows.
See him with hands out-stretcht upon the cross;
Immense compassion in his bosom glows;
He hears revilers, nor resents their scorn:
What matchless mercy in the Son of God!
When the whole human race by sin had fall'n,
He deign'd to die that they might rise again,
And share with him in the sublimest skies,
Life without death, and glory without end.

Improve your privileges while they stay,
Ye pupils, and each hour redeem, that bears
Or good or bad report of you to heav'n.
Let sin, that baneful evil to the soul,
By you be shunn'd, nor once remit your guard;
Suppress the deadly serpent in its egg.
Ye blooming plants of human race divine,
An *Ethiop* tells you 'tis your greatest foe;
Its transient sweetness turns to endless pain,
And in immense perdition sinks the soul.

On being brought from Africa to America

'Twas mercy brought me from my *Pagan* land,
Taught my benighted soul to understand
That there's a God, that there's a *Saviour* too:
Once I redemption neither sought nor knew.
Some view our sable race with scornful eye,
"Their colour is a diabolic die."
Remember, *Christians*, *Negros*, black as *Cain*,
May be refin'd, and join th' angelic train.

On the Death of the Rev. Mr. George Whitefield

1770.

Hail, happy saint, on thine immortal throne,
Possest of glory, life, and bliss unknown;
We hear no more the music of thy tongue,
Thy wonted auditories cease to throng.
Thy sermons in unequall'd accents flow'd,
And ev'ry bosom with devotion glow'd;
Thou didst in strains of eloquence refin'd
Inflame the heart, and captivate the mind.
Unhappy we the setting sun deplore,
So glorious once, but ah! it shines no more.

   Behold the prophet in his tow'ring flight!
He leaves the earth for heav'n's unmeasur'd height,
And worlds unknown receive him from our sight.
There *Whitefield* wings with rapid course his way,
And sails to *Zion* through vast seas of day.
Thy pray'rs, great saint, and thine incessant cries
Have pierc'd the bosom of thy native skies.
Thou moon hast seen, and all the stars of light,
How he has wrestled with his God by night.
He pray'd that grace in ev'ry heart might dwell,
He long'd to see *America* excel;
He charg'd its youth that ev'ry grace divine
Should with full lustre in their conduct shine;
That Saviour, which his soul did first receive,
The greatest gift that ev'n a God can give,
He freely offer'd to the num'rous throng,
That on his lips with list'ning pleasure hung.

   "Take him, ye wretched, for your only good,
Take him ye starving sinners, for your food;
Ye thirsty, come to this life-giving stream,
Ye preachers, take him for your joyful theme;
Take him my dear *Americans*, he said,
Be your complaints on his kind bosom laid:

Take him, ye *Africans*, he longs for you,
Impartial Saviour is his title due:
Wash'd in the fountain of redeeming blood,
You shall be sons, and kings, and priests to God."

   Great *Countess*,* we *Americans* revere
Thy name, and mingle in thy grief sincere;
New England deeply feels, the *Orphans* mourn,
Their more than father will no more return.

   But, though arrested by the hand of death,
Whitefield no more exerts his lab'ring breath,
Yet let us view him in th' eternal skies,
Let ev'ry heart to this bright vision rise;
While the tomb safe retains its sacred trust,
Till life divine re-animates his dust.

To the Right Honourable William, Earl of Dartmouth

His Majesty's Principal Secretary of State for North America, &c.

Hail, happy day, when, smiling like the morn,
Fair *Freedom* rose *New-England* to adorn:
The northern clime beneath her genial ray,
Dartmouth, congratulates thy blissful sway:
Elate with hope her race no longer mourns,
Each soul expands, each grateful bosom burns,
While in thine hand with pleasure we behold
The silken reins, and *Freedom's* charms unfold.
Long lost to realms beneath the northern skies
She shines supreme, while hated *faction* dies:
Soon as appear'd the *Goddess* long desir'd,
Sick at the view, she languish'd and expir'd;
Thus from the splendors of the morning light
The owl in sadness seeks the caves of night.

*The Countess of *Huntingdon*, to whom Mr. *Whitefield* was Chaplain.

No more, *America*, in mournful strain
Of wrongs, and grievance unredress'd complain,
No longer shall thou dread the iron chain,
Which wanton *Tyranny* with lawless hand
Had made, and with it meant t' enslave the land.

Should you, my lord, while you peruse my song,
Wonder from whence my love of *Freedom* sprung,
Whence flow these wishes for the common good,
By feeling hearts alone best understood,
I, young in life, by seeming cruel fate
Was snatch'd from *Afric's* fancy'd happy seat:
What pangs excruciating must molest,
What sorrows labour in my parent's breast?
Steel'd was that soul and by no misery mov'd
That from a father seiz'd his babe belov'd:
Such, such my case. And can I then but pray
Others may never feel tyrannic sway?

For favours past, great Sir, our thanks are due,
And thee we ask thy favours to renew,
Since in thy pow'r, as in thy will before,
To sooth the griefs, which thou did'st once deplore.
May heav'nly grace the sacred sanction give
To all thy works, and thou for ever live
Not only on the wings of fleeting *Fame*,
Though praise immortal crowns the patriot's name,
But to conduct to heav'ns refulgent fane,
May fiery coursers sweep th' ethereal plain,
And bear thee upwards to that blest abode,
Where, like the prophet, thou shalt find thy God.

To S. M. a young African Painter,
on seeing his Works

To show the lab'ring bosom's deep intent,
And thought in living characters to paint,
When first thy pencil did those beauties give,
And breathing figures learnt from thee to live,
How did those prospects give my soul delight,
A new creation rushing on my sight?
Still, wond'rous youth! each noble path pursue,
On deathless glories fix thine ardent view:
Still may the painter's and the poet's fire
To aid thy pencil, and thy verse conspire!
And may the charms of each seraphic theme
Conduct thy footsteps to immortal fame!
High to the blissful wonders of the skies
Elate thy soul, and raise thy wishful eyes.
Thrice happy, when exalted to survey
That splendid city, crown'd with endless day,
Whose twice six gates on radiant hinges ring:
Celestial *Salem* blooms in endless spring.

    Calm and serene thy moments glide along,
And may the muse inspire each future song!
Still, with the sweets of contemplation bless'd,
May peace with balmy wings your soul invest!
But when these shades of time are chas'd away,
And darkness ends in everlasting day,
On what seraphic pinions shall we move,
And view the landscapes in the realms above?
There shall thy tongue in heav'nly murmurs flow,
And there my muse with heav'nly transport glow:
No more to tell of *Damon*'s tender sighs,
Or rising radiance of *Aurora*'s eyes,
For nobler themes demand a nobler strain,
And purer language on th' ethereal plain.
Cease, gentle muse! the solemn gloom of night
Now seals the fair creation from my sight.

A Farewel to America

To Mrs. S. W.

I.

Adieu, *New-England's* smiling meads,
    Adieu, the flow'ry plain:
I leave thine op'ning charms, O spring,
    And tempt the roaring main.

II.

In vain for me the flow'rets rise,
    And boast their gaudy pride,
While here beneath the northern skies
    I mourn for *health* deny'd.

III.

Celestial maid of rosy hue,
    O let me feel thy reign!
I languish till thy face I view,
    Thy vanish'd joys regain.

IV.

Susannah mourns, nor can I bear
    To see the crystal show'r,
Or mark the tender falling tear
    At sad departure's hour;

V.

Not unregarding can I see
    Her soul with grief opprest:
But let no sighs, no groans for me,
    Steal from her pensive breast.

VI.

In vain the feather'd warblers sing,
 In vain the garden blooms,
And on the bosom of the spring
 Breathes out her sweet perfumes,

VII.

While for *Britannia's* distant shore
 We sweep the liquid plain,
And with astonish'd eyes explore
 The wide-extended main.

VIII.

Lo! *Health* appears! celestial dame!
 Complacent and serene,
With *Hebe's* mantle o'er her Frame,
 With soul-delighting mein.

IX.

To mark the vale where *London* lies
 With misty vapours crown'd,
Which cloud *Aurora's* thousand dyes,
 And veil her charms around,

X.

Why, *Phœbus*, moves thy car so slow?
 So slow thy rising ray?
Give us the famous town to view,
 Thou glorious king of day!

XI.

For thee, *Britannia*, I resign
 New-England's smiling fields;
To view again her charms divine,
 What joy the prospect yields!

XII.

But thou! Temptation hence away,
　　With all thy fatal train
Nor once seduce my soul away,
　　By thine enchanting strain.

XIII.

Thrice happy they, whose heav'nly shield
　　Secures their souls from harms,
And fell *Temptation* on the field
　　Of all its pow'r disarms!

Boston, May 7, 1773.

To a Gentleman of the Navy

Celestial muse! for sweetness fam'd inspire
My wondrous theme with true poetic fire,
Rochfort, for thee! And Greaves deserve my lays
The sacred tribute of ingenuous praise.
For here, true merit shuns the glare of light,
She loves oblivion, and evades the sight.
At sight of her, see dawning genius rise
And stretch her pinions to her native skies.
　Paris, for Helen's bright resistless charms,
Made Illion bleed and set the world in arms.
Had you appear'd on the Achaian shore
Troy now had stood, and Helen charm'd no more.
The Phrygian hero had resign'd the dame
For purer joys in friendship's sacred flame,
The noblest gift, and of immortal kind,
That brightens, dignifies the manly mind.
　Calliope, half gracious to my prayer,
Grants but the half and scatters half in air.
　Far in the space where ancient Albion keeps
Amidst the roarings of the sacred deeps,
Where willing forests leave their native plain,

Descend, and instant, plough the wat'ry main.
Strange to relate! with canvas wings they speed
To distant worlds; of distant worlds the dread.
The trembling natives of the peaceful plain,
Astonish'd view the heroes of the main,
Wond'ring to see two chiefs of matchless grace,
Of generous bosom, and ingenuous face,
From ocean sprung, like ocean foes to rest,
The thirst of glory burns each youthful breast.
  In virtue's cause, the muse implores for grace,
These blooming sons of Neptune's royal race;
Cerulean youths! your joint assent declare,
Virtue to rev'rence, more than mortal fair,
A crown of glory, which the muse will twine,
Immortal trophy! Rochfort shall be thine!
Thine too O Greaves! for virtue's offspring share,
Celestial friendship and the muse's care.
Yours is the song, and your's the honest praise,
Lo! Rochfort smiles, and Greaves approves my lays.

Philis's Reply to the Answer in our last by the Gentleman in the Navy

For one bright moment, heavenly goddess! shine,
Inspire my song and form the lays divine.
Rochford, attend. Beloved of Phœbus! hear,
A truer sentence never reach'd thine ear;
Struck with thy song, each vain conceit resign'd
A soft affection seiz'd my grateful mind,
While I each golden sentiment admire
In thee, the muse's bright celestial fire.
The generous plaudit 'tis not mine to claim,
A muse untutor'd, and unknown to fame.
  The heavenly sisters pour thy notes along
And crown their bard with every grace of song.
My pen, least favour'd by the tuneful nine,
Can never rival, never equal thine;
Then fix the humble Afric muse's seat

At British Homer's and Sir Isaac's feet.
Those bards whose fame in deathless strains arise
Creation's boast, and fav'rites of the skies.
    In fair description are thy powers display'd
In artless grottos, and the sylvan shade;
Charm'd with thy painting, how my bosom burns!
And pleasing Gambia on my soul returns,
With native grace in spring's luxuriant reign,
Smiles the gay mead, and Eden blooms again,
The various bower, the tuneful flowing stream,
The soft retreats, the lovers golden dream,
Her soil spontaneous, yields exhaustless stores;
For Phœbus revels on her verdant shores.
Whose flowery births, a fragrant train appear,
And crown the youth throughout the smiling year,
    There, as in Britain's favour'd isle, behold
The bending harvest ripen into gold!
Just are thy views of Afric's blissful plain,
On the warm limits of the land and main.
    Pleas'd with the theme, see sportive fancy play,
In realms devoted to the God of day!
    Europa's bard, who the great depth explor'd,
Of nature, and thro' boundless systems soar'd,
Thro' earth, thro' heaven, and hell's profound domain,
Where night eternal holds her awful reign.
But, lo! in him Britania's prophet dies,
And whence, ah! whence, shall other *Newton's* rise?
Muse, bid thy Rochford's matchless pen display
The charms of friendship in the sprightly lay:
Queen of his song, thro' all his numbers shine,
And plausive glories, goddess! shall be thine!
With partial grace thou mak'st his verse excel,
And *his* the glory to describe so well.
Cerulean bard! to thee these strains belong,
The Muse's darling and the prince of song.

December 5th, 1774.

To His Excellency General Washington

Celestial choir! enthron'd in realms of light,
Columbia's scenes of glorious toils I write.
While freedom's cause her anxious breast alarms
She flashes dreadful in refulgent arms.
See mother earth her offspring's fate bemoan,
And nations gaze at scenes before unknown!
See the bright beams of heaven's revolving light
Involv'd in sorrows and the veil of night!

The goddess comes, she moves divinely fair,
Olive and laurel bind her golden hair:
Wherever shines this native of the skies
Unnumber'd charms and recent graces rise.

Muse! bow propitious, while my pen relates
How pour her armies through a thousand gates:
As when Eolus heaven's fair face deforms,
Enwrap'd in tempest, and a night of storms;
Astonish'd ocean feels the wild uproar,
The refluent surges beat the sounding shore;
Or thick as leaves in autumn's golden reign,
Such, and so many, moves the warrior train.
In bright array they seek the work of war,
Where high unfurl'd the ensign waves in air.
Shall I to Washington their praise recite?
Enough thou know'st them in the fields of fight.
Thee, first in place and honours,—we demand
The grace and glory of thy martial band.
Fam'd for thy valour, for thy virtues more,
Hear every tongue thy guardian aid implore!

One century scarce perform'd its destin'd round,
When Gallic powers Columbia's fury found;
And so may you, whoever dares disgrace
The land of freedom's heaven-defended race!
Fix'd are the eyes of nations on the scales,
For in their hopes Columbia's arm prevails.
Anon Britannia droops the pensive head,
While round increase the rising hills of dead.
Ah! cruel blindness to Columbia's state!

Lament thy thirst of boundless power too late.
Proceed, great chief, with virtue on thy side,
The every action let the goddess guide.
A crown, a mansion, and a throne that shine,
With gold unfading, WASHINGTON! be thine.

Liberty and Peace

Lo! Freedom comes. Th' prescient Muse foretold,
All Eyes th' accomplish'd Prophecy behold:
Her Port describ'd, "*She moves divinely fair,
Olive and Laurel bind her golden Hair.*"
She, the bright Progeny of Heaven, descends,
And every Grace her sovereign Step attends;
For now kind Heaven, indulgent to our Prayer,
In smiling *Peace* resolves the Din of *War*.
Fix'd in *Columbia* her illustrious Line,
And bids in thee her future Councils shine.
To every Realm her Portals open'd wide,
Receives from each the full commercial Tide.
Each Art and Science now with rising Charms,
Th' expanding Heart with Emulation warms.
E'en great *Britannia* sees with dread Surprize,
And from the dazzl'ing Splendors turns her Eyes!
Britain, whose Navies swept th' *Atlantic* o'er,
And Thunder sent to every distant Shore:
E'en thou, in Manners cruel as thou art,
The Sword resign'd, resume the friendly Part!
For *Galia*'s Power espous'd *Columbia*'s Cause,
And new-born *Rome* shall give *Britannia* Law,
Nor unremember'd in the grateful Strain,
Shall princely *Louis'* friendly Deeds remain;
The generous Prince th' impending Vengeance eye's,
Sees the fierce Wrong, and to the rescue flies.
Perish that Thirst of boundless Power, that drew
On *Albion*'s Head the Curse to Tyrants due.
But thou appeas'd submit to Heaven's decree,
That bids this Realm of Freedom rival thee!

Now sheathe the Sword that bade the Brave attone
With guiltless Blood for Madness not their own.
Sent from th' Enjoyment of their native Shore
Ill-fated—never to behold her more!
From every Kingdom on *Europa*'s Coast
Throng'd various Troops, their Glory, Strength and Boast.
With heart-felt pity fair *Hibernia* saw
Columbia menac'd by the Tyrant's Law:
On hostile Fields fraternal Arms engage,
And mutual Deaths, all dealt with mutual Rage;
The Muse's Ear hears mother Earth deplore
Her ample Surface smoak with kindred Gore:
The hostile Field destroys the social Ties,
And ever-lasting Slumber seals their Eyes.
Columbia mourns, the haughty Foes deride,
Her Treasures plunder'd, and her Towns destroy'd:
Witness how *Charlestown*'s curling Smoaks arise,
In sable Columns to the clouded Skies!
The ample Dome, high-wrought with curious Toil,
In one sad Hour the savage Troops despoil.
Descending *Peace* the Power of War confounds;
From every Tongue cœlestial *Peace* resounds:
As from the East th' illustrious King of Day,
With rising Radiance drives the Shades away,
So Freedom comes array'd with Charms divine,
And in her Train Commerce and Plenty shine.
Britannia owns her Independent Reign,
Hibernia, *Scotia*, and the Realms of *Spain*;
And great *Germania*'s ample Coast admires
The generous Spirit that *Columbia* fires.
Auspicious Heaven shall fill with fav'ring Gales,
Where e'er *Columbia* spreads her swelling Sails:
To every Realm shall *Peace* her Charms display,
And Heavenly *Freedom* spread her golden Ray.

LEMUEL HAYNES

(1753–1833)

The Battle of Lexington

*A Poem on the inhuman Tragedy perpetrated on the 19th of April 1775 by a
Number of the Brittish Troops under the Command of Thomas Gage, which
Parricides and Ravages are shocking Displays of ministerial & tyrannic
Vengeance composed by Lemuel a young Mollato who obtained what little
knowledge he possesses, by his own Application to Letters.*

1

Some Seraph now my Breast inspire
whilst my *Urania* sings
while She would try her solemn Lyre
Upon poetic Strings.

2

Some gloomy Vale or gloomy Seat
where Sable veils the sky
Become that Tongue that would repeat
The dreadfull Tragedy

3

The Nineteenth Day of April last
We ever shall retain
As monumental of the past
most bloody shocking Scene

4

Then Tyrants fill'd with horrid Rage
A fatal Journey went
& Unmolested to engage
And slay the innocent

5

Then did we see old *Bonner* rise
And, borrowing Spite from Hell
They stride along with magic Eyes
where Sons of Freedom dwell

6

At *Lexington* they did appear
Array'd in hostile Form
And tho our Friends were peacefull there
Yet on them fell the Storm

7

Eight most unhappy Victims fell
Into the Arms of Death
unpitied by those Tribes of Hell
who curs'd them with their Breath

8

The Savage Band still march along
For *Concord* they were bound
while Oaths & Curses from their Tongue
Accent with hellish Sound

9

To prosecute their fell Desire
At *Concord* they unite
Two Sons of Freedom there expire
By their tyrannic Spite

10

Thus did our Friends endure their Rage
without a murm'ring Word
Till die they must or else engage
and join with one Accord

11

Such Pity did their Breath inspire
That long they bore the Rod
And with Reluctance they conspire
to shed the human Blood

12

But Pity could no longer sway
Tho' 't is a pow'rfull Band
For Liberty now bleeding lay
And calld them to withstand

13

The Awfull Conflict now begun
To rage with furious Pride
And Blood in great Effusion run
From many a wounded Side

14

For Liberty, each Freeman Strives
As its a Gift of God
And for it willing yield their Lives
And Seal it with their Blood

15

Thrice happy they who thus resign
Into the peacefull Grave
Much better there, in Death Confin'd
Than a Surviving Slave

16

This Motto may adorn their Tombs,
(Let tyrants come and view)
"*We rather seek these silent Rooms*
Than live as Slaves to You"

17

Now let us view our Foes awhile
who thus for Blood did thirst
See: stately Buildings fall a Spoil
To their unstoick Lust

18

Many whom Sickness did compel
To seek some Safe Retreat
Were dragged from their sheltering Cell
And mangled in the Street

19

Nor were our aged Gransires free
From their vindictive Pow'r
On yonder Ground lo: there you see
Them weltering in their Gore

20

Mothers with helpless Infants strive
T' avoid the tragic Sight
All fearfull wether yet alive
Remain'd their Soul's delight

21

Such awefull Scenes have not had Vent
Since Phillip's War begun
Nay sure a Phillip would relent
And such vile Deeds would shun

22

But Stop and see the Pow'r of God
Who lifts his Banner high
Jehovah now extends his Rod
And makes our Foes to fly

23

Altho our Numbers were but few
And they a Num'rous Throng
Yet we their Armies do pursue
And drive their Hosts along

24

One Son of Freedom could annoy
A Thousand Tyrant Fiends
And their despotick Tribe destroy
And chace them to their Dens

25

Thus did the Sons of Brittain's King
Recieve a sore Disgrace
Whilst *Sons of Freedom* join to sing
The Vict'ry they Imbrace

26

Oh! Brittain how art thou become
Infamous in our Eye
Nearly allied to antient Rome
That Seat of Popery

27

Our Fathers, tho a feeble Band
Did leave their native Place
Exiled to a desert Land
This howling Wilderness

28

A Num'rous Train of savage Brood
Did then attack them round
But still they trusted in their God
Who did their Foes confound

29

Our Fathers Blood did freely flow
To buy our Freedom here
Nor will we let our freedom go
The Price was much too dear

30

Freedom & Life, O precious Sounds
yet Freedome does excell
and we will bleed upon the ground
or keep our Freedom still

31

But oh! how can we draw the Sword
Against our native kin
Nature recoils at such a Word
And fain would quit the Scene

32

We feel compassion in our Hearts
That captivating Thing
Nor shall Compassion once depart
While Life retains her String

33

Oh England let thy Fury cease
At this convulsive Hour
Consult those Things that make for Peace
Nor foster haughty Power

34

Let Brittain's king call home his Band
of Soldiers arm'd to fight
To see a Tyrant in our Land
Is not a pleasing Sight

35

Allegiance to our King we own
And will due Homage pay
As does become his royal Throne
Yet in a *legal Way*

36

Oh Earth prepare for solemn Things
Behold an angry God
Beware to meet the King of Kings
Arm'd with an awefull Rod

37

Sin is the Cause of all our Woe
That sweet deluding ill
And till we let this darling go
There's greater Trouble still

JOEL BARLOW

(1754–1812)

Innumerable mercies acknowledged

In glad amazement, Lord, I stand,
Amidst the bounties of thy hand;
How numberless those bounties are!
How rich, how various and how fair!

But oh, what poor returns I bring!
What lifeless songs of praise I sing!
Lord, I confess, with humble shame,
My offerings scarce deserve the name.

Fain would my labouring heart devise
Some nobler gift and sacrifice;
It sinks beneath the mighty load
That I should render to my God.

To him I consecrate my praise,
And vow the remnant of my days;
Enlarge my soul with grace divine,
And make it worthier to be thine.

Give me at length an angel's tongue,
To sound thro' heaven the grateful song;
A theme so great, my voice shall raise,
And crown eternity with praise.

FROM

The Conspiracy of Kings

Hail MAN, exalted title! first and best,
On God's own image by his hand imprest;
To which at last the reas'ning race is driv'n,
And seeks anew what first it gain'd from Heav'n.

796

O MAN, my brother, how the cordial flame
Of all endearments kindles at the name!
In every clime, thy visage greets my eyes,
In every tongue thy kindred accents rise;
The thought expanding swells my heart with glee,
It finds a friend, and loves itself in thee.

    Say then, fraternal family divine,
Whom mutual wants and mutual aids combine,
Say from what source the dire delusion rose,
That souls like ours were ever made for foes;
Why earth's maternal bosom, where we tread,
To rear our mansions and receive our bread,
Should blush so often for the race she bore,
So long be drench'd with floods of filial gore;
Why to small realms for ever rest confin'd
Our great affections, meant for all mankind.
Though climes divide us; shall the stream or sea,
That forms a barrier 'twixt my friend and me,
Inspire the wish his peaceful state to mar,
And meet his falchion in the ranks of war?

    Not seas, nor climes, nor wild ambition's fire
In nations' minds could e'er the wish inspire;
Where equal rights each sober voice should guide,
No blood would stain them, and no war divide.
'Tis dark deception, 'tis the glare of state,
Man sunk in titles, lost in Small and Great;
'Tis Rank, Distinction, all the hell that springs
From those prolific monsters, Courts and Kings.
These are the vampires nurs'd on nature's spoils;
For these with pangs the starving peasant toils,
For these the earth's broad surface teems with grain,
Theirs the dread labours of the devious main;
And when the wasted world but dares refuse
The gifts oppressive and extorted dues,
They bid wild slaughter spread the gory plains,
The life-blood gushing from a thousand veins,
Erect their thrones amid the sanguine flood,
And dip their purple in the nation's blood.

The gazing crowd, of glittering State afraid,
Adore the Power their coward meanness made;
In war's short intervals, while regal shows
Still blind their reason and insult their woes.
What strange events for proud Processions call!
See kingdoms crowding to a Birth-night Ball!
See the long pomp in gorgeous glare display'd,
The tinsel'd guards, the squadron'd horse parade;
See herald's gay, with emblems on their vest,
In tissu'd robes, tall beauteous pages drest;
Amid superior ranks of splendid slaves,
Lords, Dukes and Princes, titulary knaves,
Confus'dly shine their crosses, gems and stars,
Sceptres and globes and crowns and spoils of wars.
On gilded orbs see thundering chariots roll'd,
Steeds, snorting fire, and champing bits of gold,
Prance to the trumpet's voice; while each assumes
A loftier gait, and lifts his neck of plumes.
High on a moving throne, and near the van,
The tyrant rides, the chosen scourge of man;
Clarions and flutes and drums his way prepare,
And shouting millions rend the troubled air;
Millions, whose ceaseless toils the pomp sustain,
Whose hour of stupid joy repays an age of pain.

Of these no more. From Orders, Slaves and Kings,
To thee, O MAN, my heart rebounding springs.
Behold th' ascending bliss that waits your call,
Heav'n's own bequest, the heritage of all.
Awake to wisdom, seize the proffer'd prize;
From shade to light, from grief to glory rise.
Freedom at last, with Reason in her train,
Extends o'er earth her everlasting reign;
See Gallia's sons, so late the tyrant's sport,
Machines in war and sycophants at court,
Start into men, expand their well-taught mind,
Lords of themselves and leaders of mankind.
On equal rights their base of empire lies,
On walls of wisdom see the structure rise;
Wide o'er the gazing world it towers sublime,

A modell'd form for each surrounding clime.
To useful toils they bend their noblest aim,
Make patriot views and moral views the same,
Renounce the wish of war, bid conquest cease,
Invite all men to happiness and peace,
To faith and justice rear the youthful race,
With strength exalt them and with science grace,
Till Truth's blest banners, o'er the regions hurl'd,
Shake tyrants from their thrones, and cheer the waking world.

The Hasty-Pudding

A Poem, in Three Cantos.
Written at Chambery, in Savoy, January, 1793.

Omne tulit punctum qui miscuit utile dulci.
He makes a good breakfast who mixes pudding with molasses.

CANTO I.

Ye Alps audacious, thro' the heav'ns that rise,
To cramp the day and hide me from the skies;
Ye Gallic flags, that o'er their heights unfurl'd,
Bear death to kings, and freedom to the world,
I sing not you. A softer theme I chuse,
A virgin theme, unconscious of the Muse,
But fruitful, rich, well suited to inspire
The purest frenzy of poetic fire.
  Despise it not, ye Bards to terror steel'd,
Who hurl your thunders round the epic field;
Nor ye who strain your midnight throats to sing
Joys that the vineyard and the still-house bring;
Or on some distant fair your notes employ,
And speak of raptures that you ne'er enjoy.
I sing the sweets I know, the charms I feel,
My morning incense, and my evening meal,
The sweets of Hasty-Pudding. Come, dear bowl,
Glide o'er my palate, and inspire my soul.
The milk beside thee, smoking from the kine,
Its substance mingled, married in with thine,

Shall cool and temper thy superior heat,
And save the pains of blowing while I eat.
    Oh! could the smooth, the emblematic song
Flow like thy genial juices o'er my tongue,
Could those mild morsels in my numbers chime,
And, as they roll in substance, roll in rhyme,
No more thy aukward unpoetic name
Should shun the Muse, or prejudice thy fame;
But rising grateful to th' accustom'd ear,
All Bards should catch it, and all realms revere!
    Assist me first with pious toil to trace
Thro' wrecks of time thy lineage and thy race;
Declare what lovely squaw, in days of yore,
(Ere great Columbus sought thy native shore)
First gave thee to the world; her works of fame
Have liv'd indeed, but liv'd without a name.
Some tawny Ceres, goddess of her days,
First learn'd with stones to crack the well-dry'd maize,
Thro' the rough seive to shake the golden show'r,
In boiling water stir the yellow flour:
The yellow flour, bestrew'd and stir'd with haste,
Swells in the flood and thickens to a paste,
Then puffs and wallops, rises to the brim,
Drinks the dry knobs that on the surface swim;
The knobs at last the busy ladle breaks,
And the whole mass its true consistence takes.
    Could but her sacred name, unknown so long,
Rise, like her labors, to the son of song,
To her, to them, I'd consecrate my lays,
And blow her pudding with the breath of praise.
If 'twas Oella, whom I sang before,
I here ascribe her one great virtue more.
Not thro' the rich Peruvian realms alone
The fame of Sol's sweet daughter should be known,
But o'er the world's wide climes should live secure,
Far as his rays extend, as long as they endure.
    Dear Hasty-Pudding, what unpromis'd joy
Expands my heart, to meet thee in Savoy!
Doom'd o'er the world thro' devious paths to roam,
Each clime my country, and each house my home,

My soul is sooth'd, my cares have found an end,
I greet my long-lost, unforgotten friend.
  For thee thro' Paris, that corrupted town,
How long in vain I wandered up and down,
Where shameless Bacchus, with his drenching hoard,
Cold from his cave usurps the morning board.
London is lost in smoke and steep'd in tea;
No Yankey there can lisp the name of thee;
The uncouth word, a libel on the town,
Would call a proclamation from the crown.*
For climes oblique, that fear the sun's full rays,
Chill'd in their fogs, exclude the generous maize;
A grain whose rich luxuriant growth requires
Short gentle showers, and bright etherial fires.
  But here, tho' distant from our native shore,
With mutual glee we meet and laugh once more.
The same! I know thee by that yellow face,
That strong complexion of true Indian race,
Which time can never change, nor soil impair,
Nor Alpine snows, nor Turkey's morbid air;
For endless years, thro' every mild domain,
Where grows the maize, there thou art sure to reign.
  But man, more fickle, the bold licence claims,
In different realms to give thee different names.
Thee the soft nations round the warm Levant
Polanta call, the French of course *Polante*;
Ev'n in thy native regions, how I blush
To hear the Pennsylvanians call thee *Mush*!
On Hudson's banks, while men of Belgic spawn
Insult and eat thee by the name *Suppawn*.
All spurious appellations, void of truth;
I've better known thee from my earliest youth,
Thy name is *Hasty-Pudding*! thus our sires
Were wont to greet thee fuming from their fires;
And while they argu'd in thy just defence
With logic clear, they thus explain'd the sense:—
"In *haste* the boiling cauldron, o'er the blaze,

*A certain king, at the time when this was written, was publishing proclamations to prevent American principles from being propagated in his country.

Receives and cooks the ready-powder'd maize:
In *haste* 'tis serv'd, and then in equal *haste*,
With cooling milk, we make the sweet repast.
No carving to be done, no knife to grate
The tender ear, and wound the stony plate;
But the smooth spoon, just fitted to the lip,
And taught with art the yielding mass to dip,
By frequent journeys to the bowl well stor'd,
Performs the hasty honors of the board."
Such is thy name, significant and clear,
A name, a sound to every Yankey dear,
But most to me, whose heart and palate chaste
Preserve my pure hereditary taste.

There are who strive to stamp with disrepute
The lucious food, because it feeds the brute;
In tropes of high-strain'd wit, while gaudy prigs
Compare thy nursling man to pamper'd pigs;
With sovereign scorn I treat the vulgar jest,
Nor fear to share thy bounties with the beast.
What though the generous cow gives me to quaff
The milk nutritious; am I then a calf?
Or can the genius of the noisy swine,
Tho' nurs'd on pudding, thence lay claim to mine?
Sure the sweet song, I fashion to thy praise,
Runs more melodious than the notes they raise.

My song resounding in its grateful glee,
No merit claims; I praise myself in thee.
My father lov'd thee thro' his length of days;
For thee his fields were shaded o'er with maize;
From thee what health, what vigor he possest,
Ten sturdy freemen from his loins attest;
Thy constellation rul'd my natal morn,
And all my bones were made of Indian corn.
Delicious grain! whatever form it take,
To roast or boil, to smother or to bake,
In every dish 'tis welcome still to me,
But most, my Hasty-Pudding, most in thee.

Let the green Succatash with thee contend,
Let beans and corn their sweetest juices blend,
Let butter drench them in its yellow tide,

And a long slice of bacon grace their side;
Not all the plate, how fam'd soe'er it be,
Can please my palate like a bowl of thee.
    Some talk of Hoe-cake, fair Virginia's pride,
Rich Johnny-cake this mouth has often tri'd;
Both please me well, their virtues much the same;
Alike their fabric, as allied their fame,
Except in dear New-England, where the last
Receives a dash of pumpkin in the paste,
To give it sweetness and improve the taste.
But place them all before me, smoaking hot,
The big round dumplin rolling from the pot;
The pudding of the bag, whose quivering breast,
With suet lin'd, leads on the Yankey feast;
The Charlotte brown, within whose crusty sides
A belly soft the pulpy apple hides;
The yellow bread, whose face like amber glows,
And all of Indian that the bake-pan knows—
You tempt me not—my fav'rite greets my eyes,
To that lov'd bowl my spoon by instinct flies.

CANTO II.

    To mix the food by vicious rules of art,
To kill the stomach and to sink the heart,
To make mankind to social virtue sour,
Cram o'er each dish, and be what they devour;
For this the kitchen Muse first fram'd her book,
Commanding sweat to stream from every cook;
Children no more their antic gambols tri'd,
And friends to physic wonder'd why they died.
    Not so the Yankey—his abundant feast,
With simples furnish'd, and with plainness drest,
A numerous offspring gathers round the board,
And cheers alike the servant and the lord;
Whose well-bought hunger prompts the joyous taste,
And health attends them from the short repast.
    While the full pail rewards the milk-maid's toil,
The mother sees the morning cauldron boil;
To stir the pudding next demands their care,
To spread the table and the bowls prepare;

To feed the children, as their portions cool,
And comb their heads, and send them off to school.
    Yet may the simplest dish some rules impart,
For nature scorns not all the aids of art.
Ev'n Hasty-Pudding, purest of all food,
May still be bad, indifferent, or good,
As sage experience the short process guides,
Or want of skill, or want of care presides.
Whoe'er would form it on the surest plan,
To rear the child and long sustain the man;
To shield the morals while it mends the size,
And all the powers of every food supplies,
Attend the lessons that the Muse shall bring.
Suspend your spoons, and listen while I sing.
    But since, O man! thy life and health demand
Not food alone, but labour from thy hand,
First in the field, beneath the sun's strong rays,
Ask of thy mother earth the needful maize;
She loves the race that courts her yielding soil,
And gives her bounties to the sons of toil.
    When now the ox, obedient to thy call,
Repays the loan that fill'd the winter stall,
Pursue his traces o'er the furrow'd plain,
And plant in measur'd hills the golden grain.
But when the tender germe begins to shoot,
And the green spire declares the sprouting root,
Then guard your nursling from each greedy foe,
Th' insidious worm, the all-devouring crow.
A little ashes, sprinkled round the spire,
Soon steep'd in rain, will bid the worm retire;
The feather'd robber with his hungry maw
Swift flies the field before your man of straw,
A frightful image, such as school-boys bring
When met to burn the Pope, or hang the King.
    Thrice in the season, through each verdant row
Wield the strong plow-share and the faithful hoe;
The faithful hoe, a double task that takes,
To till the summer corn, and roast the winter cakes.
    Slow springs the blade, while check'd by chilling rains,
Ere yet the sun the seat of Cancer gains;

But when his fiercest fires emblaze the land,
Then start the juices, then the roots expand;
Then, like a column of Corinthian mould,
The stalk struts upward, and the leaves unfold;
The bushy branches all the ridges fill,
Entwine their arms, and kiss from hill to hill.
Here cease to vex them, all your cares are done;
Leave the last labors to the parent sun;
Beneath his genial smiles the well-drest field,
When autumn calls, a plenteous crop shall yield.

  Now the strong foliage bears the standards high,
And shoots the tall top-gallants to the sky;
The suckling ears their silky fringes bend,
And pregnant grown, their swelling coats distend;
The loaded stalk, while still the burthen grows,
O'erhangs the space that runs between the rows;
High as a hop-field waves the silent grove,
A safe retreat for little thefts of love,
When the pledg'd roasting-ears invite the maid,
To meet her swain beneath the new-form'd shade;
His generous hand unloads the cumbrous hill,
And the green spoils her ready basket fill;
Small compensation for the two-fold bliss,
The promis'd wedding and the present kiss.

  Slight depredations these; but now the moon
Calls from his hollow tree the sly raccoon;
And while by night he bears his prize away,
The bolder squirrel labors thro' the day.
Both thieves alike, but provident of time,
A virtue rare, that almost hides their crime.
Then let them steal the little stores they can,
And fill their gran'ries from the toils of man;
We've one advantage where they take no part,—
With all their wiles they ne'er have found the art
To boil the Hasty-Pudding; here we shine
Superior far to tenants of the pine;
This envy'd boon to man shall still belong,
Unshar'd by them in substance or in song.

  At last the closing season browns the plain,
And ripe October gathers in the grain;

Deep loaded carts the spacious corn-house fill,
The sack distended marches to the mill;
The lab'ring mill beneath the burthen groans,
And show'rs the future pudding from the stones;
Till the glad house-wife greets the powder'd gold,
And the new crop exterminates the old.

CANTO III.

The days grow short; but tho' the falling sun
To the glad swain proclaims his day's work done,
Night's pleasing shades his various task prolong,
And yield new subjects to my various song.
For now, the corn-house fill'd, the harvest home,
Th' invited neighbors to the *Husking* come;
A frolic scene, where work, and mirth, and play,
Unite their charms, to chace the hours away.

Where the huge heap lies center'd in the hall,
The lamp suspended from the cheerful wall,
Brown corn-fed nymphs, and strong hard-handed beaux,
Alternate rang'd, extend in circling rows,
Assume their seats, the solid mass attack;
The dry husks rustle, and the corn-cobs crack;
The song, the laugh, alternate notes resound,
And the sweet cider trips in silence round.

The laws of Husking ev'ry wight can tell;
And sure no laws he ever keeps so well:
For each red ear a general kiss he gains,
With each smut ear he smuts the luckless swains;
But when to some sweet maid a prize is cast,
Red as her lips, and taper as her waist,
She walks the round, and culls one favor'd beau,
Who leaps, the luscious tribute to bestow.
Various the sport, as are the wits and brains
Of well-pleas'd lasses and contending swains;
Till the vast mound of corn is swept away,
And he that gets the last ear, wins the day.

Meanwhile the house-wife urges all her care,
The well-earn'd feast to hasten and prepare.
The sifted meal already waits her hand,
The milk is strain'd, the bowls in order stand,

The fire flames high; and, as a pool (that takes
The headlong stream that o'er the mill-dam breaks)
Foams, roars and rages with incessant toils,
So the vext cauldren rages, roars and boils.

First with clean salt she seasons well the food,
Then strews the flour, and thickens all the flood.
Long o'er the simmering fire she lets it stand;
To stir it well demands a stronger hand;
The husband takes his turn; and round and round
The ladle flies; at last the toil is crown'd;
When to the board the thronging huskers pour,
And take their seats as at the corn before.

I leave them to their feast. There still belong
More copious matters to my faithful song.
For rules there are, tho' ne'er unfolded yet,
Nice rules and wise, how pudding should be ate.

Some with molasses line the luscious treat,
And mix, like Bards, the useful with the sweet.
A wholesome dish, and well deserving praise,
A great resource in those bleak wintry days,
When the chill'd earth lies buried deep in snow,
And raging Boreas dries the shivering cow.

Blest-cow! thy praise shall still my notes employ,
Great source of health, the only source of joy;
Mother of Egypt's God,—but sure, for me,
Were I to leave my God, I'd worship thee.
How oft thy teats these pious hands have prest!
How oft thy bounties prove my only feast!
How oft I've fed thee with my fav'rite grain!
And roar'd, like thee, to find thy children slain!

Ye swains who know her various worth to prize,
Ah! house her well from Winter's angry skies.
Potatoes, pumpkins, should her sadness cheer,
Corn from your crib, and mashes from your beer;
When Spring returns she'll well acquit the loan,
And nurse at once your infants and her own.

Milk then with pudding I should always chuse;
To this in future I confine my Muse,
Till she in haste some farther hints unfold,
Well for the young, nor useless to the old.

First in your bowl the milk abundant take,
Then drop with care along the silver lake
Your flakes of pudding; these at first will hide
Their little bulk beneath the swelling tide;
But when their growing mass no more can sink,
When the soft island looms above the brink,
Then check your hand; you've got the portion's due,
So taught our sires, and what they taught is true.
     There is a choice in spoons. Tho' small appear
The nice distinction, yet to me 'tis clear.
The deep bowl'd Gallic spoon, contriv'd to scoop
In ample draughts the thin diluted soup,
Performs not well in those substantial things,
Whose mass adhesive to the metal clings;
Where the strong labial muscles must embrace,
The gentle curve, and sweep the hollow space.
With ease to enter and discharge the freight,
A bowl less concave but still more dilate,
Becomes the pudding best. The shape, the size,
A secret rests unknown to vulgar eyes.
Experienc'd feeders can alone impart
A rule so much above the lore of art.
These tuneful lips, that thousand spoons have tried,
With just precision could the point decide,
Tho' not in song; the muse but poorly shines
In cones, and cubes, and geometric lines.
Yet the true form, as near as she can tell,
Is that small section of a goose-egg-shell,
Which in two equal portions shall divide
The distance from the centre to the side.
     Fear not to slaver; 'tis no deadly sin.
Like the free Frenchman, from your joyous chin
Suspend the ready napkin; or, like me,
Poise with one hand your bowl upon your knee;
Just in the zenith your wise head project,
Your full spoon, rising in a line direct,
Bold as a bucket, heeds no drops that fall,
The wide mouth'd bowl will surely catch them all.

ROYALL TYLER

(1757–1826)

The Origin of Evil

An Elegy

Of man's first disobedience and the Fruit
Of that FORBIDDEN TREE, *whose mortal taste*
Brought death into the world, and all our woe:
Sing heavenly muse!

MILTON.

EVA.   *Fructus ipse est pulcher sane visu:*
      Nescio an sit ita dulcis gustatu;
      Veruntamen experiar. VAH. QUAM DULCIS EST!!!
        DIALOGI SACRI SABESTIANI CASTALIONIS.

Lovely in death the beauteous ruin lay;
And if in death still lovely, lovelier there;
Far lovelier! Pity swells the tide of love,
And will not the severe excuse a sigh?
Scorn the proud man who is asham'd to weep.
        YOUNG'S NIGHT THOUGHTS.

Proem.

Ranting topers, midnight rovers,
Cease to roar your fleshy lays;
Melancholy, moping lovers,
No more your lapsed ladies praise.

Fix your thoughts on heavenly treasure,
Let Virtue now with Wit combine;
Purge your hearts from sensual pleasure,
With Religion mix your wine.

Let each lovely *Miss* and *Madam*,
Quit the dear joys of carnal sense,
Weep the *fall* of *Eve* and *Adam*,
From their first state of Innocence.

An Elegy

In the first stillness of the even,
    When blushing day began to close,
In the blissful bowers of Eden,
    Our chaste Grand Parents sought repose.

No pair to act love's glowing passion,
    So fit, in these late days, are seen;
Since girls' shapes are spoil'd by fashion,
    And man's nerves unstrung by sin.

Eve, the fairest child of nature,
    In naked beauty stood reveal'd,
Exposing every limb and feature,
    Save those her jetty locks conceal'd.

Light and wanton curl'd her tresses
    Where each sprouting lock should grow,
Her bosom, heaving for caresses,
    Seem'd blushing berries cast on snow.

Adam, got by lusty nature,
    Form'd to delight a woman's eyes,
Stood confest in manly stature,
    The first of men in shape and size!

As *Eve* cast her arms so slender,
    His brawny chest to fondly stroke;
She seem'd an ivy tendril tender
    Sporting round a sturdy oak.

Innocent of nuptial blisses,
    Unknown to him the balm of life;
With unmeaning, wild caresses,
    Adam teaz'd his virgin wife.

As her arm Eve held him hard in,
    And toy'd him with her roving hand,
In the middle of Love's Garden,
    She saw the Tree of Knowledge stand.

Stately grew the tree forbidden,
    Rich curling tendrils grac'd its root;
In its airy pods, half hidden,
    Hung the luscious, tempting fruit.

With Love's coyest leer she view'd it,
    Then touched it with her glowing hand;
Did just touch, but not renew'd it,
    Restrain'd by the divine command.

At her guilty touch the tree seem'd
    Against the blue arch'd sky to knock;
With nervous vigour every branch beam'd,
    And swell'd the sturdy solid stock.

Softly sigh'd the rib-form'd beauty,
    "How love does new desires produce?
This pendant fruit o'ercomes my duty,
    I pant to suck its balmy juice.

"Why was this tall tree forbidden,
    So sweet and pleasant to my eyes,
Food so fit for hungry women,
    Much desir'd to make me wise?"

With sweet blandishment so civil
    She finger'd soft its velvet pods;
"Let us now know good from evil,
    Dear Adam, let us be like Gods."

With burning cheeks and eyes of fire,
    Raving and raging for the bliss,
Blushing and panting with desire,
    She glu'd her glowing lips to his.

"Threaten'd death will soon o'ertake me,
    If this forbidden tree I pluck,
But life itself will soon forsake me,
    Unless its cordial juice I suck."

Her soft hand then half embrac'd it,
  Her heaving breasts to his inclin'd,
She op'd her coral lips to taste it,
  But first she peel'd its russet rind.

In her lips she scarcely put it,
  And nibbl'd 'till its sweets she found,
Then like eager glutton took it,
  And, gorg'd with bliss, sunk on the ground.

At that hour, through all creation,
  Rode Love sublime in triumph then,
Earth, Sea, Air, gave gratulation,
  And all their offspring joy'd like them.

Fish that sported in the Gihon,
  Soaring Eagles, cooing Doves,
Leopard, Panther, Wolf and Lion,
  Reptile and Insect joy'd their loves.

Love's fierce fire seiz'd e'en the posies,
  Which deck'd the gay enammell'd mead,
Amorous pinks and wanton roses,
  Dissolv'd in love, all shed their seed!

Eve, transported beyond measure,
  Stretch'd in every vital part;
Fainting with excess of pleasure,
  For mighty knowledge rift her heart.

But when its nectar'd juice she tasted,
  Dissolving Eve could only sigh;
"I feel—I feel, my life is wasted,
  This hour I eat, and now I die."

But when she saw the tree so lofty,
   Sapless and shrunk in size so small;
Pointing she whisper'd Adam softly:
   "See! there is DEATH! and there's the FALL!"
        FINIS.

              Oh *Fruit divine!*
Sweet of *thyself*, but much *more sweet* THUS *cropt.*
                     MILTON.

Ode Composed for the Fourth of July

*Calculated for the meridian of some country towns
in Massachusetts, and Rye in Newhampshire*

Squeak the fife, and beat the drum,
INDEPENDENCE DAY has come!!
Let the roasting pig be bled.
Quick twist off the cockerel's head,
Quickly rub the pewter platter,
Heat the nutcakes fried in butter.
Set the cups and beaker glass,
The pumpkin and the apple sauce,
Send the keg to shop for brandy;
Maple sugar we have handy,
Independent, staggering Dick,
A noggin mix of *swinging thick*,
Sal, put on your ruffel skirt,
Jotham, get your *boughten* shirt,
To day we dance to tiddle diddle.
—Here comes Sambo with his fiddle;
Sambo, take a dram of whiskey,
And play up Yankee Doodle frisky.
Moll, come leave your witched tricks,
And let us have a reel of six.
Father and Mother shall make two,
Sal, Moll and I stand all a row,
Sambo, play and dance with quality;
This is the day of blest Equality.

Father and *Mother* are but men,
And Sambo—is a Citizen,
Come foot it, Sal—Moll, figure in,
And, mother, you dance up to him;
Now saw as fast as e'er you can do,
And Father, you cross o'er to Sambo.
—Thus we dance, and thus we play,
On glorious *Independent Day*—
Rub more rosin on your bow,
And let us have another go.
Zounds, as sure as eggs and bacon,
Here's ensign Sneak and uncle Deacon,
Aunt Thiah, and their Bets behind her
On blundering mare, than beetle blinder.
And there's the 'Squire too with his lady—
Sal, hold the beast, I'll take the baby.
Moll, bring the 'Squire our great arm chair,
Good folks, we're glad to see you here.
Jotham, get the great case bottle,
Your teeth can pull its corn cob stopple.
Ensign,—Deacon never mind;
'Squire, drink until your blind;
Come, here's the French—and Guillotine,
And here is good 'Squire Gallatin,
And here's each noisy Jacobin.
Here's friend Madison so hearty,
And here's confusion to the treaty.
Come, one more swig to southern Demos
Who represent our brother negroes.
Thus we drink and dance away,
This glorious INDEPENDENT DAY!

An Irregular Supplicatory Address
to the American Academies of
Arts and Sciences

Ye learned wights, who all the heights
   Of science still are soaring,
The comet's tail, or tail of mites   ·
   Sagaciously exploring.
Whose eyes, like classic bird, so round,
   All nature vast can inspect,
Now gazing Andes lofty mound,
   Now peering o'er an insect.
The maculæ of Sol detect,
   With geometric adage;
And, georgically wise, correct,
   The fungus of a cabbage.
Ye philosophic gossips, who
   Celestial scandals telling,
Tattle what night each starry beau
   Will take his brilliant belle in.
When hen peck'd Jove with long retreat,
   Flies from connubial function;
Or red coat Mars sits tete a tete,
   With Venus in conjunction.
Ye curious wights, who simpering track
   The tulips genial hours;
Lasciviously delight to act,
   As pandars to the flowers.
The genial natal hour, nor yet
   Your noblest powers arouse;
But, ghastly stems noting, sit
   CLERKS IN DEATH'S COUNTING HOUSE.
Great journalists of drizzly drops,
   Memorialists of air,
Historians of weather cocks,
   Biographers of foul and fair.
Inveterate foes to grubs, worms, flies,
   Nursing sires to weeds and swine,
O hear a suppliant's earnest cries,
   Your laurels round his wig to twine.

Oh how I yearn with you to club,
  At annual meetings, when so wise,
You trace the lineage of a grub,
  Or tender loves of Hessian flies.
Say! with you, shall I mount the seat,
  In fame's classic, georgic, charr'ot;
Be wet nurse to an infant beet,
  Foster father to a carrot?
Deign sirs to hear why now I'd reap,
  Agri-horti-cultural bays;
And what my bold pretence to seek,
  To bob my name with A.A.S.
I have two carrots in my ground,
  Each thicker than a fat man's leg;
A full grown Pumpkin, ripe and sound,
  No bigger than a pullets egg.
A peck of torpid birds I've found,
  Who've slept of centuries past four,
So meagre, mouldy, and unsound,
  You'd swear they'd sleep four centuries more.
Of petrifactions I have got
  An Indian pudding boil'd to stone;
The heart of a true Sans Culotte,
  More petrified than barber's hone,
The left eye of a non descript,
  Larger than the moon, when southfull,
Who'd sup a Kraken at a sip,
  Of Morse's Mammouth make a mouthful.
A rotten tooth which holds a peck,
  Which once crunch'd bones, or grass more pliant,
Or grac'd the jaws which erst did deck,
  Great Magnalian Mather's giant.
I keep that famous corn cob point,
  Which quickly can diseases heal,
And coax coy pain from limb or joint,
  Like stroking sticks of brass and steel.
In latitude just forty five,
  Down a dark cellar I did creep,
And, with my union rope, did strive
  To measure pecks and bushels neat.

Of kennel water I did weigh
    A pound—and thus a standard found;
For, spight of dirt, dead cats, or hay,
    This pound will always weigh a pound.
I've made a noble wriggling chair,
    In which my science I retail;
And sit, like politician rare,
    And move my snout, without my *tail*.
My darling calf now boasts in death,
    Seven legs, two tails uneven,
Who, had he puff'd a single breath,
    Had frisk'd the two, and kick'd the seven.
A new discovery I've wrote,
    Magnetic Fluid's found in flip,
My feet its variations note,
    My head the boozy needles dip.
A curious diagram I've got,
    All peppered o'er with A's and B's;
A nostrum sure to cure the rot,
    In mangy sheep—in dogs the fleas.
Whole years I've watch'd our parish vane,
    Boxing the compass, like a tar;
Whole years, with hot, cold, dry and rain,
    Like Milton's Satan, I've waged war.
I keep an obit'ary pen,
    Of men and old maids, through the town;
When death, THAT JACK KATCH, throttles them,
    I mark each CLAY COLD OBIT down.
If new discoveries wont prevail,
    Pudding, nor naturæ lusus,
If torpid birds and carrots fail,
    Your high dubbings to produce us;
My spouse, in my behalf, presents
    A certain Linguinary notion,
Which you will own well represents,
    That Arcanum—perpetual motion.

MARGARET LOWTHER PAGE

(1759–1835)

To Miss J. L.—

Indeed! dear friend, it is too True
A *Country Wife* has much to do;
No moment finds of peaceful leisure
To ope the Muses sacred Treasure
From Books and Poetry must turn
To mark *the Labours of the Churn*
Or worse than poor *Arachne*'s doom
Watch o'er the progress of the Loom
For when I would compose a Lay
Come! Mistress come! the Cotton Weigh!
Like the Dull Owl's ill-omen'd Scream
Awakes me from my pleasing dream
Proclaiming thus with dire portent
The Death of Wit, and Sentiment,
And Castles tho' e'en built in Air,
It takes us Time still to repair;
While Time Alas! for-ever flies
And thus each fond Illusion dies!
Ah yes! tis true, upon my Life!
No *Muse* was ever yet a *Wife*.
For Muses, I have heard it said
Tho' often wooed *do never wed!*
Search *All* Parnassian [   ]
Well skill'd in Heliconian [   ]
No Children's cries did e'er invade
Th'inspiring stillness of the Shade
Where underneath his favorite Tree
Apollo "wakes to extacy
The Living Lyre"! While round each Muse
Does its harmonious Notes diffuse,
The Muses too afright I ween,
In *Poultry Yards* were never seen
Nor as "I live and am a Sinner"

Were ever known to *dress a Dinner*
No future Cares on them intrude
No need have they of *Cloaths* or *Food*.
And tho' in Learning they delight
And oft' take pleasure to indite
School Mistrisses! not *they* indeed,
They never taught to *Spell* and *Read*
No thought sublime, or sally bright
Their Pupils ever put to flight!
Thus then, my friend, you see 'tis vain
Gainst Destiny I may complain
Yet never more must hope to sing
Or drink of the Castalian Spring
Destin'd to Drudge along thro' Life
[   ] *domestic Wife*.

SARAH WENTWORTH MORTON

(1759–1846)

The African Chief

See how the black ship cleaves the main,
   High bounding o'er the dark blue wave,
Remurmuring with the groans of pain,
   Deep freighted with the princely slave!

Did all the Gods of Afric sleep,
   Forgetful of their guardian love,
When the white tyrants of the deep,
   Betrayed him in the palmy grove.

A Chief of *Gambia's* golden shore,
   Whose arm the band of warriors led,
Or more—the lord of generous power,
   By whom the foodless poor were fed.

Does not the voice of reason cry,
   Claim the first right that nature gave,
From the red scourge of bondage fly,
   Nor deign to live a burdened slave.

Has not his suffering offspring clung,
   Desponding round his fettered knee;
On his worn shoulder, weeping hung,
   And urged one effort to be free!

His wife by nameless wrongs subdued,
   His bosom's friend to death resigned;
The flinty path-way drenched in blood;
   He saw with cold and phrenzied mind.

Strong in despair, then sought the plain,
   To heaven was raised his stedfast eye,
Resolved to burst the crushing chain,
   Or mid the battle's blast to die.

First of his race, he led the band,
   Guardless of danger, hurling round.
Till by his red avenging hand,
   Full many a despot stained the ground.

When erst *Messenia's* sons oppressed,
   Flew desperate to the sanguine field,
With iron cloathed each injured breast,
   And saw the cruel Spartan yield.

Did not the soul to heaven allied,
   With the proud heart as greatly swell,
As when the *Roman Decius* died,
   Or when the *Grecian victim* fell.*

Do later deeds quick rapture raise,
   The boon *Batavia's William* won,
Paoli's time-enduring praise,
   Or the yet greater *Washington*!

If these exalt thy sacred zeal,
   To hate oppression's mad controul,
For bleeding *Afric* learn to feel,
   Whose Chieftain claimed a kindred soul.

Ah, mourn the last disastrous hour,
   Lift the full eye of bootless grief,
While victory treads the sultry shore,
   And tears from hope the captive Chief.

While the hard race of *pallid hue*,
   Unpracticed in the power to feel,
Resign him to the murderous crew,
   The horrors of the quivering wheel.

Let sorrow bathe each blushing cheek,
   Bend piteous o'er the tortured slave,
Whose wrongs compassion cannot speak,
   Whose only refuge was the grave.

*Leonidas.

Memento

For My Infant, Who Lived but Eighteen Hours

As the pure snow-drop, child of April tears,
  Shook by the rough wind's desolating breath—
Scarce o'er the chilly sod its low head rears,
  And trembling dies upon the parent heath.

So my lost boy, arrayed in fancy's charms,
  Just born to mourn—with premature decay
To THE COLD TYRANT stretched his feeble arms,
  And struggling sighed his little life away.

As not in vain the early snow-drop rose,
  Though short its date, and hard the withering gale;
Since its pale bloom ethereal balm bestows,
  And cheers with vernal hope the wasted *vale*.

My perished child, dear pledge of many a pain!
  Torn from this ruffian world, in yon bright sphere,
Joins with awakened voice the cherub train,
  And pours his sweet breath on a mother's ear.

Kind dreams of morn his fairy phantom bring,
  And floating tones of extasy impart,
Soft as when Seraphs strike the heavenly string
  To charm the settled sorrow of the heart.

JOSEPH HOPKINSON

(1770–1842)

Song

Adapted to the President's March

I.

Hail COLUMBIA! happy land,
Hail ye HEROES, heav'n born band,
　Who fought and bled in Freedom's cause,
　Who fought and bled in Freedom's cause,
And when the Storm of War was gone,
Enjoy'd the Peace your Valour won,
　　Let INDEPENDENCE be our boast,
　　Ever mindful what it cost;
　　Ever grateful for the prize,
　　Let its altar reach the skies—
　　　FIRM—UNITED let us be,
　　　Rallying round our LIBERTY;
　　　As a Band of Brothers join'd,
　　　Peace and Safety we shall find.

2.

IMMORTAL PATRIOTS! rise once more,
Defend your Rights—defend your shore;
　Let no rude foe with impious hand,
　Let no rude foe with impious hand,
Invade the shrine where sacred lies,
Of toil and blood the well-earn'd prize,
　　While offering Peace, sincere and just,
　　In Heav'n we place a *manly* trust,
　　That Truth and Justice will prevail,
　　And every scheme of Bondage fail—
　　　FIRM—UNITED let us be,
　　　Rallying round our LIBERTY,
　　　As a Band of Brothers joined,
　　　Peace and Safety we shall find—

823

3.

Sound, sound, the trump of Fame,
Let WASHINGTON's great name,
    Ring through the world with loud applause,
    Ring through the world with loud applause,
Let every clime to Freedom dear,
Listen with a joyful ear—
        With equal skill with godlike pow'r,
        He governs in the fearful hour
        Of horrid war, or guides with ease
        The happier times of *honest* peace—
            FIRM—UNITED let us be,
            Rallying round our LIBERTY,
            As a Band of Brothers join'd,
            Peace and Safety we shall find.

4.

Behold THE CHIEF WHO NOW COMMANDS,
Once more, to serve his country, stands
    The Rock on which the Storm will beat,
    The Rock on which the Storm will beat,
But arm'd in virtue, firm and true,
His hopes are fix'd on Heav'n and YOU—
        When Hope was sinking in dismay,
        When glooms obscur'd Columbia's day;
        His steady mind, from changes free,
        Resolved on Death or Liberty—
            FIRM—UNITED let us be,
            Rallying round our LIBERTY,
            As a Band of Brothers join'd,
            Peace and Safety we shall find.

THOMAS GREEN FESSENDEN

(1771–1837)

Jonathan's Courtship

A Merry Tale

A merry Tale I will rehearse,
  As ever you did hear, Sir;
How Jonathan sat out so fierce,
  To see his dearest dear, Sir.
His father gave him a new suit,
  And money, Sir, in plenty;
Besides a prancing nag to boot,
  When he was one and twenty.
And more than that I'd have you know,
  That he had got some knowledge,
Enough for common use or so,
  But had not been to college.
A hundred he could count, 'tis said,
  And in the bible read, Sir,
And by good Christian parents bred,
  Could almost say the creed, sir.
One day his mother said to him,
  "Come here my son, come here,
Come fix you up so neat and trim,
  And go a courting dear."
Why what a plague does mother want?
  I snigs! I dare not go;
I shall get fun'd—and then plague on't,
  Folks will laugh at me so.
Poh! poh! fix up, for you shall go,
  And see the Deacon's Sarah;
She has a great estate you know,
  Besides she wants to marry.
Then Jonathan in best array,
  Did mount his dappled nag,
But trembling sadly all the way,
  Lest he should get the bag.

825

When he came there, as people say,
    'Twas nearly eight o'clock,
And Moll she halloo'd, "in—I say,"
    As soon as he did knock.
He made of bows 'twixt two and three,
    Just as his mother taught him,
All which were droll enough to see;
    You'd think the cramp had caught him.
Now this was all the manners he
    From home with him had brought,
Namely of bows 'twixt two and three,
    The rest he had forgot,
At length came in the Deacon's Sal,
    From milking at the barn,
And faith she was as good a girl
    As ever twisted yarn.
The ladies all, as I should guess,
    And many a lady's man,
Would wish to know about her dress,
    I'll tell them all I can.
Her wrapper gray was not so bad,
    Her apron it was blue—
One stocking on one foot she had,
    On t'other one a shoe.
Now Jonathan did scratch his head,
    When first he saw his dear,
Got up, sat down, but nothing said,
    Because he felt so queer.
Then all the folks went off to bed;
    It seem'd they took the hint.
But Jonathan was so afraid,
    Sal thought the deuce was in't.
"At length says Sal there gone you see,
    And left us here together;"
Says Jonathan "I think they be—
    'Tis very pleasant weather."
Sal cast a sheep's eye at the dunce,
    And sat towards the fire,
He muster'd courage all at once,
    And hitch'd a little nigher.

Ye young men all, and lads so smart,
   Who chance to read these verses,
His next address you'll learn by heart,
   To whisper to the lasses!
"Why Sal, I's going to say as how—
   You'll stay with me to night,
I kind o'love you Sal, I vow—
   And mother said I might."
"Well done," says Sal, "you've broke the ice,
   With very little pother,
Now Jonathan take my advice,
   And always mind your mother."
"Well Sal, I'll tell you what," says he,
   "If you will have me now,
We will be marry'd then, you see,
   You'll have our brindle cow,
And father's got a great bull calf,
   Which you shall have I vow."
"Tell him," says Sal, "he'd best, by half,
   Keep his bull calves at home."
Now Jonathan felt rather bad,
   He thought she meant to joke him,
And though he was a spunky lad,
   His courage quite forsook him.
Sal ask'd him if his heart was whole!
   His chin began to quiver;
He did not know he felt so droll,
   He guess'd he'd lost his liver.
Now Sal was scar'd out of her wits,
   To see his trepidation,
She bawl'd "he's going into fits,"
   And scamper'd like the nation,
A pail of water she did throw
   Upon her trembling lover,
Which wet the lad from top to toe,
   Like a drown'd rat all over.
Then Jonathan he hurried home.
   And since I've heard him brag, sir,
That though the jade had wet him some,
   He did not get the bag, Sir.

CHARLES BROCKDEN BROWN

(1771–1810)

Monody,
On the death of Gen. George Washington,

*Delivered at the New-York Theater,
On Monday Evening, Dec. 30, '99.*

No mimic accents now shall touch your ears,
And now no fable'd woe demand your tears;
No Hero of a visionary age,
No child of poet's phrenzy walks the stage.
'Tis not my office, now, in such a cause
As first, to cheat you of your dear applause.
'Tis no phantastic fate of Queens or Kings,
That bids your sympathy unlock its springs.
This woe is yours, it falls on every head;
This woe is yours, for *Washington is dead!*

No passing grief it is, no private woe,
That bids the universal sorrow flow.
You are not call'd to view, bereft of life,
By dread convulsion seiz'd, your child or wife,
To view a parent's feeble lamp expire;
But *Washington is dead*, his country's sire!
Not for your children's friend your tears must fall;
For *Washington is dead*, the friend of all!

Not singly we, who haunt this western shore,
Our parent, guardian, guide and friend deplore
—Not those alone who breathe this ambient air,
Are call'd to weep at this illustrious bier;
Each wat'ry bourne of this great globe afar,
Was brighten'd by this tutelary Star;
Each future age, thro wide-extended earth,
Like us, may triumph in his hour of birth;
Each age to him, its grateful dues may pay,
And join with us to mourn his fun'ral day.

But why lament the close of his career?
No cause there is that may demand a tear;
Fate gives to mortal life a narrow span,
And he, our guide and friend, was still a man.
Triumphal wreaths far rather ought to wave,
And laureate honors bloom around his grave;
For rather should ascend our hymns of praise
To Heaven, who gave him health and length of days;
Whose arm was seen amidst the deadly fray,
To open for his sword victorious way;
Who led astray from him the fateful ball,
And bade the steel on meaner crests to fall;
Who gave him for our guide, with stead fast eye,
O'er stormy waves, beneath a troublous sky;
And life dispens'd, till war's loud tempest o'er.
He safely steer'd our barque to peaceful shore.

'Twas vain that rescued from a tyrant's hand,
Sweet Liberty, consol'd his natal land;
For brief her stay where discord breathes her spell,
And not on hostile bounds she deigns to dwell.
In wide-dissevered realms new factions grow,
And call from far, or procreate the foe.
War springs afresh—rekindled flames arise,
And back the ghastly train of thraldom flies,
Nor Liberty, nor life, nor blest repose;
Nor self preserving arts his country knows.
Till join'd in vassalage to sacred laws,
One oracle directs, one centre draws;
Till all-embracing policy imparts,
Her harmony to distant, motely parts.
Till every scatter'd tribe, from end to end,
Be taught in forceful unity to blend.

Thus after foes subdued, and battles done,
The harder task was his; to make us one;
The seeds to crush, with his pacific hand,
By home-bred discord scattered thro the land.
Twas he, the darling child of bounteous fate,
That rear'd aloft the pillars of our state:

Twas he that fixed upon eternal base,
The freedom, peace and glory of his race.—
O! let no change thy glorious work befall,
Nor death betide, till death betide us all:
Firm may it stand, tho compass'd by alarms,
Tho broils intestine shake and hostile arms;
Tho the four corners of the world combine,
Against thy sons, the victory be thine!

Not to such frail and mouldering forms we trust,
As monumental stone and ivory bust,
Not to thy worshipp'd name shall alters burn,
Nor rest thy bones in consecrated urn.
No sacrificial scents perfume the air,
Nor pilgrimage be made, nor hymn nor prayer.
Thee in our country's bliss, our eyes shall trace,
Thee in the growing good of all our race;
Be taught by thee, when hostile bands are nigh,
To live for our dear country and to die.
Such rites as virtue gives and claims, be thine,
And every glowing heart, compose the shrine,
Thy fane, as most befits thy god and thee,
Not built with hands, each generous breast, shall be.

Then let us mourn, let every voice deplore,
Our county's guardian, parent now no more,
Mourn we, but let us more exalt that he,
Was born to give us life and liberty:
Let choral joys resound, and garlands wave,
That distant lands partake the boon he gave;
That freedom's banner was by him unfurl'd,
To bless each future age, and either world.

ROBERT TREAT PAINE JR.

(1773–1811)

Adams and Liberty

Written for, and sung at the fourth Anniversary of
the Massachusetts Charitable Fire Society, 1798.

Ye sons of Columbia, who bravely have fought,
    For those rights, which unstained from your Sires had
        descended,
May you long taste the blessings your valour has bought,
    And your sons reap the soil which their fathers defended.
            'Mid the reign of mild Peace,
            May your nation increase,
With the glory of Rome, and the wisdom of Greece;
    And ne'er shall the sons of Columbia be slaves,
    While the earth bears a plant, or the sea rolls its waves.

In a clime, whose rich vales feed the marts of the world,
    Whose shores are unshaken by Europe's commotion,
The trident of Commerce should never be hurled,
    To incense the legitimate powers of the ocean.
            But should pirates invade,
            Though in thunder arrayed,
Let your cannon declare the free charter of trade.
            For ne'er shall the sons, &c.

The fame of our arms, of our laws the mild sway,
    Had justly ennobled our nation in story,
'Till the dark clouds of faction obscured our young day,
    And enveloped the sun of American glory.
            But let traitors be told,
            Who their country have sold,
And bartered their God for his image in gold,
            That ne'er will the sons, &c.

While France her huge limbs bathes recumbent in blood,
    And Society's base threats with wide dissolution;

May Peace like the dove, who returned from the flood,
   Find an ark of abode in our mild constitution.
      But though Peace is our aim,
      Yet the boon we disclaim,
If bought by our Sov'reignty, Justice or Fame.
      For ne'er shall the sons, &c.

'Tis the fire of the flint, each American warms;
   Let Rome's haughty victors beware of collision,
Let them bring all the vassals of Europe in arms,
   We're a world by ourselves, and disdain a division.
      While with patriot pride,
      To our laws we're allied,
No foe can subdue us, no faction divide.
      For ne'er shall the sons, &c.

Our mountains are crowned with imperial oak;
   Whose roots, like our liberties, ages have nourished;
But long e'er our nation submits to the yoke,
   Not a tree shall be left on the field where it flourished.
      Should invasion impend,
      Every grove would descend,
From the hill-tops, they shaded, our shores to defend.
      For ne'er shall the sons, &c.

Let our patriots destroy Anarch's pestilent worm;
   Lest our Liberty's growth should be checked by corrosion;
Then let clouds thicken round us; we heed not the storm;
   Our realm fears no shock, but the earth's own explosion.
      Foes assail us in vain,
      Though their fleets bridge the main,
For our altars and laws with our lives we'll maintain.
      For ne'er shall the sons, &c.

Should the Tempest of War overshadow our land,
   Its bolts could ne'er rend Freedom's temple asunder;
For, unmoved, at its portal, would Washington stand,
   And repulse, with his Breast, the assaults of the thunder!
      His sword, from the sleep
      Of its scabbard would leap,

And conduct, with its point, ev'ry flash to the deep!
      For ne'er shall the sons, &c.

Let Fame to the world sound America's voice;
    No intrigues can her sons from their government sever;
Her pride is her Adams; her laws are his choice,
    And shall flourish, till Liberty slumbers for ever.
        Then unite heart and hand,
        Like Leonidas' band,
And swear to the God of the ocean and land;
    That ne'er shall the sons of Columbia be slaves,
    While the earth bears a plant, or the sea rolls its waves.

WILLIAM MUNFORD

(1775–1825)

The Disasters of Richland

The Author's place of residence. Written in 1795.

Fast by where roaring Roanoke
His stream doth roll o'er many a rock,
A building stands upon a hill,
Which these disasters follow still;—
Most luckless wights of all the nation,
Who make this house their habitation!
Imprimis, thro' th' unshingled top,
The waters, so uncourtly drop,
Descending on the ladies' heads,
And wet their gowns, the floor, and beds.
With these the whistling winds combine,
And in a charming concert join,
With noise of children to distract;
You'd think your very scull was crack'd.
To drive these blust'ring guests away,
Good Mr. Kennon toils all day,
To stop the window-lights with board,
Where clothes and pillows oft are stow'd.—
From room to room to make your way,
Is dang'rous on a rainy day.
The porches all are sadly falling,
And needlessly for help are calling.
While two a nat'ral death have died,
And spread their ruins far and wide,
Another, like a tree uptorn,
Whose roots high in the air are borne,
Suspended stands, with poles for prop,
No part remaining but the top;
The last, dejected, and alone
Seems it's companions' fates to moan;
Benches and banisters are gone;
The rotten sills and quaking floor

Threat him who carelessly walks o'er;
But while these evils I unfold,
A multitude remains untold,
For Satan, sure a scheme pursuing,
Brings all things on this land to ruin,
The Cats, Rats, Horses, Sheep and Hogs,
Cows, Goats, and Pigeons, Deer and Dogs,
Negroes and Overseer to plague
Unite their forces in a league.
The Cats and Rats devour the meat,
Horses and Hogs the corn and wheat,
The Cows and Sheep feed on the cotton,
The Horses tread it down to rotten;
The ruthless goats tobacco spoil,
And disappoint the lab'rer's toil;
High as they reach, they brouze and tear
The youthful trees, which flourish'd fair,
And least the ruin should diminish,
The deer takes care their work to finish.
Thus, while destruction 'round us thickens,
The dogs destroy eggs, ducks and chickens,
And Mrs. Kennon doth determine
To raise no more to feed such vermin.—
The pigeons peck the new-sown pease,
The negroes plunder all the trees,
And eat green fruit to sick'n and gripe 'em
While not a morsel's left to ripen.
The Overseer, with strife and jarrings,
Keeps all the family a warring,
And all his fuss cannot avail
Nor put in place a single nail.
Thus all the Land's a prey to foes,
At least as numerous as those,
Who Babylon in pieces trampled,
Or is perhaps quite unexampled.—
Thick weeds throughout the garden grow,
Which like a tow'ring forest shew;
With these the crop is overspread,
And scarce a plant dares lift it's head;
The fences all so wond'rous low,

That every creature in may go,
And feast him to his heart's content,
That nothing may be idly spent:
And when at last, the crop so thin
With mickle pains is gather'd in,
The wheat in roofless barns they pour,
For birds and weavil to devour,
To sun and rain expos'd 'tis laid,
Till quite destroyed, and nought is made—
The corn, because they love not eating,
They naked leave, where rains are beating,
In pens, the fence of which they leave
Down to the ground, least cows shou'd grieve.—
Tobacco, 'cause it costs so little,
The negroes think not worth a tittle?
Cut down it lies, and goes to pot,
With unregarded dust to rot.—
The people who attend the mill,
Are quarr'ling with the miller still,
Dispute accounts, and make a pother,
Which almost serves to kill my mother,
Who with her cares and doubts perplex'd,
So oft is cross'd, so often vex'd,
So often melancholy sits,
'Tis wonderful she keeps her wits.—
The picture now exactly fits,
And when to Richland house you go,
Reader, the likeness you will know.

BIOGRAPHICAL NOTES

NOTE ON THE TEXTS

ACKNOWLEDGMENTS

NOTES

INDEXES

Biographical Notes

John Adams (1705–1740)   The youngest child of a shopkeeper, John Adams was born in Boston and graduated from Harvard College in 1721. A gifted linguist with a mastery of nine languages, he was considered among Harvard's most learned graduates of the first quarter of the century. In 1727, with his uncle Matthew Adams and poet Mather Byles, he collaborated on a series of poems and essays published in the *New England Weekly Journal* under the pseudonym "Proteus Echo." In the same year, he was called to assist the Rev. Nathaniel Clap at Newport, but the two clashed, and Adams organized the short-lived rival Second Congregational Church. After four years as a Harvard tutor, he attempted twice to secure pulpits in Philadelphia, but each trial ended in failure, the second as a result of a mental breakdown. In 1736, he returned to Boston where he was a public ward until his death. A master of classical and Biblical paraphrase, Adams was the author of a powerful elegy mourning the death of the poet Jane Colman Turell. His verse was collected and published posthumously by his uncle Matthew Adams as *Poems on Several Occasions* (1745).

George Alsop (1636–c. 1673)   A royalist and Anglican born in London into the family of a successful tailor, Alsop found himself politically at odds with Oliver Cromwell's English Commonwealth. He considered the execution of King Charles I political murder and wrote as much, his candor foreclosing his chances for public employment or preferment. In 1658, at age 22, he indentured himself as a servant and was shipped to Maryland, a colonial hotbed of anti-Puritanism. He worked as secretary to royalist Thomas Stockett for four years, earned his liberty, worked in the fur trade, and returned to England in early 1664. The proprietors of Maryland engaged him to compose a promotional tract, *A Character of the Province of Maryland*, which was published in 1666. Alsop subsequently took orders in the Anglican Church and served as curate in a number of locations. The Bishop of London considered him an effective advocate of Church of England doctrine and sent him in 1670 to preach to the Quakers at the Gracechurch Street meetinghouse; his appearance provoked a riot which he barely survived. He died sometime after 1673.

John André (1750–1780)   Born in Geneva to Huguenot parents, André moved to London as an adolescent when his father's mercantile business required an English contact. In 1774, he shipped to Canada as a lieutenant in the Royal English fusiliers. He was captured by American forces at Fort St. Johns in 1775 and spent several months as a prisoner of war before being returned to General Howe as part of a prisoner exchange. His prison journal impressed Howe, who appointed him captain. During the English occupation of Philadelphia, he took up residence in Benjamin Franklin's house, pillaging its contents and shipping them back to London. He took charge of arrangements for the Meschianza, a notoriously extravagant festivity honoring

General Howe on his departure from the city. When Benedict Arnold agreed to surrender West Point to the British in exchange for cash, André served as intermediary. On the day his "Cow-Chace"—a mock-epic satirizing the American army—was published in New York's *Royal Gazette*, he was captured in disguise in the woods of New York, with the records of the traitorous plan hidden in his boot. He was executed in October 1780 before the assembled Continental Army on the command of General George Washington. Learned, artistically gifted, fluent in several languages, André inspired a martyr cult in England, admiration among the younger patriot officers, and revulsion among the common people of America.

Benjamin Banneker (1731–1806)   Banneker was born to Robert and Mary Banneky, two manumitted slaves, in the Ellicott Mills area of Maryland. Given a rudimentary education in arithmetic and letters by his family, he also benefited from the tutelage of a Quaker schoolmaster, who activated a lively interest in mathematics. Banneker labored on his family's tobacco farm for a number of years before a chance encounter with a pocket watch owned by a traveling salesman piqued his interest; using the watch as a template, he created a large wooden clock, which won him a name. For much of his adult life he worked as a maker of watches and clocks. Banneker later undertook the study of astronomy, stimulated by books lent him by John Ellicott, a surveyor for whom he worked in 1791. When he had digested the volumes sufficiently to do his own calculations of the motions of heavenly bodies, he began publishing *Benjamin Banneker's Almanac*. Funded by an abolition society, the almanac from 1792 to 1797 served as a public demonstration of African-American ingenuity and a vehicle for the abolitionist cause. The second almanac included an exchange of letters between Banneker and Thomas Jefferson on the subject of race in America. He died at his modest Maryland homestead in 1806, a lifelong bachelor.

Joel Barlow (1754–1812)   Born into a poor New England family, Barlow was educated at Moor's Charity Indian School in Hanover, New Hampshire, working as a dining hall waiter and cook's helper. He entered Dartmouth College and then Yale University, until his education was interrupted by the Revolution. He joined a patriot militia, and fought in the disastrous Battle of Long Island. At the end of his term of service, Barlow reentered Yale, finishing his degree and composing his first substantial poem, "The Prospect of Peace," for his 1778 graduation. Too much of a freethinker to be hired by the college as an instructor, Barlow served briefly as chaplain with the Third Massachusetts Brigade of the Revolutionary Army (1780–1783), until his qualms about Christian doctrine prompted his resignation. He then became a lawyer in Hartford. In 1787 he published *The Vision of Columbus*, an epic poem "designed to exhibit the importance of this country . . . as the noblest and most elevated part of the earth . . . the last and greatest theatre for the improvement of mankind." Within months, successful editions appeared in London and Paris. Barlow exploited his new international fame by going to

France as agent for the Scioto Land Company, recruiting French citizens to a settlement in the Ohio Territory. In a subsequent investigation of the company for fraud, Barlow was cleared but his reputation was so damaged that he could not return to the United States. He attached himself to the radical community in Paris, hailed the fall of the Bastille on July 14, 1789, fled to London during the Jacobin disorders, and defended the Revolution with a blistering attack on aristocracy, *Advice to the Privileged Orders* (1792), and a verse satire, *The Conspiracy of Kings* (1792). A warrant for his arrest as a radical was issued. He fled to Paris where he composed his *Letter to the National Convention of France* (1792) proposing a new constitution; the work's enthusiastic reception prompted the Assembly to make him an honorary citizen of the new Republic, an honor then granted only to George Washington and Alexander Hamilton. His status enabled him to secure publication of Thomas Paine's *The Age of Reason* (1794) while the author was in a Parisian jail. In 1793 he composed "The Hasty Pudding," a mock-epic praising the republican simplicity of New England's cherished food in contrast to the extravagances of Old World cuisine. Immediately and widely popular, it recouped his reputation in the United States. By 1796 President Washington appointed him a consul to treat with the Barbary pirates. His treaty contained the first legal admission by an agent of government that the United States was a secular state. In 1805 President Jefferson invited Barlow to return home to write a history of the United States. His arrival was marked by publication of a revised version of his 1787 epic, newly titled *The Columbiad* (1807). In 1811, President Madison appointed Barlow minister to France with a view to securing compensation for Napoleon's disruption of American shipping and trade. He died in Poland in December 1812, during the chaotic retreat of Napoleon's army from Russia.

George Berkeley (1685–1753) Berkeley was born in Kilkenny, Ireland, into a Protestant family. He entered Trinity College, Dublin, in 1700 at the age of 15, received his B.A. in 1704, and was elected to a Junior Fellowship in 1707. In 1710 he was ordained as a Church of Ireland minister. He published a series of philosophical works: *An Essay towards a New Theory of Vision* (1709), *A Treatise Concerning the Principles of Human Knowledge* (Part I, 1710), and *Three Dialogues between Hylas and Philonous* (1713). While the first of these works won Berkeley a European reputation, the radical subjectivism of *A Treatise* inspired widespread derision. From 1713 to 1721 Berkeley resided in London and toured Europe. In 1721 he published *De Motu* and *An Essay towards Preventing the Ruine of Great Britain*, a jeremiad about the decline of public morality. He returned to Ireland as a senior fellow at Trinity College and lived in Dublin until he was appointed Dean of Derry, a well-remunerated and largely ceremonial post, in 1724. While at Derry, Berkeley formed the plan of founding a college in Bermuda, described in *A Proposal for the Better Supplying of Churches in our Foreign Plantations, and for Converting the Savage American to Christianity* (1724). By 1726 Berkeley had raised substantial money for the project, secured the vote of Parliament for a much larger amount, and obtained a royal charter for his new college. Realizing that Bermuda would be an inconvenient locale for the establishment, he traveled to Newport, Rhode Island, in the fall of 1728, intending to set the foundation there. His "Verses on the Prospect of Planting Arts and Learning in America" was composed in support of this endeavor. Berkeley spent three years in Newport. Though he failed to create his college, his assistant, Samuel Johnson, went on to compose British America's first philosophical primer, *Elementa Philosophica* (1752), and to found King's College, now Columbia University. Berkeley returned to England in 1731, and published *Alciphron* (1732), a dialogue critiquing irreligious trends. He applied funds he had raised for the college to the purchase of books for Yale and Harvard. In 1734, he was appointed Bishop of Cloyne. In his last years he became convinced of the benefits of tar-water (an emulsion of water and pine tar) as a panacea; his final work, *Siris: Philosophical Reflexions and Inquiries Concerning the Virtues of Tar-water* (1744), mixed immaterialist philosophy and recipes for his curative elixir.

William Billings (1746–1800) One of the principal composers of religious music in the 18th century, Billings had no formal musical education and was notoriously scruffy in appearance and habits. Trained as a tanner in his native city of Boston, he was drawn to congregational singing and took up the practice of composition, reading popular treatises on the subject and writing out pieces according to his own intuition: "I am not confined to rules prescribed by others," he wrote in *The Continental Harmony* (1794), "yet I come near as I possibly can to a set of rules which I have carved out for myself." He sometimes composed the texts that he set, and elaborated them chorally in tiered vocal imitation, which he called "fuging." He worked as a singing master in Massachusetts and Rhode Island from as early as 1769 until his death, and founded choirs and classes which he supplied with printed collections of his compositions: *The New-England Psalm-Singer* (1770), *The Singing Master's Assistant* (1778), *The Psalm-Singer's Amusement* (1781), *The Suffolk Harmony* (1786), and *The Continental Harmony* (1794). Billings married in 1774, fathered nine children, and in 1780 bought a house in Boston; after considerable popularity in the late 1770s and early 1780s, his fortunes had by the 1790s declined to the extent that a public concert was organized in his aid.

Ann Eliza Bleecker (1752–1783) Born in New York City into a prosperous merchant family, Ann Eliza Schuyler married John J. Bleecker in 1769 and in 1771, after a brief period of residence in Poughkeepsie, set up a farm household in Tomhanick, a village 18 miles north of Albany. When Burgoyne's army invaded New York from Canada six years later, the path of their march ran toward Tomhanick. Bleecker's husband went to Albany to secure shelter for his family, but before he could return, she was forced to flee the invasion force with her two children. Reunited in Albany, the family traveled down the Hudson out of harm's way, but her youngest daughter died during the voyage, a source of despondency for the remainder of her life. After Burgoyne's defeat the family returned to their homestead, which Bleecker strove to make an outpost of politeness and refinement, in spite of "perpetual alarms from the savages." In 1781, a Tory raiding party captured her husband; though he was returned after six days, the stress of the episode caused her to miscarry. She died within two years, at age 31. In 1793 Bleecker's daughter Margaretta Faugeres, herself a noted poet, collected her mother's writings in *The Posthumous Works of Ann Eliza Bleecker in Prose and Verse.*

Robert Bolling (1738–1775) Born into an aristocratic family in Chesterfield, Virginia, the son of a planter, Robert Bolling was educated in England, at Wakefield School in Yorkshire. He enrolled in the Middle Temple, but returned to Virginia to continue his legal education, clerking in Williamsburg, after which he settled at Chellow, an inherited plantation in Buckingham County. In 1760 he unsuccessfully sought to marry, recording his efforts in verse and in a candid, often ribald diary ("A Circumstantial Account of Certain Transactions, That Once Greatly Impressed the Writer"). Bolling eventually married in 1763, and again in 1765 after his first wife died in childbirth. From 1761 to 1765 he represented Buckingham County in the House of Burgesses; in 1766, he attacked the cronyism of Virginia's General Court in the pages of the *Virginia Gazette*, precipitating widespread comment and a libel lawsuit. William Byrd III, one of the judges involved, challenged him to a duel, but both men were arrested before it was fought. Bolling's poems and prose writings appeared in magazines and newspapers on both sides of the Atlantic, but most circulated exclusively in manuscript form. He died suddenly in 1775, while attending the Third Virginia Convention.

Ned Botwood (c. 1730–1759) A native of Lancashire, Ned Botwood was Sergeant of the 47th Regiment of Foot in the Battle of Quebec during the Seven Years War. He came to America in 1750 when the regiment was deployed at Nova Scotia. He was killed on September 13, 1759, along with 68 members of his regiment at the center of the line of assault on French forces.

William Bradford (1590–1657) Born in 1590 in Austerfield, Yorkshire, Bradford was orphaned at age seven and raised by an uncle, Robert Bradford. He took to Bible reading as a boy and perfected his ability during the frequent illnesses that restricted him to his uncle's house. To further his knowledge of Christianity, he joined a local conventicle of Christian dissenters, to the distress of his guardian. When James I began the persecution of the conventicles in 1608, Bradford left with his group for Amsterdam. In 1609 the congregation moved to Leiden where Bradford became a silk weaver. In 1620 he and his wife, Dorothy, joined a segment of their community who were immigrating to America. Leaving his young son behind to be schooled by his co-religionists in Leiden, Bradford crossed the Atlantic on the *Mayflower*; Dorothy accidentally drowned shortly after their arrival at Cape Cod. After Plymouth's first governor, John Carver, died in 1621, Bradford was elected to the position, serving frequently in the office for the remainder of his life. When the Puritans arrived in Massachusetts he began a chronicle of the colony's history in a manuscript published later as *Of Plymouth Plantation*. A man of letters as well as a public figure, Bradford also composed poems, memoranda, legal documents, and letters.

Anne Bradstreet (1612–1672)   Born Anne Dudley in Northamptonshire, England, Bradstreet mastered classical Latin, Greek, and Hebrew at home, spoke passable French, knew double-entry bookkeeping, and read history, theology, and medicine. She married around 1628, came to Massachusetts with the first wave of Puritan immigrants around 1630, on the *Arabella*, living briefly in Charlestown but later moving to Boston, Newtown, Ipswich, and finally Andover in 1645. Her father, Thomas Dudley, was a Puritan soldier who served as governor of Massachusetts Bay Colony; her brother Joseph Dudley and her husband, Simon Bradstreet, also served as Massachusetts governors. She had eight children. She circulated her poetry in manuscript among her family and learned friends. Her brother-in-law the Rev. John Woodbridge conveyed one manuscript collection to England where it was published as *The Tenth Muse, Lately Sprung Up in America* (1650), winning her an avid English readership; it was the first book of original poems to be published by a woman in England and also the first by a New Englander. In 1678, six years after her death, a second collection, *Several Poems*, appeared; certain poems of a more private nature collected in her notebooks were not printed until substantially later.

Joseph Breintnall (c. 1695–1746)   Trained as a merchant by his father, David Breintnall, a native of Derby, England, Breintnall was one of Benjamin Franklin's closest associates in Philadelphia in the 1720s and 30s. In his *Autobiography* (1771–90) Franklin described him as "A Copyer of Deeds for the Scriveners; a good-natur'd friendly middle-ag'd Man, a great Lover of Poetry, reading all he could meet with, and writing some that was tolerable; very ingenious in many little Nicknackeries, and of sensible Conversation." A Quaker in good standing in his early years who was later considered a freethinker, Breintnall married in 1723. In 1729, he collaborated with Franklin on the composition of "The Busy-Body," a series of essays for the *American Weekly Mercury*. The oldest member of "the Junto," Franklin's club of young men intent on mutual improvement, Breintnall volunteered his services as secretary of the Library Company of Philadelphia, founded by the Junto in 1731, until his death. In 1735 he became sheriff of Philadelphia County. A keen amateur naturalist, he maintained a cabinet of curiosities and occupied himself by printing leaves, creating folio albums of contact images. Breintnall introduced naturalist John Bartram to the transatlantic network of botanical collectors and natural historians, and corresponded with the Royal Society in London, contributing a 1738 report on the aurora borealis. In 1746, about a month after he described for Royal Society members the harrowing ill-effects he suffered from a rattlesnake bite, he was found drowned on the banks of the Delaware River, an apparent suicide.

Henry Brooke (1678–1736) Henry Brooke was born in Norton Priory, Cheshire, the youngest son of Sir Henry Brook, a baronet. He graduated from Brasenose College, Oxford, in 1693, and spent some years in London, where he was known as a town wit. He came to America in 1702, hoping to become customs collector of Philadelphia, but his Anglican faith proved an obstacle to the appointment. The unofficial laureate of a group of gentry youth who gathered at Story's Tavern in Philadelphia, he participated in the group's riotous street war against the Quaker town watch, and in 1703 was arrested; later that year he campaigned to overthrow the reign of rude humor in taverns, composing "A Discourse upon Jesting." Settled in a position as customs collector at Lewes, on the mouth of the Delaware, he soon became a leading citizen in "The Lower Counties," the portion of Pennsylvania that later became Delaware. In 1709, he organized the inhabitants of Newcastle against a raid by a French privateer. He became speaker of the assembly for the Lower Counties in 1717, was appointed to the Governor's Council in 1721, and became associate justice of the Supreme Court for Sussex County in 1726. He was known throughout the middle colonies for his learning and conversation; his ample library included works in Greek, Latin, French, Italian, and German. He championed the aspiration of women to join the polite world. Traveling frequently from Lewes to Newcastle and Philadelphia, he was widely hailed as a paragon of gentility. He never married, living his latter years in the household of his friend the Rev. William Becket. His writings, that appeared under the cognomen "Sylvio," were collected in manuscript toward the end of his life, and he was recognized by contemporaries as the finest poet of his place and time.

Charles Brockden Brown (1771–1810) Born into a Quaker merchant family in Philadelphia, educated at the prestigious Friends' Latin School, and trained in the law, Brown abandoned his apprentice position in 1793 in favor of a career as a writer and intellectual. He joined several literary circles in Philadelphia including the Belles Lettres Club. He left Philadelphia for New York to avoid constant contact with his parents, who were disappointed with his failure to pursue a more lucrative profession. In New York he became acquainted with the circle of writers and painters who comprised the Friendly Club. Club members corresponded with the most advanced political writers in England, including William Godwin, Mary Wollstonecraft, and the young Samuel Taylor Coleridge. Brown sympathized with the feminism espoused by the English radicals, publishing *Alcuin* (1798), a dialogue on the rights of women. Living on the verge of poverty and nearly killed by yellow fever, he wrote novels in rapid succession: *Wieland* (1798), *Ormand* (1799), *Edgar Huntly* (1799), *Arthur Mervyn* (1799–1800), *Memoirs of Stephen Calvert* (1799–1800), *Clara Howard* (1801), and *Jane Talbot* (1801). In the midst of this intense period of productivity, and increasingly thereafter, he took on editorial positions, working for the New York *Monthly Magazine* (1799–1800), *The Literary Magazine* (1803–06), and *The American Register* (1807–10). He published essays and political pamphlets, planned a history of slavery, and wrote some shorter fiction that he left unpublished. Brown married Elizabeth Linn in 1804; the couple had four children. He died of tuberculosis in 1810.

Mather Byles (1707–1788)   Byles was born in Boston to saddler Joseph Byles and Elizabeth Mather; he was a grandson of Increase Mather. His father's death when he was a year old left him under the influence of his uncle Cotton Mather, who supported his education. At Harvard he distinguished himself as a literary talent, graduating in 1725 and subsequently earning a master's degree. From 1727 to 1730, he worked as a man of letters, contributing extensively to the *New England Weekly Journal*, with John and Matthew Adams, under the pseudonym "Proteus Echo," and serving as volunteer laureate of Massachusetts. He sought connection with the major figures in the English literary world, corresponding with Alexander Pope and Isaac Watts, among others. In 1730, unable to support himself by literary work, he put himself forward as candidate for various pulpits. Several cosmopolitan Congregationalist families, including that of Governor Jonathan Belcher, organized a new congregation at Brattle Street and appointed Byles their first pastor. In 1734 he married Anne Gale, Belcher's niece. His status as chief civic poet of the colony was reinforced. In 1744 his wife died, and he largely abandoned poetry writing, but he collected and published his verse as *Poems on Several Occasions*. In 1747 he married Rebecca Tailer, daughter of lieutenant-governor William Tailer. He published many of his sermons and lectures, and acquired a reputation as a wit and a punster. A Tory, he remained in Boston when it was occupied by the British during the Revolution; in 1777, returning patriots removed him from his pulpit, and he was sentenced in a public trial to banishment. The sentence was commuted to two years of house arrest. Byles spent the remainder of his life in Boston.

Thomas Clemson (fl. 1746)   A planter from Christiana Hundred in the Lower Counties of Pennsylvania (present-day Delaware), Thomas Clemson is known solely on the basis of his versified advertisement for a runaway servant, published in the *Pennsylvania Gazette*.

Benjamin Colman (1673–1747)   Born in Boston to parents who were shopkeepers, Benjamin Colman graduated from Harvard in 1692 and received his M.A. in 1695, after which he went to England and sought ordination from the London Presbytery. In 1699, a group of merchant families called him to preside over a reformed Congregationalist meeting to be housed on Brattle Street. Colman accepted amid considerable resistance to the new church from Puritan traditionalists including Increase and Cotton Mather, and began a 48-year occupation of the pulpit at the most stylish of the Reformed churches in New England. He married Jane Clark in 1700; they had three children. In

1707, he published *A Practical Discourse on the Parable of the Ten Virgins*, *The Government and Improvement of Mirth*, and an elegy on the New England theologian Samuel Willard, *A Poem on Elijah's Translation*. Colman served as fellow of Harvard from 1717 to 1728 and as an overseer from 1728 until his death, although he declined election to the presidency of Harvard in 1724. In 1731 he received an honorary Doctor of Divinity degree from the University of Glasgow. During the last years of his life he concerned himself particularly with the promotion of missionary work among the New England Indians by the Society for Promoting Christian Knowledge and the Society for the Propagation of the Gospel in Foreign Parts.

Ebenezer Cook (c. 1667–c. 1733) Cook was born in London, the son of a Maryland merchant and planter. He traveled to America in the early 1690s to manage his father's tobacco lands near the mouth of the Choptank River, on the colony's western shore. After returning to England, he published *The Sot-Weed Factor* (1708), a satirical verse account of life on the Maryland frontier and burlesque of English anti-promotion literature. Inheriting a share of the family estate after his father's death in 1712, he returned to Maryland, and during the 1720s practiced law and served as clerk of the Maryland Assembly. A self-styled poet laureate, he wrote a number of elegies memorializing the colony's leading citizens, including *Elogy on the Death of Thomas Boardley, Esq.* (1724), as well as a poem on Maryland's economy, *Sotweed Redivivus* (1730), and *The Maryland Muse* (1731), which included a revised version of *The Sot-Weed Factor* and a new verse history of Bacon's Rebellion of 1676.

Thomas Cradock (1718–1770) Son of a Staffordshire tailor, the Rev. Thomas Cradock was born in Trentham, England, in 1718. Educated at the Trentham Free School and Magdalen Hall, Oxford, he returned to his home town to teach until he was ordained as an Anglican priest and licensed as curate of Blurton in Trentham parish in 1743. Within the year he left for Maryland where he became first rector of St. Thomas Church, west of Baltimore. There he established a parish school, married Catherine Risteau, fathered four children, acquired 800 acres of land, and devoted his leisure hours to writing poetry. A champion of ecclesiastical discipline, he preached against the laxity of the colonial clergy and urged that a bishop be appointed to regulate their conduct. He composed hymns, translated the Psalms, wrote a verse drama on the death of Socrates, and composed a series of neoclassical satires on the colonial scene entitled "The Maryland Eclogues." These circulated in manuscript under his cognomen, "Jonathan Spritly, Esqr." Cradock figures humorously in Alexander Hamilton's *The History of the Ancient and Honourable Tuesday Club* (1755) as one of the "Baltimore Bards" who engage in a paper war with the Annapolis company. He would become an honorary member of the Tuesday Club. During his lifetime, Cradock gained renown for his translations of the Psalms: *A Poetical Translation of the Psalms of David* (1754) and *A New Version of the Psalms of David* (1756).

Thomas Dale (1700–1750)   Born in Hoxton, England, into a family of pharmacists, Thomas Dale studied medicine at the University of Leyden, writing his M.D. dissertation, *Dissertatio medio-botanica inauguralis de Pareira Brava et Serapia officinarum* (1723), about treatments for urinary tract disorders in women. Unable to support himself with a medical practice, he worked as a translator of Latin medical treatises, including the influential *Emmenologia* (1729), by John Friend, for the London booksellers. In 1732, facing debts and family opposition to his recent marriage, he abandoned London for Charleston, South Carolina, arriving just as yellow fever began spreading through the city. His wife, Maria, died of the fever in August of that year. Dale was remarried in 1733 to Mary Brewton, daughter of the colony's wealthiest merchant. He became a fixture of public life, serving as an assistant justice, steward of the St. George's Society (an English immigrant aid organization), an administrator of the slave detention workhouse, and an assistant justice of the Court of General Sessions; he was also a spokesman for a group that sponsored public balls and concerts, and helped to establish a theater. In 1735, he set up a pharmaceutical laboratory and gin distillery; in 1738–39, as smallpox broke out in the colony, he engaged in debates over its treatment, in the *South-Carolina Gazette*, against rival physician James Killpatrick (later Kirkpatrick). He was elected to a term in the legislature (1749–50), but found the rough and tumble of politics unsavory.

John Danforth (1660–1730)   Danforth was born in Roxbury, Massachusetts, to the Rev. Samuel and Mary Wilson Danforth. John Eliot, the Apostle to the Indians, was his father's co-pastor. Educated at Harvard, he was called to the pulpit at Dorchester in 1682; in the same year he married Elizabeth Minot, with whom he had 11 children. His father and brothers wrote verse. During the final decades of his life, he was regarded as the great literary traditionalist in New England, a last Puritan elegist, and thus became a reference point in debates over literary cosmopolitanism in the 1720s.

Samuel Davies (1723–1761)   Samuel Davies, the Presbyterian evangelist and second president of the College of New Jersey (Princeton), was born in the Lower Counties of Pennsylvania (now Delaware) to Welsh parents. Trained at the "Log College" in Chester County by Samuel Blair, Davies was licensed to preach in 1746. The next year he undertook a mission to serve the Scots-Irish population in western Virginia. His success in founding congregations and challenging the Anglican establishment in Virginia won him a reputation in Europe. His *Miscellaneous Poems, Chiefly on Divine Subjects* was published in Williamsburg in 1751. In 1753 the trustees of the newly established College of New Jersey commissioned him to travel to Great Britain to raise funds. Along with Gilbert Tennent, Davies spent 14 months traveling through England in a highly successful campaign in which Davies's skills as a sermonizer won him renown. During the Seven Years War he was a vocal champion of the imperial cause in the South, composing sermons, tracts, and poems that stirred emotions against the French. After Jonathan Edwards's death in 1759, the College of New Jersey invited Davies to preside over British America's principal New Light seminary. He served a year and a half before dying of pneumonia. A posthumous five-volume edition of Davies's sermons (1766–71), assembled by Dr. Thomas Gibbons, sealed his reputation in the history of Reformed Christian homiletics; his hymns were used in worship in England and America for over a century.

William Dawson (1704–1752) Born in Cumberland County, England, Dawson studied at Queen's College, Oxford, and began an active literary career while still an undergraduate. He received his M.A. in 1728. After his ordination in 1729, he crossed the Atlantic and became tutor and then professor of moral philosophy at William and Mary. Dawson served as chaplain of the Virginia House of Burgesses, rector of James City parish, and president of William and Mary from 1743 until his death. He circulated manuscript copies of his writings among the Tidewater elite and published occasional verse and satires in American and English periodicals. His *Poems on Several Occasions*, published (like much of his work) under his pseudonym ("a Gentleman of Virginia"), appeared from the press of William Parks in Williamsburg in 1736, the first book of poetry printed in Virginia. He died in Williamsburg.

Joseph Dumbleton (fl. 1744–1749) Nothing substantial is known about the satirist Joseph Dumbleton aside from his presence in Virginia and South Carolina during the period 1744–1749. (His authorship of an ode to the St. Patrick's Society of Charleston may indicate an Irish background, although the English town of Dumbleton is in Gloucestershire.)

Timothy Dwight (1752–1817) A grandson of Jonathan Edwards, Dwight was born in Northampton, Massachusetts, and educated at Yale, which he entered at 13. He began writing verse and literary criticism while in college, publishing *A Dissertation on the History, Eloquence, and Poetry of the Bible* in 1772, and completing *The Conquest of Canäan*, an epic in heroic couplets, in 1775. (Like much of his verse, the epic circulated in manuscript form for many years before he published it in 1785.) Dwight married in 1777, and in the same year volunteered his services as chaplain to the First Connecticut Brigade of the Continental Army. After the death of his father in 1778, he returned to Northampton where he ran two family farms; in 1781–82 he served two terms in the Massachusetts state legislature. Beginning in 1783, he was called to preach at Greenfield Hill in Fairfield, Connecticut, where his sermons earned him a wide reputation; he established Greenfield Hill Academy, an innovative, co-educational boarding school. While in Fairfield, he published *The Triumph of Infidelity* (1788), a verse satire, and *Greenfield Hill* (1794), a georgic. In 1795 he was appointed to the presidency of Yale, using his position to counter the forces of political radicalism and freethinking whose influence had widened in the wake of the French Revolution. Dwight's *Theology, Explained and Defended* was published posthumously, in five volumes, in 1818–19; he died in New Haven.

Nathaniel Evans (1742–1767)   Born into a merchant family in Philadelphia, Evans enrolled in the Philadelphia Academy with the intention of acquiring a mastery of accounting and trade. Inspired by the Academy's director, William Smith, with a love of letters and religion, he joined "The Swains," a group of young men interested in the fine arts and belles lettres. He became a close friend of poet Thomas Godfrey, Jr., and would oversee publication of Godfrey's collected verses shortly after his death in 1765. After six years of Academy schooling, Evans was apprenticed in a counting house but discovered he had no temperament for business. He returned to the College of Pennsylvania and in 1765 was awarded an M.A. In the same year, Evans traveled to England to be ordained as a minister of the Church of England and enrolled as a missionary for the Society for the Propagation of the Gospel in Foreign Parts. He returned to America as pastor to Gloucester, New Jersey, but contracted tuberculosis and died within two years. Elizabeth Graeme and William Smith collected Evans' verse and religious writings and published the posthumous *Poems on Several Occasions, with Some Other Compositions* in 1772.

Elizabeth Graeme Fergusson (1737–1801)   Daughter of a prominent Philadelphia physician, Elizabeth Graeme emerged as a literary figure in the course of her courtship and engagement with William Franklin, son of Benjamin Franklin. Writing as "Laura," she exchanged poems with others in the Delaware Valley and cultivated an extensive network of literary correspondence. After the engagement collapsed around 1757, Graeme turned to religion and undertook a translation of the Psalms. In 1764–65, she traveled to England and Scotland, where she visited the fashionable resorts, appeared before George III, met Laurence Sterne, and recorded her impressions in a literary journal. After her return she translated François Fénelon's *Télémaque*. She presided over one of the leading artistic salons in colonial America, hosting the most talented of the region's young painters, ministers, and poets— Francis Hopkinson, Thomas Godfrey, Jr., Thomas Coombe, Benjamin West, Jacob Duché, and Nathaniel Evans—in her family's Philadelphia townhouse and at Graeme Park, a family mansion north of the city. In 1772, she married Henry Hugh Fergusson, a loyalist with whom she lived at Graeme Park until 1775. Her husband returned to America after a trip to England in 1777 as a member of the British Army; although she refused to join him, he and his associates involved her in communications that incurred the anger of George Washington and sparked public questioning of her patriotism. In 1778, Graeme Park was confiscated by the patriots, and Elizabeth Graeme Fergusson exiled herself to the Pennsylvania countryside. She regained her estate in 1781 and divorced her husband, but was forced to sell much of her property. In the 1780s and 90s, she began publishing poems in magazines and newspapers.

Thomas Green Fessenden (1771–1837)   Born in Walpole, New Hampshire, the son of a minister, Fessenden attended Dartmouth College. Around 1795, he created a sensation in the college's literary clubs, defying the reigning Anglophilia with a humorous vernacular poem of thwarted love, popularly known as "Jonathan's Courtship," which became an instant literary sensation and was republished in newspapers and on broadsides throughout the United States and England. Fessenden studied law and joined the bar in Rutland, Vermont, but literary pursuits and a fascination with technology distracted him from his vocation. His penchant for investing in such inventions as hydraulic vacuums, corn mills, and "metallic tractors" (devices that purported to cure the sick by removing excess electricity from their bodies) led him to lose substantial sums in London from 1801 on. His mock-heroic account of this world of whimsical science and invention, *Terrible Tractoration!!*, won critical acclaim and sold briskly in England when published in 1803; he followed this with a successful collection of his earlier verse, *Original Poems* (1804). He returned to the United States in 1804 a literary celebrity, but with empty pockets. Becoming involved in Federalist politics, he published the anti-Jeffersonian political satire *Democracy Unveiled* (1805) and founded a short-lived newspaper, the New York *Weekly Inspector* (1806–07). From 1809 to 1822 he lived in Vermont, where he married, published a book on patent law, and worked as a newspaper editor. He later relocated to Boston, where he founded and edited the influential *New England Farmer* and served for the last two years of his life in the Massachusetts legislature.

John Fiske (1608-1677) Born in Suffolk, England, Fiske graduated from Cambridge University in 1628. A Congregationalist, he was frustrated by Anglican officials in his initial attempts to preach the Gospel and turned to the study of medicine. In 1637, he immigrated to Massachusetts with his wife and extended family; his mother died during and his first child soon after the voyage. After service as a minister and teacher in Salem and Wenham, he settled in Chelmsford, where he remained pastor until his death. He is known to have published only one work during his lifetime, *The Watering of the Olive Plant in Christ's Garden; or, A Short Catechism for the First Entrance of Our Chelmsford Children* (1657). His poetry, including a number of anagrammatic elegies written in the 1640s and 50s, remained in manuscript until his notebooks were rediscovered in the 1940s.

Benjamin Franklin (1706–1790) Born in Boston, the son of a candle and soap maker, Benjamin Franklin learned the printing trade in Boston and London. He settled in Philadelphia in 1726 and bought *The Pennsylvania Gazette* in 1729. Beginning in 1732, he published *Poor Richard's Almanack*, continuing for 25 years. He founded the American Philosophical Society in 1743, and from 1751 to 1764 served as a member of the Pennsylvania Assembly; in 1754 he proposed a plan for colonial union. In 1756 he was elected to the Royal Society after conducting a series of experiments with electricity. He represented the Pennsylvania Assembly in London (1757–62), served as Pennsylvania agent in London beginning in 1764, and by 1770 was also representing Georgia, New

Jersey, and Massachusetts. He returned to Philadelphia in 1775, serving as delegate to the Second Continental Congress. Appointed diplomatic commissioner by Congress, he traveled to France in 1776, negotiating a treaty of alliance with France in 1778 and a peace treaty with Britain in 1782. Returning to the United States in 1785, he served as president of the Pennsylvania supreme executive council (1785–88), and as a delegate to the 1788 Constitutional Convention. He died in Philadelphia. His celebrated *Autobiography*—an unfinished memoir written from 1771 to 1790—was published posthumously.

Philip Freneau (1752–1832) Born in New York City and raised in Monmouth County, New Jersey, Philip Morin Freneau graduated from the College of New Jersey (now Princeton) in 1771; at the college commencement, his friend Hugh Henry Brackenridge read *The Rising Glory of America*, a poem on which the two had collaborated. While working for a short time as a schoolteacher on Long Island, Freneau published anti-British satirical verses. He spent two years as secretary to a planter on St. Croix. Having volunteered for military service in 1778, he was captured by a British man-of-war in the Caribbean and imprisoned, later recounting his ordeal in *The British Prison-Ship* (1781). During the 1780s, Freneau worked as a postal clerk in Philadelphia; from 1784 to 1790, he captained a merchant ship in the Caribbean. He published *The Poems of Philip Freneau, Written Chiefly during the Late War* in 1786, and *The Miscellaneous Works of Mr. Philip Freneau* in 1788. Settling briefly in Middleton Point, New Jersey, where he married, in 1791 Freneau was offered a government clerkship by Thomas Jefferson and moved to Philadelphia where he founded and edited the anti-Federalist *National Gazette*. George Washington referred to him as "that rascal Freneau." Returning to New Jersey in 1793 after Jefferson lost his position as secretary of state, Freneau edited small New York and New Jersey newspapers and until 1804 occasionally worked as a captain of merchant vessels. His *Poems Written between the Years 1768 & 1794* was published in 1795; *Poems Written and Published during the American Revolutionary War* appeared in 1809.

Christopher Gardiner (c. 1596–c. 1662) Born in England into a gentry family, Gardiner briefly attended Cambridge and the Inner Temple, but left early to tour Europe. He married in England around 1620, but returned to Europe after his wife's premature death in 1624, converted to Catholicism and served in the army of the Holy Roman Empire. He bought an English estate in 1626. In 1630, having reconverted to Protestantism, he became acquainted with Sir Ferdinando Gorges of the Council for New England, and traveled to Massachusetts Bay to secure Gorges' land claims. When the Puritans learned that Gardiner, then living with a mistress, had abandoned two wives in Europe, they attempted his arrest; he fled into the wilderness, pursued by local Indians desirous of the bounty for his capture. Once seized, the Puritans found that they had no legal grounds to prosecute him, since neither wife had sworn complaint. In 1631 Gardiner removed to Kennebunc, Maine, where he stayed for several months before returning to England and initiating an unsuccessful legal proceeding, along with Thomas Morton of Merry Mount, against the Puritan settlement. The date and place of Gardiner's death are not known, but he received a land lease from the King in 1660, after the restoration of Charles II.

Thomas Godfrey Jr. (1736–1763) Godfrey was born in Philadelphia, the son of glazier Thomas Godfrey, who was a mathematical genius and member of Franklin's Junto. His anonymous submissions of verse to *The American Magazine* brought him to the attention of William Smith, provost of the College of Philadelphia, who encouraged Godfrey to join his circle of young talents, "The Swains," which included Benjamin West, Nathaniel Evans, John Green, Joseph Green, and Francis Hopkinson. Godfrey obtained a lieutenant's commission in the Pennsylvania forces and served in the expedition to Fort Duquesne; his experience of war's desolation inspired his 1758 "Epistle to a Friend, from Fort Henry." After his enlistment expired, he moved to Wilmington, North Carolina, where he was a tobacco processor and merchant. He wrote *The Prince of Parthia* (1767), a verse tragedy performed in Philadelphia; it was the first tragedy by an American author to reach the stage. Godfrey's verse characteristically celebrated friendship over love; his longest poem, *The Court of Fancy* (1762), explored the dangers of the uncontrolled imagination. He died from the effects of sunstroke while riding on a summer day. His posthumous works were collected by Nathaniel Evans and published in 1765 as *Juvenile Poems on Various Subjects, with the Prince of Parthia, a Tragedy.*

James Grainger (c. 1721–1766) Born sometime between 1721 and 1724 in Duns, Berwickshire, Scotland, the son of a tax collector, Grainger studied medicine at the University of Edinburgh, worked as a physician's apprentice and army surgeon, traveled in Europe, and in 1753 received his M.D. and secured an appointment in the Royal College of Physicians. In taverns and coffeehouses he became friendly with artists and writers such as Joshua Reynolds, Samuel Johnson, Oliver Goldsmith, James Boswell, Thomas Percy, and William Shenstone. A skilled Latinist, in 1759 he published *A Poetical Translation of the Elegies of Tibullus*. Facing bankruptcy, he moved to the island of Saint Christopher (St. Kitts), in the West Indies; within a year he married the daughter of a Nevis planter and was appointed manager of estates owned by his wife's uncle. With hundreds of African slaves under his authority, and his small savings invested in slaves, Grainger became expert in the diseases resulting from their work and living conditions, and he wrote *An Essay on the More Common West-India Diseases, and the Remedies Which That Country Itself Produces* (1764). Returning to London in 1763, he published *The Sugar-Cane* (1764), a four-canto georgic on plantation life, which won him considerable reputation; he read aloud from the poem at Joshua Reynolds' house. He died two years later on St. Kitts.

Joseph Green (1706–1780)   Born in Boston, the Harvard-trained merchant and rum distiller Joseph Green established his literary reputation with a series of parodies of the poems of the Rev. Mather Byles and the speeches of Gov. Jonathan Belcher in the 1720s and 30s. A prolific poet whose works were read in print and in manuscripts on both sides of the Atlantic, he was also a noted town wit, whose library was said to be among the largest in private hands in America. In the 1740s, his verse satirized New Light evangelical revivalism; later, his *Entertainment for a Winter's Evening* (1750) and *The Grand Arcanum Detected* (1755) mocked Boston's Freemasons. A loyalist sympathizer with extensive commercial ties to Britain, Green fled to England in 1775 with his wife (whom he had married sometime after 1742). Though many of his possessions had to be abandoned in Massachusetts, he lived comfortably in London during his final years.

Hannah Griffitts (1727–1817)   Known to the literary world as "Fidelia," Hannah Griffitts was born and lived in Philadelphia. A Quaker and an active member of a network of literary women who exchanged writings in manuscript throughout the Delaware Valley, she resided all of her life in gentry households maintained by relatives. Unmarried, she devoted herself to the care of various female members of the Norris and Griffitts families.

Jupiter Hammon (1711–c. 1806)   Hammon was born a slave to the Lloyd family of Oyster Point, Long Island, New York. Taught by the Rev. Nehemiah Bull, a Harvard College graduate, he was drawn to literature and evangelical Christianity. He was employed as a household clerk at Lloyd Manor and was given access to the manor library. His second master, Joseph Lloyd, permitted Hammon to publish his writings and preach to local African-Americans. On Christmas Day, 1760, he composed his poem "An Evening Thought. Salvation by Christ, with Penitential Cries," published as a broadside early in 1761. He issued three further poems, including his 1778 "Address to Miss Phillis Wheatly," and three religious discourses, one of which has not survived. The most influential of these tracts was *An Address to the Negroes in the State of New-York* (1787).

Charles Hansford (c. 1685–1761)   Born in Gloucester County, Virginia, and raised in neighboring York County, Hansford was trained as a blacksmith, a trade in which he worked throughout his life. In 1716, he built a mill with a brother; he married around 1723 and fathered two surviving children. Not known to have published poetry under his own name, Hansford has been credited with the authorship of some anonymous verses that appeared in 1745 in the *Virginia Gazette* ("On the Conquest of Cape Breton"). Four of his long manuscript poems, "Of Body and of Soul," "Some Reflections on My Past Life," "Brazillai," and "My Country's Worth," were shared in manuscript form among the colony's literati. Late in life, he was appointed as a reader at Kiskiack church and as a vestryman for Yorkhampton parish.

Benjamin Harris (c. 1655–c. 1720)   Harris was born in London, the son of a barber-surgeon, and served as a bookseller's apprentice from 1663 to 1670. During the 1670s he was the publisher of several religious works and a noted cookbook, *The Accomplished Ladies Delight* (1675), by Hannah Wolley. In 1679 he began an anti-Catholic newspaper, *Domestick Intelligence; or News from Both the City and Country*, which, along with other controversial tracts including *The Appeal from the Country to the City* (1679) and *A Scheme of Popish Cruelties* (1681), brought him fines and imprisonment; in 1685, after the coronation of James II, his home was raided and he was charged with sedition. He departed for Massachusetts Bay in 1686 and established the London Coffee House in Boston, which became a center of commercial activity. From the Coffee House, in 1690, Harris published Anglo-America's first newspaper, *Publick Occurrences both Foreign and Domestic*, limited to a single issue, and *The New England Primer* (c. 1690), which became the standard textbook for New England children for generations. Harris returned to London in 1694 or 1695 after the lapse of the Licensing Act in England. He produced several tracts and newspapers, including the *London Post*, which ran from 1699 to 1705. During his final years he earned a living as a seller of patent medicines.

Lemuel Haynes (1753–1833)   The abandoned child of a white woman of West Hartford, Connecticut, and an African father, Lemuel Haynes was raised as an indentured servant in the house of his foster-father and master, David Rose. Though not given a formal education, Haynes possessed an aptitude for reading and a taste for religious writing that Rose encouraged. His indenture concluded on reaching his majority, Haynes joined the "Minutemen" and fought in the early actions of the American Revolution. He memorialized the battle of Lexington in a ballad sermon. His literary work in verse and prose, including a call for the extension of freedom to slaves, "Liberty Further Extended" (1776), brought invitations to study at Dartmouth after the war ended. Haynes chose instead to read divinity and classical languages with orthodox Congregationalist clergymen in Connecticut. He proved a diligent student, was licensed to preach in 1780, and was ordained a Congregationalist minister in 1785, the first African-American anointed by a Protestant denomination in Anglo-America. A skilled preacher, an orthodox Calvinist, a Federalist, an abolitionist, and a talented controversialist, he served three congregations during his lifetime. In 1801 he published *The Nature and Importance of True Republicanism*, a tract arguing that legal slavery was inconsistent with a civil order in which human rights and public virtue were ostensibly cherished. In 1803 he was awarded an honorary M.A. by Middlebury College.

Anne Hecht (fl. 1780s)   Little is known about Anne Hecht, aside from her service as a bridesmaid to her friend Mehetible Calef in 1786. Her father was associated with the British garrison at Fort Howe, New Brunswick, in the vicinity of which many Loyalist refugees had settled after the signing of the Treaty of Paris in 1783.

Edmund Hickeringill (1631–1708)   Born in Aberford, England, and educated at Cambridge, Hickeringill began his career as a military chaplain in Scotland. During the 1650s, his religious opinions were volatile, veering from orthodox Reformed Christianity to Quakerism to deism. Publicly identified as a religious radical, he feared an anti-Puritan backlash in the wake of King Charles II's restoration to the throne in 1660 and fled to Jamaica. *Jamaica Viewed*, his widely read account of the island, was published in 1661. In the same year he avowed adherence to the beliefs of the Church of England and was ordained. Returning to England, he occupied the post of vicar at All Saints, Colchester. Despite his nominal Anglicanism, he repeatedly displayed dissenting views in pamphlets which he published in London. His rebuke of those who sought convergence between the Church of England and the Church of Rome brought him convictions for slander and even exclusion from his office during the reign of James II. He was restored to his post after the Glorious Revolution of 1688, remaining there until his death.

Archibald Home (c. 1705–1744)   Home was the third son of Sir John Home, baronet of Berwick, Scotland. Educated by private tutor, he mastered Latin and Greek. Residence in Glasgow immersed him in the Scottish literary revival led by Allan Ramsay in reaction to the 1707 Act of Union. In 1733, Home came to New York hoping to obtain a post under Governor William Cosby. He attempted to demonstrate his usefulness to Cosby's Court Party by circulating in the coffeehouses of New York City the "Memoirs of a Handspike," a satire of John Peter Zenger and the Country faction. Cosby ignored the favor, but one of Cosby's chief enemies, Lewis Morris, was struck by the artistry of the attack, approached Home, and enlisted him as protégé. In 1737, Morris became Governor of New Jersey and brought Home with him to Trenton. In quick succession Home served as deputy secretary of the province, secretary of the Provincial Council, member of His Majesty's Council, and, in 1741, Secretary of the Province. In Trenton, Home became the focal figure in a literary coterie that included Abigail Streete Coxe, David Martin, Robert Hunter Morris, Joseph Worrel, Moses Franks, and Richa Franks. His thwarted romance with Richa Franks ("Flavia"), who had promised her mother not to marry a Gentile, generated an extensive body of neoclassical poetry in which Home envisioned a pagan paradise where distinctions between Jew and Christian did not pertain and their love could flourish. Home died in 1744 before the romantic impasse could be overcome; Abigail Coxe had his verse collected in a manuscript book, *Poems on Several Occasions*, copies of which circulated in England and Scotland as well as British America.

Francis Hopkinson (1737–1791)   Born into Pennsylvania's cultural elite, Francis Hopkinson belonged to the inaugural class of the Academy of

Philadelphia. There he became a protégé of its director, Provost William Smith, and joined the "Swains," a circle of poets and painters that included Benjamin West, Thomas Godfrey, Jr., and Jacob Duché. In 1757 Hopkinson received the first B.A. awarded by the College of Philadelphia. He read law under Benjamin Chew, who engineered Hopkinson's appointment to a variety of official posts in Pennsylvania. In 1761 he was admitted to the bar of the Pennsylvania Supreme Court. His success as secretary of the treaty conference with the Indians at Lehigh prompted him to envision a future as an imperial administrator. He sailed to London in pursuit of a position, but was rebuffed as a provincial. He returned and in 1768 married Ann Borden, an ardent patriot. Serving briefly as customs collector at Newcastle, he secured an appointment at Bordentown, New Jersey, and he became established as a political force, earning appointment to the governor's council in 1774 and election to the Continental Congress in 1776. He signed the Declaration of Independence. During the Revolution, Hopkinson supplied Betsy Ross with the design of the flag of the United States and won fame for his verse satires of Tories and the British. Appointed to the Court of Admiralty of Pennsylvania in 1779, Hopkinson fought corruption in the administration of justice, incurring the wrath of American privateers who unsuccessfully attempted his impeachment. His actions vindicated, Hopkinson spent the 1780s as one of the most visible men of letters in the United States and the most conspicuous virtuoso of the polite arts. He participated in the Constitutional Convention of 1787. He died of a stroke in 1791 shortly after George Washington appointed him Federal District Judge of Pennsylvania. Three volumes of his writings, *The Miscellaneous Essays and Occasional Writings of Francis Hopkinson*, were collected and published in the year following his death.

Joseph Hopkinson (1770–1842) Son of poet and patriot Francis Hopkinson, Joseph Hopkinson was born in Philadelphia, raised in Bordentown, New Jersey, and educated at the newly reorganized University of the State of Pennsylvania. He graduated in 1786, tutoring there briefly before being granted an M.A. in 1789. He read law and in 1791 joined the bar. Hopkinson shared his father's fluency as a poet, composing lyrics that enjoyed popularity when published in magazines; his "Hail Columbia" (1798) became one of the nation's favorite patriotic songs. He served two terms in the U.S. House of Representatives from 1814 to 1819. As a lawyer he defended the men charged in the Whiskey Rebellion and successfully defended Supreme Court Justice Samuel Chase in his impeachment trial. As a federal judge, Hopkinson consolidated American copyright in his opinion in *Wheaton* v. *Peters* (1833). He served as president of the Pennsylvania Academy of Fine Arts, vice-president of the American Philosophical Society, and almost continuously from 1806 until his death as a trustee of the University of Pennsylvania.

David Humphreys (1752–1818) Born in Derby, Connecticut, the son of a Congregationalist pastor, Humphreys graduated from Yale in 1771. He earned his M.A. degree in 1774, and spent several years as master of a boarding school and as a private tutor. When the Revolution broke out he abandoned teaching to join the Continental Army. He rose quickly through the ranks, serving as aide to generals Israel Putnam, Nathanael Greene, and finally George Washington, traveling extensively with Washington between 1781 and 1783 and attaining the rank of lieutenant colonel. In 1785 he was engaged by Congress as a diplomat to assist in the United States' trade negotiations with European nations. After a brief term in the Connecticut legislature, he was again called to active duty in the Continental Army to aid in the suppression of Shays's Rebellion (1786–87). His service earned him the high regard of George Washington, for whom he worked as personal secretary (1787–88), and who appointed him Minister to Portugal in 1790, and Minister to Spain in 1796. In the wake of Shays's Rebellion, Humphreys collaborated with Joel Barlow, Lemuel Hopkins, and John Trumbull (all members of a circle later referred to as the Connecticut Wits) on *The Anarchiad* (1786–87), a Federalist satire; his *Essay on the Life of the Honorable Major General Israel Putnam* was published in 1788, and his *Poems* in 1789. After the election of Thomas Jefferson in 1800, Humphreys was recalled from office and he returned to Connecticut. He became one of New England's early industrialists, founding both wool and cotton mills. In 1802, he imported a flock of merino sheep to improve American wool quality. From 1812 to 1814 he served again in the Connecticut legislature.

Robert Hunter (1666–1734)   Grandson of Robert Hunter, the twentieth laird of Hunterston, and son of attorney James Hunter and Margaret Spalding, Hunter was born in Edinburgh. He followed a military career from 1688 until 1706, rising to the rank of lieutenant colonel and distinguishing himself as aide-de-camp to the duke of Marlborough, commander-in-chief during battles against the French at Blenheim and Ramillies. Hunter lost Marlborough's favor when he secured the surrender of Antwerp from the Spanish before Marlborough's designated victor, William Cadogan, could arrive on the scene. Retiring from military service, he married Lady Elizabeth Hay, a wealthy widow, in 1707, and associated in London with noted writers including Joseph Addison, Richard Steele, and Jonathan Swift; Steele later published his writing in *The Tatler*. Appointed lieutenant-governor of Virginia, he was taken prisoner by French pirates on his way to the colony and held captive. He was exchanged in 1709 and became governor of New York and New Jersey, then a single position, serving until 1720. While in New York he published *Androboros: A Biographical Farce* (1714), a dramatic satire directed against his opponents in the New York Assembly; the play helped turn public opinion in his favor. After seven years in London as comptroller of customs, Hunter was appointed governor of Jamaica in 1727, and served there for the remainder of his life. Most of his writings were destroyed when his papers were burned after his death.

Edward Johnson (1598–1672)   A skilled carpenter born in Canterbury, England, Johnson came to Massachusetts in the first wave of the Puritan migration. After working along the Merrimac River as an Indian trader, he returned to England, sold his family's land holdings, and then settled permanently in New England in 1637, bringing his wife, Susan, and seven children. He founded the town of Woburn, where he lived for 30 years. Orthodox in his opinions, he backed Governor John Winthrop's campaign against religious dissenters and took pride in the creation of a Bible Commonwealth in Massachusetts; to confute the criticisms of radicals in England who thought the colony a misadventure, he composed the first history of the northern Puritan settlements, *The Wonder-Working Providence of Sions Saviour in New England* (1653). He was also the author of "New England's Annoyances," a burlesque of the bad opinions of New England life then prevalent in London.

James Kirkpatrick (1696–1770)   Born (as James Killpatrick) in Carlow, near Carrickfergus, Ireland, Kirkpatrick was educated at the University of Edinburgh; he matriculated in 1708 but failed to complete a degree. His attempt to establish a medical practice in Ireland failed, and in 1717 he immigrated to South Carolina, where his uncle was a merchant. His ship was plundered by pirates en route, and he arrived in Charleston penniless. He married and established himself as a medical practitioner. Until the arrival of Thomas Dale in 1733, he exercised a near monopoly on the local manufacture and sale of drugs. When smallpox overran the colony in 1738 the rivalry between Dale and Kirkpatrick provoked extensive debate in the press, ostensibly about Kirkpatrick's application of cantharides during inoculation, though the controversy had political overtones, with Dale drawing his support from large planters and merchants, and Kirkpatrick from imperial placemen and military officers. Kirkpatrick attached himself to the expeditionary force James Oglethorpe was conducting against the Spanish in Florida; after the War of Jenkins' Ear, he sailed to London, changed his name, secured medical credentials, and attempted to become the volunteer laureate of British mercantilism, publishing a long, philosophical poem, *The Sea-Piece* (1750). His *Analysis of Innoculation* (1754) made him an international medical celebrity: he inoculated much of the royalty and aristocracy of Britain and France before he died in 1770. An interest of his latter years was the investigation of diseases common to men of letters.

Sarah Kemble Knight (1666–1727)   Relatively little is known about the life of Sarah Kemble Knight, aside from what is revealed in *The Journal of Madam Knight*, her narrative of a 1704–05 business trip from Boston to New York, first published in 1825. She was born in Boston, the daughter of a merchant, and was married, probably in the late 1680s, to a Captain Richard Knight, an older man who died in 1706, leaving her considerable property. In 1707, she was running her father's shop in Boston, copying and witnessing legal documents, keeping boarders, and possibly running a school; in 1713, after the marriage of her only daughter, she moved to New London, Connecticut, where she ran an inn and invested in real estate. She was a member of Norwich Congregational Church. On her death, she left a large estate.

Tom Law (fl. 1720s)   Tom Law has been credited with the authorship of several popular ballads dating from the 1720s, including "Lovewell's Fight" and "The Rebels Reward; or, English Courage Display'd," published in broadside form in Boston; little else is known about his life.

Richard Lewis (c. 1699–1734)   Born in Llanfair, Wales, Lewis attended Balliol College, Oxford, without taking a degree, and came to Maryland in 1718. He married in 1723, and accepted a position as schoolmaster at King William's School in Annapolis. In 1728, he published *The Mouse-Trap; or, The Battle of the Cambrians and Mice*, a translation of Edward Holdsworth's neo-Latin mock-epic *Muscipula* (1709). Other poems appeared in newspapers and magazines on both sides of the Atlantic; his widely republished "A Journey from Patapsco to Annapolis" (1730) provoked the satire of Alexander Pope for its assertion that American nature would engender a more brilliant art than that produced in the Old World. During the 1730s he sent specimens and observations of natural phenomena to Peter Collinson of the Royal Society in London.

William Livingston (1723–1790)   Born in Albany into one of New York's prominent families, William Livingston was educated at Yale; after graduation, he settled in New York City as a lawyer, mixing in politics and society. His literary reputation was established by *Philosophical Solitude*, written while an undergraduate and published in 1747. A successful lawyer, he moved in 1772 to Elizabethtown, New Jersey, where he built an estate, Liberty Hall. He served as representative of New Jersey to the Continental Congress (1774–76), brigadier general of the New Jersey militia (1775–76), and was elected first governor of the state of New Jersey, a position he held until his death. He participated in the Constitutional Convention in 1787 and worked to ensure speedy ratification in his state.

Cotton Mather (1663–1728)   Born in Boston into a dynasty of Reformed Christian ministers, Mather was educated at Harvard College (B.A. 1678, M.A. 1681), then joined his father Increase Mather at the pulpit of Second Church in Boston. Ordained in 1685, he quickly established himself as the most energetic divine of his generation. Greatly concerned with the adaptation of the elements of Reformed Christian religious practice to a society that was growing increasingly cosmopolitan and commercial, he wrote, preached, and organized religious societies to improve the piety of the citizenry. Although trained in the classics, he expressed unease with the growing prestige of neoclassical learning. He at the same time admired the advances in natural philosophy, became an American fellow of the Royal Society, and celebrated a post-Newtonian vision of providential order akin to that of British intellectuals such as Sir Richard Blackmore. Mather's early prose and poetry displayed the elaborate wit, word-play, allusion, and ornament that typified literary mannerism. Encounters with the poetry of Isaac Watts caused an expansion and simplification of his style, particularly evident in his poems after 1703. He frequently epitomized the point of sermons with a verse digest. He wrote elegies, meditations, hymns, biblical paraphrases, and occasional satires, publishing almost 500 works during his lifetime, including *Memorable Providences Relating to Witchcrafts and Possessions* (1689), *The Wonderful Works of God Commemorated* (1690), *The Wonders of the Invisible World* (1693), *Magnalia Christi Americana* (1701), *The Negro Christianized* (1706), *Bonifacius: An Essay upon the Good* (1710), *Psalterium Americanum* (1718), *The Christian Philosopher* (1721), *The Angel of Bethesda* (1724), *Parentator: Memoirs of Remarkables in the Life and the death of the Ever-Memorable Dr. Increase Mather* (1724), *Manuductio ad Ministerium* (1726), and *Agricola, or The Religious Husbandman* (1727).

Lewis Morris II (1671–1746) The orphaned son of a Welsh captain of Cromwell's army, Lewis Morris II was born in New York City in 1671. He was raised from infancy by an uncle, Lewis Morris, in New Jersey. Upon the uncle's death in 1691, Morris inherited vast tracts of land in New York and New Jersey. Educated by the Quaker savant George Keith, he displayed an early talent for writing. At 20 he was appointed judge of the Court of Sessions in East New Jersey, and a year later became a member of the Governing Council of East New Jersey, soon rising to the council's presidency. In 1702, he traveled to England and successfully petitioned Queen Anne for the consolidation of East and West Jersey into one colony, of which he was appointed governor. The appointment was immediately rescinded and the post bestowed, along with the governorship of New York, upon the Queen's dissolute cousin, Lord Cornbury. Lewis organized the opposition. When Robert Hunter was named governor of New York in 1720, Morris formed a close friendship with him; he aided Hunter in the composition of the political closet drama (*Androboros, 1714*) that turned public sentiment in Hunter's favor. Hunter appointed him Chief Justice of the Supreme Court, a post Morris held until deposed by Governor William Cosby. Morris subsequently contributed satires and screeds to John Peter Zenger's *New York Weekly Journal* and sailed to London to testify in Parliament about Cosby's corruption. In 1738, Morris was appointed governor of New Jersey. Morris's poems on affairs of state in the empire and colony expressed a profound distrust of merchants and a jaundiced view of urban democracy.

Sarah Wentworth Morton (1759–1846) Born in Boston into one of New England's wealthiest families, Sarah Apthorp was raised in Boston and in Braintree, Massachusetts. Unlike many in her extended family, she supported the patriot cause during the Revolution. In 1781 she married Perez Morton, a prominent lawyer and politician, and in 1784 the couple returned to the Apthorp mansion in Boston, which had been seized as loyalist property. They went on to raise five children together, weathering public scandal and domestic tragedy: in 1788, Frances Apthorp, Sarah's younger sister, having given birth to Perez Morton's daughter, committed suicide; Sarah's brother Charles challenged Perez Morton to a duel. Details of the scandal were reprinted in newspapers, became a subject of gossip, and reappeared in veiled form in *The Power of Sympathy* (1789), a novel by William Hill Brown. Morton began publishing her poetry in periodicals around the same time, at first as "Constantia" and later as "Philenia." She went on to write *Ouâbi, or The Virtues of Nature* (1790), *Beacon Hill* (1797), *The Virtues of Society* (1799), *My Mind and Its Thoughts* (1823), and much periodical verse on subjects both public and private. Moving with her husband to Dorchester in 1797, she entertained literary figures including Joseph Dennie, Robert Treat Paine, Jr., and Isaiah Thomas; she sat for three portraits by Gilbert Stuart, for whom she wrote "To Mr. Stuart" in 1803. She died at her childhood home in Braintree, having returned there in 1837 following the death of her husband.

Thomas Morton (c. 1580–1645) Morton was born sometime between 1580 and 1595 into a gentry family in Devonshire and educated to be a gentleman at Clifford's Inn in the Inns of Court. Lacking the cash and connections to pursue a genteel life, he sailed to America in 1624 to assist in the establishment of a trading colony at Mount Wollaston, within the limits of present-day Quincy, Massachusetts. After the departure of the settlement's leader, Morton usurped control, canceled laborers' indentures and traded guns with Native Americans to secure the colony's economic success; with the aid of newly armed Indian hunters, he established control over the regional market for game. In 1627, having renamed the colony Mare Mount, Morton erected a maypole ("after the old English custome") and invited the residents of the surrounding countryside to participate in spring revels, becoming an emblem of carnality, wickedness, and paganism in the eyes of New England's orthodox. In 1628 officials from Plymouth Plantation arrested Morton, marooned him on the Isle of Shoals, finally permitting him to leave for England. In 1629 he returned to Massachusetts, and in 1630 he was arrested again, his belongings seized and his house burned, and he was shipped to England. There he began legal proceedings against Massachusetts Bay, made petitions to various courts, and expanded these into *New English Canaan*, an account of his life in America. (Completed in 1633, the book was too controversial for English publishers and was printed instead in Amsterdam, in 1637; Parliament, believing it to be a foreign-printed outlaw tract, confiscated most copies.) Morton returned to America in 1643, living in Maine and Rhode Island; traveling into Massachusetts, he was once again arrested, spent a year in a Boston jail, and died soon afterward.

William Munford (1775–1825) Son of Colonel Robert Munford, the Revolutionary patriot and playwright, Munford was born in Mecklenburg Country, Virginia, and educated at William and Mary, where he read law. The youngest member of a Williamsburg literary coterie that included Margaret Lowther Page, John Page, St. George Tucker, and George Wythe, he published a collection of his writings, *Poems, and Compositions in Prose on Several Occasions*, in 1798. He had been elected as a representative to the House of Burgesses a year earlier, and served intermittently in the legislature and in the council of state (which advised the governor) until 1811. Munford married in 1802 and fathered eight children. To support his family, he edited and published court reports (including those of the Virginia Supreme Court of Appeals) and served as clerk of the House of Delegates; he compiled *The Revised Code of the Laws of Virginia* (1819) and *A General Index to the Virginia Law Authorities* (1819). During his leisure hours he wrote verse satires and translated the *Iliad* into English. While the translation was published posthumously (in 1846), his later poetic compositions remain in manuscript.

Mary Nelson (fl. 1769) Mary Nelson is known only from the verse advertisement "Forty Shillings Reward," published in the *Pennsylvania Chronicle* early in 1769.

John Norton Jr. (1651–1716) Born in Ipswich, Massachusetts, a nephew of the Rev. John Norton, John Norton Jr. studied divinity at Harvard College, graduating in 1671. He was called to be pastor of the church at Hingham, Massachusetts, in 1678, and married in the same year. His sole surviving contribution to religious literature was his *An Essay Tending to Promote Reformation*, published in Boston in 1708. His notable contribution to colonial New England's literary culture was his 1672 elegy for poet Anne Bradstreet, published in 1678 in her posthumous *Selected Poems.*

Urian Oakes (c. 1631–1681) Brought from England as a child during the first Puritan exodus to New England, Urian Oakes was educated at Harvard College (B.A. 1649). Orthodox in his Reformed Christianity, Oakes believed his future lay with the Bible Commonwealth being constructed by Oliver Cromwell, and in the early 1650s moved to England, where he served as a chaplain to a Puritan household, then minister at Tichfield. After the Restoration, Oakes was expelled from his pulpit, a victim of the 1662 Act of Uniformity; a military family supported him for several years until the persecutions passed and he could regain a ministerial appointment. During his English residence, he maintained his collegial bonds with his old classmates and friends in New England, composing an elegy in 1667 on the death of the Rev. Thomas Shepard, pastor of the Church at Charlestown. In 1671 Oakes accepted the position of pastor of the congregation at Cambridge, Massachusetts; in 1675, while continuing to serve the Cambridge church, he became acting president of Harvard College, which he remained until his death in 1681.

Samson Occom (1723–1792) Born in a Mohegan settlement near New London, Connecticut, Occom was converted to Christianity in 1740, during the first Great Awakening. Named to the Mohegan Council by Ben Uncas II in 1742, a scholarship from the Anglican Society for the Propagation of the Gospel enabled him, from 1743 to 1748, to attend a preparatory school run by Eleazar Wheelock in Lebanon, Connecticut. From 1749 to 1761, Occom served as schoolmaster, minister, and legal adviser to the Long Island Montauk. He married in 1751, fathering 11 children. In 1764, having preached for several years around Oneida, New York, he was employed by the Society for the Propagation of the Gospel as a missionary to the Mohegan and other Connecticut tribes. From 1765 to 1768 he traveled through England, Scotland, and Ireland, delivering hundreds of sermons and raising almost £12,000 for Indian missionary work, most of it spent in the founding of Dartmouth College. (During his tour of Great Britain he was befriended by Selina Hastings, Countess of Huntingdon, later patron of Phillis Wheatley.) Occom's ties to Wheelock and the Society for the Propagation of the Gospel were strained after he charged Wheelock with misusing funds. Around 1773, he began planning for a Christian Indian settlement, Brothertown, near Oneida, moving there finally in 1789. In 1772 he published the often reprinted *Sermon Preached at the Execution of Moses Paul*; his *Choice Collection of Hymns and Spiritual Songs* (1774) includes several hymns since attributed to him.

Jonathan Odell (1737–1818) Born in Newark, New Jersey, the son of a carpenter and the maternal grandson of Jonathan Dickinson, first president of the College of New Jersey (Princeton), Odell studied medicine at his grandfather's college. After graduation in 1754, he became master of the Princeton grammar school, but soon joined the British Army, serving for a year as a physician in the West Indies. In 1757 he earned his M.A. degree, then traveled to England, where he read for the ministry, supporting himself as a teacher. He began publishing poetry in the 1760s, took holy orders in the Church of England, and met Benjamin Franklin, who arranged for his sponsorship by the Anglican Society for the Propagation of the Gospel in America. With its support Odell returned to New Jersey in 1767, where he presided over St. Ann's Church in Burlington, New Jersey, with subsidiary appointments at St. Andrew's Church in Mount Holly and St. James's Church in Bristol, Pennsylvania. A loyalist, he remained in Burlington until late 1776: in June of that year he had visited and befriended captured English officers and written a birthday ode to the king, leading local patriots to restrict his movements, and in December patriots raided his home in search of Hessian mercenaries; his property was eventually confiscated. Fleeing to New York City, Odell served as a deputy chaplain to the British Army and also supervised the government's press and publications, becoming an effective propagandist for the loyalist cause. He wrote essays and satirical verse for loyalist newspapers. In 1779, with fellow poet and literary collaborator Joseph Stansbury, he aided in communications between John André and Benedict Arnold. Odell left New York City with the English evacuation in 1783 and eventually settled in New Brunswick, Canada, where he spent the remainder of his life as a member of the provincial council, council clerk, and in the comfortable post of provincial secretary.

George Ogilvie (c. 1753–1801) The eldest son of Alexander Ogilvie of Auchiries, Scotland, Ogilvie came to America in 1774 to serve as plantation overseer for his uncle Charles, who owned three substantial properties in South Carolina. While overseeing the construction of Myrtle Grove, a rice plantation on Crow Island in the Santee River, he began his poem "Carolina," a georgic describing plantation life; he had completed some 1400 lines of verse when the political turmoil of the Revolution interrupted his efforts. A loyalist who refused to sign an oath of allegiance to the patriot government, Ogilvie was banished and traveled back to Scotland by way of St. Eustacius. In 1779 he married his cousin Rebecca Irvine of Dumbries; the couple had 11 children. He returned to Charleston six years later to sue for reparations for seizure of property, and won his case, but found that no civil authority would enforce the verdict. Back in Scotland, he completed and published *Carolina; or, The Planter* in 1790, and took possession of Auchiries House, the family seat, in 1791. Shortly thereafter, he became comptroller of customs in Aberdeen, a post he held until his death in 1801.

John Osborn (1713–1753) Born in Sandwich, Massachusetts, the son of a Scotch-Irish schoolmaster and clergyman, John Osborn graduated from Harvard College in 1735. Failing in an attempt at a ministerial career (an early sermon, delivered at Chatham, was considered insufficiently orthodox), he studied medicine, and was invited by the college to stay on as tutor. He preferred professional and family life, moving to Middleton, Connecticut, and marrying Mary Doane of Chatham, with whom he had six children. His surviving poems include "A Whaling Song" and an "Elegiack Epistle . . . upon the Death of a Sister." In 1751, he contracted a communicable disease while treating a patient and died two years later.

Margaret Lowther Page (1759–1835) Margaret Lowther, born in New York, was already a poet when she was introduced in Martha Washington's republican court to Congressman John Page, the wealthiest man in Virginia. In 1790 she married Page and became mistress of Rosewell, an extensive plantation in the Old Dominion, and of a townhouse in Williamsburg. In Williamsburg she belonged to a literary circle that included her husband (also a poet), Theodorick Bland, and St. George Tucker. At Rosewell, she managed the household and raised children, seven from her husband's previous marriage, and five of her own, three having died in infancy. While much of her poetic production was addressed to specific individuals of her acquaintance, certain of her verses appeared in print in New York and Philadelphia magazines between 1790 and 1810. When her husband was elected governor of Virginia in 1803, she presided over his household in Richmond during his three-year term. The couple returned to Rosewell in 1805. After her husband's death in 1808, she moved permanently to Williamsburg.

Robert Treat Paine Jr. (1773–1811) Born Thomas Paine in Taunton, Massachusetts, Robert Treat Paine Jr. adopted the name of his father (a signer of the Declaration of Independence) in 1801 to avoid association with the radical writer of the same name. He graduated from Harvard, where he acquired a reputation as a scholar, but after three weeks quit the position that his father had arranged for him with one of the leading mercantile houses in

Boston. He wrote verse satires for *Massachusetts Magazine* and the *Federal Orrery* (a newspaper he founded in 1794), married an actress (after which his father barred him from the family home), worked as the master of ceremonies of a theater, and frequented taverns. His 1798 song "Adams and Liberty" (sung to "To Anacreon in Heaven," the tune that would later be adopted as the music of "The Star Spangled Banner") became highly popular. Known as a heavy drinker, he made an attempt at personal reformation after achieving literary celebrity. He read law, joined the Massachusetts bar in 1802, and practiced for a short time before resuming a dissipated life; he spent the remainder of his short life drifting.

Thomas Paine (1737–1809) Born in Thetford, England, Thomas Paine left school at 12, spent six years as an apprentice in his father's corset-making business, and served briefly as a merchant seaman. After a failed attempt to establish a corset shop, he worked for three years as an excise officer, then as a servant, a schoolteacher, and again in the excise service, from 1768 to 1774. He married twice, his first wife dying in childbirth and his second legally separating in 1774. In the same year, encouraged by Benjamin Franklin, whom he had met in London, Paine left England for Philadelphia. Early in 1776, he published an anonymous pamphlet in support of American independence, *Common Sense*, that became a widely influential bestseller. He served with the Pennsylvania militia in New Jersey and wrote "The American Crisis," the first of a series of thirteen "Crisis" essays (1776–83), along with other political articles and pamphlets. In 1781 he traveled to France to secure aid for the American war effort. In 1787, he returned to England, attempting to fund the construction of an iron bridge of his own design. With the outbreak of the French Revolution, he returned to political writing, publishing *The Rights of Man* (1791–92). Parliament suppressed the book, and Paine was tried and found guilty in absentia for treason. In France, he was made an honorary citizen, and was elected to the Convention. After the Jacobins seized power, he was jailed in Luxembourg Prison, where he worked on *The Age of Reason* (1794–95), his deistic critique of religion. Paine returned to the United States in 1802 and continued to write for the press until his death, in New York City, in 1809.

Francis Daniel Pastorius (1651–1719) Born in Sommerhausen, Germany, in present-day Bavaria, the son of a judge and burgher, Francis Daniel Pastorius attended the universities of Strasbourg, Basel, Jena, Regensburg, and Altdorf, where he received a doctor of law degree in 1676. He mastered seven languages and wrote works in German, English, and Latin. While practicing law in Frankfurt, he befriended the founder of the Pietist movement, pastor Philip Jacob Spener, and in 1682, joined Pietist associates seeking freedom of worship in a plan to immigrate to Pennsylvania, on land purchased from William Penn. The next year he led a party of Mennonites and Quakers across the Atlantic, and helped establish the new settlement of Germantown (now a neighborhood in Philadelphia). Pastorius married Anneke Klosterman in 1686, fathered two children, and became a prominent citizen of Pennsylvania, serving as justice of the peace, town clerk, mayor, and founding instructor of the school in Germantown; a two-term representative, beginning in 1687, in the Pennsylvania Assembly; author of a 1688 resolution against slave-holding adopted by the Germantown Quakers, the first such protest by a religious group in America; and author of a noted pamphlet encouraging immigration to the colony, *Circumstantial Geographical Description of Pennsylvania* (1700). Pastorius wrote profusely throughout his life in a variety of forms and on a variety of topics, in several languages; much of his poetry remains unpublished, in manuscript books.

Mary Hirst Pepperell (1708–1789)   Granddaughter of Judge Samuel Sewell and daughter of Massachusetts merchant, Grove Hirst, Mary Hirst was one of the belles of 1720s Boston. (The diary of the young Rev. Joseph Moody, the historical model for Hawthorne's protagonist in "The Minister's Black Veil," confessed his infatuation with her.) She chose to wed William Pepperell, a wealthy young landowner, merchant, shipbuilder, and military officer from Kittery, Maine. They were married in 1722 and for the next 67 years, Mary Hirst Pepperell resided at the Pepperell mansion in Kittery and exerted great social influence. She had four children, two of whom died in infancy. Her husband was made a baronet for his leadership of the conquest of Louisbourg. During the 1750s Pepperell's fortune was the largest in the northern colonies. After his death, Mary Pepperell worked to keep the reputation of her husband alive. Throughout her life she was a voluble correspondent and prolific poet, circulating verse with men and women in Boston and Portsmouth, although only one poem is known to survive.

James Revel (fl. c. 1659–1680)   It is an open question whether James Revel existed as a person, or is a later poetic personification of the "wild boy" who gets in trouble, suffers punishment, repents, and survives to warn other young men of the perils of keeping bad company. His sorrowful account of life as a transported felon in Virginia during the 1670s, at a time when white indentured servants were gradually being replaced by African slaves, contains specific details of colonial conditions that indicate that some kernel of experience stands at the center of his archetypal story. Revel's verse testimony had a long life in the London world of broadside balladry; the earliest surviving imprints of the work date from the late 18th century.

John Saffin (1626–1710)   Saffin was born into a merchant family in Exeter, England, and came with his parents to Massachusetts Bay in 1642. He was elected selectman of Scituate where his probity and business sense gave him sufficient reputation that Thomas Willett, the Plymouth magistrate (who would be appointed first mayor of New York City after its takeover from the

Dutch) consented to a match between Saffin and his daughter Martha. He moved to Boston, joined the First Church there in 1665, and established himself as a commercial and political power. He was a deputy to the General Court from 1684 to 1686, speaker of the House, and a member of the Governor's Council. In 1687, he was forced out of office for his conciliatory position toward London in struggles over the colony's charter; he moved to Rhode Island, and became the first probate judge of the newly organized Bristol County. Saffin remained a vocal participant in politics until his death, sending verse satires and admonitions to those who offended him. He kept a notebook during his latter years containing copies of his love poems to his wives, his satires against political opponents, religious meditations, notes on reading, and literary memorials of his quarrel with Samuel Sewall over the legality and morality of slavery.

George Sandys (1578–1644) Born in Bishopthorpe, York, Sandys was the youngest son of Edwin Sandys, archbishop of York. He attended Oxford and the Inns of Court, leaving to take up life as a courtier. In 1610 he embarked on a grand tour, crossing Europe into the Ottoman Empire and visiting the Holy Land, Egypt, Cyprus, Sicily, and Italy. He published his observations in a volume dedicated to Prince Charles, *A Relation of a Journey Begun Anno Dom.* 1610 (1615), which became very popular. When his niece's husband, Sir Francis Wyatt, was appointed the last governor of the Virginia under the Virginia Company Charter in 1621, Sandys became the colonial treasurer, and sailed with Wyatt to Virginia. On the voyage over, and on his plantation east of Jamestown, he continued work on his translation of Ovid's *Metamorphoses*, published in London beginning in 1626, a year after his return to England. He went on to publish other translations including *A Paraphrase Upon the Psalms of David* (1636), *A Paraphrase Upon the Divine Poems* (1638), *Christ's Passion* (1640), and *A Paraphrase Upon the Song of Solomon* (1641–42). He served on the privy council's Committee on the Plantations and as a gentleman attendant to Charles I.

George Seagood (c. 1685–1724) A 1702 graduate of Christ Church, Oxford, Seagood took holy orders in the Church of England. At Christ Church he had befriended Arthur Blackamore (c. 1679–c. 1723), a scholar who accepted an invitation in 1707 to travel to Virginia to teach at the College of William and Mary. Blackamore's descriptions of the country apparently persuaded Seagood to immigrate in 1716. The same year, Blackamore composed "Expeditio Ultramontana," a Latin verse memorial of Governor Alexander Spotswood's expedition with the Knights of the Golden Horseshoe westward into the wilds of Virginia. Seagood translated the poem into English. He became rector of Sittenbourne Parish on the Rappahanock River in 1717, enjoying a successful ministry and comfortable living until his death in 1724.

John Seccomb (1708–1792) Seccomb was born in Medford, Massachusetts. While an undergraduate at Harvard College, he became known for his witty manuscripts in prose and verse, including a burlesque on the state of college learning ("A Letter to a Gentleman, in Answer to a Latin Epistle, Written in a Very Obscure Hand") and two doggerel verses occasioned by the death of Harvard College's sweeper, Mathew Abdy. These verses became immensely popular in British America and in Great Britain, and were often reprinted and imitated. Another widely appreciated comic poem—a mock epic about the roasting of a goose illegally procured from the Boston Commons in a "Yankee Hastings"—has not survived. In 1738 Seccomb was ordained minister at Harvard, Massachusetts, where he served for almost 20 years. In 1763 he accepted the call of a congregation in Nova Scotia. A devoted angler, he delivered sermons proclaiming God's approbation of fishing.

Samuel Sewall (1652–1730) Born at Bishop Stoke in England, Samuel Sewall was brought to New England at age nine with his parents, who were fleeing the repression of Puritans after the Restoration of Charles II. He attended Harvard College, graduated in 1671, and considered a life in the ministry before marrying Hannah Hull, daughter of one of the richest men in New England, in 1676. His father-in-law set him up in business as a merchant, and the young couple lived on an estate that would give its name to the town of Brookline. In 1681 Sewall began his first public employment, overseeing the Boston printing press for the General Court of Massachusetts. He determined what was suitable for publication and whether materials should be printed at public charge. In 1691 he composed a defense of the revolt of the people of Massachusetts against the government of Sir Edmund Andros, *The Revolution in New England Justified*. Greatly interested in the possibility that the end times might be approaching, he published apocalyptic speculations: *Phaenomena quaedam Apocalyptica* (1697) and *Proposals Touching the Accomplishment of Prophecies* (1713). *The Selling of Joseph* (1700) argued that scripture showed slavery to be incompatible with the practice of Christianity. In 1671 he began to keep a journal of contemporary news and politics, continuing until his death nearly 60 years later. Sewall's diary—as detailed an account as exists of New England's changing social and political landscape during these years—chronicled his courtships and remarriages after the death of his first wife, his actions as a legislator to the Massachusetts General Court and member of the Council, his appointment as one of the judges presiding over the Salem witchcraft trials and his subsequent remorse about his role in the trials, and his pride in his son Joseph's career in the ministry.

John Singleton (fl. 1750–1767) An actor who traveled with the Lewis Hallam theatrical troupe through British America during its tours of the 1750s and 60s, John Singleton composed a celebratory poem inaugurating the theater in Williamsburg, Virginia, in 1752. He remained with the group until the late 1760s, and on Barbados during its tour of the West Indies composed *A General Description of the West Indies Islands* (1767).

John Smith (1580–1631) Born in Lincolnshire, England, the son of a tenant farmer, John Smith received a grammar school education, was apprenticed briefly to a merchant, then joined a company of soldiers fighting the Spanish in the Low Countries. He toured France with the son of a lord, then traveled through Italy, the latter journey paid for with his share of the spoils from a Venetian merchant vessel captured by his ship in the Mediterranean. In 1601, he enlisted in a Hungarian regiment and saw action against the Turks. Promoted to captain, he killed three Turkish champions in individual duels. Wounded in battle, Smith was captured and in 1603 sold to a Turkish trader, becoming a slave to an Ottoman pasha. Eventually killing his master, he escaped and returned to England in 1604. Late in 1606, he joined other colonists bound for Virginia; during the voyage, he was accused of plotting against the expedition's leaders and almost hanged at Nevis, but was later reprieved. Settling in Jamestown, Smith led surveying and supply missions, during one of which he was captured by Powhatan Indians, participated in ceremonies, and made a Powhatan chief. (He would later write he was saved from execution by the intervention of Pocahontas, but he had more probably undergone a Powhatan adoption ritual.) Smith assumed the presidency of the colony's governing council in 1608, but was forced to leave Virginia in 1609 after he was badly burned in an accident. Smith published *A Map of Virginia* in 1612. In 1614, he sailed for "Northern Virginia," surveying the coasts of Massachusetts and Maine and naming the region New England; on a second voyage in 1615, he was captured by a French privateer. Back in England, he published *A Description of New England* (1616), *New Englands Trials* (1620), *The Generall History of Virginia, New-England, and the Summer Isles* (1624), *An Accidence, or the Pathway to Experience* (1626), *The True Travels* (1630), and *Advertisements for the Unexperienced Planters of New England, or Anywhere* (1631).

William Smith (1727–1803) Smith was born in Aberdeen, Scotland, into a gentry family. Educated at the University of Aberdeen (A.M. 1747), he came to America in 1751 as tutor to the Martin family of Long Island and Antigua. During the controversy over the establishment of King's College in New York (Columbia University), he put himself forward as a candidate to lead the college, publishing a utopian tract about education, *A General Idea of the College of Mirania* (1753). The pamphlet attracted the notice of Benjamin Franklin, who installed him as director of the Academy in Philadelphia with the charge to elevate it to collegiate standing. Before assuming the post, Smith returned to England and received ordination in the Church of England. He oversaw the rechartering of the school as the Academy of Philadelphia in 1756. In Philadelphia, Smith sought out the most talented youths of the colony, fostering a circle that included the painters Benjamin West and John Green, the poets Francis Hopkinson and Nathaniel Evans, dramatist Thomas Godfrey, and the preacher Jacob Duché. He founded *The American Magazine and Monthly Chronicle of the British Colonies.* He opposed the Stamp Act but did not support independence. His Tory politics led to the dissolution of the College in 1779; during the 1780s, in Maryland, he established Washington College. By 1789, patriot resentments had receded and he was appointed provost of what was by then the University of Pennsylvania.

Joseph Stansbury (1742–1809) Born in London and educated at St. Paul's School before being apprenticed, Stansbury came to America with his wife in 1767 and established himself as the proprietor of a Philadelphia china shop. During the early years of the Revolution he published loyalist songs and verses in Philadelphia newspapers; though he signed an oath of allegiance to the patriots, he was briefly imprisoned in 1776 for his political sentiments. During the British occupation of Philadelphia, he held several minor offices, including oversight of the lottery. After the British evacuated the city, Stansbury, who had been instrumental in arranging Benedict Arnold's treason, by serving as a go-between, was again arrested for collusion with the enemy. He was able to engineer his release in a prisoner exchange and moved to New York, where he contributed satirical verses to Tory gazettes. When the Revolution ended, he burned his political writings and attempted to return to Philadelphia, but by 1783 was forced to join the loyalist exodus to Nova Scotia. After a year in England, where he sought unsuccessfully to receive a stipend for his services during the war, he returned to Philadelphia in 1785. Failing to prosper, he moved his large family in 1794 to New York, where he worked as secretary of the United Insurance Company.

James Sterling (1701–1763) Born in Downrass, Ireland, into a genteel but impoverished military family, Sterling graduated from Trinity College, Dublin, in 1720. He frequented Dublin's coffeehouses and theaters, married the actress Nancy Lyddel, and arranged for the performance and publication of his play *The Rival Generals* (1722), Ireland's first locally produced tragedy. He went to London, where he worked as a political writer, but found it difficult to earn a living. He returned to Dublin and tried, with modest success, to secure a reputation as a master of polite learning; he published a translation of Mauseus's *The Loves of Hero and Leander* (1728) and later adopted Mauseus as his cognomen. He received an M.A. degree in 1733, took holy orders, and served as chaplain of the Royal Regiment of Foot. At age 33 he published his *Poetical Works* (1734), to little acclaim; in 1736 a second tragedy, *The Parricide*, was performed at Goodman's Fields Theatre in London without success. In 1737, he immigrated to Maryland as an Anglican missionary. After holding several minor posts, he secured the rectorship of St. Paul's, in Maryland's Kent County. He joined the literary Tuesday Club, published occasional and civic verses in the *Maryland Gazette*, and became a principal contributor to William Smith's *American Magazine*.

Annis Boudinot Stockton (1736–1801) Born in Darby, Pennsylvania, the daughter of a merchant and silversmith, Annis Boudinot was educated at home. In 1753, she moved with her family to Princeton, New Jersey, where sometime in the winter of 1757–58 she married Richard Stockton, a prominent landowner with whom she had six children. Known as "Emilia" among the literati of the mid-Atlantic, she presided over a lively salon at Morven, the Stockton estate at Princeton. In 1776, the family was forced to flee their estate, which became Lord Cornwallis's headquarters; her husband, a signer of the Declaration of Independence, was imprisoned, and died in 1781. As a widow, she continued her career as a celebrated hostess and poet; her drawing room, in which she entertained Congress when it met at Princeton, became the model for Martha Washington's republican court, and she served as volunteer laureate during George Washington's presidency, regularly publishing poems on public affairs in newspapers and magazines.

Edward Taylor (c. 1642–1729)   Taylor was born into a Puritan family in Leistershire, England, and distinguished himself sufficiently at the local grammar school that he was given a position as a schoolteacher. Faced with the 1662 Act of Uniformity (which required him to swear loyalty to the Church of England) and other new anti-Puritan laws, he decided to join the second Puritan exodus to New England in 1668. In Massachusetts he enrolled in Harvard College, though he was a decade older than his fellow freshmen. He graduated in 1671 and was appointed minister of Westfield, on the colony's western frontier. In 1674 he married Elizabeth Fitch, with whom he had eight children. He served as the town's pastor, physician, and schoolteacher for the next 58 years, witnessing its transformation from a wilderness outpost to a provincial hamlet in a developed countryside. He remarried in 1689, fathering six more children. Taylor participated in the major religious controversies of the day, debating with the Rev. Solomon Stoddard whether to use the Lord's Supper as an instrument for converting the unredeemed or to exclude the unconverted from the sacrament. Taylor's particular reverence for the Lord's Supper may be seen in the series of "Preparatory Meditations" he wrote before personally partaking in it. Throughout his life Taylor wrote in verse and prose for a variety of purposes. Though he allowed only two stanzas of his extensive verse writings to appear in print, certain of his manuscripts were public, intended for circulation or for use in prayer meetings and worship; others were private, intended for his own spiritual perfection. The majority of Taylor's writings began to appear in print only in 1937.

Lucy Terry (c. 1730–1821)   Born in Africa and seized by slavers while a child, Lucy Terry was transported to Rhode Island and sold to Ebenezer Wells of Deerfield, Massachusetts. She converted to Christianity during the revivals of the late 1730s. In 1746 an Abenaki raiding party attacked Deerfield in an attempt to secure hostages for ransom. The conflict inspired Lucy Terry's sole surviving composition, "Bars Fight," which became a part of oral tradition and was eventually transcribed and published in 1855. Her freedom was purchased in 1756 by a free black farmer, Abijah Prince, whom she married; the couple moved to Guilford, Vermont, where they raised six children. She successfully pled her own case before the Vermont Supreme Court when Colonel Eli Bronson attempted the illegal seizure of the Prince family's land.

Henry Timberlake (1730–1765)   Born in Hanover county, Virginia, Timberlake volunteered for military service in 1756 and in 1758 fought against the French at Fort Duquesne. In 1760, he was appointed commander at Fort Burd, south of Pittsburgh. The next year, in the wake of a cessation of hostilities between the British and the Cherokee, he volunteered to travel into Tennessee, where he lived among the Cherokee for three months as a representative of British good faith. During a stay of three months, he courted the daughter of the Cherokee leader Ostenaca, Sakinney, who bore him a son; in 1762, he traveled with Ostenaca and a small party to London, where Ostenaca had an audience with George III, toured the city, and drew large crowds. Timberlake married, returned to America, and in 1764 accompanied another Cherokee party to London. In 1765, he published *The Memoirs of Lieut. Henry Timberlake* (*Who Accompanied the Three Cherokee Indians to England in the Year 1762*), which includes an early example of Native American song translated into English verse and remains a significant source of information about 18th-century Cherokee culture.

Benjamin Tompson (1642–1714)   Born in Braintree, Massachusetts, the son of a Puritan minister, and raised by a foster family in Charlestown after his mother's early death, Tompson graduated from Harvard College in 1662. From 1667 to 1670 he taught at the Boston Latin School (where one of his pupils was the young Cotton Mather), and then at the school in Charlestown. During these years he studied medicine; from 1674 to 1678 he worked as a physician. In 1676 he published *New Englands Crisis*, a mock-heroic account of King Philip's War, *New-Englands Tears*, and *A Funeral Tribute to . . . John Winthrope*. In 1678 he founded a school at Braintree where he taught for 22 years, also serving periodically as town clerk. In 1700 he married the wealthy Prudence Payson of Roxbury, moved to that town and served as schoolmaster for four years. In 1704 he returned to Braintree to resume work as schoolmaster, staying until 1710 when he returned permanently to Roxbury to live with his sons.

John Trumbull (1750–1831)   Born in Westbury, Connecticut, the son of a Congregationalist minister, Trumbull was granted admission to Yale College at age seven, but waited until he was 13 before attending. At Yale, he formed friendships with Timothy Dwight (with whom he wrote essays for publication in the New England papers), Joel Barlow, and David Humphreys. He graduated in 1770. In 1772 he published the first installment of his satire of contemporary manners, *The Progress of Dulness*, which he later expanded to three sections. In 1773 and 1774, having tutored at Yale and having passed the Connecticut bar, he continued legal studies in Boston with John Adams. During his time with Adams he began work on the mock epic *M'Fingal* (1775, 1782), which was republished, excerpted, and quoted ubiquitously in the press through the Revolutionary era. Trumbull married in 1776. He served in the Revolution, and when the Confederation of the United States began to unravel in the mid-1780s, collaborated with Lemuel Hopkins on the *Anarchiad*

(1786–87), a pro-Federal burlesque of manners and radical libertarian political doctrines. Trumbull represented his district in the Massachusetts state legislature and was appointed justice of the Superior Court in 1801. While a justice, he resided in Hartford until his retirement in 1825. He collected and published his poetic works in 1820. In the final years of his life he lived with a daughter in Detroit, Michigan.

St. George Tucker (1752–1827)　Born in Bermuda into a merchant family, Tucker was educated at the College of William and Mary. He read law under jurist George Wythe, and joined the Virginia bar on the eve of the American Revolution. He made his fortune during the war as a blockade runner, engaging in trade between the mainland, Bermuda, and the West Indies. In 1778 he married heiress Frances Bland Randolph. When British forces encroached into Virginia, he joined the Commonwealth militia as an officer and fought in several engagements, suffering a wound in the Battle of Guilford Courthouse. He served as a translator and liaison between the French Army and the patriot government at Yorktown. In 1788, Tucker assumed George Wythe's professorship at William and Mary; his years in Williamsburg were marked by contention with college authorities and by literary productivity nurtured in a circle of wits and writers that included John and Margaret Lowther Page, Theoderick Bland, and William Munford. As well as writing witty occasional verse, he adapted Blackstone's *Commentaries on the Laws of England* (1803) to the American legal situation, and published *A Dissertation on Slavery: With a Proposal for the Gradual Abolition of It in the State of Virginia* (1795). Tucker was a tinkerer and inventor who experimented with visual signal codes, plumbing, and telescopes. He was a charter member and officer of the Society for the Promotion of Useful Knowledge in Williamsburg. In 1804, he resigned his teaching post to become a judge on the Virginia Court of Appeals. In 1813 he accepted federal appointment on the U.S. District Court, serving until 1825.

Jane Colman Turell (1708–1735)　Jane Colman was born in Boston in 1708, where her father, the Rev. Benjamin Colman, served as first pastor of the fashionable Hollis Street Church. Home-schooled in Latin, French, and English belles lettres, she was drawn to poetry through the example of Elizabeth Singer Rowe, the English "Philomela," who was an old friend of her father. In her teens, she corresponded with a circle of Harvard-trained belletrists, including Mather Byles and John Adams, when her father became president of that institution. She married another young Harvard man, Ebenezer Turell, who took a pulpit in Medford. Jane chose not to print her compositions, circulating them in manuscript under the cognomen "Delia." She died young in childbirth and was mourned as a major loss to New England letters in a memorable elegy by the Rev. John Adams; some of her poems were printed posthumously in *Memoirs of the Life and Death of Mrs. Jane Turell* (1735). In addition to her more serious compositions, she was noted for her humorous poetry, none of which is known to have survived.

Royall Tyler (1757–1826)   The son of two old New England families, Tyler was born William Clark Tyler in Boston; he adopted his father's name in 1771, his mother having been widowed a year earlier. Tyler enrolled at Harvard College and quickly established himself as a brilliant student and mischievous personality. He graduated as valedictorian of the class of 1776, read law, and befriended painter John Trumbull and his circle. He served as a major in an unsuccessful attempt to supplant the British at Newport in 1778, then returned to the law, earning a Harvard M.A., gaining admission to the bar, and practicing in Falmouth, Maine, and later in Braintree, Massachusetts. In Braintree, where he settled in 1782, he fell in love with Abigail Adams, daughter of John and Abigail Adams. Wary of Tyler's reputation as a bon vivant, in 1785 the future president arranged for their engagement to be broken. Tyler joined the staff of General Benjamin Lincoln in 1787, and won praise for his skills as a negotiator during Lincoln's expedition against Daniel Shays and his rebel followers, earning him an appointment in negotiations between the governors of several New England states. While on a trip to confer with Governor DeWitt Clinton of New York, he composed his popular play *The Contrast* (1787), the first professionally produced American comedy; he followed up this success with a comic opera, *May Day in Town; or, New York in an Uproar* (1790). He left Boston for Vermont in 1791 and married Mary Palmer, with whom he had 11 children. In his professional life Tyler prospered, serving as assistant and later chief justice of the Vermont Supreme Court (1801–07, 1807–13), and as a law professor at the University of Vermont (1811–14). He was thwarted in his ambition to become United States senator for Vermont when he lost a special election in 1812 to Dudley Chase, speaker of the Vermont legislature. He also wrote extensively in many genres, producing poems (including verse for the popular "Colon and Spondee" columns, written with Joseph Dennie), a novel (*The Algerine Captive*, published in 1797), plays (one or two of which were produced in Boston, but which are not known to have survived), and a book of epistolary essays (*The Yankey in London*, 1809). Tyler died in Brattleboro, leaving the manuscripts of several unproduced plays including *The Island of Barrataria*, *Joseph and His Brethren*, *The Judgement of Solomon*, and *The Origin of the Feast of Purim*.

Mercy Otis Warren (1728–1814)   Born in the patriot Otis family of Barnstable, Massachusetts, Mercy Otis grew up in a household that prized intellect and public spirit. She married James Warren of Plymouth, Massachusetts, in 1754; James reveled in his wife's intelligence and encouraged her writing. He was closely involved in the political resistance to the British incursions on American liberties and served in the Massachusetts House of Representatives and the Provincial Congress; Mercy Warren found herself at the center of the debates of the day and participated in the discussions with many of the Founding Fathers. An ardent patriot, she satirized the Anglophile Tories of New England's cities in political closet dramas such as *The Adulateur* (1773) and *The Group* (1775). She was a close friend of Abigail Adams, whose Christian morality, distaste for pretension, and hunger for learning she shared.

When writing on political topics, Warren was sometimes bold to the point of tactlessness: her 1805 *History of the Rise, Progress and Termination of the American Revolution* contained several harangues aimed at central personalities of the early republic.

Phillis Wheatley (c. 1753–1784)   Brought to Boston on a slave ship in 1761, and purchased by John Wheatley, a tailor, Phillis Wheatley became the companion of John's wife, Susannah. To acquaint Phillis with the scriptures, the Wheatleys taught her to read and write. She mastered English in 16 months and could read "the most difficult Parts of the Sacred Writings, to the greatest Astonishment of all who heard her." At age 13, she began writing verse, including "To the University at Cambridge in New England." In addition to her home schooling in literary art, Wheatley sought instruction in the Christian religion under the Rev. Dr. Richard Sewall, pastor of Old South Church and member of a family long noteworthy for its antislavery beliefs. At 16 she was baptized as a communicant of Old South. Dr. Sewall died, inspiring an elegy, and shortly afterward the great evangelist and philanthropist George Whitefield died. "On the Death of the Rev. Mr. George Whitefield" was Wheatley's first published poem, appearing in 1770, when she was 16 or 17. Almost immediately she gained notice as a prodigy. Considering herself a member of the republic of letters, she corresponded with Christian belletrists, noted African-Americans, and members of the transatlantic network of abolitionists. When Phillis's ill health prompted John Wheatley to send her to England with his son, Nathaniel, in the hope that the sea voyage and foreign climate would produce an improvement in her physical condition, Wheatley made contact with the Countess of Huntingdon, Selina Hastings, one of her correspondents. A Reformed Christian philanthropist connected to the abolitionist movement, Hastings would become Wheatley's patron, ensuring that her book, *Poems on Various Subjects, Religious and Moral* (1773) was published. The book created a sensation, becoming a major document in international debates over the mental ability of Africans. In 1772 the Somerset Decision declared that the crown would not engage in the restoration of runaway slaves to their owners in Britain. Wheatley in England could have taken advantage of this legal situation; Nathaniel Wheatley, however, persuaded her to return to Boston to tend to his dying mother. Phillis did this in 1773, shortly before her book appeared. As a condition for returning, she apparently extracted the promise that he would manumit her when in America, which he did. She lived a freed woman in Boston, writing poetry and enduring the hardships of war. She married a freedman, John Peters, in 1778, and in the following year published a subscription circular for a second book. The circumstances of war and the shortage of ready cash appear to have doomed the project. Wheatley's final years were unhappy ones: she lost two children, her husband was jailed for debt, and ill health plagued her until her death in 1784.

Michael Wigglesworth (1631–1705)   Born in York, England, and brought to New Haven Colony as a boy in 1638, Wigglesworth attended Harvard College, graduating in 1651. He stayed at the college as tutor until 1654 when he began seeking a pulpit. In 1656, he was appointed minister to the church at Malden, Massachusetts, where he remained for 49 years until his death. He suffered from chronic asthma, and in 1663 the discomfort grew so great that he took a half year's leave to recover in Bermuda. Driven by the torments of his own body, he trained as a physician, acquiring skills that made him a respected healer in Massachusetts after his return. Shortly before leaving for Bermuda, Wigglesworth published *The Day of Doom* (1662), a versified elaboration of the judgment of the quick and the dead foretold in Revelation. When he returned, he found that the poem had captured the public's imagination; it would go through multiple editions during his lifetime, making him the most popular poet of 17th-century New England. Another poem, the verse jeremiad "God's Controversy with New England," made his reputation among the learned. In 1670 he published *Meat Out of the Eater*, a collection of short verses on religious themes.

Roger Williams (c. 1604–1683) Williams was born in London to a family in the cloth trade. A talented student, he captured the notice of Sir Edward Coke, who secured Williams a place in Sutton's Hospital, Charter House School. He won one of eight scholarships for excellence in Latin, Greek, and Hebrew languages offered by Pembroke College, Cambridge. He graduated in 1627 and connected with the network of East Anglian Puritans planning to move to Massachusetts Bay. Joining other Puritan immigrants to New England, he sailed in late 1630 with his new wife and arrived in the colony early in 1631. In Massachusetts Williams preached at Salem and Plymouth before being called to teach at Salem School. He was forced to surrender this post once his opposition to a civil religion became known. Controversy erupted in 1633 when the Massachusetts authorities formulated a loyalty oath to the government. Williams attacked it, arguing that an oath being a religious obligation should not be required of all men since everyone is not religiously regenerate. The civil and religious authorities ordered Williams to leave the colony. Instead of boarding a vessel to London, Williams headed southwest, settling at the headwaters of Narragansett Bay, outside of the jurisdiction of Plymouth and Massachusetts Bay. He bought land from the Narragansett chiefs Canonicus and Miantonomi and named his settlement Providence; others opposing the civil and religious order in New England were invited to join him. To protect his settlement from annexation, Roger Williams traveled to England to secure a charter that would give Providence colony status. His political connections proved valuable, for in 1643 he obtained a decree consolidating "the Providence Plantations in Narragansett Bay." While in London he also finished and published his study of American Indian languages and culture, *A Key into the Language of America* (1643). Williams's sojourn in England also saw the publication of his debate with John Cotton over the proper relation of church and state; his book *The Bloudy Tenent of Persecution, for Cause of Conscience* (1644) was embraced first by Presbyterians, and later by a host of dissenting societies in their struggles with governmental interference in worship. Upon his return to Providence Plantations, Williams set up as an Indian trader. He sailed to England again in 1651 to shore up the colony's patents. From 1654 to 1658 served as governor. He lived long enough to witness the ravages against the colony wrought by King Philip's War, 1675–76. He died while the colony was being rebuilt.

John Wilson (c. 1588–1667)   Born in Windsor, England, Wilson attended King's College, Cambridge. He sailed to Massachusetts Bay in 1630, returning to England a year later to bring his wife and others he had convinced to emigrate. From 1630 to 1667, he served as teacher and minister of the First Church of Boston. He played a large role in the establishment of Harvard College, beginning in 1636. Around the same time, his congregation was embroiled in the Antinomian controversy in response to the popular preaching of Anne Hutchinson, who was eventually condemned by church leaders and excommunicated. Wilson published a book of poetry in London in 1626, *A Song or, Story, for the Lasting Remembrance of Divers Famous Works, which God Hath Done in Our Time*, which was later reprinted in Boston; he continued writing verse in Massachusetts, and also published sermons and other religious works, including *The Day-Breaking, If Not the Sun-Rising of the Gospell with the Indians in New-England* (1647), and *The Cause of God and His People in New-England* (1663).

Christopher Witt (1675–1765)   Born in Wiltshire and trained in medicine, Dr. Christopher Witt was a physician fascinated by the mystic Johan Kelpius's "Order of Perfection." He left England in 1704 seeking the liberty to explore divine mysteries in William Penn's haven of religious tolerance, one of the 40 hermits who lived under the direction of Kelpius in the Pennsylvania wilderness. Witt lived communally with the other monks of the Wissahickon in a small log cabin and worshipped a God they believed to be immanent in Nature. The community believed in constant prayer and praise, and cultivated verse as a means of refreshing these perpetual petitions to God. Witt provided English versions of Kelpius's oracles and prayers for circulation among "seekers after perfection." When Kelpius died in 1708, at the age of about 35, Witt and five other monks remained at the hermitage for a decade. Then Witt and brother Daniel Giesler moved to Germantown where they shared a house. Witt practiced medicine and bestowed the first M.D. in Pennsylvania to John Kaign of New Jersey. His botanical garden was the most extensive in the middle colonies. He painted an oil portrait of Kelpius in 1705, built and repaired organs and virginals, designed several of Germantown's early stone houses, and constructed clockworks. He trained his mulatto slave Robert Claymore to become an expert clockmaker. Upon Witt's death in 1765 Claymore was manumitted, received Witt's furniture, a plot of land, a house, and all of Witt's clock-making tools.

Roger Wolcott (1679–1767)   Born shortly after his father Simon's house in Simsbury, Connecticut, was burned in King Philip's War, Wolcott was raised in Windsor. His father's death in 1687 left his mother, Martha, in charge of six children and an unfinished farm; she later married Daniel Clark. Roger was apprenticed to a clothier; he went into business in 1699, and was so successful that his neighbors reckoned him a rising man. He married Sarah Drake and set up a farm in 1702. He was chosen selectman for Windsor (1707), Windsor's representative for the Connecticut Assembly (1709), and Justice (1710). During the 1711 expedition against Canada, he served as commissary of Connecticut Stores. The accidental death of his son Alexander in 1711 occasioned Wolcott's first dated verse. In 1725 he published *Poetical Meditations, Being the Improvement of Some Vacant Hours*, which included religious meditations and an epic account of the history of Connecticut. He was elected deputy governor of the colony in 1741 and appointed Chief Judge of the Superior Court. In 1745, at age 67, he was commissioned a major general of the army for the expedition against Cape Breton. His leadership in the taking of Louisbourg won him an enduring reputation which bore fruit in 1750 when he was elected governor of Connecticut. He served four years.

Charles Woodmason (c.1720–c. 1777)   Woodmason, born in England, came to British America in 1752 and established himself as a planter in Winyaw, Prince Frederick Parish, South Carolina. He attempted unsuccessfully to found a scientific agricultural society, promoted Eliza Lucas Pinckney's method of cultivating indigo, and composed a georgic, "Indico," that remained unpublished because he was unable to sell enough subscriptions. He worked as warden and vestrymen in Winyaw, and served as an occasional lay preacher. Because the mercantile end of his business proved more prosperous than the planting, Woodmason moved to Charleston in 1762 with the idea of securing a position in the colonial bureaucracy. A man of letters who published poems in the London magazines, he was appointed clerk of the South Carolina Assembly. When the Stamp Act mandated the appointment of stamp collectors in the colonial capitals, Woodmason put himself forward, not anticipating the political consequences; he became so unpopular that he left for England in 1765. He was ordained an Anglican priest in 1766, and returned to South Carolina later that year as missionary to the South Carolina back country, traveling thousands of miles each year on horseback in the performance of his duties. His journal portraying the crude conditions of life on the frontier was published posthumously as *The Carolina Backcountry on the Eve of the Revolution* (1953). Woodmason moved to Virginia in 1772, to Maryland in 1773, and finally back to England in 1774. In 1776 he appealed for assistance from the bishop of London as a loyalist refugee. The date and place of his death are not known.

Susanna Wright (1697–1784)   The daughter of a Quaker minister, Susanna Wright was born in Lancashire, England, and came to Pennsylvania with her family around 1714. After some time in Philadelphia, they settled on the Susquehanna frontier, founding Wright's Ferry (now Columbia). Wright remained there for life. She ran the inn at Wright's Ferry, served as local physician, notary public, and mediator in negotiations between Pennsylvania and the Conestoga Indians. She participated in international networks of botanical exchange, pioneered silk manufacturing, painted landscapes, spoke in the Quaker meeting, and wrote poems that were shared in manuscript form throughout the middle colonies. She acquired some reputation as a woman of letters, known by the cognomen "Veneria"; her poems were read in Philadelphia's Quaker schools. Though she is not known to have traveled far from her country estate, her correspondents included Benjamin Franklin, Deborah and James Logan, Hannah Griffitts, and Benjamin Rush.

Note on the Texts

This volume contains 294 poems and excerpts from poems dating from around 1625 to 1800; it includes poems originally written in English and contemporary examples of verse translation. Most were written in those British colonies that would eventually become the United States, or after 1776 in the new nation, but a substantial minority, reflecting the more extensive geography of British America and the complexity of transatlantic lives, were written in the Caribbean or Canada, or in Great Britain by sometime residents of the American colonies.

The choice of text for each poem selected for inclusion in this volume has been made on the basis of a study of its textual history and a comparison of editions printed within the author's lifetime, along with relevant manuscripts, broadside and periodical appearances, and posthumous editions. In general, texts have been taken from the earliest book edition prepared with the author's participation; revised editions are sometimes followed, in light of the degree of authorial supervision and the stage of the writer's career at which the revisions were made, but the preference has been for the authorially approved book version closest to the date of composition. Texts from periodicals, anthologies, and posthumous sources—including modern critical editions—have been used when a poem was not printed in one of the author's books during his or her lifetime, or when such a book version is not authoritative. The texts of some or all of the poems by five writers in this volume—Henry Brooke, Joseph Green, Archibald Home, Lewis Morris II, and Margaret Lowther Page—have been prepared from original manuscripts and are published here for the first time. The texts of Christopher Witt's translations from Johannes Kelpius' German have been prepared from a published facsimile of Witt's manuscript with the kind assistance of Patrick Erben.

The following is a list of the sources of all the texts included in this volume, listed alphabetically by the authors of the poems.

John Adams. Melancholly discrib'd and dispell'd: *Poems on Several Occasions, Original and Translated* (Boston: D. Gookin, 1745), pp. 17–20.
George Alsop. The Author to His Book; "Trafique is Earth's great Atlas, that supports"; "Heavens bright Lamp, shine forth some of thy Light": *A Character of the Province of Maryland* (London: Peter Dring, 1666), pp. [ix–xii], 55, 75–80.

John André. Cow-Chace: *Cow-Chace, in Three Cantos, Published on Occasion of the Rebel General Wayne's Attack of the Refugees Block-House on Hudson's River, on Friday the 21st of July, 1780* (New York: James Rivington, 1780), pp. 3–18.

Benjamin Banneker. The Puzzle of the Hare and Hound: Silvio A. Bedini, *The Life of Benjamin Banneker: The First African-American Man of Science* (Baltimore: Maryland Historical Society, 1999), pp. 340–41.

Joel Barlow. Innumerable mercies acknowledged: *A Translation of Sundry Psalms Which Were Omitted in Doctor Watts's Version; to Which Is Added, a Number of Hymns* (Hartford: Barlow and Babcock, 1785), hymn LXV, pp. [9–10]. *from* The Conspiracy of Kings: *The Conspiracy of Kings; a Poem: Addressed to the Inhabitants of Europe, from Another Quarter of the World* (London: J. Johnson, 1792), pp. 15–19. The Hasty-Pudding: *The New York Magazine, or Literary Repository* I.1 (January 1796): 41–49.

from The Bay Psalm Book (Psalme 19, Psalme 23, Psalme 107): *The Whole Booke of Psalmes, Faithfully Translated into English Metre* (Cambridge: Stephen Day, 1640), not paginated.

George Berkeley. Verses on the Prospect of planting Arts and Learning in America: *A Miscellany, Containing Several Tracts on Various Subjects* (Dublin: George Faulkner, 1752), pp. 185–86.

William Billings. Chester: *The Singing Master's Assistant, or Key to Practical Music* (Boston: Draper and Folsom, [1778]), plate 12.

Ann Eliza Bleecker. Written in Retreat from Burgoyne; On Reading Dryden's Virgil; Return to Tomhanick: *The Posthumous Works of Ann Eliza Bleecker in Prose and Verse* (New York: T. and J. Swords, 1793), pp. 215–17, 230–31, 260–62.

Robert Bolling. Neanthe: J. A. Leo Lemay, "Southern Colonial Grotesque: Robert Bolling's 'Neanthe'," *Mississippi Quarterly* 35 (Spring 1982): 113–26. Occlusion: David S. Shields, "Literature of the Colonial South," *Resources for American Literary Study* 19.2 (1993): 221–22.

Ned Botwood. Hot Stuff: *Rivington's New York Gazetteer*, May 5, 1774, p. 2.

William Bradford. A Word to New England; Of Boston in New England: *The Collected Verse*, ed. Michael G. Runyan (St. Paul: John Colet Press, 1974), pp. 162–65, 166–73. Certain Verses left by the Honoured William Bradford, Esq;: Nathaniel Morton, *New-Englands memoriall: or, A brief relation of the most memorable and remarkable passages of the providence of God, manifested to the planters of New-England in America* (Boston: John Usher, 1669), pp. 144–45.

Anne Bradstreet. The Prologue (from *The Tenth Muse*); A Dialogue between Old England and New; The Author to her Book; Contemplations; Before the Birth of one of her Children; To my Dear and loving Husband; In memory of my dear grand-child Elizabeth Bradstreet; On my dear Grand-child Simon Bradstreet; "As weary pilgrim, now at rest"; To my dear children; May. 13. 1657; Upon my dear & loving husband his goeing into England; "In silent night when rest I took": *The Complete Works of Anne Bradstreet*, ed. Joseph R. McElrath, Jr., and Allan P. Robb (Boston: Twayne,

1981), pp. 6–8, 141–48, 167–74, 177, 179–80; 186–87, 188, 210–11, 215, 226–27, 232–33, 236–37.

Joseph Breintnall. "A plain Description of one single Street in this City": *American Weekly Mercury* 493 (June 12–19, 1729): 1. The Rape of Fewel: *Pennsylvania Gazette* 204 (October 26, 1732): 1; To the Memory of Aquila Rose, Deceas'd: Aquila Rose, *Poems on Several Occasions* (Philadelphia: Joseph Rose, 1740), pp. 3–12.

Henry Brooke. The New Metamorphosis, or, Fable of the Bald Eagle; To my Bottle-friends; Modern Politeness: David S. Shields, *Civil Tongues & Polite Letters in British America* (Chapel Hill: University of North Carolina Press, 1997), pp. 81–86, 89–90, 95–97. An Unwilling Farewell to Poesy: Manuscript collection, Commonplace Book, Richard Peters Collection, Historical Society of Pennsylvania.

Charles Brockden Brown. Monody, On the death of Gen. George Washington: *New York Commercial Advertiser*, January 2, 1800, p. 3.

Mather Byles. Hymn to Christ for our Regeneration and Resurrection The Conflagration; To Pictorio, on the Sight of His Pictures: *Poems on Several Occasions* (Boston: S. Kneeland & T. Green, 1744), pp. 100–06, 17–18, 89–93.

"Carolina, a young lady." On her Father having desired her to forbid all young Men the House: *South-Carolina Gazette* 694 (August 3, 1747): 2.

Thomas Clemson. "From Thomas Clemson ran away": *Pennsylvania Gazette*, August 7, 1746, p. 3.

"Ralpho Cobble." Learning that Cobweb of the Brain: *South-Carolina Gazette* 16 (April 15–22, 1732): 1.

Benjamin Colman. A Quarrel with Fortune: Ebenezer Turell, *The Life and Character of Reverend Benjamin Colman* (Boston: Rogers and Fowle, 1794), pp. 24–25. A Poem, on Elijahs Translation, Occasion'd by the Death of the Reverend and Learned, Mr. Samuel Willard: *A Poem on Elijahs Translation* (Boston: Benjamin Eliot, 1707), pp. 1–14.

The Convert to Tobacco. A Tale. *Gentleman's Magazine* 3 (February 1733): 92–93.

Ebenezer Cook. The Sot-Weed Factor, or A Voyage to Maryland, &c.: *The Sot-Weed Factor, or A Voyage to Maryland* (London: B. Bragg, 1708).

Thomas Cradock. Hymn for Ascension; *from* Maryland Eclogues in Imitation of Virgil's: *The Poetic Writings of Thomas Cradock, 1718–1770*, ed. David Curtis Skaggs (Newark: University of Delaware Press, 1983), pp. 124–25, 139–49.

Thomas Dale. Prologue spoken to the Orphan: *South-Carolina Gazette* 54 (February 8, 1734/35). Epilogue to the Orphan: *South-Carolina Gazette* 56 (February 22, 1734/35).

John Danforth. A few Lines to fill up a Vacant Page: *The Right Christian Temper* (Boston: Samuel Sewall, Jr., 1702), p. 29.

Samuel Davies. "What IS great God! and what IS NOT": *Miscellaneous Poems, Chiefly on Divine Subjects* (Williamsburg: William Hunter, 1751), pp. 22–23. "While o'er our guilty Land, O Lord"; "While various Rumours spread abroad": *Virginia's Danger and Remedy: Two Discourses, Occasioned by the Severe Drought in Sundry Country, and the Defeat of General Braddock* (Williamsburg: William Hunter, 1756), pp. 31–32, 51–52. The Invitations of the Gospel: *American Magazine and Monthly Chronicle* 1 (July 1758): 501. Self-Dedication at the Table of the Lord: *Hymns Adapted to Divine Worship*, ed. Thomas Gibbons (London: J. Buckland, J. Johnson, and J. Payne, 1769), vol II, pp. 192–93 (hymn XXVIII).

William Dawson. The Wager: *New York Gazette* 323 (March 27, 1749): 1–2. On the Corruptions of the Stage; To a Friend, Who Recommended a Wife to Him: *Poems on Several Occasions* (Williamsburg, Virginia: Parks, 1736), pp. 28–30, 18–19. To a Lady, on a Screen of Her Working: *Virginia Gazette*, December 10, 1736, p. 1.

A Description of a Winter's Morning. *New York Gazette and Weekly Post-Boy* 518 (January 1, 1753): 2.

Joseph Dumbleton. A Rhapsody on Rum: *Maryland Gazette*, November 1, 1749, pp. 3–4.

Timothy Dwight. *from* The Triumph of Infidelity: *The Triumph of Infidelity* ([Hartford?]: Printed in the world, 1788), pp. 16–21. *from* Greenfield Hill (Part II, The Flourishing Village): *Greenfield Hill* (New York: Childs and Swaine, 1794), pp. 30–53. *from* The Psalms of David ("Shall man, O God of light, and life"; "While life prolongs its precious light"; "I love thy Kingdom, Lord"): *The Psalms of David, Imitated in the Language of the New Testament, and Applied to the Christian Use and Worship by I. Watts, D.D. A New Edition, in the Psalms Omitted by Dr. Watts are Versified, Local Passages Are Altered, and a Number of Psalms are Versified Anew, in Proper Metres* (Hartford: Hudson and Goodwin, 1801), pp. 197–98, 199, 317–18.

Nathaniel Evans. To Benjamin Franklin, Esq; L.L.D., Occasioned by hearing him play on the Harmonica. *Poems on Several Occasions, with Some Other Compositions* (Philadelphia: John Dunlap, 1772), pp. 108–09.

Elizabeth Graeme Fergusson. To Doctor Fothergill. *Milcah Martha Moore's Book: A Commonplace Book from Revolutionary America*, eds. Catherine La Courreye Blecki and Karin A. Wulf (University Park: Pennsylvania State University Press, 1997), pp. 211–15.

Thomas Green Fessenden. Jonathan's Courtship. *Jonathan's Courtship: A Merry Tale* ([Massachusetts?: s.n., c. 1795–1810]). Broadside, American Antiquarian Society.

John Fiske. John Kotton : O, Honie Knott; John Wilson : W'on Sion-hil: *The First Century of New England Verse*, ed. Harold S. Jantz (Worcester: American Antiquarian Society, 1944), pp. 118–21, 122–23.

Benjamin Franklin. Drinking Song (To the Abbé de La Roche, at Auteuil): *Memoirs of the Life and Writings of Benjamin Franklin*, ed. William Temple Franklin, vol. 3. (London: H. Colburn, 1817–18), pp. 345–47. I Sing My Plain Country Joan: *Father Abraham's Speech to a Great Number of People, at a Vendue of Merchant-Goods; Introduced to the Publick by Poor Richard, A famous Pennsylvania Conjurer, and Almanack-Maker* (Boston: Benjamin Mecom, [1758]), p. 24. Three Precepts: *Poor Richard Improved: Being an*

Almanack and Ephemeris . . . for the Year of our Lord, 1749 (Philadelphia: B. Franklin and D. Hall, 1748), p. 31. Titles "I Sing My Plain Country Joan" and "Three Precepts" supplied for the present volume.

Philip Freneau. American Liberty: *American Liberty: A Poem* (New-York: J. Anderson, 1775). *Libera nos, Domine*—Deliver us, O Lord; Female Frailty; Stanzas Occasioned by the Ruins of a Country Inn; The Dying Indian: *The Poems of Philip Freneau, Written Chiefly during the Late War* (Philadelphia: Francis Bailey, 1786), pp. 65–66, 88–94, 235–37, 350–52. The Wild Honey Suckle; The Indian Student; Lines occasioned by a Visit to an old Indian Burying Ground: *The Miscellaneous Works of Mr. Philip Freneau, Containing His Essays, and Additional Poems* (Philadelphia: Francis Bailey, 1788), pp. 152, 69–71, 188–89. The Country Printer; To Sir Toby, a Sugar-Planter in the interior parts of Jamaica; To Mr. Blanchard: *Poems Written between the Years 1768 & 1794* (Monmouth, New Jersey: Philip Freneau, 1795), pp. 421–24, 391–92, 446–47. The Republican Genius of Europe: *Jersey Chronicle* 1.4 (May 23, 1795): 36. On a Honey Bee, Drinking from a Glass of Wine, and Drowned Therein: *Poems Written and Published during the American Revolutionary War, and Now Republished from the Original Manuscripts* (Philadelphia: Lydia R. Bailey, 1809), vol. II, pp. 97–98.

Christopher Gardiner. "Wolfes in Sheeps clothing why will ye": Thomas Morton, *New English Canaan; or, New Canaan* (Amsterdam: Jacob Frederickstam, 1637), p. 185.

Thomas Godfrey Jr. Verses Occasioned by a Young Lady's asking the Author, What Was a Cure for Love?; Epistle to a Friend, from Fort Henry; A Dithyrambic on Wine: *Juvenile Poems on Various Subjects* (Philadelphia: Henry Miller, 1765), pp. 13–14, 20–21, 34–37.

James Grainger. from *The Sugar-Cane* (Book IV: The Genius of Africa). *The Sugar-Cane: A Poem in Four Books* (London: R. and J. Dodsley, 1764), pp. 125–62.

Joseph Green. To Mr. B occasioned by his Verse, to Mr. Smibert on seeing his Pictures: Jeremy Belknap, Collection of Poetry, Belknap Papers 1720–1919. Massachusetts Historical Society. 013.9b. The Poet's Lamentation for the Loss of his Cat, which he us'd to call his Muse: *London Magazine* 1 (November 1733): 579. On Mr. B——'s singing an Hymn of his own composing: *London Magazine* 1 (November 1733): 579–80. To the Author of the Poetry in the last *Weekly Journal*: *The Boston Gazette* 743 (April 1, 1734). A True Impartial Account of the Celebration of the Prince of Orange's Nuptials at Portsmouth: Manuscript letter, Joseph Green to Captain Pollard, June 3, 1734. Smith-Carter Papers, Massachusetts Historical Society. Inscription under Revd Jn. Checkley's Picture: Ezra Stiles Literary Miscellanies, Yale University Library. "A fig for your learning": Ephraim Eliot Commonplace Book, Boston Atheneum. Mss. S151, v. 2, p. 22. The Disappointed Cooper: Pemberton Commonplace Book. Massachusetts Historical Society. MS 71.3.4. pp. 16–21. "Hail! *D—p—t* of wondrous fame": *The Boston Post-Boy* 396 (July 19, 1742): 3.

Hannah Griffitts. The female Patriots. Address'd to the Daughters of Liberty in America; To Sophronia. In answer to some Lines she directed to be wrote on my Fan; The Cits Return from the Wilderness to the City; Wrote on the last Day of February 1775; Upon reading a Book entituled Common Sense; On reading a few Paragraphs in the Crisis: *Milcah Martha Moore's Book: A Commonplace Book from Revolutionary America*, eds. Catherine La Courreye Blecki and Karin A. Wulf (University Park: Pennsylvania State University Press, 1997), pp. 172–75, 246–47, 255–56, 299–300.

Jupiter Hammon. An Address to Miss Phillis Wheatly, Ethiopian Poetess, in Boston: *An Address to Miss Phillis Wheatly* (Hartford: Watson and Goodwin? 1778). Connecticut Historical Society. Broadsides. 1778. H225a.

Charles Hansford. My Country's Worth: *The Poems of Charles Hansford*, eds. James A. Servies and Carl R. Dolmetsch (Chapel Hill: University of North Carolina Press, 1961), pp. 47–68.

Benjamin Harris. "In Adam's Fall": *New England Primer* (Boston: S. Kneeland & T. Green, 1727), from a facsimile in *The New-England Primer: A History of Its Origin an Development*, ed. Paul Leicester Ford (New York: Teachers College, Columbia University, 1962), pp. 65–68.

Lemuel Haynes. "The Battle of Lexington": Ruth Bogin, "'The Battle of Lexington': A Patriotic Ballad by Lemuel Haynes," *William and Mary Quarterly*, 42.4 (October 1985): 501-06.

Anne Hecht. Advice to Mrs. Mowat: Grace Helen Mowat, *The Diverting History of a Loyalist Town* (St. Andrews, New Brunswick: Charlotte County Cottage Craft, 1932), pp. 53–55.

Edmund Hickeringill. *from* Jamaica Viewed: *Jamaica Viewed; with all the Ports, Harbours, and Their Several Soundings, Towns, and Settlements* (London: John Williams, 1661), pp. 73–81.

Archibald Home. An Elegy on the much to be lamented Death of George Fraser of Elizabeth Town; The Ear-Ring; Black-Joke: A Song; On Killing a Book-Worm: *Poems on Several Occasions*, manuscript book, Laing Manuscripts, III, 452, University of Edinburgh Library.

Francis Hopkinson. "My gen'rous heart disdains": *Seven Songs for the Harpsichord or Forte Piano* (Philadelphia: T. Dobson, 1788), p. 12. An Epitaph for an Infant; The Battle of the Kegs; A Camp Ballad: *The Miscellaneous Essays and Occasional Writings of Francis Hopkinson*, vol. 3 (Philadelphia: T. Dobson, 1792), pp. 73, 169–73, 174–75.

Joseph Hopkinson. Song, Adapted to the President's March ("Hail Columbia!"): *Song Adapted to the President's March, Sung at the Theatre by Mr. Fox, at His Benefit* (Philadelphia: J. Ormrod, 1798), pp. 3–6.

David Humphreys. Mount-Vernon: An Ode; The Genius of America; The Monkey, Who Shaved Himself and His Friends: *Poems* (Philadelphia: Matthew Carey, 1789), pp. 57–59, 61–62, 67–68.

Robert Hunter. *from* Androboros: A Biographical Farce: *Androboros: A Biographical Farce, in Three Acts* (Monoropolis [New York]: William Bradford: 1714), pp. 7–8, 11, 14–15.

Edward Johnson. New England's Annoyances: J. A. Leo Lemay, *New England's Annoyances: America's First Folk Song* (Newark: University of

Delaware Press, 1985), pp. 17–19. "You that have seen these wondrous works by Sions Savior don": *A History of New-England. From the English Planting in the Yeere 1628 untill the yeere 1652* (London: N. Brooke, 1654), pp. 166–68.

"Poor Julian": Poor Julleyoun's Warnings to Children and Servants (Boston: B. Gray & A. Butler, 1733?). Advice from the Dead to the Living (Boston: [Thomas Fleet?], 1733?).

James Kirkpatrick. The Nonpareil: *The Sea-Piece* (London: Cooper & Buckland, 1750), pp. 139–47.

Sarah Kemble Knight. *from* The Journal of Madam Knight ("I ask thy Aid, O Potent Rum!"; "Tho' Ill at ease, A stranger and alone"): *The Journals of Madam Knight and Rev. Mr. Buckingham*, ed. Theodore Dwight (New York: Wilder and Campbell, 1825), pp. 24, 29.

Tom Law. Lovewell's Fight: "Lovewell's Fight," *Collections, Historical and Miscellaneous, and Monthly Literary Journal* (February 1824): 64–66. Originally published under the subtitle "Song"; title "Lovewell's Fight"—from the title of the article in which it appeared—has been supplied for the present volume.

Richard Lewis. To Mr. Samuel Hastings, (Ship-wright of Philadelphia) on his launching the Maryland-Merchant, a large Ship built by him at Annapolis: *The Pennsylvania Gazette* 61 (January 13, 1729–30): 1–2. A Journey from Patapsco to Annapolis: *The Pennsylvania Gazette* 131 (May 20, 1731):1–2. Food for Criticks: *The Pennsylvania Gazette* 190 (July 17, 1732): 1.

William Livingston. *from* Philosophic Solitude: *Philosophic Solitude; or, The Choice of a Rural Life* (New York: James Parker, 1747), pp. 13–19, 38–44. Proclamation ("By John Burgoyne and Burgoyne John, Esquire"): *New York Journal*, September 8, 1777.

A.L.M. A College Room: *The American Magazine and Historical Chronicle* 1 (January 1744): 213–14.

Cotton Mather. "Go then, my Dove, but now no longer *Mine!*": *Meat Out of the Eater; or, Funeral-Discourses Occasioned by the Death of Several Relatives* (Boston: Benjamin Eliot, 1703), p. 186. Gratitudinis Ergo: *Corderius Americanus: An Essay Upon the Good Education of Children* (Boston: Nicholas Boone, 1708), pp. 26–34. Singing at the Plow; The Songs of Harvest: *Agricola; or, the Religious Husbandman* (Boston: D. Henchman, 1727), pp. 21, 212.

Lewis Morris II. The Mock Monarchy; or, the Kingdom of the Apes: Robert Morris Papers, Manuscript Collection, Rutgers University Library.

Sarah Wentworth Morton. The African Chief; Memento: *My Mind and Its Thoughts, in Sketches, Fragments, and Essays* (Boston: Wells and Lilly, 1823), pp. 201–03, 255–56.

Thomas Morton. *from* New English Canaan, or New Canaan (The Authors Prologue; The Poem; The Songe): *New English Canaan; or, New Canaan* (Amsterdam: Jacob Frederickstam, 1637), pp. 10, 133, 134–35.

William Munford. The Disasters of Richland: *Poems, and Compositions in Prose on Several Occasions* (Richmond: Samuel Pleasants, 1798), pp. 175–77.

Mary Nelson. Forty Shillings Reward: *Pennsylvania Chronicle*, January 9–16, 1769.

John Norton Jr. A Funeral Elogy Upon that Pattern and Patron of Virtue, the truely pious, peerless and matchless Gentlewoman, Mrs. Anne Bradstreet: Anne Bradstreet, *Several Poems* (Boston: John Foster, 1678), pp. 252–55.

Urian Oakes. An Elegie, Upon that Reverend, Learned, Eminently Pious, and Singularly Accomplished Divine, my Ever Honoured Brother, Mr. Thomas Shepard: *An Elegie upon the Death of the Reverend Mr. Thomas Shepard* (Cambridge: Samuel Green, 1677), pp. 3–16.

Samson Occom. The Sufferings of Christ: *A Choice Collection of Hymns and Spiritual Songs*, ed. Samson Occom (New London, Connecticut: Timothy Green, 1774), pp. 78–79; A Morning Hymn; A Son's Farewell; The Slow Traveller: *Divine Hymns, or, Spiritual Songs; for the Use of Religious Assemblies and Private Christians*, ed. Joshua Smith (Exeter, New Hampshire: Stearns and Winslow, 1794), pp. 24, 44–45, 88–89.

Jonathan Odell. The Word of Congress: *Royal Gazette*, September 18, 1779, p. 2.

George Ogilvie. *from* Carolina; or, The Planter: *Carolina; or, the Planter* ([Aberdeen?], [1790?]), pp. 46–58.

John Osborn. A Whaling Song: *The Massachusetts Centinel* 6.40 (February 3, 1787): 160.

Margaret Lowther Page. To Miss J. L.—: Holograph manuscript (1790), Special Collections, Swem Library, College of William and Mary.

Robert Treat Paine Jr.. Adams and Liberty: *The Works, in Verse and Prose, of the Late Robert Treat Paine* (Boston: J. Belcher, 1812), pp. 245–47.

Thomas Paine. The Liberty Tree: *Pennsylvania Magazine*, July 1775, pp. 328–29.

Francis Daniel Pastorius. "In these Seven Languages I this my book do own"; A Token of Love and Gratitude; Rachel Preston, Hannah Hill & Mary Norris; Epibaterium, Or a hearty Congratulation to William Penn: Marion Dexter Learned, *The Life of Francis Daniel Pastorius: The Founder of Germantown* (Philadelphia: William J. Campbell, 1908), pp. 252, 199–200, 201–04, 210–15. "Delight in Books from Evening": Marion Dexter Learned, "From Pastorius' Bee-Hive or Bee-Stock," *Americana Germanica* 1.4 (1897): 106–07. "As often as some where before my Feet"; "When I solidly do ponder": *Seventeenth-Century American Poetry*, ed. Harrison T. Meserole (New York: New York University Press, 1968), pp. 294–95, 298. "If any honest Friend be pleased to walk into my poor Garden": Deliciæ Hortenses, *or Garden-Recreations, and* Voluptates Apianæ, ed. Christoph E. Schweitzer (Columbia, South Carolina: Camden House, 1982), pp. 47–49.

Mary Hirst Pepperell. A Lamentation &c. on the Death of a Child: *New England Weekly Journal* (July 30, 1733): 1.

The Petition. *The Boston Gazette, or Country Journal* 50 (March 15, 1756): 1.

The Philadelphiad. from *The Philadelphiad* (Country Clown; Quaker; The Universal Motive; Bagnio; The Emigrant; Miss Kitty Cut-a-dash): *The Philadelphiad; or, New Pictures of the City. Interspersed with a Candid*

Review and Display of Some First Rate Modern Characters of Both Sexes (Philadelphia: Kline & Reynolds, 1784), vol. I, pp. 12–13; 16–18; 18–19; 21–23; 43–44; vol II, pp. 11–12.

James Revel. The Poor Unhappy Transported Felon's Sorrowful Account of His fourteen Years Transportation at Virginia in America: *The Poor Unhappy Transported Felon's Sorrowful Account of His Fourteen Years Transportation at Virginia in America* (London: [Stonecutter Street, Fleet-Market], c. 1767–1780).

John Saffin. "Sweetly (my Dearest) I left thee asleep"; To his Excellency Joseph Dudley Eqr Gover: &c: *Seventeenth-Century American Poetry*, ed. Harrison T. Meserole (New York: New York University Press, 1968), pp. 198–99, 202–04.

George Sandys. *from* Ovid's Metamorphoses: *Ovid's Metamorphoses Englished* (London: William Stansby, 1626), pp. 108–11.

George Seagood. Mr. Blackamore's *Expeditio Ultramontana*: *Maryland Gazette* 93 (June 17–24, 1729): 1–2.

John Seccomb. Father Abbey's Will: *Weekly Rehearsal* (Boston), January 3, 1732, p. 1. Proposal to Mistress Abbey: *Weekly Rehearsal* (Boston), February 7, 1732, p. 1.

Samuel Sewall. "Once more! Our GOD, vouchsafe to Shine": Broadside (Boston: Bartholomew Green and John Allen, 1701). Upon the drying up that Ancient River, the River Merrimak. Broadside (New London, Connecticut?: Timothy Green? 1721).

John Singleton. *from* A General Description of the West-Indian Islands: *A General Description of the West-Indian Islands, as Far as Relates to the British, Dutch, and Danish Governments, from Barbados to Saint Croix* (Barbados: George Esmand & William Walker, 1767), pp. 102–118.

John Smith. The Sea Marke: *The Complete Works of Captain John Smith (1580–1631)*, ed. Philip L. Barbour (Chapel Hill: University of North Carolina Press), vol. 3, p. 265.

William Smith. The Mock Bird and Red Bird: *The Pennsylvania Gazette* 1215 (March 24, 1752): 1. The Cherry-Tree and Peach-Tree: *The New York Gazette and Weekly Post Boy* 486 (May 11, 1752): 2. The Birds of different Feather: *The New York Gazette and Weekly Post Boy* 533 (April 16, 1753): 1.

Joseph Stansbury. Verses to the Tories; The United States; To Cordelia: *The Loyal Verses of Joseph Stansbury and Doctor Jonathan Odell; relating to the American Revolution*, ed. Winthrop Sargent (Albany: J. Munsell, 1860), pp. 22–23, 89, 90–91.

James Sterling. *from* An Epistle to the Hon. Arthur Dobbs, Esq. in Europe from a Clergyman in America: *An Epistle to the Hon. Arthur Dobbs, Esq. in Europe from a Clergyman in America* (London: R. Dodsley M. Cooper, 1752), pp. 7–21.

Annis Boudinot Stockton. A Satire on the fashionable pompoons; A Sarcasm against the ladies in a newspaper; Compos'd in a dancing room; A Poetical Epistle, addressed by a Lady of New-Jersey, to her Niece, upon her Marriage, in this City; To Miss Mary Stockton; Sensibility, an Ode: *Only for the Eye of a Friend: The Poems of Annis Boudinot Stockton*, ed. Carla Mulford (Charlottesville: University Press of Virginia, 1995), pp. 72, 74–75, 90–91, 134–37, 176–77, 250–51.

Edward Taylor. from *Preparatory Meditations (First Series)* [#1, #3, #4, The Reflexion, #9, #23, #24, #32, #39, #46]; from *Preparatory Meditations (Second Series)* [#1, #4, #12, #14, #18, #24, #34, #60a, #150]; from *Gods Determinations* [The Preface; The Accusation of the Inward Man; The Glory and Grace in the Church Set Out]; Upon a Spider Catching a Fly; Upon a Wasp Child with Cold; Huswifery; The Ebb & Flow; Upon the Sweeping Flood: *The Poems of Edward Taylor*, ed. Donald E. Stanford (New Haven: Yale University Press, 1960), pp. 5, 7–8, 11–13, 14–15, 19–20, 38–39, 40–41, 83–84, 87–88, 101–02, 104–05, 111–13, 125–27, 144–46, 187–88, 354, 387–88, 409–10, 456–57, 464–65, 465–67, 467, 470, 471.

Lucy Terry. Bars Fight: Josiah Gilbert Holland, *The History of Western Massachusetts* (Springfield, Massachusetts: S. Bowles, 1855), vol. 2, part 3, p. 360.

Henry Timberlake. A Translation of the War-Song: *The Memoirs of Lieut. Henry Timberlake (Who Accompanied the Three Cherokee Indians to England in the Year 1762)* (London: J. Ridley, W. Nicoll, and C. Henderson, 1765), pp. 56–58.

Benjamin Tompson. The Grammarians Funeral; *from* New Englands Crisis; To Lord Bellamont when entering Governour of the Massachusetts; "Some of his last lines": *Benjamin Tompson, Colonial Bard: A Critical Edition*, ed. Peter White (University Park: Pennsylvania State University Press, 1980), pp. 78–80, 84–86, 157–59, 182.

John Trumbull. *from* The Progress of Dulness (*from* Part Third: The Progress of Coquetry, or The Adventures of Miss Harriet Simper): *The Progress of Dulness. Part Third, and Last: Sometimes Called, the Progress of Coquetry, or the Adventures of Miss Harriet Simper* (New Haven: Thomas and Samuel Green, 1773), pp. 9–21. *from* M'Fingal (*from* Canto III, The Liberty Pole): *M'Fingal: A Modern Epic Poem, in Four Cantos* (Hartford: Hudson & Goodwin, 1782), pp. 49–61.

St. George Tucker. A Dream on Bridecake; A Second Dream on Bridecake: *The Poems of St. George Tucker of Williamsburg, Virginia, 1752–1827*, ed. William S. Prince (New York: Vantage Press, 1977), pp. 42–45.

Jane Colman Turell. To my Muse, December 29. 1725; An Invitation into the Country; "Phoebus has thrice his Yearly Circuit run": Ebenezer Turell, *Memoirs of the Life and Death of the Pious and Ingenious Mrs. Jane Turrell*, in Benjamin Colman, *Reliquiæ Turellæ, et Lachrymæ Paternæ. The Father's Tears over his Daughter's Remains* (Boston: S. Kneeland & T. Green, 1735), pp. 74–75, 84–85, 103–04.

Royall Tyler. The Origin of Evil. An Elegy; Ode Composed for the Fourth of July; An Irregular Supplicatory Address to the American Academies of Arts and Sciences: *The Verse of Royall Tyler*, ed. Marius B. Péladeau (Charlottesville: University Press of Virginia, 1968), pp. 11–15, 47–48, 55–59.

Mercy Otis Warren. A Thought on the inestimable Blessing of Reason: Edmund M. Hayes, "The Private Poems of Mercy Otis Warren," *The New*

England Quarterly 52.3 (June 1981): 199–224. To Mr.——: *Poems, Dramatic and Miscellaneous* (Boston: I. Thomas and E. T. Andrews, 1790), pp. 195–97.

Phillis Wheatley. To Mæcenas; To the University of Cambridge, in New-England; On being brought from Africa to America; On the Death of the Rev. Mr. George Whitefield; To the Right Honorable William, Earl of Dartmouth; To S. M. a young African Painter, on seeing his Works; A Farewel to America: *Poems on Various Subjects, Religious and Moral* (London: A. Bell, 1773), pp. 9–12, 15–16, 18, 22–24, 73–75, 114–15, 119–22. To a Gentleman of the Navy: *Royal American Magazine*, December 1774, pp. 473–74. Philis's Reply to the Answer in our last by the Gentleman in the Navy: *Royal American Magazine*, January 1775, pp. 34–35. To His Excellency General Washington: *Virginia Gazette*, March 30,1776, p. 1. Liberty and Peace: Phillis Peters, *Liberty and Peace* (Boston: Warden and Russell, 1784).

Michael Wigglesworth. A Song of Emptiness; *from* The Day of Doom; God's Controversy with New-England; *from* Meat out of the Eater [Song I, "Man's Strength meer weakness is"]: *Poems of Michael Wigglesworth*, ed. Ronald A. Bosco (Lanham, MD: University Press of America, 1989), pp. 83–86; 11–37, 62–66; 88–102; 190–93. "I Walk'd and did a little Mole-hill View": *The Day of Doom* (London: J. Sims, 1673), pp. 70, 69, 70, 71 [pagination irregular].

Roger Williams. *from* A Key into the Language of America: *A Key into the Language of America*, eds. John J. Teunissen and Evelyn J. Hinz (Detroit: Wayne State University Press, 1973), pp. 99, 104–05, 133, 204, 214.

John Wilson. To God our twice-Revenger: *A Song or, Story, for the Lasting Remembrance of Divers Famous Works, which God Hath Done in Our Time* (London: R. Young for I. Bartlet, 1626), pp. 51–52. Anagram made by mr John Wilson of Boston upon the Death of Mrs Abigaill Tompson: *Handkerchiefs from Paul, Being Pious and Consolatory Verses of Puritan Massachusetts* (Cambridge: Harvard University Press, 1927), pp. 7–9.

Christopher Witt, trans. From the Hymn Book of Johannes Kelpius: Of the Wilderness of the Secret, or Private Virgin-Cross-Love; The Paradox and Seldom Contentment of the God loving Soul; Of the Power of the New Virgin-Body, Wherein the Lord himself dwelleth: "The Hymn Book of Magister Johannes Kelpius, translated by Dr. Christopher Witt," *Church Music and Musical Life in Pennsylvania in the Eighteenth Century* (Philadelphia: Pennsylvania Society of the Colonial Dames of America, 1926), vol. 1, pp. 27–43, 59–65, 91–93, 161–65.

Roger Wolcott. *from* Meditations on Man's First and Fallen Estate, and the Wonderful Love of God Exhibited in a Redeemer; *from* A Brief Account of the Agency of the Honourable John Winthrop, Esq; in the Court of King Charles the Second: *Poetical Meditations, Being the Improvement of Some Vacant Hours* (New London: T. Green, 1725), pp. 12–17, 36–57.

Charles Woodmason. To Benjamin Franklin Esq; of Philadelphia, on his Experiments and Discoveries of Electricity. *Gentleman's Magazine* 24 (February 1754): 88.

Susanna Wright. Anna Boylens Letter to King Henry the 8th; On the Bene-
    fit of Labour; On the Death of a little Girl; My own Birth Day: *Milcah
    Martha Moore's Book: A Commonplace Book from Revolutionary America*,
    eds. Catherine La Courreye Blecki & Karin A. Wulf (University Park:
    Pennsylvania State University Press, 1997), pp. 121–24, 127–28, 135–37, 147–
    49. To Eliza Norris—at Fairhill: Pattie Cowell, "'Womankind Call Reason
    to Their Aid': Susanna Wright's Verse Epistle on the Status of Women in
    Eighteenth Century America," *Signs: Journal of Women in Culture and
    Society* 6.4 (Summer 1981): 799–800.
Yankee Doodle. Yankee Doodle, or (as now christened by the Saints of New
    England), The Lexington March: Huntington Library, "Collection, Songs,
    English. *Songs*" (n.p., c. 1720–1780). The Yankey's return from Camp:
    [United States: s.n., c. 1775–1810] (broadside, American Antiquarian
    Society).

This volume presents the texts of the manuscripts, original print-
ings, and other editions chosen for inclusion here without change,
except for the correction of typographical errors or slips of the pen.
It does not attempt to reproduce nontextual features of their typo-
graphical design or certain period typographical and orthographic
conventions, such as the long "s"; the use of "u" for "v" and vice
versa (for example, "haue" for "have") or "i" for "j" (for example,
"adioyning" for "adjoyning"); the use of quotation marks at the
beginning of each line, for long quotations; marginal brackets to in-
dicate rhymed couplets or triplets; or the use of superscript charac-
ters in certain contractions ("y^{t}" for "that," for example, or "w^{ch}" for
"which"). Spelling, punctuation, and capitalization are often expres-
sive features, and they are not altered, even when inconsistent or ir-
regular. Bracketed editorial emendations used to supply letters or
words omitted from source texts because of an obvious slip of the
pen, printer's error, or damaged copy are accepted in this volume
and printed without brackets, but bracketed editorial insertions used
to clarify meaning or represent words canceled in a manuscript have
been deleted. Errata listed in the original sources have been incor-
porated into the texts.

In the case of some untitled poems, the first line, or a descriptive
phrase from the source text, is enclosed in quotation marks and used
as a title. Some of the poems in this volume were originally pub-
lished anonymously or under pseudonyms but have subsequently
been attributed to a particular author. Information about such attri-
butions is included in the Notes.

The following is a list of typographical errors, cited by page and
line number: 6.6, Irish;; 16.5, sartity; 22.11, bo; 27.26, it'h; 28.4, 'th;
66.10, Supernnuated; 68.14, Eaih; 69.12, theri; 89.21, Comdemneth;

94.11, they; 130.31, abey; 136.17, *Singers*; 136.21, *I'am*; 138.9, (Great; 138.10, (Among; 143.10, di'ed [no terminal punctuation]; 158.6, threesce; 207.23, fling.; 223.21, see,; 227.30, The; 236.28, smooth Pace; 309.5, Bu'sness; 311.19, extream / See; 315.20, Ancestors.; 336.23, increase'd; 347.6, declare / The; 347.16, Godess; 349.21, Grace'd; 354.6, place'd; 356.4, they [no terminal punctuation]; 380.28, the closely; 386.9, *perculsus*; 386.11, *bas*; 386.11, *partes*; 386.30, "Begins; 388.30, original [no terminal punctuation]; 390.2, "But; 392.10, "And; 397.18, arise / Tow'rds; 398.24, thrash; 398.27, movis; 401.34, Faints; 476.8, may; 486.35, you; 520.17, *1753*. [no closing punctuation]; 526.8, on; 558.19, Sylvania's,; 587.16, at; 608.16, thoul't; 610.17, snufflle; 617.11, Punk in; 665.35, crimes.; 681.32, *Vigil*; 686.37, Voltair's; 703.25, looss'd; 705.33, e'or; 713.10, wiews; 716.1, tempt's; 722.19, own [no closing punctuation]; 724.11, Massuchhusetts; 724.37, discover; 744.31, Havard; 769.4, tremenduous; 779.11, snatch d; 785.13, phœbus; 826.33, [no opening quotes] At; 827.9, [no opening quotes] Well; 827.9, youv'e.

ACKNOWLEDGMENTS

Great care has been taken to trace all owners of copyrighted material included in this book. If any has been inadvertently omitted or overlooked, acknowledgment will gladly be made in future printings.

Benjamin Banneker. The Puzzle of the Hare and the Hound: Silvio A. Bedini, *The Life of Benjamin Banneker: The First African-American Man of Science* (Baltimore: Maryland Historical Society, 1999), pp. 340–41. Copyright © 1991. Reprinted by permission of the Press at the Maryland Historical Society.

Robert Bolling. Neanthe: J. A. Leo Lemay, "Southern Colonial Grotesque: Robert Bolling's 'Neanthe'," *Mississippi Quarterly* 35 (Spring 1982): 113–26. Reprinted by permission. Occlusion: David S. Shields, "Literature of the Colonial South," *Resources for American Literary Study* 19.2 (1993): 221–22. Reprinted by permission.

Anne Bradstreet. The Prologue (from *The Tenth Muse*); A Dialogue between Old England and New; The Author to her Book; Contemplations; Before the Birth of one of her Children; To my Dear and loving Husband; In memory of my dear grand-child Elizabeth Bradstreet; On my dear Grand-child Simon Bradstreet; "As weary pilgrim, now at rest"; To my dear children; May. 13. 1657; Upon my dear & loving husband his goeing into England; "In silent night when rest I took": *The Complete Works of Anne Bradstreet*, ed. Joseph R. McElrath, Jr., and Allan P. Robb (Boston: Twayne, 1981), pp. 6–8, 141–48, 167–74, 177, 179–80; 186–87, 188, 210–11, 215, 226–27, 232–33, 236–37. Reprinted with permission of Gale, a division of Thompson Learning: www.thomsonrights.com.

Henry Brooke. The New Metamorphosis; To My Bottle-friends, Writ at Newcastle in Company; Modern Politeness: David S. Shields, *Civil Tongues & Polite Letters in British America* (Chapel Hill: University of North Carolina Press, 1997), pp. 81–86, 89–90, 95–97. Copyright © 1997 by the University of North Carolina Press. Used by permission of the publisher. An unwilling Farewel to Poesy: Manuscript collection, Commonplace Book, Richard Peters Collection, Historical Society of Pennsylvania. Reprinted with permission of the Historical Society of Pennsylvania.

Thomas Cradock. Hymn for Ascension; *from* Maryland Eclogues in Imitation of Virgil's: *The Poetic Writings of Thomas Cradock, 1718–1770*, ed. David Curtis Skaggs (Newark: University of Delaware Press, 1983), pp. 139–49, 124–25. Copyright © 1983 by Associated University Presses, Inc. Reprinted by permission.

Elizabeth Graeme Fergusson. To Doctor Fothergill. *Milcah Martha Moore's Book: A Commonplace Book from Revolutionary America*, eds. Catherine La Courreye Blecki and Karin A. Wulf (University Park: Pennsylvania State University Press, 1997), pp. 211–15. Copyright © 1997 by The Pennsylvania State University. All Rights Reserved. Reprinted by permission.

John Fiske. John Kotton : O, Honie Knott; John Wilson : W'on Sion-hil: From the Proceedings of the American Antiquarian Society, Vol. 53 (Oct. 1943): 334–38. Reprinted by permission.

Joseph Green. To Mr. B occasioned by his Verse, to Mr. Smibert on seeing his Pictures: Jeremy Belknap, Collection of Poetry, Belknap Papers 1720–1919. Massachusetts Historical Society. 013.9b. Jeremy Belknap Papers, 1637–1891; bulk: 1758–1799. Massachusetts Historical Society. Reprinted by permission. A True Impartial Account of the Celebration of the Prince of Orange's Nuptials at Portsmouth: Manuscript letter, Joseph Green to Captain Pollard, June 3, 1734. Smith-Carter Papers, Massachusetts Historical Society. In Joseph Green to Captain Pollard, 3 June 1734. Smith-Carter Family Papers. Massachusetts Historical Society. Reprinted by permission. Inscription under Revd Jn. Checkley's Picture: Ezra Stiles Literary Miscellanies, Beinecke Rare Book and Manuscript Library, Yale University. Reprinted by permission. The Disappointed Cooper: Pemberton Commonplace Book. Massachusetts Historical Society. MS 71.3.4. pp. 16–21. Thomas Pemberton papers, 1773–1805. Massachusetts Historical Society. Reprinted by permission.

Hannah Griffitts. The female Patriots. Address'd to the Daughters of Liberty in America; To Sophronia. In answer to some Lines she directed to be wrote on my Fan; The Cits Return from the Wilderness to the City; Wrote on the last Day of February 1775; Upon reading a Book entituled Common Sense; On reading a few Paragraphs in the Crisis: *Milcah Martha Moore's Book: A Commonplace Book from Revolutionary America*, eds. Catherine La Courreye Blecki and Karin A. Wulf (University Park: Pennsylvania State University Press, 1997), pp. 172–75, 246–47, 255–56, 299–300. Copyright © 1997 by The Pennsylvania State University. All Rights Reserved. Reprinted by permission.

Jupiter Hammon. An Address to Miss Phillis Wheatly, Ethiopian Poetess, in Boston: *An Address to Miss Phillis Wheatly* (Hartford: Watson and Goodwin, 1778). Connecticut Historical Society. Broadsides. 1778. H225a. Reprinted with permission.

Charles Hansford. My Country's Worth: *The Poems of Charles Hansford*, eds. James A. Servies and Carl R. Dolmetsch (Chapel Hill: University of North Carolina Press, 1961): 47–68. Copyright © 1961 by the Virginia Historical Society, Published by the University of North Carolina Press. Used by permission of the publisher.

Benjamin Harris. "In Adam's Fall": *New England Primer* (Boston: S. Kneeland & T. Green, 1727), from a facsimile in *The New-England Primer: A History of Its Origin an Development*, ed. Paul Leicester Ford (New York: Teachers College, Columbia University, 1962), pp. 65–68. Copyright © 1962 by Teachers College, Columbia University. Reprinted by permission of the publisher. All rights reserved.

Lemuel Haynes. "The Battle of Lexington": Ruth Bogin, " 'The Battle of Lexington': A Patriotic Ballad by Lemuel Haynes," *William and Mary Quarterly*, 42.4 (October 1985): 501–06. Reprinted by permission of Houghton Library, Harvard College Library.

Archibald Home. An Elegy on the much to be lamented Death of George Fraser of Elizabeth Town; The Ear-Ring; Black-Joke: A Song; On Killing a Book-Worm: *Poems on Several Occasions*, manuscript book, Laing Manuscripts, III, 452, University of Edinburgh Library. Reprinted by permission of Edinburgh University Library, Special Collections.

Edward Johnson. New England's Annoyances: J. A. Leo Lemay, *New England's Annoyances: America's First Folk Song* (Newark: University of Delaware Press, 1985), pp. 17–19. Copyright © 1985 by Associated University Presses, Inc. Reprinted by permission.

Lewis Morris II. The Mock Monarchy; or, the Kingdom of the Apes: Robert Morris Papers, Manuscript Collection, Rutgers University Library. Reprinted by permission of Special Collections and University Archives, Rutgers University Libraries.

Margaret Lowther Page. To Miss J. L.—: Holograph manuscript (1790), Special Collections, Swem Library, College of William and Mary. Reprinted by permission of Special Collections Research Center, Swem Library, College of William and Mary.

Francis Daniel Pastorius. "As often as some where before my Feet"; "When I solidly do ponder": *Seventeenth-Century American Poetry*, ed. Harrison T. Meserole (New York: New York University Press, 1968), pp. 294–95; 298. Copyright © 1968 by Doubleday & Company, Inc. All Rights Reserved. Reprinted by permission. "If any honest Friend be pleased to walk into my poor Garden": Deliciæ Hortenses, *or Garden-Recreations, and* Voluptates Apianæ, ed. Christoph E. Schweitzer (Columbia, South Carolina: Camden House, 1982), pp. 47–49. Courtesy of Camden House, an imprint of Boydell & Brewer Inc., Rochester, New York.

John Saffin. "Sweetly (my Dearest) I left thee asleep"; To his Excellency Joseph Dudley Eqr Gover: &c: *Seventeenth-Century American Poetry*, ed. Harrison T. Meserole (New York: New York University Press, 1968), pp. 198–99, 202–04. Copyright © 1968 by Doubleday & Company, Inc. All Rights Reserved. Reprinted by permission.

John Smith. The Sea Marke: *The Complete Works of Captain John Smith (1580–1631)*, ed. Philip L. Barbour (Chapel Hill: University of North Carolina Press), vol. 3, p. 265. Copyright © 1986 by the University of North Carolina Press. Used by permission of the publisher.

Annis Boudinot Stockton. A Satire on the fashionable pompoons; A Sarcasm against the ladies in a newspaper; Compos'd in a dancing room; A Poetical Epistle, Addressed by a Lady of New-Jersey, to her Niece, upon her Marriage, in this City; To Miss Mary Stockton; Sensibility, an Ode: *Only for the Eye of a Friend: The Poems of Annis Boudinot Stockton*, ed. Carla Mulford (Charlottesville: University Press of Virginia, 1995), pp. 72, 74–75, 90–91, 134–37, 176–77, 250–51. Copyright © 1995 by the Rector and Visitors of the University of Virginia. Reprinted by permission of the University of Virginia Press.

Edward Taylor. from *Preparatory Meditations (First Series)* [#1, #3, #4, The Reflexion, #9, #23, #24, #32, #39, #46]; from *Preparatory Meditations (Second Series)* [#1, #4, #12, #14, #18, #24, #34, #60a, #150]; from *Gods Determinations* [The Preface; The Accusation of the Inward Man; The Glory and Grace in the Church Set Out]; Upon a Spider Catching a Fly; Upon a Wasp Child with Cold; Huswifery; The Ebb & Flow; Upon the Sweeping Flood: *The Poems of Edward Taylor*, ed. Donald E. Stanford (New Haven: Yale University Press, 1960), pp. 5, 7–8, 11–13, 14–15, 19–20, 38–39, 40–41, 83–84, 87–88, 101–02, 104–05, 111–13, 125–27, 144–46, 187–88, 354, 387–88, 409–10, 456–57, 464–65, 465–67, 467, 470, 471. Copyright © 1960, renewed 1988 by Donald E. Stanford. Reprinted by permission.

Benjamin Tompson. The Grammarians Funeral; *from* New Englands Crisis; To Lord Bellamont when entering Governour of the Massachusetts; "Some of his last lines": *Benjamin Tompson, Colonial Bard: A Critical Edition*, ed. Peter White (Lanham, MD: University Park: Pennsylvania State University Press, 1980), pp. 78–80, 84–86, 157–59, 182. Copyright © 1980 by The Pennsylvania State University. All Rights Reserved.

Royall Tyler. The Origin of Evil. An Elegy; Ode Composed for the Fourth of July; An Irregular Supplicatory Address to the American Academies of Arts and Sciences: *The Verse of Royall Tyler*, ed. Marius B. Péladeau (Charlottesville: University Press of Virginia, 1968), pp. 11–15, 47–48, 55–59. Copyright © 1968. Reprinted by permission of the University of Virginia Press.

Mercy Otis Warren. A Thought on the inestimable Blessing of Reason: Edmund M. Hayes, "The Private Poems of Mercy Otis Warren," *The New England Quarterly* 52.3 (June 1981): 199–224. Reprinted by permission of the Houghton Library, Harvard University.

Michael Wigglesworth. A Song of Emptiness; *from* The Day of Doom; God's Controversy with New-England; *from* Meat out of the Eater [Song I, "Man's Strength meer weakness is"]: *Poems of Michael Wigglesworth*, ed. Ronald A. Bosco (Lanham, MD: University Press of America, 1989). Copyright © 1989 University Presses of America. Reprinted by permission.

John Wilson. Anagram made by mr John Wilson of Boston upon the Death of Mrs Abigaill Tompson: *Handkerchiefs from Paul, Being Pious and Consolatory Verses of Puritan Massachusetts* (Cambridge: Harvard University Press, 1927), pp. 7–9. Copyright © 1927 by the President and Fellows of Harvard College. Reprinted by permission of the Harvard University Press.

Christopher Witt, trans. From the Hymn Book of Johannes Kelpius: Of the Wilderness of the Secret, or Private Virgin-Cross-Love; The Paradox and Seldom Contentment of the God loving Soul; Of the Power of the New Virgin-Body, Wherein the Lord himself dwelleth: "The Hymn Book of Magister Johannes Kelpius, translated by Dr. Christopher Witt," *Church Music and Musical Life in Pennsylvania in the Eighteenth Century* (Philadelphia: Pennsylvania Society of the Colonial Dames of America, 1926), vol. 1, pp. 27–43, 59–65, 91–93, 161–65. Transcribed here with permission from The National Society of The Colonial Dames of America in The Commonwealth of Pennsylvania.

Susanna Wright. Anna Boylens Letter to King Henry the 8th; On the Benefit of Labour;

On the Death of a little Girl; My own Birth Day: *Milcah Martha Moore's Book: A Commonplace Book from Revolutionary America*, eds. Catherine La Courreye Blecki & Karin A. Wulf (University Park: Pennsylvania State University Press, 1997), pp. 121–24, 127–28, 135–37, 147–49. Copyright © 1997 by The Pennsylvania State University. All Rights Reserved. Reprinted by permission. To Eliza Norris—at Fairhill: Pattie Cowell, " 'Womankind Call Reason to Their Aid': Susanna Wright's Verse Epistle on the Status of Women in Eighteenth Century America," *Signs: Journal of Women in Culture and Society* 6.4 (Summer 1981): 799–800. Copyright © 1991. Reprinted by permission of the University of Chicago Press.

Notes

In the notes below, the reference numbers denote page and line of this volume (the line count includes titles). No note is made for material included in standard desk reference works. Quotations from Shakespeare are keyed to *The Riverside Shakespeare* (Boston: Houghton Mifflin, 1974), edited by G. Blakemore Evans. References to the Bible have been keyed to the King James Version.

For further information than is contained in the notes and references to other studies, see: Sacvan Bercovitch, ed., *The Cambridge History of American Literature, vol. 1: 1590–1820* (New York: Cambridge University Press, 1995); Pattie Cowell, ed., *Women Poets in Pre-Revolutionary America: An Anthology* (Troy, New York: Whitson, 1981); Robert Daly, *God's Altar: The World and the Flesh in Puritan Poetry* (Berkeley: University of California Press, 1978); William C. Dowling, *Poetry and Ideology in Revolutionary Connecticut* (Athens: University of Georgia, 1990); J. A. Leo Lemay, *A Calendar of American Poetry in the Colonial Newspapers and Magazines and in the Major English Magazines through 1765* (Worcester: American Antiquarian Society, 1972); J. A. Leo Lemay, *Men of Letters in Colonial Maryland* (Knoxville: University of Tennessee Press, 1972); James Levernier and Douglas Wilmes, eds., *American Writers before 1800: A Biographical and Critical Dictionary* (Westport, Connecticut: Greenwood Press, 1983); Harrison T. Meserole, ed., *Seventeenth-Century American Poetry* (New York: New York University Press, 1968); Ivy Schweitzer, *The Work of Self-Representation: Lyric Poetry in Colonial New England* (Chapel Hill: University of North Carolina Press 1991); David S. Shields, *Civil Tongues and Polite Letters in British America* (Chapel Hill: University of North Carolina Press, 1997). For information about early American poetry written in languages other than English, see: Leo M. Kaiser, ed., *Early American Latin Verse, 1625–1825* (Chicago: Bolchazy-Carducci, 1984); Henry C. Murphy, ed., *Anthology of New Netherland, or Translations from the Early Dutch Poets of New York* (New York: s.n., 1865); J. Riis Owre, "Alonso de Escobedo and 'La Florida'," *Hispania* 47.2 (May 1964): 242–50; Gordon Sayre, "Plotting the Natchez Massacre: Le Page du Pratz, Dumont de Montigny, Chateaubriand," *Early American Literature* 37.3 (2002): 381–412; J. J. Stoudt, ed., *Pennsylvania German Poetry, 1685–1830* (Allentown: Pennsylvania German Folklore Society, 1956); Gaspar Pérez de Villagrá (Miguel Encinias, Alfred Rodríguez,

& Joseph P. Sánchez, ed. & tr.), *Historia de la Nueva México, 1610* (Albuquerque: University of New Mexico Press, 1992)

The editor wishes to thank Debra Hecht for her assistance with translations from the Greek and Latin, and Patrick Erben for his review of the notes on Francis Daniel Pastorius and Christopher Witt.

1.5–6   FROM *The Sixth Booke*]   Lines 53–145.

1.7   Both settle to their tasks apart]   Prior to the excerpt printed in this volume, Pallas Minerva, the goddess of weaving (among other arts), is offended when Arachne, a skilled weaver, fails to credit her influence. Appearing in the form of an old woman, Pallas tricks Minerva into challenging her to a contest of skill.

1.34   murrion]   Morion, a metal helmet.

1.35   *Ægis*]   Zeus's shield or breastplate.

4.27–6.10   *The Poem* . . . to Hymen, &c.]   "The Poem" and "The Songe" originally appeared in a chapter of Thomas Morton's *New English Canaan* (1637) entitled "Of the Revells of New Canaan," which describes the occasion of their composition and offers explanatory comments:

> The Inhabitants of Pasonagessit (having translated the name of their habitation from that ancient Salvage name to Ma-re Mount; and being resolved to have the new name confirmed for a memorial to after ages) did devise amongst themselves to have it performed in a solemne manner with Revells, & merriment after the old English custom: prepared to sett up a Maypole upon the festivall day of Philip and Jacob; & therefore brewed a barrell of excellent beare, & provided a case of bottles to be spent, with other good cheare, for all commers of that day. And because they would have it in a compleat forme, they had prepared a song fitting to the time and present occasion. And upon Mayday they brought the Maypole to the place appointed, with drumes, gunnes, pistols, and other fitting instruments, for that purpose; and there erected it with the help of Salvages, that came thither of purpose to see the manner of our Revells. A goodly pine tree of 80. foote longe, was reared up, with a pair of buckshorns nayled one somewhat neare unto the top of it: where it stood as a faire sea marke for directions; how to finde out the way to mine Hoste of Mare-Mount.
>
> And because it should more fully appeare to what end it was placed there, they had a poem in readines made, which was fixed to the Maypole, to shew the new name confirmed upon that plantation; which, allthough it were made according to the occurrents of the time, it being Enigmatically composed, pusselled the Separatists most pitifully to expound it, which (for the better information of the reader) I have here inserted. [*The Poem*]

The setting up of this Maypole was a lamentable spectacle to the precise separatists: that lived at new Plimmouth. They termed it an Idoll; yea they called it the Calfe of Horeb: and stood at defiance with the place, naming it Mount Dagon; threatning to make it a woefull mount and not a merry mount.

The Riddle, for want of Oedipus, they could not expound, onely they made some explication of part of it, and sayd it was meant by Samson Job, the carpenter of the Ship that brought over a woman to her husband, that had bin there longe before; and thrived so well, that hee sent for her and her children to come to him; where shortly after hee died, having no reason but because of the sound of those two words: when as (the truth is) the man they applyed it to was altogether unknowne to the Author.

There was likewise a merry song made, which (to make their Revells more fashionable) was sung with a Corus, every man bearing his part; which they performed in a daunce, hand in hand about the Maypole, whiles one of the Company sung, and filled out the good liquor like gammedes and Jupiter. [*The Songe*]

This harmless mirth made by younge men (that lived in hope to have wifes brought over to them, that would save them a laboure to make a voyage to fetch any over) was much distasted, of the precise Seperatists; that keepe much a doe, about the tyth of Mint and Cummin; troubling their braines more then reason would require about things that are indifferent: and from that time sought occasion against my honest Host of Ma-re Mount to overthrow his ondertakings, and to destroy his plantation quite and cleane. But because they presumed with their imaginary gifts (which they have out of Phaos box) they could expound hidden misteries (to convince them of blindnes as well in this, as in other matters of more consequence) I will illustrate the poem, according to the true intent of the authors of these Revells, so much distasted by those Moles.

Oedipus is generally receaved for the absolute reader of riddles who is invoked: Silla and Caribdis are two dangerous places for seamen to incounter, neere unto vennice, & have bin by poets formerly resembled to man and wife. The like licence of the author challenged for a paire of his nomination, the one lamenting for the losse of the other as Niobe for her children. Amphitrite is an arme of the Sea, by which the newes was carried up and down, of a rich widow, now to be tane up or laid downe. By Triton is the fame spread, that caused the Suters to muster; (as it had bin to Penelope of Greece) and the coast lying circuler, all our passage to and froe, is made more convenient by Sea, then Land. Many aimed at this marke; but hee that played Proteus best and could comply with her humor must be the man, that would carry her, & hee had need have Samsons strength to deale with a Dallila: and as much patience as Job that should come there, for a thing that I did observe in the life time of the former.

But marriage and hanging (they say) comes by desteny, and Scogans choice tis better none at all. Hee that played Proteus (with the helpe of Priapus) put their noses out of joynt as the Proverbe is.

And this the whole company of the Revellers at Ma-re Mount, knew to be the true sence and exposition of the riddle: that was fixed to the Maypole, which the Seperatists were at defiance with some of them affirmed, that the first institution thereof, was in memory of a whore; not knowing that is was a Trophe erected at first, in honor of Maia, the Lady of learning which they despise; vilifying the two universities with uncivile terms; accounting for what is there obtained by studdy is but unnecessary learning; not considering that learninge does inable mens mindes to converse with climents of a higher nature then is to be found within the habitation of the Mole.

4.31   Niobe] In Greek mythology, a mortal woman who commits suicide, or turns to stone while weeping, after the murder of her children.

4.32–5.2   Amphitrites . . . Triton] Amphitrite, a sea goddess in classical mythology, was mother of Triton, messenger of the sea, by Neptune (Poseidon), the sea god.

5.9   Cupids beautious mother] Aphrodite or Venus, associated in classical mythology with love, beauty, and fertility.

5.10   Scogans choise] A choice among unappealing alternatives: John Scoggin (fl. 1480), legendary court jester to Edward IV and putative author of *The Jestes of Skoggyn* (c. 1570), was supposed to have evaded a death sentence when, given the choice of a tree from which to hang, he was unable to pick one.

5.13   Esculapius] In classical mythology, god of medicine.

5.16   Cithareas] Cytherea, another name for Aphrodite or Venus (from Cythera, an island where she was worshipped).

5.22   Iô] A Greek and Latin exclamation of joy or triumph.

8.33   *The whore*] The whore of Babylon, an allegorical figure for the Catholic church.

8.34–9.8   Long were they hid . . . reveng'd them all.] Guy Fawkes (1570–1606) and others plotted unsuccessfully to blow up Westminster Palace during the opening session of Parliament, in November 1605.

10.11   Tyth] Tithe, a tenth part.

12.6   Hooker, Winthrop, Cotton] The Rev. Thomas Hooker (1586–1647), minister of the First Church of Hartford, Connecticut; John Winthrop (1585–1649), governor of the Massachusetts Bay Colony for a number of terms between 1630 and 1649; the Rev. John Cotton (1585–1652), a prominent Boston minister.

14.3–4   faithful Wilson . . . Norton] The Rev. John Wilson (1588–1667), minister of the First Church of Boston from 1630 until his death; the Rev. John Norton (1606–1663), a Boston minister from 1653 until his death.

16.3–14   Wolfes . . . devoure.] When he published this sonnet in *New English Canaan* (1637), Thomas Morton offered the following comments on its occasion:

> Sir Christopher was gone with a guide (a Salvage) into the inland parts for discovery: but, before hee was returned, hee met with a Salvage that told the guide, Sir Christopher would be killed: Master Temperwell (who had now found out matter against him) would have him dead, or alive. This hee related; and would have the gentleman not to goe to the place appointed, because of the danger, that was supposed.
>
> But Sir Christopher was nothing dismaid: hee would on, whatsoever come of it; and so met with the Salvages: and betweene them was a terrible skermish: But they had the worst of it, and hee scaped well enough.
>
> The guide was glad of it, and learnd of his fellowes that they were promised a great reward, for what they should doe in this imployment.
>
> Which thing (when Sir Christopher understood,) hee gave thanks to God; and after (upon this occasion, to sollace himself) in his table booke, hee composed this sonnet, which I have here inserted for a memoriall . . .
>
> This Sonnet the Gentleman composed, as a testimony of his love towards them, that were so ill affected towards him; from whome they might have receaved much good, if they had bin so wise to have imbraced him in a loving fashion.
>
> But they despise the helpe, that shall come from a carnall man (as they termed him) who (after his retorne from those designes) finding how they had used him with such disrespect, tooke shipping, and disposed of himselfe for England, and discovered their practises in those parts towards his Majesties true harted Subjects, which they made wery of their aboade in those parts.

30.4   *A Key . . . America*] Williams' verses originally appeared as codas to the following chapters in *A Key into the Language of America* (1643): "Of Salutation," "Of Eating and Entertainment," "Of Their Persons and Parts of Body," "Of Their Government and Justice," and "Concerning Their Coyne."

35.1–3   *Reverendo viro Domino . . . observando*] To a man most worthy of reverence, Lord John Wilson, most faithful pastor of the Boston Church, brother and friend most worthy of recognition.

35.15–16   Tuus . . . addictissimus] Yours with sympathy and great devotion.

36.14   *Bartas*] Guillaume de Salluste Du Bartas (1544–1590), French Protestant epic poet.

36.27–28   that fluent . . . *Greek / Who* lisp'd at first] Demosthenes (384–322 BCE), Greek orator and statesman.

37.13   those nine] The muses.

38.34   *Hengist*] Invited into England by Celtish ruler Vortigern to fight the Picts, the legendary Hengist (d. 488?) turned against the Celts and founded his own dynasty in Kent.

38.37   *Canutus*] Canute I (c. 995–1035), Viking king of England.

39.5   *Maud,* and *Stephen* . . . contend?] Maud (1101–1167), also known as Empress Matilda, and Stephen of Blois (c. 1096–1154) fought to succeed Henry I after his death in 1135, provoking a lengthy civil war (1139–53).

39.8   *Edward*] Edward II (1307–1327) was deposed in 1327.

39.11   from the red . . . Roses sprung] The houses of Lancaster and York fought the War of the Roses from 1455 to 1485.

39.12–13   *Richmonds* ayd . . . Boar?] Henry Tudor, earl of Richmond (1457–1509), became Henry VII after his defeat of Richard III (1452–1485), whose heraldic symbol was the boar.

39.31   *Alcies* Son, and *Henries* Daughter] Stephen and Maud (see note 39.5).

39.33–34   *John* . . . bring] During the First Barons' War (1215–1217), a group of barons invited Louis VIII (1187–1226), King of France, to replace King John (1199–1216) on the throne.

39.36   *Lancastrians*] See note 39.11.

39.39   Duke . . . *March*] Edmund Plantagenet (1341–1402) and Roger de Mortimer (1287–1330).

41.3–4   *Edwards* Babes . . . O *Jane*] Young royals who died in the Tower of London: Edward V (1470–1483?) and Richard Shrewsbury, duke of York (1473–1483), sons of Edward IV; Edward Plantagenet, 17th earl of Warwick (1475–1499), son of the first duke of Clarence, imprisoned from 1485 to 1499; Lady Jane Grey (1537–1554), executed for treason.

41.34   strong *Rochel*] La Rochelle, a fortified Huguenot city in western France, was besieged by Catholic forces in 1572–73 and again in 1627–28.

42.24–25   *Strafford* . . . *Laud*] Thomas Wentworth, first earl of Strafford (1593–1641), and William Laud (1573–1645), archbishop of Canterbury, both executed for treason.

44.1   *Gideon*]   Cf. Judges 7:18–19.

44.2   *Mero's* curse]   Cf. Judges 5:23.

44.14   *Essex* . . . son thou art]   Robert Devereux, third earl of Essex (1591–1646); his father, the second earl, was executed for treason.

44.19   sturdy *Tyburn* loaded]   The Tyburn gallows, in London.

44.39   Pursevants and Catchpoles]   Officers-of-arms and sheriff's officers.

45.32–36   *her Book* . . . publick view]   *The Tenth Muse, Lately Sprung Up in America* (1650), which had been published in London without Bradstreet's prior knowledge.

50.15   Land of *Nod*]   Cf. Genesis 4:16.

52.13   *Thetis* house]   The sea (in Greek mythology, Thetis was a sea nymph).

63.37   Idalian]   Of Idalium, a city in Cyprus sacred to Venus.

64.10   *Joseph Dudley*]   Dudley (1647–1720) served as governor of Massachusetts from 1702 to 1715. In 1703 he removed John Saffin from the council, prompting Saffin's verse epistle.

64.17–23   that Noble Bassa . . . Atchievements]   Ottoman emperors distracted from affairs of state by the beauty of a Christian captive appear with many variations in dramatic and fictional works, including William Painter's *Palace of Pleasure* (1566), Thomas Goffe's *The Courageous Turke* (1618/32), and Gilbert Swinhoe's *The Tragedy of the Unhappy Fair Irene* (1658).

65.18   Lord Burleigh]   William Cecil Burleigh (1520–1596), a principal adviser to Elizabeth I.

72.25–28   The *Eastern Conquerour* . . . subdue]   Alexander the Great (356–323 BCE).

73.16   unweeting]   Unwitting.

74.21   *Omnia praetereunt praeter amare Deum.*]   All things pass except the love of God.

108.7   lins]   Ceases.

111.27–30   Quod Deus omnipotens . . . Lector Amice]   What God almighty warns you with a ruler's voice, / What the prophets proclaim unto you, crying in unison, / And what I with many tears testify concerning God's wrath, / Do not, dear reader, consider lightly.

114.29   Our Governour]   John Endecott (1588–1665), governor of Massachusetts from 1655 until his death.

115.6   pight]   Pitch, set up.

115.20   amate]   Dismay, dishearten.

120.20   sweale]   Melt, waste away.

128.10   'I Walk'd . . . *Mole-hill* view]   This poem was first published in a London edition of *The Day of Doom* (J. Sims, 1673) not known to have been authorized by Wigglesworth himself, and some scholars have suggested that it may not have been written by him. For further information, see O. M. Brack Jr., "Michael Wigglesworth and the Attribution of 'I Walk'd and Did a Little Molehill View,'" *Seventeenth Century News* 28 (1970): 41–44.

130.15   *Pelion* on *Ossa* build]   In Greek mythology, Otus and Ephialtes attempted to reach heaven and challenge the gods by piling Mt. Ossa on Mt. Olympus, and then Mt. Pelion on Mt. Ossa.

137.30   *Momus*]   In Greek mythology, god of ridicule.

140.13   Father *Wilsons*]   John Wilson (c. 1588–1667), a Boston pastor.

142.7   *LEVERET*]   John Leverett (1662–1724), president of Harvard from 1707 to 1724.

144.3   *His Book*]   *A Character of the Province of Maryland* (1666).

144.27   Col'nel *Pride*]   In December 1648, Thomas Pride (d. 1658) commanded troops that forcibly prevented royalist and Presbyterian members of the House of Commons from taking their seats, leaving a majority in favor of Republican government; the event is known as "Pride's Purge."

146.11   Heavens bright lamp]   In *A Character of the Province of Maryland*, Alsop's poem appeared at the conclusion of a letter "To my much Honored Friend Mr. T.B.":

> Sir,
>
> I have lived with sorrow to see the Anointed of the Lord tore from his Throne by the hands of Paricides, and in contempt haled, in the view of God, Angels and Men, upon a publick Theatre, and there murthered. I have seen the sacred Temple of the Almighty, in scorn by Schismaticks made the Receptacle of Theeves and Robbers; and those Religious Prayers, that in devotion Evening and Morning were offered up as a Sacrifice to our God, rent by Sacrilegious hands, and made no other use of, then sold to Brothel-houses to light Tobacco with.
>
> Who then can stay, or will, to see things of so great weight steer'd by such barbarous Hounds as these: First, were there an *Egypt* to go down to, I would involve my Liberty to them, upon condition ne're more to see my Country. What? live in silence under the sway of such base actions, is to give consent; and though the lowness of my present Estate and Condition, with the hazard I put my future dayes upon, might plead a just excuse for me to stay at home; but Heavens forbid: I'le rather serve in Chains, and draw the Plough with Animals, till death shall stop and say, *It is enough*. Sir, if you stay behind, I wish you

well: I am bound for *Mary-Land*, this day I have made some entrance into my intended Voyage, and when I have done more, you shall know of it. I have here inclosed what you of me desired, but truly trouble, discontent and business, have so amazed my senses, that what to write, or where to write, I conceive my self almost as uncapable as he that never did write. What you'le find will be *Ex tempore*, without the use of premeditation; and though there may want something of a flourishing stile to dress them forth, yet I'm certain there wants nothing of truth, will, and desire.

146.26   *Oliver* and *Joan*]   Oliver Cromwell (1599–1658) and his wife Elizabeth (1598–1665), often called Joan.

146.35   our King]   Charles I (1600–1649).

147.3   Conventicks]   Dissenters.

147.30   Great *Charles* . . . his own]   Charles II (1630–1685), in exile after his father's execution.

147.32   Vale]   Farewell.

148.15   *Lillies*]   William Lily (1468?–1522), author of *Absolutissimus de octo orationis partium constructione libellus* (c. 1513) and *Rudimenta grammatices* (c. 1527).

150.2   *De Tristibus*]   *Tristia*, a poem Ovid wrote after he was exiled from Rome in 8 CE.

150.13   *Sic Maestus Cecinit*]   Thus sang the afflicted one.

150.26   Cimnels]   Biscuits.

150.29   *poor Robins Almanack*]   A popular English almanac, first published around 1662.

151.17   *Jonakin*]   Johnnycake.

151.39   snib'd]   Rebuffed.

153.1   *Lord Bellamont*]   Richard Coote (1636–1701), first earl of Bellamont.

153.30   Chicataubuts]   Chickataubut (d. 1632), a sachem of the region around Weymouth, Massachusetts.

154.6   Emmett]   Ant.

154.9   Fam'd Agawam]   Cf. *The Simple Cobbler of Agawam in America* (1644), a satirical essay by Nathaniel Ward (1578–1652).

154.26   to fetch a Kid]   In 1699, Bellamont arrested William Kidd (c. 1645–1701), who had been accused of piracy.

156.3–5   *The Poor Unhappy . . . America*]   Though not published until the second half of the 18th century, this poem may have been composed around 1680. For further information, see John Melville Jennings, "The Poor Unhappy Transported Felon's Sorrowful Account of His Fourteen Years Transportation at Virginia in America," *Virginia Magazine of History and Biography* 56 (1948): 180–94.

166.19 Garzia Horti] Cf. *Aromatum et simplicium aliquot Medicamentorum apud Indos nascentium* (1563), a work on the medicinal plants of India by Garcia da Orta (c. 1501–1568).

166.32 Catholicons] Panaceas; cf. also the *Catholicon*, a widely reprinted 13th-century Latin dictionary.

167.6 Palma Christi] *Ricinus communis*, a large shrub with palmate leaves from which castor oil is obtained (literally, "palm of Christ").

167.8 Unguent Apostolorum] Apostolic ointment, so called because it had twelve ingredients.

169.31 Spagyrist] Alchemist.

170.3 Aurum Vitae] Living gold, a red-colored medicine.

174.19 Wine-fats] Wine-presses.

176.22 Skeg] Nail; part of a ship's keel; species of oat.

176.32 gastard] Gastered: terrified, devastated.

178.3 Shalm] A wind instrument, antecedent of the modern oboe.

178.4 Shoshannim . . . Michtams] Shoshannim: a musical instrument or musical form referred to in Psalms 45, 60, 69, and 80. Michtams: "golden" or "hidden" psalms, of which there are six (cf. Psalms 16, 56–60).

185.19–20 ἐσκήνωσεν ἐν ἡμῖν] He dwelt among us.

186.14 Feast of Booths] During Sukkot, also known as the Feast of Booths or the Feast of Tabernacles, the observant build temporary huts recalling the habitations of the Israelites in the desert, after the Exodus.

192.11 Squitchen] Escutcheon.

192.16 fet] Fetched.

193.16 fleere] Mock, deride.

195.19 froppish] Peevish, contrary.

198.11 Fulling] A finishing process in the manufacture of woolen cloth.

200.3 In these Seven . . . do own] In Pastorius's *Beehive* manuscript, these lines follow the work's title, given in seven languages: Greek, Latin, English, Dutch, German, Italian, and French. A marginal gloss in Pastorius' manuscript reads "vide infra p. 7 num": "see within, page number 7."

200.14–19   Freund . . . seyn.]   Friend, *whatever you find, return,* / Otherwise people will call you a thief / And in this life and the next / Follows nothing but the pains of hell. / God Himself gave us this law / Do unto others what you would have them do unto you.

200.20   Quod Tibi . . . Aliis]   Do unto others as you would have done unto you.

200.21   *A Token . . . Gratitude*]   Written on August 20, 1714, the first of a series of poems commemorating Pastorius's arrival in Philadelphia with his late friend Thomas Lloyd (1640–1694) on August 20, 1683. The poems are addressed to Lloyd's daughters Hannah Hill, Rachel Preston, and Mary Norris.

200.27   Charities of old]   The three graces (Greek: charites).

200.33   Thrums]   Tufts of thread.

201.11   John De la Val]   John Delaval (d. 1693), a Philadelphia merchant, the first husband of Lloyd's daughter Hannah Hill.

202.23   George Keith]   A longtime Quaker who had served as headmaster of the Friends School in Philadelphia, Keith (c. 1638–1716) broke with his coreligionists in the early 1690s, formed a group of "Christian Quakers," and later attempted to win converts to the Anglican faith.

202.28   *Fortunante . . . Palmam*]   With God willing, piety at last brings the palm of victory.

203.2   my former Sheet]   Cf. "A Token of Love and Gratitude," pages 200–02 in this volume.

204.20–21   Utopia . . . by Thomas Morus]   Cf. *Utopia* (1516) by Sir Thomas More (1478–1535).

204.39   Francia Orientalis : Wallia Septentrionalis.]   Eastern France: Northern Wales.

205.29   Bull of Bashan]   Cf. Psalm 22: 12–13.

205.38   Vox Bovis, non Hominis.]   The voice of a cow, not of man.

206.16   Simonides]   Simonides of Ceos (c. 556–468 BCE), lyric poet.

207.26   Ut . . . pungant.]   So that they anoint rather than sting.

207.27–28   Das . . . frumm.]   That be the sum of all books: / Believe in Christ, and live piously.

207.29   Ex Fide Vita.]   Life from faith.

208.16   Braganza]   A town and region in northeast Portugal.

208.35   Nep]   Catmint, *Nepeta cataria*.

209.12   Animus sine . . . *Horat.*]   Mind quick moving without weight. Cf. Horace, *Epistles*, I.xii.13: "animus sine corpore velox" ("mind quick moving without body").

209.13   *Epibaterium*]   The Entrance.

209.20–21   Ter Fortunatus . . . tuus!]   May your third approach to the Indians be thrice fortunate, happy, and favorable, William!

211.18–21   Juxta Ovidium . . . tamen]   After Ovid, love of money grows, etc. (cf. Juvenal, Satire XIV, "crescit amor nummi, quantum ipsa pecunia crevit": the love of money grows as wealth itself has grown). And while zeal for silver rules in our city, caring about money has robbed brotherly love of its name. One responds, brother Romulus, brother Abimeleck, brother Esau, brother Cain, and brother Jehoram all have brothers; in spite of all this, it's a rare grace.

211.40–41   Onomastical Observations]   Pastorius's numbered observations on the origins of proper names appear throughout his manuscripts.

212.1   Kuster, Keith & Budd]   Henry Bernhard Koster (1662–1749) and Thomas Budd (1649–c. 1699) sided with George Keith (c. 1638–1716) in his schismatic arguments against certain tenets of Quakerism.

213.23   black Loyol]   Saint Ignatius of Loyola (1491–1556), founder of the Jesuit order.

213.29   acer Eremi . . . benè]   Translated in the text that follows: God Almighty [. . .] Wilderness.

213.36   Veritas . . . Latrat]   Translated in the text that follows: All Devilish [. . .] Lurking-holes.

213.38   Vult . . . Latere]   Translated in the text that follows: Whenas [. . .] the Poles.

213.40–41   Wahrheit . . . untergeht]   Truth stands like a palm tree. / When your lying disappears.

214.7–9   Je conclus . . . d'Allemand.]   I conclude, / Here, and in Heaven Penn is Welcome! / For to have everything, one must also have a little German.

214.14–24   Penn . . . Papist]   Penn means in Welsh a head, in Low German a quill, / Which one uses for writing; the head devises either / Something good or evil, and with it the Queen / Forces both rich and poor to pay her tribute / No, if I was granted a wish, I would that my quill / Had such an impact that everyone would submit / As an obedient member to Jesus Christ / Who is the only head of the true church / Then there would be no Heathen, nor Jew, nor Papist.

214.26   *Distichon*]   Distich, verse couplet.

214.27   *Sit Pax . . . Salus!*]   Peace be with the one who enters, and health with the one who returns!

214.28–30   Mit Fried . . . tecum.]   With peace inside; with happiness outside! / Go into the house from the garden, Friend, / And wish for me what I wish for you. God be with you.

214.32   Svaviter . . . Profani!]   The good one is pleasantly received, but the evil ones, may they stay away! (Cf. *Aeneid*, VI.258: "O procul este, profani.")

214.33–34   Die guten . . . fromm]   Good people are welcome here: I love no one who is not pious.

215.1–3   Janua . . . procacem.]   Our door is open; sweet friends come in! / You who are evil, I said farewell to you a long time ago. / I hate the liar and cannot stand the fresh and forward one.

215.4–6   Nun Die . . . reüen.]   Now, those who only enjoy with their hearts and eyes, / But who shrink from using their hands, / A company thus inclined I shall never resent.

215.7–8   Hic Argus . . . Invide.]   Let be here be Argus, not Briareus. / Look, don't envy. (In Greek mythology, Argus was a hundred-eyed giant, a watchman, and Briareus one of three Hecatonchires or hundred-handed giants.)

215.9–12   Quisquis . . . feras.]   Whoever you are who crawl furtively through these our gardens, / Beware of touching my fruits with a deceitful hand; / If you don't obey, may God do everything that I hope so that you, / Along with all our apples, bear all evils.

216.7   Panaretes]   All-virtuous (Greek: *panaretos*).

217.10   *Maro*'s]   Virgil's.

217.26   *Thespian*]   From Thespiae, an ancient Greek city where the muses were worshipped.

218.33   *Omnia . . . Gentis*]   Let all the wonders of the Roman people be silent.

219.5   *A little before . . . Massachusetts*]   Sewall's diary entry for Jan 2, 1701, records the occasion for which this poem was composed: "Just about break a day Jacob Amsden and 3 other trumpeters gave a blast with the trumpets on the Common near Mr. Alford's. Then went to the Green Chamber and sounded there till about sunrise. Bell man said these verses a little before break-a-day which I printed and gave them. The trumpeters cost me five pieces ⅜—."

222.15–18   The *Royal Oak* . . . Majestie.]   In 1651, during the English Civil War, Charles II (1630–1685) hid in an oak tree on the grounds of Boscobel House to evade capture by Commonwealth troops.

225.3–16   Go then . . . ALL.]   The poem was originally published as an epigram to a funeral sermon, *Death Made Happy and Easy*, distributed at the funeral of Mather's first wife, Abigail, in 1702.

225.19–20   *Augusto perstringere . . . queat.*]   To bind in a noble song praises / That no power of eloquence can celebrate.

225.23   stabb'd *Cassian*]   St. Cassian of Imola (d. 363?), Christian saint who had been stabbed by his students with their metal styluses.

226.26   *Loretto*-Table]   The Santa Casa di Loreto, a Marian shrine in Loreto, Italy.

227.19   CORLET's]   Elijah Corlet (c. 1610–1687), longtime master of the grammar school in Cambridge, Massachusetts.

227.27   *Lilly*]   William Lily (c. 1468–1522), English scholar whose grammar texts were widely used in schools.

227.31   *Tullies Offices*]   *De Officiis* ("On Duties," 44 BCE), by Roman philosopher and orator Marcus Tullius Cicero (106–43 BCE).

227.37–38   Young *Austin* . . . had:]   Cf. Augustine's *Confessions* (397–398), book 1.

228.1   *Textors Epistles*]   The *Epistolae* of Johannes Ravisius Textor (1470–1524), often used in the teaching of Latin.

228.5   *Nestors*]   An elder statesman of the Trojan war.

229.37   *Macrobius*]   Ambrosius Theodosius Macrobius, Roman philosopher and grammarian (fl. 395–423 CE).

230.6   DAVENPORT]   John Davenport (1597–1670), cofounder of the New Haven Colony.

230.18   in *Ferio*]   A form of syllogism.

230.38-39   *Et Tumulum* . . . Daphn.)]   Virgil, Eclogue V. 42 (the lament for Daphnis): "And build a tomb, and on the burial mound as well, this verse."

231.1–232.6   *EPITAPHIUM* . . . primam.]   Epitaph / Ezekiel Cheever / Schoolmaster / First of New Haven; / Then of Ipswich; / After of Charlestown / Last of Boston / Whose / Learning and Virtue / You know, if you be a New Englander, / You honor, if you be not a foreigner; / GRAMMARIAN / from whom talk is not only pure but / also pious; / RHETORICIAN / from whom speech is elegant / not only to men in public / but he also showers / Most effective speeches on God in public /

POET / from whom not only songs are composed / But he also / Sings Celestial hymns and angelic odes, / They learn, / Who wish to learn; / A LAMP / from whom has been kindled / Who can count / How many lights of the Churches? / AND / He carries off the corpus of Theology with him / Most experienced THEOLOGIAN / He placed his own body less dear to him. / He lived 94 years. / He taught 70 years. / He died in 1708 A.D. / And because he is able to die / He awaits and desires / The first resurrection of the holy ones / for Immortality / Honor is owed first.

234.5–11   I ask thy Aid . . . comes!]   This poem is taken from Knight's journal entry of October 3, 1704, which gives the following account of its occasion:

Being come to mr. Havens', I was very civilly Received, and courteously entertained, in a clean comfortable House; and the Good woman was very active in helping off my Ridign clothes, and then ask't what I would eat. I told her I had some Chocolett, if shee would prepare it; which with the help of some Milk, and a little clean brass Kettle, she soon effected to my satisfaction. I then betook me to my Apartment, which was a little Room parted from the Kitchen by a single bord partition; where, after I had noted the Occurrances of the past day, I went to bed, which, tho' pretty hard, Yet neet and handsome. But I could get no sleep, because of the Clamor of some of the Town tope-ers in next Room, Who were entred into a strong debate concerning the Signifycation of the name of their Country, (*viz.*) *Narraganset.* One said it was named so by the Indians, because there grew a Brier there, of a prodigious Highth and bigness, the like hardly ever known, called by the Indians Narragansett; And quotes an Indian of so Barberous a name for his Author, that I could not write it. His Antagonist Replyd no—It was from a Spring it had its name, which hee well knew where it was, which was extreem cold in summer, and as Hott as could be imagined in the winter, which was much resorted too by the natives, and by then called Narragansett, (Hott and Cold,) and that was the originall of their places name—with a thousand Impertinences not worth notice, which He utter'd with such a Roreing voice and Thundering blows with the fist of wickedness on the Table, that it peirced my very head. I heartily fretted, and wish't 'um tongue tyed; but with as little succes as a freind of mine once, who was (as shee said) kept a whole night awake, on a Jorny, by a country Left. and a Sergent, Insigne and a Deacon, contriving how to bring a triangle into a Square. They kept calling for tother Gill, which while they were swallowing was some Intermission; But presently, like Oyle to fire, encreased the flame. I set my Candle on a Chest by the bedside, and setting up, fell to my old way of composing my Resentments, in the following manner: . . . And I know not but my wishes took effect; for the dispute soon ended with 'tother Dram; and so Good night!

234.12–23   Tho' Ill . . . Dreem]   Knight's journal entry of October 4, 1704, introduces this poem with the following comments:

From hence we proceeded (about ten forenoon) through the Narragansett country, pretty Leisurely; and about one afternoon come to Paukataug River, which was about two hundred paces over, and now very high, and no way over to to'ther side but this. I darid not venture to Ride thro, my courage at best in such cases but small, And now at the Lowest Ebb, by reason of my weary, very weary, hungry and uneasy Circumstances. So takeing leave of my company, tho' with no little Reluctance, that I could not proceed with them on my Jorny, Stop at a little cottage Just by the River, to wait the Waters falling, which the old man that lived there said would be in a little time, and he would conduct me safe over. This little Hutt was one of the wretchedest I ever saw a habitation for human creatures. It was suported with shores enclosed with Clapboards, laid on Lengthways, and so much asunder, that the Light come throu' every where; the doore tyed on with a cord in the place of hinges; The floor the bear earth; no windows but such as the tin covering afforded, nor any furniture but a Bedd with a glass Bottle hanging at the head on't; an earthan cupp, a small pewter Bason, A Bord with sticks to stand on, instead of a table, and a block or two in the corner instead of chairs. The family were the old man, his wife and two Children; aall and every part being the picture of poverty. Notwithstanding both the Hutt and its Inhabitance were very clean and tydee: to the crossing the Old Proverb, that bare walls make giddy hows-wifes.

I Blest myselfe that I was not one of this misserable crew; and the Impressions their wretchedness formed in me caused mee on the very Spott to say:

239.3   *Sot-Weed*]   Tobacco.

240.21   Tripple Tree]   The gallows.

241.6   As *Sol* fell into *Thetis* lap]   As the sun fell into the sea.

242.6   on the Fret]   Fermenting.

242.22   *Indian* Gun]   Pipe.

245.32–33   Orsin's]   In Samuel Butler's mock-heroic *Hudibras* (1663–78), Orsin is a bear keeper.

247.2   *Balaam's* Ass . . . kick'd]   Cf. Numbers 22: 22–23.

248.37–38   *A Groat ad purgandus Rhenes*]   A worthless purge for the kidneys.

254.14   *Lanctre-Looe*]   Langteraloo, or loo; a card game.

254.22   *Pam*]   The jack of clubs (a trump card, in some versions of loo).

254.28   Froes]   Women.

254.38   *Bridewell* or *Newgate*]   London prisons.

255.10   *Adam's* Ale]   Water.

255.30   *Goodwin-Sands*]   A sand bank on the coast of the English Channel.

257.11   *Galen* . . . Lord *Cook*]   Galen (129–c. 200), ancient Greek physi-
cian; Edward Coke (1552–1634), author of widely influential legal texts.

257.29   St. *Mary's* once]   Annapolis replaced St. Mary's as Maryland's
capital in 1694.

258.16–29   I left this dreadful Curse . . . Chast.]   When he revised "The
Sot-Weed Factor" for publication in 1731, Cook replaced "this dreadful
Curse" with a "Wish," as follows:

> This Wish proceeded from my Mind,
>
> > *If any Youngster cross the Ocean,*
> > *To sell his Wares—may he with Caution*
> > *Before he pays, receive each Hogshead,*
> > *Lest he be cheated by some Dogshead,*
> > *Both of his Goods and his Tobacco;*
> > *And then like me, he shall not lack-woe.*
> > *And may that Land where Hospitality*
> > *Is every Planter's darling Quality,*
> > *Be by each Trader kindly us'd.*
> > *And may no Trader be abus'd;*
> > *Then each of them shall deal with Pleasure,*
> > *And each encrease the other's Treasure.*

259.19   groats]   English coins valued at four pence; small sums.

260.9   moile]   Toil.

260.30   Elizian plaines]   The Elysian fields, in classical mythology the
final resting place of the honored dead.

261.17   rapperees]   Bandits, freebooters.

261.37   a Governour]   Richard Nicolla (1624–1672), military governor of
New York from 1664 to 1668.

262.33   The chieftain]   Sir Edmund Andros (1637–1714), governor of New
England from 1686 to 1689 and also of New York and the Jerseys from 1688
to 1689.

266.20   The chieftain]   Benjamin Fletcher (1640–1703), governor of New
York from 1692 to 1697.

269.24   N C]   *Nolo contestare*, without objection.

271.24   *Samuel Willard*] Willard (1640–1707) was a minister in Groton and later at Boston's Old South Church; he served as president of Harvard from 1701 until his death.

280.3   *Lovewell's Fight*] When first published in February 1824, "Lovewell's Fight" was prefaced as follows: "The following Song was written about one hundred years since, to commemorate one of the most fierce and obstinate battles which had been fought with the Indians. For many years, it was sung throughout a considerable portion of New-Hampshire and Massachusetts, and probably served more than any thing else to keep in remembrance the circumstances of this desperate engagement." John Lovewell (1691–1725) died during an expedition against the Abenaki on May 8, 1725.

280.10   Pigwacket] Near present-day Fryeburg, Maine.

284.3   *the Hymn-Book . . . Kelpius*] The 1705 manuscript hymn-book of Johannes Kelpius (c. 1673–1708), at the Historical Society of Pennsylvania, contains musical scores and German texts of Kelpius's hymns in the hand of Christina Warmer, a Germantown tailor, with facing English translations by Christopher Witt. The English title of the book is *The Lamenting Voice of the Hidden Love, at the time when she lay in Misery & forsaken; and oprest by the multitude of her Enemies. Composed by one In Kumber.*

297.27   [ ]] The brackets indicate that part of the original manuscript is illegible.

298.2   leer] Empty.

299.16–17   Southwark . . . the Rules] A region of central London, Southwark was home of the King's Bench Prison, often used for debtors; some prisoners purchased "Liberty of the Rules" and were able to live in a circumscribed area outside the prison.

300.4–5   Pyrgopolinices . . . Alcides] Pyrgopolynices, a "braggart soldier" in the comedy *Miles Gloriosus* (c. 206 BCE), by Titus Maccius Plautus (254–184 BCE); Bombardomachides, a similar character in Abraham Cowley's play *Naufragium Ioculare* (1638); Orgoglio, a giant (from the Italian for "Pride") in *The Faerie Queene* (1590–96) by Edmund Spenser (c. 1552–1599); Pantagruel, another giant, son of Gargantua, who appears in novels (1532–1564) by François Rabelais (c. 1494–1553); Roland, a hero of medieval legend featured in works including *La Chanson de Roland* (c. 1140–1170); Alcides, another name for Heracles, preeminent hero of Greek mythology.

302.1   Oroonoke] Tobacco.

302.14   Idalium, or Paphos] Cities in Cyprus associated with the goddess Aphrodite or Venus.

304.33–305.4   as Epigram makes known . . . Owl dead] Cf. the *Greek Anthology*, Book XI, epigrams 186 (Nicarchus: "The night-raven's song bodes death, but when Demophilus sings the night-raven itself dies") and

255 (Palladas: "Snub-nosed Memphis danced the parts of Daphne and Niobe, Daphne as if he were wooden, and Niobe as if he were of stone").

305.11   see Wycherly] William Wycherley (1640–1716).

305.32   Toland] John Toland (1670–1722), a freethinker and author of many works critical of religious institutions.

305.36   Faustina and Cuzzone] Faustina Bordoni (1693–1781) and Francesca Cuzzoni (1700–1770), prima donnas whose intense rivalry divided London society; in June 1727 they came to blows on stage.

307.20   Acrisius wakeful Care] In Greek mythology, Acrisius imprisoned his daughter Danaë after it was prophesied a grandchild would slay him. Zeus, taking the form of a shower of gold, impregnated her, and her son Perseus eventually fulfilled the prophecy by accident.

307.21   Atalanta] In Greek mythology, Atalanta's suitor Hippomenes was able to outrun her, and win her hand, having distracted her with three golden apples.

308.1–4   Tale of Lesbia . . . Tragedy:] In his Carmen 2, Catullus (c. 84–c. 54 BCE) laments the death of his lover Lesbia's pet sparrow; Martial (40–c. 102 CE), in his Epigrams (cix), compares his friend Publius' dog Issa to Catullus' sparrow.

314.9   *Sasacus*] Sassacus (c. 1560–1637), Pequot sachem.

314.33   *Norton . . . Surprise*] In separate incidents regarded as inciting causes of the 1637 Pequot War, captains John Norton and John Stone were killed on a slaving voyage on the Connecticut River in 1634, and John Oldham (1592–1636) while on a trading voyage to Block Island, by tributary clients of the Pequot.

315.2   *Endicott*] John Endecott (c. 1588–1665), magistrate and later governor of the Massachusetts Bay Colony.

317.1   *Panime*] Pagan.

319.32   *Mason*] John Mason (c. 1600–1672), commander of the Connecticut Colony expedition against the Pequot in 1637.

320.3   *Hooker*] Thomas Hooker (1586–1647), a founder of the Connecticut Colony.

320.5   *Uncass*] Uncas (c. 1588–1682), Pequot sachem who broke with his tribe in 1637, becoming leader of the Mohegans.

321.3   *Underhill*] John Underhill (1609–1672), captain of the Massachusetts Bay Colony militia.

322.2   *Miaantinomohs*] Miantonomoh (c. 1565–1643), Narragansett chief.

323.35   an *Alta*] A halt.

327.6–7   Black Prince]   Edward of Woodstock, Prince of Wales (1330–1376).

327.26   King *Philip*]   Philip II of Spain (1527–1598).

327.29   *Howards . . . Drake*]   Lord High Admiral Charles Howard (1536–1624), Admiral Thomas Howard (1561–1626), Lord Henry Seymour (fl. 1588), and Francis Drake (1540–1596), naval commanders who defended England against the Spanish Armada in 1588.

331.31   a Carter . . . as now]   Col. Charles Carter (1707–1764), a leading advocate for the relocation of Virginia's capital from Williamsburg, was a son of Robert "King" Carter (1663–1732).

332.11   Middle Plantation]   The tract of land on which Williamsburg was built.

332.33   Corinthian brass]   An alloy produced at Corinth, said to be of gold, silver, and copper.

336.19   Dinwiddie]   Robert Dinwiddie (1693–1770) served as lieutenant governor of Virginia from 1751 to 1758.

337.1   great Camden's skill]   William Camden (1551–1623), an English historian.

338.23   Norton]   John Norton (1719–1777), a Yorktown merchant.

339.8   Carter Burwell's part]   Burwell (1716–1756) served in the Virginia House of Burgesses from 1742 to 1756.

339.15   Prince Eugene]   François Eugène, Prince of Savoy (1663–1763).

339.22–24   Nat . . . Grymes's]   Nathaniel Burwell (b. 1750) was the son of Carter Burwell and Lucy Ludwell Grymes.

339.32   the engine . . . Sidney fell]   Sir Philip Sidney (1554–1586) died from a bullet wound during the Battle of Zutphen.

339.36   Titus]   Flavius Sabinus Vespasianus Titus (40–81 CE), Roman emperor from 79 until his death.

344.13   Selimus . . . Bajazett]   Selim I (1467–1520), son of Bayezid II (1481–1512); both fought against the Mamluks of Egypt.

347.3–5   *Mr. Blackamore's . . . Governour*]   On its first appearance in print (in *The Maryland Gazette*, June 17–24, 1729), this poem was introduced with the following letter from "Ecclesiasticus" to printer and editor William Parks:

> Mr. *Parks*,
>
> The *College* at *Williamsburgh* is obliged to pay Two Copies of Latin Verses, to the Governour, every Fifth of *November*, as Quit-Rent for Land. The *November* after Col. *Spotswood*, and his Train, return'd

from the Progress amongst the Mountains (when the *Tramontane Order* was instituted) Mr. *Blair*, the President, chose for his Subject, The Suppression of the *Late Rebellion*; and Mr. *Blackamore*, the Humanity Professor, composed an excellent Poem on this *Mountain Expedition*; which the late Rev. Mr. *George Seagood* turn'd into *English*.

I have sent you the Translation, which (having gain'd the Applause of several good Judges) may probably contribute to the Satisfaction of your Correspondents, that are poetically inclined.

Arthur Blackamore (c. 1679–c. 1723), born in London, was master of the Grammar School at the College of William and Mary; his original Latin poem, written in 1716, is not known to be extant.

347.7 *Northern* Civil War] The First Jacobite Rebellion of 1715.

347.10 *Spotswood*] Alexander Spotswood (c. 1676–1740), acting governor of Virginia. His expedition into the mountains of northern Virginia took place in 1716.

348.36 *Rapidanna*] The Rapidan River, a tributary of the Rappahannock.

349.8 *Germanna*] A settlement near present-day Culpeper, Virginia, begun in 1714.

349.17 *George's* Hill] Present-day High Top Mountain, Greene County, Virginia.

350.24 the *Jolly God*] Bacchus, Roman god of intoxication.

350.25 *Pomona*] In Roman mythology, goddess of fruit trees and orchards.

351.2 antidated] Antedated, occurring prematurely.

353.3 "*A plain . . . City*"] This poem was published anonymously in "The Busy-Body," No. 18, a regular column in *The American Weekly Mercury* to which Joseph Breintnall and Benjamin Franklin both contributed. The poem has been attributed to Breintnall, and the title is taken from the introduction to the poem, reprinted below:

> *One Science only will one Genious fit;*
> *So vast is Art, so narrow Human Wit:*
> *Not only bounded to peculiar Arts,*
> *But oft in those, confin'd to single Parts.*
> Pope's Essay on Crit.

I was t'other Day repeating to a Friend the Lines I have chosen for the Motto of my present Paper, and speaking it as my Opinion, That Art, vast as it is, seems no where so near a Match for Nature as in Poetry and Painting, You should say, reply'd my Friend, That in these Sciences Nature is best imitated or described—For there is no Creating

Power in Art. All we can pretend to in our Works, is to set in an advantageous View, and explain to one another, those of Nature. Yet I confess in Poetical Descriptions we may go beyond the Truth, in some Particulars, as in Painting Faces a fine Beauty may be flatter'd—Perhaps, added he, my Words may seem perplex——but you will allow, when you consider in what Manner our Ideas of Arts are brought to the Mind, where for every distinct Thing there is a distinct Name adapted by the Artists, that we can much more easily comprehend those than the inscrutable Works of Nature, in which we may deily descry Thousand nameless Novelties (a Trifle to the exhaustless Whole) And Multitude of them that receive Appellations in one Country according to the Learning and Humour of the Discoverers, have, in may be very different Names confer'd upon 'em in outher Countries, at the same Time.

I did not design said I, to run into these Speculations—I only thought to observe to you, the difficulty of Writing a Compleat Poem, and how the ancient Poets excell'd by substituting Persons for Things, striking on suprizing Hyperboles, and superlatively characterizing the most minute Matters that were capable of illustrating and aggrandizing their Works.

He agreed to this, and added that the Fame would always be given to the Ancients, the Moderns ever be esteem'd no better than their imitators or Copiers, and that the Composition is as mean on our Side as the Writer to the Dictator; besides which our vastly different Religion denies us the Use of the grand Ornaments the Greek and Roman poets shined in, and are graced with to this Day: Yet an explicit Account, or naked Relation of any Place or Thing may as well be given at this time as could have been in any past Age.

This Discourse of ours, did not deter my Friend from thinking of the Muses, if he did not invoke them. He has writ and presented me with a Copy of Verses; which he says is a plain Description of one single Street in this City; the Whole Town being too great a Task for his Leisure.

I freely bestow his Lines on my Readers, for their Approbation or Condemnation.

353.7   the Street]   High Street, now known as Market Street.

353.15   Cæsarea's Pine tree Land]   New Jersey.

355.16   *Palatine*]   From the Palatine (Pfalz) region of Germany; a large emigration from the region began in 1709, and many Palatines settled in Pennsylvania.

355.22   pickthank]   One who "picks a thank"; a sycophant or tale-bearer.

362.6   *Charon*]   In Greek mythology, the ferryman of Hades.

365.18   *Bendall's* Board]   Bendall's Dock, a Boston marketplace named after Edward Bendall (1607–1631), a ferryman.

365.25   *Helicon*]   In Greek mythology, a mountain whose springs were sacred to the Muses.

366.7   *Claudian*'s Muse]   Cf. "Phoenix," by Claudius Claudianus (fl. 395–404).

366.28   TOWNSHEND'S]   George Townshend (1715/16–1769), a British naval officer who served as commander of the fleet at Jamaica from 1748 to 1752, was Kirkpatrick's patron; *The Sea-Piece* (1750), in which "The Nonpareil" was first published, was dedicated to him, and "The Nonpareil" was "Humbly Inscribed to the Honorable Miss Townshend."

369.6   *Catesby*]   Mark Catesby (1683–1749), author of *Natural History of Carolina, Florida and the Bahama Islands* (1743).

369.8   DART]   Hannah Dart, mistress of Maryville Plantation in South Carolina, and amateur biologist.

369.28   *Juno*'s Bird]   The peacock.

371.3   *Anna Boylens*]   Anne Boleyn (c. 1504–1536), the second wife of Henry VIII.

376.5   *My own Birth Day*]   In the margins of the original manuscript of this poem, in *Milcah Martha Moore's Book*, is a comment by Hannah Griffitts: "Soft moving Language, deep Reflection strong / Compose thy pow'rful Harmony of Song. Fidelia."

376.7   *Few . . . my Life been*]   Cf. Genesis 47:9.

378.35   fey]   Fatal, deadly.

386.8–15   *Me vero primum . . . Geor.* 2]   Virgil, *Georgics*, II, 475–77, 483–86: "But as for me—first above all, may the sweet Muses whose holy emblems, struck by a mighty love, I bear, take me to themselves, and show me the paths and the stars of the sky . . . But if the chill blood about my heart bar me from reaching these realms of nature, let my delight be the country, and the running streams amid the dells—may I love the waters and the woods, though I shall be inglorious."

386.28   Anne-Arundel]   Anne Arundell (1615–1649), wife of Lord Baltimore, founder of the Maryland Colony.

388.26   Philomel]   The nightingale.

389.14–15   that *bard . . . The phœnix]   See note 366.7.

396.10–12   *Hic sunt . . . ævo.* Virg.]   Virgil, *Eclogues* X, 42–43: "Here are cold springs, Lycoris, here soft meadows, here woodland; here, with thee, time alone would wear me away."

396.14   castalian or pierian well]   Ancient springs associated with poetic inspiration.

398.27   mavis]   *Turdus philomelos*, the song thrush.

401.3   the *Orphan*]   *The Orphan, or The Unhappy Marriage* (1680), a tragedy by Thomas Otway (1652–1685).

405.4   *Arthur Dobbs*]   Dobbs (1689–1765), author of *Essay on the Trade and Improvement of Ireland* (1728–30), served as governor of North Carolina from 1754 to 1765.

407.1   *Euxines*]   The Black Sea.

407.5   *Eurus'* Blast]   In Greek mythology, the east wind.

410.15   *Copac*'s Laws]   Manco Capac, legendary first king of Cuzco and lawgiver to the Incas.

410.22–23   Blest Prince! . . . regal Line!]   The recently deceased Frederick, Prince of Wales (1707–1751), who had been in line of succession to the British throne.

411.8   *Him* . . . mortal Part]   George II (1683–1760).

411.9   *Her* . . . faithful Heart]   Caroline of Ansbach, Queen Caroline (1683–1737).

411.13   *Her* . . . soaring Soul!]   Princess Augusta of Saxe-Gotha, Princess of Wales (1719–1772).

411.16   the lov'd *Youth*]   George III (1738–1820).

411.25   Aval]   Endorsed, guaranteed.

411.27   *Hides* or *Sallusts*]   Edward Hyde (1609–1674) and Gaius Sallustis Crispus (86–34 BCE), historians.

412.2   *Ophirs*]   Old Testament port noted for its wealth; cf. 1 Kings 9:26–28, 10:11, 22; 2 Chronicles 8:17–18, 9:10.

413.5   *Dare jura Maritis*, Hor.]   Horace, *Ars Poetica*, line 398: "To give rules for wedded life."

413.35   *Meroz*]   Cf. Judges 5:23. ("Curse ye Meroz, said the angel of the LORD, curse ye bitterly the inhabitants thereof, because they came not to the help of the LORD, to the help of the LORD against the mighty.")

414.5   *Lycurgus'*]   Legendary Spartan lawgiver (c. 700–630 BCE).

414.29–30   As *France*'s King . . . came down]   Cf. the nursery rhyme: "The King of France went up the hill / With twenty thousand men; / The King of France came down the hill, / And ne'er went up again."

418.4–5   near that Spring . . . *Totapotamoy*'s Renown] Totopotomoy Creek, in Hanover County, Virginia; Totopotomoi (c. 1625–1656) was a Paumankey chief.

418.8   Phiz] Face, visage.

418.31   *Nicholas*] Francis Nicholson (1655–1728), governor or acting governor of New York, Virginia (1690–92), Maryland, Nova Scotia, and South Carolina.

420.4   *Row*] Nicholas Rowe (1674–1718), English dramatist.

421.1   Macheath] Character in *The Beggar's Opera* (1728), by John Gay (1685–1732).

422.4   *Henley*'s] John Henley (1692-1759), known as "Orator Henley."

425.7   Dawty's gane] Favorite's gone.

425.8   Wae] Woe.

425.12   thrawn] Twisted.

425.16   mair] More.

425.22   sik kittle] Such ticklish.

425.24   sawt] Salt.

425.25   kent] Knew.

425.25   ilka] Every.

425.26   Wad shaw] Would show.

426.3   sat the Gait a Sooming] Seat the way a swimming.

426.6   Waughts] Draughts.

426.7   Wha] Who.

426.7   Bairns] Children.

426.9   Speer] Question.

426.16   Baith] Both.

426.17   fae] Foe.

426.23   mais things] Most weighs.

426.24   nae] Not.

426.30   pang'd] Crammed.

428.27   Bumpers] Drinking vessels filled to the brim.

429.19   Desunt Catera] The rest is missing.

430.3–4   *Mr. B . . . Pictures*] The "Pictorio" of Mather Byles's "To Pictorio, on the Sight of His Pictures" (see pages 448–50 in this volume) was John Smibert (1688–1751), one of New England's earliest portrait painters.

430.19   *Felis . . . Adolescentis.*] A certain cat who was the delight of a certain young boy.

434.1–2   *the Poetry . . .* Journal] "To Thee, my Fair, I string the Lyre," attributed to Mather Byles, appeared anonymously in the *New-England Weekly Journal* on March 25, 1734.

434.18   *Finis coronat opus*] The ending crowns the work.

435.5   The Chief] Jonathan Belcher (1682–1757), governor of Massachusetts Bay Colony and New Hampshire from 1730 to 1741.

435.7–8   the News . . . takeing Spouse] Anne, Princess Royal (1709–1759) married William IV of Orange on March 25, 1734.

436.19   Brimer] Brimmer, a cup or goblet.

437.17   *Mr. W. C.*] William Cooper (1694–1743), who shared the pulpit at Boston's Brattle Church with the Rev. Benjamin Colman, beginning in 1716.

438.15–17   all hands . . . great undertaking] George Whitefield (1714–1770), Gilbert Tennent (1703–1764), James Davenport (1716–1757), Daniel Rogers (1707–1785), Andrew Croswell (1708–1785), and Ephraim Bound (d. 1765), preachers associated with the first Great Awakening.

439.9   More-head] John Moorhead (1703–1774), pastor of the Scotch-Irish Presbyterian Church in Boston from 1730 to 1774.

439.20   Ash-ly] Jonathan Ashley (1712–1780), pastor at Deerfield, Massachusetts.

440.17   *D—p—t*] James Davenport (see note 438.15–17).

441.8   *Cantant Cicadæ per Æstatem*] The cicadas sing all summer long.

441.15–16   *Leges . . . insuper*] The recent laws, and the laws to come, are proper.

441.26   *Ne sutor, ultra Cripidam*] Literally, "Let not the cobbler, beyond the shoe"; let the cobbler stick to his last.

441.30   *per Magnum fas*] By divine decree.

441.34   *Honi soit qui Mal y pence*] Old French, "Shame on him who thinks evil of it."

442.15   *Si talis, qualis, sit non Compos*] If he turns out to be insane.

443.3–4   *Drinking Song . . . Auteuil*] Franklin included his "Drinking Song" in a letter (1779?) to the Abbé de la Roche, with the following comment: "I have run over, my dear friend, the little book of poetry by

M. Helvetius, with which you presented me. The poem on *Happiness* pleased me so much, and brought to my recollection a little drinking song which I wrote forty years ago upon the same subject, and which is nearly on the same plan, with many of the same thoughts, but very concisely expressed."

448.1   *Pictorio*]   John Smibert (1688–1751), Scottish-born portrait painter who immigrated to Bermuda with George Berkeley in 1728, intending to teach painting, and later settled in Boston.

454.18   *Orinda's* Fame]   Katherine Philips (1631–1664), Anglo-Welsh poet known by the pseudonym "Orinda."

458.3   *A Lamentation . . . Child*]   First published anonymously, this poem was introduced as follows: "The following Lines, (compos'd by a tender Mother, not far from this Place,) on the Death of a most forward, amiable and hopeful Child, was lately left with us for a Publication, without her Knowledge, and without the least Alteration."

466.5   *Disce Tubo . . . Fumos*]   "Teach your children how to smoke a pipe," title of a poem in Robert Prior's *Lusus Westmonasterienses* (1730).

466.25   Cambro Briton]   Welshman.

485.7   *Maryland Eclogues . . . Virgil's*]   The title page of Cradock's manuscript continues: "By Jonathan Spritly, Esqr. / Formerly a Worthy Member of the Assembly / Revis'd & Corrected by his / Friend Sly Boots." In the margins of the manuscript, Cradock transcribed passages, amounting to almost the entire text, of Virgil's first eclogue.

485.19   Chunk]   "A small Planter's Pipe which some of the Clergy don't disdain to make use of" (author's note).

485.22   Bacon]   "The chief Food of the Marylanders" (author's note).

485.25   D——y]   "A numerous Family in the Province" (author's note).

485.31   He made me Parson]   "Too just an Insinuation, that the true merit of a Clergyman is not considered here in his Promotion" (author's note).

486.3   Their Hate . . . Parsons]   "The name of a Clergyman almost scandalous here; which proceeds from two Causes: the ill Conduct of some of them & the vast numbers of Roman Catholicks & Quakers, who, however wide in their Points of Belief & doctring, both of them heartily join in aspersing the Teachers and Members Church of England" (author's note).

486.7   *white oak*]   "A particular kind of oak very plentiful in this Province" (author's note).

486.10–11   My Vestry . . . Door.]   "The Vestries in Virginia have it in their Pow'r, if the minister behaves ill, to get rid of him; which the Maryland Vestries have not" (author's note).

486.15   A—] "What Countryman my friend means, I can't exactly tell; however, am of opinion he had no Intention of aspersing any Country" (author's note).

486.20   W——n . . . D–ll?] "These really are Gentlemen that bring a great discredit on their Funtion" (author's note).

486.36   The Cause is plain] "The philosophy of this I don't pretend to assert; but I think Experience is plainly on our Side" (author's note).

487.7   my Lord's] "Lord B[altimore,] Proprietary of Maryland, who has all the Livings in his own Gift" (author's note).

487.9   puts up . . . Pray'r] "A very just Satyr I think on our Clergy for putting his lordship in our Pray'rs on a par with the Royal Family" (author's note).

487.15   Forties] "The Clergy's Income is by forty Pound W[eight] of Tobacco a Head; & indeed little enough for those that are worthy of it; tho' occasion is taken from the Ill behaviour of some to represent their Income as a great Burthen on the Country" (author's note).

487.18   *Locusts*] "A wood that grows by the Waterside, remarkable for its Hardness & it's long Continuance so that it is made use of much in their Gardens &c." (author's note).

487.31   Mast] Fruit and nuts of forest trees used as food for swine.

487.33   *Potomack's*] "A fine large River, that divides Virginia & Maryland, tis reckond twenty miles wide at it's Mouth" (author's note).

487.35   gen'rous] "Gen'rous indeed, since his Church Favours fall without Distinction, on any that ask for them" (author's note).

488.4–5   *Go* preach . . . *Planters* here?] "Ten to one! a great deal more Purpose; tho' tis observable all over America, Christianity makes very small Progress among the Indians, which is owing no doubt to the scandalous Lives of it's pretended Professors among them" (author's note).

488.10–12   No more . . . swill;] "I'm sorry to say, the Satyr here too just. Indeed Ecclesiastical Authority is much wanted here; & till proper measures are taken, there will be some among the Clergy, whose Lives will be a Scandal to the rest" (author's note).

488.17   Bumbo] "Rum, Water and Sugar without Acid" (author's note).

488.19   Cyder] "Cider very plentiful in this Country: but tis observable that the Trees bear but ev'ry other Year. We must suppose this then to be the scarce year" (author's note).

488.23   Frogs;] "The frogs here are of various Kinds & have notes as various, which on a summer's Ev'ning make a musick not disagreable" (author's note).

492.30   my Melvil] Robert Melvil or Melville (1723–1809), an army officer who in 1763 was appointed governor of the Ceded Islands (Grenada, the Grenadines, Tobago, Dominica, and St. Vincent) after military success during the Seven Years' War.

493.34   Papaws] Generic name for slaves from an area of the Slave Coast straddling the present border between Benin and Togo; also spelled *Pawpaws, Papas, Popos,* or *Paupahs.*

493.36   Rey] The Rio del Rey, on the northern border of what is now Cameroon.

494.17   Cormantee] Generic name given to slaves from the vicinity of Koromantin, on the Gold Coast, in what is now Ghana; also spelled *Coromantee, Koromantee, Kromante,* or *Kromantee.*

494.34   Minnah] El Mina or Elmina, a coastal town in present-day Ghana.

495.2   Moco-nation] Also spelled *Moko,* a generic name for Africans from what is now northwestern Cameroon.

495.4   Mundingo] A large region around the upper Niger, formerly the Mali Empire, inhabited by the Mandingo or Mandinkan-speaking peoples.

495.13   Quanza's lucid stream] The river Cuanza, in Angola.

495.19   Ethiop] Generic term for all black Africans.

495.21   Machaon] In Greek mythology, a surgeon, son of Esculapius.

495.23   sempre-vive] *Sempervivum,* a genus of succulents.

496.20   Pæan] In Greek mythology, physician to the gods.

500.23   defœdations] Defilings, befoulings.

501.13   "melt . . . hectic fire."] Cf. "The Art of Preserving Health" (1744), a long poem by John Armstrong (1709–1799).

501.34   Strabo] Greek historian and philosopher (c. 63 BCE–c. 24 CE), author of the encyclopedic *Geographica* (7–23 CE).

502.13   Enna] A region in central Sicily.

503.2   Eurus] Greek god of the east wind.

503.6   Lusitania] A Roman province including parts of present-day Portugal and Spain.

504.38 . . . 505.34   Dr. Stork . . . publication] Cf. *Safe and Efficacious Remedies in the Cure of Many Obstinate Diseases* (1763), by Anton Störck (1731–1803).

505.20   Iërne's] Ireland's.

506.19   Ogilvy's America] Cf. John Ogilby, *America; being the Latest and Most Accurate Description of the New World* (1670).

508.4   Phæacia's isle] An island in Greek mythology, the last visited by Odysseus before his return to Ithaca.

508.7   Pomona's] In Greek mythology, goddess of orchards and fruit trees.

508.15   "Insuperable . . . shade"] Cf. Milton, *Paradise Lost*, IV.138.

509.15–16   Jones . . . Palladio] Inigo Jones (1573–1652), Christopher Wren (1632–1723), and Andrea Palladio (1508–1580), architects.

513.11–17   Gallic Lewis' . . . mild laws] Louis XIV (1638–1715), king of France; his 1685 *Code Noir* sanctioned and regulated the institution of slavery, including provisions that slaves could not be tortured, murdered, or allowed to fall ill without treatment by their masters.

513.16   Themis] In Greek mythology, a goddess personifying order, custom, and law.

523.18–21   *Prior* . . . pious *South*] Matthew Prior (1664–1721), a lyric poet; Euclid, a Greek mathematician whose *Elements* (c. 300 BCE) was a standard text; John Wilmot (1647–1680), second earl of Rochester, author of bawdy and satirical poetry; John Tillotson (1630–1694), Archbishop of Canterbury, author of many volumes of sermons; Robert South (1634–1716), theologian.

523.30   *Arateens*] Arretines, a type of Roman pottery.

523.32   *Joan* . . . Punchanello] Punch and Judy.

523.33   *Vernon*'s siege of *Porto-Bello*] Edward Vernon (1684–1757) commanded the fleet that captured the Spanish fort at Porto Bello, in what is now Panama, in 1739.

524.3   Pope's new *Dunciad* & *Garth*] Alexander Pope's *Dunciad*, first published in 1728, appeared in revised and expanded form in 1729, 1742, and 1743. Samuel Garth (1661–1719) wrote the satirical poem *The Dispensary* (1699).

529.4–5   *Nec prius* . . . MET.] Ovid, *Metamorphoses*, VII.569: "Drinking, thirst is not quenched sooner than life."

533.20   *Xantippe*] Wife of Socrates, a proverbial scold or nag.

534.16   *Tully*] See note 227.31.

535.5   *Hymeneans*] Songs of the marriage bed.

538.10   *Proclamation*] Livingston's poem was one of many parodies of a proclamation issued by General John Burgoyne on June 20, 1777, prior to the Battle of Saratoga. It began: "By John Burgoyne Esq'r; Lieut Gen'l of His

Majesties Armies in America., Col. of the Queens Reg't of Lt. Dragoons, Governor of Fort William in North Britain, one of the Representatives of the Commons of Great Britain in Parliament, and Commanding an Army and Fleet employed on an expedition from Canada &c &c &c."

538.23   *North*'s]   Frederick North (1732–1792), Tory prime minister of Great Britain, 1770–82.

540.25   'Squire *Carleton* my *Sancho*]   Burgoyne had been appointed second in command to Major-General Guy Carleton (1724–1808) in 1775, and assumed full command of the Saratoga expedition in 1777.

541.5–6   *Sir William*'s . . . blunders]   Sir William Howe (1729–1814), commander-in-chief of British forces, chose to occupy Philadelphia instead of aiding Burgoyne's assault as originally planned.

541.13–18   King Pigmalion . . . cut his throat]   Cf. *Aeneid*, I.347–52.

541.37   *Haman*]   Cf. Esther, 7:6–10.

542.17   *procul a fulmine*]   From *Procul a Jove, procul a fulmine*, a Latin proverb: The farther away from Jove, the less to fear his thunderbolts.

543.3–547.5   *The Sufferings* . . . King]   Attributed to Occom by Joanna Brooks; see "Six Hymns by Samson Occom," *Early American Literature* 38.1 (2003): 67–87.

550.5–7   *Cantando* . . . VIRG.]   Cf. Virgil, *Eclogues* III, 25, 28–29: *Menalcas*: You beat him singing? *Damoetas*: Well, would you have us try together, taking turns, what each can do?

558.12   Taxables]   Tea, paper, glass, and paints, among other commodites, were newly taxed under the Townshend Act of 1767.

558.15–16   Grenville . . . Tea]   Prime minister and chancellor of the exchecquer George Grenville (1712–1770) passed the American Revenue Act, or Sugar Act, in 1764.

559.24   *Cits*]   Citizens.

561.27   *Common Sense*]   Thomas Paine's *Common Sense* was first published in January 1776.

562.1   Oliverian]   Partisan of Oliver Cromwell.

570.3   *Bars Fight*]   The poem commemorates an Indian raid at a point called "The Bars," near Deerfield, Massachusetts.

571.6   the Hero . . . Quebec]   General James Wolfe (1727–1759), leader of the 1759 British assault against Quebec.

571.8   giving leg-bail]   Escaping from custody by flight; cutting and running.

571.15   Vaudreuil] Pierre François de Rigaud, Marquis de Vaudreuil-Cavagnal (1698–1778), French colonial governor and commander-in-chief of French forces.

571.23–26   forty-seventh . . . Lascelles] A French privateer having captured the uniforms of the 47th regiment of foot, the regiment purchased replacements from troops under the command of William Shirley (1694–1771). Montcalm is Louis-Joseph, Marquis de Montcalm (1712–1759), military commander of French forces at Quebec; Lascelles is General Peregrine Lascelles (1684–1772), commander of the 47th. Ned Botwood, according to a note published with the poem in *Rivington's New York Gazetteer*, "was killed, sword in hand, at the attack of the French entrenchments, on the 31st of July, that year [1759]."

571.29   Monckton and Townshend] Robert Monckton (1726–1782) and Isaac Townsend (1684–1756).

572.3   *A Translation of the War-Song*] Introducing this translation (in *The Memoirs of Lieut. Henry Timberlake, Who Accompanied the Three Cherokee Indians to England in the Year 1762*, 1765), Timberlake writes that the Cherokee "have . . . a sort of loose poetry, as the war-songs, love-songs, &c. Of the latter many contain no more than that the young man loves the woman, and will be uneasy, according to their own expression, if he does not obtain her. Of the former I shall present the following specimen, without the original in Cherokee, on account of the expletive syllables, merely introduced for the music, and not the sense, just like the folderols of many old English songs."

577.10   * ——*] Nathaniel Evans (see pages 641 and 850 in this volume).

578.4   Cott] Cottage.

590.10   the neat capital] Christiansted.

597.18–24   Corybantian brass . . . Rhea] In Greek mythology, the corybantes and the dactyls of Mount Ida were both associated with the worship of Rhea, an Earth Mother.

597.26   "Unused to the melting mood,"] Cf. Shakespeare, *Othello*, V.ii.349.

600.21   Sir William] William Howe (see note 541.5–6).

600.24   Mrs. L——g] Elizabeth (Lloyd) Loring, reputed to have been Howe's mistress during his Philadelphia sojourn.

600.30   Sir Erskine] General William Erskine, a British staff officer.

604.4–5   *Tartaream* . . . Virgil] *Aeneid*, VII.514: "Blasts the voice of hell."

605.7   Charles Thompson] Thompson (1729–1824) was secretary of the Continental Congress from 1774 to 1789.

605.10–23   There dwelt in Norriton's . . . Rittenhouse became] Ritten-
house (1732–1796), an astronomer, inventor, and mathematician from Norri-
ton, Pennsylvania, served as a delegate to the Pennsylvania constitutional
convention in 1776 and as Pennsylvania treasurer (1779–87).

605.30   Duffield] George Duffield (1732–1790), one of the joint chap-
lains of Congress.

605.38   Tim Matlack] Matlack (1730–1829), a Quaker merchant, served
as a Pennsylvania delegate to the Continental Congress in 1780.

606.32   Tucker] Thomas Tucker (1745–1828), delegate to the Continen-
tal Congress from South Carolina in 1787 and 1788.

607.10   Shippen . . . Yates] William Shippen (1712–1801), a leading citi-
zen of Pennsylvania, was delegate to the Continental Congress in 1779 and
1780; Abraham Yates (1724–1796), a New York political writer and public ser-
vant, was a delegate in 1778 and 1779.

607.11   Green and Gates] Nathaniel Greene (1742–1786), major general
in the Continental Army; Horatio Gates (1726–1806), general in the Conti-
nental Army.

607.16   Poughkeepsie's Lord] George Clinton (1739–1812) served as
New York's governor from 1777 (when Poughkeepsie was briefly its capital)
to 1795; he was elected to the second Continental Congress in 1775.

607.19   Heath] William Heath (1737–1814), brigadier general in the Con-
tinental Army.

607.24   Mifflin] Thomas Mifflin (1744–1800), quartermaster general of
the Continental Army from 1775 to 1777.

607.34   Roberdeau] Daniel Roberdeau (1727–1795), merchant and
brigadier general in the Pennsylvania militia.

607.39   Joe Reed] Joseph Reed (1741–1785), lawyer and general in the
Continental Army; Pennsylvania delegate to the Continental Congress in 1777.

608.4   thy father] Robert Gates, customs collector at Greenwich.

608.18   Where, where is Sinclair] Arthur St. Clair (c. 1734–1818) was a
delegate (1785–87) and ninth president of the Continental Congress. In 1777,
while serving in the Continental Army, forces under his command failed to
arrive in the defense of Fort Ticonderoga as they had been ordered; a 1778
court-martial acquitted him of wrongdoing.

608.28–35   Schuyler . . . court-martials] Philip Schuyler (1733–1804)
was elected to the Continental Congress in 1775 and served as a major gen-
eral in the Continental Army from 1775 to 1779, after which he returned to
the Continental Congress for the sessions of 1779 and 1780. A 1778 court-
martial cleared his name of improper conduct for his part in the loss of Fort

Ticonderoga. John Bradstreet (1714–1774), one of Schuyler's mentors, was also a close companion of Schuyler's wife, Catherine (1734–1803).

609.1   Sullivan]   John Sullivan (1741–1795), New Hampshire delegate to the first Continental Congress and a major general in the Continental Army.

610.11   Cacus]   In Greek mythology, a fire-breathing monster.

610.37   Suffolk's infamous resolve]   In 1774, leaders of Suffolk County, Massachusetts, drafted resolutions calling for the raising of local militias and the boycott of British goods.

611.16–17   Saint —— . . . Canadian land—]   In 1776, the Continental Congress sent Benjamin Franklin, Samuel Chase (1741–1811), and two priests, John Theodore Carroll (1735–1815) and his cousin Charles (1737–1832) to Quebec to enlist the aid of the French Canadians.

611.24   McWhorter, Spencer]   In 1775, Presbyterian clergymen Elihu Spencer (1721–1784) and Alexander McWhorter (1734–1807) were sent by Congress to North Carolina in the hope of gaining the allegiance of the Scotch Highlanders.

612.13   Grubstreet]   A street in London that became synonymous with literary hack-work.

612.15   Old ——]   Robert Aitken (1735–1802), who hired Paine as editor of his *Pennsylvania Magazine* soon after his arrival in Philadelphia.

613.26   Wayne . . . Lee]   Brigadier General Anthony Wayne (1745–1796) and Major General Charles Lee (1731–1782), both of the Continental Army.

614.3   *Liberty Tree*]   Originally published under the pseudonym "Atlanticus."

614.5   Tune . . . *Greeks.*]   Song from *The Choice Spirits' Chaplet* (1761) by George Alexander Stevens (1710?–1784).

621.4   *Doctor Fothergill*]   John Fothergill (1712–1780), a Quaker physician from London, was the patron of American botanists John and William Bartram.

622.38   Harvey]   William Harvey (1578–1657), British physician, author of the 1628 *Exercitatio Anatomica de Motu Cordis et Sanguinis in Animalibus* (*An Anatomical Exercise on the Motion of the Heart and Blood in Animals*).

623.3   Hunter]   William Hunter (1717–1783), Scottish anatomist and physician.

625.19   Pulpitier]   Pulpiteer, preacher.

625.23   Scalade]   Scaling the walls of a fort with a ladder.

625.28–30   Argus . . . at last]   In Greek mythology, Argus was lulled to sleep and slain by Hermes.

626.36   yellowboys]   Gold coins.

628.38   feazy]   Cf. *feaze*, unravel; *feeze up*, work into a passion.

629.32   Devoirs]   Civilities; duties.

629.33   Gurge]   Whirlpool.

629.36   Scarborough]   Colonel Edmund Scarborough (1617–1671) led attacks against a number of Indian tribes in eastern Virginia in the 1650s.

629.40   qui scavaient vivre]   Who knew how to live.

631.15   villous]   Hairy.

632.9   Ramscalian, Drazel, draffy]   Ramscallion, wretch; slut; worthless, full of draff or dregs.

632.11   Wherrets]   Sharp blows.

632.15   rory]   Dewy.

633.25   *A toute Outrance*]   To the final limit.

634.20   Chamade]   Signal made for a parley by the beat of a drum.

635.1   Fear, like Colier's]   The Rev. Jeremy Collier (1650–1726), a theater critic and clergyman, notoriously offered last-minute absolution to assassins Sir John Friend and Sir William Parkyns prior to their 1696 executions.

635.12   Surry, the *venire*]   A writ directing the summons of prospective jurors, or a panel of such jurors, from Surry County, Virginia.

635.23   Lob's Pound]   Prison, jail.

635.24   capot]   In piquet, a winning of tricks by which others are defeated or made *capot*.

635.26   Favonius]   Roman god of the west wind (in Greek mythology, Zephyrus).

635.30   Cochin]   Princely state in southwest India.

637.38   Paphian Queen]   Venus.

638.4   Maia's Son]   Hermes, Greek god of measure, invention, boundaries, shepherds, athletics, cunning, and wit.

638.5   that Maid]   Helen of Troy.

641.23   Urania's . . . art]   In Greek mythology, Urania was one of the nine muses and a patron of astronomy.

647.7–14   TANNER . . . *Bergen* Cows]   On July 20, 1780, George Washington sent a force led by General Anthony Wayne (1745–1796), a former tanner, to destroy a blockhouse at Bull's Ferry, New Jersey, and capture cattle and horses on nearby Bergen's Neck.

647.21   soupaan] Supawn, hasty pudding.

647.24–25   Major *Lee* . . . cannon.] Major Henry Lee (1756–1818), a noted cavalry leader not involved in the engagement at Bull's Ferry, and Colonel Thomas Proctor (1739–1806), artillery commander.

648.2   Freedom's Pole] A liberty pole located between Nyack, New York, and Orangetown, New Jersey.

648.15   IO] A celebratory exclamation in classical literature, and in classical mythology the name of a goddess who is transformed by Zeus into a white cow.

648.16   the Gen'ral's] George Washington's.

649.22–650.2   *Irvine's* nod . . . Pill.] Colonel William Irvine (1741–1804), a physician who fought at Bull's Ferry, had been a prisoner of war in Canada; Brigadier General James Irvine (1735–1819), a hatter, had been wounded and captured in battle at Chestnut Hill, Pennsylvania.

650.8   *Stirling*] William Alexander (1726–1783), an American major-general, claimed himself the Earl of Stirling, a title denied him by the House of Lords.

651.15–17   "In Valour's phrenzy . . . *Harrison*] Alexander Hamilton (1757–1804) and Robert Harrison (1745–1790) were Washington's military secretaries; during his 1778 court-martial, General Charles Lee (1732–1782) described Hamilton at one point in battle as "much flustered and in a sort of phrenzy of valor."

651.21   The fate of *Withrington*] Cf. the traditional English "Ballad of Chevy Chase," which in one version reads: "For Witherington needs I must waite, / As one in doleful dumpes; / For when his legs were smitten off, / He fought upon his stumpes."

653.27   *Cunningham*] William Cunningham (1738–1791), provost marshal of New York.

655.13   Poor Parson *Caldwell*] The Rev. James Caldwell (1734–1781), a Presbyterian minister from Elizabethtown, New Jersey, and Patriot soldier; in the months prior to the events described in the poem, his house and church had been burned and his wife killed.

656.7–8   pretty *Susan* . . . paper] Susannah Livingston (b. 1748), author of occasional anonymous contributions to the *New-Jersey Gazette*, published in Chatham.

657.34   *Joan of Nokes*] An adaptation of "John of Noakes," a generic name.

667.4–10   *Pamela* . . . *Lovelace*] Characters in the novels *Pamela* (1740), *History of Sir Charles Grandison* (1754), and *Clarissa; or the History of a Young Lady* (1748), by Samuel Richardson (1689–1761).

668.25   Satan's walking-staff in Milton] Cf. *Paradise Lost*, I. 292–96.

669.31   Gage's] General Thomas Gage (1719–1787), commander in chief of British forces in North America from 1763 to 1775.

671.34   Arnold] Benedict Arnold (1741–1801), general in the Continental Army.

672.32   friar Bacon's brazen head] An oracular brass head owned, according to legend, by Roger Bacon (c. 1214–1294), English Franciscan philosopher and alchemist; cf. Robert Greene, *Honourable History of Friar Bacon and Friar Bungay* (1594).

673.2–4   Shakespeare's . . . you."] Cf. *The Tempest*, III.ii.108.

674.25   Hutchinson] Thomas Hutchinson (1711–1780), governor of Massachusetts from 1771 to 1774.

675.5   Smith's] William Smith (1728–1793), Chief Justice of New York.

675.16   North . . . Tryon] Frederick North (1732–1792), prime minister of Great Britain, 1770–82; John Stuart, 3rd Earl of Bute (1713–1792), prime minister of Great Britain, 1762–63; William Tryon (1729–1788), governor of New York, 1771–80.

675.18   Galloway] Joseph Galloway (1731–1803), a delegate from Pennsylvania to the Continental Congress in 1774, opposed American independence and in 1778 moved to London.

684.8   kennel's] Gutter's.

684.12–14   Scotia's realms . . . Hume] Cf. David Hume (1711–1776), Scottish philosopher.

685.14   Chihohamti's] Shih Huang-ti (259–09 BCE).

685.33   LORD KAIMS's sketches] *Sketches of the History of Man* (1776), by Henry Home, Lord Kames (1696–1782), Scottish philosopher.

686.2   Behmen] Jacob Boehme (1575–1624), German mystic.

686.28   Socinus] Faustus Socinus (1539–1604), Italian religious reformer.

686.36   GARTH's alphabetical prophecies] Cf. *The Dispensary* (1699), a satiric poem by Samuel Garth (1661–1719).

687.16   Priestly] Joseph Priestly (1733–1804), British scientist and theologian.

695.5   HOME seek . . . vales] See note 685.33.

695.6   MONBODDO . . . tails] In *The Origin and Progress of Man and Language* (1773–92), James Burnett, Lord Monboddo (1714–1799), notoriously claimed it "probable . . . that there is a race or nation of men with tails."

695.32   "Te-Deum!"]   A hymn of praise to God sung as part of a liturgy.

695.35   Vertumnus]   In Roman mythology, god of the seasons and of vegetative growth.

696.34   Tartarus]   In Greek mythology, a primal deity and the deepest level of the underworld.

698.16   Mæonian star]   Homer, sometimes supposed to have been born in Maeonia, in what is now northwestern Turkey.

698.19   Dilworth's knots]   Thomas Dilworth (d. 1780) wrote *The Schoolmaster's Assistant* (1744) and *A New Guide to the English Tongue* (1751), widely reprinted schoolbooks.

708.26   *Bishop Horne on these verses*]   Cf. *Commentary on the Psalms* (1771), by George Horne (1730–1792).

714.10   *Penseroso . . . L'legroe's*]   Cf. "Il Penseroso" and "L'Allegro," a pair of poems (c. 1631–32) by John Milton (1608–1674).

714.11   *Melpomene* in *Thalia*'s part]   In Greek mythology, the muses of tragedy and comedy.

716.37   A glaring instance . . . Americans]   General Benedict Arnold (1741–1801) had plotted to betray the Continental Army in 1780.

722.11   [ ]]   The brackets indicate that a part of Hecht's manuscript is illegible.

723.4–5   *Sit mihi . . .* VIRG.]   Cf. *Aeneid*, VI.264 ("May I be allowed to tell what I have heard").

723.6–8   *Jove fix'd . . .* POPE]   From Book XVII of Homer's *Odyssey*, as translated in 1726 by Alexander Pope (1688–1744).

723.29   Bellona]   Roman goddess of war.

724.23   a Stuart's reign]   Charles I, King of England, Scotland, and Ireland from 1625 to 1649.

726.30   Havanna's bloody siege]   British forces successfully laid siege to Havana in 1762, during the Seven Years' War.

726.34   Gibraltar's action]   British and Dutch troops captured Gibraltar in 1704, during the War of Spanish Succession.

727.34   Xerxes . . . waves]   Xerxes the Great (fl. 485–465 BCE), having failed to bridge the Hellespont during an attempted invasion of Greece, is reported to have ordered that the water be given 300 lashes.

729.19   Diomede]   A hero of the Trojan war.

729.20–22   As when he fought . . . day,]   Washington served during the French and Indian War under General Edward Braddock (1695?–1755), who was killed in battle.

730.30   WARREN]   Dr. Joseph Warren (1741–1775), a leading patriot who
died in the Battle of Bunker Hill.

732.1   *Libera nos, Domine . . . Lord*]   Later retitled "A Political Litany"
by Freneau.

732.15–16   valiant Dunmore . . . city]   John Murray, 4th Earl of Dun-
more (1730–1809), was governor of Virginia from 1771 to 1776, during which
time he raided Williamsburg's public stores.

732.17   Montague]   George Montagu (1750–1829), British admiral during
the early years of the Revolutionary War.

732.23   Tryon]   William Tryon (1729–1788), colonial governor of New
York from 1771 to 1780; he fled the city in October 1775, returning with the
British occupation in September 1776.

732.27   lord *North*]   Frederick North (1732–1792), prime minister of
Great Britain, 1770–82.

740.20   *Debemur morti nos, nostraque.*]   Horace, *Ars Poetica*, l. 63: "We
are destined to death—we and all things ours."

743.15–17   *Rura mihi . . .* GEORG. II. V. 483]   "Let my delight be the
country, and the running streams amid the dells—may I love the waters and
woods, though I shall be inglorious."

753.9   EBOE's]   "A small negro kingdom near the river Senegal" (Fre-
neau's note, in a later edition of this poem).

754.2   LIGUANEE]   "The mountains northward of Kingston" (Freneau's
note, in a later edition of this poem).

754.5   *Mr. Blanchard*]   Jean-Pierre Blanchard (1753–1809), French aviation
pioneer.

754.25   INSKEEP's coach]   Philadelphia's principal stagecoach to New
York, which departed from a tavern run by John Inskeep (1757–1834).

760.8   *Tune, the watry god*]   Cf. "Neptune's Resignation," an English
naval ballad (1759) with lyrics by John Wignell (d. 1774) and music by John
Worgan (1724–1790); it begins "The wat'ry God, great Neptune, lay."

763.3–766.14   *A Dream . . . Sept. 20. 1777*]   "The following dreams,"
Tucker notes in his manuscript, "were written at the wedding of Mr. Nelson
and Miss Cary, and were produced for the entertainment of the company
each morning when they assembled at breakfast; the ceremony of putting
bridecake under the head at night having been previously observed by the
whole company."

772.17   Lemnean God]   Hephaestus, Greek god of technology.

772.25   Liber . . . Queen]   Liber was a Roman god of husbandry and
crops, and Ceres, his consort, sometimes crowned with ears of corn.

774.3   *Mæcenas*]   Patron (d. 8 BCE) of Horace and Virgil.

774.20–23   When great *Patroclus* . . . stern Pelides]   Cf. *Iliad*, book XVI. Achilles, son of Peleus, was sometimes referred to as Pelides.

774.27   *Mantuan* Sage]   Virgil.

775.26   *University of Cambridge*]   Harvard.

780.1   *S. M.*]   Scipio Moorhead (fl. 1773), believed to have painted a portrait of Wheatley from which the frontispiece of her *Poems on Various Subjects, Religious and Moral* (1773) was engraved.

781.2   *Mrs. S.W.*]   Susannah Wheatley (d. 1774), the wife of Wheatley's owner.

782.14   *Hebe's*]   Greek goddess of eternal youth.

783.12   *To a Gentleman of the Navy*]   This poem first appeared, without a title, in the December 1774 issue of the *Royal American Magazine*. It was introduced with the following comments:

> By particular request we insert the following Poem addressed by Philis, (a young *Affrican*, of surprising genius) to a gentleman of the navy, with his reply.
> By this single instance may be seen, the importance of education. —— Uncultivated nature is much the same in every part of the globe. It is probable *Europe* and *Affrica* would be alike *savage* or *polite* in the same circumstances; though, it may be questioned, whether men who have no *artificial* wants, are capable of becoming so ferocious as those, who, by faring *sumptuously every day*, are reduced to a habit of thinking it is necessary to *their* happiness, to plunder the whole human race.

Wheatley's poem was followed by the gentleman's "Answer":

> Celestial muse! sublimest of the nine,
> Assist my song, and dictate every line:
> Inspire me once, nor with imperfect lays,
> To sing this great, this lovely virgins praise:
> But yet, alas! what tribute can I bring,
> WH—TL—Y but smiles, whilst I thus faintly sing,
>   Behold with reverence, and with joy adore;
> The lovely daughter of the Affric shore,
> Where every grace, and every virtue join,
> That kindles friendship and makes love divine;
> In hue as diff'rent as in souls above;
> The rest of mortals who in vain have strove,
> Th' immortal wreathe, the muse's gift to share,
> Which heav'n reserv'd for this angelic fair.
>   Blest be the guilded shore, the happy land,
> Where spring and autumn gently hand in hand;

O'er shady forests that scarce know a bound,
In vivid blaze alternately dance round:
Where cancers torrid heat the soul inspires;
With strains divine and true poetic fires;
(Far from the reach of Hudson's chilly bay)
Where cheerful phoebus makes all nature gay;
Where sweet refreshing breezes gently fan;
The flow'ry path, the ever verdent lawn,
The artless grottos, and the soft retreats;
"At once the loevr and the muse's seats."
Where nature taught, (tho' strange it is to tell,)
Her flowing pencil Europe to excell.
Britania's glory long hath fill'd the skies;
Whilst other nations, tho; with envious eyes,
Have view'd her growing greatness, and the rules,
That's long been taught in her untainted schools:
Where great Sir Isaac! whose immortal name;
Still shines the brightest on the seat of fame;
By ways and methods never known before;
The sacred depth of nature did explore:
And like a God, on philosophic wings;
Rode with the planets thro' their circling rings:
Surveying nature with a curious eye,
And viewing other systems in the sky.
    Where nature's bard with true poetic lays,
The pristine state of paradise displays,
And with a genius that's but very rare
Describes the first the only happy pair
That in terrestrial mansions ever reign'd,
View'd happiness now lost, and now regain'd,
Unravel'd all the battles of the Gods,
And view'd old night below the antipodes.
On his imperious throne, with awful sway,
Commanding regions yet unknown today,
    Or where those lofty bards have dwelt so long,
That ravish'd Europe with their heavenly song,
    But now this blissful clime, this happy land,
That all the neighboring nations did command;
Whose royal navy neptunes waves did sweep,
Reign'd Prince alone, and sov'reign of the deep:
No more can boast, but of the power to kill,
By force of arms, or diabolic skill.
For softer strains we quickly must repair
To Whetly's song, for Wheatly is the fair;
That has the art, which art could ne'er acquire;
To dress each sentence with seraphic fire.

> Her wondrous virtues I could ne'er express!
> To paint her charms, would only make them less.

785.1   British Homer's and Sir Isaac's]   John Milton (1608–1674) and Sir Isaac Newton (1643–1727).

787.9–10   *"She moves . . . Hair."*]   Cf. "To His Excellency General Washington," page 786.10–11 in this volume.

790.2   old *Bonner*]   Edmund Bonner (c. 1500–1569), bishop of London, was notorious for his persecution of heretics during the reign of Mary I.

799.10   *The Hasty-Pudding*]   Barlow's Preface to the poem reads as follows:

> A simplicity in diet, whether it be considered with reference to the happiness of individuals or the prosperity of a nation, is of more consequence that we are apt to imagine. In recommending so important an object to the rational part of mankind, I wish it were in my power to do it in such a manner as would be likely to gain their attention. I am sensible that it is one of those subjects in which example has infinitely more power that the most convincing arguments or the highest charms of poetry. Goldsmith's *Deserted Village*, though possessing these two advantages in a greater degree than any other work of the kind, has not prevented villages in England from being deserted. The apparent interest of the rich individuals, who form the taste as well as the laws in that country, has been against him; and with that interest it has been vain to contend.
>
> The vicious habits which in this little piece I endeavour to combat, seem to me not so difficult to cure. No class of people has any *interest* in supporting them; unless it be the interest which certain families may feel in vying with each other in sumptuous entertainments. There may indeed be some instances of depraved appetites, which no arguments will conquer; but these must be rare. There are very few persons but what would always prefer a plain dish for themselves, and would prefer it likewise for their guests, if there were no risk of reputation in the case. This difficulty can only be removed by example; and the example should proceed from those whose situation enables them to take the lead in forming the manners of a nation. Persons of this description in America, I should hope, are neither above nor below the influence of truth and reason, when conveyed in language suited to the subject.
>
> Whether the manner I have chosen to address my arguments to them be such as to promise any success is what I cannot decide. But I certainly had hopes of doing some good, or I should not have taken the pains of putting so many rhymes together.—The example of the domestic virtues has doubtless a great effect. I only wish to rank

simplicity of diet among the virtues. In that case I should hope it will be cherished and more esteemed by others than it is at present.

800.31   Oella, whom I sang before] Mama Oella, wife of Manco Capac, legendary Peruvian lawgiver; Barlow refers to and includes an extensive historical footnote on the pair in Book II of his epic poem *The Vision of Columbus* (1787).

809.5–9   *Of man's . . .* MILTON] *Paradise Lost*, I. 1–3, 7.

809.10–13   EVA . . . CASTALIONIS] Cf. Sebastian Castalion, *Dialogorum Sacrorum Libri Quatuor* (1576):
    EVE.   The fruit is indeed beautiful to the sight:
            I do not know whether it is likewise so sweet to taste;
            Yet I will taste it. OH! HOW SWEET IT IS!!!

809.14–19   *Lovely . . .* THOUGHTS] Edward Young, *The Complaint; or, Night Thoughts on Life, Death and Immortality* (1742), III. 104–08.

812.13   the Gihon] A river in the Garden of Eden (cf. Genesis 2:13).

813.6–8   Oh *Fruit . . .* MILTON] *Paradise Lost*, V.67–68.

813.9   *Ode . . . July*] Originally published in *The Newhampshire and Vermont Journal*, July 19, 1796, under the pseudonym "Colon and Spondee," a literary partnership for which Tyler ("Spondee") supplied the verse and his friend Joseph Dennie the prose.

814.27   the treaty] The Jay Treaty, signed in 1794 and debated in Congress in 1795–96.

816.28   Morse's Mammouth] Jedidiah Morse (1761–1826) refers to the discovery of fossil mammoths in several of his publications, including *The American Geography* (1789).

816.32   Magnalian Mather's giant] Cotton Mather (1663–1728) discusses giants in his *Magnalia Christi Americana* (1702), Book VI, Chapter 7.

817.27   JACK KATCH] Jack Ketch (d. 1686), an executioner during the reign of Charles II whose name became synonymous with death and the gallows.

817.30   naturæ lusus] Joke of nature, monstrosity.

818.3   *Miss J. L.—*] Judith Lomax (1774–1828), Page's niece by marriage. Lomax wrote a poem in reply, "To Mrs. Page of Rosewell," and later published it in her collection *The Notes of an American Lyre* (1813).

818.26–27   Parnassian . . . [ ]] The brackets indicate areas of Page's manuscript that have been damaged.

818.31–32   "wakes to extacy . . . Lyre"] Cf. line 48 of the "Elegy Written in a Country Churchyard" (1751), by Thomas Gray (1716–1771).

820.3   *The African Chief*]   "Taken in arms, fighting for his freedom, and inhumanly butchered by his conquerors! This affecting event was fully delineated in the various gazettes of the period." (Morton's note.)

821.5   *Messenia's*]   "The *Messenians* being conquered by the *Spartans*, and agreeably to the custom of the age, the miserable remnant led into slavery, under these circumstances were so inhumanly oppressed, that rising, and united in arms, they seized upon a Spartan fortress and after innumerable injuries, inflicted and reciprocated, finally obtained their freedom." (Morton's note.)

821.14   *Batavia's William*]   William I of Orange-Nassau (1533–1584), leader of the Dutch revolt against the Spanish.

821.15   *Paoli's*]   Pasquale Paoli (1725–1807), leader of the Corsican independence movement.

831.3   *Adams*]   John Adams (1735–1826), second president of the United States, 1797–1801.

Index of Titles and First Lines

A Bran, a Chaff, a very Barly yawn, 183

A Cooper there was, he work'd at his trade, 437

A fig for your learning, I tell you the Town, 437

A Man who own'd a barber's shop, 761

A merry Tale I will rehearse, 825

A NEW CREATION charms the ravish'd sight, 421

A Pritty BIRD did lately please my sight, 458

A True Friend came to see Johann in his Recesses, 284

Adam from Paradise expell'd, 373

Adams and Liberty, 831

Address to Miss Phillis Wheatley . . . , An, 477

Adieu, *New-England's* smiling meads, 781

Advice from the Dead to the Living, 473

Advice to Mrs. Mowat, 720

African Chief, The, 820

Ages our Land a barbarous Desart stood, 448

Alas, deare Mother, fairest Queen, and best, 38

Alas how blind must be to Temporal things the Eye, 297

All things within this fading world hath end, 55

Aloofe, aloofe, and come no neare, 7

American Liberty, A Poem, 723

Anagram made by mr John Willson . . . , 9

And must we part? 306

Androboros: A Biographical Farce, 235

Anna Boylens Letter to King Henry the 8th, 371

Arabia's Bird, it's spicy Tomb and Nest, 366

Artful Painter, by this Plan, 549

As Happiness must ever be our Aim, 621

As often as some where before my Feet, 207

As spring the winter doth succeed, 59

As the pure snow-drop, child of April tears, 822

As weary pilgrim, now at rest, 57

Ask not why hearts turn Magazines of passions, 216

At *Delaware*'s broad stream, the View begin, 353

At length the wintry horrors disappear, 386

At Pungoteague a Planter erst, 625

August 'twas the twenty-fifth, 570

Author to her Book, The, 45

Author to His Book, The, 144

Bagnio, 716

Bars Fight, 570

Battle of Lexington, The, 789

Battle of the Kegs, The, 599

Bay Psalm Book, The, 23

Before the Birth of one of her Children, 55

Believe me, Love, this vagrant life, 644

Beneath the shade of these wide-spreading Trees, 485

Beside a stream, that never yet ran dry, 747

Birds of different Feather, The, 554

Black-Joke: A Song, 428

Both settle to their tasks apart: both spread, 1

Brief Account of the Agency of the Honourable John Winthrop . . . , A, 313

Brother Ephraim sold his Cow, 616

But now the wand'ring muse, returning, points, 590

By broad Potowmack's azure tide, 758

By *John Burgoyne* and *Burgoyne John*, Esquire, 538

By Science taught, on silken wings, 754

By various Arts we thus attempt to please, 402

Camp Ballad, A, 602
Carolina; or, The Planter, 767
Celestial choir! enthron'd in realms of light, 786
Celestial muse! for sweetness fam'd inspire, 783
Certain Verses left by the Honoured William Bradford *Esq. . . . ,* 14
Cherry-Tree and Peach-Tree, The, 552
Chester, 646
Cits Return from the Wilderness to the City, The, 559
College Room, A, 523
Come, each death-doing dog who dare venture his neck, 571
Come! let Mirth our hours employ, 578
Come, ye Brave, by Fortune wounded, 643
Come Gentle *Muse,* and once more lend thine aid, 454
"Come hither, *Harriet,* pretty Miss, 657
Compos'd in a dancing room, 583
Condemn'd by Fate to way-ward Curse, 239
Conflagration, The, 450
Conspiracy of Kings, The, 796
Contemplations, 46
Convert to Tobacco, The, 466
Could I envy Maria I certainly shou'd, 587
Count me not liquorish if my Soule do pine, 189
Country Clown, 713
Country Printer, The, 747
Cow-Chace, 647

Day of Doom, The, 74
Dear girls, since you the task impose, 763
Delight in Books from Evening, 207
Description of a Winter's Morning, A, 548
Dialogue between Old England and New, A, 38
Did Ever Lord such noble house mentain, 169
Disappointed Cooper, The, 437
Disasters of Richland, The, 834
Dithyrambic on Wine, A, 578
Dream on Bridecake, A, 763

Drinking Song, 443
Dull, Dull indeed! What shall it e're be thus? 180
Dying Indian, The, 740

Ear-Ring, The, 427
Ebb and Flow, The, 198
Eight Parts of *Speech* this Day wear *Mourning Gowns,* 148
Elegie Upon . . . Mr. Thomas Shepard, An, 132
Elegy On the much to be lamented Death of George Fraser . . . , An, 425
Emigrant, The, 717
Emperors and kings! in vain you strive, 755
Enough, the Bible is by wits arraign'd, 684
Epibaterium, Or a hearty Congratulation to William Penn, 209
Epilogue to the Orphan, 402
Epistle to a Friend; from Fort Henry, 577
Epistle to the Hon. Arthur Dobbs . . . , An, 405
Epitaph for an Infant, An, 599

Fair flower, that dost so comely grow, 742
Fair Venus calls, her voice obey, 443
Fair Verna! loveliest village of the west, 688
Farewel dear babe, my hearts too much content, 56
Farewel to America, A, 781
Fast by where roaring Roanoke, 834
Father Abbey's Will, 459
Father and I went down to camp, 618
Female Frailty, 733
female Patriots, The, 558
few Lines to fill up a Vacant Page, A, 224
Flourishing Village, The, 687
Food for Criticks, 396
For one bright moment, heavenly goddess! shine, 784
For which good Patriots these sev'ral years did long, 209
Forty Shillings Reward, 564

From a junto that labour for absolute power, 732

From anxious Thoughts of every future Ill, 371

From Climes remote, but not to Thee unknown, 405

From me, my Dear, O seek not to receive, 576

From my years young in dayes of Youth, 14

From Susquehanna's utmost springs, 743

From the Hymn-Book of Johannes Kelpius, 284

From the soft Shades, and from the balmy Sweets, 454

From Thomas Clemson ran away, 526

From where his lofty head TALHEO rears, 577

Funeral Elegy, Upon . . . Anne Bradstreet, A, 216

Gallants attend and hear a friend, 599

General Description of the West-Indian Islands, A, 590

Genius of Africk! whether thou bestrid'st, 492

Genius of America, The, 760

Go then, my DOVE, but now no longer *Mine!* 225

God's controversy with New-England, III

Gods Determinations, 191

Good christian Reader judge me not, III

Grammarians Funeral, The, 148

Gratitudinis Ergo, 225

Great Spirit, hail!—confusion's angry sire, 529

Greenfield Hill, 687

Had Caesar took this useful Hint, 561

Hail! *D—p—t* of wondrous fame, 440

Hail, happy day, when, smiling like the morn, 778

Hail, happy saint, on thine immortal throne, 777

Hail, happy shades! tho' clad with heavy snows, 682

Hail! once again, dear natal Seats, 559

Hail COLUMBIA! happy land, 823

Hail MAN, exalted title! first and best, 796

Hail RALEIGH! Venerable Shade, 466

Halfe Dead: and rotten at the Coare: my Lord! 182

Hasty-Pudding, The, 799

Having, with searching eye, remark'd ere while, 767

He springs, he rises from the ground, 484

Heavens bright Lamp, shine forth some of thy Light, 146

Hot Stuff, 571

How dull the age when ladies must express—, 581

How sweet a Lord is mine? If any should, 164

Huswifery, 198

Hymn for Ascension, 484

Hymn to Christ for our Regeneration and Resurrection, 447

i am gon to all bliss, 9

I ask thy Aid, O Potent Rum! 234

I feel this World too mean, and low, 155

I hear the Gospel's joyful sound, 545

I love thy Kingdom, Lord, 711

I own, the Match, you recommend, 421

I Sing My Plain Country Joan, 444

I Sing the MAN, by Heav'ns peculiar Grace, 271

I Stroll'd one day into a room, 523

I Walk'd and did a little *Mole-hill* view, 128

If any honest Friend be pleased to walk into my poor Garden, 214

If art & industry should doe as much, 4

If ever two were one, then surely we, 555

If there exists a HELL—the case is clear—, 752

Illustrious Bard! (whoe'er thou art,), 434

In a chariot of light from the regions of day, 614

In *Adam's* Fall, 221

In *David's* psalms, an oversight, 432

In glad amazement, Lord, I stand, 796

In grateful wonder lost, long had we view'd, 641

In Jesus loving frind! What love does thou inherit! 293

In memory of my dear grand-child Elizabeth Bradstreet, 56

In pious princes golden Days, 259

In silent night when rest I took, 61

In some calm Midnight, when no whisp'ring Breeze, 450

In spite of all the learn'd have said, 746

In these Seven Languages I this my Book do own, 200

In Things of moment, on thy self depend, 446

In vain you talk of shady bowers, 733

Indeed! dear friend, it is too True, 818

Indian Student, The, 743

Infinity, when all things it beheld, 191

Innumerable mercies acknowledged, 796

Inscription under Revd. Jn. Checkley's Picture, 437

Invitation into the Country, An, 454

Invitations of the Gospel, The, 520

Irregular Supplicatory Address to the American Academies of Arts and Sciences, An, 815

I've neither Reserve or aversion to Man, 559

Jamaica Viewed, 67

Jersey! Lament in briny tears, 425

John! had thy Sickness snatch'd thee from our Sight, 437

John Kotton: O, Honie knott, 32

John Wilson: W'on Sion-hil, 35

Jonathan's Courtship, 825

Journal of Madam Knight, The, 234

Journey from Patapsco to Annapolis, A, 386

Just from the plough observe the country clown, 713

Just one and thirty years, or (says one, I know who,), 200

Key into the Language of America, A, 30

Lamentation &c. On the Death of a Child, A, 458

Last Wednesday morn, at break of day, 564

Learning that Cobweb of the Brain, 403

Let ardent heroes seek renown in arms, 531

Let other Pens th' ungrateful News declare, 347

Let others muse on sublunary things, 489

Let tyrants shake their iron rod, 646

Lexington March, The, 616

Libera nos, Domine—Deliver us, O Lord, 732

Liberty and Peace, 787

Liberty Pole, The, 668

Liberty Tree, 614

Lines occasioned by a Visit to an old Indian Burying Ground, 746

Lo! Freedom comes. Th' prescient Muse foretold, 787

Long did *Euphrates* make us glad, 210

Long did the Stage with nervous Sense delight, 420

Long since I bad the pleasing Muse adieu, 380

Lord, art thou at the Table Head above, 168

LORD, I am thine, entirely thine, 521

Lovewell's Fight, 280

Mæcenas, you, beneath the myrtle shade, 774

Make me, O Lord, thy Spining Wheele compleate, 198

Make room, oh! ye kingdoms in hist'ry renowned, 602

Maryland Eclogues in Imitation of Virgil's, 485

May. 13. 1657, 59

Meat out of the Eater, 124

Meditation 1 (First Series), 164

Meditation 1 (Second Series), 178

Meditation 3 (First Series), 164

Meditation 4 (First Series), 166

Meditation 4 (Second Series), 179

Meditation 9 (First Series), 169

Meditation 12 (Second Series), 180

Meditation 14 (Second Series), 182

Meditation 18 (Second Series), 183

Meditation 23 (First Series), 170

Meditation 24 (First Series), 172

Meditation 24 (Second Series), 185

Meditation 32 (First Series), 173

Meditation 34 (Second Series), 187

Meditation 39 (First Series), 175

Meditation 46 (First Series), 176

Meditation 60a (Second Series), 189

Meditation 150 (Second Series), 190

Meditations on Man's First and Fallen Estate . . . , 310

Melancholly discrib'd and dispell'd, 423

Memento, 822

Men's Strength meer Weakness is, 124

M'Fingal, 668

Michy, the Hero of my Rhyme, 299

Miss Kitty Cut-a-dash, 718

Mistress A——y, / To you I fly, 462

Mock Bird and Red Bird, The, 550

Mock Monarchy, The, 259

Modern Politeness, 304

Money answers every thing, 310

Monkey, Who Shaved Himself and His Friends, The, 761

Monody, On the death of Gen. George Washington, 828

Morning Hymn, A, 544

Mount Vernon: An Ode, 758

Mr. Blackmore's Expeditio Ultramontana, 347

Muse, sing the Man, whose overclouded Head, 423

My Blessed Lord, how doth thy Beautious Spouse, 190

My Country's Worth, 329

My gen'rous heart disdains, 598

My Gracious Lord, I would thee glory doe, 179

My *Heart*, how very *Hard* its grown! 232

My humble Muse Sad, and in lonely State, 64

My loving countrymen pray lend an ear, 156

My own Birth Day, 376

My Silver Chest a Sparke of Love up locks, 166

My Sin! my Sin, My God, these Cursed Dregs, 175

My Soul would gazing all amazed stand, 185

Nay, may I, Lord, believe it? Shall my Skeg, 176

Neanthe, 625

New England's Annoyances, 17

New England's annoyances you that would know them, 17

New Englands Crisis, 150

New English Canaan, or New Canaan, 4

New Metamorphosis, The, 299

No mimic accents now shall touch your ears, 828

No sooner come, but gone, and fal'n asleep, 57

Nonpareil, The, 366

Now arm'd with ministerial ire, 668

Now cease *these* tears, lay gentle *Virgil* by, 681

Now the shades of night are gone, 544

Now this War at length is o'er, 643

O Come you pious youth! adore, 477

O give yee thanks unto the Lord, 25

O thou most high who rulest All, 60

Observe that foot, how nice the shoe it fits, 718

Occlusion, 639

Ode Composed for the Fourth of July, 813

Of ancient streams presume no more to tell, 396

Of Boston in New England, 12

Of the Power of the New Virgin-Body . . . , 297

Of the Wilderness of the Secret, or Private Virgin-Cross-Love, 284

Of their *Chloes* and *Phyllises* Poets may prate, 444

Of worthy Captain Lovewell, I purpose now to sing, 280

Oft', O ye Muses! to delightful Scenes, 357

Oh! happy soul how fast you go, 546

Oh! that I were a Poet now in grain! 132

Oh! that Id had a tear to've quencht that flame, 199

Oh Boston, though thou now art grown, 12

Oh Leaden heeld. Lord, give, forgive I pray, 178

Oh New England, thou canst not boast, 12

On a Honey Bee, Drinking from a Glass of Wine, and Drowned Therein, 756

On being brought from Africa to America, 776

On her Father having desired her to forbid all young Men the House, 528

On killing a Book-Worm, 429

On Mr. B——s's singing an Hymn of his own composing, 432

On my dear Grand-child Simon Bradstreet, 57

On reading a few Paragraphs in the Crisis, 562

On Reading Dryden's Virgil, 681

On the Benefit of Labour, 373

On the Corruptions of the Stage, 420

On the Death of a little Girl, 374

On the Death of the Rev. Mr. George Whitefield, 777

"On yonder lake I spread the sail no more! 740

Once more! Our GOD, vouchsafe to Shine, 219

Once more Bellona, forc'd upon the stage, 723

Opress'd with grief, in heavy strains I mourn, 430

Origin of Evil, The, 809

Ovid has sweetly sung how mighty Jove, 427

Ovid's Metamorphoses, 1

Paine, tho' thy Tongue may now run glibber, 562

Paradox and Seldom Contentment of the God loving Soul, The, 293

Petition, The, 549

Philadelphiad, The, 713

Philis's Reply to the Answer in our last by the Gentleman in the Navy, 784

Philosophic Solitude, 531

Phoebus has thrice his Yearly Circuit run, 456

"plain Description of one single Street in this City, A," 353

Poem, on Elijahs Translation . . . , A, 271

Poetical Epistle, addressed by a Lady of New-Jersey . . . , A, 584

Poet's Lamentation for the Loss of his Cat . . . , The, 430

Poor Julleyoun now doth cry aloud, 470

Poor Julleyoun's Warnings to Children and Servants, 470

Poor Unhappy Transported Felon's Sorrowful Account . . . , The, 156

Preparatory Meditations (First Series), 164

Preparatory Meditations (Second Series), 178

Proclamation, 538

Progress of Dulness, The, 657

Prologue, The, 36

Prologue spoken to the Orphan, 401

Proposal to Mistress Abbey, 462

Psalm LXXXVIII, 708

Psalm CXXXVII, 711

Psalme 19, 23

Psalme 23, 24

Psalme 107, 25

Psalms of David, The, 708

Puzzle of the Hare and Hound, The, 574

Quaker, 714

Quarrel with Fortune, A, 271

Rachel Preston, Hannah Hill & Mary Norris, 202

Ranting topers, midnight rovers, 809

Rape of Fewel, The, 354

Reflexion, The, 168

Republican Genius of Europe, The, 755

Return to Tomhanick, 682

Rhapsody on Rum, A, 529

Sarcasm against the ladies in a newspaper . . . , A, 582

Satire on the fashionable pompoons worn by the ladies . . . , A, 581

Sea Marke, The, 7

Second Dream on Bridecake, A, 764

See how the black ship cleaves the main, 820

See the lone emigrant just come on shore, 717

Self-Dedication at the Table of the Lord, 521

Sensibility, an ode, 588

Shall man, O God of light, and life, 708

Since Adam, by our first fair Mother won, 377

Since the Men from a Party, or fear of a Frown, 558

Since the single state, 720

Singing at the Plow, 232

Sleep on, sweet babe! no dreams annoy thy rest, 599

Slow Traveller, The, 546

So have I seen a little silly Fly, 271

Some Birds, (it is no News to tell), 550

Some Seraph now my Breast inspire, 789

Sometimes now past in the Autumnal Tide, 46

Song, 823

Song of Emptiness, A, 71

Songs of Harvest, The, 233

Son's Farewell, A, 545

Sot-Weed Factor, The, 239

Squeak the fife, and beat the drum, 813

Stanzas Occasioned by the Ruins of a Country Inn, 739

Still was the night, Serene and Bright, 74

Sufferings of Christ, The, 543

Sugar-Cane, The, 492

Suppose this Earthy globe a Cocoe Nut, 187

Sweet Sensibility Celestial power, 588

Sweetly (my dearest) I left thee asleep, 63

Tenth Muse, The, 36

The ambling *Quaker* glides along the street, 714

The Bare that breaths the Northern blast, 196

The *Bees* so fam'd for Feats of War, 235

The bleak North-west with nipping rigour reigns, 548

The bleak Norwest begins his dreaded Reign, 354

The Chief, to whose extended sway, 435

The Courteous *Pagan* shall condemne, 30

The *English* Settlements when thus begun, 313

The heavens doe declare, 23

The little Bird at break of Day, 374

The Lord to mee a shepheard is, 24

The Muse, disgusted at an Age and Clime, 346

The times wherein old *Pompion* was a Saint, 150

The Vizard drop'd, see Subtilty prevail, 561

The various ills that have happen'd to Man, 428

The Wine and Company are good, 303

The word of Congress, like a round of beef, 604

That most men have a great respect and love, 329

This Book by Any yet unread, 58

This Day take warning young and old, 473

Tho' ill at ease, A stranger and alone, 234

Tho you have stop'd the muses tongue, 583

Thou, born to sip the lake or spring, 756

Thou ill-form'd offspring of my feeble brain, 45

Thou sorrow, venom Elfe, 195

Though short, far short, my pen of the sublime, 567

Thought on the inestimable Blessing of Reason, A, 566

Three Precepts, 446

Throughout the Saviour's Life we trace, 543

Thy Grace, Dear Lord's my golden Wrack, I finde, 173

"'Tis from high life high characters we trace, 715

Tis not the Till'd, Poor, Lifeless *Earth*, 233

To a Friend, Who recommended a Wife to him, 421

To a Gentleman of the Navy, 783

To a Lady, on a Screen of Her Working, 421

To Benjamin Franklin . . . ("In grateful wonder lost, long had we view'd"), 641

To Benjamin Franklin . . . ("Let others muse on sublunary things"), 489

To Cordelia, 644

To Doctor Fothergill, 621

To drive the kine one summer's morn, 647

To Eliza Norris—at Fairhill, 377

To God our twice-Revenger, 8

To His Excellency General Washington, 786

To his Excellency Joseph Dudley . . . , 64

To Lord Bellamont when entering Governour of the Massachusetts, 153

To Mæcenas, 774

To Miss J. L.——, 818

To Miss Mary Stockton, 587

To Mr. ——, 567

To Mr. B occasioned by his Verse . . . , 430

To Mr. Blanchard, 754

To Mr. Samuel Hastings . . . , 380

To my Bottle-friends, 303

To my Dear and loving Husband, 55

To my dear children, 58

To my dear Wife, 459

To my Muse . . . , 454

To Pictorio, on the Sight of his Pictures, 448

To please Mankind enough I've writ, 639

To S. M. a young African Painter, on seeing his Works, 780

To show the lab'ring bosom's deep intent, 780

To sing of Wars, of Captaines, and of Kings, 36

To Sir Toby, 752

To Sophronia, 559

To the Author of the Poetry in the last Weekly Journal, 434

To the Memory of Aquila Rose, Deceas'd, 357

To the Right Honourable William, Earl of Dartmouth, 778

To the University of Cambridge, in New-England, 775

To Thee, my LORD, I lift the Song, 447

To-day the living streams of grace, 520

Token of Love and Gratitude, A, 200

Trafique is Earth's great *Atlas*, that supports, 146

Translation of the War-Song, A, 572

Trees once could speak, some Authors say, 552

Triumph of Fidelity, The, 684

True Impartial Account . . . of the Prince of Orange's Nuptials . . . , The, 435

Turn we to view the Bagnio's horrid scene, 716

'Twas mercy brought me from my *Pagan* land, 776

Two Sparks were earnest in Debate, 413

Under the Line that equal's night and day, 67

Unhappy Bard! sprung in such Gothic Times, 430

United States, The, 643

Universal Motive, The, 715

unwilling Farewell to Poesy, An, 306

Upon a Spider Catching a Fly, 195

Upon a Wasp Child with Cold, 196

Upon my dear & loving husband his goeing into England, 60

Upon reading a Book entitled Common Sense, 561

Upon the drying-up that Ancient River, the River Merrimak, 220

Upon the Sweeping Flood . . . , 199

Vain, frail, short liv'd, and miserable Man, 71

Vermine accurst, how couldst thou thus abuse, 429

Verses Occasioned by a Young Lady . . . , 576

Verses on the Prospect of planting Arts and Learning in America, 346

Verses to the Tories, 643

Wager, The, 413

Was it for this, with thee a pleasing load, 680

Was there a Palace of Pure Gold, all Ston'de, 172

We saw, but oh! how sad we were to see, 8

Well! my lov'd Niece, I hear the bustle's o'er, 584

Well—sure no mortal e'er was cursed, 764

Were few & Evil stil'd the Patriarchs Days, 376

Were I sole sov'reign of rare Fancies now, 153

Whaling Song, A, 481

What IS great *God*! And what IS NOT, 516

What is it moves within my soul, 566

What Love is this of thine, that Cannot bee, 164

When fair Intention has been slighted, 554

When filial Words describe a Daughter's Grief, 528

When first *Apollo* got my brain with Childe, 144

When first Columbus touch'd this distant Shore, 401

When first thou on me Lord wrought'st thy Sweet Print, 198

When fleecy skies have Cloth'd the ground, 574

When I solidly do ponder, 207

When Jah so rare a Gem pleas'd to distrayne, 35

When spring returns with western gales, 481

Where now these mingled ruins ly, 739

Where spirits dwell and shad'wy forms, 760

Where'er the earth's enlighten'd by the sun, 572

While an intrinsic ardor prompts to write, 775

While life prolongs its precious light, 710

While o'er our guilty Land, O Lord, 517

While various Rumours spread abroad, 519

Wild Honey Suckle, The, 742

With Joy erst while, (when knotty doubts arose), 32

Wo worth the Days! The Days I spent, 224

Wolfes in Sheeps clothing why will ye, 16

Woman are books in which we often spy, 582

Word of Congress, The, 604

Word to New England, A, 12

Would God I in that Golden City were, 170

Written in the Retreat from Burgoyne, 680

Wrote on the last Day of February 1775, 561

Yankee Doodle, 616

Yankey's return from Camp, The, 618

Ye Alps audacious, thro' the heav'ns that arise, 799

Ye learned wights, who all the heights, 815

Ye sons of Columbia, who bravely have fought, 831

You that are *Men*, & Thoughts of *Manhood* know, 225

You that have seen these wondrous works by *Sions* Savior don, 20

Young Dapper once had some pretence, 304

Your kindness wherewithal my last years Meeters met, 202

Index of Poets

Adams, John, 423
Alsop, George, 144
Andre, John, 647

Banneker, Benjamin, 574
Barlow, Joel, 796
Berkeley, George, 346
Billings, William, 646
Bleecker, Ann Eliza, 680
Bolling, Robert, 625
Botwood, Ned, 571
Bradford, William, 12
Bradstreet, Anne, 36
Breintnall, Joseph, 353
Brooke, Henry, 299
Brown, Charles Brockden, 828
Byles, Mather, 447

"Carolina, a Young Lady," 528
Clemson, Thomas, 526
"Cobble, Ralpho," 403
Colman, Benjamin, 271
Cook, Ebenezer, 239
Cradock, Thomas, 484

Dale, Thomas, 401
Danforth, John, 224
Davies, Samuel, 516
Dawson, William, 413
Dumbleton, Joseph, 529
Dwight, Timothy, 684

Evans, Nathaniel, 641

Fergusson, Elizabeth Graeme, 621
Fessenden, Thomas Green, 825
Fiske, John, 32

Franklin, Benjamin, 443
Freneau, Philip, 723

Gardiner, Christopher, 16
Godfrey, Thomas, Jr., 576
Grainger, James, 492
Green, Joseph, 430
Griffitts, Hannah, 558

Hammon, Jupiter, 477
Hansford, Charles, 329
Harris, Benjamin, 221
Haynes, Lemuel, 789
Hecht, Anne, 720
Hickeringill, Edmund, 67
Home, Archibald, 425
Hopkinson, Francis, 598
Hopkinson, Joseph, 823
Humphreys, David, 758
Hunter, Robert, 235

Johnson, Edward, 17

Kirkpatrick, James, 366
Knight, Sarah Kemble, 234

Law, Tom, 280
Lewis, Richard, 380
Livingston, William, 531

M., A.L., 523
Mather, Cotton, 225
Morris, Lewis, II, 259
Morton, Sarah Wentworth, 820
Morton, Thomas, 4
Munford, William, 834

Nelson, Mary, 564
Norton, John, Jr., 216

Oakes, Urian, 132
Occom, Samson, 543
Odell, Jonathan, 604
Ogilvie, George, 767
Osborn, John, 481

Page, Margaret Lowther, 818
Paine, Robert Treat, Jr., 831
Paine, Thomas, 614
Pastorious, Francis Daniel, 200
Pepperell, Mary Hirst, 458
"Poor Julian," 470

Revel, James, 156

Saffin, John, 63
Sandys, George, 1
Seagood, George, 347
Seccomb, John, 459
Sewall, Samuel, 219
Singleton, John, 590
Smith, John, 7
Smith, William, 550

Stansbury, Joseph, 643
Sterling, James, 405
Stockton, Annis Boudinot, 581

Taylor, Edward, 164
Terry, Lucy, 570
Timberlake, Henry, 572
Tompson, Benjamin, 148
Trumbull, John, 657
Tucker, St. George, 763
Turell, Jane Colman, 454
Tyler, Royall, 809

Warren, Mercy Otis, 566
Wheatley, Phillis, 774
Wigglesworth, Michael, 71
Williams, Roger, 30
Wilson, John, 8
Witt, Christopher, 284
Wolcott, Roger, 310
Woodmason, Charles, 489
Wright, Susanna, 371

THE LIBRARY OF AMERICA SERIES

The Library of America fosters appreciation and pride in America's literary heritage by publishing, and keeping permanently in print, authoritative editions of America's best and most significant writing. An independent nonprofit organization, it was founded in 1979 with seed money from the National Endowment for the Humanities and the Ford Foundation.

1. Herman Melville, *Typee, Omoo, Mardi* (1982)
2. Nathaniel Hawthorne, *Tales and Sketches* (1982)
3. Walt Whitman, *Poetry and Prose* (1982)
4. Harriet Beecher Stowe, *Three Novels* (1982)
5. Mark Twain, *Mississippi Writings* (1982)
6. Jack London, *Novels and Stories* (1982)
7. Jack London, *Novels and Social Writings* (1982)
8. William Dean Howells, *Novels 1875–1886* (1982)
9. Herman Melville, *Redburn, White-Jacket, Moby-Dick* (1983)
10. Nathaniel Hawthorne, *Collected Novels* (1983)
11. Francis Parkman, *France and England in North America*, vol. I (1983)
12. Francis Parkman, *France and England in North America*, vol. II (1983)
13. Henry James, *Novels 1871–1880* (1983)
14. Henry Adams, *Novels, Mont Saint Michel, The Education* (1983)
15. Ralph Waldo Emerson, *Essays and Lectures* (1983)
16. Washington Irving, *History, Tales and Sketches* (1983)
17. Thomas Jefferson, *Writings* (1984)
18. Stephen Crane, *Prose and Poetry* (1984)
19. Edgar Allan Poe, *Poetry and Tales* (1984)
20. Edgar Allan Poe, *Essays and Reviews* (1984)
21. Mark Twain, *The Innocents Abroad, Roughing It* (1984)
22. Henry James, *Literary Criticism: Essays, American & English Writers* (1984)
23. Henry James, *Literary Criticism: European Writers & The Prefaces* (1984)
24. Herman Melville, *Pierre, Israel Potter, The Confidence-Man, Tales & Billy Budd* (1985)
25. William Faulkner, *Novels 1930–1935* (1985)
26. James Fenimore Cooper, *The Leatherstocking Tales*, vol. I (1985)
27. James Fenimore Cooper, *The Leatherstocking Tales*, vol. II (1985)
28. Henry David Thoreau, *A Week, Walden, The Maine Woods, Cape Cod* (1985)
29. Henry James, *Novels 1881–1886* (1985)
30. Edith Wharton, *Novels* (1986)
31. Henry Adams, *History of the U.S. during the Administrations of Jefferson* (1986)
32. Henry Adams, *History of the U.S. during the Administrations of Madison* (1986)
33. Frank Norris, *Novels and Essays* (1986)
34. W.E.B. Du Bois, *Writings* (1986)
35. Willa Cather, *Early Novels and Stories* (1987)
36. Theodore Dreiser, *Sister Carrie, Jennie Gerhardt, Twelve Men* (1987)
37A. Benjamin Franklin, *Silence Dogood, The Busy-Body, & Early Writings* (1987)
37B. Benjamin Franklin, *Autobiography, Poor Richard, & Later Writings* (1987)
38. William James, *Writings 1902–1910* (1987)
39. Flannery O'Connor, *Collected Works* (1988)
40. Eugene O'Neill, *Complete Plays 1913–1920* (1988)
41. Eugene O'Neill, *Complete Plays 1920–1931* (1988)
42. Eugene O'Neill, *Complete Plays 1932–1943* (1988)
43. Henry James, *Novels 1886–1890* (1989)
44. William Dean Howells, *Novels 1886–1888* (1989)
45. Abraham Lincoln, *Speeches and Writings 1832–1858* (1989)
46. Abraham Lincoln, *Speeches and Writings 1859–1865* (1989)
47. Edith Wharton, *Novellas and Other Writings* (1990)
48. William Faulkner, *Novels 1936–1940* (1990)
49. Willa Cather, *Later Novels* (1990)

50. Ulysses S. Grant, *Memoirs and Selected Letters* (1990)
51. William Tecumseh Sherman, *Memoirs* (1990)
52. Washington Irving, *Bracebridge Hall, Tales of a Traveller, The Alhambra* (1991)
53. Francis Parkman, *The Oregon Trail, The Conspiracy of Pontiac* (1991)
54. James Fenimore Cooper, *Sea Tales: The Pilot, The Red Rover* (1991)
55. Richard Wright, *Early Works* (1991)
56. Richard Wright, *Later Works* (1991)
57. Willa Cather, *Stories, Poems, and Other Writings* (1992)
58. William James, *Writings 1878–1899* (1992)
59. Sinclair Lewis, *Main Street & Babbitt* (1992)
60. Mark Twain, *Collected Tales, Sketches, Speeches, & Essays 1852–1890* (1992)
61. Mark Twain, *Collected Tales, Sketches, Speeches, & Essays 1891–1910* (1992)
62. *The Debate on the Constitution: Part One* (1993)
63. *The Debate on the Constitution: Part Two* (1993)
64. Henry James, *Collected Travel Writings: Great Britain & America* (1993)
65. Henry James, *Collected Travel Writings: The Continent* (1993)
66. *American Poetry: The Nineteenth Century,* Vol. 1 (1993)
67. *American Poetry: The Nineteenth Century,* Vol. 2 (1993)
68. Frederick Douglass, *Autobiographies* (1994)
69. Sarah Orne Jewett, *Novels and Stories* (1994)
70. Ralph Waldo Emerson, *Collected Poems and Translations* (1994)
71. Mark Twain, *Historical Romances* (1994)
72. John Steinbeck, *Novels and Stories 1932–1937* (1994)
73. William Faulkner, *Novels 1942–1954* (1994)
74. Zora Neale Hurston, *Novels and Stories* (1995)
75. Zora Neale Hurston, *Folklore, Memoirs, and Other Writings* (1995)
76. Thomas Paine, *Collected Writings* (1995)
77. *Reporting World War II: American Journalism 1938–1944* (1995)
78. *Reporting World War II: American Journalism 1944–1946* (1995)
79. Raymond Chandler, *Stories and Early Novels* (1995)
80. Raymond Chandler, *Later Novels and Other Writings* (1995)
81. Robert Frost, *Collected Poems, Prose, & Plays* (1995)
82. Henry James, *Complete Stories 1892–1898* (1996)
83. Henry James, *Complete Stories 1898–1910* (1996)
84. William Bartram, *Travels and Other Writings* (1996)
85. John Dos Passos, *U.S.A.* (1996)
86. John Steinbeck, *The Grapes of Wrath and Other Writings 1936–1941* (1996)
87. Vladimir Nabokov, *Novels and Memoirs 1941–1951* (1996)
88. Vladimir Nabokov, *Novels 1955–1962* (1996)
89. Vladimir Nabokov, *Novels 1969–1974* (1996)
90. James Thurber, *Writings and Drawings* (1996)
91. George Washington, *Writings* (1997)
92. John Muir, *Nature Writings* (1997)
93. Nathanael West, *Novels and Other Writings* (1997)
94. *Crime Novels: American Noir of the 1930s and 40s* (1997)
95. *Crime Novels: American Noir of the 1950s* (1997)
96. Wallace Stevens, *Collected Poetry and Prose* (1997)
97. James Baldwin, *Early Novels and Stories* (1998)
98. James Baldwin, *Collected Essays* (1998)
99. Gertrude Stein, *Writings 1903–1932* (1998)
100. Gertrude Stein, *Writings 1932–1946* (1998)
101. Eudora Welty, *Complete Novels* (1998)
102. Eudora Welty, *Stories, Essays, & Memoir* (1998)
103. Charles Brockden Brown, *Three Gothic Novels* (1998)
104. *Reporting Vietnam: American Journalism 1959–1969* (1998)
105. *Reporting Vietnam: American Journalism 1969–1975* (1998)
106. Henry James, *Complete Stories 1874–1884* (1999)

107. Henry James, *Complete Stories 1884–1891* (1999)
108. *American Sermons: The Pilgrims to Martin Luther King Jr.* (1999)
109. James Madison, *Writings* (1999)
110. Dashiell Hammett, *Complete Novels* (1999)
111. Henry James, *Complete Stories 1864–1874* (1999)
112. William Faulkner, *Novels 1957–1962* (1999)
113. John James Audubon, *Writings & Drawings* (1999)
114. *Slave Narratives* (2000)
115. *American Poetry: The Twentieth Century,* Vol. 1 (2000)
116. *American Poetry: The Twentieth Century,* Vol. 2 (2000)
117. F. Scott Fitzgerald, *Novels and Stories 1920–1922* (2000)
118. Henry Wadsworth Longfellow, *Poems and Other Writings* (2000)
119. Tennessee Williams, *Plays 1937–1955* (2000)
120. Tennessee Williams, *Plays 1957–1980* (2000)
121. Edith Wharton, *Collected Stories 1891–1910* (2001)
122. Edith Wharton, *Collected Stories 1911–1937* (2001)
123. *The American Revolution: Writings from the War of Independence* (2001)
124. Henry David Thoreau, *Collected Essays and Poems* (2001)
125. Dashiell Hammett, *Crime Stories and Other Writings* (2001)
126. Dawn Powell, *Novels 1930–1942* (2001)
127. Dawn Powell, *Novels 1944–1962* (2001)
128. Carson McCullers, *Complete Novels* (2001)
129. Alexander Hamilton, *Writings* (2001)
130. Mark Twain, *The Gilded Age and Later Novels* (2002)
131. Charles W. Chesnutt, *Stories, Novels, and Essays* (2002)
132. John Steinbeck, *Novels 1942–1952* (2002)
133. Sinclair Lewis, *Arrowsmith, Elmer Gantry, Dodsworth* (2002)
134. Paul Bowles, *The Sheltering Sky, Let It Come Down, The Spider's House* (2002)
135. Paul Bowles, *Collected Stories & Later Writings* (2002)
136. Kate Chopin, *Complete Novels & Stories* (2002)
137. *Reporting Civil Rights: American Journalism 1941–1963* (2003)
138. *Reporting Civil Rights: American Journalism 1963–1973* (2003)
139. Henry James, *Novels 1896–1899* (2003)
140. Theodore Dreiser, *An American Tragedy* (2003)
141. Saul Bellow, *Novels 1944–1953* (2003)
142. John Dos Passos, *Novels 1920–1925* (2003)
143. John Dos Passos, *Travel Books and Other Writings* (2003)
144. Ezra Pound, *Poems and Translations* (2003)
145. James Weldon Johnson, *Writings* (2004)
146. Washington Irving, *Three Western Narratives* (2004)
147. Alexis de Tocqueville, *Democracy in America* (2004)
148. James T. Farrell, *Studs Lonigan: A Trilogy* (2004)
149. Isaac Bashevis Singer, *Collected Stories I* (2004)
150. Isaac Bashevis Singer, *Collected Stories II* (2004)
151. Isaac Bashevis Singer, *Collected Stories III* (2004)
152. Kaufman & Co., *Broadway Comedies* (2004)
153. Theodore Roosevelt, *The Rough Riders, An Autobiography* (2004)
154. Theodore Roosevelt, *Letters and Speeches* (2004)
155. H. P. Lovecraft, *Tales* (2005)
156. Louisa May Alcott, *Little Women, Little Men, Jo's Boys* (2005)
157. Philip Roth, *Novels & Stories 1959–1962* (2005)
158. Philip Roth, *Novels 1967–1972* (2005)
159. James Agee, *Let Us Now Praise Famous Men, A Death in the Family* (2005)
160. James Agee, *Film Writing & Selected Journalism* (2005)
161. Richard Henry Dana, Jr., *Two Years Before the Mast & Other Voyages* (2005)
162. Henry James, *Novels 1901–1902* (2006)
163. Arthur Miller, *Collected Plays 1944–1961* (2006)

164. William Faulkner, *Novels 1926–1929* (2006)
165. Philip Roth, *Novels 1973–1977* (2006)
166. *American Speeches: Part One* (2006)
167. *American Speeches: Part Two* (2006)
168. Hart Crane, *Complete Poems & Selected Letters* (2006)
169. Saul Bellow, *Novels 1956–1964* (2007)
170. John Steinbeck, *Travels with Charley and Later Novels* (2007)
171. Capt. John Smith, *Writings with Other Narratives* (2007)
172. Thornton Wilder, *Collected Plays & Writings on Theater* (2007)
173. Philip K. Dick, *Four Novels of the 1960s* (2007)
174. Jack Kerouac, *Road Novels 1957–1960* (2007)
175. Philip Roth, *Zuckerman Bound* (2007)
176. Edmund Wilson, *Literary Essays & Reviews of the 1920s & 30s* (2007)
177. Edmund Wilson, *Literary Essays & Reviews of the 1930s & 40s* (2007)
178. *American Poetry: The 17th & 18th Centuries* (2007)

This book is set in 10 point Linotron Galliard,
a face designed for photocomposition by Matthew Carter
and based on the sixteenth-century face Granjon. The paper
is acid-free lightweight opaque and meets the requirements
for permanence of the American National Standards Institute.
The binding material is Brillianta, a woven rayon cloth made
by Van Heek-Scholco Textielfabrieken, Holland. Compo-
sition by Dedicated Business Services. Printing by
Malloy Incorporated. Binding by Dekker Book-
binding. Designed by Bruce Campbell.